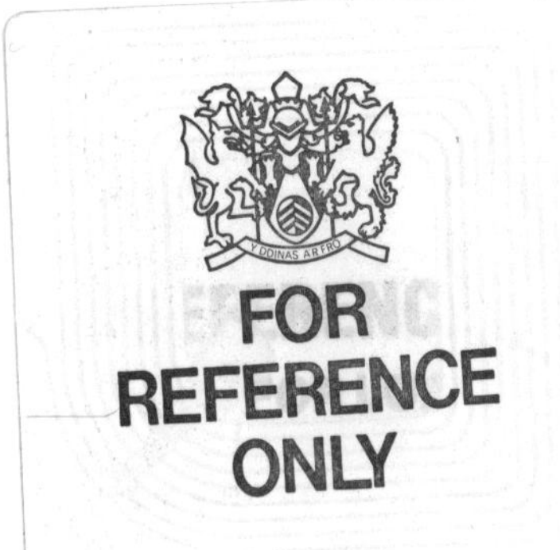
FOR
REFERENCE
ONLY

D1612934

Digest of Welsh Historical Statistics
Volume 1

Crynhoad o Ystadegau Hanesyddol Cymru
Cyfrol 1

By
Gan **John Williams**

Department of Economic and Social History,
University College of Wales, Aberystwyth

First published 1985

Printed in Wales for The Welsh Office
by Mid Wales Litho Ltd., Griffithstown, Pontypool
O/N 85/32 800 Dec 85

ISBN 0 86348 120 5

Cover design and illustrative material compiled by Steven Knowles, Cartographic Services, Welsh Office

CONTENTS

Volume I

	Page
General Introduction	viii
1. POPULATION	1
1. Estimates of population, 1570-1750; and totals and intercensal change, by sex, Wales and each county, 1801-1971.	6
2. Number of females per thousand males, Wales and each county, 1801-1971.	25
3. Age and marital condition, by sex, Wales, 1841-1971.	26
4. Area. Wales and each county, 1841-1971.	40
5. Population of Registration counties, 1841-1911.	41
6. Comparative area and population of Registration, Ancient and Administrative counties, 1891.	43
7. Parish register returns of baptisms, burials and marriages, Wales, 1700-1840.	44
8. Estimated mid-year population, by sex, Wales, 1841-1974.	46
9. Estimated mid-year population, total, each county, 1903-74.	50
10. Deaths. Number of deaths (by sex), crude death rates and infant mortality, Wales, 1838-1974.	53
11. Births. Number of births (by sex), and birth-rate per thousand population, Wales, 1839-1974.	57
12. Marriages. Number of marriages and rate per thousand population, Wales, 1839-1974.	61
13. Population of towns, 1801-1971.	62
14. Migration. Net migration and natural increase, number and per cent for each inter-censal period, Wales, and each county, 1841-1971.	68
15. Migration. Number born in Wales and living in United States, 1850-1970.	76
16. Language. Number of Welsh speakers, by sex, Wales and each county and county borough, 1891-1971.	78
17. Language. Welsh speakers as percentage of total population over 3 years of age, Wales and each county and county borough, 1891-1971.	86
18. Language. Welsh-speaking population, by age, Wales, 1901-71.	87
2. LABOUR	89
1. Occupations, by sex, Wales, 1801-1971.	95
2. Occupations, by sex, each county, 1801-1971.	103
3. Employment. Estimated number of persons insured against unemployment, 1922-47; estimated number of employees, 1948-74; and numbers in employment, 1922-39, 1951-74, Wales.	133
4. Number of employees by sex and industry, Wales, 1939-74.	135
5. Number and percentage unemployed, by sex, each month, Wales, 1923-75.	142
6. Vacancies unfilled, by sex, Wales, 1949-74.	157
7. Unemployment by age groups and duration, Wales, 1935-75.	158
8. Number of persons placed in employment by employment exchanges and youth employment services, Wales, 1948-74.	162
9. Number of Trades Councils and number of trade union members represented, Wales, 1894-1924.	163
10. Total number of workpeople affected by, and days lost through, disputes, Wales (and U.K.), 1891-1913.	164
11. Disputes by industry, Wales and U.K., various dates, 1899-1974.	165
3. WAGES, EARNINGS AND CONSUMER EXPENDITURE	167
1. Coal. Percentage changes in miners' wage-rates, South Wales, 1848-1939	172
2. Coal. Average earnings, 1840-1974; average earnings per shift, North Wales, 1888, 1914, 1918-46 (quarterly); and South Wales, 1840-1914 (occasional dates) and 1918-46 (quarterly); and South Wales (per shift, weekly) 1945-75.	175
3. Agriculture. Nominal weekly wages, occasional dates, 1788-1882; average weekly earnings, occasional dates, by county, 1867-1917; minimum rates, by county, 1918-39; weekly earnings and hours, Wales, 1967-75.	178
4. Police. Maximum and minimum rates of pay of police constables, by county, 1902-14.	181
5. Building. Hours and rates per hour building trades, main towns, 1894-1914 and 1936.	182
6. Engineering and ship-repairing. Rates for different trades, main ports, 1880-1968.	184
7. Rates of pay and hours for printing trades, main towns, 1850-1968: cabinet makers, 1901-14.	187
8. Average weekly and hourly earnings, and average hours, manual workers over 20 in manufacturing, all industries, and selected individual industries, Wales, 1960-74.	189
9. Household income and expenditure, Wales and U.K., 1953-4 and 1961-73.	192
4. AGRICULTURE	193
1. Acreage of crops, Wales, 1867-1974.	197
2. Acreage of crops, each county, 1867-1973.	203
3. Livestock, Wales, 1867-1974.	217
4. Livestock, each county, 1867-1973.	226
5. Estimated production of principal crops, Wales, 1886-1974.	234
6. Estimated yields of principal crops, Wales, 1886-1974.	236
7. Size of agricultural holdings, Wales, 1875-1973.	238
8. Size of agricultural holdings, each county, 1875-1973.	240
9. Workers on agricultural holdings, Wales, 1921-74.	254
10. Workers on agricultural holdings, each county, 1921-73.	256
11. Prices. Wheat, barley and oats in selected markets, 1794-1920; meat prices at Bangor, 1828-1907; salt butter at Carmarthen, 1811-1913. Annual averages.	282
12. Agricultural machinery, Wales, 1942-72.	286
13. Milk. Number of producers and Sales under Marketing Scheme, Wales, 1934-74.	287
14. Fishing. Landings at Welsh ports. Quantity and value, 1886-1974.	288
15. Forestry. Woodland area, Wales, 1924 and 1938-75 (and figures for 'Woods' various dates 1871-1905).	291

Page

5. COAL 293
  1. Output and number of collieries, North Wales and South Wales, 1854-78. 297
  2. Output, numbers employed and output per head, by region and county, 1874-1945. 289
  3. Output, number employed and productivity, North Wales and South Wales, 1945-74. 307
  4. Output of anthracite, South Wales and U.K., 1854-1974. 310
  5. Output from government open-cast workings, South Wales, 1943-72. 311
  6. Output and number employed, South Wales as a percentage of U.K., 1874-1974. 312
  7. Shipments (Coastal and Foreign) from South Wales ports, 1816-74. 314
  8. Shipments (Coastal, Foreign and Bunkers) of coal from South Wales ports, and South Wales shipments as a percentage of U.K., 1874-1937. 315
  9. Shipments. Exports of coal, coke and patent fuel from South Wales ports, 1854-1937. 316
  10. Shipments. Foreign and coastal shipments from each port (Cardiff, Swansea, Newport, Llanelli, Milford, Neath, Porthcawl), various dates, 1780-1974. 318
  11. Colliery deaths, number and rate, underground and total, South Wales, 1853-1974; and North Wales (number only), 1853-1938. 332
  12. Mechanisation. Number, type and work done by mechanical coal cutters; number of coal conveyers; and amount of electricity used in mines, North Wales and South Wales, 1900-45. 334
  13. Mechanisation. Percentage of coal output cut and conveyed by machinery (1937-60); and percentage power-loaded (1947-75), South Wales, 1937-75. 336
  14. Prices. Average pit head prices, North Wales and South Wales, 1878-1938; and f.o.b. prices for steam coal (large and small), South Wales, 1840-1934. 337
  15. Costs and proceeds. Average wage coal, total cost and proceeds, per ton, North Wales and South Wales, 1917-74. 338
  16. The number and annual output of members of the Coal Owners' Association, 1863-1946. 340
  17. Output from Aberdare parish, 1844-1874; and coal carried by the Taff Vale Railway, 1841-1921. 341
  18. Output of coke and number of coke ovens, South Wales, 1905-74. 342

6. IRON AND STEEL 343
  1. Iron. Number of works and furnaces, North Wales and South Wales, 1740-1974. 346
  2. Amount and value of iron ore mined in North Wales, 1855-1920, and South Wales, 1855-1971. 350
  3. Pig iron production, North Wales, 1740-1919, and South Wales, 1740-1974. 352
  4. Production of pig-iron, by type, South Wales, 1886-1974. 354
  5. Production of steel ingots and castings, by type of furnace, South Wales, 1878-86; 1920-74. 355
  6. Tinplate. Average number of mills working, 1869-1937, and total production, 1834-1974, United Kingdom. 356
  7. Prices (per ton). Bar iron (Newport), 1803-23, 1866-77; Bar iron (London), 1812-40; Pig iron, 1802-23, 1863-80; Railway iron, 1843-52; Tinplate bars, 1913-43. 357
  8. Prices (per box, f.o.b. Swansea), tinplate, 1827-1943. 359

Volume II

7. LEAD, COPPER, SLATE ETC. 1
  1. Output of copper ore, tons, by main counties and Wales, 1855-1919. 5
  2. Copper ore sold at Swansea ticketings, 1804-81; and imports of copper ore and unwrought copper to Swansea, 1832-74, and Llanelli, 1832-98. 6
  3. Lead ore. Output and number of mines recording sales, by main counties and Wales, 1845-1948. 8
  4. Zinc ore. Output, main counties and Wales, 1854-1938; Bluestone, output, Anglesey, 1863-1917. 11
  5. Slate and slate slabs. Output, main counties, 1882-1938; and Wales, 1882-1974. 13
  6. Gold and silver, output, Wales, 1854-1920. 14
  7. Limestone, sandstone and igneous rocks, output, Wales, 1895-1974. 15
  8. Employment. Numbers employed in metalliferous mines, Wales and each county, 1872-1926. 16
  9. Employment. Numbers employed in slate mines and quarries, Wales and each county, 1884-1926. 18
  10. Employment. Deaths in metalliferous mines and quarries, North Wales and South Wales, 1873-1926. 20
  11. Price of lead, 1620-1765, and of lead ore, 1662-1809 and 1859-82. 21

8. TRANSPORT 23
  1. Canals. Mileage and costs at opening, South Wales and North Wales, 1700-1945. 28
  2. Canals. Iron carried on the Monmouthshire, 1802-40, and Glamorganshire, 1817-40, canals. 31
  3. Railways. Mileage, traffic and capital, 1848-1938. 32
  4. Roads. Mileage, Wales, 1860-1974. 42
  5. Road vehicles. Licences current, by type, Wales, 1926-74. 45
  6. Ports. Total tonnage of coasting vessels belonging to main ports, 1709-51. 46
  7. Ports. Foreign trade, value of imports and exports, Wales and main ports, 1857-1972; shipping registered at main ports, 1814, 1815, 1829. 48
  8. Ports. Cargo traffic through main ports, 1911-74. 55
  9. Ports. Cargo traffic, by type of cargo, main ports, 1922-74. 57

Page

10. Ports. Shipping movements: Cardiff, arrivals and departures, 1841-86; main ports, arrivals 1911-38; arrivals and departures, foreign and coastal, 1946-71. 60
11. Civil aviation. Movement, by type, passengers and freight carried, Welsh air ports, 1938-74. 64
12. Communication. Number of letters and parcels posted, 1938-75: number of broadcast receiving licences in force, 1954-75, Wales. 64

9. HOUSING 65
1. Number of houses, inhabited, uninhabited (and building, 1811-1921), Wales and each county, 1801-1971. 69
2. (a) Number of private households, Wales and each county, 1801-1901; (b) number of private households, dwellings, rooms and density of occupation, Wales and each county, 1911-71. 73
3. Number of rooms occupied by private households, Wales and each county, 1911-71. 74
4. Brick production: (a) return of duties paid on bricks, Wales and regions, 1829-49; (b) number of bricks and amount of duty paid, Wales and each county, 1836-46. 77
5. Number of house plans approved, by town, South Wales, 1851-1914. 79
6. Estimated costs of building plans passed by Urban Districts, by type of building, Wales, quarterly, 1909-39. 82
7. Total number of houses built in inter-war years, Wales and each county, total of 1919-40. 88
8. Number of houses authorised, under construction and completed, local authority and private enterprise, Wales, 1919-39 and 1946-74, each county, 1919-39 and 1957-74 and county boroughs, 1919-39; number of houses demolished, 1947-74. 89
9. Decisions on planning applications, by type of development, Wales, 1962-72. 107
10. Houses completed, by number of bedrooms, public and (from 1963) private sectors, houses and flats, Wales, 1945-74. 114
11. Government financial contributions, new houses and improvement grants, Wales, 1950-74. 116
12. Number of conversions and improvements, approved for grant, by public and private sector, Wales, 1955-74. 117
13. Prices and costs, Wales, 1958-74. 118

10. MISCELLANEOUS: TOURISM, PARLIAMENTARY ELECTIONS, SOCIAL SERVICES AND CRIME 121
1. Tourism. Percentage of holiday-makers staying in each country for one night or more on holidays in Great Britain (British holiday-makers only). 126
2. Election results. All parliamentary elections and by-elections, Wales, 1832-1974. 127
3. Health Service. Number of doctors and persons supplying drugs, for insured persons, Wales, 1918-74. 150
4. Health Service. Number of medical and dental practitioners, and number of hospital staff, Wales, 1949-74. 151

Page

5. Health Service. Hospitals. Number of beds, available and occupied, Wales, 1931-8, 1948-75; and number of out-patients, Wales, 1948-75. 152
6. Health Service. Gross expenditure, Wales, by category, 1950-75. 153
7. Health Service. Local authority services, number of users, etc., Wales, 1931-75. 155
8. Social Services. Non-contributory pensions, number payable, 1909-65; National assistance, number of cases, 1936-65; Supplementary benefits, number in payment, 1966-74, Wales. 157
9. Social Services. Contributory pensions, benefits and allowances, Wales, 1926-75. 159
10. Social Services. National health insurance, receipts, etc., 1912-44; claims and insured persons absent from work, 1949-75, Wales. 161
11. Social Services. Family allowances. Number of families receiving and number of children for whom allowances were paid, Wales, 1948-75. 162
12. Crime. Indictable offences known to police, Wales, 1857-1974; persons prosecuted for non-indictable offences, Wales, 1893-1974. 164
13. Crime. Assizes and Quarter Sessions. Number of persons brought for trial, 1805-1974; offences classified, 1834-1918; number convicted, 1834-74, Wales. 166
14. Crime. Courts of summary jurisdiction. Number brought for trial 1857-1918; number a) tried and b) found guilty of indictable offences, 1893-1918; 1949-74, Wales. 168
15. Public Utilities. Tramways, Wales, 1880-1938. 169
16. Public Utilities. Gas, Wales, 1882-1939. 170

11. LOCAL GOVERNMENT 171
1. Poor law expenditure and receipts, Wales, 1748-1937. 174
2. Number of paupers relieved, indoor and outdoor, Wales, 1840-1939. 178
3. Income, Wales and each county, 1792-1937. 181
4. Expenditure, Wales and each county, 1792-1937. 185
5. Income and expenditure, Wales, 1957-74. 192
6. Expenditure on highways, 1812-1914, police, 1857-1914 and eduction, 1903-14, Wales. 193

12. EDUCATION 195
1. Schools. Number of schools, Wales, various dates, 1818-67; Monmouthshire, 1600-1870; and works schools, 1700-1890. 201
2. Schools. Church of England elementary schools under government inspection, Wales, 1850-62; British schools, total and inspected, Wales and South Wales, various dates, 1843-71. 205
3. Schools, by type of school, Wales, 1877-1976. 206
4. Schools, by responsible body, Wales, 1879-1971. 210
5. Pupils. Number of pupils in day and Sunday schools, Wales, various dates, 1818-67. 212
6. Pupils. Number on register, by type of school, Wales, 1877-1976. 214

Page

7. Pupils. Number of pupils in maintained schools, by sex, Wales, 1898-1976. 217
8. School leavers by age of leaving, A. from Public and Elementary schools, 1920-38; B. from Secondary Schools on the grant list, 1909-38; andC. school leavers, by sex and reason, 1947-74, Wales. 219
9. Teachers. Number of full-time teachers, by type of school, Wales, 1851-1973. 222
10. Teachers. Full-time teachers, by qualification, Wales, 1851-1973. 225
11. Teachers. Teachers in training, Wales, 1865-1974. 227
12. Finance. Total net expenditure on elementary education, Wales, 1873-1938; net expenditure on education, Wales, 1951-75. 231
13. Examinations. Number of candidates and passes, Central Welsh Board 1900-50; and Welsh Joint Education Committee, 1951-74. 236
14. University. Number of full-time degree and diploma students, by College and by sex, 1893-1972. 238
15. University. Origin (by Wales, other G.B., and over-seas) of full-time degree students of University of Wales, 1921-75. 242
16. University. Staff of University of Wales, by grade, 1908-74. 243
17. University. Finance. Total current income and expenditure by institution, University of Wales, 1893-1974. 244

13. RELIGION 249
1. Church of England, number of incumbents, by diocese, Wales, 1832, 1879-90. 256
2. Church in Wales (before 1920, Church of England), number of incumbents, baptisms, Easter communicants and Sunday scholars, by diocese, Wales, 1885-1974. 257
3. Church in Wales, number of churches, by diocese, Wales, various dates, 1832-1973. 267
4. Nonconformist Congregations, by county, 1672, 1716 and 1742. 267
5. Baptists. Number of churches, members and Sunday scholars, by associations, various dates, 1839-65. 268
6. Baptists. A. Members. Various dates, 1669-1860; B. Number of churches, chapels, pastors, members, Sunday school scholars and baptisms, Wales and each county, 1861-1972. 271
7. Calvinistic Methodists. Number of chapels, churches, ministers, lay preachers, communicants, Sabbath scholars and adherents, each county, 1860, 1885-1973, Wales, 1855-1972. 294
8. Methodists. Number of members, by districts and Wales, 1767-1968. 323
9. Congregationalists and Welsh Independents. Number of churches, ministers, members and Sabbath scholars, by counties and Wales, various dates 1861-91, and 1897-1975. 328
10. Roman Catholics. Number of clergy and churches (from 1838), schools, Catholics, baptisms, marriages and conversions (from 1911), Wales and by diocese, various dates, 1838-1974. 346
11. Religious Census of 1851, summary table for Wales (1) 352
12. Communicants, by county and denomination, 1905 353
13. Marriages, by type of rite, quinquennially, Wales, 1839-1972 354

MAPS

1. Administrative Areas, 1971 355
2. Wales and the Marches 356

Preface

In the last couple of decades Welsh historical studies have flourished. The present volume is not offered as part of that very welcome development: it was rather conceived with the more modest aim of providing a service for those working on the history of modern Wales. It arose from a belief that the quantitative element is a necessary and important part of the historical record; from an awareness that it was an aspect that was particularly inaccessible for scholars of Welsh history; and from a conviction that some encouragement in the use of quantitative material was necessary.

It was fortunate that my then colleagues in the Department of Economics at U.C.W. Aberystwyth sufficiently shared my views as to allow me research assistance. I am most grateful to them and also the the Social Science Research Council (as it then was) for funding a research officer. These two institutions generously provided the crucial opportunities.

None the less the vigour with which these opportunities were exploited depended entirely on how effectively the researchers used the couple of years to which funding was limited. In this respect I was exceptionally lucky. The two young researchers, Rosemary Oakley (as she then was) and Trevor Boyns, did far more than could reasonably have been asked of them. They were terrier-like in their pursuit of material, meticulously painstaking in its arrangement, careful in indicating its limitations, ingenious in suggesting improvisation, and were enjoyable and stimulating colleagues. Such virtues as the work possesses derives mostly from their efforts and I am conscious that much has been lost because of the necessity to reduce, merge or manipulate much of what they had done.

For a variety of reasons this work has taken a somewhat tortuous path towards publication. It is thus with especial gratitude that I acknowledge the assistance of the Welsh Office in enormously facilitating the final stages. If, as is hoped, the work will be of some use to scholars its appearance owes much to the Welsh Office and to the enthusiastic assistance and support given by Ed Swires-Hennessy, their survey statistician. I am grateful, too, to John Rhys of the University of Wales Press for his ready acceptance of this arrangement. If the standard of accuracy fails to reach the normal high standards of Welsh Office statistical publications the responsibility is entirely mine; as is the fault for any shortfall from the normal production standards, the copy not having been originally prepared for this form of publication.

Certainly none of the responsibility for any shortcomings would rest with those who have executed a difficult and tedious typing job with remarkable accuracy and cheerfulness. Rosemary Law, Susan Cadman and Pam Davies bore the brunt of this and, in particular, Rosemary Law gave freely of her time and skill in the final substantial task of correcting and adapting the typescript for a different mode of publication. Similarly, Dot Jones has, over a considerable period of time, sunk a great deal of effort into the enterprise not least in the demanding task of checking and preparing the typescript for publication.

The task of compiling a set of historical statistics for Wales was one which was undertaken with the greatest reluctance. It was attempted because of the continuous personal frustration induced by lengthy searches for quite basic statistical information. It was attempted because this seemed a general experience amongst those working in Welsh history. It was attempted because the preferred solution to the problem (i.e. that someone else should undertake the task) remained as remote as ever. The reluctance was reinforced by an acute appreciation of the difficulties involved and of being inadequately qualified for the task. Misgivings on these last two counts have mostly been confirmed.

The obvious model for a work of this kind is provided by the two volumes devoted to British historical statistics.[1] The general outline follows the same pattern as the British volumes. Each section has a brief introduction which is intended to provide some explanatory remarks, not on the general subject of the section, but on the particular statistical series which have been provided. These comments will not be, and are not intended to be very helpful to those who are already expert in the given area, but it is hoped that non-specialists will be able to gain some idea of the nature of the sources upon which the tables are based, obtain an indication of the reliability of the figures, and - perhaps most important - be warned about their limitations. Each section also has a short bibliography, which is largely confined to listing those works which have been of direct use in compiling the tables and/or contain comment upon statistical material. No attempt has been made to provide a bibliography of the numerous more general works which have been consulted: interested readers are referred to the second edition of the Bibliography of the History of Wales published by the University of Wales Press in 1962 and its later supplements.

In some respects substantial effort has been expended in an attempt to follow the model provided by the volumes on British historical statistics as exactly as possible. Naturally it would be pleasing to reach the same standards of accuracy and clarity but, more operationally, the aim was to facilitate comparisons between the figures relating to Wales and those relating to Britain. The limitations of the material, however, often frustrated such attempts but, beyond this, there are other substantial departures from the model provided by the British volumes. It might help potential users to offer some brief comments on these departures, some of which have been deliberate and some have been more or less involuntary.

The deliberate deviations are of three main kinds. In the first place, a greater attention has been given to statistics of a non-economic, or less explicitly economic, nature. This is justified, if justification is needed, by the growth of the new social history and its readiness to use quantitative material and techniques; and by the extent to which economic historians and economists have increasingly recognised that most questions cannot be satisfactorily resolved simply on the basis of a small number of exclusively economic variables. Such recognition has naturally been strongest in the case of relatively long-run issues, where the assumption that 'other things remain equal' becomes increasingly questionable: but part of the justification for a volume such as the present lies precisely in the assistance it can give in tackling issues of a relatively long-run nature. In the second place, more detail has sometimes been given than was contained in the British volumes. Thus, for example, a greater range of statistical information is included on the coal industry, because of its peculiar importance for

1. Mitchell, B.R. and Deane, P., Abstract of British Historical Statistics, 1962; and Mitchell, B.R. and Jones, H.G., Second Abstract of British Historical Statistics, 1971.

Wales. Conversely, much less information (or none at all) is included for sectors or industries (like cotton manufacture) which were unimportant or non-existant in Wales. And thirdly, substantially more information has been included on a local, and especially a county, basis. For many issues the aggregate figures for Wales are inadequate or even mis-leading. The division between the industrial and the rural is perhaps especially significant within Wales, whilst communications have tended to run east-west, rather than north-south, making Wales less integrated as a national unit. It is hoped that a greater inclusion of information on a county basis will offer investigators more flexibility in using the material.

The involuntary deviations from the British model are more numerous and regrettable. Mostly they arise from the, till recently, deeply-entrenched tendency for administrators (and others) to lump Wales in with England. Scotland and Ireland are usually separately designated but the historical investigator for Wales is perpetually balked by the irritating phenomenon of 'England and Wales'. In some cases it has been possible to separate out the figures for Wales. It would be possible in many other cases to make reasonable estimates for Wales: but, in general, such calculations have not been presented here because of the intention to confine attention, apart from a few indices, to making available raw data. In other cases, the problems seem insurmountable. Thus any reasonable approximation for the total external trade of Wales seems beyond our reach: the bulk of such trade - imports and exports - was with England and is unrecorded. Other areas are not beyond reach, but would demand a degree of fundamental research which was impossible to undertake with the time and resources available. There is a great deal of empirical evidence concerning prices in Wales. It appears as incidental material in government and other official records and reports, it recurs in a wide variety of farm, business and household accounts and manuscripts; and it appears in a wide range of local newspapers and secondary writings. But it is scattered, patchy, sporadic and unsystematic: substantial and sustained research would be needed to collect and organise it into meaningful economic trends. There is thus no separate section on prices in the present volume, but wherever a reasonably consistent series was available for a particular sector (for coal, for example, and some farm products) it has been included with the other material for that sector. A similar situation exists for wages but it was judged that, despite the gaps and shortcomings, enough usable material existed to justify a separate section (Section 3) especially since good figures exist on the topic for recent years.

The reference to recent years prompts comment upon a number of more general limitations to the present work. The starting date for some of the basic demographic tables is at the beginning of the nineteenth century and a few isolated tables, for example dealing with iron and coal, lap back into the eighteenth century. But in most areas reasonably consistent and continuous series for Wales can only be obtained from around the middle of the nineteenth century at the earliest. Often the starting-point is much later since the figures are frequently a by-product of two late-flowering processes: the extension of government activity into new areas of social interest, and the pursuit of active regional policies. At the other end of the chronological scale the cut-off date has normally been made around 1974. This marked the re-organisation of local government in Wales and it would have been impossible, as well as being historically meaningless, to have converted all the earlier data to coincide with the radically different administrative basis. A related problem concerns the decimilisation of money. Apart from some marginal re-adjustments in the years immediately around the change-over in 1971, the figures have normally been left as they were originally expressed.

Another significant limitation is that there are occasional gaps and omissions in the tables. For example, table 8 in the section on education gives information on school leavers but there are gaps for 1923 and 1924 because the volume relating for Wales was not published in those years and the department was unable to provide the figures or to give information from which they could be calculated. A number of such gaps have been filled often with the help of the appropriate government department, and most of the remaining gaps of this kind are irritating rather than serious. That they are more or less unavoidable if Wales is the unit arises from the fact, already mentioned, that in some cases a total for Wales can only be obtained by extracting and aggregating more detailed figures; and if the details are not available for any particular year no total can be provided. It is this aspect which largely accounts for the two more serious periods of omission covering the two world wars. Very little was published on a county or regional basis during these periods, and at the level of detail required it seems that much of the necessary information was either not collected at all or has not been retained.

A more general point concerns the kind of statistics which have been included in this volume. The overwhelming emphasis has been on the collection of 'raw' statistics. In general, therefore, the aim has been to avoid processing or manipulating the basic data in order to construct indices of various kinds or to convert the collected figures into indicators of concepts (like national income) for which no consciously-constructed contemporary figures exist. Of course, it is not meant to imply by this that each statistic given existed in exactly that form in the original document or report from which it was constructed. On the contrary, one of the persistent obstacles to be overcome was that there was no figure for Wales directly available. In many cases such a figure was only reached by summing up figures which could be obtained for, say, each Welsh county, or - to cite a particularly tricky case - each Welsh railway (raising the ultimately unanswerable question of 'What is a Welsh railway?'). Where any substantial aggregation of this sort has been undertaken it has been noted in the introduction to the particular section since it obviously involves an additional source of possible error. But the general point remains: the statistics have not normally been processed in a way which would alter their original form. It was felt that the over-riding priority was to present the basic figures: partly, indeed, to provide material but part of the motivation for, and justification of, such an enterprise was precisely to aid - and perhaps even encourage those who wish to process the statistics, and adapt them so that a wider range of social and economic concepts can be brought to bear upon Welsh history.

Chapter 1
Population

The obvious starting point for any collection of historical statistics is with the basic demographic material. In this respect, reasonable reliability essentially dates from the taking of the first census in 1801.[1] Fortunately, it is possible to secure from the outset separate figures for Wales on the fundamental issue of the size of the total population and its breakdown by sex. Table 1 presents this information and is preceded by some estimates of the population for earlier years made by John Rickman, who directed the first three censuses. Rickman's estimates depend on some strong and arbitrary assumptions: the wide differences in the estimates thus produced mainly serve to underline the problems involved. The table includes the same information on the total population (by sex) for each county. In the same way, Table 2 which gives the proportion of females to males at each decennial census, does so for Wales and each of the counties.

The inclusion of fuller information on a county basis requires some care in interpretation as the definition of 'county' tended to shift from time to time.[2] Up to 1891 the county figures refer either to Ancient counties or to Registration counties; after 1891 they refer either to Registration counties or, most usually, to Administrative counties. In Wales the division into ancient counties began with the formation of Pembroke as a County Palatine in 1138 and was largely completed by Henry VIII. Some small changes were made under an Act of 1844. The registration counties originated with the civil registration of births, marriages and deaths in 1837. In general registration districts were formed out of Poor Law unions, which themselves had been formed under the 1834 Act by combining together groups of parishes for poor law purposes. Registration counties were formed by grouping together registration districts and the resulting areas did not always coincide exactly with the ancient counties. Administrative counties were formed as a result of the Local Government Acts of 1888 and 1894. In Wales the administrative counties largely coincided with the ancient counties: but both differed sharply from the registration counties. The differences and some indication of their significance are indicated in Tables 4 to 6. From 1841, it is possible to present a break-down of the population of Wales by age, and in Table 3 this has been combined, from 1851, with a break-down by marital status.

The early censuses attempted to obtain information on births, marriages and deaths by asking clergymen to compile figures from their parish registers. The 1801 census attempted to secure this information for the preceding century by calling for information on baptisms and burials for every tenth year up to 1780 and annually thereafter, and for the number of marriages for each year from 1754. There are many deficiencies in the results. In many cases the parish registers were missing or had serious gaps: some clergymen failed to make returns; and others doubtless made errors in doing so, especially perhaps in Wales where the quality of the Anglican clergy was not high. Some of these difficulties were less acute for material collected in later censuses covering c.1800 to 1840, but throughout it is impossible to know just what proportion of the total population was represented in the parish registers. How many deaths were registered as Anglican burials, and how many births were registered in the church, and did these proportions change over time? In these respects some of the conditions in Wales (language, extent

---

1. It should be noted, however, that there is general agreement that the censuses of 1801 and, to a lesser extent, 1811 left out a significant part of the population. There is no way of knowing just how many were not counted but it seems likely that at least 5 per cent in 1801 and 3 per cent in 1811 could be taken as reasonable indicators. A J Taylor, 'The Taking of the Census, 1801-1951', British Medical Journal, 1951; J T Krause, 'Changes in English Fertility and Mortality, 1781-1850', EHR, XI, 1958. No attempt has been made to correct the figures given in the actual census except in so far as any particular figure was revised by a later census.

2. In addition, of course, the inaccuracies inherent in the taking of a census increase as the area considered becomes smaller in size. M Drake, 'The Census 1801-1891' in E A Wrigley (ed.) Nineteenth Century Society, and P M Tillott, 'Sources of Inaccuracy in the 1851 and 1861 Census' in Ibid.

of Nonconformity) make it unlikely that estimates made of these variables for England[1] can simply be transferred to Wales. There are many pitfalls, therefore, but Table 7 does present a basic part of the evidence for any studies on Welsh population in the eighteenth century, a subject on which surprisingly little work has been done.

The introduction of the civil registration of births, marriages and deaths in 1837 substantially improved knowledge in these areas. The improvement was, however, spread over time as registration gradually became more comprehensive in its coverage and more accurate in the information provided. However, the shortcomings, and hence the improvements, were particularly marked in the earliest years and thereafter present no serious general problems. There are problems more specific to Wales. In particular, the registrar general's reports do not give separate estimates for Wales of the mid-year population before 1878. Thus relating the figures on births, marriages and deaths to total population for each year in the earlier period requires a prior calculation of the population for the inter-censal years. This calculation has been made for the years between 1841 and 1878 and included in Table 8.[2] The basis for the calculation is the assumption of a constant rate of growth of population for the inter-censal years. Thus the growth between the census years has been allocated to each year by using an annual compound rate which sums up to the decadal rate. Such procedures obviously do not give a precise indication of the actual mid-year population (nor, of course, do the later official estimates of the Registrar-General). Any errors will clearly affect the accuracy of the death, birth and marriage-rates shown in Tables 10, 11 and 12, which are based upon the estimates of the annual population. It is, however, not thought that such errors will be significant especially as the main determinant of the rates for deaths, births and marriages are the fluctuations in the number of deaths, births and marriages rather than the (proportionately small) errors in the estimation of the total population. And fortunately, the actual number of deaths, births and marriages has been directly obtained and, with time, became increasingly more reliable. A further small source of error rises from the differences in the area covered. Thus figures based on the census relate to administrative Wales whilst the figures on the number of births and deaths relate, until 1910, to the Welsh Registration Division or to the sum of the registration counties, and the number of marriages remains based on that area until 1938. There are, as Tables 4 - 6 indicate, small differences between these areas and that used for the overall population figures for Wales.

Table 13 gives information on the population of towns in Wales since 1801. It needs to be interpreted with much caution. What constitutes the 'proper' area of a town at any particular time is not an easy question to determine and it is certain that it would be impossible always to obtain the information on population for such an area. The figures in the table relate solely to the administrative area, but they do include the changes, both geographical and verbal, in that concept. It is hoped that the approach allows some flexibility (not making the area of each town conform exactly with the area as it was on one particular date) whilst the needs of consistency for comparison is met by attempting to include figures on both the old and new basis at the time of any change in the administrative area. For the early censuses there are particular difficulties over giving the populations of towns. Only a few places are so designated in the census and places which later featured as towns often did not have the same boundaries as the parishes by which they had been earlier designated. In addition to uncertainties about boundary changes, it is known that at least the first three censuses underestimated the true size of the population but the population figures for towns and parishes, unlike those for counties, were not revised later except in the cases of Swansea and Merthyr - the major towns in Wales at the time.

Tables 14 and 15 bring together some information on two broad aspects of migration. It is not possible, over any length of time, to get figures of the total numbers moving into and out of Wales (and each county). Table 14, however, attempts to indicate

---

1. See, e.g., J T Krause, loc. cit.

2. Similar information for each county can only be obtained from 1903 and is given in Table 9.

the net size of such population movements and also expresses them as a percentage of the total population to indicate changes in the relative magnitudes over time and between counties. It needs to be emphasized that the migration figures are obtained as a residual (by subtracting the figures for natural increase from the total intercensal change); as such they are liable to an additional margin of error. No full and continuous series has been found for the number of Welsh people migrating overseas. Occasional scattered figures of variable quality have been collected but it was felt that only the number of Welsh people in the United States provided a sufficiently consistent and continuous series to be worth reproducing. Fortunately, for the half century or so before the first world war there are good reasons[1] for believing that the scale of migration from Wales was relatively modest.

Finally, there are three tables relating to language. All these go back to 1891 when, for the first time, the census in Wales included a question on ability to speak Welsh. As often happens when a new topic is introduced into the census, the first result was not fully satisfactory. In particular the census authorities judged that, because the wording led to some misunderstanding, the response over-stated the number of monoglot Welsh speakers. Comparisons between the 1891 figures of monoglot Welsh-speakers and those for later censuses thus demands care - for this and other reasons given in the foot-notes to Table 16. These cautionary words also apply to the other two tables dealing with language. Table 17 converts the absolute numbers into percentages and, like the preceding table, gives the information for each county and county borough. The variations within Wales on this topic are so marked and so significant as to make such a break-down imperative. The final language table looks at the age-distribution of Welsh-speakers over this period of eighty years.

---

1. These have been well-analysed by Brinley Thomas, 'Wales and the Atlantic Economy', Scottish Journal of Political Economy, November 1959 and re-printed in B.Thomas (ed.) The Welsh Economy, Cardiff, 1962.

BOOKS AND THESES

M.W. Flinn — British Population Growth, 1700-1850, 1970.

D.V. Glass and D.E.C. Eversley (eds) — Population in History, 1965.

D.V. Glass (ed) — Numbering the People, Farnborough, 1973.

D.V. Glass (ed) — The Population Controversy, Farnborough, 1973.

P.N. Jones — 'Aspects of the population and settlement geography of the South Wales coalfield, 1850-1926', Ph.D. thesis, Birmingham, 1965.

W. King — 'A Statistical study of the rural population of Wales in the nineteenth and twentieth centuries', U. of W. thesis 1929.

D.C. Marsh — The Changing Social Structure of England and Wales, rev. edn. 1965.

Butt Philip — The Welsh Question, Cardiff,1975.

B. Thomas — Migration and Economic Growth, Cambridge, 1954.

B. Thomas (ed) — The Welsh Economy, Cardiff, 1962.

E.A. Wrigley — Population and History, 1969.

E.A. Wrigley (ed) — Nineteenth Century Society, Cambridge, 1972.

E.A. Wrigley and R.S. Schofield — The Population History of England, 1541-1871, 1981.

ARTICLES

D. Williams — 'A Note on the Population of Wales, 1536-1801', B.B.C.S., viii, 1936.

D. Williams — 'Some figures relating to emigration from Wales', B.B.C.S., vii 1935, viii 1936.

D.V. Glass — 'A Note on the under-registration of births in Britain in the nineteenth century', Pop. Studies, v, 1951-2.

J.T. Krause — 'Changes in English Fertility and Mortality, 1781-1850', E.H.R. 2nd, series, xi.

B. Thomas — 'The Migration of labour into the Glamorgan coalfield 1861-1911', Economica, 1930.

GOVERNMENT AND OFFICIAL PUBLICATIONS

Reports and *Abstracts* of the Census of Great Britain, 1801-51 (in *sessional papers*)

Reports and *Tables* of the Census of England and Wales, 1861-1971 (in *sessional papers* to 1911, then as non-parliamentary papers)

Registrar General Annual Reports, 1838-1920 (non-parliamentary papers till 1851, then in *sessional papers*, 1920 again non-parliamentary)

Registrar General Statistical Review, 1921-73 (non-parliamentary papers)

Guides to Official Sources, no.2: Census Reports of Great Britain, 1801-1931

Royal Commission on Land in Wales, *Appendix*, S.P. 1896,

Royal Commission on Population, 1949.

Office of Population, Censuses and Surveys, *Population Estimates* 1974 revised, 1975 provisional (Series PP1 no.1)

Office of Population, Censuses and Surveys, *Population Trends*, 1975; quarterly

U.S. Census of Population

Report of departmental committee to enquire into position of the Welsh language, 1927

Report on the Welsh language today, Council for Wales and Mon., 1963

The Legal Status of the Welsh Language, Report of the Hughes-Parry Committee, 1965

POPULATION 1. ESTIMATES OF POPULATION 1570 - 1750.

a) WALES (1)

	Population according to : 1) Baptisms	2) Burials	3) Marriages	Population according to ave. of 1,2 & 3
1570	323,665	402,227	541,546	422,479
1600	343,879	335,282	374,631	351,264
1630	387,177	393,627	344,957	375,254
1670	325,681	453,617	356,085	378,461
1700	324,426	424,855	426,560	391,947
1750	464,362	387,875	500,745	450,994

b) COUNTIES. (2)

	1700	1750
Anglesey	22,800	26,900
Brecon	27,200	29,400
Caernarvonshire	25,300	32,000
Cardiganshire	49,700	62,000
Carmarthenshire	24,800	36,200
Denbigh	39,700	46,900
Flint	19,500	29,700
Glamorgan	49,700	55,200
Merioneth	23,800	30,900
Monmouth	39,700	40,600
Montgomery	27,400	37,000
Pembroke	41,300	44,800
Radnor	15,300	19,200
WALES	406,200	489,900

1). Richman's estimates, published in 1841 Census (Enumeration 1 pp 34-37 of preface). The estimates were obtained by assuming in the years 1570, 1600, 1630 etc. the same proportion of baptisms, burials and marriages to the existing population as in 1800 and 1801. For each of the years given, the figures were calculated by averaging the entries in the parish registers over a period of three years (e.g. 1570 was based on the average number of entries for 1569, 1570 and 1571).

2). 1811 Census - Preliminary Observations - pp xxviii - xxx

POPULATION 1. TOTAL POPULATION AND INTERCENSAL CHANGES BY SEX, WALES 1801 - 1971.

	POPULATION			INTERCENSAL CHANGE					
				AMOUNT			PER CENT.		
Date of Census	Males	Females	Total	M	F	T	M	F	T
1801 March 9/10	279,407	307,838	587,245						
1811 May 26/27	322,371	350,969	673,340	42,964	43,131	86,105	15.38	14.01	14.66
1821 May 27/28	390,735	403,419	794,154	68,364	52,450	120,714	21.21	14.94	17.93
1831 May 29/30	445,702	458,698	904,400	54,967	55,279	110,246	14.07	13.70	13.88
1841 June 6/7	518,372	527,701	1,046,073	72,670	69,003	141,673	16.30	15.04	15.66
1851 March 30/31	581,840	581,299	1,163,139	63,468	53,598	117,066	12.24	10.16	11.19
1861 April 7/8	641,652	644,761	1,280,413	59,812	63,462	123,274	10.28	10.92	10.60
1871 April 2/3	706,048	706,535	1,412,583	64,396	61,774	126,170	10.04	9.58	9.81
1881 April 3/4	786,322	785,458	1,571,780	80,274	78,923	159,157	11.37	11.17	11.27
1891 (1) April 5/6 (a)	892,256	879,195	1,771,451	105,934	93,737	199,671	13.47	11.93	12.70
1891 (b)	892,256	879,195	1,771,451						
1901 March 31/Ap.1	1,011,458	1,001,418	2,012,876 (2)	119,202	122,223	241,425	13.36	13.90	13.63
1911 April 2/3	1,231,739	1,189,182	2,420,921	220,281	187,764	408,045	21.78	18.75	20.27
1921 June 19/20	1,329,994	1,326,480	2,656,474	98,255	137,298	235,553	7.98	11.55	9.73
1931 April 26/27	1,293,805	1,299,527	2,593,332	-36,189	-26,953	-63,142	-2.72	-2.03	-2.38
1939 Mid-year	1,228,000	1,259,000	2,487,000	-65,805	-40,527	-106,332	-5.09	-3.12	-4.10
1951 April 8/9	1,270,103	1,328,572	2,598,675	42,103	69,572	111,675	3.43	5.53	4.49
1961 April 23/24	1,291,764	1,352,259	2,644,023	21,661	23,687	45,348	1.71	1.78	1.75
1971 April 25/26	1,327,507	1,403,697	2,731,204	35,743	51,438	87,181	2.77	3.80	3.30

NOTES

1) 1891 (a) Ancient County
(b) Administrative County

All figures 1801-81 for Ancient Counties
All figures 1901-71 for Administrative Counties

2) Boundary change 1891/1901 :-
Sum of counties in 1891, for areas as constituted 1901, is 1,771,430

The source for all figures for Table 1 is the Census Returns 1801-1971.

POPULATION 1. TOTAL POPULATION AND INTERCENSAL CHANGES BY SEX, ANGLESEY 1801 - 1971.

	POPULATION			INTERCENSAL CHANGE					
				AMOUNT			PER CENT.		
Date of Census	Males	Females	Total	M	F	T	M	F	T
1801 March 9/10	15,775	18,031	33,806						
1811 May 26/27	17,444	19,601	37,045	1,669	1,570	3,239	10.58	8.71	9.58
1821 May 27/28	21,784	23,279	45,063	4,340	3,678	8,018	24.88	18.76	21.64
1831 May 29/30	23,475	24,850	48,325	1,691	1,571	3,262	7.76	6.75	7.24
1841 June 6/7	24,374	26,517	50,891	899	1,667	2,566	3.83	6.71	5.31
1851 March 30/31	28,101	29,226	57,327	3,727	2,709	6,436	15.29	10.22	12.65
1861 April 7/8	26,294	28,315	54,609	-1,807	-911	-2,718	-6.43	-3.12	-4.70
1871 April 2/3	24,400	26,640	51,040	-1,894	-1,675	-3,569	-7.20	-5.92	-6.54
1881 April 3/4	25,103	26,313	51,416	703	-327	376	2.88	-1.23	0.74
1891 (1) April 5/6 (a)	23,941	26,157	50,098	-1,162	-156	-1,318	-4.63	-0.59	-2.56
1891 (b)	23,941	26,157	50,098						
1901 March 31/April 1	24,487	26,119	50,606	546	-38	508	2.28	-0.15	1.01
1911 April 2/3	24,598	26,330	50,928	111	211	322	0.45	0.81	0.64
1921 June 19/20	24,746	26,998	51,744	148	668	816	0.60	2.54	1.60
1931 April 26/27	23,642	25,387	49,029	-1,104	-1,611	-2,715	-4.46	-5.97	-5.25
1939 Mid-year			46,500			-2,529			-5.16
1951 April 8/9	24,505	26,155	50,660	863	768	4,160	3.65	3.03	8.95
1961 April 23/24	25,328	26,377	51,705	823	222	1,045	3.36	0.85	2.06
1971 April 25/26	29,411	30,350	59,761	4,083	3,973	8,056	16.12	15.06	15.58

NOTES.

1) 1891 (a) Ancient County
(b) Administrative County

All figures 1801-81 for Ancient Counties
All figures 1901-71 for Administrative Counties.

POPULATION 1. TOTAL POPULATION AND INTERCENSAL CHANGES BY SEX, BRECONSHIRE 1801 - 1971.

	POPULATION			INTERCENSAL CHANGE					
				AMOUNT			PER CENT.		
Date of Census	Males	Females	Total	M	F	T	M	F	T
1801 March 9/10	15,709	16,616	32,325						
1811 May 26/27	18,507	19,228	37,735	2,798	2,612	5,410	17.81	15.72	16.74
1821 May 27/28	22,066	21,760	43,826	3,559	2,532	6,091	19.23	13.17	16.14
1831 May 29/30	23,896	23,867	47.763	1,830	2,107	3,937	8.29	9.68	8.98
1841 June 6/7	28.074	27,529	55,603	4,178	3,662	7.840	17.48	15.34	16.41
1851 March 30/31	31,314	30,160	61 474	3,240	2,631	5,871	11.54	9.56	10.56
1861 April 7/8	31,052	30,575	61,627	-262	415	153	-0.84	1.38	0.25
1871 April 2/3	29,928	29,973	59,901	-1,124	-602	-1,726	-3.62	-1.97	-2.80
1881 April 3/4	28,861	28.885	57,746	-1,067	-1,088	-2,155	-3.57	-3.63	-3.60
1891 (1) April 5/6 (a)	28,509	28,522	57,031	-352	-363	-715	-1.22	-1.26	-1.24
1891 (b)	25,633	25,760	51,393						
1901 March 31/Ap.1	27,499	26,714	54,213	1,866	954	2,820	7.28	3.70	5.49
1911 April 2/3	30,366	28,921	59,287	2,867	2,207	5,074	10,43	8.26	9.36
1921 June 19/20	31,030	30,192	61,222	664	1,271	1,935	2.19	4.39	3.26
1931 April 26/27	29,302	28,473	57,775	-1,728	-1,719	-3,447	-5.57	-5.69	-5.63
1939 Mid-year	..	..	52,540			-5,235			-9.06
1951 April 8/9	28,596	27,912	56,508	-706	-561	3,968	-2.41	-1.97	7.55
1961 April 23/24	27,892	27,293	55,185	-704	-619	-1,323	-2.46	-2.22	-2.34
1971 April 25/26	26,606	26,771	53,377	-1,286	-522	-1,808	-4.61	-1.91	-3.28

NOTES.

1) 1891 (a) Ancient County
(b) Administrative County

All figures 1801-81 for Ancient Counties
All figures 1901-71 for Administrative Counties.

POPULATION 1. TOTAL POPULATION AND INTERCENSAL CHANGES BY SEX, CAERNARVONSHIRE 1801 - 1971.

	POPULATION			INTERCENSAL CHANGE					
				AMOUNT			PER CENT.		
Date of Census	Males	Females	Total	M	F	T	M	F	T
1801 March 9/10	19,586	21,935	41,521						
1811 May 26/27	23,525	26,130	49,655	3,939	4,195	8,134	20.11	19.12	19.59
1821 May 27/28	28,553	29,546	58,099	5,028	3,416	8,444	21.37	13.07	17.01
1831 May 29/30	32,343	34,475	66,818	3,790	4,929	8,719	13.27	16.68	15.01
1841 June 6/7	39,625	41,468	81,093	7,282	6,993	14,275	22.51	20.28	21.36
1851 March 30/31	42,978	44,892	87,870	3,353	3,424	6,777	8.46	8.26	8.36
1861 April 7/8	46,820	48,874	95,694	3,842	3,982	7,824	8.94	8.87	8.90
1871 April 2/3	51,874	54,247	106,121 (3)	5,054	5,373	10,427	10.79	10.99	10.90
1881 April 3/4	58,735	60,614	119,349	6,861	6,367	13,228	13.23	11.74	12.47
1891 (1) April 5/6 (a)	56,496	61,708	118,204	-2,239	1,094	1,145	-3.81	1.80	-0.96
1891 (b)	56,047	61,186	117,233 (4)						
1901 March 31/Ap.1	60,392	65,257	125,649 (4)	4,345	4,071	8,416	7.75	6.65	7.18
1911 April 2/3	59,379	65,664	125,043	-1,013	407	-606	-1.68	0.62	-0.48
1921 June 19/20	59,999	70,976	130,975 (5)	620	5,312	5,932	-1.04	8.09	4.74
1931 April 26/27	56,721	64,108	120,829 (5)	-3,278	-6,868	-10,146	5.46	-9.68	-7.75
1939 Mid-year			118,950			- 1,879			-1.56
1951 April 8/9	57,243	66,897	124,140	522	2,789	5,190	0.92	4.35	4.36
1961 April 23/24	56,175	65,592	121,767	-1,068	-1,305	- 2,373	1.87	-1.95	-1.91
1971 April 25/26	57,274	65,790	123,064	1,099	198	1,297	1.96	0.30	1.07

NOTES

1) 1891 (a) Ancient County
(b) Administrative County

All figures 1801-81 for Ancient Counties
All figures 1901-71 for Administrative Counties.

3) 106,121 given in 1871 Census.
106,282 first appears in 1881 Census, General Report - no explanation given. This figure appears on all subsequent censuses - but only as a total - no breakdown into Male and Female.

4) Boundary change 1891/1901 :-
The figure for 1891, for the area as constituted in 1901, is 117,586.

5) Boundary change 1921/3 :-
The figure for 1921, for the area as constituted in 1931, is 128,183. This makes the intercensal change - 7,354.

Similar figures for the county as constituted 1931 :-

1891	115,886
1901	123,481
1911	122,588
1921	128.183

(Source :- 1971 Census County Reports).

POPULATION 1. TOTAL POPULATION AND INTERCENSAL CHANGES BY SEX. CARDIGANSHIRE 1801 -1971.

	POPULATION			INTERCENSAL CHANGE					
				AMOUNT			PER CENT.		
Date of Census	Males	Females	Total	M	F	T	M	F	T
1801 March 9/10	20,408	22,548	42,956						
1811 May 26/27	23,759	26,501	50,260	3,351	3,953	7,304	16.42	17.53	17.00
1821 May 27/28	27,898	29,886	57,784	4,139	3,385	7,524	17.42	12.77	14.97
1831 May 29/30	30,868	33,912	64,780	2,970	4,026	6,996	10.65	13.47	12.11
1841 June 6/7	32,215	36,551	65,766	1,347	2,639	3,986	4.36	7.78	6.15
1851 March 30/31	32,961	37,835	70.796	746	1,284	2,030	2.32	3.51	2.95
1861 April 7/8	33,126	39,119	72.245	165	1,284	1,449	0.50	3.39	2.05
1871 April 2/3	33,396	40.045	73,441	270	926	1,196	0.82	2.37	1.66
1881 April 3/4	31,575	38,695	70,270	-1,821	-1,350	-3,171	-5.45	-3.37	-4.32
1891 (1) April 5/6 (a)	27,365	35,265	62,630	-4,210	-3,430	-7,640	-13.33	-8.86	-10.87
1891 (b)	27,731	35,735	63,467						
1901 March 31/Ap.1	26,877	34,201	61,078	-854	-1,535	-2,389	-3.08	4.30	3.76
1911 April 2/3	26,918	32,961	59,879	41	-1,240	-1,199	0.15	-3.63	-1.96
1921 June 19/20	27,844	33,037	60,881	926	76	1,002	3.44	0.23	1.67
1931 April 26/27	25,428	29,756	55,184	-2,416	-3,281	-5,697	-8.68	-9.93	-9.36
1939 Mid-year			51,650			-3,534			-6.40
1951 April 8/9	25,014	28,264	53,278	-414	-1,492	1,628	-1.63	-5.01	3.15
1961 April 23/24	26,004	27,644	53,648	990	-620	370	3.96	-2.19	0.69
1971 April 25/26	26,528	28,354	54,882	524	710	1,234	2.02	2.57	2.30

NOTES

1) 1891 (a) Ancient County
(b) Administrative County

All figures 1801-81 for Ancient Counties
All figures 1901-71 for Administrative Counties.

POPULATION 1. TOTAL POPULATION AND INTERCENSAL CHANGES BY SEX, CARMARTHENSHIRE 1801 - 1971.

	POPULATION			INTERCENSAL CHANGE					
				AMOUNT			PER CENT.		
Date of Census	Males	Females	Total	M	F	T	M	F	T
1801 March 9/10	31,439	35,878	67,317						
1811 May 26/27	36,080	41,137	77,217	4,641	5,259	9,900	14.76	14.66	14.71
1821 May 27/28	43,577	46,662	90,239	7,497	5,525	13,022	20.78	13.43	16.86
1831 May 29/30	48,683	52,057	100,740	5,106	5,395	10,501	11.72	11.56	11.64
1841 June 6/7	50,676	55,650	106,326	1,993	3,593	5,586	4.09	6.90	5.54
1851 March 30/31	53,076	57,556	110,632	2,400	1,906	4,306	4.74	3.42	4.05
1861 April 7/8	53,229	58,567	111,796	153	1,011	1,164	0.29	1.76	1.05
1871 April 2/3	54,921	60,789	115,710	1,692	2,222	3,914	3.18	3.79	3.50
1881 April 3/4	59,709	65,155	124,864	4,788	4,366	9,154	8.72	7.18	7.91
1891 (1) April 5/6 (a)	62,316	68,250	130,566	2,607	3,095	5,702	4.37	4.75	4.57
1891 (b)	62,316	68,250	130,566						
1901 March 31/Ap.1	64,627	70,701	135 328	2,311	2,451	4,762	3.71	3.59	3.65
1911 April 2/3	80,045	80 361	160,406	15,418	9,660	25,078	23.86	13.66.	18.53
1921 June 19/20	86.731	88.342	175,073	6,686	7,981	14,667	8.35	9.93	9.14
1931 April 26/27	88 923	90,177	179,100	2,192	1,835	4,027	2.53	2.08	2.30
1939 Mid-year			171,980			-7,120			-3.98
1951 April 8/9	84,313	87,721	172,034	-4,610	-2,456	54	-5.18	-2.72	0.03
1961 April 23/24	81,950	86,058	168,008	-2,363	-1,663	-4,026	-2.80	-1.90	-2.34
1971 April 25/26	78,552	83,980	162,562	-3,368	-2,078	-5,446	-4.11	-2.41	-3,24

NOTES

1) 1891 (a) Ancient County
(b) Administrative County

All figures 1801-81 for Ancient Counties
All figures 1901-71 for Administrative Counties.

POPULATION 1. TOTAL POPULATION AND INTERNCENSAL CHANGES BY SEX, DENBIGHSHIRE. 1801 - 1971.

	POPULATION			INTERCENSAL CHANGE					
				AMOUNT			PER CENT.		
Date of Census	Males	Females	Total	M	F	T	M	F	T
1801 March 9/10	29,268	31,031	60,299						
1811 May 26/27	31,139	33,110	64,249	1,871	2,079	3,950	6.39	6.70	6.55
1821 May 27/28	37,932	38,496	76,428	6,793	5,386	12,179	21.82	16.27	18.96
1831 May 29/30	41,153	41,512	82,665	3,221	3,016	6,237	8,49	7.83	8.16
1841 June 6/7	44,236	44,242	88,478	3,083	2,730	5,813	7.49	6.58	7.03
1851 March 30/31	46,708	45,875	92,583	2,472	1,633	4,105	5.59	3.69	4.64
1861 April 7/8	51,098	49,680	100,778	4,390	3,805	8,195	9.40	8.29	8.85
1871 April 2/3	52,866	52,236	105,102 (6)	1,768	2,556	4,324	3.46	5.14	4.29
1881 April 3/4	56,428	55,312	111 740	3,562	3,076	6,638	6.74	5.89	6.32
1891 (1) April 5/6 (a)	59,569	58,303	117,872	3,141	2,991	6,132	5.57	5.41	5.49
1891 (b)	60,018	58,825	118 843 (7)						
1901 March 31/Ap.1	65,969	65,613	131,582 (7)	5,951	6,788	12,739	9.92	11.54	10.72
1911 April 2/3	72,208	72,575	144,783	6,239	6,962	13,201	9.46	10.61	10.03
1921 June 19/20	75,393	79,449	154,842 (8)	3,185	5,874	10,059	4.41	8.09	6.95
1931 April 26/27	77,404	80,244	157,648 (8)	2,011	795	2,806	2.67	1.00	1.81
1939 Mid-year			156,920			-728			-0.46
1951 April 8/9	81,681	89,045	170,726	4,277	8,801	13,806	5.53	10.97	8.80
1961 April 23/24	52,990	91,161	174,151	1,309	2,116	3,425	1.60	2.38	2.01
1971 April 25/26	88,471	96,721	185, 192	5,481	5,560	11,041	6.60	6.10	6.34

NOTES

1) 1891 (a) Ancient County
(b) Administative County

All figures 1801-81 for Ancient Counties
All figures 1901-71 for Administrative Counties.

6) 105,102 given in 1871 Census. Same figure given in 1881 Census Preliminary Report. 104,941 first appears in 1881, General Report - either as a result of an error, or reworking of previous figures - no explanation given.

7) Boundary change 1891/1901 :-
The figure for 1891, for area as constituted in 1901, is 118,979.

8) Boundary change 1921/31 :-
The figure for 1921, for area as constituted in 1931, is 157,634. Intercensal change, relating to this figure is 14 instead of 2,806.

Figures for the county as constituted in 1931 :-

1891	120,679
1901	133,750
1911	147,238
1921	157,634

POPULATION 1. TOTAL POPULATION AND INTERCENSAL CHANGES BY SEX. FLINTSHIRE 1801 - 1971.

	POPULATION				INTERCENSAL CHANGE					
					AMOUNT			PER CENT.		
Date of Census	Males	Females	Total		M	F	T	M	F	T
1801 March 9/10	19,462	20,007	39,469							
1811 May 26/27	22,436	23,501	45,937		2,974	3,491	6,468	15.28	17.45	16.39
1821 May 27/28	26,783	27,110	53,893		4,347	3,609	7,956	19.33	15.36	17.32
1831 May 29/30	30,029	30,215	60,244		3,246	3,105	6,351	12.12	11.45	11.78
1841 June 6/7	33,808	33,111	66,919		3,779	2,896	6,675	12.58	9.58	11.08
1851 March 30/31	34,452	33,704	68,156		644	593	1,237	1.90	1.79	1.85
1861 April 7/8	34,812	34,925	69,737		360	1,221	1,581	1.04	3.62	2.32
1871 April 2/3	38,350	37,962	76,312		3,538	3,037	6,575	10.16	8.70	9.43
1881 April 3/4	40,409	40,178	80,587		2,059	2,216	4,275	5.37	5.84	5.60
1891 (1) April 5/6 (a)	38,242	39,035	77,277		-2,167	-1,143	-3,310	-5.36	-2.84	-4.11
1891 (b)	38,242	39,035	77,277	(10)						
1901 March 31/Ap.1	40,370	41,115	81,485	(10)	2,128	2,080	4,208	5.56	5.33	5.45
1911 April 2/3	45,780	46,925	92,705		5,410	5,810	11,220	13.40	14.13	13.77
1921 June 19/20	51,220	55,397	106,617		5,440	8,472	13,912	11.88	18.05	15.01
1931 April 26/27	54,757	58,132	112,889		3,537	2,735	6,272	6.91	4.94	5.88
1939 Mid-year			121,900				9,011			7.98
1951 April 8/9	71,047	74,232	145,279		16,290	16,100	23,379	29,75	27,70	19.18
1961 April 23/24	72,266	77,816	150,082		1,219	3,584	4,803	1.72	4.83	3.31.
1971 April 25/26	84,704	91,065	175,769		12,438	13,249	25,687	17.21	17.03	17.12

NOTES

1) 1891 (a) Ancient County
(b) Administrative County

All figures 1801-31 for Ancient Counties
All figures 1901-71 for Administrative Cpunties.

10) Boundary change 1891/1901 :-

Figure for 1891, for area as constituted in 1901, is 77,041.

POPULATION 1. TOTAL POPULATION AND INTERCENSAL CHANGES BY SEX. GLAMORGAN 1801 - 1971.

	POPULATION			INTERCENSAL CHANGE					
				AMOUNT			PER CENT.		
Date of Census	Males	Females	Total	M	F	T	M	F	T
1801 March 9/10	33,902	36,977	70,879						
1811 May 26/27	41,365	43,702	85,067	7,463	6,925	14,188	22.01	18.73	20.02
1821 May 27/28	50,795	51,278	102,073	9,430	7.576	17,006	22.80	17.34	19.99
1831 May 29/30	63,284	63,328	126,612	12,489	12,050	24,539	24.59	23.50	24.04
1841 June 6/7	87,869	83 319	171 188	24.585	19,991	44.576	38.85	31.57	35.21
1851 March 30/31	120,748	111,101	231,849	32,879	27,782	60,661	37.42	33.34	35.44
1861 April 7/8	163,499	154,253	317,752	42,751	43,152	85,903	35.41	38.84	37.05
1871 April 2/3	205,660	192,199	397,859	42,161	37,946	80,107	25.79	24.60	25.21
1881 April 3/4	262,579	248,854	511,433	56,919	56,655	113,574	27.68	29.48	28.55
1891 April (1) 5/6 (a)	360,250	326,968	687,218	97,671	78,114	175,785	37.20	31.39	34.37
1891 (b)	360,250	326,968	687,218						
1901 March 31/Ap.1	443,762	416,169	859,931	83,512	89,201	172,713	23.18	27.28	25.13
1911 April 2/3	582,180	538,730	1,120,910	138,418	122,561	260,979	31.19	29.45	30.35
1921 June 19/20	637,627	614,854	1,252,481	55,447	76,124	131,571	9.52	14.13	11.74
1931 April 26/27	616,849	608,868	1,225,717 (11)	-20,778	-5,986	-26,764	-3.26	-0.97	-2.14
1939 Mid-year			1,157,640			-68,077			-5.55
1951 April 8/9	587,717	614,864	1,202,581 (11)	-29,132	5,996	44,941	-0.47	0.98	3.88
1961 April 23/24	600,450	629,278	1,229,728 (12)	12,733	14,414	27,147	2.17	2.34	2.26
1971 April 25/26	612,047	646,683	1,258,730 (12)	11,597	17,405	29,002	1.93	2.77	2.36

NOTES.

1) 1891 (a) Ancient County
(b) Administrative County

All figures 1801-81 for Ancient Counties
All figures 1901-71 for Administrative Counties

11) Boundary Changes 1931/51 :-

The figure for 1931. for the area as constituted in 1951, is 1.229.069. The intercensal change, using this figure, is - 26,484.

Figures for previous years, for areas as constituted immediately before the boundary changes of 1st April 1951 :-

1891	687,758
1901	860,510
1911	1,121,840
1921	1,253,728
1931	1,229,065
1951	1,202,491

12) Boundary Change 1961/71.

Figures for previous years, for areas as constituted 1971 :-

1951	1,202,591
1961	1,229,707

POPULATION 1. TOTAL POPULATION AND INTERCENSAL CHANGES BY SEX, MERIONETH 1801 - 1971.

	POPULATION			INTERCENSAL CHANGE					
				AMOUNT			PER CENT.		
Date of Census	Males	Females	Total	M	F	T	M	F	T
1801 March 9/10	13,896	15,610	29,506						
1811 May 26/27	14,308	16,546	30.854	412	936	1,348	2.92	6.00	4.57
1821 May 27/28	16,479	17,903	34.382	2,171	1,357	3,528	15.17	8.20	11.43
1831 May 29/30	17,194	18,121	25.315	715	218	933	4.34	1.22	2.71
1841 June 6/7	19,279	20.053	39,332	2,085	1,932	4,017	12.13	10.66	11.37
1851 March 30/31	19 151	19,692	38,843	-128	-361	-489	-0.66	-1.80	1.24
1861 April 7/8	19,145	19,818	38,963	-6	126	120	-0.03	0.64	0.31
1871 April 2/3	23,261	23,337	46,598	4,116	3,519	7,635	21.50	17.76	19.60
1881 April 3/4	26,269	25,769	52,038	3,008	2,432	5,440	12.93	10.42	11.67
1891 (1) April 5/6 (a)	24,035	25,177	49,212	-2,234	-592	-2,826	-8.50	-2.30	-5.43
1891 (b)	24,035	25,177	49,212 (13)						
1901 March 31/Ap.1	23,824	25,028	48,852	-211	-149	-360	-0.88	-0.59	-0.73
1911 April 2/3	21,802	23,763	45,565	-2,022	-1,265	-3,287	-8.49	-5.05	-6.73
1921 June 19/20	21,035	24,052	45,087	-767	289	-478	-3.52	1.22	-1.05
1931 April 26/27	20,938	22,263	43,201	-97	-1,789	-1,886	-0.46	-7.44	-4.18
1939 Mid-year			39,860			-3,341			-7.73
1951 April 8/9	20,940	20,525	41,465	2	-1,738	1,605	0.01	-7.81	4.03
1961 April 23/24	18,797	19,513	38,310	-2,143	-1,012	-3.155	-10.23	-4.93	-7.61
1971 April 25/26	16,764	18,566	35,330	-2,033	-947	-2,980	-10.82	-4.85	-7.78

NOTES

1) 1891 (a) Ancient County
(b) Administrative County

All figures 1801-81 for Ancient Counties
All figures 1901-71 for Administrative Counties

13) Boundary Change 1891/1901 :-

Figure for 1891, for area as constituted in 1901, is 48,859.

POPULATION 1. TOTAL POPULATION AND INTERCENSAL CHANGES BY SEX. MONMOUTH 1801 - 1971.

	POPULATION				INTERCENSAL CHANGE					
					AMOUNT			PER CENT.		
Date of Census	Males	Females	Total		M	F	T	M	F	T
1801 March 9/10	22,159	23,409	45,568							
1811 May 26/27	30,976	31,129	62,105		8,817	7,720	16,537	39.79	32.98	36.29
1821 May 27/28	39,214	36,587	75,801		8,238	5,458	13,696	25.59	17.53	22.05
1831 May 29/30	51,090	47,036	95,126		11,876	10,449	22,325	30.29	28.56	29.45
1841 June 6/7	70,608	63,760	134,368		19,518	16,724	36,242	38.20	35.56	36.93
1851 March 30/31	82,349	75,069	157,418		11,741	11,309	23,050	16.63	17.74	17.15
1861 April 7/8	89,637	84,996	174,633		7,288	9,927	17,215	8.85	13.22	10.94
1871 April 2/3	101,448	94,000	195,448		11,811	9,004	20,815	13.18	10.59	11.92
1881 April 3/4	108,262	103,005	211,267		6,814	9,005	15,819	6.72	9.58	8.09
1891 April 5/6 (a) (1)	130,757	121,659	252,416		22,495	18,654	41,149	20.78	18.11	19.48
1891 (b)	133,633	124,421	258,054	(14)						
1901 March 31/Ap.1	153 384	144.692	298.076	(14)	19.751	20,271	40,022	14.78	16.29	15.51
1911 April 2/3	207,429	188.290	395,719		54,045	43,598	97.643	35.24	30.13	32.76
1921 June 19/20	232.402	218 392	450.794		24,973	30,102	55,075	12.04	15.99	13.92
1931 April 26/27	222,438	212,520	434,958	(15)	-9,964	-5,872	-15,836	-4.29	-2.69	-3.51
1939 Mid-year			399,640				-35,318			-8.12
1951 April 8/9	210,997	214,118	425,115	(15)	-11,441	1,598	25,475	-5.14	0.75	6.37
1961 April 23/24	222,060	222,619	444,679	(16)	11,063	8,501	19,564	5.24	-3.97	4.60
1971 April 25/26	228,009	234,162	462,171	(16)	5,949	11,543	17,492	2.68	5.19	3.93

NOTES

1) 1891 (a) Ancient County
(b) Administrative County

All figures 1801-81 for Ancient Counties
All figures 1901-71 for Administrative Counties

14) Boundary change 1891/1901 :-
Sum of counties in 1891, for areas as constituted 1901, is 258,133

15) Boundary change 1931/51 :-

Figure for 1931, for area as constituted at 31st March, 1951, is 431,610; this makes the intercensal change - 6,495.

Figures for previous years, for area as constituted at 31st March, 1951 :-

1891	257,593
1901	297 497
1911	394,789
1921	449,547
1931	431,610

(Source :- 1971 Census)

There was also a boundary change 1st April 1951. The figure for 31st March 1951 is 425,205.

16) Boundary change :- 1961/71.

Figures for 1961 and 1951, for areas as constituted in 1971 are : -

1951	425,105
1961	444,700

POPULATION 1. TOTAL POPULATION AND INTERCENSAL CHANGES BY SEX. MONTGOMERYSHIRE 1801 - 1971.

	POPULATION			INTERCENSAL CHANGE					
				AMOUNT			PER CENT.		
Date of Census	Males	Females	Total	M	F	T	M	F	T
1801 March 9/10	23,008	25,176	48,184						
1811 May 26/27	25,493	26,691	52,184	2,485	1,515	4,000	10.80	6.02	8.30
1821 May 27/28	29,918	30,327	60,245	4,425	3,636	8,061	17.36	13.62	15.45
1831 May 29/30	33,233	33,611	66,844	3,315	3,284	6,599	11.08	10.83	10.95
1841 June 6/7	34,475	35,132	69,607	1,242	1,521	2,763	3.74	4.53	4.13
1851 March 30/31	33,634	33,701	67,335	-841	-1,431	-2,272	-2.44	-4.07	-3.26
1861 April 7/8	33,870	33,049	66,919	236	-652	-416	0.70	-1.93	-0.62
1871 April 2/3	34,095	33,528	67,623	225	479	704	0.66	1.45	1.05
1881 April 3/4	33,004	32,714	65,718	-1,091	-814	-1,905	-3.20	-2.43	-2.82
1891 (1) April 5/6 (a)	28,222	29,781	58,003	-4,782	-2,933	-7,715	-14.49	-8.97	-11.74
1891 (b)	28,222	29,781	58,003						
1901 March 31/Ap.1	26,790	28,111	54,901	-1,432	-1,670	-3,102	-5.07	-5.61	-5.35
1911 April 2/3	26,232	26,914	53,146	-558	-1,197	-1,755	-2.08	-4.26	-3.20
1921 June 19/20	25,469	25,794	51,263	-763	-1,120	-1,883	-2.91	-4.16	-3.54
1931 April 26/27	24,030	24,443	48,473	-1,439	-1,351	-2,790	-5.65	-5.24	-5.44
1939 Mid-year			44,830			-3,643			-7.52
1951 April 8/9	22,902	23,088	45,990	-1,128	-1,355	1,160	-4.69	-5.54	2.59
1961 April 23/24	22,077	22,088	44,165	-825	1,000	-1,825	-3.60	-4.33	-3.97
1971 April 25/26	21,469	21,650	43,119	-608	-438	-1,046	-2.75	-1.92	2.37

NOTES

1) 1891 (a) Ancient County
(b) Administrative County

All figures 1801-81 for Ancient Counties
All figures 1901-71 for Administrative Counties

POPULATION 1. TOTAL POPULATION AND INTERCENSAL CHANGES BY SEX. PEMBROKESHIRE 1801 - 1971.

	POPULATION			INTERCENSAL CHANGE AMOUNT			PER CENT.		
Date of Census	Males	Females	Total	M	F	T	M	F	T
1801. March 9/10	25,400	30 874	56,280						
1811 May 26/27	27,453	33 162	60,615	2,047	2,288	4,335	8.06	7.41	7.70
1821 May 27/28	34,430	39,358	73,788	6,977	6,196	13,173	25,43	18.68	21.73
1831 May 29/30	37,952	43,473	81,425	3,522	4,115	7,637	10.23	10.46	10.35
1841 June 6/7	40,250	47,794	88,044	2,298	4,321	6,619	6.06	9.94	8.13
1851 March 30/31	43,675	50,465	94,140	3,425	2,671	6,096	8.51	5.59	6.92
1861 April 7/8	45,930	50,348	96,278	2,255	-117	2,138	5.16	-0.23	2.27
1871 April 2/3	42,782	49,216	91,998	-3,148	-1,132	-4,280	-6.85	-2.25	-4.45
1881 April 3/4	43,449	48,375	91,824	667	-841	-174	1.56	-1.71	-0.19
1891 (1) April 5/6 (a)	41,685	47,448	89,133	-1,764	-927	-2,691	-4.06	-1.92	-2.93
1891 (b)	41,319	46,977	88,296						
1901 March 31/Ap.1	41,617	46,277	87,894	298	-700	-402	0.72	-1.49	-0.46
1911 April 2/3	43,462	46,498	89,960	1,845	221	2,066	4.43	0.48	2.35
1921 June 19/20	45,046	46,932	91,978	1,584	434	2,018	3.64	0.93	2.24
1931 April 26/27	42,808	44 398	87,206	-2,238	-2,534	-4,772	-4.97	-5.40	-5.19
1939 Mid-year			83,270			-3,936			-4.51
1951 April 8/9	45.041	45,865	90,906	2,233	1,467	7,636	5.22	3.30	7.97
1961 April 23/24	46.601	47.523	94,124	1,560	1,658	3,218	3.46	3.61	3.54
1971 April 25/26	48,569	50,399	98,968	1,968	2,876	4,844	4.22	6.05	5.15

NOTES

1) 1891 (a) Ancient County
(b) Administrative County

All figures 1801-81 for Ancient Counties
All figures 1901-71 for Administrative Counties

POPULATION 1. TOTAL POPULATION AND INTERCENSAL CHANGES BY SEX. RADNORSHIRE 1801 - 1971.

	POPULATION			INTERCENSAL CHANGE					
				AMOUNT			PER CENT.		
Date of Census	Males	Females	Total	M	F	T	M	F	T
1801 March 9/10	9,389	9,746	19,135						
1811 May 26/27	9,886	10,531	20,417	497	785	1,282	5.29	8.05	6.70
1821 May 27/28	11,306	11,227	22,533	1,420	696	2,116	14.36	6.61	10.36
1831 May 29/30	12,502	12,241	24,743	1,196	1,014	2,210	10.58	9.03	9.81
1841 June 6/7	12,883	12,575	25,458	381	334	715	3.05	2.73	2.89
1851 March 30/31	12,693	12 023	24,716	-190	-552	-742	-1.47	4.39	-2.91
1861 April 7/8	13.140	12.242	25,382	447	219	666	3.52	1.82	2.69
1871 April 2/3	13,067	12,363	25,430	-73	121	48	-0.56	0.99	0.19
1881 April 3/4	11,939	11,589	23,528	-1,128	-774	-1,902	-8.63	-6.26	-7.48
1891 April 5/6 (a) (1)	10,869	10,922	21,791	-1,070	-667	-1,737	-8.96	-5.76	-7.38
1891 (b)	10,869	10,922	21,791						
1901 March 31/Ap.1	11,860	11,421	23,281	991	499	1,490	9.12	4.57	6.84
1911 April 2/3	11,340	11,250	23,590	-520	-171	-691	-4.38	-1.50	-2.97
1921 June 19/20	11,452	12,065	23,517	112	815	927	0.99	7.24	4.10
1931 April 26/27	10,565	10,758	21,323	-887	1,307	2,194	-7.75	-10.83	-9.33
1939 Mid-year			19,520			-1,803			-8.46
1951 April 8/9	10,107	9,886	19,993	-458	-872	473	-4.34	-8.11	2.42
1961 April 23/24	9,174	9,297	18,471	-933	-589	-1,522	-9.23	-5.96	-7.61
1971 April 25/26	9,073	9,206	18,279	-101	-91	-192	-1.10	-0.98	-1.04

NOTES

1) 1891 (a) Ancient County
(b) Administrative County

All figures 1801-81 for Ancient Counties
All figures 1901-71 for Administrative Counties

POPULATION 2. Females per 1,000 Males. Wales and each County 1801 - 1971.

	WALES	ANGL.	BRECS.	CAERNS.	CARDS.	CARMS.	DENBS.	FLINTS.	GLAM.	MERION.	MONS.	MONTS.	PEMBS.	RAD.
1801	1101.75	1143.01.	1057.74	1119.93	1104.86	1141.19	1060.24	1028.00	1090.70	1123.34	1056.41	1094.23	1215.22.	1038.02
1811	1088.71	1123.65	1038.96	1110.73	1115.41	1140.16	1063.30	1047.47	1056.50	1156.42	1004.94	1046.99	1207.96	1065.24
1821	1032.46	1068.62	986.13	1034.78	1071.26	1070.79	1014.87	1012.21	1008.51	1086.41	933.01	1013.67	1143.13	993.01
1831	1029.16	1058.57	998.79	1065.92	1098.61	1069.31	1008.72	1006.19	1000.70	1053.91	920.65	1011.37	1145.47	979.12
1841	1018·00	1087.92	980.59	1046.51	1134.60	1098.15	1000.14	979.38	948.22	1040.15	903.01	1019.06	1187.43	976.09
1851	999.07	1040.30	963.15	1044.53	1147.87	1084.41	982.17	978.29	920.11	1028.25	911.60	1001.99	1155.47	947.22
1861	1004.85	1076.86	984.64	1043.87	1180.92	1100.33	972.25	1003.25	943.45	1035.15	948.22	975.76	1096.19	931.66
1871	1000.69	1091.80	1001.50	1045.75	1199.10	1106.84	988.08	989.88	934.55	1003.27	926.58	983.37	1150.39	946.12
1881	998.90	1048.20	1000.83	1031.99	1225.49	1091.21	980.22.	994.28	947.73	980.97	951.44	991.21	1113.37	970.68
1891[1] a	985.36	1092.56	1000.46	1092.25	1288.69	1095.22	978.75	1020.74	907.61	1047.51	930.42	1055.24	1138.25	1004.88
1891 b	985.36	1092.56	1004.95	1091.69	1288.67	1095.22	980.12	1020.74	907.61	1047.51	931.06	1055.24	1136.93	1004.88
1901	990.07	1066.65	971.45	1080.56	1272.50	1094.12	994.60	1018.45	937.82	1050.54	943.33	1049.31	1111.97	962.98
1911	965.45	1070.41	952.41	1105.85	1224.50	1003.95	1005.08	1025.01	925.37	1089.95	907.73	1026.00	1069.85	992.06
1921	997.36	1091.01	972.99	1182.95	1186.50	1018.57	1053.80	1081.55	964.28	1143.43	939.72	1012.76	1041.87	1053.53
1931	1004.42	1073.81	971.71	1130.23	1170.21	1014.10	1036.69	1061.64	987.06	1063.28	955.41	1017.19	1037.14.	1018.27
1939	1025.24	1073.81	971.71	1130.23	1170.21	1014.10	1036.69	1061.64	987.06	1063.28	955.41	1017.19	1037.14	1018.27
1951	1046.03	1067.33	976.08	1168.65	1129.93	1040.42	1090.16	1044.83	1046.19	980.18	1014.79	1008.12	1018.29	978.13
1961	1046.83	1041.42	978.52	1167.64	1063.07	1050.13	1098.46	1076.80	1048.01	1038.09	1002.52	1000.50	1019.78	1013.41
1971	1057.39	1031.93	1006.20	1148.69	1068.83	1068.69	1093.25	1075.10	1056.59	1107.49	1029.99	1008.43	1037.68	1014.66

The general notes on Sources etc. of Table 1 apply for Table 2.

Notes.

1. 1891 a) Ancient County. b) Administrative County. All figures for 1801-81 are on basis of Ancient Counties, and for 1901-71 on basis of Administrative counties.

POPULATION 3. AGE AND MARITAL CONDITION, BY SEX, WALES 1841 - 1971

1841

Age last birthday	PERSONS	MALES Total	MALES S	MALES M	MALES W	MALES D	FEMALES Total	FEMALES S	FEMALES M	FEMALES W	FEMALES D
all ages	1,001,199	495,187	..	..	..	..	506,012	..	..	..	..
0-4	134,124	67,277	..	..	..	..	66,847	..	..	..	..
5-9	121,646	61,289	..	..	..	..	60,357	..	..	..	..
10-14	110,733	56,346	..	..	..	..	54,387	..	..	..	..
15-19	104,905	52,311	..	..	..	..	52,594	..	..	..	..
20-24	97,592	47,958	..	..	..	..	49,631	..	..	..	..
25-29	81,161	40,486	..	..	..	..	40,675	..	..	..	..
30-34	69,415	34,803	..	..	..	..	34,612	..	..	..	..
35-39	53,128	26,878	..	..	..	..	26,250	..	..	..	..
40-44	50,308	25,026	..	..	..	..	25,282	..	..	..	..
45-49	39,655	19,244	..	..	..	..	20,411	..	..	..	..
50-54	39,508	18,992	..	..	..	..	20,516	..	..	..	..
55-59	27,281	13,021	..	..	..	..	14,260	..	..	..	..
60-64	29,849	13,694	..	..	..	..	16,155	..	..	..	..
65-69	18,197	8,200	..	..	..	..	9,920	..	..	..	..
70-74	15,109	6,659	..	..	..	..	8,450	..	..	..	..
75-79	9,074	3,941	..	..	..	..	5,133	..	..	..	..
80-84	6,422	2,585	..	..	..	..	3,837	..	..	..	..
85-89	2,379	943	..	..	..	..	1,436	..	..	..	..
90-94	731	253	..	..	..	..	478	..	..	..	..
95-99	182	56	..	..	..	..	126	..	..	..	..
100+	41	11	..	..	..	..	30	..	..	..	..
not specified	1,916	1,609	..	..	..	..	307	..	..	..	..

POPULATION 3. AGE AND MARITAL CONDITION, BY SEX, WALES 1841-1971

1851

Age last birthday	PERSONS	MARITAL CONDITION									
		MALES					FEMALES				
		Total	S	M	W	D	Total	S	M	W	D
all ages	1,188,914	594,793	382,568	189,580	22,645		594,121	358,364	192,256	43,501	
0-4	155,860	78,910	78,910				76,950	76,950			
5-9	144,119	72,680	72,680				71,439	71,439			
10-14	130,488	66.215	66,215				64,273	64,273			
15-19	116,767	59,352	59,194	155	3		57,415	56,467	939	9	
20-24	106,817	53,588	45,404	8,061	123		53,229	38,890	14,098	241	
25-29	92,298	46,121	23,774	21,828	519		46,177	19,127	26,218	832	
30-34	80,004	40,764	12,466	27,270	1,028		39,240	9,270	28,485	1,485	
35-39	70,384	35,891	7,332	27,153	1,406		34,493	5,677	26,804	2,012	
40-44	60,639	30,708	4,969	24,036	1,703		29,931	3,777	23,593	2,561	
45-49	50,720	25,406	3,471	20,256	1,679		25,314	2,741	19,563	3,010	
50-54	45,337	22,723	2,697	17,899	2,127		22,614	2,320	16,465	3,829	
55-59	36,247	17,739	1,833	13,801	2,105		18,508	1,822	12,532	4,154	
60-64	34,117	16,088	1,461	11,874	2,753		18,029	1,813	10,417	5,799	
65-69	23,810	10,899	890	7,590	2,419		12,911	1,276	6,319	5,316	
70-74	18,715	8,367	648	5,177	2,542		10,348	1,069	3,903	5,376	
75-79	12,029	5,185	346	2,817	2,022		6,844	736	1,952	4,156	
80-84	6,988	2,802	183	1.234	1,385		4,186	483	759	2,944	
85-89	2,580	1,009	71	343	595		1,571	159	169	1,243	
90-94	777	272	20	63	189		505	66	29	410	
95-99	179	66	4	21	41		113	9	9	95	
100+	39	8		2	6		31		2	29	

POPULATION 3. AGE AND MARITAL CONDITION, BY SEX, WALES 1841-1971

1861

Age last birthday	PERSONS	MARITAL CONDITION									
		MALES					FEMALES				
		Total	S	M	W	D	Total	S	M	W	D
all ages	1,312,834	655,145	411,386	218,511	25,248		657,689	388,689	220,287	48,713	
0-4	176,635	88,791	88,791				87,844	87,844			
5-9	155,503	78,323	78,323				77,180	77,180			
10-14	141,154	71,912	71,912				69,242	69,242			
15-19	130,282	66,581	66,320	255	6		63,701	62,234	1,451	16	
20-24	116,721	57,528	47,053	10,330	145		59,193	41,061	17,843	289	
25-29	97,531	48,137	22,139	25,435	563		49,394	18,245	39,256	893	
30-34	86,979	43,399	11,549	30,871	979		43,580	9,529	32,355	1,696	
35-39	76,510	38,267	7,139	29,820	1,308		38,243	5,974	30,001	2,268	
40-44	68,978	35,076	5,384	28,011	1,681		33,902	4,174	26,716	3,012	
45-49	61,200	30,563	3,617	24,915	2,031		30,637	3,192	23,813	3,632	
50-54	52,885	26,643	2,929	21,269	2,445		26,242	2,605	19,268	4,369	
55-59	40,592	20,387	2,006	15,942	2,439		20,205	1,875	13,693	4,637	
60-64	37,316	18,232	1,850	13,220	3,162		19,084	1,891	10,834	6,359	
65-69	26,188	12,232	1,046	8,400	2,786		13,956	1,253	6,906	5,797	
70-74	20,352	9,098	676	5,554	2,868		11,254	1,113	4,242	5,899	
75-79	13,051	5,687	382	2,852	2,453		7,364	672	1,938	4,754	
80-84	7,317	2,971	197	1,210	1,564		4,346	409	730	3,207	
85-89	2,691	1,037	58	350	629		1,654	115	195	1,344	
90-94	751	236	13	66	157		515	60	36	419	
95-99	171	37	2	9	26		134	19	10	105	
100+	27	8		2	6		19	2		17	

POPULATION 3. AGE AND MARITAL CONDITION, BY SEX, WALES 1841-1971

1871

Age last birthday	PERSONS	MARITAL CONDITION									
		MALES					FEMALES				
		Total	S	M	W	D	Total	S	M	W	D
all ages	1,421,670	710,601	447 173	235.931	27,497		711,069	418,212	238,079	54,778	
0-4	193,659	97,232	97,232				96,427	96,427			
5-9	174,139	87,819	87,819				86,320	86,320			
10-14	155,524	78,680	78,680				76,844	76,844			
15-19	137,607	71,174	70,843	329	2		66,433	64,635	1,785	13	
20-24	121,386	61,358	49,300	11,915	143		60,028	40,318	19,386	324	
25-29	105,114	51,966	23,618	27,735	613		53,148	19,201	32,822	1,125	
30-34	92,838	45,874	12,558	32,248	1,068		46,964	9,940	35,023	2,001	
35-39	79,679	39,648	7,272	30,994	1,382		40,031	6,194	31,309	2,528	
40-44	72,628	36,166	5,368	29,068	1,730		36,462	4,423	28,645	3,394	
45-49	64,654	32,138	3,907	26,171	2,060		32,516	3,311	25,020	4,185	
50-54	57,983	29,230	3,308	23,325	2,597		28,753	2,827	20,920	5,006	
55-59	47,905	23,996	2,400	18,813	2,783		23,909	2,127	16,113	5,669	
60-64	42,021	20,465	2,043	15,018	3,404		21,556	2,100	12,279	7,177	
65-69	29,153	13,784	1,267	9,334	3,183		15,369	1,327	7,428	6,614	
70-74	21,799	10,198	848	6,043	3,307		11,601	1,017	4,252	6,332	
75-79	13,601	6,126	435	3,137	2,554		7,475	628	2,038	4,809	
80-84	8,049	3,296	202	1,348	1,746		4,753	392	841	3,520	
85-89	2,942	1,144	59	370	715		1,798	140	173	1,485	
90-94	801	259	13	67	179		542	37	40	465	
95-99	167	43		16	27		124	4	5	115	
100+	21	5	1		4		16			16	

POPULATION 3. AGE AND MARITAL CONDITION, BY SEX, WALES 1841-1971

1881

Age last birthday	PERSONS	MALES Total	MALES S	MALES M	MALES W	MALES D	FEMALES Total	FEMALES S	FEMALES M	FEMALES W	FEMALES D
all ages	1,577,559	789,074	501,012	258,345	29,717		788,485	467,154	260,792	60,539	
0-4	212,181	106,165	106,165				106,016	106,016			
5-9	197,015	98,897	98,897				98,118	98,118			
10-14	176,895	89,239	89,239				87,656	87,656			
15-19	156,490	81,230	80,899	326	5		75,260	73,531	1,713	16	
20-24	136,099	69,143	56,135	12,832	176		66,956	44,671	21,956	329	
25-29	117,376	59,429)	40,434	68,395	1,886		57,947)	30,309	74,855	3,038	
30-34	101,541	51,286)					50.255)				
35-39	89,355	44,595)	14,051	66,883	3,593		44,760)	11,648	67,078	6,659	
40-44	80,557	39,932)					40,625)				
45-49	68,927	33,695)	7,425	51,976	4,952		35,232)	6,775	49,254	10,706	
50-54	62,161	30,658)					31,503)				
55-59	50,660	24,922)	4,678	35,796	6,742		25,738)	4,532	30,160	14,640	
60-64	45,888	22,294)					23,594)				
65-69	33,316	15,709)	3,089	22,137	12,363		17,607)	3,898	15,776	25,151	
70-74	23,836	10,977)					12,859)				
75-79	14,368	6,405)					7,963)				
80-84	7,384	3,143)					4,241)				
85-89	2,675	1,079)					1,596)				
90-94	652	229)					423)				
95-99	157	39)					118)				
100+	26	8)					18)				

POPULATION 3. AGE AND MARITAL CONDITION, BY SEX, WALES 1841-1971

1891

Age last birthday	PERSONS	MARITAL CONDITION									
		MALES					FEMALES				
		Total	S	M	W	D	Total	S	M	W	D
all ages	1.776,405	894,509	569,214	292,235	33,060		881,896	522,319	292,686	76,891	
0-4	221,351	110,600					110,751				
5-9	207,391	104,049					103,342				
10-14	197,227	99,072					98,155				
15-19	185,409	96,944	96,513	423	8		88,465	86,268	2,187	10	
20-24	166,349	85,517	70,185	15,148	184		80,832	54,476	26,114	242	
25-29	141,702	72,336)	52,680	79,238	1,818		69,366)	38,627	86,016	2,791	
30-34	119,468	61,400)					58,068)				
35-39	104,857	54,022)					50,835)				
		)	18,159	77,858	3,988		)	13,501	74,883	6,714	
40-44	90,246	45,983)					44,263)				
45-49	79,966	39,763)	9,205	59,298	5,921		40,203)	7,910	55,695	12,107	
50-54	70,170	34,661)					35,509)				
55-59	54,729	26,777)					27,952)				
		)	5,302	37.247	7,382		)	5,028	31,761	16,598	
60-64	48,589	23,154)					25,435)				
65-69	36,034	16,742)					19,292)				
70-74	25,851	11,811)					14,040)				
75-79	15,892	7.059)					8,833)				
		)	3,449	23,023	13,759		)	4,261	16,030	28,429	
80-84	7,778	3,296)					4,482)				
85-89	2,683	1,060)					1,623)				
90-94	586	223)					363)				
95-99	105	34)					71)				
100+	22	6)					16)				

POPULATION 3. AGE AND MARITAL CONDITION, BY SEX, WALES 1841-1971

1901

Age last birthday	PERSONS	MALES Total	MALES S	MALES M	MALES W	MALES D	FEMALES Total	FEMALES S	FEMALES M	FEMALES W	FEMALES D
all ages	2,012,876	1,011,458	634,499	339,802			1,001,418	567,904	342,719		
0-4	245,231	122,496	122,496				122,735	122,735			
5-9	229,638	114,806	114,806				114,832	114,832			
10-14	209,570	105,178	105,178				104,392	104,392			
15-19	198,104	101,931	101,636	291	4		96,173	94,211	1,954	8	
20-24	187,107	93,861	78,908	14,812	141		93,426	64,929	28,104	213	
25-29	172,581	87,258	65,750	96,247	2,074		85,323	48,231	107,589	2,721	
30-34	150,031	76,813					73,218				
35-39	129,407	66,663	23,340	94,424	4,383		62,744	17,658	90,502	6,826	
40-44	107,726	55,484					52,242				
45-49	93,202	47,739	12,099	69,041	6,824		45,463	9,358	62,706	12,689	
50-54	79,515	40,225					39,290				
55-59	63,831	31,335	6,339	42,165	8,939		32,496	5,931	35,927	18,921	
60-64	54,391	26,108					28,283				
65-69	38,184	17,784	2,953	18,127	8,827		20,400	3,275	13,345	18,457	
70-74	26,800	12,123					14,677				
75-79	16,302	7,129	863	4,385	5,154		9,173	1,247	2,459	10,177	
80-84	7,983	3,273					4,170				
85-89	2,593	1,018	131	310	811		1,575	166	133	1,722	
90-94	570	199					371				
95-99	95	27					68				
100+	15	8					7				

POPULATION 3. AGE AND MARITAL CONDITION, BY SEX, WALES 1841-1971

1911

Age last birthday	PERSONS	MALES Total	MALES S	MALES M	MALES W	MALES D	FEMALES Total	FEMALES S	FEMALES M	FEMALES W	FEMALES D
all ages	2,420,921	1,231,739	765 543	421.421			1,189,182	686,399	423,827		
0-4	285,428	143,089	143.089				142,339	142,339			
5-9	269,636	135 161	135 161				134,475	134,475			
10-14	242,394	121.123	121,123				121,271	121,271			
15-19	228,879	117,700	117,432	263	5		111,179	109,123	2,033	23	
20-24	214,805	111,350	95,325	15,863	162		103,455	71,839	31,432	184	
25-29	205,179	106,587	56,545	49,336	706		98,592	37,262	60,502	828	
30-34	187,313	96,786	31,147	64,138	1,501		90,527	20,332	68,426	1,769	
35-39	171,568	89,622	20,501	66,807	2,314		81,946	13,768	65,303	2,875	
40-44	144,344	75,225	13,674	58,538	3,013		69,119	9,655	55,237	4,227	
45-49	121,505	63,281	10,052	49,425	3,804		58,224	7,461	44,870	5,893	
50-54	97,897	50,487	7,295	38,601	4,591		47,410	5,588	34,175	7,647	
55-59	77,798	39,808	5,053	29,710	5,045		37,990	4,039	24,944	9,007	
60-64	61,382	30,685	3,851	21,192	5,642		30,697	3,169	17,105	10,423	
65-69	48,485	23,021	2,659	14,460	5,902		25,464	2,468	11,114	11,882	
70-74	33,918	15,147	1,522	8,122	5,503		18,771	1,915	5,796	11,060	
75-79	18,282	7,928	725	3,507	3,696		10,354	1,014	2,161	7,179	
80-84	8,480	3,383	288	1,174	1,921		5,097	502	612	3,983	
85-89	2,916	1,103	82	250	771		1,813	141	105	1,567	
90-94	613	223	15	31	177		390	32	10	348	
95-99	85	27	3	4	20		58	5	2	51	
100+	14	3	1		2		11	1		10	

POPULATION 3. AGE AND MARITAL CONDITION, BY SEX, WALES 1841-1971

1921

Age last birthday	PERSONS	MARITAL CONDITION									
		MALES					FEMALES				
		Total	S	M	W	D	Total	S	M	W	D
all ages	2,656,474	1,329,994	778,357	503,027	48,180	430	1,326,480	727,198	505,314	93,665	303
0-4	265,165	134,329	134,329				130,836	130.836			
5-9	271,387	136,507	136,507				134,880	134,880			
10-14	273,253	136,794	136,794				136,459	136,459			
15-19	254,136	128,879	128,378	490	11		125,257	122,124	3,120	11	2
20-24	222,823	109,860	90,534	19,159	150	17	112,963	76,199	36,371	384	9
25-29	210,168	102,578	50,240	51,616	685	37	107,590	39,477	66,198	1,873	42
30-34	193,014	95,558	26,446	67,756	1,285	71	97,456	22,108	72,216	3,086	46
35-39	185,295	92,766	18,625	72,117	1,956	68	92,529	15,821	72,441	4,230	37
40-44	170,006	85,204	14,527	68,027	2,590	60	84,802	12,236	67,282	5,236	48
45-49	158,380	82,168	12,709	65,531	3,877	51	76,212	10,114	59,291	6,770	37
50-54	131,294	68,037	9,759	53,402	4,831	45	63,257	7,964	46,608	8,658	27
55-59	104,175	53,666	7,295	40,695	5,652	24	50,509	6,024	34,025	10,431	29
60-64	79,481	39,922	5,133	28,444	6,318	27	39,559	4,779	22,833	11,937	10
65-69	60,351	29,774	3,549	19,303	6,909	13	30,577	3,425	13,961	13,183	8
70-74	39,416	18,160	1,992	10,125	6,032	11	21,256	2,434	7,157	11,660	5
75-79	23,185	9,984	985	4,529	4,468	2	13,201	1,404	2,840	8,956	1
80-84	10,744	4,333	408	1,502	2,420	3	6,411	661	795	4,955	
85-89	3,399	1,246	125	280	841		2,153	192	151	1,810	
90-94	677	195	20	45	129	1	482	56	21	403	2
95+	125	34	2	6	26		91	5	4	82	

POPULATION 3. AGE AND MARITAL CONDITION, BY SEX, WALES 1841-1971

1931

Age last birthday	PERSONS	MALES Total	MALES S	MALES M	MALES W	MALES D	FEMALES Total	FEMALES S	FEMALES M	FEMALES W	FEMALES D
all ages	2,593,332	1,293,805	711,328	528,803	53,120	554	1,299,527	660,289	535,069	103,541	
0-4	204,591	103,003	103,003				101,588	101,588			
5-9	243,196	122,865	122,865				120,331	120,331			
10-14	242,436	122,547	122,547				119,889	119,889			
15-19	227,529	118,940	118,658	278	4		108,589	106,134	2,448	7	
20-24	210,244	106,025	92,958	12,981	84	2	104,219	74,170	29,873	165	11
25-29	206,236	101,837	52,875	48,423	515	24	104,399	40,954	62,672	706	67
30-34	193,843	94,387	25,538	67,661	1,121	67	99,456	22,783	74,819	1,761	93
35-39	182,289	88,119	15,830	70,614	1,581	94	94,170	16,268	74,302	3,486	114
40-44	168,469	82,743	12,032	68,310	2,322	79	85,726	12,989	67,268	5,364	105
45-49	160,023	79,498	11,008	65,148	3,260	82	80,525	10,849	62,196	7,400	80
50-54	146,942	73,180	9,752	58,848	4,513	67	73,762	9,413	54,677	9,604	68
55-59	129,647	66,293	8,539	51,411	6,295	48	63,354	7,772	43,478	12,068	36
60-64	102,992	52,254	6,474	38 040	7,708	32	50,738	6,137	30,447	14,129	25
65-69	77,361	38,285	4,738	25,159	8,360	28	39,076	4,832	18,556	15,675	13
70-74	51,284	23,963	2,678	13,736	7,531	18	27,321	3,363	9,684	14,264	10
75-79	28,801	13.014	1,294	6,001	5,710	9	15,787	1,779	3,522	10,482	4
80-84	12,500	5,118	393	1,781	2,941	3	7,382	736	910	5,734	2
85-89	3,977	1,434	117	357	959	1	2,543	236	194	2,113	
90-94	832	259	24	49	186		573	56	20	497	
95+	140	41	5	6	30		99	10	3	86	

POPULATION 3. AGE AND MARITAL CONDITION, BY SEX, WALES 1841-1971

1951

Age last birthday	PERSONS	MARITAL CONDITION									
		MALES					FEMALES				
		Total	S	M	W	D	Total	S	M	W	D
all ages	2,598,675	1,270,103	580,313	635,056	51,133	3,601	1,328,572	542,799	642,297	138,541	4,935
0-4	221,268	113,035	113,035				108,233	108,233			
5-9	191,358	97,529	97,529				93,829	93,829			
10-14	177,866	90,561	90,561				87,305	87,305			
15-19	166,627	81,951	81,596	352		3	84,676	80,945	3,721	7	3
20-24	171,009	84,364	66,296	18,013	33	22	86,645	45,769	40,668	112	96
25-29	194,700	97,486	38,046	58,973	210	257	97,214	21,343	74,688	580	603
30-34	181,281	89,437	19,816	68,660	454	507	91,844	13,432	76,144	1,384	884
35-39	188,934	93,810	14,981	77,341	812	676	95,124	12,224	79,507	2,476	917
40-44	191,030	94,808	12,477	80,448	1,252	631	96,222	13,048	78,568	3,835	771
45-49	186,277	91,840	10,998	78,407	1,923	512	94,437	13,428	74,262	6,122	625
50-54	170,762	81,854	8,852	69,687	2,914	401	88,908	11,920	66,144	10,423	421
55-59	148,072	69,402	7,028	58,087	4,049	238	78,670	10,436	53,143	14,822	269
60-64	127,930	59,005	5,949	46,975	5,909	172	68,925	9,660	39,584	19,511	170
65-69	107,880	49,342	5,309	36,073	7,862	98	58,538	7,872	28,036	22,532	98
70-74	83,942	37,433	4,101	23,971	9,311	50	46,509	6,231	17,169	23,063	46
75-79	53,961	24,073	2,494	12,808	8,748	23	29,888	4,111	7,789	17,962	26
80-84	25,238	10,432	935	4,221	5,267	9	14,806	2,098	2,330	10,374	4
85-89	8,459	3,123	265	907	1,950	1	5,336	716	453	4,166	1
90-94	1,818	553	37	126	390		1,265	177	73	1,015	
95+	263	65	8	7	49	1	198	22	18	157	

POPULATION 3. AGE AND MARITAL CONDITION, BY SEX, WALES 1841-1971

1961

Age last birthday	PERSONS	MARITAL CONDITION									
		MALES					FEMALES				
		Total	S	M	W	D	Total	S	M	W	D
all ages	2,644,023	1,291,764	580,204	663,702	43,062	4,796	1,352,259	523,652	666,424	154,702	7,481
0-4	205,544	105,390	105,390				100,154	100,154			
5-9	193,170	98,655	98,655				94,515	94,515			
10-14	219,284	112,029	112,029				107,255	107,255			
15-19	185,851	94,937	93,859	1,077	1		90,914	84,721	6,189	4	
20-24	157,676	80,432	56,720	23,668	13	31	77,244	32,064	45,001	80	99
25-29	155,076	79,176	24,809	54,091	78	198	75,900	10,698	64,584	234	384
30-34	165,934	83,752	16,055	67,138	185	374	82,182	8,452	72,452	575	703
35-39	187,649	94,293	14,277	78,922	415	679	93,356	8,617	82,240	1,308	1,191
40-44	176,455	86,813	10,951	74,389	705	768	89,642	8,536	76,965	2,882	1,259
45-49	181,263	89,695	10,217	77,367	1,327	784	91,568	9,288	75,865	5,181	1,234
50-54	181,246	89,019	9,661	76,378	2,227	753	92,227	10,828	71,218	9,164	1,017
55-59	169,748	81,790	8,560	69,115	3,571	544	87,958	11,457	61,128	14,627	746
60-64	147,366	67,027	6,582	55,042	5,048	355	80,339	10,761	47,600	21,529	449
65-69	119,920	51,464	4,932	39.969	6,393	170	68,456	9,232	32,617	26,375	232
70-74	89,680	36,716	3,556	25,735	7,339	86	52,964	7,578	18,484	26,795	107
75-79	59,735	23,276	2,331	13,713	7,189	43	36,459	5,079	8,445	22,891	44
80-84	32,976	12,099	1,145	5,466	5,477	11	20,877	2,891	2,978	14,997	11
85-89	12,373	4,306	382	1,422	2,502		8,067	1,185	587	6,290	5
90-94	2,680	804	85	190	529		1,876	283	64	1,529	
95+	397	91	8	20	63		306	58	7	241	

POPULATION 3. AGE AND MARITAL CONDITION, BY SEX, WALES 1841-1971

1971

Age last birthday	PERSONS	MARITAL CONDITION									
		MALES					FEMALES				
		Total	S	M	W	D	Total	S	M	W	D
all ages	2,731,205	1,327,505	587,040	688,935	41,595	9,940	1,403,695	523,595	692,725	173,015	14,365
0-4	214,790	109,965	109,965				104,825	104,825			
5-9	225,240	115,730	115,730				109,510	109,510			
10-14	207,025	106,325	106,325				100,700	100,700			
15-19	188,885	96,235	94,085	2,145			92,650	84,125	8,505	15	5
20-24	197,685	100,535	62,200	38,125	25	180	97,150	36,590	59,900	100	560
25-29	167,615	84,555	20,980	62,745	70	760	83,060	9,400	71,925	245	1,490
30-34	153,960	78,365	11,340	65,780	110	1,135	75,595	5,370	68,105	425	1,690
35-39	152,355	76,780	9,365	65,935	250	1,225	75,575	4,840	68,175	925	1,640
40-44	163,060	81,630	9,790	70,000	560	1,280	81,430	5,585	72,030	2,150	1,660
45-49	181,635	90,180	10,440	77,205	1,175	1,355	91,460	6,795	78,315	4,395	1,955
50-54	168,705	82,000	8,435	70,560	1,780	1,225	86,700	7,155	69,945	7,950	1,655
55-59	168,635	81,100	8,070	68,935	3,060	1,035	87,540	8,030	63,950	14,155	1,405
60-64	162,605	75,510	7,225	62,790	4,660	830	87,100	9,845	54,355	21,800	1,095
65-69	142,710	63,020	5,840	49,990	6,685	510	79,690	10,310	39,525	29,155	700
70-74	107,070	42,550	3,685	30,895	7,725	250	64,520	8,565	23,115	32,525	315
75-79	68,970	24,630	2,075	15,500	6,950	105	44,340	6,005	10,295	27,915	130
80-84	38,755	12,355	975	6,260	5,085	35	26,400	3,765	3,590	19,000	45
85-89	16,110	4,670	395	1,730	2,535	10	11,445	1,610	825	8,990	15
90-94	4,535	1,155	90	275	790		3,380	470	145	2,760	5
95+	855	220	20	60	145		635	95	30	515	

GENERAL NOTES.

i) Sources. Census Reports. 1841 : Age Table. Summary of Wales :
1851 : Ages etc. 2; 1861 : Vol.11 Welsh Division
Tables 1 and 7; 1871 : Ages etc. Welsh Division
Tables 1 and 7; 1881 : Ages etc. Wales and Mon.
Tables 1 and 7; 1891 : Ages etc. Welsh Division
Tables 1 and 4; 1901 : County Tables 23 and 27
1911 : County Tables 17 and 19
1921 - 51 : General Tables
1961 - 71 : Age, Marital Condition and General Tables.

POPULATION 4. AREA - WALES AND EACH COUNTY, 1841 - 1971 (acres)

	Ang.	Brecs.	Caerns.	Cards.	Carms.	Denbs.	Flints.	Glam.	Mer.	Mon.	Mont.	Pembs.	Rad.	WALES.	
1841	173,440	482,560	348,160	432,000	623,630	405,120	156,160	506,880	424,320	317,440	536,960	390,400	272,640	5,069,710	1841
1851	193,453	460,158	370,273	443,387	606,331	386,052	184,905	547,494	385,291	368,399	483,323	401,691	272,128	5,102,885	1851
1861	193,453	460,158	370,273	443,387	606,331	386,052	184,905	547,494	368,291	368,399	483,323	401,691	272,128	5,102,885	1861
1871	193,511	460,158	369,482	443,387	606,172	392,005	169,162	547,070	385,291	368,399	485,351	393,682	276,552	5,090,222	1871
1881	193,511	460,158	369,477	443,387	594,405	425,038	161,807	516,959	384,717	370,350	495,089	391,181	276,552	5,141,225	1881
1891 (a)	175,836	475,224	361,097	440,630	587,816	423,477	164,050	516,959	427,810	341,688	510,111	395,151	301,164	5,121,013	1891
1891 (b)	175,836	469,894	360,138	443,071	587,816	424,435	164,051	516,966	427,810	347,011	510,111	392,710	301,164	5,121,013	1891
1901	176,630	469,301	365,986 (1)	443,071	587,816	426,084 (1)	163,025 (1)	518,863	422,018 (1)	349,712 (1)	510,111	392,710	301,164	5,121,013	1901
1911	176,630	469,281	365,986	443,189	588,472	426,084	163,025	518,865	422,372	349,552	510,110	393,003	301,165	5,127,734	1911
1921	176,630	469,281	366,005	443,189	588,472	426,080	163,707	520,456	422,372	349,552	510,110	393,003	301,165	5,130,022	1921
1931	176,694	469,281	364,108 (1)	443,189	588,472	427,977 (1)	163,707	520,456	422,372	349,569	510,110	393,003	301,165	5,130,103	1931
1951	176,694	469,281	364,108	443,189	588,472	427,977	163,707	523,244 (1)	422,372	346,781 (1)	510,110	393,007	301,165	5,130,107	1951
1961	176,694	469,281	364,108	443,189	588,472	427,977	163,707	523,244	422,372	346,781	510,110	393,007	301,165	5,130,107	1961
1971	176,692	469,280	364,109	443,190	588,503	427,981	164,053	523,235	422,372	346,775	510,111	393,166	301,167	5,130,634	1971

Notes. (1) Boundary change since previous census; for details of the population effected - see Table 1.

General Notes.

Census Reports.

(i) Sources : 1841 Census Emuneration - County Tables
1851 Census Enumeration 1, Summary Tables, Table 111.
1861 Census General Report, Table 1
1871 Census General Report, App. A Table 20
1881-91 Census Area, Houses and Population Vol 1, County Tables, Table 7
1901 Census Summary Tables, Table XV.
1911-71 County Reports
Figures for Wales are totals of county figures.

(ii) The county figures relate to ancient counties for 1841-91 (a); and to administrative counties for 1891 (b) - 1971. The changes in county areas are not only due to boundary changes: they can also reflect more accurate measurement or land reclamation. The 1871 figures have been converted from hectares to acres.

Population of Registration Counties as constituted at time of each census, 1841-1911.

	1841			1851			1861			1871		
	M.	F.	Total	M.	F	Total	M	F	Total	M.	F.	Total
Anglesey	18,271	19,835	38,106	21,172	22,071	43,243	18,501	19,656	38,157	16,890	18,237	35,127
Brecon	27,858	27,562	55,420	29,993	29,185	59,178	29,640	29,220	58,860	28,494	28,438	56,932
Caernarvon	42,272	44,481	86,753	46,472	48,202	94,674	50,420	53,118	103,538	54,077	57,301	111,378
Cardigan	44,492	51,510	96,002	45,155	52,459	97,614	44,446	52,955	97,401	44,247	53,622	97,869
Carmarthen	42,694	46,865	89,559	45,519	49,153	94,672	46,149	50,502	96,651	48,350	53,031	101,381
Denbigh	45,826	46,210	92,036	48,639	48,276	96,915	52,508	51,838	104,346	52,389	52,775	105,164
Flint	20,673	20,125	40,798	20,787	20,260	41,047	19,997	19,944	39,941	22,119	21,398	43,517
Glamorgan	91,430	86,620	178,050	125,087	115,008	240,095	167,835	158,419	326,254	209,616	196,182	405,798
Merioneth	25,061	25,389	50,713	25,652	25,918	51,307	26,308	26,922	53,230	30,765	30,742	61,507
Monmouth	79,034	71,987	151,021	93,301	84.829	177,130	101,010	95,967	196,977	113,862	105,846	219,708
Montgomery	39,488	40,268	79,756	38,541	38,601	77,142	38,887	38,036	76,923	39,507	38,893	78,400
Pembroke	36,401	42,156	78,557	39,620	44,852	84,472	42,388	45,302	87,690	39,474	44,399	83,873
Radnor	16,116	15,660	31,776	16 118	15,307	31,425	17,056	15,810	32,866	10,811	10,205	21,016
WALES	529,616	538,931	1,068,547	594,793	594,121	1,188,914	655,145	657,689	1,312,834	710,601	711,069	1,421,670

	1881			1891			1901			1911		
Anglesey	17,190	17,951	35,141	16,322	17,897	34,219	16,821	17,987	34,808	16,980	18,379	35,359
Brecon	26,991	28,438	54,140	26,333	26,539	52,872	26,970	26,981	53,951	28,308	28,062	56,370
Caernarvon	60,742	63,039	123,781	59,731	65,854	125,585	65,368	71,868	137,236	66,619	75,148	141,767
Cardigan	42,717	52,420	95,137	37,992	48,391	86,383	36,603	46,104	82,707	36,526	44,243	80,769
Carmarthen	53,489	57,766	111,255	56,922	61,702	118,624	59,339	64,231	123,570	76,017	75,033	151,050
Denbigh	56,501	56,439	112,940	58,433	58,265	116,698	63,351	63,107	126,458	68,298	68,512	136,810
Flint	23,217	22,557	45,774	21,373	21,192	42,565	21,129	21,132	42,261	35,440	34,282	69,722
Glamorgan	266,128	252,255	518,383	363,252	329,820	693,072	447,103	419,147	866,250	587,666	543,002	1,130,668
Merioneth	34,350	33,928	68,278	31,841	32,885	64,726	31,504	32,744	64,248	29,076	31,204	60,280
Monmouth	119,965	114,367	234,332	142,332	132,910	275,242	162,737	154,127	316,864	216,906	197,760	414,666
Montgomery	38,295	37,901	76,196	32,721	34,576	67,297	31,195	32,799	63,994	30,536	31,665	62,201
Pembroke	40,085	43,594	83,679	38,771	43,232	82,003	39,356	43,068	82,424	41,219	43,655	84,874
Radnor	9,404	9,119	18,523	8,486	8,633	17,119	10,711	9,530	20,241	8,796	8,709	17,505
WALES	789,074	788,485	1,577,559	894,509	881 896	1,776,405	1,012,187	1,082,825	2,015,012	1,242,387	1,201,654	2,444,041

General Notes.

i) Sources. Census Reports : 1841, Enumeration, County Tables.

1851, Enumeration 11 Welsh Division pp 4-5
1861, Vol. 1 Wales and Monmouth p.700
1871, Area, Houses and Inhabitants 11. Wales and Monmouth, Table 1 p.527
1881, Area, Houses and Population 11. Wales and Monmouth, Table 1 p.625
1891, Area, Houses and Population 11. Wales and Monmouth, Table 1 p.1067
1901, County Tables, 1.
1911, County Tables, 2.

Population 6. Comparative Area and Population of Registration. Ancient and Administrative Counties, 1891.

	Area, 1891			Population, 1891		
	Ancient	Registration	Administrative	Ancient	Registration	Administrative
		Statute Acres				
Anglesey	175,836	120,199	175,836	50,098	34,219	50,098
Breconshire	475,224	458,652	469,894	57,031	52,872	51,393
Caernarvonshire	361,097	322,135	360,138	118,204	125,585	117,233
Cardiganshire	440,630	595,285	443,071	62,630	86,383	63,467
Carmarthenshire	587,816	478,717	587,816	130,566	118,624	130,566
Denbighshire	423,477	386,416	424,435	117,872	116,698	118,843
Flintshire	164,050	73,380	164,051	77,277	42,565	77,277
Glamorganshire	516,959	576,308	516,966	687,218	693,072	687,218
Merionethshire	427,810	525,802	427,810	49,212	64,726	49,212
Monmouthshire	341,688	394,424	347,018	252,416	275,242	258,054
Montgomeryshire	510,111	589,846	510,111	58,003	67,297	58,003
Pembrokeshire	395,151	357,110	392,710	89,133	82,003	88,296
Radnorshire	301,164	238,715	301,164	21,791	17,119	21,791
WALES	5,121,013	5,116,997	5,121,013	1,771,451	1,776,405	1,771,451

General Notes.

i) Source : 1891 Census Report General Tables 6 and 7.

Population 7 - PARISH REGISTER RETURNS OF BAPTISMS, BURIALS AND MARRIAGES, WALES, 1700 - 1840.

	BAPTISMS	BURIALS	MARRIAGES
1700	9,174	7,997	
1710	9,058	7,655	
1720	9,707	7,981	
1730	10,077	9,499	
1740	10,286	8,152	
1750	11,105	7,327	
1754			2,587
1755			3,016
1756			2,984
1757			2,880
1758			2,967
1759			3,348
1760			3,507
1761			3,446
1762			3,364
1763			3,393
1764			3,480
1765			3,514
1766			3,277
1767			3,200
1768			3,485
1769			3,569
1770	11,884	9,261	3,577
1771			3,484
1772			3,510
1773			4,127
1774			3,557
1775			3,729
1776			4,183
1777			3,784
1778			3,574
1779			3,751
1780	13,452	9,081	3,778
1781	12,993	9,399	3,734
1782	12,482	9,661	3,545
1783	12,440	10,362	3,634
1784	12,701	11,451	3,697
1785	13.554	10,249	4,093
1786	12,941	9,024	4,017
1787	13,435	8,681	3,936
1788	14,261	9,174	3,931
1789	14,068	8,706	3,910
1790	13,709	8,402	3,753
1791	13,576	8,576	3,803
1792	14,073	9,316	3,785
1793	13,708	9,936	3,876
1794	13,807	8,686	3,846
1795	13,440	9,393	3,605
1796	13,419	9,502	3,798
1797	14,385	8,952	4,101
1798	14,294	8,669	4,002
1799	14,097	8,646	3,957
1800	12,659	9,845	3,497
1801(1)	12,708	11,396	3,655
1802	15,279	10.620	4,925
1803	16,497	10,752	5,659
1804	16,254	9,984	5,152
1805	16,158	10,256	4,827
1806	16,235	9,901	4,781
1807	16,715	10,866	5,139

	BAPTISMS	BURIALS	MARRIAGES
1808	16,663	10,767	5,145
1809	16,509	9,650	5,049
1810	16,747	10,724	4,743
1811 (2)	16,654	9,615	4,888
1812	16,082	9,738	4,648
1813	17,147	9,997	5,091
1814	17,732	10,868	5,307
1815	17,904	10 065	5,664
1816	17,373	10,975	5,181
1817	16,272	11 569	4,923
1818	15,506	12,535	4,807
1819	16,627	12,587	5,322
1820	16,920	10,653	5,679
1821 (3)	18,031	10,454	5,914
1822	18,150	10,826	5,595
1823	17,582	12,781	5,556
1824	17,423	12,654	5,451
1825	17,268	12,750	6,128
1826	18,570	12,503	6,321
1827	17,527	12,276	6,266
1828	18,252	12,727	6,458
1829	17,470	13,741	6,374
1830	16,416	13,076	6,090
1831 (4)	16 034	13,915	6,032
1832	15 514	15,461	6,424
1833	16 361	15.329	6,919
1834	16 790	14,704	7,421
1835	16,845	14,488	7,238
1836	17,232	16,037	7,525

	BAPTISMS	BURIALS	MARRIAGES
1837	17,471	18,527	6,976
1838	16,397	16,752	6,954
1839	15,868	16,313	7,295
1840	15,207	17,548	6,893

General Notes.

i) Sources. Census Reports, Parish Registers, 1801 - 41.

ii) The figures for 1700 - 1800 are subject to wide margins of error. Whilst this is generally true, it is probably especially the case for Wales because of such factors as the generally unsatisfactory quality of many of the Anglican clergy in Wales during the eighteenth century, and also because whereas Rickman re-calculated the figures for England and Wales for 1700 - 1800, no separate revision was made for Wales alone. From 1800 onwards, the figures are presumed to be much more reliable. At least returns did reach all churches and were completed by the incumbents. There were of course, still inaccuracies because of the deficiencies in the parish registers themselves and also because of errors made in extracting and copying the information. Some estimate of these short-comings is made in Notes 1 - 4 below.

Notes.

1) 1801 - 10 Average number of unentered :

a) baptisms - 1,609
b) burials - 649

2) 1811 - 20

Average number of unentered :

a) baptisms - 2,633
Burials - 823

3) 1821 - 30 Average number of unentered :

a) baptisms - 3,513
b) burials - 1,101

4) 1831 - 40 Average number of unentered :

a) baptisms - 3,386
b) burials - 1,414
c) marriages . 277

Number of illegitimate children born 1830 - 1,581.

Population 8. Estimated mid-year population, by sex, Wales 1841 - 1974.

	Males	Females	Total	Thousands
1841	518.4	527.7	1,046.1	
1842	524.4	532.8	1,057.2	
1843	530.5	538.0	1,068.5	
1844	536.6	543.2	1,079.9	
1845	542.9	548.5	1,091.0	
1846	549.2	553.9	1,103.0	
1847	555.6	559.2	1,114.8	
1848	562.0	564.7	1,126.7	
1849	568.6	570.2	1,138.7	
1850	575.2	575.7	1,150.9	
1851	581.8	581.3	1,163.1	
1852	587.7	587.4	1,174.9	
1853	593.3	593.5	1,186.8	
1854	599.2	599.7	1,198.8	
1855	605.1	605.9	1,211.0	
1856	611.0	612.2	1,223.2	
1857	617.0	618.6	1,235.6	
1858	623.1	625.0	1,248.1	
1859	629.2	631.5	1,260.8	
1860	635.4	638.1	1,273.5	
1861	641.7	644.8	1,286.4	
1862	647.8	650.7	1,298.5	
1863	654.0	656.7	1,310.7	
1864	660.3	662.7	1,323.0	
1865	666.7	668.8	1,335.5	
1866	673.1	674.9	1,348.0	
1867	679.5	681.1	1,360.7	
1868	686.1	687.4	1,373.5	
1869	692.7	693.7	1,386.4	
1870	699.3	700.1	1,399.4	
1871	706.0	706.5	1,412.6	
1872	713.7	714.1	1,427.7	
1873	721.4	721.7	1,443.1	
1874	729.2	729.3	1,458.5	
1875	737.1	737.1	1,474.2	
1876	745.1	744.9	1,490.0	
1877	753.2	752.9	1,506.0	
1878	761.3	760.9	1,522.2	
1879	769.6	769.0	1,538.6	
1880	777.9	777.2	1,555.1	
1881	786.3	785.5	1,571.8	

Population 8. Estimated mid-year population, by sex, Wales 1841 - 1974.

			Total	Thousands
1882	..	..	1,537.8	
1883	..	..	1,614.0	
1884	..	..	1,630.3	
1885	..	..	1,646.7	
1886	..	..	1,663.2	
1887	..	..	1,679.8	
1888	..	..	1,696.5	
1889	..	..	1,713.1	
1890	..	..	1,760.4	
1891	..	..	1,781.4	
1892	..	..	1,803.0	
1893	..	..	1,824.9	
1894	..	..	1,846.8	
1895	..	..	1,869.1	
1896	..	..	1,891.6	
1897	..	..	1,814.4	
1898	..	..	1,937.5	
1899	..	..	1,960.9	
1900	..	..	1,995.9	
1901	1,013,589	1,004,417	2,018.0	
1902	1,026,149	1,017,301	2,043.5	
1903	1,050,500	1,040,981	2,091.5	
1904	1,063,508	1,054,285	2,117.8	
1905	1,076,658	1,067,732	2,144.4	
1906	1,089,953	1,081,321	2,171.3	
1907	1,103,392	942,460	2,045.9	
1908	1,116,980	1,108,941	2,225.9	
1909	1,130,716	1,123,144	2,253.9	
1910	1,225,180	1,184,990	2,410.2	
1911	1,237,545	1,194,127	2,431.7	
1912	1,260,911	1,214,048	2,475.0	
1913	1,284,519	1,234,171	2,518.7	
1914	1,287,091	1,236,362	2,523.5	
1915	..	..	2,425.0	
1916	..	..	2,573.1	
1917	..	..	2,653.5	
1918	..	..	2,614.8	
1919	..	..	2,654.3	
1920	..	..	2,627.8	
1921	..	..	2,657.7	
1922	..	..	2,686.1	
1923	..	..	2,704.0	
1924	..	..	2,730.2	

Population 8. Estimated mid-year population, by sex, Wales 1841-1974.

	Males	Females	Total	Thousands
1925	..	..	2,736.8	
1926	..	..	2,731.2	
1927	..	..	2,723.6	
1928	..	..	2,687.3	
1929	..	..	2,677.1	
1930	..	..	2,628.9	
1931	..	..	2,593.3	
1932	1,290.2	1,291.7	2,581.9	
1933	1,283.8	1,284.3	2,568.1	
1934	1,276.4	1,278.0	2,554.4	
1935	1,270.6	1,267.1	2,537.7	
1936	1,259.4	1,257.5	2,516.9	
1937	1,242.1	1,236.9	2,479.0	
1938	1,235.7	1,230.1	2,465.8	
1939	1,228.0	1,259.0	2,487.0	
1940	1,186.0	1,337.0	2,523.0	
1941	1,180.0	1,423.0	2,603.0	
1942	..	..	2,525.6	
1943	..	..	2,455.9	
1944	..	..	2,449.5	
1945	..	..	2,422.3	
1946	..	..	2,473.4	
1947	..	..	2,501.0	
1948	1,246.0	1,306.0	2,552.0	
1949	1,258.0	1,313.0	2,571.0	
1950	1,282.0	1,317.0	2,599.0	
1951	1,269.0	1,318.0	2,587.0	
1952	1,270.0	1,318.0	2,588.0	
1953	1,275.0	1,319.0	2,594.0	
1954	1,272.0	1,329.0	2,601.0	
1955	1,275.0	1,328.0	2,603.0	
1956	1,279.0	1,329.0	2,608.0	
1957	1,281.0	1,330.0	2,611.0	
1958	1,282.0	1,333.0	2,615.0	
1959	1,286.0	1,337.0	2,623.0	
1960	1,291.0	1,338.0	2,629.0	
1961	1,296.0	1,334.0	2,630.0	
1962	1,310.0	1,341.0	2,651.0	
1963	1,310.3	1,351.8	2,662.1	
1964	1,309.9	1,366.4	2,676.3	
1965	1,318.2	1,374.6	2,692.8	
1966	1,323.0	1,378.2	2,701.2	
1967	1,328.0	1,381.9	2,709.9	
1968	1,325.1	1,394.9	2,720.0	

Population 8. Estimated mid-year population, by sex, Wales 1841-1974.

	Males	Females	Total	Thousands
1969	1,328.3	1,396.2	2,724.5	
1970	1,322.4	1,401.5	2,723.9	
1971	1,324.5	1,400.7	2,725.2	
1972	1,327.4	1,407.3	2,734.7	
1973	1,333.5	1,415.8	2,749.3	
1974	1,337.7	1,419.5	2,757.2	

General Notes.

i) Sources. Census Reports, 1841 - 81; Registrar General: Annual Reports, 1878 - 1920; Registrar General: Statistical Review, 1921 - 73; Population Estimates, 1974.

ii) From 1841 to 1878 the Registrar General's reports do not give a separate estimate for Wales. For these years, and up to 1881 an estimate has been made by taking the census figures for each decade and allowing the difference between the individual years on the assumption of a constant (compound) rate of growth. From 1881 the Registrar General's figures have been used, although these only give the estimate of the total population until 1900.

iii) Until 1910 the Registrar General's figures relate to the Welsh Registration division; from 1911 on they are for Wales. The estimated figures mentioned in note ii) above are for Wales.

Estimated mid-year population, total, each County, 1903 - 74.

	Ang.	Brecs.	Caerns.	Cards.	Carms.	Denbs.	Flints.	Glam.	Mer.	Mon.	Mont.	Pembs.	Rad.
1903	35,000	54,023	140,098	82,021	125,100	129,235	61,130	906,917	64,278	326,707	63,332	82,761	20,979
1904	35,092	54,065	141,399	81,730	125,805	130,495	61,405	925,203	64,304	231,153	63,048	82,782	21,312
1905	35,188	54,112	142,718	81,447	126,526	131,773	61,687	943,628	64,336	335,643	62,772	82,912	21,648
1906	35,288	54,166	144,055	81,172	127,260	133,041	61,978	962,194	64,374	340,180	62,501	83,051	21,987
1907	35,392	54,225	145,411	80,906	128,011	134,380	62,275	980,905	64,420	344,762	62,235	83,198	22,329
1908	35,500	54,290	146,785	80,647	128,776	135,708	62,578	999,765	64,473	349,393	61,976	83,355	22,675
1909	35,612	54,361	148,177	80,394	129,556	137,054	62,889	1,018,778	64,532	354,070	61,722	83,520	23,022
1910	35,324	56,189	141,419	80,920	148,914	136,004	69,014	1,110,011	60,603	407,033	62,343	84,677	17,719
1911	50,936	59,421	125,027	59,847	161,067	145,131	93,001	1,128,186	45,478	398,292	53,100	90,014	22,572
1912	50,971	59,959	124,963	59,720	163,727	146,531	94,191	1,155,471	45,130	408,650	52,914	90,234	22,498
1913	51,004	60,502	124,899	59,592	166,414	147,947	95,394	1,383,441	44,777	419,116	52,725	90,455	22,424
1914	51,008	60,561	124,890	59,578	166,707	148,100	95 525	1,386,489	44,739	431,821	52,705	90,480	22,416
1915	49,647	58,389	116,633	57,323	163.622	140.756	92,944	1,138,977	42,378	404,261	50,473	87,825	21,771
1916[1]	48,029	56,175	112,115	55,270	160.587	136,955	90.478	1,115,496	40.432	395.368	48,553	84,552	20,917
1917[1]	47,027	55,135	104,574	53 698	167 240	136,468	93,057	1,122.713	38,633	408,101	47,950	86,056	19,799
1918[1]	47,755	53,639	103,419	51,573	159,280	134,156	91,315	1,102,257[2]	37,375	403,473	46,426	82,307	20,396
1919[1]	47,592	55,147	111,830	55,897	169,746	141,756	95,099	1,232,808	39,781	442,467	48,787	86,277	20,881
1920	50,952	60,472	121,812	57,666	174,999	150,515	101,218	1,254,555	41,740	450,936	50,714	90,717	21,530
1921	51,202	61,069	121,989	57,654	176,667	151,716	102,077	1,267,758	41,783	457,658	50,950	91,480	21,656
1922	51,493	61,644	122,088	57,704	178,743	152,552	102,572	1,288,367	41,951	464,085	51,087	91,978	21,857
1923	51,940	61,900	120,213[3]	57,860	180,060	155,737[3]	103,380	1,298,560	42,320	466,590	51,240	92,140	22,089
1924	52,290	63,320	120,250	58,290	181,550	158,160	104,900	1,267,040	43,710	470,150	51,640	92,670	22,200
1925	52,290	62,260	119,970	57,970	181,930	158,640	105,460	1,316,820	42,950	471,980	51,900	92,290	22,290
1926	52,500	61,580	119,810	58,410	182,470	159,290	106,970	1,312,690	43,640	469,030	52,070	90,430	22,330
1927	52,060	61,340	120,150	57,860	182,190	159,580	108,750	1,305,000	43,980	468,700	52,120	89,630	22,200

	Ang.	Brecs.	Caerns.	Cards.	Carms.	Denbs.	Flints.	Glam.	Mer.	Mon.	Mont.	Pembs.	Rad.
1928	51,340	60,180	123,900	56,060	180,100	160,020	111,300	1,280,400	44,000	458,520	50,960	88,610	21,920
1929	51,330	59,450	123,670	56,070	181,280	159,540	112,390	1,273,890	44,110	445,870	50,140	87,790	21,570
1930	49,620	58,220	120,600	55,350	180,600	158,100	112,300	1,249,020	43,090	445,100	48,920	86,820	21,140
1931	48,350	57,270	118,480	54,750	180,080	157,230	112,480	1,230,480	42,370	437,010	47,980	86,020	20,820
1932	48,590	57,030	119,580	54,840	179,290	157,300	112,900	1,221,190	42,120	433,590	47,950	86,490	20,970
1933	48,240	56,660	119,500	54,080	177,950	156,500	113,750	1,215,340	41,760	430,050	47,380	86,040	20,850
1934	47,950	56,150	119,400	53,950	177,350	156,700	114,950	1,206,950	41,500	426,550	46,700	85,650	20,600
1935	47,600	55,400	119,400	53,800	176,900	156,400	116,000	1,197,200	41,300	421,900	46,200	85,100	20,500
1936	47,280	54,600	119,520	53,680	176,390	157,090	117,770	1,182,590	41,030	417,140	45,950	83,700	20,140
1937	46,720	53,500	118,880	52,770	174,090	156,950	119,540	1,159,400	40,330	408,510	45,270	83,270	19,770
1938	46,530	53,060	118,590	52,120	172,700	156,840	121,020	1,154,960 [4]	39,970	402,380 [4]	44,890	83,200	19,540
1939	46,500	52,540	118,950	51,650	171,980	156,920	121,900	1,157,640	39,860	399,640	44,830	83,270	19,520
1940	48,390	54,830	127,540	55,960	172,920	167,540	130,720	1,160,900	41,610	412,650	46,600	86,320	20,420
1941	50,200	58,840	141,520	58,840	180,390	180,950	140,100	1,159,340	44,720	423,790	49,450	92,200	22,660
1942	49,480	55,470	137,000	56,390	172,180	175,850	137,440	1,126,500	42,800	411,150	47,850	91,270	22,220
1943	47,300	53,250	131,870	54,160	165,810	169,250	131,590	1,102,840	41,290	403,000	46,280	87,870	21,390
1944	47,080	52,350	126,620	53,540	164,490	164,630	127,260	1,118,750	40,040	404,410	45,480	84,340	20,510
1945	46,070	51,560	121,700	51,690	162,670	162,390	125,670	1,114,760	38,860	400,030	44,680	82,690	19,510
1946	46,940	51,540	122,190	51,580	165,070	165,020	131,870	1,143,890	38,790	408,790	45,280	83,580	18,860
1947	47,150	53,121	123,135	52,609	168,400	165,365	135,000	1,155,770	38,375	413,200	44,775	84,451	19,679
1948	49,130	53,802	124,607	53,632	170,200	167,493	138,300	1,183,440	39,166	420,800	45,544	86,108	20,288
1949	49,300	54,159	123,348	54,001	170,800	168,452	140,300	1,194,680	38,838	424,300	45,762	86,599	20,261
1950	50,060	56,426	123,824	53,993	171,730	169,686	145,080	1,204,790	40,543	426,940	45,837	89,887	20,404
1951	50,980	55,700	123,300	54,210	170,600	170,400	145,700	1,195,980 [5]	41,170	422,720 [5]	45,520	90,740	19,980
1952	50,960	56,200	122,500	53,240	170,700	170,700	145,700	1,198,000	41,070	423,100	45,070	91,040	19,720
1953	51.100	55,700	122,600	53,550	170,900	170,400	145,100	1,203,400	40,850	423,700	45,010	92,090	19,600
1954	51,280	55,500	123,200	53,750	171,100	170,500	145,800	1,207,000	40,190	425,400	45,090	92,750	19,440
1955	51,600	55,700	123,100	53,600	170,800	170,300	146,100	1,207,000	40,000	426,500	45,100	93,800	19,400
1956	51,660	56,300	122,700	53,450	170,400	170,700	146,000	1,209,000	40,580	428,300	44,940	94,260	19,210
1957	51,990	56,300	122,100	53,400	170,300	169,500	147,200	1,213,500	39,080	429,900	44,930	93,670	19,130

	Ang.	Brecs.	Caerns.	Cards.	Carms.	Denbs.	Flints.	Glam.	Mer.	Mon.	Mont.	Pembs.	Rad.
1958	52,100	56,000	121,600	53,000	169,300	170,000	146,600	1,219,000	38,100	431,700	44,800	93,700	19,100
1959	52,300	55,800	121,200	53,100	168,700	170,200	147,000	1,224,000	38,600	433,500	44,800	94,600	19,200
1960	52,070	55,470	121,400	53,280	168,250	169,810	148,060	1,227,750	39,140	435,730	44,720	94,580	19,160
1961	51,710	55,290	119,510	53,210	166,800	172,500	149,240	1,226,960	37,740	442,200	44,060	93,380	18,410
1962	51,430	54,460	120,460	53,390	167,110	174,180	150,430	1,236,980	38,360	449,370	43,690	93,050	18,430
1963	51,830	54,390	120,560	53,260	166,560	174,680	152,310	1,241,980	38,390	451,440	43,660	94,660	18,370
1964	53,650	54,320	119,820	53,250	166,600	176,840	155,150	1,244,290	38,870	456,230	43,720	95,350	18,300
1965	55,460	54,460	120,030	53,330	166,320	178,480	158,240	1,250,470	38,270	459,850	43,690	95,920	18,240
1966	55,950	54,470	120,050	53,410	165,650	179,150	160,560	1,252,010	37,750	463,150	43,700	97,060	18,300
1967	56,670	54,230	119,720	53,430	165,110	179,780	163,110	1,255,090 (6)	37,710	464,840 (6)	43,590	98,330	18,320
1968	57,800	55,120	120,770	53,710	164,790	181,440	166,160	1,258,320	37,530	462,990	42,800	100,360	18,210
1969	58,210	54,940	120,620	53,500	163,600	182,050	169,210	1,258,450	37,700	463,990	42,870	101,150	18,250
1970	60,000	54,690	121,500	53,180	164,300	182,860	173,070	1,259,200	37,450	464,560	43,270	101,200	18,590
1971	60,170	52,910	122,410	56,160	163,170	184,830	176,830	1,252,970	34,810	461,670	43,110	97,870	18,270
1972	60,590	53,020	122,530	54,300	162,530	186,100	179,950	1,254,260	34,710	463,190	43,320	98,420	18,530
1973	62,020	52,730	122,790	55,430	162,770	187,820	183,650	1,264,160	34,690	462,210	43,580	98,760	18,670
1974	63,200	53,000	123,400	57,200	163,100	188,800	187,000	1,264,800	34,400	461,700	43,900	99,800	19,000

General Notes.

i) Sources. Registrar General : Annual Report, 1903 - 20; Registrar General : Statistical Review, 1921 - 75

ii) Until 1910 the figures relate to the registration counties; after this date to the administrative counties.

Notes.

1) Civilian population.
2) Adjusted to allow for boundary changes in 1918.
3) 1923. 1,892 acres and 2,792 persons (1921 census) transferred from Caernarvonshire to Denbighshire.
4) 1938. Population after boundary change made during year estimated to be : Glamorgan 1,156,130 ; Monmouthshire 401,210.
5) 1951. 712 acres and 90 persons (1951 census) transferred from Monmouth to Glamorgan (Cardiff C.B.)
6) 1967. 30 acres and 10 persons (1961 census) transferred from Monmouth to Glamorgan; and 4 acres and 31 persons (1961 census) transferred from Glamorgan to Monmouth.

POPULATION 10 Deaths. Number of Deaths (by sex), Crude death-rates and infant mortality,[1]

Wales 1838 - 1974

	Deaths			Crude death rate per 1,000	Infant Deaths	
	Males	Females	Total		Number	Rate per 1,000 Births
1838	10,870	10,205	21,075		3,859	
1839	10.350	9,811	20,161		3,759	125.5
1840	11,160	0,701	21,861		3,990	127.0
1841	10.712	10,382	21,094	20.2	3,912	121.0
1842	9,849	9,642	19,631	18.6	3,794	117.0
1843	10,153	9,782	19,795	18.5	3,713	112.6
1844	11,305	9,878	22,183	20.5	4,047	119.9
1845	11,304	10,821	22,125	20.3	3,859	117.0
1846	11,550	10,821	22,371	20.3	4,313	122.2
1847	13,552	12,725	26,277	23.6	4,997	147.4
1848	12,693	12,137	24,830	22.0	4,573	129.6
1849	15,304	14,056	29,360	25.8	4,947	136.4
1850	11,757	11,528	23,285	20.2	4,452	120.3
1851	12,361	11,577	23,938	20.6	4,773	126.9
1852	12,880	12,212	25,092	21.4	5,127	134.8
1853	13,662	12,965	26,627	22.4	5,279	139.0
1854	13,836	12,850	26,685	22.3	5,325	133.5
1855	14,064	13,475	27,539	22.7	5,377	133.2
1856	12,911	11,800	24,711	20.2	5,310	125.1
1857	13,243	12,142	25,385	20.5	5,361	124.6
1858	15,208	14,123	29,331	23.5	6,191	145.4
1859	14,674	14,105	28,779	22.8	5,996	131.9
1860	14,214	13,640	27,854	21.9	5,915	133.1
1861	14,077	13,217	27,294	21.2	5,554	128.3
1862	14,106	13,450	27,556	21.2	5,683	126.5
1863	14,515	13,644	28,159	21.5	5,698	124.5
1864	16,323	15,252	31,575	23.9	6,132	129.5
1865	16,550	15,336	31,886	23.9	6,663	139.6
1866	16,195	15,299	31,494	23.4	6,126	125.7
1867	14,958	13,856	28,814	21.2	6,221	128.5
1868	14,539	13,309	27,848	20.3	6,024	121.7
1869	15,279	13,808	29,087	21.0	6,127	125.5
1870	15,997	14,610	30,607	21.9	6,380	130.2
1871	15,698	14,254	29,952	21.2	6,239	126.2
1872	15,914	14,189	30,103	21.1	6,243	125.1
1873	15,930	14,692	30,622	21.2	6,644	130.9
1874	17,718	16,129	33,847	23.2	7,508	138.7
1875	17,265	16,183	33,448	22.7	7,506	138.6
1876	16,054	14,697	30,751	20.6	6,982	126.2
1877	16,450	15,211	31,661	21.0	6,939	127.3
1878	16,560	15,499	32,059	21.1	7,270	136.7
1879	16,277	15,097	31,374	20.5	6,388	122.0

POPULATION 10 Deaths. Number of Deaths (by sex), Crude death-rates and infant mortality,(1)

Wales 1838 - 1974

	Deaths			Crude death rate per 1,000	Infant Deaths	
	Males	Females	Total		Number	Rate per 1,000 Births
1880	16,977	15,081	32,058	20.5	6,875	133.9
1881	15,827	14,323	30,150	19.1	6,272	119.9
1882	15,566	14,418	29,984	19.5	6,466	122.7
1883	16,898	15,759	32,657	20.2	7,165	136.8
1884	16,446	14,938	31,384	19.3	7,003	129.9
1885	16,776	15,632	32,408	19.7	7,200	131.7
1886	17,730	16,185	33,915	20.4	8,215	150.1
1887	16,696	15,534	32,230	19.2	7,288	136.2
1888	16,362	14,861	31,223	18.4	6,704	124.3
1889	16,525	15,338	31,863	18.6	7,724	144.0
1890	17,996	16,405	34,401	19.5	8,264	150.1
1891	20,788	18,773	39,561	22.2	8,965	151.2
1892	18,622	16,790	35,412	19.6	8,824	149.5
1893	18,765	17,491	36,256	19.9	9,742	158.4
1894	17,020	15,598	32,618	17.7	8,323	141.8
1895	19,340	17,902	37,242	19.9	10,296	165.5
1896	17,519	16,653	34,172	18.1	9,378	151.0
1897	18,245	16,884	35,129	19.4	9,581	155.6
1898	17,915	16,924	34,839	18.0	9,607	154.2
1899	19,266	18,241	37,507	19.1	10,558	174.0
1900	19,196	17,822	37,018	18.5	9,303	150.2
1901	19,344	17,825	37,170	18.4	10,210	161.5
1902	18,582	17,062	35,644	17.4	9,159	140.0
1903	17,811	16,542	34,353	16.4	8,860	134.0
1904	18,838	17,635	36,473	17.2	9,925	148.3
1905	19,165	17,473	36,638	17.1	9,433	141.0
1906	18,199	16,911	35,110	16.2	9,129	137.5
1907	18,482	16,987	35,469	17.3	8,222	125.2
1908	19,218	17,643	36,861	16.6	9,452	137.1
1909	18,405	16,762	35,167	15.6	7,865	113.0
1910	18,430	16,527	34,957	14.5	8,076	117.3
1911	18,921	17,297	36,218	14.9	9,158	135
1912	17,376	16,299	33,675	13.6	7,077	106
1913	18,388	16,312	34,700	13.8	7,907	117
1914	18,976	16,843	35,819	14.2	7,499	110
1915	19,413	18,050	37,463	15.4	7,167	112
1916	17,619	16,089	33,708	14.3	5,512	92
1917	16,886	15,228	32,114	13.5	5,024	92
1918	20,183	18,426	38,609	16.5	5,366	95
1919	17,574	16,242	33,816	13.3	5,039	92
1920			33,559	12.8	6,026	86
1921	16,797	15,241	32,038	12.1	5,794	87
1922	18,270	16,516	34,786	13.0	4,926	75
1923	16,677	14,860	31,537	11.7	4,309	74
1924	17,210	15,609	32,819	12.0	4,402	77

POPULATION 10 Deaths. Number of Deaths (by sex), Crude death-rates and infant mortality,[1] Wales 1838 - 1974

	Deaths			Crude Death Rate per 1,000	Infant Deaths	
	Males	Females	Total		Number	Rate per 1,000 Births
1925	17,499	15,842	33,341	12.2	4,479	82
1926	16,335	14,663	30,998	11.4	3,757	71
1927	17,703	15,732	33,435	12.3	3,798	81
1928	16,845	15,077	31,922	11.9	3,383	72
1929	17,584	15,954	33,538	12.5	3,240	77
1930	16,219	14,612	30,831	11.7	2,924	67
1931	17,518	15,866	33,384	12.9	3,141	74
1932	17,002	15,547	32,549	12.6	2,828	69
1933	17,724	15,886	33,610	13.1	2,926	74
1934	16,680 (2)	15,049	31,729	12.4	2,578	65
1935	17,139	15,099	32,238	12.7	2,479	63
1936	17,502	15,191	32,693	13.0	2,343	62
1937	17,626	15,571	33,197	13.4	2,324	63
1938	17,071	14,703	31,774 (3)	12.9	2,135	57
1939	17,836 (4)	15,464	33,300 (3)	13.4.	2,247	60
1940	19,069	16,516	35,585	14.1	2,614	65
1941	19,190	16,647	35,837	13.8	2,886	70
1942	16,754	14,606	31,360	12.4	2,435	58
1943	16,851	14,618	31,469	12.8	2,218	52
1944	16,495	14,492	30,987	12.7	2,246	49
1945	16,985	14,907	31,892	13.2	2,296	54
1946	16,842	14,705	31,547	12.8	2,139	47
1947	17,898	15,393	33,291	13.3	2,543	49
1948	16,225	13,870	30,095	11.8	1,885	39
1949	17,305	14,804	32,109	12.5	1,762	39
1950	17,910	15,385	33,295	12.8	1,528	35
1951	19,422	16,583	36,005	13.9	1,502	36
1952	16,985	14,020	31,005	12.0	1,377	33
1953	17,117	14,275	31,392	12.1	1,299	31
1954	17,830	14,992	32,822	12.6	1,271	32
1955	18,528	15,410	33,938	13.0	1,219	31
1956	17,548	14,890	32,438	12.4	1,174	29
1957	17,767	14,929	32,696	12.5	1,183	28
1958	17,604	15,038	32,642	12.5	1,126	27
1959	17,318	14,816	32,134	12.3	1,113	26
1960	17,716	14,999	32,715	12.4	1,117	25
1961	18,160	15,545	33,705	12.8	1,079	24
1962	18,160	15,621	33,781	12.7	1,150	25
1963	18,554	16,209	34,763	13.1	1,156	25
1964	17,607	15,139	32,746	12.2	1,154	24
1965	17,667	15,395	33,062	12.3	940	20
1966	18,599	16,044	34,643	12.8	911	20
1967	17,704	15,456	33,160 (5)	12.2	813	19
1968	18,327	16,565	34,892	12.8	867	20
1969	19,139	16,814	35,953	13.2	826	19

POPULATION 10 Deaths. Number of Deaths (by sex), Crude death-rates and infant mortality,(1)

Wales 1838 - 1974

	Deaths			Crude death rate per 1,000	Infant Deaths	
	Males	Females	Total		Number	Rate per 1,000 Births
1970	18,363	16,635	34,998	12.8	794	19
1971	18,131	16,686	34,817	12.8	794	18
1972	19,143	16,857	36,000	13.2	639	16
1973	18,574	17,252	35,826	13.0	615	16
1974	18,403	17,231	35,634	12.9	617	17

General Notes.

i) Sources. Registrar General. Annual Report, 1845 - 1920, Abstract of Births and Deaths;

Registrar General. Statistical Review, 1921 - 1974

ii) Up to 1910 the figures given by the Registrar General relate to the Welsh Registration division: from 1911 onwards they relate to Wales.

iii) For the years before 1910 the crude death rate and the infant mortality rates have been separately calculated. Up to 1910 the Resistrar General's reports do not give these rates for Wales, although they do give such rates separately for North Wales, South Wales and Monmouthshire. The rates given in the table have been calculated as follows: the crude death rate has been obtained by relating the number of deaths to the estimated mid-year population as given in Table 8, the infant mortality rate by relating the infant deaths to the total of births as given in Table 10.

Notes

1. The infant mortality rates are based on the number of live births occurring in the same year, except forthe period 1931 to 1956 when they are based on the births to which they relate in the current and preceding years.

2. Excludes 265 deaths in Gresford colliery disaster. These deaths were not actually registered until 1938-9.

3. Welsh Digest of Statistics gives 31,941 for 1938 and 33,398 for 1939 to include those mentioned in note 2. above.

4. Deaths of civilians only for September 1939 to end of 1949 (males); and June 1941 to end of 1949 (females).

5. Figures include 141 deaths resulting from Aberfan disaster of 1966 but registered in 1967.

POPULATION 11 Number of Births and Birth-rates, Wales 1839 - 1974.

	Legitimate		Illegitimate		Total	Crude rate per 1,000 population.
	Males	Females	Males	Females		
1839 (1)	15,826	15,120			30,946	
1840	16,204	15,208			31,412	
1841	16,607	15,755			32,362	30.9 (2)
1842	15,632	14,603	1,139	1,065	32,439	30.7
1843	16,921	16,067			32,988	30.9
1844	17,451	16,308			33,759	31.3
1845	15,734	14,717	1,241	1,285	32,977	30.2
1846	16,999	15,926	1,238	1,138	35,301	32.0
1847	16,216	15,325	1,208	1,146	33,895	30.4
1848	16,927	15,910	1,206	1,235	35,278	31.3
1849	17,438	16,220	1,369	1,233	36,260	31.8
1850	17,656	16,742	1,320	1,286	37,004	32.2
1851	17,836	17,058	1,377	1,350	37,621	32.3
1852	18,169	17,134	1,408	1,319	38,030	32.4
1853	18,189	17,164	1,397	1,254	38,004	32.0
1854	19,203	17,955	1,447	1,282	39,887	33.3
1855	19,118	18,477	1,466	1,316	40,377	33.3
1856	20,363	19,241	1,405	1,426	42,435	34.7
1857	20,551	19,637	1,472	1,371	43,031	34.8
1858	20,445	19,278	1,468	1,391	42,582	34.1
1859	21,725	20,751	1,563	1,430	45,469	36.1
1860	21,245	20,271	1,466	1,474	44,456	34.9
1861	20,688	19,809	1,406	1,389	43,292	33.7
1862	21,318	20.477	1,612	1,520	44,927	34.6
1863	22,011	20.509	1,704	1,531	45,755	34.9
1864	22,633	21,421	1,692	1,606	47,352	35.8
1865	22,612	21,834	1,647	1,642	47,735	35.7
1866	23,375	22,139	1,660	1,574	48,748	26.2
1867	23,152	22,178	1,612	1,484	48,426	35.6
1868	23,681	22,579	1,608	1,615	49,483	36.0
1869	23,416	22,206	1,619	1,575	48,816	35.2
1870	23,444	22,519	1,582	1,445	48,990	35.0
1871	23,577	22,795	1,574	1,487	49,433	35.0
1872	23,998	22,818	1,576	1,509	49,901	35.0
1873	24,633	23,382	1,401	1,356	50,772	35.2
1874	26,199	25,064	1,483	1,384	54,130	37.1
1875	26,248	25,189	1,420	1,289	54,146	36.7
1876	27,086	25,468	1,392	1,360	55,306	37.1
1877	26,259	25,533	1,416	1,320	54,528	36.2
1878	25,734	24,747	1,395	1,314	53,190	35.0
1879	25,250	24,358	1,453	1,336	52,397	34.2
1880	24,888	23,825	1,349	1,294	51,356	32.8
1881	25.426	24,168	1,402	1,334	52,330	33.1
1882	25.584	24,408	1.370	1,342	52,704	34.3
1883	25,340	24,381	1,343	1,303	52,367	32.4
1884	26 288	25,035	1,305	1,284	53,912	33.1

POPULATION 11 Number of Births and Birth-rates, Wales 1839 - 1974.

	Legitimate		Illegitimate		Total	Crude rate per 1,000 population.
	Males	Females	Males	Females		
1885	26,530	25,395	1,417	1,331	54,673	33.2
1886	26,750	25,288	1.386	1,315	54,739	33.0
1887	26,142	24,743	1,331	1,277	53,493	31.8
1888	26,151	25,152	1,364	1,278	53,945	31.8
1889	26,222	24,887	1,334	1,227	53,670	31.3
1890	26,905	25,729	1,223	1,191	55,048	31.3
1891	29,181	27,618	1,254	1,241	59,294	33.3
1892	28,860	27,871	1,197	1,097	59,025	32.7
1893	29,991	29,036	1,233	1,258	61,518	33.7
1894	28,815	27,445	1,177	1,247	58,684	31.8
1895	30,609	29,186	1,178	1,238	62,211	33.3
1896	30,333	29,282	1,291	1,185	62,091	32.8
1897	30,316	28,907	1,172	1,180	61,575	33.9
1898	30,096	29,779	1,269	1,174	62,318	32.2
1899	29,925	28,526	1,144	1,068	60,663	30.9
1900	30,429	29,134	1,188	1,176	61,927	31.0
1901	31,204	29,828	1,121	1,080	63,233	31.3
1902	32,395	30,715	1,136	1,171	65,417	32.0
1903	32,418	31,405	1,205	1,113	66,141	31.6
1904	32,801	31,702	1,252	1,154	66,909	31.6
1905	33,062	31,361	1,260	1,205	66,888	31.2
1906	32,708	31,271	1,248	1,173	66,400	30.6
1907	32,153	31,159	1,182	1,168	65,662	32.1
1908	34,115	32.423	1.200	1,185	68,923	31.1
1909	34,156	32,968	1,281	1,258	69,663	30.1
1910	33,851	32,570	1,256	1,191	68,868	28.6
1911	32,987	32,033	1,349	1,247	67,616	27.8
1912	32,741	31,499	1,357	1,334	66,931	27.0
1913	33,176	32,035	1,377	1,268	67,856	26.9
1914	33,465	31,992	1,293	1,321	68,071	27.0
1915	31,377	29,868	1,333	1,284	63,862	25.3
1916	29,083	28,121	1,275	1,229	59,708	23.2
1917	26,749	25,389	1,235	1,146	54,519	20.5
1918	27,457	26,237	1,382	1,274	56,350	21.6
1919	26,936	25,304	1,362	1,346	54,948	20.7
1920	34,416	32,783	1,556	1,537	70,292	26.7
1921	32,780	31,025	1,404	1,339	66,548	25.0
1922	28,868	27,467	1,261	1,115	58,711	21.9
1923	28,752	27,451	1,171	1,074	58,448	21.6
1924	28,350	26,885	1,098	1,093	57,426	21.0
1925	27,068	25,840	1,024	1,003	54,935	20.1
1926	25,698	24,888	1,045	1,006	52,637	19.3
1927	22,732	22,164	954	1,023	46,873	17.2
1928	22,812	21,862	1,048	974	46,696	17.4
1929	21,717	20.860	984	1,034	44,595	16.7

POPULATION 11 Number of Births and Birth-rates, Wales 1839 - 1974.

	Legitimate		Illegitimate		Total	Crude rate per 1,000 population.
	Males	Females	Males	Females		
1930	21,433	20,505	1,015	988	43,941	16.7
1931	20.734	19 677	1,003	916	42,330	16.3
1932	20,097	19.055	907	814	40,873	15.8
1933	19,400	18,316	874	834	39,424	15.4
1934	19,607	18,678	869	802	39,956	15.6
1935	19,437	18,145	810	795	39,187	15.4
1936	18,774	17,683	722	730	37,909	15.1
1937	18,434	17,281	773	687	37,175	15.0
1938	18,482	17,681	743	719	37,625	15.3
1939	18,502	17,498	730	672	37,402	15.2
1940	19,318	18,494	768	739	39,319	15.6
1941	19,503	18,597	906	880	39,886	15.3
1942	21,205	19,891	1,030	1,004	43,130	17.1
1943	21,148	19,769	1.172	1,181	43,270	17.6
1944	22,395	21,322	1,532	1,481	46,730	19.1
1945	19,615	18,639	1,685	1,576	41,515	17.1
1946	23,051	21,869	1,331	1,315	47,566	19.2
1947	25,238	23,716	1,146	1,063	51,163	20.4
1948	23,185	21,968	1,037	985	47,175	18.5
1949	22,013	20,585	883	856	44,337	17.2
1950	21,141	19,893	863	879	42,776	16.5
1951	20,351	19,360	787	772	41,270	16.0
1952	20,358	19,419	837	774	41,388	16.0
1953	20,602	19,272	878	776	41,528	16.0
1954	19,864	18,984	728	680	40,256	15.5
1955	19,149	18,378	726	623	38,876	14.9
1956	20,348	19,100	758	709	40,915	15.7
1957	20,711	19,505	710	719	41,645	15.9
1958	21,095	19,889	768	708	42,460	16.2
1959	21,069	19,648	783	762	42,262	16.1
1965	22,583	21.043	1,439	1,227	46,292	17.2
1966	21,608	20.419	1,433	1,406	44,866	16.6
1967	20,964	19,741	1,534	1,467	43,706	16.1
1968	20,981	20,072	1,618	1,536	44,207	16.3
1969	20,583	19,516	1,483	1,500	43,082	15.8
1960	21,831	20,633	854	829	44,147	16.8
1961	22,247	20,842	916	918	44,923	17.1
1962	22,225	21,083	1,054	1,020	45,382	17.1
1963	22,969	21,806	1,169	1,094	47,038	17.7
1964	22,921	22,008	1,360	1,213	47,502	17.7
1970	20,525	19,097	1,432	1,433	42,487	15.5
1971	20,670	19,318	1,600	1,468	43,056	15.8
1972	19,104	17,785	1,588	1,478	39,955	14.6
1973	17,849	16,877	1,483	1,388	37,597	13.7
1974	33,216		2,990		36,206	13.1

General Notes.

i) Sources. Registrar General. Annual Report, 1845 - 1920 (the report for 1845 gives figures for 1839 - 1845);
Registrar General. Statistical Review, 1921 - 74.

ii) Up to 1910 the figures given by the Registrar General relate to the Welsh Registration division; from 1911 onwards they relate to Wales.

iii) Before 1910 the Registrar General's reports do not give a birth rate for Wales, although they do give such rates separately for North Wales; South Wales; and Monmouthshire. The rates in the table have been calculated by relating the number of births to the estimated mid-year population as given in Table 8. It should be noted that from 1841-81, the estimates of the total population have been derived from the census estimates for Wales; from 1882 - 1910 they are the figures given by the Registrar General and based on the Welsh Registration division.

Notes.

1. For 1839 - 41 and 1843 - 44 no separate figures are given for illegitimate births, which are included in the figures for legitimate births.

2. For 1839 - 45, The Registrar General's report also gives figures for the birth-rate for Wales. They are :

1839, 29.8	1840, 29.8	1841, 30.3
1842, 29.6	1843, 30.0	1844, 30.3
1845, 29.2		

The difference between these and the calculated figures included in the table for 1841 - 45 result from a) the difference between Wales and the Welsh registration district, and b) the greater deficiencies of registration figures generally in the earlier years.

Population 12 Marriages, Number of Marriages and Rate per Thousand Population Wales, 1839-1974

	Marriages	Rate per 1,000 population
1839	7,847	
1840	7,765	
1841	7,409	14.2
1842	7,350	13.9
1843	7,143	13.4
1844	7,649	14.2
1845	8,304	15.2
1846	9,122	16.5
1847	8,368	15.0
1848	8,433	15.0
1849	8,609	15.1
1850	9,323	16.2
1851	9,195	15.8
1852	9,272	15.8
1853	9,904	16.7
1854	9,911	16.5
1855	9,721	16.1
1856	10,292	16.8
1857	10,195	16.5
1858	9,550	15.3
1859	10,419	16.5
1860	10,009	15.7
1861	9,482	14.7
1862	9,842	15.2
1863	10,570	16.1
1864	11,274	17.0
1865	11,279	16.9
1866	11,285	16.7
1867	10,725	15.8
1868	10,303	15.0
1869	10,504	15.2
1870	10,953	15.7
1871	11,002	15.6
1872	12,126	17.0
1873	12,765	17.7
1874	12,844	17.6
1875	11,856	16.1
1876	11,619	15.6
1877	11,055	14.7
1878	10,562	13.9
1879	10,130	13.2
1880	10,952	14.0
1881	11,283	14.3
1882	11,744	15.3
1883	12,254	15.2
1884	12,226	15.0
1885	11,751	14.3
1886	11,382	13.7
1887	12,018	14.3
1888	12,290	14.5
1889	13,462	15.7
1890	14,457	16.4
1891	14,615	16.4
1892	14,564	16.2
1893	13,652	15.0
1894	14,683	15.9
1895	14,203	15.2
1896	14,752	15.6
1897	15,047	16.6
1898	14,074	14.3
1899	15,563	15.9
1900	16,214	16.2
1901	16,377	16.2
1902	16,133	15.8
1903	16,256	15.5
1904	16,175	15.3
1905	16,331	15.2
1906	17,007	15.7
1907	17,538	17.1
1908	17,592	15.8
1909	17,260	15.3
1910	17,062	14.2
1911	17,918	14.7
1912	18,192	14.7
1913	19,371	15.4
1914	20,052	15.8
1915	21,479	16.7
1916	17,342	13.4
1917	16,587	12.4
1918	17,056	13.0
1919	24,397	18.3
1920	25,667	19.4
1921	20,939	15.6
1922	19,922	14.7
1923	20,133	14.9
1924	19,729	14.5
1925	19,334	14.1
1926	16,320	12.0
1927	19,508	14.3
1928	18,706	13.9
1929	19,147	14.3
1930	19,216	14.6
1931	18,926	14.4
1932	19,368	14.9
1933	20,058	15.5
1934	21,095	16.4
1935	20,839	16.3
1936	20,580	16.2
1937	20,354	16.4
1938	20,012	16.2
1939	23,401	19.0
1940	26,291	20.8
1941	24,700	19.0
1942	23,769	18.8
1943	19,278	15.7
1944	18,371	15.0
1945	23,791	19.6
1946	23,354	18.9
1947	23,448	18.8
1948	23,265	18.2
1949	22,108	17.2
1950	20,813	16.0
1951	20,759	16.0
1952	20,590	15.9
1953	19,967	15.4
1954	19,578	15.1
1955	21,273	16.3
1956	20,301	15.6
1957	19,729	15.1
1958	19,277	14.7
1959	19,198	14.6
1960	19,341	14.7
1961	19,619	14.9
1962	19,302	14.6
1963	19,468	14.6
1964	19,892	14.9
1965	20,020	14.9
1966	20,659	15.3
1967	20,749	15.3
1968	22,353	16.4
1969	21,753	16.0
1970	23,058	16.9
1971	22,424	16.5
1972	22,725	16.6
1973	22,292	16.2
1974	21,252	15.3

General Notes

(i) Sources. Registrar General Annual Report, 1845-1920 (1845 report gives figures for 1839-45); Registrar General Statistical Review, 1921-74.

(ii) Up to 1938 the figures relate to the Welsh registration division: from 1939 on they are for Wales.

(iii) Before 1914 (and for 1923-30) the Registrar General's reports and reviews do not give a marriage rate for Wales, although from 1853-1910 they do give separate rates for South Wales: North Wales and Monmouthshire. The rates in the table have been calculated by relating the number of marriages to the estimated mid-year population as given in Table 8. For some years (up to 1881; 1910-13 and 1923-30) this means that the number of marriages based on the Welsh registration division is related to the total population based on administrative Wales. The margin of inaccuracy thus introduced is, especially after the earliest years, very slight.

Population 13. Population of Towns, 1801-1971

TOWN		1801	1811	1821	1831	1841	1851	1861	1871	1881	1891	1901	1911	1921	1931	1951	1961	1971
Anglesey:																		
BEAUMARIS	B., M.B.				2,675	2,701	2,599	2,558	2,291	2,239	2,202	2,326	2,231	1,841	1,710	2,134	1,962	2,102
HOLYHEAD	Town, Borough	2,132	3,005	4,071	4,282	3,869												
	P.B, U.S.D., U.D.					2,974	5,622	6,193	7,191	8,680	8,745	10,079	10,636	11,761	10,700	10,563	10,412	10,620
Breconshire:																		
BRECON	Town, M.B.	2,576	3,196	4,193	5,026	5,701	5,673	5,235	5,845	6,247	5,646	5,875	5,908	5,646	5,332	6,470	5,766	6,304
Caernarvonshire:																		
BANGOR	City	1,770	2,383	3,579	4,751	7,232												
	P.B.					5,058	6,338	6,738	9,859									
	U.S.D.								7,939	8,247								
(incorp. 1883)	M.B.									9,005	9,892	11,269	11,236	11,029	10,960			
	M.B.(new boundaries)														11,163	12,822	13,993	14,558
CAERNARVON	Parish[3] B.[3]	3,626	4,595	5,788	7,642	9,192												
	Borough, M.B.					8,001	8,674	8,512	9,449	10,258	9,804	9,760	9,119	8,307	8,469	9,271	9,055	9,260
CONWAY	P.B.					1,828	2,105	2,523	2,620									
(incorp. 1876)	M.B.								2,512	3,254	3,442	4,681	5,242	6,506[1]				
	M.B.(new boundaries)													7,964	8,772			
	M.B.(" ")														8,826	10,239	11,183	12,206
LLANDUDNO	U.S.D., U.D.								3,695	4,839[4]	7,348	9,279	10,469	19,281[1]	13,679			
	U.D.(new boundaries)														15,703	16,715	17,904	19,077
Cardiganshire:																		
ABERYSTWYTH	Chapelry	1,758	2,264	3,556	4,128	4,916												
	Borough, M.B.					4,975	5,231	5,641	6,898	7,088	6,725	8,014	8,411					
	M.B.(new boundaries)												8,794	11,211[1]	9,473	9,315	10,427	10,688
Carmarthenshire:																		
CARMARTHEN	Town, B., M.B.	5,548	7,275	8,906	9,955	9,526	10,524	9,993	10,488	10,514	10,300							
	M.B.(new boundaries)										10,338	10,025	10,221	10,011	10,310	12,114	13,247	13,081
LLANELLI[6]	B.	2,072	2,791	2,621	4,173	6,846	8,415	11,084	13,958									
(M.B. 1913)	U.S.D., U.D., M.B.								15,021	19,760	23,937	25,617	32,071	36,520	38,416	34,476	29,979	26,383
Denbighshire:																		
COLWYN BAY	U.S.D., U.D.									2,418	4,754	8,689	12,630	18,774[1]				
	U.D.(new boundaries)													21,566	20,886			
	M.B.														20,823	22,283	23,201	25,564
WREXHAM	Township, P.B., M.B.	2,575[7]	4,524[7]	4,795	5,484	5,831	6,714	7,562	8,576	10,978	12,552	14,966	18,377	18,703	18,569			
	M.B.(new boundaries)														23,639	30,967	35,438	39,052
Flintshire:																		
FLINT	B., M.B.	1,961	1,433	1,612	2,216	2,860	3,296	3,428	4,269	5,096	5,247	4,625	5,472	6,298	7,655	14,267	13,707	14,662
MOLD	P.B.					3,557	3,432	3,735	4,534									
	L.Bd., U.S.D., U.D.							-	3,978	4,320	4,457	4,263	4,873	4,659	5,137			
	U.D.(new boundaries)														5,260	6,434	6,894	8,251

TOWN		1801	1811	1821	1831	1841	1851	1861	1871	1881	1891	1901	1911	1921	1931	1951	1961	1971
Flintshire:																		
RHYL	U.S.D., U.D.								4,500	6,029	6,491	8,473	9,005	13,490[1]				
	U.D.(new boundaries)													13,968	13,485	18,868	21,737	21,821
Glamorgan:																		
CARDIFF	Town, B., M.B.	1,870	2,457	3,521	6,187	10,077	18,351	32,954	39,536									
	M.B.(new boundaries), C.B.								57,363	82,761	128,915	164,333	182,259	200,184				
	C.B.(new boundaries)													219,580	223,589[5]			
	C.B.(new boundaries)														226,937	243,632	256,582	
	C.B.(new boundaries)																283,998	279,111
MERTHYR	Parish, L.Bd., U.S.D.	7,705	11,104	17,404	22,083	34,977	46,378	49,794	51,949	48,861	58,080							
(C.B. 1908)	U.D., C.B.										59,004	69,228	80,990	80,116	71,108	61,142	59,039	55,317
SWANSEA	Town, B.	6,099	8,196	10,255	13,694	16,787												
	M.B.	10,117[9]	11,963[9]	14,896[9]	19,672[9]	24,604[9]	31,461	41,606										
	M.B.[8]							40,802	51,702	65,597								
	C.B.									76,430	90,349							
	C.B.(new boundaries)										91,034	94,537	114,663					
	C.B.(new boundaries)												143,997	157,554	164,797	160,988	167,322	173,413
ABERAVON[10]	Parish, B., M.B.	275	321	365	573	1,290	2,380	2,916	3,574	4,859	6,300	7,553	10,505	15,370[10]				
PORT TALBOT[10]	M.B.													40,005	40,678	44,115	51,322	50,729
ABERDARE	L.Bd., U.S.D., U.D.							-	36,112	33,804	38,431	43,365	50,830	55,007	48,746	40,932	39,155	37,775
BRITON FERRY[11]	L.Bd., U.S.D., U.D.								4,803	6,061	5,778	6,973	8,472	9,165)				
NEATH[11]	Parish	2,502	2,740	2,823	4,043	4,970	5,778								(11)			
	B., M.B.					4,967	5,841	6,810	9,319	10,409	11,113	13,720	17,586	18,928)				
	M.B.(new boundaries)													32,712	33,340	32,284	30,935	28,619
BRIDGEND	L.Bd, U.S.D., U.D.							-	3,539	4,153	4,676	6,062						
	U.D.(new boundaries)											6,299	8,021	9,199	10,029	13,643	15,174	14,544
BARRY	U.S.D., U.D.									494	13,278	27,030	33,763	38,945	38,891			
(M.B. 1939)	M.B.														38,925	40,990	42,084	41,681
CAERPHILLY	U.D.										8,064	15,835	32,844	36,896	35,768			
	U.D.(new boundaries)														35,024	35,189	35,997	40,788
GELLIGAER	U.D.											17,242	35,521	43,121	41,043	36,169	34,656	33,705
GLYNCORRWG	Hamlet, C.P.	102	116	124	133	136	93	322	734	1,288	2,277[12]							
	C.P.(new boundaries)									1,648	3,522							
(1893)	U.D.										3,683	6,452	8,688	10,771	10,203	9,240	9,368	8,647
LLWCHWR	U.D.													24,752	26,626	25,882	25,013	26,864
MAESTEG	U.S.D., U.D.								7,667	8,310	9,417	15,012	24,977	28,917	25,570	23,141	21,625	20,971
MOUNTAIN ASH	L.Bd, U.S.D.							-	7,457	10,295	17,590							
	U.D.										17,826	31,093	42,246	43,287	38,386	31,521	29,575	27,856

TOWN		1801	1811	1821	1831	1841	1851	1861	1871	1881	1891	1901	1911	1921	1931	1951	1961	1971
OGMORE & GARW	U.S.D., U.D.									6,894	13,800	19,907	26,741	30,174	26,981	22,631	20,985	19,477
PENARTH	Parish	72	75	77	68	110	105	1,406	2,612									
	U.S.D., U.D.								3,104	6,228	12,424	14,228	15,488	17,104	17,719			
	U.D. (new boundaries)															18,544[13]	20,896	24,000
PONTYPRIDD	U.S.D.								11,000[2]	12,317	19,969							
	U.D.										24,763	32,316	43,211	47,184	42,717	38,633	35,494	34,608
PORTHCAWL	U.D.										1,758	1,872	3,444	6,642*	6,447	9,521	11,086	14,103
RHONDDA[14]	Parish	542	973	985	1,047	1,363	1,998	3,857	17,777									
(M.B. 1935-51)	U.S.D., U.D., M.B.								23,950	55,632	88,351	113,735	152,781	162,717	141,346	111,389	100,287[19]	
	M.B. (new boundaries)[6]																100,369	88,994
Merionethshire:																		
FFESTINIOG	Parish, U.S.D., U.D.	732	961	1,168	1,648	3,138	3,460	4,553	8,055	11,274	11,073	11,435	9,674	8,138	9,078	6,920	6,708	5,751
Monmouthshire:																		
NEWPORT[15]	B., M.B.	1,135	2,346	4,000	7,062	10,492	19,323	23,249	27,069	35,313								
	C.B.									38,469	54,707	67,270	83,691	92,358	89,203			
	C.B. (new boundaries)														98,447	105,547		
	C.B. (new boundaries)															106,420	108,123	
	C.B. (new boundaries)																109,087	112,286
ABERGAVENNY	Parish	1,472	3,036															
	Parish		2,815	3,388	3,940	4,689	5,204											
	"town", Impt D., U.S.D., M.B.						4,797	4,621	4,803	6,941	7,743	7,795	8,511	9,010	8,608			
(M.B. 1899)	M.B. (new boundaries)														8,813	8,848	9,624	9,401
ABERSYCHAN[18]	L.Bd, U.S.D., U.D.							-	14,569	13,496	15,296	17,768	24,656	27,087	25,748			
PANTEG[18]	L.Bd., U.S.D.								2,761	3,321								
	U.S.D. (new boundaries), U.D.									5,539	6,479	7,484	10,098	10,985	11,499	(18)		
PONTYPOOL[18]	"town", L.Bd., U.S.D., U.D.						3,708	4,661	4,834	5,244	5,842	6,126	6,452	6,881	6,790			
	U.D. (new boundaries)														43,910	42,703	39,930	37,030
ABERTILLERY	U.S.D.								5,696	6,003	9,138							
	U.D.										10,846	21,945	35,415	38,805	31,803			
	U.D. (new boundaries)														31,755	27,620	25,146	21,142
BEDWELLTY	U.S.D.									3,622	6,773							
	U.D.										6,743	9,988	22,547	31,088	30,074			
	U.D. (new boundaries)														30,970	28,830	27,307	25,331
BLAENAVON	L.Bd., U.S.D.							-	9,376	9,451								
	U.S.D. (new boundaries) U.D.									9,522	11,452	10,869	12,010	12,469	11,076	9,779	8,451	7,186
CHEPSTOW	Town						4,295	3,364										
	L.Bd., U.S.D., U.D.							3,455	3,347	3,591	3,378	3,067	2,953					
	U.D. (new boundaries)												3,048	5,143	4,302	5,283	6,091	8,082
CWBRAN	(1935) U.D.														11,756	13,166	22,486	31,670

TOWN		1801	1811	1821	1831	1841	1851	1861	1871	1881	1891	1901	1911	1921	1931	1951	1961	1971
EBBW VALE	U.S.D.								14,505[2]	14,700	17,034							
	U.D.										17,312	20,994	30,541	35,381	31,686	29,220	28,627	26,069
MYNYDDISLWYN	(1903) U.D.											3,337	9,980	14,900	16,204			
	U.D. (new boundaries)														15,136	14,434	15,464	15,380
NANTYGLO & BLAINA	U.S.D., U.D.									9,267	12,410	13,489	15,395	16,448	13,189	11,442	10,959	10,628
RHYMNEY	U.S.D., U.D.								8,138	8,663	7,733	7,915	11,449	11,690	10,506	9,137	8,861	8,059
RISCA	U.S.D.								5,396[2]	5,540								
	U.S.D. (new boundaries), U.D.									5,556	7,783	9,661	14,149	16,745	16,605	15,130	13,955	15,837
TREDEGAR	"town"						8,305	9,383	12,389									
	U.S.D., U.D.								16,989	18,771	17,341	18,497	23,601	25,110	23,192	20,376	19,835	17,962
Montgomeryshire:																		
NEWTOWN & LLANLLWCHIAN[16]	Parish, U.S.D., U.D.	1,665	2,724	3,593	6,555	6,842	6,559	6,086	5,886	7,170	6,610	6,500	6,068	5,666	5,154	5,431	5,517	6,115
WELSHPOOL	Town, B., M.B.	2,872	3,440	4,255	5,255	6,185	6,564	7,304	6,983[17]	7,107	6,501	6,121	5,917	5,682	5,639	6,036	6,330	7,030
Pembrokeshire:																		
HAVERFORDWEST	Town, B., M.B.	2,880	3,093	2,280	3,915	5,941	6,580	7,019	6,622	6,398	6,179	6,007	5,919	5,756	6,121			
	M.B. (new boundaries)														6,134	7,267	8,892	9,104
MILFORDHAVEN	P.B.					2,377	2,837	3,007	2,836									
	U.S.D., U.D.								3,348	3,812	4,070	5,102	6,399	7,772	10,104			
	U.D. (new boundaries)														10,679	11,710		
	U.D. (new boundaries)															12,159	12,802	13,751
PEMBROKE	B., M.B.	1,842[13]	2,415	2,527	6,511	7,412	10,107	15,071	13,704	14,156	14,978	15,853	15,673	15,472	12,009	12,296	12,751	14,197

General Notes

(i) Sources. Census Returns, 1801-1971. The scattered nature of the information prompts a more specific indication of the major sources in each census:

1801-31	Enumeration. County Tables
1841	Enumeration. County table and Appendix I
1851	Enumeration 2. Welsh Division County tables and pp. 84-9 for P.Bs. and M.Bs.
1861	Volume I. Welsh Division. County tables and p. XXI Table IX.
1871	Area etc. Vol. I Table VII " " Vol. II County tables.
1881	Area etc. Vol. I Table VI " " Vol. II Table II and County tables.
1891	Area etc. Vol. I Table VI " " Vol II Table II
1901	Summary Tables, XI Wales and Mon. County tables.
1911	Administrative Areas, Table 10.
1921	General Tables, 10.
1931	General Tables, 8B.
1951	General Tables, 8.
1961	Age and General Tables, Table 7. For 1921-61 boundary changes were checked in County Tables.
1971	County Tables.

(ii) No attempt has been made to calculate at each census date the population of the particular geographical area covered by any particular town at one given date. The figures given throughout relate solely to the administrative areas, and may thus not always reflect the true growth of an urban area.

As far as possible, however, figures have been taken in a consistent basis for each town. In some cases, this presents no problem- figures are available throughout for the same area even though there may be a change in the administrative unit. For example, an urban sanitary district may become an urban district but still cover the same area. In other cases it has been impossible to obtain figures on a continuously consistent basis. Such breaks in continuity are indicated by starting a new line. For the year of change-over two sets of figures have been given to facilitate comparison.

(iii) The administrative units to which the figures relate are indicated after the name of each town and in the line or lines below where there is a break in continuity, where more than one type of unit is given on the same line, these units are consecutive, not concurrent, but the actual area involved remains the same. The types of administrative units with, where applicable, the abbreviations used are as follows:

Parish)
Town) used 1801-41 and, in a few cases,
Borough) 1851-71;

'Town' used 1851-61 for Pontypool, Tredegar, Chepstow and Abergavenny. The limits were defined by the Superintendent Registrar of the Division;

M.B.(Municipal Borough) used 1851-1971;

C.B. (County Borough) used 1891-1971;

Insp.D. (Improvement Commissioners District) used 1871 only;

L.Bd. (Local Board District) used 1871 only;

U.S.D. (Urban Sanitary District) used 1881-91;

U.D. (Urban District) used 1901-1971;

P.B. (Parliamentary Borough) used 1841-71.

(iv) The figures in italics (or under-lined) are taken from the census following the date for which they are given, and relate to the administrative unit at the later date. All other figures are from the census of the year for which they are given, and relate to the administrative unit as constituted at that year.

(v) 1801-41. For some towns figures are readily obtained for these years: they are described in the census as towns or boroughs and distinguished from the parishes. In a few other cases the boundaries of a town seem to have been the same as the parish under which it appeared in the early censuses. In most cases, however, parish boundaries do not coincide with the boundaries of what later became towns.

For this reason no figures aregiven for 1801-41 for many of the towns included in the table. And caution is needed in interpreting any figures which are given for 1801-41. Partly because it is often impossible to tell if the figures disguise boundary changes but also, and more important, because the figures in the first three censuses under-estimated the true size of the population. The county population figures were later revised but (with the exceptions of Merthyr and Swansea) the figures for towns and parishes were not revised.

Notes

1. 1921 Towns where the size of the population was inflated by summer visitors:

	%	
Aberystwyth	19.9)	
Colwyn Bay	15.7)	
Conway	5.0)	excess of enumerated over estimated
Llandudno	33.1)	resident population expressed as a
Porthcawl	16.7)	percentage of the former.
Rhyl	22.7)	

2. These are only approximate figures, given in 1881.

3. Parish of Llanbeblig, which includes Borough of Carnarvon, and the townships of Bont Newydd and Treflan.

4. The figure 4,807 is given for 1881 in 1891; however, no boundary change is indicated. 4,807 may be a revision or an error.

5. The figures given for Penarth and Cardiff for 1951 do not reflect a boundary change by which a small part of Penarth was transferred to Cardiff on 1 April 1951. Because the 1931 census records were lost in 1941, it was not possible to recalculate the 1931 figures for the area as constituted in 1951.
The Cardiff figures do, however, take account of a boundary change in 1938.

6. The Llanelli figures for 1801 and 1811 reflect later (1851) attempts to put population on same boundary basis.

7. The figures given for 1811-31 are the totals of the figures for Wrexham Regis and Wrexham Abbot for these years, since the population of these two parishes corresponded with that of Wrexham Parliamentary Borough in 1841. The figure for 1801, however, is only that for Wrexham Regis, since Wrexham Abbot is not given in the Census for this year; this accounts for the apparently large increase in population between 1801 and 1811.

8. No boundary change between 1861 and 1871 is mentioned in the 1871 census, but the large difference in the figures given for 1861 in the 1861 and 1871 censuses would seem to indicate a change - unless there was an error or a revision in 1871.

9. The figures for 1801-41 are taken from the 1851 census and relate as nearly as possible to the area as constituted in 1851.

10. November 1921: Aberavon M.B. changed to Port Talbot M.B. and area enlarged considerably.

11. November 1922: Neath M.B. took in all of Briton Ferry U.D., as well as part of Port Talbot, Neath R.D. and Llantwit Lower.

12. The figure in black is the population of the area in 1891, for the area as in 1881. It has been calculated from figures in the 1891 census.

13. Sum of the two parishes making up the borough of Pembroke.

14. Called Ystradyfodwg until 1891.

15. All figures for Newport 1801-51 are taken from the 1851 census, and may be for the area as constituted in 1851, since they differ considerably from the figures given in the individual censuses. There was a boundary change at some time before 1851. The 1821 figure is an estimate made by Rickman in 1831.

16. The present U.D. is Newtown and Llanllwchian. The U.S.D. covered the same area. The two parishes were added together to obtain the figures 1801-71; together they are the same area as the U.S.D. and U.D.

17. 1881 census gives 7,199 as population for 1871, but does not indicate any boundary change.

18. April 1935: Pontypool took in all Panteg U.D. and almost all Abersychan U.D. (25,621 people). The rest of Abersychan went to Abercarn U.D.

19. 1971 census gives Rhondda M.B. as 100,369 for 1961, but does not indicate a boundary change. In fact, the adjacent R.D. of Llantrisant and Llantwit Fardre is shown as losing 82 people (1961) between 1961 and 1971, the same amount as Rhondda gained. Presumably there was a boundary change which has not been noted in 1971 census tables.

Population 14. Migration. Net migration and natural increase, number and per cent for each inter-censal period, Wales and each county, 1841-1971.

WALES

Dates	1. Total Change		2. Natural Increase		3. Net Migration (1-2)	
	Amount	per cent	Amount	per cent	Amount	per cent
1841-51	+120,367	+11.26	+111,312	+10.42	+9,055	+0.85
1851-61	+126,137	+10.63	+145,951	+12.30	-19,814	-1.67
1861-71	+125,669	+9.70	+175,204	+13.52	-49,535	-3.82
1871-81	+157,151	+11.06	+209,284	+14.73	-52,133	-3.67
1881-91	+198,872	+12.61	+216,666	+13.73	-17,794	-1.13
1891 - 1901	+240,202	+13.53	+249,552	+14.06	-9,350	-0.53
1901 - 11	+408,754	+20.10	+310,262	+15.26	+98,492	+4.84
1911-21	+235,553	+9.73	+280,472	+11.59	-44,919	-1.86
1921-31	-63,142	-2.38	+205,565	+7.74	-268,707	-10.12
1931-51	+5,343	+0.21	+186,807	+7.20	-181,464	-7.00
1951-61	+45,348	+1.75	+86,960	+3.35	-41,612	-1.60
1961-71	+87,181	+3.30	+107,782	+4.08	-20.601	-0.78

These figures have been calculated making allowance for the following boundary changes:

1851-61	Loss of 2,217 people (1851) - from Denbigh to England
1861-71	Loss of 16,833 people (1861) - from Denbigh and Radnor
1871-81	Loss of 1,262 people (1871) - from Radnor
1881-91	Loss of 26 people (1881)
1891-1901	Loss of 1,595 people (1891) from Montgomery and Denbigh
1901-1911	Gain of 18,275 people (1901) to Flint

ANGLESEY

Dates	1. Total Change		2. Natural Increase		3. Net Migration (1-2)	
	Amount	per cent	Amount	per cent	Amount	per cent
1841-51	+5,137	+13.48	+3,935	+10.33	+1,202	+3.15
1851-61	-1,575	-3.96	+3,384	+8.52	-4,959	-12.48
1861-71	-3,030	-7.94	+1,963	+5.14	-4,993	-13.09
1871-81	+14	+0.04	+2,432	+6.92	-2,418	-6.88
1881-91	-903	-2.57	+2,320	+6.61	-3,223	-9.18
1891-1901	+589	+1.72	+2,127	+6.22	-1,538	-4.49
1901-11	+551	+1.58	+2,439	+7.01	-1,888	-5.42
1911-21	+816	+1.60	+2,210	+4.34	-1,394	-2.74
1921-31	-2,715	-5.25	+1,187	+2.29	-3,902	-7.54
1931-51	+1,631	+3.33	+914	+1.86	+717	+1.46
1951-61	+1,045	+2.06	+967	+1.91	+78	+0.15
1961-71	+8,056	+15.58	+3,009	+5.82	+5,047	+9.76

These figures have been calculated making allowance for the following boundary changes:

1851-61	Population loss to Caernarvonshire (3,511 people, 1851)
1881-91	Population loss to Caernarvo shire (19 people, 1851 Census)

BRECONSHIRE

Dates	1. Total Change		2. Natural Increase		3. Net Migration (1-2)	
	Amount	per cent	Amount	per cent	Amount	per cent
1841-51	+3,758	+6.78	+6,124	+11.05	-2,366	-4.27
1851-61	-318	-0.54	+6,300	+10.65	-6,618	-11.18
1861-71	-1,928	-3.28	+7,057	+11.99	-8,985	-15.27
1871-81	-2,792	-4.90	+6.683	+11.74	-9,475	-16.64
1881-91	-1.268	-2.34	+5,691	+10.51	-6,959	-12.85
1891-1901	-94	-0.17	+5,485	+10.15	-5,579	-10.32
1901-11	+2,419	+4.48	+5,944	+11.02	-3,525	-6.53
1911-21	+1,935	+3.26	+5,629	+9.49	-3,694	-6.23
1921-31	-3,447	-5.63	+3,824	+6.25	-7,271	-11.88
1931-51	-1,267	-2.19	+2,968	+5.14	-4,235	-7.33
1951-61	-1,323	-2.34	+1,340	+2.37	-2,663	-4.71
1961-71	-1,808	-3.28	+463	+0.84	-2,271	-4.12

These figures have been calculated making allowance for the following boundary changes:

1891-1901 Gains of population (1,173 in 1891) from Carmarthen and Monmouth.

CAERNARVONSHIRE

Dates	1. Total Change		2. Natural Increase		3. Net Migration (1-2)	
	Amount	per cent	Amount	per cent	Amount	per cent
1841-51	+7,921	+9.13	+10,453	+12.05	-2,532	-2.92
1851-61	+5,353	+5.45	+9,820	+10.00	-4,467	-4.55
1861-71	+7,840	+7.57	+10,462	+10.10	-2,622	-2.53
1871-81	+12,403	+11.14	+11,188	+10.05	+1,215	+1.09
1881-91	+1,785	+1.44	+10,244	+8.27	-8,459	-6.83
1891-1901	+11,651	+9.28	+8,839	+7.04	+2,812	+2.24
1901-11	+4,531	+3.30	+9,424	+6.87	-4,893	-3.57
1911-21	+5,932	+4.74	+1,855	+1.48	+4,077	+3.26
1921-31	-7,354	-5.74	+721	+0.56	-8,075	-6.30
1931-51	+3,311	+2.74	-1,475	-1.22	+4,786	+3.96
1951-61	-2,373	-1.91	-1,925	-1.55	-448	-0.36
1961-71	+1,297	+1.07	-1,284	-1.05	+2,581	+2.12

These figures have been calculated making allowance for the following boundary changes:

1851-61 Gain of population (3,511 people in 1851) from Anglesey

1881-91 Gain of population (19 people in 1881) from Anglesey

1921-31 Loss of population (2,792 people in 1921)

CARDIGANSHIRE

Dates	1. Total Change		2. Natural Increase		3. Net Migration (1-2)	
	Amount	per cent	Amount	per cent	Amount	per cent
1841-51	+1,612	+1.68	+11,040	+11.50	-9,428	-9.82
1851-61	-213	-0.22	+9,100	+9.32	-9,313	-9.54
1861-71	+468	+0.48	+10,628	+10.91	-10,160	-10.43
1871-81	-2,732	-2.79	+8,582	+8.77	-11,314	-11.56
1881-91	-8,754	-9.20	+6,968	+7.32	-15,722	-16.53
1891-1901	-3,676	-4.26	+3,592	+4.16	-7,268	-8.41
1901-11	-1,938	-2.34	+1,809	+2.19	-3,747	-4.53
1911-21	+1,002	+1.67	-582	-0.97	+1,584	+2.65
1921-31	-5,697	-9.36	-962	-1.58	-4,735	-7.78
1931-51	-1,906	-3.45	-3,164	-5.73	+1,258	+2.28
1951-61	+370	+0.69	-1,020	-1.91	+1,390	+2.61
1961-71	+1,234	+2.30	-828	-1.54	+2,062	+3.84

These figures have been calculated making allowance for the following boundary changes:

NIL

CARMARTHENSHIRE

Dates	1. Total Change		2. Natural Increase		3. Net Migration (1-2	
	Amount	per cent	Amount	per cent	Amount	per cent
1841-51	+5,113	+5.71	+11,588	+12.94	-6,475	-7.23
1851-61	+1,979	+2.09	+15,803	+16.69	-13,824	-14.60
1861-71	+4,730	+4.89	+12,961	+13.41	-8,231	-8.52
1871-81	+9,874	+9.74	+15,326	+15.12	-5,452	-5.38
1881-91	+7,369	+6.62	+15,239	+13.70	-7,870	-7.07
1891-1901	+5,794	+4.92	+14,382	+12.22	-8,588	-7.30
1901-11	+27,480	+22.24	+16,816	+13.61	+10,664	+8.63
1911-21	+14,667	+9.14	+17,615	+10.98	-2,948	-1.84
1921-31	+4,027	+2.30	+12,129	+6.93	-8,102	-4.63
1931-51	-7,066	-3.95	+7,794	+4.35	-14,860	-8.30
1951-61	-4,026	-2.34	+1,632	+0.95	-5,658	-3.29
1961-71	-5,446	-3.24	-345	-0.21	-5,101	-3.04

These figures have been calculated making allowance for the following boundary changes:

1891-1901 Loss of population (903 people in 1891) to Brecon

DENBIGHSHIRE

Dates	1. Total Change		2. Natural Increase		3. Net Migration (1-2	
	Amount	per cent	Amount	per cent	Amount	per cent
1841-51	+4,879	+5.30	+3,327	+3.61	+1,552	+1.69
1851-61	+9,648	+10.19	+9,286	+9.81	+362	+0.38
1861-71	+5,721	+5.75	+11,845	+11.91	-6,124	-6.16
1871-81	+7,776	+7.39	+11,893	+11.31	-4,117	-3.91
1881-91	+3,716	+3.29	+11,172	+9.89	-7,456	-6.60
1891-1901	+11,355	+9.87	+12,582	+10.93	-1,227	-1.07
1901-11	+10,352	+8.19	+13,706	+10.84	-3,354	-2.65
1911-21	+10,059	+6.95	+12,178	+8.41	-2,119	-1.46
1921-31	+14	+0.01	+8,329	+5.28	-8,315	-5.27
1931-51	+13,078	+8.30	+8,551	+5.42	+4,527	-2.87
1951-61	+3,425	+2.01	+3,028	+1.77	+397	+0.23
1961-71	+11,041	+6.34	+4,594	+2.64	+6,447	+3.70

These figures have been calculated making allowance for the following boundary changes:

1851-61 Loss of population (2,217 people in 1851) to England
1861-71 Loss of population (4,903 people in 1861) to Cheshire
1881-91 Gain of population (42 people in 1881) from Merioneth
1891-1901 Loss of population (1,595 people in 1891)
1921-31 Gain of population (2,792 people in 1921)

FLINTSHIRE

Dates	1. Total Change		2. Natural Increase		3. Net Migration (1-2)	
	Amount	per cent	Amount	per cent	Amount	per cent
1841-51	+249	+0.61	+4,650	+11.40	-4,401	-10.79
1851-61	-1,106	-2.69	+3,275	+7.98	-4,381	-10.67
1861-71	+3,576	+8.95	+4,555	+11.40	-979	-2.45
1871-81	+2,257	+5.19	+5,466	+12.56	-3,209	-7.37
1881-91	-3,209	-7.01	+4,592	+10.03	-7,801	-17.04
1891-1901	-304	-0.71	+4,064	+9.55	-4,368	-10.26
1901-11	+9,186	+15.17	+7,613	+12.58	+1,573	+2.60
1911-21	+13,912	+15.01	+8,386	+9.05	+5,526	+ 5.96
1921-31	+6,272	+5.88	+6,863	+6.44	-591	-0.55
1931-51	+32,390	+28.69	+11,052	+9.79	+21,338	+18.90
1951-61	+4,803	+3.31	+5,679	+3.91	-876	-0.60
1961-71	+25,687	+17.12	+8,358	+5.57	+17,329	+11.55

These figures have been calculated making allowance for the following boundary changes:

1901-11 Gain of population (18,275 in 1901) from Cheshire

GLAMORGANSHIRE

Dates	1. Total Change		2. Natural Increase		3. Net Migration (1-2)	
	Amount	per cent	Amount	per cent	Amount	per cent
1841-51	+62,045	+34.85	+20,170	+11.33	+41,875	+23.52
1851-61	+86,159	+35.89	+41,924	+17.46	+44,235	+18.42
1861-71	+79,544	+24.38	+60,563	+18.56	+18,981	+5.82
1871-81	+112,585	+27.74	+82,276	+20.28	+30,309	+7.47
1881-91	+174,689	+33.70	+97,222	+18.75	+77,467	+14.94
1891-1901	+173,718	+25.09	+132,748	+19.17	+40,970	+5.92
1901 - 11	+264,418	+30.52	+172,297	+19.89	+92,121	+10.63
1911-21	+131,571	+11.74	+167,840	+14.97	-36,269	-3.24
1921-31	-26,764	-2.14	+118,292	+9.44	-145,056	-11.58
1931-51	-26,484	-2.15	+104,687	+8.52	-131,171	-10.67
1951-61	+27,147	+2.26	+50,980	+4.24	-23,833	-1.98
1961-71	+29,023	+2.36	+59,116	+4.81	-30,093	-2.45

These figures have been calculated making allowance for the following boundary changes:

1891-1901 Loss of population (640 people, 1891) to Monmouthshire
1931-51 Gain of population (3,348 people, 1931)
1961-71 Loss of population (21 people, 1961)

MERIONETHSHIRE

Dates	1. Total Change		2. Natural Increase		3. Net Migration (1-2)	
	Amount	per cent	Amount	per cent	Amount	per cent
1841-51	+594	+1.17	+4,781	+9.43	-4,187	-8.26
1851-61	+1,923	+3.75	+4,703	+9.17	-2,780	-5.42
1861-71	+8,277	+15.55	+6,534	+12.28	+1,743	+3.27
1871-81	+6,771	+11.01	+8,319	+13.53	-1,548	-2.52
1881-91	-3,511	-5.15	+7,202	+10.55	-10,713	-15.70
1891-1901	-357	-0.55	+4,871	+7.54	-5,228	-8.09
1901 - 11	-3,968	-6.18	+4,397	+6.84	-8,365	-13.02
1911-21	-478	-1.05	+492	+1.08	-970	-2.13
1921-31	-1,886	-4.18	+559	+1.24	-2,445	-5.42
1931-51	-1,736	-4.02	-730	-1.69	-1,006	-2.33
1951-61	-3,155	-7.61	-199	-0.48	-2,956	-7.13
1961-71	-2,980	-7.78	+138	+0.36	-3,118	-8.14

These figures have been calculated making allowance for the following boundary changes:

1881-1891 Population loss (41 people, 1881) to Denbigh
1891-1901 Population loss (121 people, 1891)

MONMOUTHSHIRE

Dates	1. Total Change		2. Natural Increase		3. Net Migration (1-2)	
	Amount	per cent	Amount	per cent	Amount	per cent
1841-51	+26,109	+17.29	+16,509	+10.93	+9,600	+6.36
1851-61	+19,847	+11.20	+25,956	+14.65	-6,109	-3.45
1861-71	+22,731	+11.54	+29,919	+15.19	-7,188	-3.65
1871-81	+14,624	+6.66	+36,349	+16.54	-21,725	-9.89
1881-91	+40,938	+17.47	+37,237	+15.89	+3,701	+1.58
1891-1901	+41,252	+14.97	+46,387	+16.83	-5,135	-1.86
1901 - 11	+97,802	+30.87	+63,394	+20.01	+34,408	+10.86
1911-21	+55,075	+13.92	+63,205	+15.97	-8,130	-2.05
1921-31	-15,836	-3.51	+46,790	+10.38	-62,626	-13.89
1931-51	-6,495	-1.50	+46,503	+10.77	-52,998	-12.28
1951-61	+19,564	+4.60	+21,184	+4.98	-1,620	-0.38
1961-71	+17,471	+3.93	+28,414	+6.39	-10,943	-2.46

These figures have been calculated making allowance for the following boundary changes:

1881-91 Loss of population (28 people in 1881)
1891-1901 Gain of population (370 people in 1891)
1931-51 Loss of population (3,348 people in 1931)
1961-71 Gain of population (21 people in 1961)

MONTGOMERYSHIRE

Dates	1. Total Change		2. Natural Increase		3. Net Migration (1-2)	
	Amount	per cent	Amount	per cent	Amount	per cent
1841-51	-2,614	-3.28	+5,009	+6.28	-7,623	-9.56
1851-61	-219	-0.28	+7,116	+9.22	-7,335	-9.51
1861-71	+1,477	+1.92	+8,117	+10.55	-6,640	-8.63
1871-81	-2,204	-2.81	+8,961	+11.43	-11,165	-14.24
1881-91	-8,900	-11.68	+6,886	+9.04	-15,786	-20.72
1891-1901	-3,424	-5.08	+5,263	+7.81	-8,687	-12.89
1901 - 11	-1,793	-2.80	+4,808	+7.51	-6,601	-10.32
1911-21	-1,883	-3.54	+2,636	+4.96	-4,519	-8.50
1921-31	-2,790	-5.44	+2,205	+4.30	-4,995	-9.74
1931-51	-2,483	-5.12	+1,799	+3.71	-4,282	-8.83
1951-61	-1,825	-3.97	+1,481	+3.22	-3,306	-7.19
1961-71	-1,046	-2.37	+954	+2.16	-2,000	-4.53

These figures have been calculated making allowance for the following boundary changes:

1891-1901 Gain of population (121 people in 1891)

76,196 is the population figure given for 1881 in 1881
76,197 is the population figure given for 1881 in 1891
but probably an error rather than a boundary change.

PEMBROKESHIRE

Dates	1. Total Change		2. Natural Increase		3. Net Migration (1-2)	
	Amount	per cent	Amount	per cent	Amount	per cent
1841-51	+5,915	+7.53	+10,622	+13.52	-4,707	-5.99
1851-61	+3,218	+3.81	+8,965	+10.61	-5,747	-6.80
1861-71	-3,817	-4.35	+10,009	+11.41	-13,826	-15.77
1871-81	-194	-0.23	+9,198	+10.97	-9,392	-11.20
1881-91	-1,676	-2.00	+9,914	+11.85	-11,590	-13.85
1891-1901	+421	+0.51	+7,629	+9.30	-7,208	-8.79
1901 - 11	+2,450	+2.97	+7,922	+9.61	-5,472	-6.64
1911-21	+2,018	+2.24	+6,962	+7.74	-4,944	-5.50
1921-31	-4,772	-5.19	+4,546	+4.94	-9,318	-10.13
1931-51	+3,700	+4.24	+5,644	+6.47	-1,944	-2.23
1951-61	+3,218	+3.54	+4,670	+5.14	-1,452	-1.60
1961-71	+4,844	+5.15	+4,937	+5.25	-93	-0.10

These figures have been calculated making allowance for the following boundary changes:

NIL

RADNORSHIRE

Dates	1. Total Change		2. Natural Increase		3. Net Migration (1-2)	
	Amount	per cent	Amount	per cent	Amount	per cent
1841-51	-351	-1.70	+3,403	+10.71	-3,754	-11.81
1851-61	+1,441	+4.59	+4,330	+13.78	-2,889	-9.19
1861-71	+80	+0.38	+3,236	+15.46	-3,156	-15.07
1871-81	-1,231	-6.23	+2,479	+12.55	-3,710	-18.78
1881-91	-1,404	-7.58	+2,019	+10.90	-3,423	-18.48
1891-1901	+3,122 (1)	+18.24	+2,085	+12.18	+1,037	+6.06
1901 - 11	-2,736	-13.52	+1,951	+9.64	-4,687	-23.16
1911-21	+927	+4.10	+1,617	+7.16	-690	-3.05
1921-31	-2,194	-9.33	+1,082	+4.60	-3,276	-13.93
1931-51	-1,330	-6.24	+1,008	+4.73	-2,338	-10.96
1951-61	-1,522	-7.61	+260	+1.30	-1,782	-8.91
1961-71	-192	-1.04	+256	+1.39	-448	-2.43

These figures have been calculated making allowance for the following boundary changes:

1861-71 Loss of population (11,930 people in 1861) to Hereford

1871-81 Loss of population (1,262 people in 1871) to Hereford

1. "At the date of the recent census, the population of the county was augmented by a large number of men temporarily engaged in the construction of new waterworks for the corporation of Birmingham. These men, together with their families, account for the abnormal increase in the population of the county". (1901 census, County Tables, Radnor, Table 1 - footnote)

General Notes

(i) Sources. Census Reports, 1851-1971; Registrar General Annual Reports, 1841-1920 and Statistical Review, 1921-71.

(ii) Most of the figures in these tables have been separately calculated from material in the censuses and the Registrar General's annual reports (later statistical reviews).
The figures in column 1 (Total Change) have been calculated from the population figures in the censuses, taking into account boundary changes between the censuses.
For 1841-1911 the figures relate to the registration counties (and, for Wales, to the Welsh Registration Division) because until 1911 the natural increase figures are only available for registration counties.
For 1921-71 the figures relate to administrative counties.

Boundary changes mean that the figures for one census are not always directly comparable with those of the next. In all cases where there has been a boundary change, the population increase or decrease has been calculated from the figures relating to the population of the county as constituted at the later date. Thus the population of Anglesey in 1851 was 43,243 and in 1861 it was 38,157. But between 1851 and 1861 there was a boundary change so that the population of the county in 1851, for the 1861 area, was 39,732. The inter-censal change is the difference between 39,732 and 38,157.

The implicit assumption of this method of calculating the total change in population is that the boundary change took place at the beginning of the inter-censal period. However, the registrar-general's annual figures of births and deaths (from which the Natural Increase figures of column 2 have been calculated) relate to the original area until the actual date of any boundary change. In a few cases this could be a significant source of error.

All boundary changes and the numbers involved have been noted on the relevant tables.

(iii) With the exceptions noted below, the figures in column 2 (Natural Increase) have been calculated by subtracting the total deaths in the ten years between censuses from the total births. For strict accuracy these figures should relate to the exact period between the censuses, e.g. from April 1811 to June 1921. However, it is not possible to obtain quarterly figures for births and deaths by counties before 1921, or for 1961, and thus all figures in column 2 relate to ten complete years - the whole year of the census and the nine following years, e.g. 1881-90 inclusive.

The exceptions arise because the figures for natural increase for the counties for 1851-81 and 1891-21 were taken directly from the figures given in the censuses and not calculated from the registrar-general's reports. Hence these figures presumably relate to the exact period between censuses and not to the calendar years.
No allowance has been made in the period 1841-71 for the under-registration of births.

(iv) The figures in column 3 (migration) are simply the difference between columns 1 and 2 (i.e. the total inter-censal change in population minus the natural increase.

(v) The percentages are of the relevant total population at the beginning of each ten-year period.

Population 15. Migration. Number born in Wales and living in United States, 1850-1970

Date	Population of U.S. born in Wales	Welsh migrants to U.S. in intercensal period
1850	29,868	..
1860	45,763[1]	..
1870	74,533	..
1880	83,302	..
1890	100,079	12,640
1900	93,586	11,219
1910	82,488	18,631
1920	67,066	15,379
1930	60,203[1][2]	17,267
1940	35,360	..
1950	30,060	..
1960	23,469	..
1970	17,014	..

General Notes

i) Sources. Historical Statistics of the United States for U.S. population born in Wales, 1850-1950; U.S. Censuses for 1960, 1970 and notes 1 and 2; B. Thomas, The Welsh Economy, p11, for Welsh migrants to U.S., 1890-1930.

ii) The figures in the two columns of the table are not directly comparable, partly because they are drawn from different sources but mainly because they measure different things. Thus the difference between the column indicating the number of Welsh migrants and the numbers indicated in note 2 is accounted for by the deaths of immigrants, re-emigration, etc.

Notes

1. An indication of the distribution by states is given below for 1860 and 1930.

	1860	1930
Alabama	11	141
Arizona	-	139
Arkansas	10	51
California	1,262	4,111
Colorado (3)	38	1,061
Connecticut	176	581
Delaware	30	45
District of Columbia	28	116
Florida	6	289
Georgia	56	83
Idaho	-	355
Illinois	1,528	3,277
Indiana	226	934
Iowa	913	1,183
Kansas	163	785
Kentucky	420	114
Louisiana	97	66
Maine	88	137
Maryland	701	477
Massachusetts	320	1,358
Michigan	348	2,236
Minnesota	422	582
Mississippi	21	18
Missouri	305	573
Montana	-	580
Nebraska (3)	128	383
Nevada (3)	21	67
New Hampshire	14	72
New Jersey	371	1,532
New Mexico (3)	2	99
New York	7,998	7,037
North Carolina	20	35
North Dakota (3)	-	111
Ohio	8,365	6,897
Oklahoma	-	235
Oregon	32	592
Pennsylvania	13,101	17,767
Rhode Island	19	224
South Carolina	11	13
South Dakota	-	265
Tennessee	86	104
Texas	48	260
Utah (3)	945	862
Vermont	384	462
Virginia	584	132
Washington (3)	11	1,694
West Virginia	-	607
Wisconsin	6,454	1,241
Wyoming	-	222

2. Of these, 32,189 were males and 28,016 were females. It is also possible to break-down the figure for 1930 by year of migration:

	Males	Females	Total
1900 or earlier	17,340	16,070	33,410
1901-10	4,947	3,452	8,399
1911-14	2,143	1,767	3,910
1915-19	654	690	1,344
1920-24	2,567	2,079	4,646
1925-29	2,929	2,331	5,260
1930 (to Apr 1st)	128	100	228
unknown	1,481	1,527	3,008

3. These were territories, not states, in 1860; the figure given for North Dakota is that for the whole Dakota Territory.

Population 16. Language. Number of Welsh speakers, by sex, Wales and each county and county borough, 1891-1971

	Population aged 3yrs & over			Welsh-speaking			Speaking both English & Welsh			Total Welsh Speakers		
	Persons	Males	Females	Persons	Males	Females	Persons	Males	Females	Persons	Males	Females
						WALES						
1891[1]	1,685,614	..	..	508,036	..	..	402,253	..	..	910,289[2]	..	..
1901	1,864,696	937,236	927,460	280,905	137,333	143,572	648,919	324,539	324,380	929,824[2]	461,872	467,952
1911	2,247,927	1,144,694	1,103,233	190,292	92,737	97,555	787,074	395,907	391,167	977,366[2]	488,644	488,722
1921	2,486,740	1,243,768	1,242,972	155,989	76,591	79,389	766,103	381,966	384,137	922,092[2]	458,557	463,535
1931	2,472,378	1,232,580	1,239,798	97,932	48,629	49,303	811,329	407,428	403,901	909,261	456,057	453,204
1951[3]	2,472,429	1,205,506	1,266,923	41,155	19,528	21,627	673,531	328,033	345,498	714,686	347,561	367,125
1961	2,518,711	1,227,512	1,291,199	26,223	13,542	12,681	629,799	301,747	328,032	656,002	315,289	340,713
1971[4]	2,602,955	1,261,705	1,341,255	32,725	15,865	16,860	509,700	239,925	269,775	542,425	255,790	286,630
						ANGLESEY						
1891[1]	32,836	..	..	23,200	..	..	7,201	..	..	30,401	..	..
1901	47,504	22,884	24,620	22,791	11,295	11,496	20,763	9,469	11,267	43,554	20,791	22,763
1911	48,095	23,148	24,947	17,434	8,702	8,732	25,232	11,742	13,490	42,666	20,444	22,222
1921	48,876	23,296	25,580	15,133	7,603	7,530	26,364	12,430	13,934	41,497	20,033	21,464
1931	46,940	22,551	24,389	11,231	5,733	5,498	29,813	14,233	15,580	41,044	19,966	21,078
1951[3]	48,178	23,231	24,947	4,623	2,240	2,383	33,820	16,243	17,577	38,443	18,483	19,960
1961	49,156	24,029	25,127	2,765	1,454	1,311	34,336	16,384	17,952	37,101	17,838	19,263
1971[4]	56,450	27,660	28,790	2,555	1,275	1,280	34,530	16,615	17,915	37,090	17,890	19,195
						BRECONSHIRE						
1891[1]	50,335	..	..	5,228	..	..	13,699	..	..	18,927	..	..
1901	50,409	25,573	24,836	4,674	2,292	2,382	18,445	9,325	9,120	23,119	11,617	11,502
1911	55,315	28,319	26,996	3,015	1,476	1,539	19,881	10,226	9,655	22,896	11,702	11,194
1921	57,540	29,135	28,405	2,603	1,293	1,310	18,806	9,662	9,144	21,409	10,955	10,454
1931	55,153	27,930	27,223	1,104	555	549	19,443	10,021	9,422	20,547	10,576	9,971
1951[3]	53,909	27,275	26,634	295	127	168	16,044	8,068	7,976	16,339	8,195	8,144
1961	52,855	26,736	26,119	333	174	159	14,517	7,154	7,363	14,850	7,328	7,522
1971[4]	51,185	25,460	25,725	555	245	305	11,150	5,345	5,810	11,705	5,590	6,115

	Population aged 3yrs & over			Welsh-speaking			Speaking both English & Welsh			Total Welsh Speakers		
	Persons	Males	Females	Persons	Males	Females	Persons	Males	Females	Persons	Males	Females
						CAERNARVONSHIRE						
1891 (1)	120,314	..	..	78,780	..	..	28,330	..	..	107,110	..	..
1901	117,647	53,364	61,268	55,955	28,089	27,866	49,746	23,041	26,305	105,701	51,130	54,171
1911	118,344	56 034	62,310	42,097	21,291	20,806	59,150	27,579	31,571	101,247	48,870	52,377
1921	124,960	56,915	68,045	32,701	16,220	16,481	60,986	28,380	32,606	93,687	44,600	49,087
1931	116,013	54,332	61,681	24,873	12,658	12,215	67,024	31,916	35,108	91,897	44,574	47,323
1951 (3)	118,824	54,472	64,352	10,552	5,247	5,305	74,563	35,023	39,540	85,115	40,270	44,845
1961	116,932	53,715	63,217	5,768	2,947	2,821	74,118	34,530	39,588	79,886	37,477	42,409
1971 (4)	117,960	54,645	63,315	5,125	2,540	2,585	67,980	31,695	36,285	73,105	34,235	38,870
						CARDIGANSHIRE						
1891 (1)	82,979	..	..	61,624	..	..	17,111	..	..	78,735	..	..
1901	57,664	25,147	32,517	29,081	12,036	17,045	24,557	11,257	13,300	53,638	23,293	30,345
1911	57,039	25,537	31,502	19,497	8,078	11,419	21,580	14,508	17,702	41,077	22,586	28,491
1921	58,018	26,400	31,618	15,158	6,526	8,632	32,444	15,335	17,109	47,602	21,861	25,741
1931	53,186	24,404	28,782	10,612	4,696	5,916	35,679	16,614	19,065	46,291	21,310	24,981
1951 (3)	51,110	23,937	27,173	3,803	1,677	2,126	36,839	17,422	19,417	40,642	19,099	21,543
1961	51,460	24,890	26,570	2,402	1,206	1,196	36,112	17,133	18,979	38,514	18,339	20,175
1971 (4)	52,900	25,545	27,355	1,960	985	975	33,820	16,060	17,760	35,780	17,045	18,735
						CARMARTHENSHIRE						
1891 (1)	112,685	..	..	63,345	..	..	36,937	..	..	100,282	..	..
1901	126,166	60,102	66,064	44,901	20,409	24,492	69,046	33,674	35,372	113,947	54,083	59,864
1911	149,691	74,721	74,970	30,705	13,882	16,823	96,531	48,187	48,344	127,236	62,069	65,167
1921	164,319	81,331	82,988	27,063	12,664	14,399	108,424	53,956	54,468	135,487	66,620	68,867
1931	171,445	85,068	86,377	15,728	7,312	8,416	125,410	62,904	62,506	141,138	70,216	70,922
1951 (3)	164,681	80,585	84,096	7,302	3,305	3,997	119,993	58,863	61,130	127,295	62,168	65,127
1961	161,099	78,428	82,671	3,976	1,986	1,990	116,963	56,736	60,227	120,939	58,722	62,217
1971 (4)	156,075	75,260	80,820	4,500	2,250	2,250	99,325	47,505	51,815	103,825	49,760	54,065

Population 16 contd.

	Population aged 3yrs & over			Welsh-speaking			Speaking both English & Welsh			Total Welsh Speakers		
	Persons	Males	Females	Persons	Males	Females	Persons	Males	Females	Persons	Males	Females
						DENBIGHSHIRE						
1891 (1)	111,191	..	..	37,195	..	..	35,030	..	..	72,225	..	..
1901	122,195	61,281	60,914	22,366	11,788	10,578	53,238	26,827	26,411	75,604	38,615	36,989
1911	135,607	67,674	67,933	13,637	7,267	6,370	63,224	32,023	31,201	76,861	39,290	37,571
1921	145,939	70,870	75,069	12,380	6,576	5,804	58,174	28,960	29,214	70,554	35,536	35,018
1931	150,656	73,875	76,781	8,113	4,451	3,662	64,979	32,668	32,311	73,092	37,119	35,973
1951 (3)	162,556	77,400	85,156	3,725	1,876	1,849	58,777	29,045	29,732	62,502	30,921	31,581
1961	166,336	78,898	87,438	2,184	1,130	1,054	55,739	27,266	28,473	57,921	28,396	29,527
1971 (4)	176,475	83,990	92,485	3,170	1,560	1,610	46,385	22,160	24,225	49,555	23,720	25,835
						FLINTSHIRE						
1891 (1)	40,601	..	..	10,484	..	..	16,879	..	..	27,361	..	..
1901	75,931	37,549	38,382	5,722	3,075	2,647	31,568	15,542	16,026	37,290	18,617	18,673
1911	86,570	42,682	43,888	2,946	1,570	1,376	33,587	16,794	16,793	36,533	18,364	18,169
1921	100,362	48,088	52,274	2,323	1,263	1,060	30,513	15,168	15,345	32,836	16,431	16,405
1931	107,581	52,106	55,475	1,028	543	485	33,048	16,653	16,395	34,076	17,196	16,880
1951 (3)	138,133	67,404	70,729	401	175	226	28,720	14,196	14,524	29,121	14,371	14,750
1961	142,882	68,538	74,344	366	189	177	26,840	12,991	13,849	27,206	13,180	14,026
1971 (4)	166,645	80,045	86,600	1,400	635	765	23,025	10,935	12,090	24,425	11,570	12,855
						GLAMORGANSHIRE (A.C. & C.B.s)						
1891 (1)	653,889	..	..	142,346	..	..	177,726	..	..	320,072	..	..
1901	791,847	409,769	382,078	52,493	27,416	25,077	292,399	151,587	140,812	344,892	179,003	165,889
1911	1,033,717	538,343	495,374	31,719	16,199	15,520	361,973	187,504	174,469	393,692	203,703	189,989
1921	1,167,969	594,697	573,272	25,540	12,955	12,585	343,357	175,000	168,357	368,897	195,955	180,942
1931	1,166,998	587,126	579,872	9 129	4,455	4,674	346,244	177,637	168,607	355,373	182,092	173,281
1951 (3)	1,142,791	557,228	585,563	3,457	1,479	1,978	228,265	111,360	116,905	231,725	112,839	118,883
1961	1,169,943	569,998	599,945	4,144	2,185	1,959	197,001	93,211	103,790	201,145	95,396	105,749
1971 (4)	1,199,205	581,455	617,750	8,665	3,980	4,685	132,380	60,005	72,375	141,045	63,990	77,055

Population 16 contd.

	Population aged 3yrs & over			Welsh-speaking			Speaking both English & Welsh			Total Welsh Speakers		
	Persons	Males	Females	Persons	Males	Females	Persons	Males	Females	Persons	Males	Females
						MERIONETHSHIRE						
1891 (1)	61,903	..	..	45,856	..	..	12,023	..	..	57,879	..	..
1901	45,631	22,261	23,370	23,081	11,630	11,451	19,674	9,373	10,301	42,755	21,003	21,752
1911	43,209	20,627	22,582	15,857	7,905	7,952	23,119	10,861	12,258	38,976	18,766	20,210
1921	42,806	19,891	22,915	12,699	6,358	6,341	22,455	10,620	11,835	35,154	16,978	18,176
1931	41,312	20,001	21,311	9,113	4,706	4,407	26,431	12,769	13,662	35,544	17,475	18,069
1951 (3)	39,734	20,054	19,680	3,663	1,783	1,880	26,303	12,576	13,727	29,966	14,359	15,607
1961	36,585	17,905	18,680	2,016	1,083	933	25,759	12,274	13,485	27,775	13,357	14,418
1971 (4)	33,865	16,025	17,835	2,640	1,335	1,310	22,255	10,530	11,725	24,895	11,860	13,035
						MONMOUTHSHIRE (A.C. & C.B.s)						
1891 (1)	260,033	..	..	9,816	..	..	29,743	..	..	39,559	..	..
1901	274,415	141,484	132,931	2,013	1,037	976	33,677	17,429	16,248	35,690	18,466	17,224
1911	364,590	191,605	172,985	1,496	782	714	33,751	17,832	15,919	35,147	18,614	16,633
1921	418,845	216,143	202,702	973	513	460	25,976	13,509	12,467	26,949	14,022	12,927
1931	413,191	211,428	201,763	514	282	232	24,449	12,932	11,517	24,963	13,215	11,749
1951 (3)	403,237	199,795	203,442	551	252	299	13,566	6,982	6,584	14,117	7,234	6,883
1961	422,411	210,548	211,863	889	481	408	13,546	6,793	6,753	14,435	7,274	7,161
1971 (4)	439,160	216,180	222,980	630	285	345	8,635	4,240	4,395	9,260	4,525	4,735
						MONTGOMERYSHIRE						
1891 (1)	64,359	..	..	16,414	..	..	15,846	..	..	32,260	..	..
1901	51,310	24,985	26,325	7,980	3,977	4,003	16,361	7,906	8,455	24,341	11,883	12,458
1911	50,008	24,659	25,349	5,367	2,730	2,637	17,039	8,347	8,692	22,406	11,077	11,329
1921	48,370	23,990	24,380	4,289	2,225	2,064	16,152	8,097	8,055	20,441	10,322	10,119
1931	46,267	22,913	23,354	3,152	1,667	1,485	15,693	7,860	7,833	18,845	9,527	9,318
1951 (3)	43,745	21,747	21,998	1,407	737	670	13,933	7,091	6,842	15,340	7,828	7,512
1961	42,107	21,012	21,095	553	288	265	13,050	6,657	6,393	13,603	6,945	6,658
1971 (4)	41,230	20,535	20,695	540	280	260	11,050	5,605	5,445	11,590	5,885	5,705

Population 16 contd.

	Population aged 3yrs & over			Welsh-speaking			Speaking both English & Welsh			Total Welsh Speakers		
	Persons	Males	Females	Persons	Males	Females	Persons	Males	Females	Persons	Males	Females
						PEMBROKESHIRE						
1891 (1)	78,163	..	..	13,673	..	..	10,804	..	..	24,477	..	..
1901	82,223	38,778	43,445	9,797	4,251	5,546	18,536	8,370	10,166	28,333	12,621	15,712
1911	84,463	40,694	43,769	6,511	2,852	3,659	20,879	9,735	11,144	27,390	12,587	14,803
1921	86,423	42,199	44,224	5,024	2,345	2,679	21,169	10,212	10,957	26,193	12,557	13,636
1931	83,274	40,780	42,494	3,328	1,565	1,763	22,149	10,745	11,404	25,477	12,310	13,167
1951 (3)	86,398	42,703	43,695	1,362	624	738	21,865	10,722	11,143	23,227	11,346	11,881
1961	89,326	44,082	45,244	811	412	399	21,024	10,250	10,774	21,835	10,662	11,173
1971 (4)	94,300	46,215	48,085	950	470	475	18,545	8,950	9,595	19,490	9,420	10,070
						RADNORSHIRE						
1891 (1)	16,326	..	..	75	..	..	924	..	..	999	..	..
1901	21,754	11,059	10,695	51	38	13	1,309	712	597	1,360	750	610
1911	21,279	10,651	10,628	11	3	8	1,128	569	559	1,139	572	567
1921	22,313	10,813	11,500	103	50	53	1,283	637	646	1,386	687	699
1931	20,362	10,066	10,296	7	6	1	967	476	491	974	482	492
1951 (3)	19,133	9,675	9,458	14	6	8	843	442	401	857	448	409
1961	17,619	8,733	8,886	16	7	9	774	368	406	790	375	415
1971 (4)	17,510	8,685	8,825	30	15	15	625	285	340	655	300	355

	Population aged 3yrs & over			Welsh-speaking			Speaking both English & Welsh			Total Welsh Speakers		
	Persons	Males	Females	Persons	Males	Females	Persons	Males	Females	Persons	Males	Females
						CARDIFF C.B.						
1891 (1)	164,134	..	..	3,120	..	..	19,395	..	..	22,515	..	..
1901	151,925	75,496	76,429	329	172	157	12,066	5,697	6,269	12,395	5,869	6,426
1911	170,016	83,552	86,464	262	118	144	11,053	5,192	5,861	11,315	5,310	6,005
1921	188,499	93,689	94,810	512	393	119	8,930	4,296	4,634	9,442	4,689	4,753
1931	213,120	102,034	111,086	169	77	92	10,693	4,977	5,716	10,862	5,054	5,808
1951 (3)	230,478	108,731	121,747	136	56	80	9,487	4,476	5,011	9,623	4,532	5,091
1961	243,246	116,778	126,468	362	192	170	11,183	5,112	6,071	11,545	5,304	6,241
1971 (4)	266,495	127,575	138,915	975	465	505	11,960	5,340	6,615	12,930	5,810	7,125
						MERTHYR TYDFIL C.B.						
1891 (1)	110,569	..	..	35,244	..	..	39,812	..	..	75,056	..	..
1901	63,681	34,291	29,390	4,630	2,468	2,162	31,763	16,535	15,228	36,393	19,003	17,390
1911	74,597	39,778	34,819	2,643	1,405	1,238	34,826	18,098	16,728	37,469	19,503	17,966
1921	74,627	38,351	36,276	1,752	887	865	29,196	14,674	14,522	30,948	15,561	15,387
1931	67,970	34,748	33,222	587	274	313	26,439	13,431	13,008	27,026	13,705	13,321
1951 (3)	58,058	28,293	29,765	217	85	132	14,321	6,916	7,405	14,538	7,001	7,537
1961	56,244	27,541	28,703	318	161	157	10,851	5,059	5,792	11,169	5,220	5,949
1971 (4)	52,725	25,615	27,110	480	215	265	5,465	2,340	3,125	5,945	2,555	3,390
						RHONDDA U.D.						
1891 (1)	..	..	..	..	..	..	..	..	..	..	..	..
1901	103,740	57,292	46,448	11,841	6,458	5,383	54,906	30,117	24,789	66,747	36,575	30,172
1911	139,235	76,424	62,811	6,100	3,187	2,913	70,696	38,154	32,542	76,796	41,341	35,455
1921	150,680	79,227	71,453	4,448	2,240	2,208	64,071	33,502	30,569	68,519	35,742	32,777
1931	134,603	70,650	63,953	1,462	706	756	61,062	31,936	29,126	62,524	32,642	29,882
1951 (3)	106,098	51,757	54,341	440	168	272	30,775	14,714	16,061	31,215	14,882	16,333
1961	95,846	46,518	49,328	492	248	244	22,741	10,432	12,309	23,233	10,680	12,553
1971 (4)	85,140	41,040	44,100	650	255	390	10,645	4,370	6,275	11,295	4,630	6,665

Population 16 contd.

	Population aged 3yrs & over			Welsh-speaking			Speaking both English & Welsh			Total Welsh Speakers		
	Persons	Males	Females	Persons	Males	Females	Persons	Males	Females	Persons	Males	Females
SWANSEA C.B.												
1891 (1)	107,963	..	..	22,417	..	..	27,229	..	..	49,646	..	..
1901	87,885	42,792	45,093	2,861	1,334	1,527	25,567	12,073	13,494	28,428	13,407	15,021
1911	106,776	53,907	52,869	2,031	940	1,073	26,860	12,955	13,905	28,873	13,895	14,978
1921	147,894	73,165	74,729	2,571	1,243	1,328	39,648	19,411	20,237	42,219	20,654	21,565
1931	156,679	76,625	80,054	815	368	447	42,047	20,750	21,297	42,862	21,118	21,744
1951 (3)	153,372	74,160	79,212	224	82	142	30,511	14,564	15,947	30,735	14,646	16,089
1961	159,344	77,153	82,191	526	276	250	27,421	12,803	14,618	27,947	13,079	14,868
1971 (4)	165,720	80,015	85,705	1,005	455	550	20,425	9,195	11,230	21,430	9,645	11,780
NEWPORT C.B.												
1891 (1)	91,222	..	..	2,240	..	..	8,164	..	..	10,404	..	..
1901	62,181	30,843	31,338	55	35	20	2,215	1,129	1,086	2,270	1,164	1,106
1911	77,686	39,187	38,499	26	14	12	2,032	1,072	960	2,058	1,086	972
1921	86,378	43,092	43,286	32	13	9	1,833	915	918	1,865	928	937
1931	84,854	41,674	43,180	42	24	18	1,779	920	859	1,821	944	877
1951 (3)	100,152	48,618	51,534	48	23	25	1,732	896	836	1,780	919	861
1961	102,608	50,781	51,827	129	76	53	2,092	1,072	1,020	2,221	1,148	1,073
1971 (4)	106,540	51,890	54,650	70	35	35	1,720	850	870	1,790	885	905

General Notes

(i) Sources. Census Reports, 1891-1971. 1891, Ages etc., p. 561; 1901, Summary Tables, table L11 and County Tables, table 40; 1911, vol. xii, tables 1 and 2; 1921, General Tables, tables 54 and 56; 1931, General Tables, tables 39 and 41; 1951 and 1961, Report on Welsh-speaking population: 1971, Report on Welsh Language.

Notes

1. Figures for 1891 are not directly comparable with those for later years for three reasons:

   (a) The question was not fully understood, resulting in a substantial overstatement of the number of people speaking Welsh only. The total Welsh speakers figure is more accurate.

   (b) Figures are for all the population aged two years and over, instead of three years and over, as in all the years 1901-71.

   (c) Figures are for registration counties, not administrative counties. The effect of this is most marked on the figures for the towns, where figures are for registration districts, not the county boroughs as in later years.

2. In 1891-1921, there were the following numbers of people for whom no statement of language spoken was made:-

1891	12,833	1911	38,930
1901	2,757	1921	86,907

   The large number of people failing to reply in 1921 was attributed in 1921 Census report to the number of summer visitors in Wales at the time, but (in the 1931 census report) it was attributed to the fact that since the question was 'Can you speak Welsh only/English and Welsh/ English only?', many people, able to speak Welsh and/or English and other languages could not, technically answer the question. For this reason the question was altered in 1931 and people merely had to state if they could speak Welsh, or Welsh and English.

3. "In 1951 only, a rule was introduced in the checking of forms the effect of which was to regard a person who claimed to speak Welsh only but who personally completed and signed a schedule in English, as able to speak both languages, and this reduced the number of persons counted as speaking Welsh only in that census". (1971 Census, Report on Language spoken in Wales, p. vii).

4. In the 1971 Census, all numbers were rounded to the nearest 5 since they were rounded independently, totals will not always agree with the individual figures.

Population 17. Language. Welsh speakers as a percentage of total population over 3 years of age[1], Wales, and each county and county borough, 1891-1971

	Welsh Only								Total Welsh Speakers							
	1891	1901	1911	1921	1931	1951	1961	1971	1891	1901	1911	1921	1931	1951	1961	1971
WALES	30.3	15.1	8.5	6.3	4.0	1.7	1.0	1.3	54.4	49.9	43.5	37.1	36.8	28.9	26.0	20.9
Anglesey	71.4	48.0	36.2	31.0	23.9	9.6	5.6	4.5	93.5	91.7	88.7	84.9	87.4	79.8	75.5	65.7
Brecon	10.4	9.3	5.6	4.5	2.0	0.5	0.6	1.1	37.7	45.9	41.5	37.2	37.3	30.3	28.1	22.9
Caernarvon	65.7	47.7	35.6	26.2	21.4	8.9	4.9	4.3	89.3	89.6	85.6	75.0	79.2	71.7	68.3	61.9
Cardigan	74.4	50.4	34.2	26.1	20.0	7.4	4.7	3.7	95.0	93.0	89.6	82.1	87.1	79.5	74.9	67.6
Carmarthen	56.4	35.6	20.5	16.5	9.2	4.4	2.5	2.9	89.3	90.4	84.9	82.4	82.3	77.3	75.1	66.5
Denbigh	33.3	18.6	10.1	8.5	5.4	2.3	1.3	1.8	64.7	62.2	56.7	48.4	48.5	38.5	34.8	28.1
Flint	26.0	7.5	3.4	2.3	1.0	0.3	0.3	0.8	67.8	49.1	42.2	32.7	31.7	21.1	19.1	14.6
Glamorgan[2]	21.9	6.6	3.1	2.2	0.8	0.3	0.4	0.7	49.2	43.5	38.1	31.6	30.5	20.3	17.2	11.7
Merioneth	72.8	50.6	36.7	29.7	22.1	9.2	5.5	7.8	92.3	93.7	90.3	82.1	86.1	75.4	75.9	73.5
Monmouth[2]	3.8	0.7	0.4	0.2	0.1	0.1	0.2	0.1	15.3	13.0	9.6	6.4	6.0	3.5	3.4	2.1
Montgomery	25.6	15.6	10.7	8.9	6.8	3.2	1.3	1.3	50.3	47.5	44.8	42.3	40.7	35.1	32.3	28.1
Pembroke	17.8	11.9	7.7	5.8	4.0	1.6	0.9	1.0	31.9	34.4	32.8	30.3	30.6	26.9	24.4	20.7
Radnor	0.5	0.2	0.1	0.5	0.0	0.1	0.1	0.2	6.0	5.8	5.4	6.3	4.7	4.5	4.5	3.8
Cardiff	1.9	0.2	0.2	0.3	0.1	0.1	0.1	0.4	13.8	8.1	6.7	5.0	5.1	4.2	4.7	4.9
Merthyr	32.1	7.3	3.5	2.3	0.9	0.4	0.6	0.9	68.3	57.1	50.2	41.4	39.8	25.1	19.9	11.3
Rhondda	..	11.4	4.4	3.0	1.1	0.4	0.5	1.1	..	64.3	55.2	45.5	46.5	29.4	24.2	13.6
Swansea	20.9	3.3	1.9	1.7	0.5	0.1	0.3	0.6	46.2	32.4	27.1	28.5	27.3	20.0	17.5	12.9
Newport	2.4	0.1	0.0	0.0	0.0	0.0	0.1	0.1	11.5	3.7	2.6	2.1	2.1	1.7	2.1	1.7

General Notes

i) Sources. As in table 16, except for 1891 the fuller figures in the R.C. on Land in Wales and Monmouthshire, 1896, p 293 have been used. They differ very slightly from the census figures.

ii) The figures relate to the areas as constituted at the date of each census.

Notes

1. In 1891 as percentage of population aged over 2 years.
2. These figures include those for the county boroughs given below.

Population 18. Language. Welsh-speaking population, by age, Wales, 1901-71

Age last birthday	Population aged 3yrs and over						
	1901 (1)	1911	1921	1931	1951	1961	1971
PERSONS							
3+	1,864,696	2,247,927	2,486,740	2,472,378	2,472,429	2,518,711	2,602,955
3-4		112,434	95,431	83,637	95,022	80,253	86,545
5-9	536,259 (3-14)	269,636	271,387	243,196	191,358	193,168	225,240
10-14		242,394	273,253	242,436	177,866	219,281	207,025
15-24	385,211	443,684	476,959	437,773	337,636	343,524	386,565
25-44	559,745	708,404	758,483	750,837	755,945	685,107	636,990
45-64	290,939	358,582	473,330	539,604	633,041	679,618	681,585
65+	92,542	112,793	137,897	174,895	281,561	317,760	379,010
MALES							
3+	937,236	1,144,694	1,243,768	1,232,580	1,205,506	1,227,512	1,261.705
3-4		56,044	48,103	41,778	48,438	41,148	44,160
5-9	268,258 (3-14)	135,161	136,507	122,865	97,529	98,654	115,730
10-14		121,123	136,794	122,547	90,561	112,028	106,325
15-24	195,792	229,050	238,739	224,965	166,315	175,368	196,765
25-44	286,218	368,220	376,106	367,086	375,541	344,030	321,330
45-64	145,407	184,261	243,793	271,225	302,101	327,529	328,785
65+	41,561	50,835	63,726	82,114	125,021	128,755	148,600
FEMALES							
3+	927,460	1,103,233	1,242,972	1,239,798	1,266,923	1,291,199	1,341,255
3-4		56,390	47,328	41,859	46,584	39,105	42,385
5-9	268,001 (3-14)	134,475	134,880	120,331	93,829	94,514	109,510
10-14		121,271	136,459	119,889	87,305	107,253	100,700
15-24	189,419	214,634	238,220	212,808	171,321	168,156	189,800
25-44	273,527	340,184	382,377	383,751	380,404	341,077	315,655
45-64	145,532	174,321	229,537	268,379	330,940	352,089	352,795
65+	50,981	61,958	74,171	92,781	156,540	189,005	230,410

Age last birthday	Speaking Welsh only						
	1901	1911	1921	1931	1951 (2)	1961	1971
PERSONS							
3+	280,905	190,292	155,989	97,932	41,155	26,223	32,725
3-4		14,594	10,685	7,999	5,670	3,807	3,435
5-9	84,917 (3-14)	26,267	21,244	14,850	7,973	4,084	3,000
10-14		14,609	12,917	7,014	2,843	1,295	1,765
15-24	40,228	20,506	17,039	8,654	3,082	1,546	2,725
25-44	70,540	44,005	32,139	15,877	6,087	3,158	5,100
45-64	57,858	45,063	39,092	24,629	7,627	6,592	8,970
65+	27,362	25,248	22,873	18,909	7,873	5,741	7,725
MALES							
3+	137,333	92,737	76,591	48,629	19,528	13,542	15,865
3-4		7,371	5,449	4,105	2,924	2,045	1,855
5-9	43,554 (3-14)	13,500	11,052	7,742	4,194	2,191	1,625
10-14		7,717	6,732	3,747	1,545	666	835
15-24	21,604	11,212	9,307	5,084	1,772	841	1,450
25-44	34,669	21,797	15,703	7,952	2,799	1,746	2,630
45-64	26,636	21,213	18,958	11,938	3,157	3,535	4,330
65+	10,870	9,927	9.390	8,061	3,137	2,518	3,135
FEMALES							
3+	143,572	97,555	79,398	49,303	21,627	12,681	16,860
3-4		7,223	5,236	3,894	2,746	1,762	1,580
5-9	41,363 (3-14)	12,767	10,192	7,108	3,779	1,893	1,375
10-14		6,892	6,185	3,267	1,298	629	930
15-24	18,624	9,294	7,732	3,570	1,310	705	1,270
25-44	35,871	22,208	16,436	7,925	3,288	1,412	2,470
45-64	31,222	23,850	20,134	12,691	4,470	3,057	4,640
65+	16,492	15,321	13,483	10,848	4,736	3,223	4,590

Age last birthday	1901	1911	1921	1931	1951	1961	1971
	Speaking both English and Welsh						
				PERSONS			
3+	648,919	787,074	766,103	811,329	673,531	629,779	509,700
3-4		19,596	14,817	10,465	8,065	6,681	6,305
5-9	145,977	71,285	58,565	49,836	30,461	28,331	29,615
10-14		81,666	75,190	66,676	36,724	41,456	33,430
15-24	144,204	159,694	147,325	137,736	73,917	69,944	58,770
25-44	214,045	267,664	248,168	264,716	201,159	155,541	111,755
45-64	112,551	144,577	173,409	213,483	216,485	215,280	160,110
65+	32,142	42,592	48,629	68,417	106,720	112,546	109,710
				MALES			
3+	324,539	395,907	381,966	407,428	328,033	301,747	239,925
3-4		9,597	7,429	5,216	4,017	3,337	3,110
5-9	72,370	35,159	28,845	24,793	14,956	13,966	14,710
10-14		40,171	37,253	33,218	18,190	20,657	16,325
15-24	71,492	79,969	92,915	70,300	35,352	34,635	28,635
25-44	108,985	137,170	122,937	131,880	101,084	78,106	56,290
45-64	56,515	74,022	89,510	109,007	105,354	104,517	77,700
65+	15,177	19,819	23,077	33,014	49,080	46,529	43,155
				FEMALES			
3+	324,380	391,167	384,137	403,901	345,498	328,032	269,775
3-4		9,999	7,388	5,249	4,048	3,344	3,200
5-9	73,607	36,126	29,720	25,043	15,505	14,365	14,905
10-14		41,495	37,937	33,458	18,534	20,799	17,105
15-24	72,712	79,725	74,410	67,436	38,565	35,309	30,135
25-44	105,060	130,494	125,231	132,836	100,075	77,435	55,465
45-64	56,036	70,555	83,899	104,476	111,131	110,763	82,410
65+	16,965	22,773	25,552	35,403	57,640	66,017	66,555

General Notes

(i) Sources. Census Reports, 1901-71. The 1891 Census report does not give details of the ages of Welsh-speakers.

Notes

1. The summary table for 1901 does not give details for the age-groups, 3-4 5-9 and 10-14, but the county tables for that year do give a break-down.

2. When schedules were checked in 1951 people who claimed to be Welsh only speakers but who personally completed the schedule in English were counted as speaking both languages.

Chapter 2
Labour

Information on the occupational distribution of the population has been collected as part of each census. In each, moreover, the figures are given, or can be calculated, separately for Wales. Table 1 seeks to present this information. There are, however, quite sharp variations in the occupational pattern of different parts of Wales, variations which tend to be submerged in the aggregates. For this reason a more detailed analysis by county has been included in Table 2.

For both tables the information given in the early years is of limited value. Indeed, there is general recognition that the occupational figures contained in the census report for 1801 are more or less worthless. The censuses of 1811-1831 are limited in that the analysis is by families, rather than persons, and the classification is only made between three very broad groups. Within these constraints, however, the exercise seems to have been generally reliable and useful. The 1831 figures were, for males over 20, broken down into eight categories whilst the 1841 census attempted to conduct a full survey of occupations. Neither of these makes possible a satisfactory comparison with the findings of later censuses. They have therefore only been used as a basis for comparison with 1811 and 1821.

By 1851 the basic occupational classification had been given a form which was recognisably modern. But although the broad outline of the classification has not changed greatly, there are substantial hazards in making comparisons over time. There is, for example, a tendency for the accuracy and reliability of the census information on occupations to improve over time with the accumulation of experience. The pace of such improvement was naturally especially rapid in the early years. In addition the attempt to place the results for a number of years on the same basis[1] has necessarily involved the moving around of groups, sometimes quite large, between occupational orders. Again the necessary movements were larger in the earlier years - 1851, 1861 and 1871. Every care has been taken to make the figures as consistent as possible and usually the decisions involve much less doubt and ambiguity in practice than might be expected from an abstract description of the process. Mostly this is because the occupational groups used are very broad: excluding the retired and unoccupied there are only 22 occupational orders in the tables for 1851-1911 and still only 26 orders for the period from 1921 to 1971.

In general, therefore, the breadth of the categories used allows comparisons over time to be made with reasonable confidence. There are, however, occasions when there are - or seem to be - more serious breaks in the series. The most significant of these occurs between 1911 and 1921 because of a substantial change in the form of the occupational census at that time. Until 1911 the categorisation which had been used had been of a semi-industrial, semi-occupational type: but since 1921 two separate studies, one of the industrial distribution of the working population and one of the occupational distribution, have been published at each census. Direct comparisons between pre-1911 and post-1921 figures are clearly hazardous, but the extent of the dislocation varies substantially as between the different occupational orders. Thus some of the orders - like Agriculture, and Mining and Quarrying, where the industrial and occupational groupings largely coincided - were virtually unaffected by the change. On the other hand it is not possible to get a 1911 figure to correspond to the 1921 order of Administrators and Managers because until 1911 such persons were inextricably mixed up with others under a variety of industries and occupations. Fortunately, in the case of Wales the former groups, where comparisons are still possible across the 1911-21 break, are much the more important.

---

1. The figures for the census returns for 1851-1911 have been re-arranged on the basis of the 1911 classification; and those for 1921-71 on the basis of the 1951 classification.

Other significant breaks occur between 1871 and 1881, and between 1951 and 1961. Before 1881 retired persons were included in their previous occupations; from 1881 retired persons (except for Army, Navy, Medical Practitioners and Clergymen) were enumerated in the 'Unoccupied' order. It has been pointed out that the effect of this was, for Britain as a whole, relatively small.(1) It was entirely so for Wales. In 1891, for example, the number of retired persons or pensioners was 13,000 or 2.3 per cent of the total working population, the effects of which would be very tiny when distributed over the 22 occupational orders. Thus there seems to be little reason, so far as Wales is concerned, for attaching any particular cautions to making comparisons between 1871 and 1881, except for the 'Unoccupied'. Even for that order a more important change occurred in 1891 when the returns shifted from including all persons, to referring only to persons over the age of ten. The break between 1951 and 1961 is more difficult to judge because the 1961 census made little attempt to assess the significance of the classification changes which were introduced. There must therefore be some uncertainty but there do not seem to be strong grounds for thinking that any serious distortions were introduced in the series for Wales. Again, a more important development arises because the figures of the various censuses refer to persons of different ages - persons over 12 in 1921, over 13 in 1931 and thereafter over 15.

The figures for occupations go a long way back. Additional information on employment and unemployment is of a more recent date. No really comprehensive information is available, even for the United Kingdom as a whole, before the early 1920s. The provision of compulsory insurance for most manual, and many non-manual workers made possible such general coverage and dates from the end of 1920 but, partly because of initial classification problems, most series start in 1922 or 1923. Fortunately the Ministry of Labour from the outset recorded some of the information on a regional basis. Tables 3 - 7 thus give continuous series, apart from the disruption of the second world war, for the main indicators on employment and unemployment in Wales for a period of a little over fifty years.

The number of insured persons from 1922 to 1947 (Table 3A) leaves out various groups of employees. In particular those who were (like those in banking and insurance) included in special schemes do not figure in the tables at all before 1947. Others (like those in agriculture and domestic service, where the insurance scheme only applied from 1936 and 1938 respectively) are only included from 1939 onwards. In some cases these exclusions are unavoidable because no regional break-down was provided for these groups. The exclusions do, however, increase the consistency of coverage, although there are still breaks in 1927 and 1939 because of variations in the age-range covered.(1)

The major break, however, occurs in 1948.(2) From that year onwards the coverage is much more comprehensive because the national insurance scheme applied to all persons working for employers regardless of age, occupation or number of hours worked. The figures do not include employers and self-employed persons, or serving members of H.M. Forces. There remain many obstacles to the attainment of complete accuracy. Until 1971 the estimates were mainly based on counts of national insurance cards due for exchange in June and (since 1955) voluntary returns by employers of insurance cards held by them in June. These latter have been particularly useful in re-allocating to the appropriate region the cards held by those firms who keep the cards of all their employees at a central office, though some may be working elsewhere. In addition establishments near to regional boundaries may exchange cards at offices across the boundary and attempts are made to take such cases into account.(3)

---

1. Mitchell, B.R. and Deane, P. Abstract of British Historical Statistics, Cambridge, 1962, p. 56.

---

1. The details of these various qualifications are indicated in the notes to Table 3.

2. Details are given in British Labour Statistics: Historical Abstracts, App. B, pp. 414-5.

3. A fuller discussion of these and other problems is given in Ministry of Labour Gazette, January 1965 and July 1966.

The errors arising from such problems are, however, relatively small, and the table is probably reliable enough for both year-to-year comparisons and for indicating long-period shifts. It is helpful, too, that for the period after 1948 it is possible to distinguish between the numbers of male and female employees since one of the outstanding characteristics of the generation following the second world war in Wales was the stagnation and decline in the number of male employees and the relatively large increase in the number of female employees.

It is more difficult to secure consistency as between tables. Tables 3B and 4 should give the same figure for the total number of employees, but these totals diverge somewhat for the years 1951-4 and 1959-63. Partly this is because the total figures, given in Table 3B, have sometimes been revised to take account of some of the problems listed above but it has not always been possible to incorporate these revisions into the more detailed industry by industry allocations given in Table 4. For the years 1951-4, for example, Table 3B used the figures given in British Labour Statistics: Historical Abstract which revised the figures originally given in the Ministry of Labour Gazettes to make allowance for insurance cards held in central offices but relative to people working in different regions: but the industrial analysis of Table 4 could not be so revised.[1] The much smaller differences for the years 1959-63 have not been traced to any particular problem. Table 3 is the more reliable source for the total number of employees. The main purpose of Table 4 is to indicate the industrial distribution of the male and female labour force in Wales. For this purpose it is fortunate that, even for those years where the total diverges from that given in Table 3, the effect of the discrepancy is reduced once it is distributed over the various industries. No industrial break-down of the number of employees in Wales has been discovered for the inter-war years. The figures have been re-worked to put them all on the basis of the 1968 Standard Industrial Classification.

1. Ministry of Labour Gazette, January 1975.

A general point to be emphasized about all the employment figures is that it is not easy to reconcile statistics taken from different sources even when they appear to relate to the same problem. In particular there are often discrepancies between Census and Department of Employment (Ministry of Labour) figures. There is a difference in coverage: in general the census is much more comprehensive especially before 1948 when the insured persons, to whom most of the Ministry's figures related, excluded substantial categories of the total workforce. There is also some variation in definitions as, indeed, there is within each series over time. Thus the Census definition of 'working population' shifts substantially in 1881 and such changes demand care in the construction and interpretation of continuous series.[1]

The main series on unemployment are contained in Table 5. Before 1948 the basis for the first part of this table, relating to the numbers unemployed, is a little different from that of the second part, relating to the percentage unemployed. The monthly figure of the number unemployed showed the numbers of those who, by signing the register at the employment exchanges, indicated that they were seeking employment and were capable of, and available for, work. The figures in the series include all unemployed persons on the registers of employment exchanges irrespective of whether they were insured under the Unemployment Insurance Acts. The percentage series is based on the number of insured workers unemployed as obtained from a count of the number of unemployed books lodged at the employment exchanges. There is a break in both series at 1948 because of the much more comprehensive coverage of the national insurance act. Thereafter both series, numbers and percentages, relate to the number of persons (with a few small exceptions) on the registers of employment exchanges and youth employment offices who were unemployed and available for work on the day of the monthly count. The analysis of the unemployed by age and duration, Table 7,

1. Buxton, N.K. and MacKay, D.I., British Employment Statistics, Ch.1. gives an excellent guide to these problems.

refers only to the wholly unemployed. A useful article in the Gazette for August 1968 comments on the significance and shortcomings of the figures on the duration of unemployment.

Table 6 shows the number of unfilled vacancies and relates to vacancies notified to local employment offices and youth employment (service careers) offices. They exclude all vacancies which were not so notified, which normally meant the exclusion of over half of all vacancies.[1] It is clear, therefore, that Table 6 cannot be taken as a measure of the total number of vacancies at any particular time nor of the total extent to which the immediate manpower needs of employers were unsatisfied. Changes in the series do, however, probably give a reasonable reflection of changes in the pressure of demand in the labour market. Similarly, the statistics of placings, Table 8, does not purport to measure the total number of workers engaged by employers. The figures refer only to those persons placed in employment by local employment offices and youth employment (service careers) offices.

The information available on labour organisations is disappointingly meagre. Partly this is because the official collection of labour statistics was a comparatively late development in Britain: it is not until the last decade of the nineteenth century that the first industrial nation collected statistics on trade unions and industrial disputes. Most of the difficulty, however, stems from more cogent, specific and persistent problems. By the time information on trade unions began to be collected there were very few such organisations which originated in, and were confined to, Wales. Most Welsh trade unionists were members of branches of unions which were organised on a UK basis. Few of the official figures were published on a regional basis and there was no separate trade union body for Wales, like the Scottish TUC which was formed in 1897. Nor did Wales, for most individual unions, form a separate administrative unit. Table 9 gives a series for thirty years after 1894 of the number and membership of Trades Councils. The Trades Councils are loose federations of the branches of the different trade unions within a particular area and provided a forum for the discussion of problems common to trade unionists generally and possibly for the initiation and organisation of common action on local industrial and political issues. Their authority was always limited since the individual unions were naturally reluctant to share any control over their particular members and policies. However, they were during these years often involved in uniting the political activities of the various trade unions in their town or district.

On industrial disputes the Labour Department of the Board of Trade began encouragingly enough with a regional break-down of the number of work people affected and the number of days lost. The series, however, ends in 1913 and comprehensive regional figures are not again available until 1955. The available figures are given in Tables 10 and 11.

---

1. Until March 1950, however, the Control of Engagement Order meant that most labour engagements had to be made through local offices and, to a lesser extent, the operation of the Notification of Vacancies Order had a similar effect from February 1952 to May 1956.

BOOKS AND THESES

N.K. Buxton and D.I. Mackay — British Employment Statistics: a guide to sources and methods, 1977.

K.G.J.C. Knowles — Strikes, Oxford, 1952.

W.R. Garside — The Measurement of Unemployment, Oxford, 1980.

S. and B. Webb — The History of Trade Unionism, 1920 ed.

E.A. Wrigley (ed) — Nineteenth Century Society, Cambridge, 1972 (Chapter by W.A. Armstrong, 'The Use of information about occupation.')

ARTICLES

J. Bellamy — 'A note on occupation statistics in British censuses', Pop.St., vi, 1953.

J. Bellamy — 'Occupations in Kingston upon Hull, 1841-1948', Yorkshire Bulletin, 4, 1952.

J. Sykes — 'Employment and Unemployment in Regions and the Development Areas', Scot JPE 7, 1959.

D. Jones — 'Some Notes on the Census of Occupations for England and Wales', JRSS., LXXVIII, 1915.

D.I. Mackay and N.K. Buxton — 'A view of Regional Labour Statistics', JRSS., CXXVIII, 1965.

L.J. Williams and T. Boyns — 'Occupations in Wales, 1851-1971', Bull. of Econ. Res., 29, 1977.

GOVERNMENT AND OFFICIAL PUBLICATIONS

Reports and Abstracts of the Census of Great Britain, 1801-51 (in Sessional Papers)

Reports and Tables of the Census of England and Wales, 1861-1971 (in Sessional Papers till 1911, and then issued as non-parliamentary papers).

Report on Strikes and Lock-outs (in Sessional Papers, 1889 to 1914-16, annually).

Abstract of Labour Statistics, (in Sessional Papers, 22 issues between 1893 and 1936).

Labour Gazette, 1893-1976. (Called Board of Trade Labour Gazette from 1905-18; Ministry of Labour Gazette, 1923-68; Employment and Productivity Gazette, 1968-70; Department of Employment Gazette, 1971-).

Guides to Official Sources : No.1. Labour Statistics, revised, 1958.

Department of Employment and Productivity. British Labour Statistics: Historical Abstract, 1868-1968, 1969.

Department of Employment, British Labour Statistics : Year Book, annually since 1969.

Ministry of Labour, Tables relating to Employment and Unemployment in Great Britain, 1948, 1949 and 1950, 1951.

Wales and Monmouthshire. Reports on Government action in Wales, Sessional Papers, 1946-

Digest of Welsh Statistics, annually since 1954.

Abstract of Regional Statistics, annually since 1965.

LABOUR 1. Occupations, Wales, 1801-1971

A. 1801-41

	Persons	Number of Families			Males over 20[1]	
	1801	1811	1821	1831	1831	1841
Agriculture	201,933	78,661	80,245	78,809	95,162	80,395
Trade, Manufactures and Handicraft	59,362	40,856	47,827	53,328	49,444	68,084
Others	291,790	22,787	32,756	54,312	50,100	81,779[2]

1. The figures for Males over 20 for 1831 and 1841 refer to Wales excluding Monmouthshire.

2. For 1831 and 1841, 'Others' can be broken down into:

	1831	1841
Capitalists, Bankers, Professional and other educated men	5,204	9,714
Non-agricultural labourers	31,571	43,673
Male servants	2,145	5,804
Others	11,180	22,588

LABOUR 1. Occupations, Wales, 1801-1971

B. 1851-1921

CLASS	MALES 1851	1861	1871	1881	1891	1901	1911	1921[1]	FEMALES 1851	1861	1871	1881	1891	1901	1911	1921[1]
1 General or Local Government	2,742	3,227	4,222	4,179	5.736	7,934	11,311	11,504	148	228	322	380	787	1,478	2,743	3.239
2 Defence	2,644	3,466	3,400	3,207	2,859	3,195	3,000	4,933	-	-	-	-	-	-	-	-
3 Professional Occupations	6,820	7,861	9,047	12,413	14,814	18,519	22,367	24,802	1,870	2,900	3,862	6,512	10,147	14,406	18,453	23,911
4 Domestic Offices or Services	5,259	5,587	6,133	10,240	4,848	11,459	14,792	8,024	41,948	68,817	83,896	88,221	105,390	88,878	90,496	78,481
5 Commercial Occupations	1,921	3,518	5,427	9,673	13,880	19,635	27,057	35,336	138	50	119	148	298	941	2,269	13,363
6 Conveyance of Men, Goods & Messages	16,144	22,937	26,547	36,644	52,027	69,751	85,481	94,401	496	301	318	416	434	652	683	4,214
7 Agriculture	135,443	131,330	111,815	100,023	98,999	91,668	95,966	94,739	33,748	18,023	13,541	10,731	9,294	12,359	20,181	11,355
8 Fishing	769	747	961	895	1,013	1,234	1,282	1,879	-	12	114	86	116	110	68	35
9 Mines & Quarries	65,398	77,348	89,656	101,675	144,705	188,958	256,250	278,003	1,816	1,485	1,986	1,320	802	343	268	175
10 Metals, Machines, Implements & Conveyances	35,659	47,945	53,727	55,503	62,451	68,033	90,845	100,889	2,127	2,652	3,134	3,710	4,549	2,411	3,525	4,586
11 Precious Metals, Jewels, Watches, Instruments & Games	693	926	1,037	1,121	1.449	1,751	2,191	1,274	10	47	75	91	133	181	286	50
12 Building & Works of Construction	26,102	32,225	33,603	39,871	44.040	52,048	59,958	61,040	645	968	332	58	66	35	27	173
13 Wood, Furniture, Fittings and Decorations	5,526	5,979	5,512	5,241	5,291	5,933	7,716	8,347	175	139	174	190	243	247	483	300
14 Brick, Cement, Pottery and Glass	1,341	1,576	1,608	2,133	2,803	4,440	5,096	3,040	244	467	644	707	678	498	484	483
15 Chemicals, Oil, Grease, Soap, Resin, etc.	1,152	1,384	1,837	2,161	2,409	2,414	3,331	1,793	52	51	104	123	156	190	373	96
16 Skins, Leather, Hair and Feathers	2,156	2,175	1,763	1,886	1,956	1,895	1,995	1,496	77	78	58	64	71	74	130	160
17 Paper, Print, Books and Stationery	1,095	1,435	1,944	2,513	3,360	4,193	4,966	3,824	143	189	288	520	825	1,331	1,933	1,272
18 Textile Fabrics	8,275	7,167	7,122	7,294	7,669	7,256	6,856	2,165	3,616	2,862	2,517	2,843	4,059	5,539	7,358	2,882
19 Dress	21,473	20,189	18,142	15,785	15,673	15,938	17,643	9,557	27,117	32,809	29,886	26,296	32,898	32,145	33,507	18,132
20 Food, Tobacco, Drink and Lodging	14,710	17,055	19,078	21,016	26,579	34,346	44,422	14,658	8,707	8,130	8,187	9,561	18,377	16,383	28,287	17,596
21 Gas, Water, Electricity, Sanitary Work	106	290	478	689	1,148	2,125	3,665	2,890	4	2	3	9	5	1	1	15
22 Other, General and Undefined Workers	30,530	33,161	61,274	55,477	62,253	43,024	42,404	115,813	2,781	2,413	3,320	2,771	2,580	2,222	4,126	32,631
TOTAL OCCUPIED	385,958	427,528	468,503	489,639	575,962	655,749	808,594	880,407	125,862	142,623	152,880	154,757	191,908	180,424	215,681	213,149
23 Unoccupied etc.	208,835	227,617	246,268	299,435	103,898	118,407	144,895	123,643	468,259	515,066	558,189	633,702	475,895	583,427	696,687	792,497

1. The figures for 1921 represent an attempt to redistribute the information from the 1921 census on the same basis as was used for 1851-1911

LABOUR 1. Occupations, Wales, 1801-1971

C. 1911-71

	MALES						FEMALES					
	1911[1]	1921	1931	1951	1961	1971	1911[1]	1921	1931	1951	1961	1971
1 Fishing	1,282	1,879	2,379	1,334	730	470	68	35	18	3	-	20
2 Agriculture	102,371	95,480	92,510	79,457	61,230	45,130	20,192	11,355	8,606	10,267	6,470	7,620
3 Gas, Coke and Chemicals	1,342	5,011	3,489	9,408	11,440	12,090	229	102	81	1,348	1,420	1,020
4 Metal Manufacturing and Engineering	94,436	98,558	81,449	112,430	142,370	160,120	3,839	4,527	1,627	7,345	13,910	19,550
5 Mining and Quarrying	256,250	274,682	234,554	110,000	79,470	36,500	268	146	32	32	20	60
6 Woodworkers (+ Cork and Cane)	23,325	20,575	17,770	19,667	17,580	17,330	493	170	72	225	300	470
7 Leather Workers, Fur Dressers	9,057	5,544	4,897	3,325	2,130	1,620	1,007	211	132	1,011	800	1,390
8 Textile Workers	6,856	1,876	1,291	1,892	1,530	2,850	7,358	1,629	2,237	2,106	2,050	2,120
9 Clothing Workers	8,030	6,342	4,718	3,131	1,930	2,220	32,464	19,436	10,447	13,156	11,710	13,130
10 Food, Drink and Tobacco	8,549	8,824	8,878	7,534	10,930	9,170	1,976	2,609	1,912	2,831	3,150	3,690
11 Paper and Printing	4,966	3,824	3,768	3,170	3,940	4,850	1,933	1,272	1,120	1,291	1,700	2,410
12 Building and Contracting	35,928	38,735	43,227	63,098	30,690	31,900	20	100	42	81	20	80
13 Makers of Other Products (Rubber, Plastics etc.)	50	5,671	3,833	2,695	6,450	9,950	10	216	160	1,395	3,940	5,240
14 Painters and Decorators	6,652	8,019	8,503	12,113	12,410	11,820	2	82	85	397	540	480
15 Stationary Engine and Crane Drivers	14,826	20,203	20,965	22,472	26,990	25,970	-	-	23	150	130	170
16 Labourers (n.e.c.)	23,145	39,264	42,371	67,736	77,120	72,350	77	446	131	17,988	5,260	6,150
17 Transport and Communication	89,720	88,674	94,774	86,167	74,660	64,080	2,679	2,920	2,597	5,353	4,800	5,830
18 Warehousemen, Storekeepers Packers, Bottlers etc.	212	5,727	6,880	12,972	18,190	19,870	6	1,294	1,552	4,416	6,470	8,480
19 Clerical Workers	16,695	21,746	25,986	36,715	45,320	41,300	2,763	12,303	13,179	45,393	63,600	85,420
20 Sales Workers	49,683	59,026	77,211	60,996	58,440	50,780	15,995	32,191	34,165	42,219	52,180	54,050
21 Services, Sport and Recreation (inc. Personal Sevice)	20,393	21,730	25,877	31,960	34,680	39,510	106,719	94,827	98,234	67,059	67,590	95,230
22 Administrators and Managers	-	9,578	4,510	15,681	21,480	28,680	-	3,323	198	1,357	1,190	2,410
23 Professional, Technical Workers, Artists	21,282	22,117	23,829	37,326	56,720	66,140	16,854	22,536	23,580	30,334	39,530	48,850
24 Armed Forces	3,000	4,933	2,746	20,776	11,640	7,450	-	-	-	641	230	290
25 Inadequately Described Occupations	4,448	9,349	34,187	8,567	18,390	16,200	245	936	5,763	2,465	7,980	22,480
26 Glass, Ceramics, Cement	5,096	3,040	2,070	2,901	2,580	2,040	484	483	146	498	560	590
TOTAL OCCUPIED	807,594	880,407	872,672	833,523	829,040	780,390	215,681	213,149	206,139	259,361	295,550	387,230
27 Retired and Unoccupied	144,895	123,643	95,533	135,455	154,470	215,095	696,687	792.497	773,655	779,844	759,050	701,430

1. The Figures for 1911 represent an attempt to redistribute the information from the 1911 Census on the same basis as that used for 1921-1971

Key to reclassification of census categories, 1851 - 1911

	1911 and 1901	1891 and 1881[1]	1871 and 1861[2]	1851
(1) General or Local Government	I	I	I	I
(2) Defence	II	II	II	II
(3) Professional Occupations	III	III(except 4 - Students)	III(except 3 - Chemist, Druggist)	III(1,2,3,4,5), IV, XI(2,3 - except Musical Instrument Maker,4,5,6,7, 15 - Surveyor
(4) Domestic Offices or Services	IV	IV + VII(Gamekeeper)	V + IX(Gamekeeper)	VI(1,2) + X(Gamekeeper)
(5) Commercial Occupations	V	V	VI(1)	VII(except House Proprietor, and Pawnbroker down to Hawker, Pedlar)
(6) Conveyance of Men, Goods, Messages	VI	VI	VII	VIII
(7) Agriculture	VII	VII(except Gamekeeper)	VIII,IX(except Fisherman and Gamekeeper)	IX, X(except Fisherman and Gamekeeper)
(8) Fishing	VIII	VIII	IX(Fisherman)	X(Fisherman)
(9) Mines and Quarries	IX	XXI(1,2 except Gas Works service, 3 Stone Quarriers to Clay, Sand Gravel, Chalk + Dealers + Others)	XV(1,2 except Chimney Sweep & Gas Works Service, 3 Stone Quarrier to Clay Labourer and Others)	XIV(1 except Gas Works Service, 2 Stone Quarrier to Limestone Burner + other workers in Stone, Clay) + XIV(9,10,11,12,13,14)*
(10) Metal, Machines, Implements & Conveyances	X	X(1,2,3 Electrical Apparatus Makers,5,7), XI(2(a)), XII(1), XIII, XXI(8,9,10,11,12)	X(6,9,10,11,13), XV(9,10,11, 12,13,14)	XI(8,10,11,12,14,16), XIV(9,10,11, 12,13,14)*
(11) Precious metals,Jewels, Watches, Instruments and Games	XI	X(3 except Electrical Apparatus Maker,4,6,8), XXI(7)	X(2,5,7,8), XV(8)	XI(3 Musical Instrument Maker,9), XIV(7,8)
(12) Building and Works of Construction	XII	XI(1),XXI(3 Well Sinker,Borer and Paviour, Road Labourer to Plate-layer	X(14),XV(3 Railway Labourer to Road Labourer)	VII(House Proprietor),XI(15 except Surveyor),XIII(13 Paper Hanger), XIV(2 Marble Mason,Road to Railway Labourer)
(13) Wood, Furniture, Fittings and Decorations	XIII	XI(2 except (a),3),XX(2,3)	X(4,15),XIV(1 French Polisher, 2,3,4)	XIII(3 French Polisher,4,5,6,7,8, 9,10)
(14) Brick, Cement Pottery and Glass	XIV	XXI(3 Plaster, Cement to Brick, Tile,4)	XV(3 Brick,Maker,Dealer,4,5), XIV(1 Japonner)	XIV(2 Brick,Maker,Dealer,3,4)
(15) Chemicals, Oil, Grease, Soap, Resin, etc.	XV	XIV,XIX(1 except Bone,Horn,Ivory, etc.), XX(1), XXI(5)	III(3 Chemist,Druggist),X(16), XIII(1),XIV(1 except Japonner and French Polisher),XV(6)	III(6),XI(17),XII(2),XIII(3 except French Polisher),XIV(5)
(16) Skins, Leather, Hair and Feathers	XVI	XII(2), XIX(2,3)	X(12), XIII(2,3)	XI(13), XII(3,4,5)
(17) Paper, Prints, Books and Stationary	XVII	IX, XX(4)	X(1,3),XIV(5 except Rag Gatherer, Dealer)	XI(1),XIII(3 except Paper Hanger)
(18) Textile Fabrics	XVIII	XVII	XI(1,2,3,4,6)	XII(6,7),XIII(11,12)
(19) Dress	XIX	XVIII	XI(5)	VI(3)
(20) Food, Tobacco, Drink and Lodging	XX	XV,XVI	XII	XII(1),XIII(1,2)

(21) Gas, Water, Electricity, Sanitary Work	XXI	XXI(2 Gas,Works,Service,6),XXIII except Chimney Sweep & Rag Gatherer,Dealer)	XV(2 Gas,Works,Service,3 Scavenger & Dust Collector,7)	XIV(1 Gas,Works,Service,6)
(22) Other General and Undefined Workers	XXII	XXII,XXIII(Chimney Sweep and Rag, Gatherer,Dealer),XIX(1 Bone,Horn, etc.)	XIV(5 Rag,Gatherer,Dealer), VI(2),XVI,XV(2 Chimney Sweep)	VII(Pawnbroker to Hawker,Pedlar), XIV(1 Chimney Sweep),XV
(23) Unoccupied, etc.	XXIII	XXIV,III(4 Students)	IV, XVII, XVIII	V, XVI, XVII, XVIII

Note:

2(a) - Locksmith, Bellhanger

1. Except:
   3. III
   7. VII,VIII(except Fisherman, Gamekeeper, Knacker and Catsmeat Dealer)
   8. VIII(Fisherman)
   20. XV,XVI,VIII(Knacker,Catsmeat Dealer)
   23. XXIV

2. Except:
   3. III(except 3(b))
   10. Includes X(16)
   15. III(3(b)) and X(17) instead of X(16)

* The majority of the categories and headings in this group are included in order (10). However, those refering to miners of various sorts are included in order (9), i.e. XIV(9 Copper Miners,10 Tin Miners, 12 Lead Miners and 14 Iron Miners) are included in order (9).

Key to reclassification of census categories, 1921 - 1971

	1961 and 1971[1]	1951	1931	1921
(1) Fishing	000 of order I	I	I	I
(2) Agriculture	Order I (except 000)	II + XXII(861)	II + XXVII(860)	II + XXVII(910)
(3) Gas, Coke & Chemicals	III	V	IV, VI	IV, VI
(4) Metal Manufacturing & Engineering	V, VI, VII	VI	VII, VIII, IX, X, XIX(504)	VII, VIII, IX, X
(5) Mining & Quarrying	II	III	III	III
(6) Woodworkers(+ Cane & Cork)	VIII	XI	XV(sub-order 1)	XV(sub-order 1) - less French Polishers
(7) Leather Workers, Fur Dressers	IX	VIII	XI, XIII(352-6)	XI, XIII(412-15)
(8) Textile Workers	X	VII	XII	XII
(9) Clothing Workers	XI	IX	XIII(except 352-6) + XV(sub-order 2)	XIII(except 412-15) + XV(sub-order 2)
(10) Food, Drink & Tobacco	XII	X	XIV	XIV
(11) Paper & Printing	XIII	XII	XVI, XVII	XVI
(12) Building & Contracting	XV	XIV	XVIII	XVII
(13) Makers of Other Products (rubber, plastics etc.)	XIV	XIII	XX, XXI	XIX, XX
(14) Painters & Decorators	XVI	XV	XIX(less 504)	XVIII + XV(French Polishers)
(15) Stationary Engine, & Crane, Drivers, etc.	XVII	XXV	XXX, XXXI(915)	XXX
(16) Labourers (n.e.c.)	XVIII	XXVI	XXXI(920, 930)	XXXI(967, 970, 971)
(17) Transport & Communication	XIX	XVII	XXII	XXII
(18) Warehousemen, Storekeepers, Packers, Bottlers, etc.	XX	XXIV	XXIX	XXIX
(19) Clerical Workers	XXI	XXIII	XXVIII(883, 884, 889)	XXVIII(939, 933)
(20) Sales Workers	XXII	XVIII	XXIII	XXIII
(21) Service, Sport & Recreation (includes personal service)	XXIII, XXV(294)	XX(sub-order 2), XXI, XXII(except 861)	XXIV(750, 751),XXVI, XXXI(913,914), XXVII(except 860)	XXVI, XXVII(except 910), XXIV(808-9),XXXI(987)
(22) Administrators & Managers	XXIV	XVI	XXIV(sub-order 1 except 743,750-1),XXVIII(880-1)	XXVIII(930-1), XXIV(800-805)
(23) Professional, Technical Workers, Artists	XXV (except 294)	XIX	XXV, XXVIII(882)	XXV, XXVIII(932)
(24) Armed Forces	XXVI	XX(sub-order 1)	XXIV(sub-order 2)	XXIV(sub-order 2)
(25) Inadequately Described Occupations	XXVII	XXVII	XXXI(except 913-15,920, 930), XXIV(743)	XXXI(except 967,970-1, 987), XXI
(26) Retired and Unoccupied	XXVIII	XXVIII	XXXII	XXXII
(27) Glass, Ceramics, Cement	IV	IV	V	V

Note: 1. Except:
21. XXIII,XXV(207)
23. XXV(except 207)

LABOUR 1. Occupations, Wales, 1801-1971

General Notes

1. Sources: Census Reports, 1801-1971

Table A. 1801-41

2. There is an apparent decline in the number occupied in Agriculture between 1831 and 1841. The census authorities thought this was mis-leading. They believed that some farm servants kept in farm houses were returned as domestic servants in 1841 but had been included amongst agricultural labourers in 1831. If allowance had been made for this they thought there would have been a small increase in the numbers occupied in Agriculture between 1831 and 1841. Census Report, 1841, p.15.

Table B. 1851-1911

3. A table follows these notes to indicate how the information on occupations given in each census from 1851 to 1911 has been allocated to ensure as much comparability as possible.

4. Up to 1871 persons described as 'retired' from any stated occupation were classed to that occupation. Only the residue of those described as 'retired' without any indication of former occupation were classified as 'Unoccupied'. From 1881 onwards all such retired persons (except officers in the army and navy, and, until 1911, clergymen and medical practitioners) were included with the 'Unoccupied', as also were inmates of workhouses over 60 years of age, and inmates of lunatic asylums of whatever age. At the same time clerks in industry and commerce (except those employed by the civil service, army, navy, law, banks and railways) were no longer enumerated with the particular branch of industry in which they worked, but were classed as 'Commercial Clerks'. Similarly messengers, errand boys and porters (except those employed by the civil service or the railways) were classed under these general headings rather than attributed to a particular industry.

5. In the census for 1871 order IV is: 'wives and women engaged in household duties but also assisting in certain cases in the husband's business'. Because it is impossible to break down this group to get any idea of the number who were thus 'assisting', all those enumerated under this order have been placed in the 'unoccupied' class. The same problem, with the addition of 'relatives and children', occurs in 1861 and the same procedure has been followed.

6. Until 1891 'Children' were included in the unoccupied class. There is some ambiguity, however, over the age up to which they were classed as 'children'. 1881 is the only year for which an age for children is given: in that year the Unoccupied included children under 5 years of age, as well as persons of Rank, Property etc. After 1891 children were excluded altogether and for 1891, 1901 and 1911 this referred to children under 10; for 1921 to those under 12. The exclusion must be at least part of the explanation for the sharp drop in the Unoccupied order in 1891.

7. In 1851, 1861 and 1871 the censuses enumerated groups which it called 'House Proprietors' and 'Land Proprietors' but, as a foot-note to the 1871 census recognised, most such proprietors returned themsleves under a different profession or occupation. These categories disappear after 1871. Until then there is a good case for re-allocating them to the 'Unoccupied'. Instead, they have been left in the occupational order to which they were originally allocated, namely Building and Agriculture respectively. Land proprietors, both male and female, are small relative to the agricultural order, and male house proprietors are small relative to the building order. But female house proprietors actually form the majority of females in Building: if they were excluded the number of females in Building in 1851, 1861 and 1871 would be 20; 12; and 42 respectively.

The total numbers involved were:

	Land Proprietors		House Proprietors	
	Male	Female	Male	Female
1851	973	713	290	625
1861	904	867	342	956
1871	864	464	114	290

8. In 1891 'Domestic Coachman, Groom' is taken out of order 4 and included amongst 'Coachman, Cabman, Groom, Horsebreaker', in order 6. No separate figures are available to adjust for this change. In 1901 'Domestic Coachman, Groom' is again separately identified and returned to order 4. 'Domestic Coachman' in 1901 numbered 2,910. In addition, 'Domestic Gardener' is also taken out of order 4 in 1891 and included amongst 'Gardener, Nurseryman, Seedman' in order 7. Again, no separate figure is available to adjust for this change. In 1901 'Domestic Gardener' is back in order 4. The numbers of Domestic gardeners in 1881 and 1901 were 3,917 and 3,579. The figures given are for males (the number of females in these groups is very tiny), and these changes probably account for the sharp drop in the number of males in order 4 in 1891).

9. As some might expect, a problem arises with students. Before 1891 only small specific groups are identified ('Law student', Medical student, Assistant') and these are included in order 3 (Professional). In 1901 and 1911 they cannot be separated out and are included with the 'Unoccupied'. In 1891 a general class of students is given. The census authorities put these in 'Professional', but they have been re-allocated to secure consistency with 1901-11. The number involved is relatively large (M, 5,080; F, 4,746) and if more detail had been given some of these might have been left in the 'professional' order.

10. 'Coalheavers' cannot be confidently singled out. From 1901 they were included in order 6, 'Conveyance of Men, Goods and Messages'. Before this they were included in the order for Mines and Quarries. They have been left in this form.

11. A table follows these notes to indicate how the information on occupations given in each decennial census from 1921 to 1971 has been allocated to ensure as much comparability as possible.

12. The Census Report for 1921 asserted that 'the returns of occupation in this census have been tabulated under a scheme differing so much from those in use previously as to preclude the possibility of an exact comparison with previous census results'. In particular, several broad groups, such as general labourers, dealers and owners, were separated whereas they had previously been classed in the industry they worked in as determined by the raw material with which they worked.

13. The figures for 1921 relate to persons 12 years old or over; those for 1931 to persons 14 years old and over: and from 1951 on to persons 15 years old and over.

LABOUR 2. Occupations, by sex, each county, 1801-1971

A. 1801-31

	Families chiefly employed in Agriculture				Families chiefly employed in Trade, Manufacturers and Handicrafts				All other families			
	1801(1)	1811	1821	1831	1801(1)	1811	1821	1831	1801(1)	1811	1821	1831
Anglesey	9,766	5,376	6,187	5,314	2,614	1,453	1,702	2,141	19,228	877	1,936	2,673
Brecon	14,346	4,667	4,039	3,959	4,204	2,239	3,703	2,954	11,864	1,013	1,280	2,935
Caernarvon	12,808	6,667	6,890	5,778	4,234	2,687	2,649	2,997	17,342	833	1,939	5,778
Cardigan	16,511	5,864	6,312	7,246	2,896	1,913	2,501	3,243	23,497	3,519	3,258	3,163
Carmarthen	32,862	9,878	9,628	9,987	4,343	5,256	4,823	5,299	29,672	949	3,941	5,433
Denbigh	21,104	7,973	8,625	8,135	6,960	3,447	4,399	4,478	25,747	2,283	2,653	4,537
Flint	10,332	4.086	4,421	4,660	6,989	3,009	3,531	3,101	20,536	2,645	2,659	4,377
Glamorgan	18,515	8,217	7,126	6,814	6,903	7,915	8,336	8,929	39,964	2,563	4,852	10,368
Merioneth	10,308	3,619	3,570	3,583	2,711	1,270	1,434	1,815	16,398	1,928	2,275	1,960
Monmouth	12,871	5,815	6,020	5,614	5,540	4,812	6,147	8,626	25,217	1,916	1,955	5,671
Montgomery	13,802	6,369	6,594	6,610	6,233	3,164	3,882	4,198	25,561	772	1,580	2,599
Pembroke	20,088	7,189	7,651	7,974	4,846	2,848	3,779	4,519	30,075	2,900	3,772	4,102
Radnor	8,620	2,941	3,182	3,135	889	843	941	1,028	6,689	584	656	716
WALES	201,933	78,661	80,245	78,809	59,362	40,856	47,827	53,328	291,790	22,782	32,756	54,312

1. The figures for 1801 refer to persons: those for 1811, 1821 and 1831 to families. The 1801 figures are not considered to be very reliable.

LABOUR 2. Occupations, by sex, each county, 1801-1971

B. 1841

	1841	ANGLESEY	BRECON	CAERNARVON	CARDIGAN	CARMARTHEN	DENBIGH	FLINT	GLAMORGAN	MERIONETH	MONMOUTH	MONTGOMERY	PEMBROKE	RADNOR	WALES
	MALES														
1.	Persons engaged in Commerce, Trade & Manufacture	3,480	5,222	5,677	4,875	8,071	7,463	5,742	21,685	2,685	16,131	6,166	6,785	1,769	95,292
2.	Persons engaged in Agriculture	7,088	5,325	9,330	8,393	13,267	10,934	5,210	9,757	5,348	8,196	9,763	9,047	4,337	105,995
3,	Labourers[1]	1,258	5,001	5,713	1,486	3,040	4,400	5,561	18,407	1,709	15,800	1,103	2,222	232	65,932
4.	Army	7	209	15	11	36	10	10	291	6	641	83	36	6	1,361
5.	Navy & Merchant Seaman Shore	403	55	808	387	305	64	443	1,435	165	356	89	876	8	5,394
6.	Professional Persons[2]	91	158	186	177	278	207	161	401	83	271	176	250	64	2,503
7.	Other Educated Persons	66	139	167	123	304	270	251	657	95	475	169	189	39	2,944
8.	Persons engaged in the Government Civil Service[3]	43	20	47	39	45	39	25	115	17	65	27	82	6	570
9.	Parochial, Town & Church Officers[4] (incl. Police & Law Officers)	31	40	38	34	61	72	44	115	27	79	62	87	21	711
10.	Domestic Servants	470	506	490	1,212	1,068	1,292	1,126	1,364	393	1,874	787	1,413	368	12,363
11.	Persons returned as independent	175	398	401	431	658	512	281	895	285	712	414	627	291	5,368
12.	Almspeople, Pensioners, Paupers, Lunatics & Prisoners	177	180	149	241	340	286	145	353	122	423	387	400	63	3,230
	FEMALES														
1.	Persons engaged in Commerce, Trade & Manufacture	620	567	601	782	999	871	645	2,713	491	1,510	1,384	1,098	201	13,482
2.	Persons engaged in Agriculture	632	264	483	603	1,244	507	281	329	329	489	466	423	272	6,322
3.	Labourers	78	417	86	110	389	239	140	962	92	988	163	548	74	4,286
4.	Army	-	-	-	-	-	-	-	-	-	-	-	-	-	-
5.	Navy & Merchant Seamen or Shore	-	-	-	-	-	-	-	-	-	-	-	-	-	-
6.	Professional Persons[2]	5	5	6	3	6	7	6	13	3	9	3	1	-	67
7.	Other Educated Persons	26	34	33	20	80	75	67	136	21	116	32	85	12	737
8,	Persons engaged in the Government Civil Service	6	-	1	2	2	2	3	3	2	3	2	1	2	29
9.	Parochial, Town & Church Officers (incl. Police & Law Officers)	-	5	2	4	8	4	3	8	3	8	3	6	4	58
10.	Domestic Servants	2,516	3,200	4,632	4,653	7,010	5,376	3,144	7,779	2,630	5,682	4,223	6,002	1,562	58,409
11.	Persons returned as independent	919	907	1,880	1,762	2,944	1,456	971	3,176	758	1,910	763	2,520	554	20,520
12.	Almspeople, Pensioners, Paupers, Lunatics & Prisoners	541	213	252	424	691	645	250	501	333	314	477	543	117	5,301

General Notes

i) Source: Table inserted between pp 52 and 53 of '1841 Population Abstract - Occupations: England and Wales'.

Notes

1. This column includes Labourers whose employment is not otherwise specified; also 'Miners, Quarriers, Porters, Messengers, and other persons variously engaged in Laborious occupations', for a list of whom see Table page 53, part III (p 56).

2. The order is divided into three groups: clerical, legal and medical. The aggregate figures for Wales allocates all professional persons under 'males'; but the county tables make it possible to allocate those occupied in the third group, medicine, into males and females. This has been done, but it is a minor source of error because the aggregate total for Wales in the original tables is greater than the sum of the counties. The discrepancy arises in the clerical group. A footnote to the summary table explains (p 285) that 'Considerable difficulty has occured in ascertaining the number of Clergymen in England and Wales correctly, in consequence of the word 'Clerk' being equally applicable to Clergymen and to a large class of persons employed by Bankers, Merchants, and professional men. The above results (i.e. those relating to Wales as a whole) have been arrived at after a careful examination and correction of the tables returned under these heads in the several counties.'

3. Exclusive of many persons who have returned themselves simply as Clerks, Messengers, etc., and many who are also engaged in Trade, etc.

4. Exclusive of many persons who are likewise engaged in Trade and Professions.

LABOUR 2. Occupations, by sex, each county, 1801-1971

C. 1851-1921

Occupational Distribution of the Population: Anglesey

CLASS	MALES 1851	1861	1871	1881	1891	1901	1911	1921[1]	FEMALES 1851	1861	1871	1881	1891	1901	1911	1921[1]
1 General or Local Government	64	83	88	92	114	218	283	199	4	3	10	11	19	46	52	62
2 Defence	51	41	47	46	50	174	93	152	-	-	-	-	-	-	-	-
3 Professional Occupations	219	217	223	254	277	471	541	584	39	47	67	100	155	276	402	520
4 Domestic Offices or Services	95	279	133	145	107	537	468	196	1,221	2,112	2,397	1,813	2,546	2,986	2,806	2,364
5 Commercial Occupations	55	71	77	107	117	189	249	456	1	-	3	2	3	3	11	116[2]
6 Conveyance of Men, Goods and Messages	845	1,249	1,031	1,661	1,492	2,567	2,456	3,020	12	4	6	21	20	24	16	82
7 Agriculture	6,535	5,186	4,602	4,444	4,505	6,118	6,234	6,094	1,470	489	531	390	429	759	1,069	600
8 Fishing	38	37	47	52	35	48	69	46	-	-	-	-	-	-	-	-
9 Mines & Quarries	1,072	822	531	389	221	836	718	535	65	1	3	15	8	7	3	1
10 Metals, Machines, Implements & Conveyances	458	563	461	464	438	694	664	914	-	49	47	11	6	3	12	2
11 Precious Metals, Jewels, Watches, Instruments & Games	35	23	19	21	23	31	36	17	-	-	3	-	1	9	6	-
12 Building & Works of Construction	1,180	750	811	867	765	1,404	1,278	1,305	16	11	6	3	2	-	2	3
13 Wood, Furniture, Fittings and Decorations	91	78	65	59	52	74	87	108	-	1	1	1	-	4	3	3
14 Brick, Cement, Pottery & Glass	30	30	25	10	13	18	21	17	8	3	4	2	3	9	6	-
15 Chemicals, Oil, Grease, Soap, Resin, etc.	43	39	46	35	56	56	53	13	1	1	2	3	-	1	3	5
16 Skins, Leather, Hair and Feathers	73	76	46	51	46	48	34	31	-	2	-	4	2	-	3	3
17 Paper, Print, Books & Stationery	13	17	22	25	23	33	37	39	2	1	1	5	7	10	18	6
18 Textile Fabrics	263	169	133	116	112	157	144	58	62	28	39	34	50	128	133	39
19 Dress	852	695	581	462	385	438	393	255	960	902	839	692	716	927	756	380
20 Food, Tobacco, Drink and Lodging	495	437	436	416	499	804	848	275	308	256	274	262	365	489	703	413
21 Gas, Water, Electricity, Sanitary Work	3	7	10	7	10	25	41	26	-	-	-	1	-	-	-	-
22 Other, General & Undefined Workers	727	714	1,644	1,296	892	940	994	2,052	135	84	126	131	65	45	109	590
TOTAL OCCUPIED	13,237	11,583	11,185	11,109	10,232	15,880	15,741	16,392	4,304	3,994	4,359	3,501	4,397	5,726	6,113	5,189
23 Unoccupied etc.	7,935	6,918	5,812	6,171	2,293	3,361	3,721	2,877	17,767	15,662	13,877	14,450	9,872	15,264	15,361	16,418

1. The figures for 1921 represent an attempt to redistribute the information from the 1921 census on the same basis as was used for 1851-1911

2. 110 of these are 'other clerks'

Occupational Distribution of thePopulation: Breconshire

CLASS	MALES 1851	1861	1871	1881	1891	1901	1911	1921[1]	FEMALES 1851	1861	1871	1881	1891	1901	1911	1921[1]
1 General or Local Government	93	146	158	161	187	229	305	227	12	20	22	23	36	66	95	89
2 Defence	330	55	323	319	263	190	213	203	-	-	-	-	-	-	-	-
3 Professional Occupations	404	435	450	497	472	551	565	575	74	137	171	218	268	372	468	649
4 Domestic Offices or Services	367	356	406	590	229	520	709	202	2,166	2,992	3,782	3,582	3,938	2,946	2,910	2,191
5 Commercial Occupations	58	93	129	212	214	336	429	553	1	3	2	2	6	15	27	140[2]
6 Conveyance of Men, Goods and Messages	235	269	354	695	934	1,199	1,270	1,453	31	21	12	15	11	13	11	57
7 Agriculture	8,171	8,260	7,193	5,997	5,991	4,838	4,834	4,810	1,748	1,367	543	342	379	453	832	407
8 Fishing	6	17	5	5	5	2	3	1	-	-	-	-	-	-	-	-
9 Mines & Quarries	3,584	3,330	2,679	2,412	3,092	4,160	5,945	6,456	101	102	107	56	18	14	9	2
10 Metals, Machines, Implements & Conveyances	1,523	1,636	1,432	910	752	952	896	1,188	152	130	83	12	16	15	34	38
11 Precious Metals, Jewels, Watches, Instruments & Games	34	42	38	38	48	40	43	14	-	1	3	1	1	2	7	1
12 Building & Works of Construction	1,186	1,596	1,535	1,467	1,481	1,982	1,762	1,624	37	63	22	1	1	2	1	3
13 Wood, Furniture, Fittings and Decorations	302	291	267	200	145	136	121	204	7	5	5	7	3	11	4	1
14 Brick, Cement, Pottery & Glass	46	25	29	36	30	57	89	41	3	18	16	44	19	13	17	8
15 Chemicals, Oil, Grease, Soap, Resin, etc.	50	42	46	42	39	63	63	21	3	2	4	1	1	2	3	1
16 Skins, Leather, Hair and Feathers	125	124	87	87	63	59	62	48	-	1	1	-	-	-	1	-
17 Paper, Print, Books & Stationery	57	37	55	63	88	95	111	94	7	5	6	23	24	27	34	10
18 Textile Fabrics	286	221	254	199	196	190	138	37	97	66	76	67	106	98	142	15
19 Dress	1,124	987	848	684	533	494	498	267	1,497	1,573	1,208	760	857	786	763	398
20 Food, Tobacco, Drink and Lodging	835	828	856	734	801	864	1,061	367	458	353	316	334	480	500	788	402
21 Gas, Water, Electricity, Sanitary Work	4	17	13	18	22	35	67	62	-	-	-	-	-	1	-	1
22 Other, General & Undefined Workers	1,342	1,164	1,867	1,481	1,435	1,310	888	2,244	108	120	130	94	88	53	72	638
TOTAL OCCUPIED	20,162	19,971	19,183	16,847	17,020	18,302	20,072	20,691	6,502	6,979	6,509	5,582	6,252	5,389	6,218	5,051
23 Unoccupied etc.	9,831	9,669	9,470	10,144	3,189	3,114	3,718	3,125	22,683	22,241	21,929	21,547	14,164	15,247	16,285	18,036

1. The figures for 1921 represent an attempt to redistribute the information from the 1921 census on the same basis as was used for 1851-1911

2. Includes 121 'other clerks'

LABOUR 2.

Occupational Distribution of thePopulation: Caernarvon

CLASS	MALES 1851	1861	1871	1881	1891	1901	1911	1921 (1)	FEMALES 1851	1861	1871	1881	1891	1901	1911	1921 (1)
1 General or Local Government	139	234	306	324	423	566	753	746	11	16	17	21	62	106	156	249
2 Defence	50	91	106	128	162	89	59	70	-	-	-	-	-	-	-	-
3 Professional Occupations	524	683	764	1,090	1,288	1,450	1,621	2,038	101	189	252	447	796	882	1,043	1,686
4 Domestic Offices or Services	383	447	518	1,075	490	892	1,103	599	3,561	6,830	7,800	8,581	9,920	7,529	6,807	6,314
5 Commercial Occupations	109	223	327	668	780	1,012	1,157	2,346	15	6	10	24	30	66	117	981 (2)
6 Conveyance of Men, Goods and Messages	1,981	2,367	2,389	2,474	3,139	3,820	3,664	4,648	47	23	22	24	25	47	37	252
7 Agriculture	11,694	11,403	9,644	8,995	9,442	7,446	7,606	7,965	2,661	1,181	1,013	916	799	857	1,309	761
8 Fishing	61	71	102	160	119	141	149	195	-	-	-	1	1	2	1	1
9 Mines & Quarries	5,698	7,687	8,278	10,463	9,296	12,098	11,172	6,060	2	12	7	32	15	24	30	7
10 Metals, Machines, Implements & Conveyances	1,136	1,393	1,210	1,271	1,274	1,579	1,535	2,301	10	2	5	12	10	21	31	44
11 Precious Metals, Jewels, Watches, Instruments & Games	59	68	89	108	123	143	142	79	1	2	9	11	14	34	32	10
12 Building & Works of Construction	2,057	2,488	2,771	3,500	3,337	3,688	3,267	5,523	37	59	26	6	3	1	1	18
13 Wood, Furniture, Fittings and Decorations	281	289	284	259	238	285	301	360	9	2	6	9	33	17	28	12
14 Brick, Cement, Pottery & Glass	69	67	82	79	53	98	81	83	10	7	9	7	12	9	15	18
15 Chemicals, Oil, Grease, Soap, Resin, etc.	101	92	104	99	110	119	144	59	3	2	5	4	3	3	16	5
16 Skins, Leather, Hair and Feathers	144	136	113	116	112	97	83	64	6	1	-	1	2	4	10	9
17 Paper, Print, Books & Stationery	118	140	185	277	325	326	365	303	2	9	12	27	34	58	83	53
18 Textile Fabrics	504	484	518	503	526	555	512	184	111	163	251	228	265	237	341	186
19 Dress	1,715	1,623	1,466	1,384	1,275	1,199	1,151	668	2,063	2,489	2,374	2,339	2,487	2,163	1,902	984
20 Food, Tobacco, Drink and Lodging	984	1,177	1,341	1,604	2,017	2,329	2,591	925	614	756	849	1,077	1,911	1,714	2,647	2,070
21 Gas, Water, Electricity, Sanitary Work	7	21	26	49	53	92	179	146	-	-	-	-	-	-	-	2
22 Other, General & Undefined Workers	1,747	1,586	4,588	3,454	2,962	2,173	1,984	5,603	220	190	252	244	189	154	223	1,891
TOTAL OCCUPIED	29,561	32,770	35,673	38,080	37,544	40,197	39,619	40,965	9,484	11,941	12,919	14,011	16,611	13,928	14,829	15,553
23 Unoccupied etc.	16,911	17,650	18,866	22,662	8,564	7,259	7,936	6,911	38,718	41,177	44,382	49,028	35,832	38,675	38,999	43,432

1. The figures for 1921 represent an attempt to redistribute the information from the 1921 census on the same basis as was used for 1851-1911

2. 936 of these are 'other clerks'

LABOUR 2.

Occupational Distribution of thePopulation: Cardigan

CLASS	MALES 1851	1861	1871	1881	1891	1901	1911	1921[1]	FEMALES 1851	1861	1871	1881	1891	1901	1911	1921[1]
1 General or Local Government	169	165	199	249	243	261	340	244	151	26	25	43	74	100	148	118
2 Defence	158	106	90	91	95	79	22	27	-	-	-	-	-	-	-	-
3 Professional Occupations	535	554	671	813	857	762	792	1,040	67	98	111	205	309	368	459	601
4 Domestic Offices or Services	344	318	434	488	254	428	466	206	2,601	5,969	7,139	6,898	7,697	4,575	3,680	2,725
5 Commercial Occupations	102	104	155	247	266	284	364	627	8	4	4	10	10	16	21	241[2]
6 Conveyance of Men, Goods and Messages	1,074	1,081	1,094	975	1,139	933	1,014	1,599	29	19	17	22	17	16	9	123
7 Agriculture	13,460	14,370	12,734	11,681	11,039	7,238	7,914	7,509	4,868	2,692	2,575	2,348	1,992	1,487	2,571	1,282
8 Fishing	84	87	69	63	59	30	51	56	-	-	-	3	-	-	-	1
9 Mines & Quarries	1,883	2,358	2,504	1,972	1,126	873	788	1,677	9	5	70	151	21	7	3	1
10 Metals, Machines, Implements & Conveyances	850	1,018	858	835	770	678	640	700	258	345	238	8	26	6	19	8
11 Precious Metals, Jewels, Watches, Instruments & Games	50	57	59	61	65	56	71	35	-	-	8	6	8	5	10	-
12 Building & Works of Construction	1,931	2,074	2,150	2,164	1,892	1,817	1,626	1,406	19	41	11	4	7	1	1	6
13 Wood, Furniture, Fittings and Decorations	309	347	276	260	246	134	155	206	3	7	5	6	3	3	6	1
14 Brick, Cement, Pottery & Glass	23	17	23	29	19	22	24	31	8	11	5	6	15	15	11	2
15 Chemicals, Oil, Grease, Soap, Resin, etc.	53	60	87	76	65	44	52	7	10	6	15	1	2	5	8	-
16 Skins, Leather, Hair and Feathers	178	178	161	160	141	101	62	57	4	7	2	8	6	1	-	2
17 Paper, Print, Books & Stationery	31	61	54	72	90	112	105	110	3	3	6	8	17	20	21	22
18 Textile Fabrics	750	720	739	870	1,126	528	437	162	405	252	188	224	349	249	245	106
19 Dress	1,896	1,662	1,421	1,229	1,099	705	648	439	2,116	2,574	2,676	2,660	2,591	1,405	1,276	624
20 Food, Tobacco, Drink and Lodging	722	823	922	910	1,021	854	966	362	607	678	662	829	1,052	866	1,304	927
21 Gas, Water, Electricity, Sanitary Work	3	4	7	8	8	16	35	22	-	-	-	-	-	-	-	-
22 Other, General & Undefined Workers	2,635	1,242	2,244	1,570	1,136	820	848	2,025	445	165	255	216	116	54	121	728
TOTAL OCCUPIED	27,240	27,406	27,468	24,823	22,756	16,775	17,420	18,547	11,475	12,902	14,012	13,656	14,312	9,199	9,913	7,518
23 Unoccupied etc.	17,915	17,040	17,296	17,894	5,916	4,177	4,452	3,744	40,984	40,053	39,610	38,764	24,841	19,114	17,929	19,993

1. The figures for 1921 represent an attempt to redistribute the information from the 1921 census on the same basis as was used for 1851-1911

2. 230 of these are 'other clerks'

Occupational Distribution of the Population: Carmarthen

CLASS	MALES 1851	1861	1871	1881	1891	1901	1911	1921[1]	FEMALES 1851	1861	1871	1881	1891	1901	1911	1921[1]
1 General or Local Government	196	206	274	274	367	529	698	581	10	10	13	26	51	131	177	152
2 Defence	310	87	83	72	59	141	49	41	-	-	-	-	-	-	-	-
3 Professional Occupations	544	648	687	894	980	1,278	1,389	1,603	135	184	205	364	523	769	996	1,249
4 Domestic Offices or Services	305	286	377	553	329	654	823	330	3,322	5,501	6,653	6,492	7,885	7,024	6,189	4,512
5 Commercial Occupations	118	188	287	559	638	809	1,190	1,655	7	1	11	4	13	22	71	464[2]
6 Conveyance of Men, Goods and Messages	781	1,142	1,196	1,388	2,006	2,894	3,747	4,207	31	14	29	39	15	32	28	214
7 Agriculture	12,937	12,228	10,311	9,191	8,966	10,746	11,284	10,698	4,398	3,192	2,196	1,616	1,444	2,797	4,019	2,377
8 Fishing	123	111	101	104	106	79	88	81	-	5	43	20	39	73	36	19
9 Mines & Quarries	2,793	3,400	3,242	3,163	4,305	6,798	11,340	14,644	24	34	46	29	18	3	13	2
10 Metals, Machines, Implements & Conveyances	1,971	2,588	4,001	5,476	7,835	6,331	9,505	9,898	67	142	298	766	1,184	620	893	1,243
11 Precious Metals, Jewels, Watches, Instruments & Games	49	48	62	62	71	107	92	38	2	3	1	4	6	9	8	-
12 Building & Works of Construction	2,162	2,317	2,253	2,536	2,512	3,032	4,272	3,776	29	42	16	2	4	3	4	10
13 Wood, Furniture, Fittings and Decorations	436	437	408	364	401	444	651	621	17	10	16	7	13	12	23	30
14 Brick, Cement, Pottery & Glass	135	172	151	166	203	258	358	212	48	74	97	79	67	65	62	52
15 Chemicals, Oil, Grease, Soap, Resin, etc.	108	100	147	175	198	176	194	86	2	2	9	16	7	9	12	22
16 Skins, Leather, Hair and Feathers	160	152	123	128	118	137	114	90	7	16	11	11	5	4	8	2
17 Paper, Print, Books & Stationery	111	129	158	157	186	202	215	158	8	12	14	28	28	36	65	30
18 Textile Fabrics	638	662	766	831	828	1,112	914	406	264	158	142	137	225	644	731	329
19 Dress	1,801	1,579	1,423	1,194	1,200	1,349	1,373	773	2,120	2,644	2,192	2,061	2,779	2,864	3,315	1,778
20 Food, Tobacco, Drink and Lodging	953	1,064	1,121	1,199	1,411	1,743	2,189	736	807	702	636	730	1,103	1,128	1,930	770
21 Gas, Water, Electricity, Sanitary Work	6	13	26	35	54	120	138	194	1	-	-	1	1	-	-	-
22 Other, General & Undefined Workers	1,304	1,303	2,820	2,663	2,366	1,831	2,516	6,638	255	160	263	176	116	94	231	1,916
TOTAL OCCUPIED	27,941	28,860	30,452	31,184	35,139	40,770	53,139	57,466	11,554	12,906	12,891	12,608	15,526	16,339	18,811	15,171
23 Unoccupied etc.	17,578	17,289	18,333	22,305	7,410	8,632	9,690	8,068	37,599	37,596	40,140	45,158	31,624	38,963	44,174	52,102

1. The figures for 1921 represent an attempt to redistribute the information from the 1921 census on the same basis as was used for 1851-1911

2. 407 of these are 'other clerks'

LABOUR 2.

Occupational Distribution of the Population: Denbigh

CLASS	MALES 1851	1861	1871	1881	1891	1901	1911	1921[1]	FEMALES 1851	1861	1871	1881	1891	1901	1911	1921[1]
1 General or Local Government	161	225	315	304	375	479	654	559	18	21	35	39	54	94	135	199
2 Defence	102	109	110	412	284	333	238	306	-	-	-	-	-	-	-	-
3 Professional Occupations	699	756	818	1,101	1,173	1,354	1,598	1,657	187	269	317	504	722	940	1,280	1,670
4 Domestic Offices or Services	688	825	812	1,338	513	1,355	1,714	632	3,852	5,817	7,111	7,078	7,979	6,966	7,095	6,335
5 Commercial Occupations	137	282	405	648	741	1,116	1,451	2,003	3	3	37	10	10	63	128	739[2]
6 Conveyance of Men, Goods and Messages	573	814	833	1,008	2,009	2,417	2,899	3,825	62	41	34	26	32	39	39	183
7 Agriculture	14,099	13,504	10,581	9,453	9,511	9,555	10,143	9,861	3,015	1,824	993	684	601	935	1,576	920
8 Fishing	18	20	11	22	14	5	6	9	-	1	3	-	3	-	-	-
9 Mines & Quarries	4,637	6,434	7,033	7,719	8,850	10,647	11,978	13,447	115	34	58	57	38	9	5	4
10 Metals, Machines, Implements & Conveyances	1,750	2,258	1,885	1,587	1,636	2,107	2,350	2,910	6	6	20	9	9	50	16	38
11 Precious Metals, Jewels, Watches, Instruments & Games	46	60	60	77	82	123	143	95	1	2	6	7	13	12	18	6
12 Building & Works of Construction	1,822	2,336	2,384	2,823	2,656	3,449	3,388	3,627	55	77	20	1	1	1	-	7
13 Wood, Furniture, Fittings and Decorations	422	416	350	338	301	355	496	597	22	5	17	12	17	11	21	29
14 Brick, Cement, Pottery & Glass	138	218	232	512	815	1,479	1,207	760	10	8	8	15	30	24	18	38
15 Chemicals, Oil, Grease, Soap, Resin, etc.	124	140	111	105	128	168	197	143	5	5	8	14	7	8	36	8
16 Skins, Leather, Hair and Feathers	272	285	183	265	311	341	440	282	14	6	7	8	24	33	60	67
17 Paper, Print, Books & Stationery	128	196	233	253	294	306	319	246	24	55	47	64	65	77	100	39
18 Textile Fabrics	399	356	371	349	359	516	470	149	73	100	95	80	128	160	266	130
19 Dress	2,084	1,922	1,579	1,288	1,196	1,076	1,114	655	2,250	2,274	1,787	1,565	1,750	1,712	1,618	923
20 Food, Tobacco, Drink and Lodging	1,465	1,594	1,759	1,947	2,145	2,598	3,073	1,035	854	609	632	759	1,151	1,228	1,983	1,654
21 Gas, Water, Electricity, Sanitary Work	9	27	57	50	69	119	171	133	-	1	2	-	-	-	-	2
22 Other, General & Undefined Workers	1,669	2,090	4,120	4,001	3,950	2,748	2,696	6,861	185	170	230	224	122	113	216	1,871
TOTAL OCCUPIED	31,442	34,867	34,640	35,600	37,412	42,646	46,745	49,792	10,751	11,328	11,467	11,156	12,756	12,475	14,610	14,862
23 Unoccupied etc.	17,197	17,641	18,147	20,901	7,446	8,288	9,940	8,397	37,525	40,510	41,308	45,283	32,140	38,236	42,524	47,519

1. The figures for 1921 represent an attempt to redistribute the information from the 1921 census on the same basis as was used for 1851-1911

2. 689 of these are 'other clerks'

LABOUR 2.

Occupational Distribution of the Population: Flint

CLASS	MALES 1851	1861	1871	1881	1891	1901	1911	1921 (1)	FEMALES 1851	1861	1871	1881	1891	1901	1911	1921 (1)
1 General or Local Government	59	76	104	104	125	312	412	437	7	9	18	16	27	65	111	146
2 Defence	30	23	51	47	12	48	46	302	-	-	-	-	-	-	-	-
3 Professional Occupations	195	209	238	353	355	782	975	1,110	67	99	123	183	256	676	912	1,125
4 Domestic Offices or Services	226	221	219	366	113	717	903	364	1,455	2,071	2,411	2,148	2,434	4,000	4,109	3,879
5 Commercial Occupations	81	101	152	249	231	628	918	1,481	23	3	2	2	6	18	47	501 (2)
6 Conveyance of Men, Goods and Messages	520	563	558	662	901	2,309	2,350	2,831	35	22	25	29	15	27	31	171
7 Agriculture	3,178	2,897	2,590	2,231	2,259	4,719	5,155	5,183	713	272	258	191	155	446	825	543
8 Fishing	47	24	34	30	47	57	58	67	-	-	1	3	1	4	-	-
9 Mines & Quarries	3,541	3,492	3,868	3,503	3,430	4,776	5,057	4,545	8	7	13	16	6	4	5	1
10 Metals, Machines, Implements & Conveyances	1,135	1,174	1,058	1,132	1,110	2,412	4,409	5,139	14	6	5	45	35	24	32	56
11 Precious Metals, Jewels, Watches, Instruments & Games	24	24	31	19	21	50	68	52	-	1	1	2	8	6	14	2
12 Building & Works of Construction	710	732	827	946	886	2,380	2,237	2,605	24	37	7	5	-	-	1	8
13 Wood, Furniture, Fittings and Decorations	220	222	196	202	160	189	243	351	31	1	4	6	6	6	7	4
14 Brick, Cement, Pottery & Glass	175	141	157	220	245	883	788	497	4	2	3	5	7	7	15	38
15 Chemicals, Oil, Grease, Soap, Resin, etc.	54	148	340	671	640	401	551	212	1	-	2	1	2	2	12	8
16 Skins, Leather, Hair and Feathers	63	54	55	48	37	65	60	56	-	1	-	1	-	-	-	8
17 Paper, Print, Books & Stationery	73	86	119	171	198	308	350	236	31	34	63	92	115	131	170	87
18 Textile Fabrics	191	206	158	156	156	219	461	432	80	229	74	131	213	183	458	763
19 Dress	588	519	436	358	290	484	534	318	706	793	620	591	624	1,004	972	571
20 Food, Tobacco, Drink and Lodging	606	628	696	665	740	1,600	1,911	726	347	272	236	280	369	881	1,317	1,136
21 Gas, Water, Electricity, Sanitary Work	8	6	13	20	22	64	87	133	-	-	1	1	-	-	-	-
22 Other, General & Undefined Workers	1,285	1,530	2,523	2,150	1,713	2,114	1,786	6,239	74	70	100	95	63	113	185	1,380
TOTAL OCCUPIED	13,009	13,076	14,540	14,303	13,691	25,517	29,359	33,316	3,620	3,929	3,967	3,843	4,342	7,597	9,223	10,427
23 Unoccupied etc.	7,778	6,921	7,696	8,914	2,729	5,647	6,440	5,483	16,640	16,015	17,431	18,714	11,769	24,388	27,671	32,614

1. The figures for 1921 represent an attempt to redistribute the information from the 1921 census on the same basis as was used for 1851-1911

2. 453 of these are 'other clerks'

Occupational Distribution of the Population: Glamorgan

MALES

CLASS	1851	1861	1871	1881	1891	1901	1911	1921[1]
1 General or Local Government	389	705	1,084	1,275	2,134	3,135	5,047	6,014
2 Defence	323	235	276	454	329	615	611	1,105
3 Professional Occupations	1,275	1,618	2,266	3,674	5,268	7,388	9,622	10,745
4 Domestic Offices or Services	686	745	899	2,140	1,330	2,856	4,271	3,560
5 Commercial Occupations	608	1,411	2,326	4,464	7,684	11,248	15,886	19,179
6 Conveyance of Men, Goods and Messages	5,629	8,889	12,674	17,663	26,812	38,167	48,376	51,241
7 Agriculture	13,139	12,753	11,394	10,015	10,102	8,990	9,489	9,796
8 Fishing	98	92	288	171	113	107	229	374
9 Mines & Quarries	22,320	30,257	37,364	48,380	82,160	107,859	150,694	163,399
10 Metals, Machines, Implements & Conveyances	13,670	20,030	24,460	26,709	31,025	36,096	48,461	52,564
11 Precious Metals, Jewels, Watches, Instruments & Games	165	347	418	409	641	822	1,106	653
12 Building & Works of Construction	6,320	8,717	9,711	13,195	18,385	20,700	26,441	25,293
13 Wood, Furniture, Fittings and Decorations	1,310	1,466	1,601	1,840	2,204	2,870	3,921	3,776
14 Brick, Cement, Pottery & Glass	346	459	452	627	771	839	1,459	774
15 Chemicals, Oil, Grease, Soap, Resin, etc.	275	369	524	585	757	1,010	1,485	953
16 Skins, Leather, Hair and Feathers	318	364	370	408	506	507	594	455
17 Paper, Print, Books & Stationery	209	356	597	871	1,360	1,953	2,424	1,895
18 Textile Fabrics	1,099	1,215	1,557	1,705	1,971	2,168	2,169	383
19 Dress	3,982	4,344	4,482	4,383	5,330	6,263	7,749	4,029
20 Food, Tobacco, Drink and Lodging	3,291	4,527	5,646	7,004	10,414	15,049	21,156	6,644
21 Gas, Water, Electricity, Sanitary Work	22	102	195	281	563	1,115	2,022	1,518
22 Other, General & Undefined Workers	9,313	11,775	20,409	21,235	30,319	20,259	19,970	56,747
TOTAL OCCUPIED	84,787	110,776	139,912	167,488	240,178	290,016	383,182	421,097
23 Unoccupied etc.	40,300	57,059	70,623	98,640	35,769	46,962	62,575	54,554

FEMALES

CLASS	1851	1861	1871	1881	1891	1901	1911	1921[1]
1 General or Local Government	15	33	66	65	194	444	1,065	1,370
2 Defence	-	-	-	-	-	-	-	-
3 Professional Occupations	397	774	1,296	2,437	4,243	6,435	8,297	10,760
4 Domestic Offices or Services	8,834	13,964	19,595	23,999	31,793	29,268	33,079	29,950
5 Commercial Occupations	51	12	27	44	128	527	1,404	7,596[2]
6 Conveyance of Men, Goods and Messages	74	30	48	112	183	318	363	2,167
7 Agriculture	3,030	1,475	1,133	946	779	792	1,579	990
8 Fishing	-	6	14	18	33	3	28	10
9 Mines & Quarries	678	571	798	558	349	112	92	119
10 Metals, Machines, Implements & Conveyances	888	1,274	1,677	2,095	2,640	1,499	2,157	2,754
11 Precious Metals, Jewels, Watches, Instruments & Games	2	26	20	32	43	63	114	25
12 Building & Works of Construction	186	272	112	12	37	22	11	92
13 Wood, Furniture, Fittings and Decorations	24	60	63	71	104	128	281	181
14 Brick, Cement, Pottery & Glass	105	202	337	345	350	227	225	241
15 Chemicals, Oil, Grease, Soap, Resin, etc.	12	9	35	69	120	136	221	28
16 Skins, Leather, Hair and Feathers	8	9	8	13	23	24	35	46
17 Paper, Print, Books & Stationery	15	30	61	165	327	666	1,020	719
18 Textile Fabrics	331	285	468	672	1,214	2,254	3,133	763
19 Dress	5,696	8,343	8,663	8,450	12,812	13,532	15,376	8,766
20 Food, Tobacco, Drink and Lodging	1,941	1,986	2,174	2,582	7,573	5,564	10,906	6,575
21 Gas, Water, Electricity, Sanitary Work	2	1	-	-	1	-	1	9
22 Other, General & Undefined Workers	604	712	1,024	860	1,209	1,100	2,022	16,066
TOTAL OCCUPIED	22,893	30,074	37,619	43,545	64,155	63,114	81,409	89,227
23 Unoccupied etc.	92,115	128,345	158,563	208,710	178,624	245,444	320,998	366,298

1. The figures for 1921 represent an attempt to redistribute the information from the 1921 census on the same basis as was used for 1851-1911

2. 6,969 of these are 'other clerks'

Occupational Distribution of the Population: Merioneth

CLASS	MALES 1851	1861	1871	1881	1891	1901	1911	1921 (1)	FEMALES 1851	1861	1871	1881	1891	1901	1911	1921
1 General or Local Government	62	107	152	168	217	230	254	218	8	13	15	20	36	41	76	101
2 Defence	55	30	28	15	19	26	33	19	-	-	-	-	-	-	-	-
3 Professional Occupations	295	361	455	641	698	565	546	604	50	65	100	192	301	366	388	494
4 Domestic Offices or Services	237	208	315	555	266	450	506	200	1,659	3,222	4,246	4,314	4,715	2,942	2,575	2,313
5 Commercial Occupations	39	76	158	311	319	251	296	581	-	4	8	6	11	9	15	211 (2)
6 Conveyance of Men, Goods and Messages	436	646	787	878	1,150	1,020	987	1,099	31	22	27	15	9	7	12	84
7 Agriculture	8,492	8,233	7,611	6,776	6,750	4,561	4,728	4,659	2,155	962	769	632	605	574	901	458
8 Fishing	6	7	12	8	12	8	6	15	-	-	1	-	1	-	-	-
9 Mines & Quarries	1,658	2,506	4,220	5,072	4,723	4,489	3,368	2,447	6	5	14	9	4	6	4	2
10 Metals, Machines, Implements & Conveyances	582	636	639	659	608	413	367	537	7	4	4	5	4	1	9	11
11 Precious Metals, Jewels, Watches, Instruments & Games	38	27	36	46	64	33	38	29	-	1	2	7	3	1	1	1
12 Building & Works of Construction	772	1,008	1,555	2,096	1,390	1,207	1,228	1,492	14	20	10	-	4	-	-	4
13 Wood, Furniture, Fittings and Decorations	157	173	150	139	138	84	81	112	5	1	3	3	1	3	6	2
14 Brick, Cement, Pottery & Glass	27	38	77	103	128	9	6	6	8	6	6	6	14	12	13	-
15 Chemicals, Oil, Grease, Soap, Resin, etc.	36	34	49	40	54	39	51	8	1	2	3	1	3	-	8	2
16 Skins, Leather, Hair and Feathers	120	130	86	114	138	81	82	81	6	1	1	5	1	1	2	2
17 Paper, Print, Books & Stationery	38	55	77	111	129	109	102	86	2	4	3	9	17	14	14	11
18 Textile Fabrics	643	576	534	557	543	258	185	35	183	139	101	85	92	82	83	28
19 Dress	906	873	846	711	633	432	376	211	1,005	1,116	1,119	908	1,082	767	683	332
20 Food, Tobacco, Drink and Lodging	498	557	684	783	816	736	739	228	322	285	298	420	671	569	857	655
21 Gas, Water, Electricity, Sanitary Work	-	6	12	13	19	23	41	30	-	-	-	-	-	-	-	-
22 Other, General & Undefined Workers	936	974	1,762	1,916	1,342	551	542	1,569	80	52	91	105	40	40	75	519
TOTAL OCCUPIED	16,033	17,261	20,410	21,712	20,066	15,575	14,562	14,266	5,542	5,924	6,821	6,742	7,614	5,435	5,722	5,230
23 Unoccupied etc.	9,356	9,047	10,520	12,638	4,240	3,131	3,151	2,383	20,376	20,998	23,921	27,180	17,884	14,465	13,813	14,507

1. The figures for 1921 represent an attempt to redistribute the information from the 1921 census on the same basis as was used for 1851-1911

2. 204 of these are 'other clerks'

Occupational Distribution of the Population: Monmouth

MALES

CLASS	1851	1861	1871	1881	1891	1901	1911	1921[1]
1 General or Local Government	309	476	582	637	832	1,071	1,453	1,543
2 Defence	513	176	642[2]	201	319	730	222	1,580
3 Professional Occupations	974	1,101	1,171	1,579	1,975	2,330	3,023	3,169
4 Domestic Offices or Services	851	725	942	1,383	601	1,576	2,071	1,111
5 Commercial Occupations	393	665	988	1,576	2,168	2,939	4,087	4,947
6 Conveyance of Men, Goods and Messages	2,301	3,386	3,753	6,663	9,412	10,492	14,426	14,971
7 Agriculture	13,311	13,053	10,668	9,516	9,484	7,439	7,819	7,875
8 Fishing	85	76	69	60	76	34	23	27
9 Mines & Quarries	15,771	14,429	16,565	16,208	25,993	34,951	53,504	62,038
10 Metals, Machines, Implements & Conveyances	10,038	13,249	14,739	13,089	13,402	12,794	18,147	20,397
11 Precious Metals, Jewels, Watches, Instruments & Games	97	124	134	161	201	221	310	179
12 Building & Works of Construction	4,187	4,723	5,288	5,694	6,776	7,314	9,956	9,767
13 Wood, Furniture, Fittings and Decorations	1,028	1,124	1,151	906	913	940	1,211	1,260
14 Brick, Cement, Pottery & Glass	257	289	275	266	440	691	947	554
15 Chemicals, Oil, Grease, Soap, Resin, etc.	164	188	231	205	233	228	388	282
16 Skins, Leather, Hair and Feathers	268	248	218	193	191	209	212	135
17 Paper, Print, Books & Stationery	204	213	297	332	461	502	679	467
18 Textile Fabrics	535	518	543	495	569	529	531	82
19 Dress	2,973	2,702	2,390	1,927	1,847	1,843	2,293	990
20 Food, Tobacco, Drink and Lodging	2,502	2,919	3,242	3,399	4,287	5,074	6,870	2,347
21 Gas, Water, Electricity, Sanitary Work	33	62	87	142	264	418	715	524
22 Other, General & Undefined Workers	6,370	6,751	12,863	10,236	12,063	6,500	6,928	19,211
TOTAL OCCUPIED	63,164	67,197	77,321	74,868	92,507	98,825	135,815	153,456
23 Unoccupied etc.	29,137	33,813	36,924	45,097	15,277	16,965	22,057	19,187

FEMALES

CLASS	1851	1861	1871	1881	1891	1901	1911	1921[1]
1 General or Local Government	18	31	54	63	128	199	456	499
2 Defence	-	-	-	-	-	-	-	-
3 Professional Occupations	427	614	744	1,204	1,727	2,326	2,951	3,587
4 Domestic Offices or Services	6,213	8,501	10,407	11,130	13,313	10,407	12,102	10,889
5 Commercial Occupations	13	-	8	27	59	157	361	1,893[3]
6 Conveyance of Men, Goods and Messages	56	44	58	60	71	96	99	688
7 Agriculture	2,088	991	684	540	450	475	940	678
8 Fishing	-	-	-	-	-	-	-	-
9 Mines & Quarries	525	586	636	346	283	140	86	35
10 Metals, Machines, Implements & Conveyances	653	587	715	732	597	159	294	380
11 Precious Metals, Jewels, Watches, Instruments & Games	1	7	18	10	19	26	54	3
12 Building & Works of Construction	156	226	61	15	3	3	4	20
13 Wood, Furniture, Fittings and Decorations	40	31	44	46	36	41	89	28
14 Brick, Cement, Pottery & Glass	30	124	143	182	140	100	79	85
15 Chemicals, Oil, Grease, Soap, Resin, etc.	5	12	6	6	6	21	49	13
16 Skins, Leather, Hair and Feathers	6	11	13	6	5	6	5	17
17 Paper, Print, Books & Stationery	41	18	60	67	142	238	336	260
18 Textile Fabrics	122	156	222	302	513	670	964	157
19 Dress	4,296	5,105	4,503	3,282	4,073	3,950	4,132	2,091
20 Food, Tobacco, Drink and Lodging	1,142	938	976	1,039	2,015	1,836	3,484	1,826
21 Gas, Water, Electricity, Sanitary Work	1	-	-	6	3	-	-	-
22 Other, General & Undefined Workers	340	430	504	415	432	341	649	5,218
TOTAL OCCUPIED	16,173	18,412	19,856	19,478	24,015	21,191	27,134	28,367
23 Unoccupied etc.	68,656	77,555	85,990	94,889	74,235	85,827	112,392	131,474

1. The figures for 1921 represent an attempt to redistribute the information from the 1921 census on the same basis as was used for 1851-1911

2. Includes 507 soldiers

3. 1,694 of these are 'other clerks'

Occupational Distribution of the Population: Montgomery

CLASS	MALES 1851	1861	1871	1881	1891	1901	1911	1921[1]	FEMALES 1851	1861	1871	1881	1891	1901	1911	1921[1]
1 General or Local Government	113	159	208	213	242	269	325	182	10	15	19	24	47	56	73	83
2 Defence	87	61	74	139	63	37	24	20	-	-	-	-	-	-	-	-
3 Professional Occupations	430	481	538	682	600	529	554	488	89	148	171	261	306	315	395	458
4 Domestic Offices or Services	403	446	445	752	299	579	671	175	2,631	4,606	5,184	4,950	5,025	3,162	3,129	2,281
5 Commercial Occupations	63	128	181	281	326	305	348	458	-	4	4	7	9	13	24	160[2]
6 Conveyance of Men, Goods and Messages	393	603	490	543	915	960	1,013	1,261	40	26	29	24	14	11	13	59
7 Agriculture	14,289	13,613	11,838	10,769	10,231	8,344	8,501	8,190	3,031	1,267	983	769	608	774	1,543	679
8 Fishing	4	5	10	8	11	5	2	2	-	-	-	-	-	-	-	-
9 Mines & Quarries	1,250	1,441	2,341	1,683	839	488	517	815	9	2	127	16	5	4	9	-
10 Metals, Machines, Implements & Conveyances	936	1,019	906	857	770	656	630	601	63	91	23	8	13	5	13	3
11 Precious Metals, Jewels, Watches, Instruments & Games	36	40	38	43	41	45	44	33	-	-	2	8	7	3	3	1
12 Building & Works of Construction	1,230	2,019	1,674	1,763	1,427	1,398	1,306	1,635	30	16	9	4	3	1	-	-
13 Wood, Furniture, Fittings and Decorations	352	411	332	264	195	150	130	310	3	3	4	8	10	4	6	2
14 Brick, Cement, Pottery & Glass	63	69	66	65	45	44	52	34	6	7	10	5	7	3	7	1
15 Chemicals, Oil, Grease, Soap, Resin, etc.	45	63	59	41	52	27	36	2	4	2	3	2	1	-	1	1
16 Skins, Leather, Hair and Feathers	218	212	140	157	143	110	117	121	4	-	1	6	1	1	2	1
17 Paper, Print, Books & Stationery	40	51	59	73	86	103	92	60	2	6	3	13	13	13	22	4
18 Textile Fabrics	2,426	1,496	1,031	1,006	910	594	521	132	1,678	1,092	706	757	721	511	450	288
19 Dress	1,463	1,326	1,246	955	817	583	513	355	1,645	1,697	1,350	1,010	1,155	940	777	386
20 Food, Tobacco, Drink and Lodging	1,083	1,060	1,159	1,088	1,014	933	948	324	506	389	397	441	557	413	617	268
21 Gas, Water, Electricity, Sanitary Work	3	10	13	40	26	34	50	24	-	-	-	-	-	-	-	-
22 Other, General & Undefined Workers	581	1,097	2,743	2,363	1,717	1,083	861	1,843	118	92	142	99	72	56	71	462
TOTAL OCCUPIED	25,508	25,846	25,789	23,785	20,769	17,276	17,255	17,065	9,869	9,463	9,167	8,412	8,574	6,285	7,155	5,137
23 Unoccupied etc.	13,033	13,041	13,916	14,510	4,353	3,551	3,520	2,747	28,732	28,573	29,726	29,489	18,269	15,849	14,523	15,116

1. The figures for 1921 represent an attempt to redistribute the information from the 1921 census on the same basis as was used for 1851-1911

2. 147 of these are 'other clerk

LABOUR 2.

Occupational Distribution of the Population: Pembroke

CLASS	MALES 1851	1861	1871	1881	1891	1901	1911	1921[1]	FEMALES 1851	1861	1871	1881	1891	1901	1911	1921[1]
General or Local Government	944	570	694	321	411	514	645	462	14	23	22	25	51	106	162	139
Defence	608	2,423	1,552	1,279	1,200	723	1,375	1,100	-	-	-	-	-	-	-	-
Professional Occupations	544	601	641	694	705	812	885	879	171	213	259	322	446	548	678	863
Domestic Offices or Services	437	506	462	630	242	602	710	295	3,321	5,270	5,796	5,882	6,567	5,388	4,519	3,359
Commercial Occupations	125	144	208	319	342	408	559	836	14	10	3	8	12	19	31	233[2]
Conveyance of Men, Goods and Messages	1,306	1,841	1,314	1,939	1,907	2,554	2,851	3,663	35	21	7	22	19	19	18	104
Agriculture	9,666	9,186	8,443	7,609	7,524	7,790	8,308	8,308	3,298	1,886	1,652	1,215	935	1,667	2,514	1,459
Fishing	199	200	213	211	416	718	598	1,005	-	-	52	41	38	28	3	4
Mines & Quarries	1,139	1,105	870	666	619	831	1,017	1,648	273	126	103	35	36	13	8	1
Metals, Machines, Implements & Conveyances	1,232	1,949	1,874	2,337	2,677	3,071	2,974	3,471	6	10	16	7	7	5	15	6
Precious Metals, Jewels, Watches, Instruments & Games	51	47	47	64	57	65	74	38	-	3	2	2	9	5	14	1
Building & Works of Construction	1,873	2,502	2,100	2,275	2,012	2,595	2,493	2,322	33	82	29	5	1	1	1	1
Wood, Furniture, Fittings and Decorations	405	477	336	346	252	218	263	317	9	9	6	14	15	5	7	7
Brick, Cement, Pottery & Glass	15	9	28	16	37	36	61	28	4	2	4	8	12	10	11	-
Chemicals, Oil, Grease, Soap, Resin, etc.	76	89	79	78	69	64	100	6	3	7	12	5	3	2	3	3
Skins, Leather, Hair and Feathers	130	132	147	127	121	108	99	53	21	21	12	1	2	-	2	2
Paper, Print, Books & Stationery	65	82	83	96	103	115	129	97	5	12	12	16	30	32	40	26
8 Textile Fabrics	449	425	431	449	417	360	315	96	182	173	131	102	135	268	358	76
9 Dress	1,486	1,348	1,108	962	867	844	805	497	2,121	2,646	2,230	1,724	1,695	1,837	1,702	787
0 Food, Tobacco, Drink and Lodging	878	1,001	979	1,018	1,131	1,357	1,646	513	677	786	660	721	979	932	1,262	543
1 Gas, Water, Electricity, Sanitary Work	6	13	17	21	34	42	80	60	-	-	-	-	-	-	-	-
2 Other, General & Undefined Workers	2,036	2,339	3,001	2,671	2,051	2,023	2,096	3,972	165	138	175	97	56	46	127	1,106
TOTAL OCCUPIED	23,670	26,989	24,885	24,128	23,194	25,850	28,083	29,666	10,352	11,438	11,183	10,252	11,048	10,931	11,475	8,720
3 Unoccupied etc.	15,950	15,399	14,847	15,957	5,648	5,997	6,217	4,889	34,500	33,864	33,216	33,342	22,351	25,803	26,001	27,982

1. The figures for 1921 represent an attempt to redistribute the information from the 1921 census on the same basis as was used for 1851-1911

2. 215 of these are 'other clerks'

Occupational Distribution of the Population: Radnor

MALES

CLASS	1851	1861	1871	1881	1891	1901	1911	1921 (1)
1 General or Local Government	44	75	58	57	66	121	142	92
2 Defence	27	29	18	4	4	10	15	8
3 Professional Occupations	182	197	125	141	166	247	256	310
4 Domestic Offices or Services	237	225	171	225	75	293	377	154
5 Commercial Occupations	33	32	34	32	54	110	123	214
6 Conveyance of Men, Goods and Messages	70	87	74	95	211	419	428	583
7 Agriculture	6,472	6,644	4,206	3,346	3,195	3,884	3,951	3,791
8 Fishing	-	-	-	1	-	-	-	1
9 Mines & Quarries	52	87	61	45	51	152	152	292
10 Metals, Machines, Implements & Conveyances	378	432	204	177	154	250	267	269
11 Precious Metals, Jewels, Watches, Instruments & Games	9	19	6	12	12	15	24	12
12 Building & Works of Construction	672	963	544	545	521	1,082	704	665
13 Wood, Furniture, Fittings and Decorations	213	248	96	64	46	54	56	125
14 Brick, Cement, Pottery & Glass	17	42	11	4	4	6	3	3
15 Chemicals, Oil, Grease, Soap, Resin, etc.	23	20	14	9	8	19	17	1
16 Skins, Leather, Hair and Feathers	87	84	34	32	29	32	36	23
17 Paper, Print, Books & Stationery	8	12	5	12	17	29	38	33
18 Textile Fabrics	92	119	87	58	46	70	59	9
19 Dress	603	573	316	248	201	228	196	100
20 Food, Tobacco, Drink and Lodging	398	440	237	249	283	405	424	176
21 Gas, Water, Electricity, Sanitary Work	2	2	2	5	4	22	39	18
22 Other, General & Undefined Workers	585	596	690	441	307	672	295	809
TOTAL OCCUPIED	10,204	10,926	7,045	5,802	5,454	8,120	7,602	7,688
23 Unoccupied etc.	5,914	6,130	3,818	3,602	1,064	1,323	1,478	1,278

FEMALES

CLASS	1851	1861	1871	1881	1891	1901	1911	1921
1 General or Local Government	6	8	6	4	8	24	37	32
2 Defence	-	-	-	-	-	-	-	-
3 Professional Occupations	66	63	46	75	95	133	184	249
4 Domestic Offices or Services	1,112	1,962	1,375	1,354	1,578	1,685	1,496	1,369
5 Commercial Occupations	2	-	-	2	1	13	12	88
6 Conveyance of Men, Goods and Messages	13	14	4	7	3	3	7	30
7 Agriculture	1,273	423	213	142	118	343	503	201
8 Fishing	-	-	-	-	-	-	-	-
9 Mines & Quarries	1	-	4	-	1	-	1	-
10 Metals, Machines, Implements & Conveyances	3	6	3	-	2	3	-	3
11 Precious Metals, Jewels, Watches, Instruments & Games	3	1	-	1	1	6	5	-
12 Building & Works of Construction	9	22	3	-	-	-	1	1
13 Wood, Furniture, Fittings and Decorations	5	4	-	-	2	2	2	-
14 Brick, Cement, Pottery & Glass	-	3	2	3	2	4	5	-
15 Chemicals, Oil, Grease, Soap, Resin, etc.	2	1	-	-	1	1	1	-
16 Skins, Leather, Hair and Feathers	1	2	2	-	-	-	2	1
17 Paper, Print, Books & Stationery	1	-	-	3	6	9	10	5
18 Textile Fabrics	28	21	23	24	48	55	54	2
19 Dress	642	653	325	254	277	258	235	112
20 Food, Tobacco, Drink and Lodging	124	120	77	87	151	263	489	357
21 Gas, Water, Electricity, Sanitary Work	-	-	-	-	-	-	-	1
22 Other, General & Undefined Workers	52	30	28	15	12	13	25	246
TOTAL OCCUPIED	3,343	3,333	2,111	1,971	2,306	2,815	3,069	2,697
23 Unoccupied etc.	11,964	12,477	8,094	7,148	4,290	6,152	6,017	7,006

1. The figures for 1921 represent an attempt to redistribute the information from the 1921 census on the same basis as was used for 1851-1911

2. 85 of these are 'other clerks'

ABOUR 2. Occupations, by sex, each county, 1801-1971

D. 1911-71

Occupational Distribution of the Population: Anglesey

	MALES						FEMALES					
	1911 (1)	1921	1931	1951	1961	1971	1911 (1)	1921	1931	1951	1961	1971
1 Fishing	69	46	21	23	30	-	-	-	1	-	-	-
2 Agriculture	6,489	6,136	5,433	4,195	2,910	1,770	1,069	600	493	427	280	380
3 Gas, Coke and Chemicals	15	13	14	18	50	60	1	3	-	-	-	20
4 Metal Manufacturing and Engineering	735	873	652	1,200	1,560	2,670	19	2	2	76	60	310
5 Mining and Quarrying	718	534	507	191	40	50	3	1	-	1	-	-
6 Woodworkers (+ Cork and Cane)	624	562	539	477	500	580	3	2	2	8	-	-
7 Leather Workers, Fur Dressers	199	143	106	50	10	-	24	3	1	1	10	-
8 Textile Workers	144	31	12	3	-	180	133	16	4	5	-	40
9 Clothing Workers	198	175	91	40	20	10	733	405	173	57	90	210
10 Food, Drink and Tobacco	151	181	203	180	180	140	22	47	30	44	20	90
11 Paper and Printing	37	39	35	18	50	70	18	6	3	2	-	20
12 Building and Contracting	568	646	1,029	1,506	520	790	1	1	-	4	-	10
13 Makers of Other Products (Rubber, Plastics etc.)	-	90	41	31	40	70	-	3	-	13	40	140
14 Painters and Decorators	152	176	180	292	240	330	-	1	-	6	10	-
15 Stationary Engine and Crane Drivers	27	87	73	118	110	400	-	-	-	-	-	-
16 Labourers (n.e.c.)	801	885	962	599	1,300	1,710	-	3	5	210	20	40
17 Transport and Communication	2,695	2,968	2,632	2,195	2,030	1,580	58	67	51	109	50	100
18 Warehousemen, Storekeepers Packers, Bottlers etc.	2	52	62	127	190	260	-	15	6	22	10	100
19 Clerical Workers	126	282	326	517	870	600	19	110	121	535	860	1,360
20 Sales Workers	941	1,120	1,311	1,011	1,210	870	450	571	528	623	860	960
21 Services, Sport and Recreation (inc. Personal Service)	347	351	433	665	850	1,070	3,178	2,760	2,659	1,516	1,420	1,890
22 Administrators and Managers	..	164	111	269	500	510	..	63	2	15	20	60
23 Professional, Technical Workers, Artists	545	529	484	722	1,160	1,440	372	490	430	527	590	1,040
24 Armed Forces	93	152	7	1,050	1,420	1,110	-	-	-	17	-	20
25 Inadequately Described Occupations	44	140	231	235	230	260	4	20	49	89	110	440
26 Glass, Ceramics, Cement	21	17	18	9	-	-	6	-	-	1	-	-
TOTAL OCCUPIED	15,741	16,392	15,513	15,741	16,020	16,530	6,113	5,189	4,560	4,308	4,450	7,230
27 Retired and Unoccupied	3,721	2,877	2,488	3,128	3,380	4,180	15,361	16,418	15,424	16,193	16,050	15,900

Occupational Distribution of the Population: Brecon

	MALES						FEMALES					
	1911[(1)]	1921	1931	1951	1961	1971	1911[(1)]	1921	1931	1951	1961	197
1 Fishing	3	1	-	1	10	10	-	-	-	-	-	-
2 Agriculture	5,214	4,853	4,779	3,838	2,940	2,280	832	407	334	428	290	310
3 Gas, Coke and Chemicals	26	36	38	135	160	130	2	2	3	18	30	10
4 Metal Manufacturing and Engineering	930	1,171	913	1,586	2,170	2,470	41	36	8	166	660	610
5 Mining and Quarrying	5,945	6,441	5,712	2,851	2,080	820	9	1	-	-	-	-
6 Woodworkers (+ Cork and Cane)	615	532	416	450	350	480	4	1	1	-	-	10
7 Leather Workers, Fur Dressers	305	178	137	102	50	70	39	8	5	16	20	40
8 Textile Workers	138	36	28	69	40	60	142	3	10	20	-	160
9 Clothing Workers	208	144	93	44	-	20	721	403	178	208	200	270
10 Food, Drink and Tobacco	180	190	193	151	230	160	14	23	12	54	10	40
11 Paper and Printing	111	94	89	50	70	90	34	10	8	8	-	10
12 Building and Contracting	1,136	1,134	1,090	1,527	440	550	1	2	-	4	-	-
13 Makers of Other Products (Rubber, Plastics etc.)	1	62	53	28	190	170	-	4	1	10	30	70
14 Painters and Decorators	154	131	137	194	150	210	-	-	-	15	-	-
15 Stationary Engine and Crane Drivers	230	293	310	416	560	550	-	-	-	1	-	-
16 Labourers (n.e.c.)	455	773	770	899	1,340	1,190	-	1	-	320	110	110
17 Transport and Communication	1,579	1,391	1,370	1,365	1,010	1,050	82	53	67	104	120	80
18 Warehousemen, Storekeepers Packers, Bottlers etc.	1	62	65	168	260	350	-	4	3	38	50	100
19 Clerical Workers	246	358	408	575	910	700	49	121	137	627	1,010	1,450
20 Sales Workers	1,083	1,226	1,458	1,088	970	990	396	646	616	800	810	770
21 Services, Sport and Recreation (inc. Personal Service)	564	446	542	656	680	770	3,379	2,581	2,557	1,517	1,350	2,220
22 Administrators and Managers	..	171	92	284	340	400	..	91	2	19	10	20
23 Professional, Technical Workers, Artists	560	544	621	843	1,290	1,210	448	637	624	708	1,050	1,330
24 Armed Forces	213	203	208	1,572	1,320	540	-	-	-	8	-	-
25 Inadequately Described Occupations	86	180	323	155	490	330	8	9	42	48	200	360
26 Glass, Ceramics, Cement	89	41	14	28	40	20	17	8	6	2	-	10
TOTAL OCCUPIED	20,072	20,691	19,859	19,075	18,090	15,620	6,218	5,051	4,614	5,139	5,950	7,980
27 Retired and Unoccupied	3,718	3,125	2,361	3,145	3,780	4,440	16,285	18,036	17,048	16,800	15,530	12,920

LABOUR 2.

Occupational Distribution of the Population; Caernarvon

	MALES						FEMALES					
	1911(1)	1921	1931	1951	1961	1971	1911(1)	1921	1931	1951	1961	1971
1 Fishing	149	195	114	98	50	120	1	1	-	1	-	-
2 Agriculture	8,121	8,029	7,003	5,743	3,940	2,580	1,309	761	518	600	280	260
3 Gas, Coke and Chemicals	32	83	62	111	30	120	4	4	1	21	10	30
4 Metal Manufacturing and Engineering	1,750	2,368	2,051	3,358	4,150	4,820	63	49	45	177	390	550
5 Mining and Quarrying	11,172	6,032	5,689	3,607	1,650	430	30	7	1	1	-	-
6 Woodworkers (+ Cork and Cane)	1,339	1,204	1,136	993	770	900	28	6	2	2	-	-
7 Leather Workers, Fur Dressers	564	343	309	194	110	30	62	11	5	17	-	40
8 Textile Workers	512	171	64	27	10	210	341	91	33	16	20	120
9 Clothing Workers	527	430	293	111	30	50	1,847	1,081	457	322	520	420
10 Food, Drink and Tobacco	432	560	513	417	670	510	44	172	94	141	180	80
11 Paper and Printing	365	303	272	176	170	200	83	53	55	27	10	40
12 Building and Contracting	1,647	4,020	4,623	3,196	1,360	1,530	-	17	14	7	-	-
13 Makers of Other Products (Rubber, Plastics etc.)	-	139	67	105	380	800	-	8	5	13	30	140
14 Painters and Decorators	522	539	543	681	560	530	1	2	3	9	10	20
15 Stationary Engine and Crane Drivers	334	307	330	319	420	480	-	-	-	1	20	-
16 Labourers (n.e.c.)	1,328	1,699	2,096	1,587	2,900	2,540	-	5	4	291	90	130
17 Transport and Communication	4,259	4,476	4,283	3,921	3,410	2,590	164	192	149	293	160	200
18 Warehousemen, Storekeepers Packers, Bottlers etc.	7	172	157	340	510	610	-	60	32	69	130	140
19 Clerical Workers	717	1,368	1,165	1,657	1,840	1,550	138	939	656	1,796	2,120	2,690
20 Sales Workers	2,781	4,207	4,264	3,647	3,480	3,020	985	1,886	1,880	2,227	2,580	2,870
21 Services, Sport and Recreation (inc. Personal Service)	1,179	1,278	1,513	2,329	2,090	2,690	8,718	8,312	7,785	5,570	4,240	4,940
22 Administrators and Managers	..	729	243	799	970	1,010	..	265	14	75	100	60
23 Professional, Technical Workers, Artists	1,546	1,795	1,493	1,985	2,530	2,770	985	1,588	1,280	1,810	2,320	2,160
24 Armed Forces	59	70	24	315	60	90	-	-	-	11	10	-
25 Inadequately Described Occupations	196	365	716	479	1,280	1,090	11	25	147	169	410	1,230
26 Glass, Ceramics, Cement	81	83	44	80	140	10	15	18	1	6	10	-
TOTAL OCCUPIED	39,619	40,965	39,067	36,275	33,510	31,280	14,829	15,553	13,181	13,672	13,640	16,120
27 Retired and Unoccupied	7,936	6,911	5,164	7,910	9,430	10,860	38,999	43,432	38,740	40,688	38,720	34,520

Occupational Distribution of the Population: Cardigan

	MALES						FEMALES					
	1911[1]	1921	1931	1951	1961	1971	1911[1]	1921	1931	1951	1961	1971
1 Fishing	51	56	35	26	30	50	-	1	-	-	-	-
2 Agriculture	8,090	7,531	7,141	6,545	5,220	4,210	2,573	1,282	1,015	1,059	500	810
3 Gas, Coke and Chemicals	11	13	9	30	-	-	-	-	-	-	-	-
4 Metal Manufacturing and Engineering	674	720	537	818	920	1,100	28	6	1	14	20	-
5 Mining and Quarrying	788	1,669	378	61	110	40	3	1	-	-	-	-
6 Woodworkers (+ Cork and Cane)	842	607	555	375	450	310	8	2	-	1	-	10
7 Leather Workers, Fur Dressers	308	195	183	87	60	-	19	4	-	2	-	-
8 Textile Workers	437	158	102	15	20	10	245	48	22	6	-	20
9 Clothing Workers	368	314	190	37	30	10	1,251	680	315	93	30	200
10 Food, Drink and Tobacco	169	202	175	187	230	170	44	36	25	38	30	40
11 Paper and Printing	105	110	110	96	120	100	21	22	21	17	10	20
12 Building and Contracting	845	849	1,163	1,433	720	890	-	4	1	2	-	10
13 Makers of Other Products (Rubber, Plastics etc.)	-	34	22	28	50	80	-	3	2	-	-	10
14 Painters and Decorators	141	141	160	204	220	230	-	1	-	-	-	-
15 Stationary Engine and Crane Drivers	34	47	27	100	190	180	-	-	-	-	-	-
16 Labourers (n.e.c.)	639	631	718	338	1,040	850	1	4	3	13	20	10
17 Transport and Communication	1,296	1,549	1,557	1,449	1,300	1,120	136	117	126	130	80	90
18 Warehousemen, Storekeepers Packers, Bottlers etc.	5	50	41	96	140	150	-	6	1	7	40	-
19 Clerical Workers	204	364	321	561	690	570	37	231	192	615	820	1,160
20 Sales Workers	1,047	1,490	1,647	1,262	1,270	1,020	533	722	595	757	940	910
21 Services, Sport and Recreation (inc. Personal Service)	470	445	542	627	710	810	4,555	3,633	3,306	1,728	1,380	1,910
22 Administrators and Managers	..	242	115	271	290	310	..	119	9	23	30	70
23 Professional, Technical Workers, Artists	801	966	727	1,093	1,560	1,730	440	583	639	783	1,020	1,050
24 Armed Forces	22	27	14	80	100	190	-	-	-	3	-	-
25 Inadequately Described Occupations	49	106	194	121	410	400	8	11	25	26	110	280
26 Glass, Ceramics, Cement	24	31	1	1	-	20	11	2	1	1	-	10
TOTAL OCCUPIED	17,420	18,547	16,664	15,941	15,880	14,550	9,913	7,518	6,299	5,318	5,030	5,190
27 Retired and Unoccupied	4,452	3,744	3,235	3,765	4,000	5,190	17,929	19,993	17,955	17,701	16,810	15,390

BOUR 2.

Occupational Distribution of the Population: Carmarthen

	MALES						FEMALES					
	1911 (1)	1921	1931	1951	1961	1971	1911 (1)	1921	1931	1951	1961	1971
Fishing	88	81	78	24	20	20	36	19	12	-	-	-
Agriculture	11,610	10,726	10,736	9,647	7,770	5,950	4,024	2,377	1,956	2,007	1,400	1,830
Gas, Coke and Chemicals	41	154	78	399	640	190	-	22	3	14	20	-
Metal Manufacturing and Engineering	9,667	9,834	8,796	8,329	8,450	9,620	900	1,241	483	744	1,140	2,020
Mining and Quarrying	11,340	14,573	13,723	6,117	5,490	3,080	13	2	1	1	-	-
Woodworkers (+ Cork and Cane)	2,077	1,537	1,429	1,387	1,010	1,010	25	26	6	35	50	70
Leather Workers, Fur Dressers	677	412	388	190	90	50	65	11	2	56	20	120
Textile Workers	914	400	278	136	80	70	731	241	156	136	150	190
Clothing Workers	694	467	356	98	60	20	3,255	1,859	978	372	220	390
Food, Drink and Tobacco	321	380	430	538	660	870	88	97	75	153	240	330
Paper and Printing	215	158	176	105	100	160	65	30	17	13	30	10
Building and Contracting	2,493	2,490	2,982	4,865	1,900	1,550	3	4	1	2	10	10
Makers of Other Products (Rubber, Plastics etc.)	-	171	190	94	180	390	-	5	7	27	160	230
Painters and Decorators	323	303	370	573	640	570	1	8	12	9	150	60
Stationary Engine and Crane Drivers	1,007	1,405	1,594	1,615	1,660	1,830	-	-	7	6	20	-
Labourers (n.e.c.)	1,155	2,142	2,403	4,783	4,920	4,000	2	39	4	1,341	220	200
Transport and Communication	4,197	3,874	4,603	5,193	5,020	3,850	180	154	188	300	300	200
Warehousemen, Storekeepers Packers, Bottlers etc.	8	333	471	914	980	1,480	-	60	77	232	320	460
Clerical Workers	2,782	1,060	1,376	2,105	2,250	2,250	87	407	476	2,041	2,970	3,350
Sales Workers	2,490	3,166	4,281	3,723	3,777	2,760	1,200	1,896	2,010	2,523	2,870	2,860
Services, Sport and Recreation (inc. Personal Service)	1,061	1,070	1,257	1,598	1,770	1,810	7,150	5,226	5,395	3,818	3,660	5,150
Administrators and Managers	..	497	237	852	1,110	1,240	..	154	10	69	40	80
Professional, Technical Workers, Artists	1,414	1,516	1,581	2,468	4,010	3,370	906	1,205	1,424	1,929	2,530	2,670
Armed Forces	49	41	26	325	110	90	-	-	-	8	-	-
Inadequately Described Occupations	158	464	2,811	477	1,040	930	18	36	802	167	540	1,640
Glass, Ceramics, Cement	358	212	141	195	130	220	62	52	9	71	150	200
TOTAL OCCUPIED	53,139	57,466	60,791	56,750	54,110	47,380	18,811	15,171	14,111	16,074	17,210	22,070
Retired and Unoccupied	9,690	8,068	6,699	9,373	10,990	14,710	44,174	52,102	54,672	54,299	52,460	46,020

Occupational Distribution of the Population: Denbigh

	MALES						FEMALES					
	1911[1]	1921	1931	1951	1961	1971	1911[1]	1921	1931	1951	1961	1971
1 Fishing	6	9	3	5	10	-	-	-	-	-	-	-
2 Agriculture	11,027	10,016	9,674	8,229	5,740	4,620	1,576	920	630	980	560	600
3 Gas, Coke and Chemicals	44	248	216	953	1,020	1,040	25	7	1	49	160	90
4 Metal Manufacturing and Engineering	2,532	2,989	2,644	5,283	6,960	8,620	34	42	21	169	470	990
5 Mining and Quarrying	11,978	13,334	12,574	7,026	4,940	2,050	5	4	2	3	-	-
6 Woodworkers (+ Cork and Cane)	1,545	1,380	1,326	1,318	1,190	1,430	21	14	13	15	10	20
7 Leather Workers, Fur Dressers	916	574	457	373	340	250	108	70	34	75	20	40
8 Textile Workers	470	144	81	157	190	230	266	59	31	244	390	60
9 Clothing Workers	486	403	293	182	140	150	1,565	998	573	652	790	1,110
10 Food, Drink and Tobacco	712	651	631	585	800	750	67	197	171	330	170	160
11 Paper and Printing	319	246	245	126	190	180	100	39	43	44	70	180
12 Building and Contracting	1,887	2,170	2,964	4,179	2,200	2,290	-	2	1	4	-	10
13 Makers of Other Products (Rubber, Plastics etc.)	2	205	177	152	250	850	-	12	11	31	210	350
14 Painters and Decorators	432	515	647	826	700	780	-	11	27	25	60	50
15 Stationary Engine and Crane Drivers	701	902	803	1,038	1,150	1,250	-	-	-	4	-	10
16 Labourers (n.e.c.)	1,500	2,257	3,095	2,880	4,540	5,110	1	14	12	711	280	350
17 Transport and Communication	3,644	3,604	4,298	4,411	4,160	3,830	141	152	152	304	290	400
18 Warehousemen, Storekeepers Packers, Bottlers etc.	5	221	224	589	870	840	-	31	23	297	540	850
19 Clerical Workers	827	1,114	1,313	2,143	2,560	2,210	148	692	727	2,655	3,600	5,080
20 Sales Workers	3,224	3,978	4,976	4,462	3,950	3,820	939	1,825	2,090	2,939	3,520	3,470
21 Services, Sport and Recreation (inc. Personal Service)	1,310	1,166	1,805	2,330	2,280	2,620	8,409	7,859	8,614	5,403	4,780	6,340
22 Administrators and Managers	..	530	277	1,045	1,350	1,590	..	211	12	86	120	170
23 Professional, Technical Workers, Artists	1,537	1,510	1,681	2,734	3,940	4,190	1,182	1,600	1,774	2,362	3,320	3,860
24 Armed Forces	238	306	322	886	370	150	-	-	-	191	-	-
25 Inadequately Described Occupations	196	560	1,522	422	1,220	1,050	5	65	213	122	610	1,490
26 Glass, Ceramics, Cement	1,207	760	624	456	410	340	18	38	36	37	50	40
TOTAL OCCUPIED	46,745	49,792	52,872	52,790	51,470	50,240	14,610	14,862	15,211	17,732	20,020	25,720
27 Retired and Unoccupied	9,940	8,397	6,397	9,387	10,710	15,460	42,524	47,519	47,285	52,788	52,020	49,890

LABOUR 2.

Occupational Distribution of the Population : Flint

	MALES						FEMALES					
	1911[1]	1921	1931	1951	1961	1971	1911[1]	1921	1931	1951	1961	1971
1 Fishing	58	67	57	25	10	10	-	-	-	-	-	-
2 Agriculture	5,598	5,234	5,194	4,880	3,640	2,540	825	543	415	712	500	470
3 Gas, Coke and Chemicals	428	271	1,217	2,388	1,720	2,180	9	8	39	499	190	330
4 Metal Manufacturing and Engineering	4,522	5,112	4,088	5,994	8,540	10,390	46	53	16	111	150	310
5 Mining and Quarrying	5,057	4,481	3,325	1,674	900	700	5	-	2	-	-	-
6 Woodworkers (+ Cork and Cane)	944	920	951	1,256	1,100	1,170	8	2	1	41	120	120
7 Leather Workers, Fur Dressers	314	234	215	155	70	20	33	9	15	13	-	-
8 Textile Workers	461	406	304	204	190	450	458	701	1,633	627	500	470
9 Clothing Workers	192	187	157	122	50	50	938	634	361	433	450	660
10 Food, Drink and Tobacco	308	399	442	390	700	450	26	75	73	186	170	100
11 Paper and Printing	350	236	240	202	200	400	170	87	80	130	170	250
12 Building and Contracting	1,249	1,603	2,158	3,531	1,830	1,930	-	7	3	2	-	-
13 Makers of Other Products (Rubber, Plastics etc.)	1	199	101	96	130	360	-	7	2	5	10	80
14 Painters and Decorators	268	315	426	777	860	630	-	1	1	33	20	-
15 Stationary Engine and Crane Drivers	489	751	725	1,299	2,010	1,890	-	-	-	14	-	30
16 Labourers (n.e.c.)	1,011	2,678	3,190	5,273	5,760	5,980	1	17	5	536	260	410
17 Transport and Communication	2,753	2,510	3,232	3,675	3,190	3,640	118	124	121	273	320	340
18 Warehousemen, Storekeepers Packers, Bottlers etc.	2	321	389	704	1,160	1,210	-	47	100	293	360	550
19 Clerical Workers	556	853	1,100	1,947	2,410	2,590	69	462	473	2,513	3,590	5,970
20 Sales Workers	2,028	2,687	3,667	3,238	3,010	2,950	685	1,331	1,454	2,387	2,950	3,280
21 Services, Sport and Recreation (inc. Personal Service)	844	1,244	1,264	2,319	1,870	2,350	4,968	5,027	5,285	4,275	4,350	6,290
22 Administrators and Managers	..	392	181	820	1,250	1,830	..	152	9	69	50	140
23 Professional, Technical Workers, Artists	992	961	1,097	1,999	2,680	4,550	845	1,042	1,177	1,790	2,450	2,760
24 Armed Forces	46	302	473	3,281	1,180	990	-	-	-	10	20	50
25 Inadequately Described Occupations	100	456	2,477	594	1,540	860	4	60	354	192	650	1,310
26 Glass, Ceramics, Cement	788	497	348	344	400	240	15	38	5	33	80	40
TOTAL OCCUPIED	29,359	33,316	37,018	47,187	46,400	50,360	9,223	10,427	11,624	15,177	17,360	23,960
27 Retired and Unoccupied	6,440	5,483	4,468	7,087	8,670	13,060	27,671	32,614	33,303	42,619	43,870	46,060

Occupational Distribution of the Population: Glamorgan

	MALES						FEMALES					
	1911[1]	1921	1931	1951	1961	1971	1911[1]	1921	1931	1951	1961	197
1 Fishing	229	374	458	297	100	100	28	10	2	1	-	10
2 Agriculture	10,842	9,883	10,137	8,576	7,030	5,130	1,582	990	617	899	650	730
3 Gas, Coke and Chemicals	560	3,369	1,332	2,720	4,230	4,730	162	49	14	222	320	170
4 Metal Manufacturing and Engineering	50,484	50,921	43,060	59,963	74,000	80,880	2,298	2,701	853	4,395	8,030	10,070
5 Mining and Quarrying	150,694	160,949	136,240	61,463	44,000	19,940	92	92	18	17	-	60
6 Woodworkers (+ Cork and Cane)	10,251	8,599	7,260	9,284	7,500	7,560	283	96	34	104	80	210
7 Leather Workers, Fur Dressers	3,505	2,128	1,957	1,521	870	820	425	62	52	730	640	870
8 Textile Workers	2,169	224	216	807	560	1,210	3,133	195	160	700	580	810
9 Clothing Workers	3,427	2,856	2,302	2,051	1,280	1,580	14,894	9,395	5,495	8,487	6,930	6,870
10 Food, Drink and Tobacco	4,266	4,178	4,059	3,445	5,150	4,110	1,196	1,435	1,068	1,292	1,560	1,860
11 Paper and Printing	2,424	1,895	1,866	1,850	2,240	2,600	1,020	719	650	851	1,110	1,330
12 Building and Contracting	16,354	15,415	16,507	28,296	14,540	14,780	10	44	13	43	10	20
13 Makers of Other Products (Rubber, Plastics etc.)	42	3,252	2,389	1,703	3,980	5,390	8	125	120	991	2,520	3,040
14 Painters and Decorators	3,083	4,018	4,161	6,098	6,730	6,090	-	51	33	188	230	280
15 Stationary Engine and Crane Drivers	8,680	11,679	12,215	11,955	14,070	12,120	-	-	9	93	60	80
16 Labourers (n.e.c.)	10,276	18,118	18,594	33,364	35,820	31,770	62	247	61	10,885	3,330	3,570
17 Transport and Communication	47,813	47,983	50,567	43,014	35,990	30,870	1,063	1,422	1,134	2,369	2,010	3,010
18 Warehousemen, Storekeepers Packers, Bottlers etc.	161	3,258	3,992	7,059	9,950	10,080	4	745	971	2,393	3,570	4,140
19 Clerical Workers	9,724	11,952	14,573	19,669	23,340	22,090	1,605	6,987	7,919	25,354	35,090	45,870
20 Sales Workers	24,952	28,391	38,804	30,052	29,070	24,900	7,088	15,829	17,283	20,445	25,570	25,980
21 Services, Sport and Recreation (inc. Personal Service)	9,749	10,573	12,678	14,455	16,100	18,070	38,644	35,822	38,992	27,699	29,920	42,710
22 Administrators and Managers	..	4,751	2,205	8,105	10,900	15,170	..	1,397	101	746	570	1,310
23 Professional, Technical Workers, Artists	8,914	9,400	10,829	17,350	25,650	31,960	7,460	10,015	10,550	13,606	17,360	22,750
24 Armed Forces	611	1,105	509	7,456	4,270	3,300	-	-	-	241	120	150
25 Inadequately Described Occupations	2,511	5,052	17,945	4,311	7,440	7,670	127	558	3,310	1,080	3,100	10,260
26 Glass, Ceramics, Cement	1,459	774	516	1,176	710	450	225	241	70	290	260	250
TOTAL OCCUPIED	383,182	421,097	415,371	386,040	385,520	363,370	81,409	89,227	89,529	124,121	143,620	186,410
27 Retired and Unoccupied	62,575	54,554	42,122	60,096	67,340	94,980	320,998	366,298	362,421	354,431	344,050	315,560

Occupational Distribution of the Population: Merioneth

	MALES						FEMALES					
	1911(1)	1921	1931	1951	1961	1971	1911(1)	1921	1931	1951	1961	1971
1 Fishing	6	15	7	3	10	10	-	-	-	-	-	-
2 Agriculture	5,020	4,725	4,417	3,493	2,470	1,780	901	458	281	402	190	200
3 Gas, Coke and Chemicals	11	7	38	99	90	80	5	2	12	94	70	50
4 Metal Manufacturing and Engineering	417	575	480	666	960	1,220	10	10	12	18	10	100
5 Mining and Quarrying	3,368	2,447	1,925	1,058	530	190	4	2	-	-	20	-
6 Woodworkers (+ Cork and Cane)	433	342	320	246	580	190	6	1	-	1	-	-
7 Leather Workers, Fur Dressers	272	169	131	47	30	20	33	5	1	1	-	-
8 Textile Workers	185	35	31	16	-	-	83	16	6	43	-	30
9 Clothing Workers	159	130	72	23	-	10	649	342	146	98	90	160
10 Food, Drink and Tobacco	103	138	145	157	120	170	9	45	39	62	60	-
11 Paper and Printing	102	86	79	48	40	30	14	11	18	22	10	20
12 Building and Contracting	744	1,105	1,724	1,206	570	510	-	4	-	1	-	-
13 Makers of Other Products (Rubber, Plastics etc.)	-	20	12	16	40	20	-	2	-	-	-	20
14 Painters and Decorators	125	127	137	156	90	170	-	-	-	1	-	-
15 Stationary Engine and Crane Drivers	78	81	114	146	210	280	-	-	-	1	-	-
16 Labourers (n.e.c.)	368	440	891	348	750	810	-	-	2	53	20	10
17 Transport and Communication	1,233	1,072	1,039	1,129	960	760	76	80	53	91	80	10
18 Warehousemen, Storekeepers Packers, Bottlers etc.	1	27	23	70	80	130	-	4	20	44	40	90
19 Clerical Workers	158	343	258	379	680	350	22	206	119	359	570	680
20 Sales Workers	838	1,195	1,186	886	950	610	403	516	479	527	590	670
21 Services, Sport and Recreation (inc. Personal Service)	318	308	355	534	800	680	3,122	2,934	2,527	1,486	1,150	1,590
22 Administrators and Managers	..	211	71	192	260	280	..	104	8	20	40	20
23 Professional, Technical Workers, Artists	543	557	485	627	920	620	370	483	441	497	660	670
24 Armed Forces	33	19	184	2,696	400	20	-	-	-	2	-	-
25 Inadequately Described Occupations	41	86	179	102	430	300	2	5	50	32	170	410
26 Glass, Ceramics, Cement	6	6	4	4	-	-	13	-	1	1	-	-
TOTAL OCCUPIED	14,562	14,266	14,307	14,347	11,970	9,240	5,722	5,230	4,215	3,856	3,770	4,760
27 Retired and Unoccupied	3,151	2,383	1,859	2,490	2,620	3,330	13,813	14,507	13,337	12,641	11,880	10,250

Occupational Distribution of the Population: Monmouth

	MALES						FEMALES					
	1911 (1)	1921	1931	1951	1961	1971	1911 (1)	1921	1931	1951	1961	1971
1 Fishing	23	27	24	13	20	-	-	-	-	-	-	-
2 Agriculture	8,700	7,930	7,851	6,382	5,040	3,690	940	678	399	599	310	480
3 Gas, Coke and Chemicals	144	793	429	2,427	3,300	3,260	19	3	8	424	620	300
4 Metal Manufacturing and Engineering	18,647	19,846	15,937	21,462	29,710	31,920	350	375	182	1,363	2,730	3,960
5 Mining and Quarrying	53,504	61,486	53,057	25,603	19,570	9,030	86	35	6	9	-	-
6 Woodworkers (+ Cork and Cane)	3,484	2,903	2,286	2,515	3,030	2,460	91	12	10	13	30	10
7 Leather Workers, Fur Dressers	1,175	620	592	383	280	260	135	19	14	36	30	190
8 Textile Workers	531	49	44	401	380	370	964	28	17	159	150	130
9 Clothing Workers	931	605	453	319	270	250	3,965	2,222	1,022	2,123	2,220	2,350
10 Food, Drink and Tobacco	1,314	1,360	1,462	996	1,440	1,250	403	408	262	420	650	870
11 Paper and Printing	679	467	465	381	590	840	336	260	198	165	290	480
12 Building and Contracting	6,484	6,486	5,835	8,845	4,750	4,740	3	13	8	7	-	10
13 Makers of Other Products (Rubber, Plastics etc.)	2	1,055	634	382	1,050	1,400	2	40	10	300	890	1,080
14 Painters and Decorators	1,088	1,343	1,354	1,754	1,740	1,640	-	7	5	82	60	60
15 Stationary Engine and Crane Drivers	3,015	4,318	4,489	4,959	6,020	6,060	-	-	7	29	30	50
16 Labourers (n.e.c.)	3,121	6,755	6,714	15,295	14,380	14,210	10	100	31	3,375	840	1,160
17 Transport and Communication	15,045	14,108	15,726	14,432	13,230	10,820	400	384	335	946	1,030	1,040
18 Warehousemen, Storekeepers Packers, Bottlers etc.	18	863	1,029	2,144	3,330	3,980	2	304	301	935	1,310	1,880
19 Clerical Workers	2,597	3,167	4,069	5,654	7,070	6,280	479	1,701	1,880	7,177	10,430	14,110
20 Sales Workers	7,394	7,976	11,347	8,259	7,350	7,210	2,065	5,177	5,485	6,868	8,700	9,280
21 Services, Sport and Recreation (inc. Personal Service)	3,153	3,527	3,938	4,599	5,190	6,260	14,092	12,512	13,099	9,541	11,560	16,340
22 Administrators and Managers	..	1,295	711	2,337	3,600	5,080	..	508	23	180	160	380
23 Professional, Technical Workers, Artists	2,732	2,828	3,367	5,493	9,650	11,030	2,677	3,384	3,737	4,642	6,040	8,250
24 Armed Forces	222	1,580	342	1,145	470	450	-	-	-	20	-	10
25 Inadequately Described Occupations	865	1,515	6,991	1,263	3,010	2,370	36	112	675	418	1,630	3,780
26 Glass, Ceramics, Cement	947	554	329	564	650	690	79	85	17	56	10	30
TOTAL OCCUPIED	135,815	153,456	149,475	138,007	145,120	135,550	27,134	28,367	27,731	39,887	49,720	66,230
27 Retired and Unoccupied	22,057	19,189	14,237	20,611	24,420	33,780	112,392	131,474	127,175	124,353	121,200	112,550

ABOUR 2. Occupational Distribution of the Population : Montgomery

	MALES						FEMALES					
	1911 (1)	1921	1931	1951	1961	1971	1911 (1)	1921	1931	1951	1961	1971
Fishing	2	2	-	-	10	-	-	-	-	-	-	-
Agriculture	8,896	8,260	8,134	7,111	5,910	4,080	1,543	679	614	820	400	540
Gas, Coke and Chemicals	7	10	12	25	30	20	1	1	-	-	-	10
Metal Manufacturing and Engineering	585	668	516	976	1,120	1,820	15	3	1	61	170	280
Mining and Quarrying	517	806	381	114	40	-	9	-	-	-	-	-
Woodworkers (+ Cork and Cane)	625	696	443	347	370	290	7	3	-	3	10	10
Leather Workers, Fur Dressers	323	269	184	121	190	60	17	2	2	60	60	70
Textile Workers	521	132	81	7	-	10	450	195	122	9	180	50
Clothing Workers	277	210	114	34	-	-	759	478	320	146	90	170
Food, Drink and Tobacco	203	191	205	155	180	120	15	23	17	34	30	30
Paper and Printing	92	60	73	41	60	90	22	4	5	5	-	20
Building and Contracting	769	1,085	1,056	1,312	610	550	-	-	1	1	-	-
Makers of Other Products (Rubber, Plastics etc.)	2	17	12	10	40	50	-	1	-	1	-	-
Painters and Decorators	138	115	114	121	110	200	-	-	2	28	-	-
Stationary Engine and Crane Drivers	58	47	38	87	110	220	-	-	-	1	-	-
Labourers (n.e.c.)	651	758	695	566	1,030	930	-	3	1	104	30	20
Transport and Communication	1,377	1,206	1,179	1,253	1,150	1,050	64	48	58	121	90	80
Warehousemen, Storekeepers Packers, Bottlers etc.	1	55	56	147	120	290	-	11	10	39	10	70
Clerical Workers	222	295	347	395	440	490	43	147	164	529	780	1,080
Sales Workers	915	1,070	1,266	975	1,020	710	369	454	450	530	700	620
Services, Sport and Recreation (inc. Personal Service)	407	331	424	406	550	490	3,456	2,536	2,512	1,362	1,320	1,820
Administrators and Managers	..	158	87	212	310	340	..	85	2	24	20	40
Professional, Technical Workers, Artists	528	445	420	587	1,020	620	370	447	466	480	740	700
Armed Forces	24	20	12	68	20	10	-	-	-	2	-	-
Inadequately Described Occupations	63	125	254	99	320	240	8	16	40	36	110	130
Glass, Ceramics, Cement	52	34	22	16	40	40	7	1	-	-	-	-
TOTAL OCCUPIED	17,255	17,065	16,125	15,185	14,800	12,720	7,155	5,137	4,787	4,396	4,740	5,740
Retired and Unoccupied	3,520	2,747	1,947	2,431	2,680	3,440	14,523	15,116	14,006	13,665	12,740	11,150

LABOUR 2.

Occupational Distribution of the Population: Pembroke

	MALES						FEMALES					
	1911[1]	1921	1931	1951	1961	1971	1911[1]	1921	1931	1951	1961	197[illegible]
1 Fishing	598	1,005	1,581	819	420	150	3	4	3	1	-	1[illegible]
2 Agriculture	8,625	8,333	8,291	7,693	6,060	4,360	2,515	1,459	1,170	1,076	830	81[illegible]
3 Gas, Coke and Chemicals	23	4	33	95	150	280	1	1	-	7	-	1[illegible]
4 Metal Manufacturing and Engineering	3,226	3,189	1,536	2,449	3,370	4,200	30	6	2	44	70	26[illegible]
5 Mining and Quarrying	1,017	1,647	903	131	20	110	8	1	2	-	-	
6 Woodworkers (+ Cork and Cane)	1,211	1,031	896	838	610	800	7	5	2	2	-	[illegible]
7 Leather Workers, Fur Dressers	369	215	184	75	30	40	34	4	1	4	-	1[illegible]
8 Textile Workers	315	81	49	50	60	20	358	34	43	141	80	3[illegible]
9 Clothing Workers	468	357	251	59	50	20	1,664	829	381	138	70	25[illegible]
10 Food, Drink and Tobacco	299	309	341	286	470	400	34	49	36	68	20	9[illegible]
11 Paper and Printing	129	97	92	58	90	70	40	26	19	5	-	2[illegible]
12 Building and Contracting	1,388	1,290	1,594	2,521	1,060	1,560	1	1	-	2	-	1[illegible]
13 Makers of Other Products (Rubber, Plastics etc.)	-	411	131	34	80	320	-	5	1	1	50	7[illegible]
14 Painters and Decorators	141	238	205	370	300	390	-	-	1	1	-	1[illegible]
15 Stationary Engine and Crane Drivers	150	257	227	342	420	590	-	-	-	-	-	[illegible]
16 Labourers (n.e.c.)	1,616	1,859	1,964	1,685	2,930	2,790	-	13	2	135	40	1[illegible]
17 Transport and Communication	3,219	3,368	3,793	3,599	2,700	2,520	162	99	121	265	230	23[illegible]
18 Warehousemen, Storekeepers Packers, Bottlers etc.	1	295	356	594	570	450	-	5	8	40	80	8[illegible]
19 Clerical Workers	460	479	625	972	1,820	1,390	46	215	242	1,000	1,470	2,15[illegible]
20 Sales Workers	1,635	1,947	2,459	1,973	2,040	1,630	747	1,093	1,122	1,376	1,850	2,08[illegible]
21 Services, Sport and Recreation (inc. Personal Service)	742	718	848	1,199	1,550	1,730	5,179	3,891	4,059	2,386	1,890	3,32[illegible]
22 Administrators and Managers	..	361	142	427	490	740	..	140	5	22	30	4[illegible]
23 Professional, Technical Workers, Artists	919	797	826	1,159	1,890	2,300	623	824	812	983	1,180	1,31[illegible]
24 Armed Forces	1,375	1,100	620	1,845	1,890	480	-	-	-	127	80	6[illegible]
25 Inadequately Described Occupations	96	250	490	264	830	620	12	16	55	64	260	1,05[illegible]
26 Glass, Ceramics, Cement	61	28	8	19	60	-	11	-	-	-	-	1[illegible]
TOTAL OCCUPIED	28,083	29,666	28,445	29,556	29,960	27,960	11,475	8,720	8,087	7,888	8,230	12,02[illegible]
27 Retired and Unoccupied	6,217	4,889	3,727	4,875	5,400	7,070	26,001	27,982	26,086	27,676	28,290	26,51[illegible]

ABOUR 2.

Occupational Distribution of the Population: Radnor

		MALES						FEMALES					
		1911[1]	1921	1931	1951	1961	1971	1911[1]	1921	1931	1951	1961	1971
	Fishing	-	1	1	-	10	-	-	-	-	-	-	-
:	Agriculture	4,139	3,824	3,720	3,125	2,560	2,140	503	201	164	258	280	200
3	Gas, Coke and Chemicals	-	10	11	8	20	-	-	-	-	-	-	-
4	Metal Manufacturing and Engineering	267	292	239	346	460	390	5	3	1	7	10	90
5	Mining and Quarrying	152	283	140	104	100	60	1	-	-	-	-	-
6	Woodworkers (+ Cork and Cane)	335	262	213	181	120	150	2	-	1	-	-	10
7	Leather Workers, Fur Dressers	130	64	54	27	-	-	13	3	-	-	-	10
3	Textile Workers	59	9	1	-	-	30	54	2	-	-	-	10
9	Clothing Workers	93	64	53	11	-	50	223	110	48	27	10	70
)	Food, Drink and Tobacco	91	85	79	47	100	70	14	2	10	9	10	-
1	Paper and Printing	38	33	26	19	20	20	10	5	3	2	-	10
2	Building and Contracting	364	442	502	681	190	230	1	1	-	2	-	-
3	Makers of Other Products (Rubber, Plastics etc.)	-	16	4	16	40	50	-	1	1	3	-	10
4	Painters and Decorators	85	58	69	67	70	50	-	-	1	-	-	-
5	Stationary Engine and Crane Drivers	23	29	20	78	60	120	-	-	-	-	-	-
6	Labourers (n.e.c.)	224	269	279	119	410	460	-	-	1	14	-	30
7	Transport and Communication	610	565	495	531	510	400	35	28	42	48	40	20
3	Warehousemen, Storekeepers Packers, Bottlers etc.	-	18	15	20	30	40	-	2	-	7	10	20
9	Clerical Workers	76	111	105	141	190	230	21	85	73	192	290	470
0	Sales Workers	355	573	545	420	350	290	135	245	173	217	240	300
1	Services, Sport and Recreation (inc. Personal Service)	249	273	278	243	240	160	1,869	1,734	1,444	758	570	710
2	Administrators and Managers	..	77	38	68	110	180	..	34	1	9	-	20
3	Professional, Technical Workers, Artists	251	269	218	266	420	350	176	238	226	217	270	300
4	Armed Forces	15	8	5	57	30	30	-	-	-	1	-	-
5	Inadequately Described Occupations	43	50	54	45	150	80	2	3	1	22	80	100
6	Glass, Ceramics, Cement	3	3	1	9	-	10	5	-	-	-	-	-
	TOTAL OCCUPIED	7,602	7,688	7,165	6,629	6,190	5,590	3,069	2,697	2,190	1,793	1,810	2,380
27	Retired and Unoccupied	1,478	1,278	829	1,157	1,050	1,570	6,017	7,006	6,203	5,990	5,430	4,630

Sources Census Reports, 1801-1971

Notes The notes to Table 1. apply.

The relevant county figures for notes 7 and 9 of Table 1 are:

		Land Proprietors			House Proprietors			Students
		1851	1861	1871	1851	1861	1871	1891
Anglesey	M	20	26	25	3	15	5	141
	F	40	25	4	16	11	5	84
Brecon	M	62	62	60	20	31	11	190
	F	39	46	28	36	63	19	135
Caernarvon	M	58	55	62	10	16	10	652
	F	48	63	38	35	58	21	441
Cardigan	M	69	79	115	8	9	1	610
	F	63	73	55	19	41	9	276
Carmarthen	M	90	98	62	19	19	9	530
	F	68	105	60	27	41	12	369
Denbigh	M	129	92	60	32	21	12	398
	F	97	110	53	53	77	19	287
Flint	M	19	21	20	13	12	3	138
	F	24	17	11	22	36	7	99
Glamorgan	M	131	102	87	88	110	39	1,370
	F	87	100	46	185	270	102	1,892
Merioneth	M	39	40	33	5	8	2	257
	F	27	26	17	14	20	8	176
Monmouth	M	136	125	114	66	74	12	425
	F	93	115	60	150	222	52	641
Montgomery	M	84	70	68	7	13	2	127
	F	55	72	30	28	15	7	123
Pembroke	M	78	81	93	14	10	7	218
	F	54	86	46	33	81	27	190
Radnor	M	58	53	65	5	4	18	24
	F	18	29	16	7	21	2	33

A (i) Estimated numbers of persons insured against unemployment in July of each year, Wales 1922-47.

(ii) Number of insured persons in employment in June of each year, Wales, 1922-39.

Thousands

Date	A(i)[1]	A(ii)[3]
1922	606	548
1923	618	583
1924	625	586
1925	623	520
1926	629	(4)
1927	629	516
1927	608	499
1928	592	463
1929	583	477
1930	592	443
1931	606	414
1932	619	387
1933	621	409
1934	622	416
1935	618	428
1936	611	425
1937	610	484
1938	617	460
1939	620	524[5]
1939	696	
1943	721	
1945	678[2]	
1946	727	
1947	731	

B (i) Number of employees (employed and unemployed) each mid-year, Wales, 1948-74.

(ii) Number of employees in employment at each mid-year, Wales, 1951-74.

Thousands

Date	B(i)[6]			B(ii)		
	M	F	T	M	F	T
1948	683	236	919			
1949	681	236	917			
1950	683	240	923			
1951	685	247	932	671	241	912
1952	684	250	934	670	242	912
1953	690	254	944	675	247	921
1954	684	260	944	671	254	925
1955	680	266	946	671	261	932
1956	684	272	956	673	267	940
1957	686	271	957	673	264	937
1958	683	270	953	662	261	923
1959	682	276	958	662	267	928
1960	684	285	969	669	278	948
1961	685	289	974	672	284	957
1962	686	296	982	668	289	958
1963	690	300	990	669	292	962
1964	686	311	997	672	305	977
1964	687	312	999	673	306	979
1965	685	321	1,006	670	316	985
1966	680	327	1,007	664	322	986
1967	667	320	987	640	312	952
1968	658	327	985	629	320	950
1969[8]	647[7]	324	971	618	319	936
1969[8]	649[7]	327	976	620	322	942
1970	635	332	967	608	327	935
1971[9]	636[8]	334	970	603	327	930
1971[9]	662[8]	339	1,002	629	333	962
1972	667	350	1,016	630	342	973
1973	663	369	1,032	636	364	1,000
1974	649	376	1,025	621	371	992

General Notes

(i) Sources. Ministry of Labour Gazette; British Labour Statistics, Historical Abstract, 1886-1968; Ministry of Labour, Tables relating to Employment and Unemployment in Great Britain. 1948, 1949 and 1950, 1951; British Labour Statistics, Year Books 1970-.

Notes

1. 1922-27 Insured persons aged over 16; 1927-1939 Insured persons aged 16-64; 1939-47 Males aged 14-64, Females aged 14-59. For 1922-47 persons insured under the special scheme for the banking and insurance industries are excluded because these figures are available only on a U.K. basis. Also excluded up to 1939 were (i) persons under 16 included in the insurance scheme from September 1934, (ii) those included in a scheme for agriculture, horticulture and forestry begun in May 1936, and (iii) domestic workers who were brought within the Unemployment Insurance Acts for the first time in April 1938.

2. From 1940 non-manual workers with a rate of renumeration exceeding £250 but not exceeding £420 per year were included, and women over 60 were excluded. Domestic workers and those under the agricultural scheme are included in the figures for 1945-7, and a revised 1939 fugure on the same basis is also given.

3. The general qualifications of note 1. apply. The number of insured workers in employment was obtained by deducting from the figures under A(i) the number of such persons recorded as unemployed in June.

4. Figures were not given for June 1926 because employment was affected by the prolonged national stoppage of work in the coal industry.

5. Not strictly comparable with earlier figures as it included domestic workers.

6. From 1948 the basis of the figures changes. They are based on the count of insurance cards under the national insurance scheme, under which cards had to be held for all persons working for employers, irrespective of age, occupation or the number of hours worked per week.

7. A new method of calculating regional employment estimates was introduced in 1965. Two figures are given for 1964, the first for comparison with earlier years, the second for comparison with later years.

8. From 1969 fuller information was available on the location of employees in the distributive trades. Two figures are given, the first for comparison with earlier years, the second for comparison with later years.

9. Until 1971 the figures were derived mainly from counts of national insurance cards. In 1971 a new system was introduced which relied upon returns from employers (i.e. a census of employment). The first figure for 1971 is on the old system of a card count basis: the second is on the new basis of a census.

LABOUR 4. Estimated number of insured employees (employed and unemployed), by sex and industry, Wales, 1939-74

Figures in thousands at July of each year

		MALES				FEMALES			
		1939	1945	1946	1947	1939	1945	1946	1947
1	Agriculture and Fishing	24.9	24.3	26.7	26.9	0.8	0.8	4.2	3.6
2	Mining and Quarrying	182.8	128.7	131.2	127.3	0.3	1.2	1.3	1.4
3	Food, Drink and Tobacco	9.8	8.2	9.7	10.5	5.4	4.9	5.5	5.7
4	Non-metallic Mining Products	4.2	3.1	3.9	4.6	0.1	0.2	0.3	0.2
5	Chemicals, Paints, Oils	3.7	32.2	18.3	13.7	0.4	28.5	13.2	5.9
6	Metal Manufacture	69.7	50.8	56.2	62.6	3.2	11.5	9.7	8.2
7	Engineering, etc.	10.3	22.8	17.7	18.1	1.1	15.6	8.3	5.1
8	Shipbuilding and Ship Repairing	4.5	8.9	8.6	7.8	-	0.5	0.3	0.2
9	Construction and Repair of Vehicles	6.5	16.9	14.3	15.5	0.7	10.6	5.1	3.5
10	Other Metal Industries	9.3	10.1	13.2	15.9	3.1	10.7	11.9	13.6
11	Textiles	4.2	3.3	4.5	5.9	2.8	3.3	3.4	3.9
12	Leather, Leather Goods and Fur	0.6	0.6	0.7	0.9	0.2	0.6	0.7	0.9
13	Clothing	1.8	1.6	1.9	2.3	4.4	5.0	6.7	8.0
14	Bricks, Pottery, Glass	5.9	2.5	4.1	4.7	0.2	0.5	0.5	0.6
15	Woodworking etc.	4.4	3.5	4.3	4.9	0.5	1.6	0.8	0.6
16	Paper, Painting etc.	4.5	2.5	3.3	3.9	1.8	1.7	2.0	2.3
17	Other Manufacturing Industries	1.3	0.9	1.7	2.3	0.8	1.3	2.6	3.3
18	Building and Civil Eng. Construction	89.5	20.1	41.8	58.5	0.3	0.5	0.6	0.6
19	Gas, Water, Electricity	8.0	5.4	7.4	8.6	0.4	0.9	0.8	0.7
20	Transport and Communication	46.6	46.0	50.7	51.4	0.8	7.5	6.3	4.0
21	Distributive Trades	55.2	27.0	33.7	36.7	35.7	37.4	38.3	38.3
22	Commerce and Finance	2.2	0.8	1.0	1.1	0.7	0.8	0.8	0.8
23	Miscellaneous	52.1	49.1	59.4	63.4	30.4	54.3	54.5	53.5
	TOTAL	602.1	469.6(1)	520.1(1)	553.6(1)	93.9	204.2(1)	178.5(1)	165.5(1)

MALES

	1948	1949	1950	1951	1952	1953	1954	1955	1956	1957	1958	1959	1960	1961	1962	1963	1964	1965
1 Agriculture, Forestry & Fishing	37.72	37.63	34.23	29.1	29.2	27.9	27.9	27.8	25.3	24.5	23.8	24.0	22.0	21.0	20.1	19.9	17.6	15.5
2 Mining and Quarrying	139.89	137.64	133.29	135.5	136.5	137.1	133.6	131.1	126.8	129.0	128.6	120.6	110.0	104.5	101.2	99.7	94.7	88.5
Coal Mining	128.53	126.26	121.90	124.6	125.6	126.5	123.5	121.7	117.7	119.8	119.6	113.7	102.5	97.4	94.5	93.1	88.3	82.4
Iron Ore Mining & Quarrying	0.30	0.30	0.32	0.3	0.3	0.4	0.4	0.5	0.5	0.6	0.6)		)	)	)	)	)	)
Stone Quarrying & Mining	5.81	5.73	5.83	5.5	5.4	5.1	5.0	4.4	4.5	4.3	4.4)	6.9	) 6.3	) 6.0	) 5.8	) 5.6	)5.4	) 5.2
Slate Quarrying & Mining	4.65	4.66	4.55	4.3	4.2	4.1	3.8	3.6	3.3	3.5	3.3)		)	)	)	)	)	)
3 Food, Drink & Tobacco	13.50	13.93	14.33	14.7	15.0	14.9	15.3	15.0	15.1	14.8	14.9	12.9	13.0	12.7	12.6	13.1	12.7	12.3
4 Coal & Petroleum Products	4.14	4.51	4.58	5.1	5.2	5.9	6.3	5.9	6.5	6.5	6.4	6.2	6.6	6.6	6.7	6.6	6.5	6.8
5 Chemicals & Allied Industries	12.07	11.54	12.05	13.6	13.6	13.9	14.4	15.0	15.6	16.8	15.0	16.0	14.8	14.7	13.7	13.3	13.0	13.3
6 Metal Manufacture	71.47	72.46	73.68	74.8	75.7	75.1	75.3	78.0	82.4	84.4	81.0	77.6	83.3	85.0	81.7	84.7	88.4	87.9
7 Mechanical Engineering	15.75	16.44	16.66	14.2	14.2	15.5	15.0	18.3	19.1	19.0	18.7	13.8	15.4	18.0	17.5	17.6	17.6	19.0
8 Instrument Engineering	1.53	1.73	1.93	1.7	1.6	1.8	2.1	2.2	2.3	2.3	2.3	2.4	2.0	2.1	2.2	2.3	2.3	2.2
9 Electrical Engineering	5.70	5.82	6.47	7.5	8.8	8.6	8.6	10.1	9.8	10.5	11.0	12.0	13.3	13.5	14.2	14.3	14.0	14.7
10 Shipbuilding & Marine Engineering	9.26	8.49	7.40	6.8	6.9	7.7	7.2	7.6	7.4	7.3	6.9	6.3	5.7	5.0	5.0	4.6	4.1	4.2
11 Vehicles	11.64	13.35	14.07	17.0	18.2	17.3	16.3	16.6	16.6	15.0	14.7	12.4	14.9	14.4	14.0	13.9	14.6	14.9
12 Metal Goods not elsewhere specified	9.62	9.78	9.86	9.8	10.2	11.4	10.7	11.1	11.2	11.1	11.8	13.1	13.1	14.8	13.7	13.8	14.4	16.2
13 Textiles	8.13	9.97	10.98	10.8	9.0	9.8	10.6	11.3	11.4	11.7	10.8	10.6	11.0	11.0	11.3	11.6	12.1	12.3
14 Leather, Leather Goods & Fur	1.00	0.64	1.01	1.0	0.9	1.1	1.1	1.1	1.0	1.1	1.1	1.2	1.1	1.1	1.0	1.1	1.0	1.0
15 Clothing & Footwear	1.79	2.06	2.17	2.3	2.3	2.2	2.2	2.3	2.0	2.1	2.0	1.9	2.1	2.0	2.0	2.2	2.2	2.3
16 Bricks, Pottery, Glass, Cement, etc.	9.69	9.65	9.75	10.6	10.6	10.5	10.7	10.6	10.3	10.1	10.3	8.3	8.8	9.2	8.9	8.7	9.1	9.9
17 Timber, Furniture, etc.	5.12	5.58	6.19	7.1	6.6	6.7	6.2	6.3	6.0	5.8	5.6	5.5	5.3	5.4	5.5	5.5	5.4	5.6
18 Paper, Printing & Publishing	4.46	4.52	4.68	4.9	5.3	5.1	5.1	5.3	5.5	6.2	6.5	6.1	6.2	7.1	7.3	7.8	8.1	7.5
19 Other Manufacturing Industries	2.13	2.58	3.15	3.5	3.8	4.3	4.6	4.8	4.9	5.4	5.6	6.1	6.4	6.3	6.6	7.1	7.6	8.4
20 Construction	64.95	63.70	63.21	63.6	62.3	61.7	57.3	61.6	60.8	59.4	60.1	68.7	73.8	78.3	78.1	77.2	79.1	77.4
21 Gas, Electricity & Water	12.34	13.39	14.62	15.7	15.6	17.0	17.4	17.5	17.2	17.8	18.4	18.0	17.4	17.6	18.5	19.0	19.5	20.2
22 Transport & Communication	84.05	84.61	85.22	80.5	79.0	76.8	74.5	76.0	75.9	76.2	75.6	75.9(2)	73.0(2)	72.2(2)	72.9(2)	69.1(2)	67.6	64.0
23 Distributive Trades	43.09	43.06	41.32	39.8	37.3	38.9	41.5	38.7	42.2	41.8	42.9	46.3	47.9	47.1	47.9	49.7	47.0	48.3
24 Insurance, Banking, Finance & Business Services	7.26	6.88	6.74	6.5	6.5	6.3	5.9	7.4	7.6	7.6	7.8	8.4	8.3	8.4	8.5	8.5	8.6	9.0
25 Professional & Scientific Services	20.96	19.83	22.27	22.9	22.9	23.9	24.3	23.9	24.9	25.7	26.3	27.5	29.0	30.0	31.2	32.1	33.6	36.1
26 Miscellaneous Services	26.93	24.26	26.31	24.3	23.7	25.4	25.4	25.5	26.1	25.9	27.0	29.7	30.1	30.3	32.0	33.0	34.1	34.6
27 Public Administration & Defence	53.30	51.39	52.25	47.8	48.4	48.6	48.9	49.4	49.6	49.4	50.0	48.1	47.9	49.2	50.1	52.4	49.0	50.4
Persons not classified by industry	—	—	—	0.8	1.0	0.6	0.6	0.6	0.5	0.6	0.8	0.5	0.2	0.2	0.2	0.1	0.1	1.5
TOTAL	682.94	680.65	682.81	671.6	670.3	676.0	669.0	681.0	684.0	681.0	683.0	680.0(2)	683.0(2)	688.0(2)	685.0(2)	689.0	684.0	684.0

1966	1967	1968	1969[4]	1970	1971[3]	1971[3]	1972	1973	1974
15.2	14.5	12.8	12.7	11.7	10.4	21.2	20.9	21.4	20.6
79.6	75.0	66.6	60.3	55.0	49.3	51.0	48.4	45.5	42.9
73.8	69.3	61.3	55.3	50.1	45.2	47.4	44.8	42.1	39.2
)4.9	)4.4	)3.9	)3.9	)3.9	)3.0	).. [5]	)2.7	)2.6	)2.8
12.6	12.3	12.1	(11.4) 11.9	12.7	13.0	12.3	12.8	12.2	11.6
6.8	6.6	6.7	6.8	6.8	7.7	5.4	5.3	5.4	5.4
14.3	15.0	14.0	(13.9) 12.4	13.8	13.9	12.3	12.7	12.3	13.1
87.1	86.2	86.0	(87.6) 87.7	88.5	81.5	85.3	81.2	79.5	77.9
20.4	23.0	25.5	(25.7) 26.0	28.4	27.8	25.3	23.2	23.3	23.5
1.9	2.1	2.2	(2.3) 1.9	2.0	2.0	2.1	2.0	2.4	2.8
15.3	14.8	15.4	(15.6) 15.7	17.5	17.2	17.8	18.0	18.1	19.2
4.1	3.3	2.8	2.5	2.5	1.6	1.4	1.7	1.7	1.7
16.0	16.3	15.9	(17.4) 18.3	19.1	20.5	20.6	20.6	21.4	21.5
16.4	16.8	17.1	(18.2) 17.3	17.5	17.7	17.1	16.8	17.1	17.3
12.2	11.8	11.8	13.0	13.4	14.7	13.0	13.0	12.7	12.5
1.1	1.0	0.9	1.0	0.8	0.9	..	..	..	..
2.4	2.4	2.4	2.5	2.4	2.3	2.4	2.5	2.6	2.7
9.7	10.0	9.9	(9.6) 9.4	9.1	9.6	9.2	9.2	10.2	10.0
5.9	6.5	7.9	(7.8) 7.9	7.9	7.7	7.0	7.2	7.8	7.3
8.3	8.5	8.7	(9.2) 9.3	9.6	9.4	8.9	8.8	8.8	8.9
7.4	7.2	8.1	(8.6) 9.9	11.4	11.3	10.8	11.1	12.5	13.6
82.0	78.7	76.9	(73.5) 73.4	68.7	74.8	74.0	80.5	77.2	72.4
20.6	20.8	20.2	20.1	18.7	18.6	17.6	16.6	16.4	16.6
60.3	59.2	58.3	(55.2) 55.1	54.6	54.8	56.8	55.9	54.7	53.8
46.5	43.1	41.7	(40.1) 42.7	39.3	39.3	43.9	44.5	45.0	44.4
9.1	9.3	9.1	(9.1) 9.7	9.4	9.5	11.9	11.9	12.4	12.4
36.3	36.2	38.4	(38.5) 38.6	36.4	39.1	42.2	44.4	44.8	45.2
35.7	32.8	35.4	(33.7) 33.0	30.9	32.6	35.3	37.5	38.9	38.6
50.8	51.9	49.1	47.9	47.2	45.7	53.8	55.4	54.9	49.1
1.5	2.1	2.3	2.5	2.8	2.9	2.9	3.5	3.3	3.2
680.1	667.5	658.4	(647.0) 649.5	635.3	635.8	662	666	663	649

FEMALES

	1948	1949	1950	1951	1952	1953	1954	1955	1956	1957	1958	1959	1960	1961	1962	1963	1964	1965	1966
1 Agriculture, Forestry & Fishing	5.55	4.90	4.02	3.5	3.0	3.4	3.2	3.0	3.0	3.0	2.6	2.9	2.7	2.4	2.3	2.7	2.1	1.8	2.2
2 Mining and Quarrying	1.62	1.70	2.14	2.1	2.3	2.5	2.7	2.7	2.6	2.8	2.9	3.3	3.0	3.0	2.9	2.9	2.9	2.8	2.9
Coal Mining	1.45	1.55	1.98	1.9	2.2	2.3	2.5	2.5	2.4	2.6	2.7	3.0	2.8	2.8	2.7	2.7	2.7	2.6	2.6
Iron Ore Mining & Quarrying	-	-	-	-	-	-	-	-	-	-	-	)	)	)	)	)	)	)	)
Stone Quarrying & Mining	0.13	0.12	0.12	0.1	0.1	0.2	0.2	0.2	0.2	0.2	0.2	)0.3	)0.2	)0.2	)0.2	)0.2	)0.2	)0.2	)0.2
Slate Quarrying & Mining	0.03	0.01	0.02	-	-	-	-	-	-	-	-	)	)	)	)	)	)	)	)
3 Food, Drink & Tobacco	6.75	7.50	7.99	8.5	9.2	9.8	10.1	10.4	10.3	10.3	10.4	8.7	8.8	8.8	8.9	9.2	9.0	9.5	9.6
4 Coal & Petroleum Products	0.25	0.33	0.27	0.3	0.2	0.3	0.3	0.3	0.3	0.4	0.3	0.3	0.3	0.3	0.3	0.3	0.3	0.3	0.6
5 Chemicals & Allied Industries	3.24	2.69	2.57	3.1	3.9	3.9	4.2	4.6	4.5	3.9	3.4	3.7	3.6	3.4	3.4	3.5	3.6	4.0	4.1
6 Metal Manufacture	8.14	7.86	8.44	8.3	8.9	7.6	7.4	7.1	7.5	7.2	6.4	6.4	6.5	6.7	6.6	6.9	7.2	7.1	7.0
7 Mechanical Engineering	2.60	2.31	2.33	2.8	2.8	2.7	3.1	3.1	3.3	3.2	3.2	2.5	3.1	3.4	3.8	4.0	4.2	4.4	4.4
8 Instrument Engineering	1.30	1.69	1.61	1.7	1.7	1.8	1.8	2.1	1.9	2.1	2.2	2.2	2.2	2.3	2.3	2.1	2.2	2.2	2.1
9 Electrical Engineering	5.32	4.76	4.92	6.1	6.5	6.2	6.3	7.6	7.4	7.6	7.9	9.1	9.9	9.6	10.2	11.0	12.4	11.7	12.7
10 Shipbuilding & Marine Engineering	0.24	0.26	0.20	0.2	0.3	0.2	0.2	0.3	0.3	0.2	0.2	0.4	0.3	0.4	0.3	0.3	0.3	0.3	0.4
11 Vehicles	3.76	3.14	3.44	4.0	4.4	3.8	3.5	4.1	3.8	3.3	3.5	3.2	3.8	3.1	3.4	3.7	3.8	4.5	4.1
12 Metal Goods not elsewhere specified	7.05	7.76	7.71	8.5	8.3	8.9	9.0	8.8	9.2	8.6	8.1	8.1	8.3	8.6	7.7	7.4	8.0	8.2	8.3
13 Textiles	4.46	5.18	5.44	5.3	4.5	5.0	5.7	5.5	5.6	5.7	5.5	5.7	6.0	6.0	5.9	5.6	5.8	5.4	5.5
14 Leather, Leather Goods & Fur	0.65	0.70	0.84	0.9	0.9	1.0	0.9	1.1	1.0	1.0	0.9	0.9	1.0	1.0	1.0	1.0	0.9	1.0	1.0
15 Clothing & Footwear	8.48	10.55	12.12	12.7	12.8	13.4	12.9	13.7	14.2	13.0	12.1	10.8	11.6	12.2	12.7	12.4	12.7	12.9	13.5
16 Bricks, Pottery, Glass, Cement, etc.	1.21	1.50	1.34	1.7	1.5	1.3	1.5	1.6	1.4	1.6	1.4	1.3	1.4	1.3	1.5	1.4	1.5	1.6	1.7
17 Timber, Furniture, etc.	0.72	0.87	0.99	1.0	1.0	1.2	1.2	1.2	1.2	1.1	1.0	0.9	0.9	0.9	0.9	0.8	0.9	0.9	1.1
18 Paper, Printing & Publishing	2.04	2.15	2.39	2.3	2.4	2.5	2.7	2.9	2.8	3.1	3.0	2.9	3.1	3.4	3.6	4.0	4.1	3.9	4.1
19 Other Manufacturing Industries	3.04	3.49	3.70	4.5	4.5	4.7	5.6	5.7	4.7	5.1	4.9	5.3	5.9	5.7	5.9	6.4	6.8	7.3	8.1
20 Construction	1.09	0.77	0.78	1.1	1.2	1.2	1.6	1.5	1.6	1.7	1.9	2.0	2.3	2.2	2.4	2.6	2.5	2.6	2.8
21 Gas, Electricity & Water	1.07	1.43	1.55	1.8	1.9	2.0	1.9	2.0	2.0	2.2	2.2	2.2	2.2	2.3	2.4	2.5	3.0	2.8	2.9
22 Transport & Communication	9.35	9.10	9.32	9.3	9.5	9.4	9.7	10.0	9.9	10.0	9.5	9.7	9.7	10.3	10.3	9.8	9.9	10.3	10.7
23 Distributive Trades	39.32	41.83	41.00	41.3	43.2	44.8	46.5	48.7	51.3	51.6	50.4	54.3	56.0	57.2	59.7	61.4	59.7	62.3	60.0
24 Insurance, Banking, Finance & Business Services	3.20	3.05	3.11	3.2	3.3	3.4	3.4	4.4	4.7	5.0	5.3	5.6	5.8	6.0	6.4	6.1	6.8	7.4	7.6
25 Professional & Scientific Services	37.71	38.65	40.12	42.7	41.7	44.0	45.1	45.4	47.6	48.3	50.0	60.6	62.7	64.8	67.2	68.0	72.8	77.3	81.9
26 Miscellaneous Services	56.55	53.04	54.29	50.3	51.2	50.6	50.4	52.2	52.9	52.4	53.4	45.8	45.8	45.2	45.5	44.8	48.5	49.7	50.3
27 Public Administration & Defence	19.54	17.65	16.49	15.3	14.8	14.4	15.1	15.0	15.9	15.6	16.4	14.5	14.1	14.4	15.5	16.2	15.1	15.5	16.4
Persons not classified by industry	-	-	-	-	-	-	-	-	0.1	-	-	-	-	-	-	-	-	1.3	1.5
TOTAL	235.35	235.74	240.45	242.1	245.9	250.0	256.0	265.0	271.0	270.0	269.0	273.0	281.0	285.0	293.0	297.0	307.0	319.0	327.2

1967	1968	1969[4]	1970	1971[3]	1971[3]	1972	1973	1974
1.9	1.9	1.7	1.7	1.7	7.2	6.4	7.1	7.1
2.4	2.5	2.0	2.0	1.7	1.6	1.5	1.4	1.5
2.1	2.2	1.7	1.8	1.5	1.4	1.3	1.2	1.3
)0.2	)0.2	)0.2	)0.2	)0.2	) ..[5]	)0.1	)0.1	) -
9.2	8.9	(8.6) 8.9	9.6	9.7	8.5	8.8	8.1	8.2
0.3	0.4	(0.4) 0.3	0.3	0.4	0.3	0.3	0.3	-
4.4	3.7	(4.0) 3.6	3.9	3.8	2.9	3.4	3.8	4.2
7.0	6.9	(6.8) 7.0	6.7	6.7	6.6	6.1	5.9	6.3
4.6	4.7	(4.8) 4.9	5.1	5.0	4.2	3.9	4.1	4.6
1.8	1.9	(2.4) 2.2	2.1	1.7	1.6	1.5	1.7	1.9
12.3	13.4	(13.2) 13.6	15.3	14.1	14.2	13.9	15.9	16.7
0.2	0.2	0.2	0.2	0.1	0.1	0.1	0.1	-
3.7	3.8	(5.0) 5.2	5.2	5.6	5.2	4.9	5.4	5.2
7.7	7.8	(7.1) 7.0	7.5	7.2	6.6	6.2	6.4	6.6
5.4	6.0	6.1	6.2	5.8	4.8	4.8	4.5	4.5
0.8	0.8	0.8	0.7	0.7	1.2	1.2	1.5	..
13.3	13.1	14.3	13.9	14.9	13.2	13.5	13.9	14.0
1.6	1.5	1.6	1.6	1.9	1.6	1.7	1.8	2.1
1.5	1.4	1.4	1.6	1.7	1.4	1.6	1.7	1.7
4.2	4.2	4.6	5.0	4.6	4.0	3.8	4.1	4.2
8.4	9.0	8.9	10.1	9.0	8.2	8.7	9.9	11.7
2.5	2.6	2.6	2.6	2.8	3.3	3.5	3.6	3.5
2.9	3.0	2.8	3.1	2.9	2.9	2.8	2.9	3.0
11.5	10.5	(10.2) 9.8	10.4	10.4	8.6	8.8	8.5	8.6
56.9	56.1	(55.5) 58.5	56.5	56.1	55.6	56.3	59.1	58.4
7.2	7.5	(7.7) 9.6	10.0	10.6	12.2	12.2	13.9	13.6
81.9	86.3	(87.7) 87.9	89.2	91.5	93.1	97.3	101.7	102.7
47.4	48.5	(44.5) 42.6	41.5	44.1	44.9	48.9	54.2	55.3
17.6	18.4	(18.0) 18.1	19.1	18.1	24.6	26.6	27.4	28.4
1.5	1.6	1.2	1.2	1.3	1.4	1.6	1.4	1.4
319.7	326.9	(324.0) 327.4	332.4	334.3	340	350	370	376

General Notes

(i) Sources. For 1939, 1945 and 1946: Wales and Monmouthshire, Reports on Government Action, 1945-6, Cd. 6938, 1947-48, Cd. 7267. For 1947-50: Min. of Lab. and Nat. Service, Tables Relating to Employment and Unemployment in Great Britain, 1947, 1948 and 1951. For 1951: provided direct by Dept. of Employment. For 1952-71: Digest of Welsh Statistics, 1952-71. For 1971-4: British Labour Statistics, Yearbook, 1971-4.

(ii) The total number of employees given in this table for 1951-54 does not agree with that given in Table 3. A change in the method of counting national insurance cards was introduced in 1955. The change allowed better estimates to be made of the number of persons employed in each of the regions. For the total figures, as given in Table 3, the 1955 adjustments were applied retrospectively to the years 1951-54, but it was not possible to allocate retrospectively for each of the industrial groups, as given in Table 4.

(iii) The figures from 1948 on have, where necessary, been reworked to have them all on the basis of the 1968 standard Industrial Classification. In general there were official revisions of the figures from 1959 on, so the re-working has mainly been on the figures for 1948-58. The main changes were:

Order iv. For 1948-58 the constituent parts of this Order included under 'Chemical and allied trades' as: 'Gas-ovens and by-product works'· 'Mineral oil refining': and 'Other oils, greases, glues etc.' These three minimum list heading have thus been extracted from 1948-58 tables to make Order iv for those years.

Order vi. For 1948-58, 'Iron and steel forgings, not elsewhere specified' and 'Brass manufactures' have been taken out of 'Metal goods, not elsewhere specified' and put in this Order.

Order vii, ix and x have been created out of the 1948-58 category, 'Engineering, Shipbuilding and electrical goods' as follows: Order x is 'Shipbuilding and ship-repairing' plus 'Marine Engineering': Order ix is from 'Electrical machinery' down to 'Other electrical goods': Order vii is the remainder of the 1948-58 category of 'Engineering, Shipbuilding and electrical goods'.

Order viii has been formed by adding together the 1948-58 totals for the minimum list headings 'Scientific, surgical and photogra hic instruments etc' and 'Manufacture and repair of Watches and Clocks'.

Order xi is the Vehicles category for 1948-58 less the minimum list heading 'Motor repairers and garages' which in the 1968 S.I.C. is included in Order xxvi.

Order xii is the same as that given in 1948-58 under the same name ('Metal goods not elsewhere specified') except that it includes 'Iron and steel forgings n.e.s'., 'Brass manufacturers' (see note on Order vi) and 'Engineers, small tools and garages'.

(iii) Order xv is the 1948-58 category 'Clothing and Footwear' except for 'Repair of boots and shoes' which is included in Order xxvi.

Order xxvi. See notes on Orders xi and xv and add in 'Entertainment and Sport'.

Notes

1. In 1945, 1946 and 1947 the figures exclude persons classified as unsuitable for ordinary employment and insured ex-members of the Forces on demobilisation leave. These classes are included in the following figures which show the estimated total numbers (in thousands) of insured persons in the Wales region.

mid-	M	F
1939	602	94
1945	473	205
1946	547	180
1947	565	166

There is an additional complication for 1946 and 1947 where the total figure given in the table is greater than the sum of the various industry groups. In 1946 this is because the total figure includes a number of ex-members of the Forces who had had no employment since release on discharge (and hence could not be allocated to an industry) but were on the register for employment.

In 1947 the excess of the totals over the sum of the figures for the individual industries is due to the inclusion of (a) a number of ex-members of the Forces who had had no employment since release or discharge and were registered for employment, and (b) a number of ex-colliery workers who were no longer fit for employment in coal mining and were therefore excluded from the unemployment figures in that industry.

2. The figures for Order xxii (Transport and Communications) for males were in 1965 revised for the years 1959 to 1963 inclusive to include a category of industrial civil servants engaged in the Post Office, but who did not hold insurance cards. The total male figures for these years had also to be revised because of this adjustment. See Min. of Lab. Gazette, Feb. 1965.

3. There is a break in the series in 1971 because of a change in the method of obtaining employment figures. For comparison two sets of figures are given for 1971. The first, on the old basis, relates to figures based on counts of National Insurance cards. The second, on the new basis are derived from an annual census of employment and are obtained by addingthese figures to the numbers unemployed for each industry group. The changes are explained in two articles in the employment Gazette which are re-printed as Appendix I to the 1972 Yearbook of British Labour Statistics.

4. Where applicable two figures are given for 1969: one (in brackets) on the basis of the 1958 S.I.C., the other on the basis of the 1969 S.I.C.

5. From 1971 on figures of the total number of employees are obtained by adding the separately published numbers for 'in employment' and 'unemployed'. But the published data on the 'unemployed' is only given for the main headings. The Ministry kindly supplied the information for these sub-groups for 1972-4, but those for 1971 were not available.

LABOUR 5. Unemployment. Number and Percentage, by sex, each month 1923-75. Wales

Date	Number unemployed				Percent unemployed		
	Men	Women	Juveniles	Total	Men	Women	Total
1923 Jan	45,936	3,217	2,973	52,126	..	..	..
Feb	43,745	3,064	2,760	49,569	..	..	8.0
Mar	38,990	2,782	2,462	44,234	..	..	..
Apr	34,881	2,854	2,552	40,287	..	..	..
May	31,993	2,158	2,125	36,276	..	..	6.1
June	31,540	2,267	1,920	35,727	..	..	..
July	29,001	2,184	2,213	33,398	..	..	..
Aug	29,602	2,356	2,249	34,207	..	..	5.7
Sept	31,278	2,607	2,261	36,146	..	..	..
Oct	32,233	2,863	2,220	37,316	..	..	..
Nov	31,321	2,917	2,066	36,304	..	..	5.8
Dec	29,992	2,853	1,916	34,761	..	..	..
Ave	34,209	2,677	2,310	39,196	..	..	6.4
1924 Jan	62,895	3,575	3,579	70,049	..	..	..
Feb	29,362	3,263	2,267	34,892	..	..	5.8
Mar	26,468	2,933	1,935	31,336	..	..	..
Apr	26,306	2,640	2,295	31,241	..	..	..
May	31,013	2,546	2,613	36,172	..	..	5.9
June	33,059	2,338	2,116	37,513	.	..	..
July	35,968	2,167	2,217	40,352	.	..	..
Aug	53,117	2,381	3,418	58,916	..	..	8.3
Sept	68,690	2,961	4,038	75,689	..	..	..
Oct	79,194	3,402	4,594	87,190	..	..	..
Nov	72,704	3,745	3,758	80,207	..	..	12.8
Dec	81,045	4,486	3,996	89,527	..	..	..
Ave	49,985	3,036	3,069	56,090	..	..	8.6

LABOUR 5. Unemployment. Number and Percentage, by sex, each month 1923-75. Wales

Date	Number unemployed				Percent unemployed		
	Men	Women	Juveniles	Total	Men	Women	Total
1925 Jan	79,838	4,866	4,916	89,620	..	..	..
Feb	89,972	4,424	4,827	99,223	..	..	16.0
Mar	80,849	4,132	4,891	89,872	..	..	..
Apr	83,327	3,876	5,003	92,206	..	..	..
May	80,880	3,347	4,582	88,809	..	..	14.2
June	93,074	2,970	4,644	100,688	..	..	..
July	75,408	2,599	3,514	81,521	..	..	..
Aug	122,907	3,029	6,606	132,542	..	..	20.4
Sept	152,830	3,139	8,077	164,046	..	..	..
Oct	131,739	3,398	7,030	142,167	..	..	..
Nov	91,068	3,225	4,112	98,405	..	..	17.2
Dec	76,792	2,607	3,143	82,542	..	..	..
Ave	96,557	3,468	5,112	105,137	..	..	16.5
1926 Jan	80,994	3,638	4,118	88,750	..	..	..
Feb	73,039	3,396	3,786	80,221	..	..	13.1
Mar	68,017	3,222	3,151	74,390	..	..	..
Apr	62,052	3,142	3,474	68,668	..	..	..
May	122,302	6,140	6,800	135,242(1)	..	..	21.5
June	125,052	6,462	6,663	138,150	..	..	..
July	119,775	6,308	6,207	132,290	..	..	..
Aug	120,350	5,774	6,080	132,204	..	..	21.3
Sept	116,461	6,318	5,921	128,700	21.5	12.0	20.6
Oct	118,957	6,712	5,687	131,356	21.9	13.7	21.1
Nov	119,765	6,341	5,087	131,193	22.2	13.3	21.4
Dec	121,363	4,220	4,944	130,527	18.5	9.2	17.6
Ave	104,011	5,139	5,160	114,308	..	..	18.0

LABOUR 5. Unemployment. Number and Percentage, by sex, each month 1923-75. Wales

Date	Number unemployed				Percent unemployed		
	Men	Women	Juveniles	Total	Men	Women	Total
1927 Jan	127,216	4,027	5,531	136,774	23.1	8.5	21.8
Feb	105,133	3,302	4,172	112,607	19.6	7.2	18.5
Mar	98,229	3,064	3,878	105,171	17.5	5.8	16.5
Apr	84,062	2,781	3,640	90,483	15.7	5.2	14.7
May	102,289	2,956	4,045	109,290	16.7	5.3	15.6
June	110,631	3,733	4,567	118,931	19.4	5.4	18.1
July	111,942	2,824	4,952	119,718	20.7	5.0	19.2
Aug	118,188	3,106	5,598	126,892	21.1	5.7	19.7
Sept	127,382	3,703	5,949	137,034	23.7	7.0	22.2
Oct	137,375	4,006	6,690	148,071	24.8	7.4	23.2
Nov	129,934	3,994	6,232	140,160	22.9	7.5	21.5
Dec	152,909	4,375	6,351	163,635	25.0	6.6	23.3
Ave	117,108	3,489	5,134	125,731	20.9	6.4	19.5
1928 Jan[2]	133,183	4,387	7,305	144,875	26.3	8.9	24.6
Feb	122,075	4,307	6,549	132,931	25.0	9.5	23.5
Mar	114,635	3,700	5,948	124,283	22.1	7.1	20.7
Apr[3]	109,722	3,348	6,246	119,316	20.8	6.2	19.5
May	117,667	3,883	6,493	128,043	22.5	6.7	21.0
June	120,932	3,064	5,136	129,132	23.0	5.1	21.3
July[4]	133,296	3,357	5,568	142,221	26.7	5.1	24.6
Aug	122,829	3,770	5,752	132,351	22.7	5.7	21.1
Sept	128,534	4,161	6,204	138,899	24.3	7.3	22.7
Oct	140,200	5,206	7,023	152,429	27.5	9.2	25.8
Nov	144,578	5,667	7,161	157,406	28.1	10.3	26.3
Dec	136,705	5,944	6,300	148,949	24.3	9.0	22.8
Ave	127,030	4,233	6,307	137,570	24.4	7.5	22.8

LABOUR 5. Unemployment. Number and Percentage, by sex, each month 1923-75. Wales

Date	Number unemployed				Percent unemployed		
	Men	Women	Juveniles	Total	Men	Women	Total
1929 Jan	113,675	5,640	6,241	125,556	22.8	10.6	21.6
Feb	118,103	5,669	6,098	129,870	22.8	10.5	21.6
Mar	99,480	4,337	4,733	108,550	19.4	7.7	18.2
Apr	93,726	4,693	5,452	103,871	18.1	7.7	17.1
May	95,127	4,206	5,062	104,395	18.5	7.3	17.4
June	105,494	4,055	5,271	114,820	19.1	7.0	17.9
July	105,874	4,488	5,370	115,732	19.8	6.3	18.5
Aug	94,340	4,073	5,372	103,785	18.4	7.4	17.3
Sept	102,454	4,743	6,105	113,302	20.8	8.8	19.6
Oct	104,370	5,674	6,252	116,296	20.7	10.4	19.7
Nov	110,797	6,302	6,004	123,103	21.8	11.2	20.8
Dec	120,084	6,892	6,030	133,006	21.9	10.2	20.7
Ave	105,294	5,064	5,666	116,024	20.3	8.8	19.2
1930 Jan	104,278	7,019	6,547	117,844	20.5	12.5	19.7
Feb	110,139	7,373	6,405	123,917	21.7	13.4	20.9
Mar[5]	137,894	7,328	7,075	152,297	25.1	14.1	23.9
Apr	131,258	7,191	7,374	145,823	25.9	13.0	24.6
May	148,900	6,720	8,312	163,932	29.4	11.8	27.7
June	143,288	6,159	7,701	157,148	27.1	10.7	25.5
July	152,261	6,296	7,895	166,452	28.7	10.7	26.9
Aug	137,887	6,493	7,546	151,926	27.3	11.8	25.7
Sept	152,814	8,288	8,580	169,682	29.3	14.3	27.7
Oct	164,395	8,897	9,066	182,358	31.9	16.0	30.3
Nov	154,107	9,434	8,593	172,134	29.9	17.1	28.6
Dec	175,874	10,693	8,588	195,155	32.6	18.7	31.2
Ave	142,758	7,658	7,807	158,222	27.5	13.7	26.0

LABOUR 5. Unemployment. Number and Percentage, by sex, each month 1923-75. Wales

Date		Number unemployed				Percent unemployed		
		Men	Women	Juveniles	Total	Men	Women	Total
1931	Jan	164,542	10,937	9,613	185,092	31.9	19.8	30.6
	Feb	173,417	11,185	9,221	193,823	33.6	20.1	32.2
	Mar	169,100	9,904	8,547	187,551	33.0	18.3	31.5
	Apr	169,020	10,151	9,131	188,302	32.7	17.7	31.2
	May	173,088	9,385	8,297	190,770	36.1	16.3	34.1
	June	177,512	8,890	8,247	194,649	34.4	15.8	32.5
	July	178,618	9,012	8,230	195,860	34.7	15.8	32.8
	Aug	183,912	9,347	8,958	202,217	35.4	16.3	33.5
	Sept	186,934	11,074	9,589	207,597	36.2	18.5	34.4
	Oct (6)	184,308	11,766	9,388	205,462	35.0	19.3	33.3
	Nov	188,971	10,631	9,616	209,218	35.5	19.0	33.7
	Dec	176,324	9,775	8,321	194,420	33.4	17.5	31.7
	Ave	177,146	10,171	8,930	196,247	34.3	17.9	32.6
1932	Jan	194,704	10,637	10,290	215,631	37.0	18.5	35.1
	Feb	193,953	10,541	9,892	214,386	36.9	17.9	34.9
	Mar	184,588	9,968	9,176	203,732	35.1	16.5	33.1
	Apr	195,062	9,937	10,010	215,009	37.0	16.4	34.9
	May	192,816	9,228	9,423	211,467	36.6	15.4	34.3
	June	215,314	9,242	10,173	234,729	40.9	15.3	38.2
	July	218,336	8,959	10,346	237,641	41.6	14.9	38.8
	Aug	224,591	9,116	10,872	244,579	42.8	15.3	39.9
	Sept	214,506	10,148	10,537	235,191	40.7	16.8	38.2
	Oct	219,173	11,016	10,508	240,697	40.6	18.1	38.3
	Nov	219,787	11,617	10,307	241,711	40.6	18.8	38.3
	Dec	214,677	10,651	9,448	234,776	39.5	17.2	37.2
	Ave	207,292	10,088	10,082	227,462	39.1	16.8	36.8

LABOUR 5. Unemployment. Number and Percentage, by sex, each month 1923-75. Wales

Date		Number unemployed				Percent unemployed		
		Men	Women	Juveniles	Total	Men	Women	Total
1933	Jan	213,357	11,914	10,072	235,343	39.2	19.4	37.2
	Feb	202,403	11,409	9,650	223,462	37.3	19.0	35.4
	Mar	203,230	11,790	9,661	224,681	37.5	19.1	35.6
	Apr	206,652	10,713	9,623	226,988	38.0	17.7	35.9
	May	201,577	9,930	9,316	220,823	37.1	15.6	34.9
	June	199,707	8,158	8,785	216,650	36.8	13.0	34.3
	July	201,823	7,820	8,689	218,332	37.2	12.6	34.6
	Aug	196,058	7,732	8,181	211,971	36.0	12.8	33.6
	Sept	189,003	8,579	8,582	206,164	34.7	14.2	32.5
	Oct	201,185	9,670	9,148	220,003	36.8	15.7	34.6
	Nov	193,974	9,820	8,629	212,423	35.5	16.1	33.4
	Dec	196,974	8,901	7,563	213,438	35.9	14.3	33.6
	Ave	200,495	9,703	8,992	219,190	36.8	15.8	34.6
1934	Jan	201,341	10,497	10,023	221,861	36.8	17.4	34.7
	Feb	195,745	10,433	9,925	216,103	35.7	17.2	33.8
	Mar	193,900	9,542	9,098	212,540	35.4	15.4	33.3
	Apr	192,755	9,063	9,855	211,673	35.2	14.4	33.0
	May	185,798	7,822	9,019	202,639	33.8	12.3	31.5
	June	195,911	7,138	8,865	211,914	35.8	11.4	33.2
	July	190,662	6,746	8,109	205,517	34.8	10.9	32.3
	Aug	181,980	6,827	8,649	197,456	33.1	11.3	30.8
	Sept (7)	174,237	7,820	10,667	192,734	31.7	13.1	29.7
	Oct	186,703	9,353	12,298	208,354	33.9	15.5	32.0
	Nov	186,090	9,571	12,491	208,152	33.8	16.0	31.9
	Dec	187,389	8,838	11,981	208,208	34.0	14.6	31.9
	Ave	189,376	8,638	10,082	208,096	34.5	14.1	32.3

LABOUR 5. Unemployment. Number and Percentage, by sex, each month 1923-75. Wales

Date		Number unemployed				Percent unemployed		
		Men	Women	Juveniles	Total	Men	Women	Total
1935	Jan[8]	188,288	10,702	14,979	213,969	34.1	17.8	32.4
	Feb	196,539	10,756	15,328	222,623	35.7	18.1	33.8
	Mar	190,300	10,104	14,755	215,159	34.5	16.5	32.6
	Apr	188,122	8,996	14,920	212,038	34.1	14.7	32.0
	May	184,613	8,337	15,240	208,190	33.5	13.5	31.4
	June	181,129	6,924	15,097	203,150	32.8	11.3	30.6
	July	176,217	6,842	13,897	196,956	32.0	11.1	29.8
	Aug	174,825	7,858	14,469	197,152	31.9	13.1	29.9
	Sept	182,098	8,373	16,727	207,198	33.2	13.9	31.1
	Oct	178,655	9,358	16,194	204,207	32.7	15.5	30.9
	Nov	174,862	9,819	15,427	200,108	32.0	16.4	30.3
	Dec	169,680	8,598	14,462	192,740	31.0	14.3	29.2
	Ave	182,111	8,889	15,125	206,124	33.1	14.7	31.2
1936	Jan	180,071	10,813	17,455	208,339	33.0	18.0	31.4
	Feb	184,505	10,886	18,301	213,692	33.8	18.1	32.2
	Mar	187,202	10,180	17,761	215,143	34.5	17.0	32.6
	Apr	180,073	9,143	17,641	206,857	33.1	15.0	31.2
	May	173,456	8,130	17,311	198,897	31.9	13.6	29.9
	June	175,098	7,463	16,255	198,816	32.2	12.5	30.1
	July	166,393	6,902	14,619	187,914	30.6	11.5	28.5
	Aug	158,844	7,015	14,676	180,535	29.2	12.0	27.4
	Sept	158,520	8,639	16,445	183,604	29.2	14.6	27.6
	Oct	159,521	9,641	15,850	185,012	29.9	16.1	28.3
	Nov[9]	153,448	9,665	14,744	177,857	28.4	15.1	27.0
	Dec	151,504	8,846	13,536	173,886	27.8	14.4	26.3
	Ave	169,053	8,944	16,216	194,213	31.1	14.8	29.4

LABOUR 5. Unemployment. Number and Percentage, by sex, each month 1923-75. Wales

Date		Number unemployed				Percent unemployed		
		Men	Women	Juveniles	Total	Men	Women	Total
1937	Jan	149,259	10,224	15,017	174,500	27.5	17.3	26.3
	Feb	147,179	10,010	14,416	171,605	27.2	16.8	26.0
	Mar	140,781	9,946	13,232	163,959	25.9	15.7	24.7
	Apr	131,110	8,763	13,347	153,220	24.2	14.0	23.1
	May	128,874	7,222	12,462	148,558	23.8	12.1	22.5
	June	118,935	6,639	10,928	136,502	21.9	11.1	20.7
	July	113,633	6,690	10,255	130,578	21.0	11.3	19.9
	Aug	114,329	6,549	11,252	132,130	21.1	11.2	20.0
	Sept	112,182	7,019	12,376	131,577	20.6	11.8	19.6
	Oct	120,270	8,945	12,546	141,761	22.2	14.7	21.3
	Nov	118,956	9,546	12,007	140,509	21.9	15.7	21.2
	Dec	125,217	8,990	11,386	145,593	23.0	14.2	21.9
	Ave	117,810	8,379	12,435	147,541	23.4	13.8	22.3
1938	Jan	133,816	10,886	13,999	158,701	24.7	17.5	23.8
	Feb	131,834	11,681	14,276	157,791	24.4	18.9	23.0
	Mar	135,401	11,221	13,902	160,524	25.3	18.1	24.4
	Apr[10]	144,659	10,595	13,937	169,191	27.1	16.8	25.9
	May	152,280	9,817	15,074	177,171	28.4	15.7	26.9
	June	146,456	8,939	14,205	169,600	27.3	14.4	25.8
	July	139,934	8,396	12,826	161,156	26.2	13.5	24.7
	Aug	136,054	8,793	13,262	158,109	25.5	14.3	24.2
	Sept	139,247	9,173	14,689	163,109	26.1	14.9	24.8
	Oct	133,809	11,275	14,221	159,305	24.6	16.7	23.6
	Nov	141,516	11,934	13,854	167,304	26.0	17.4	24.9
	Dec	145,517	11,208	13,404	170,129	26.6	16.2	25.3
	Ave	140,044	10,327	13,971	164,341	26.0	16.2	24.8

LABOUR 5. Unemployment. Number and Percentage, by sex, each month 1923-75. Wales

Date		Number unemployed				Percent unemployed		
		Men	Women	Juveniles	Total	Men	Women	Total
1939	Jan	145,867	12,919	14,913	173,699	26.7	18.7	25.7
	Feb	146,873	12,929	14,996	174,798	26.9	18.7	25.9
	Mar	130,877	11,966	12.760	155,603	23.9	16.9	23.0
	Apr	120,572	10,098	11,641	142,311	22.0	14.2	21.0
	May	103,978	9,318	10,478	123,774	18.8	13.1	18.1
	June	97,951	7,409	9,143	114,503	17.7	10.5	16.8
	July	91,102	7,234	7,993	106,329	16.5	9.9	15.7
	Aug	86,736	7,419	8,470	102,625	15.8	10.8	15.2
	Sept[11]	75,396	14,144	11,478	101,018	13.9	17.6	14.3
	Oct	80,759	16,096	11,703	108,558	14.7	18.9	15.3
	Nov	83,418	15,955	11,128	110,501	15.2	17.6	15.5
	Dec	86,967	14,344	10,114	111,425	15.7	16.5	15.8
	Ave	104,208	11,653	11,235	127,095	19.0	15.3	18.5
1940	Jan	91,062	14,562	10,584	116,208	16.6	17.3	16.7
	Feb	96,661	13,757	10,566	120,984	17.6	16.6	17.5
	Mar	78,048	12,322	8,713	99,083	14.3	14.4	14.3
	Apr	73,058	11,071	8,299	92,428	13.4	13.1	13.4
	May	62,712	10,023	6,974	79,709	11.5	11.0	11.4
	June	50,253	11,071	6,523	67,847	9.2	10.0	9.3
	July	60,195	12,557	7,826	80,578	11.3	11.3	11.3
	Aug	54,891	11,981	8,598	75,470	10.4	11.5	10.5
	Sept[12]	55,223	12,291	8,535	76,049	..	..	10.6
	Oct	59,133	14,729	9,636	83,498	..	..	..
	Nov	69,356	14,818	10,282	94,456	..	..	..
	Dec	63,555	14,176	9,253	86,984	..	..	..
	Ave	67,846	11,947	8,816	89,441	..	..	..

LABOUR 5. Unemployment. Number and Percentage, by sex, each month 1923-75. Wales

Date		Number unemployed				Percent unemployed		
		Men	Women	Juveniles	Total	Men	Women	Total
1941	Jan	55,167	13,410	9,479	78,056	..	..	..
	Feb	47,227	12,835	8,396	68,458	..	..	..
	Mar	37,108	12,168	7,085	56,361	..	..	..
	Apr	32,767	10,612	6,651	50,030	..	..	..
	May	29,223	10,086	6,436	45,745	..	..	..
	June	23,566	8,007	5,320	36,893	..	..	..
	July	25,231	6,465	4,765	36,461	..	..	..
	Aug	21,727	5,735	5,102	32,564	..	..	..
	Sept	14,804	4,906	4,307	24,017	..	..	..
	Oct	13,778	4,489	3,898	22,165	..	..	..
	Nov	14,161	4,347	3,671	22,179	..	..	..
	Dec	13,203	4,310	3,179	20,692	..	..	..
	Ave	27,330	8,114	5,691	41,135	..	..	..
1942	Jan	13,499	3,193	3,173	19,865	..	..	..
	Feb[13]	12,774	2,877	2,739	18,390	..	..	..
	Mar	7,967	2,681	2,495	13,143	..	..	..
	Apr	8,550	2,118	2,861	13,529	..	..	..
	May	9,933	1,973	2,853	14,759	..	..	..
	June	9,820	1,964	2,437	14,221	..	..	..
	July	8,895	1,807	2,326	13,028	..	..	..
	Aug	9,091	1,701	3,004	13,796	..	..	..
	Sept	7,963	1,842	3,041	12,846	..	..	..
	Oct	7,942	2,065	3,093	13,100	..	..	..
	Nov	8,122	1,863	2,403	12,388	..	..	..
	Dec	7,552	1,421	1,966	10,939	..	..	..
	Ave	9,342	2,125	2,699	14,167	..	..	..

LABOUR 5. Unemployment. Number and Percentage, by sex, each month 1923-75. Wales

Date		Number unemployed				Percent unemployed		
		Men	Women	Juveniles	Total	Men	Women	Total
1943	Jan	7,122	1,311	2,424	10,857	..	..	..
	Feb	..	..	..	..	..	..	..
	Mar	..	..	..	..	..	..	..
	Apr	7,840	2,223	1,921	11,984	..	..	..
	May	..	..	..	..	..	..	..
	June	..	..	..	..	..	..	..
	July	6,637	1,313	1,706	9,656	..	..	..
	Aug	..	..	..	..	..	..	..
	Sept	..	..	..	..	..	..	..
	Oct	6,694	1,648	2,340	10,682	..	..	..
	Nov	..	..	..	..	..	..	..
	Dec	..	..	..	..	..	..	..
	Ave	7,073	1,624	2,098	10,795	..	..	..
1944	Jan	7,302	1,462	2,385	11,149	..	..	..
	Feb	..	..	..	..	..	..	..
	Mar	..	..	..	..	..	..	..
	Apr	6,497	1,579	2,090	10,166	..	..	..
	May	..	..	..	..	..	..	..
	June	..	..	..	..	..	..	..
	July	6,362	1,545	1,473	9,380	..	..	..
	Aug	..	..	..	..	..	..	..
	Sept	..	..	..	..	..	..	..
	Oct	7,269	1,989	2,149	11,407	..	..	..
	Nov	..	..	..	..	..	..	..
	Dec	..	..	..	..	..	..	..
	Ave	6,858	1,644	2,024	10,526	..	..	..

LABOUR 5. Unemployment. Number and Percentage, by sex, each month 1923-75. Wales

Date		Number unemployed				Percent unemployed		
		Men	Women	Juveniles	Total	Men	Women	Total
1945	Jan	8,601	2,679	2,347	13,627	..	..	..
	Feb	..	..	..	..	..	..	..
	Mar	..	..	..	..	..	..	..
	Apr	8,171	3,106	2,338	13,615	..	..	..
	May	..	..	..	..	..	..	..
	June	..	..	..	..	..	..	..
	July (14)	12,454	7,870	2,039	22,363	..	..	..
	Aug	16,308	11,154	..	27,462	3.5	5.5	4.0
	Sept	18,752	17,836	1,915	38,503	4.0	9.5	6.0
	Oct	25,092	27,264	2,363	54,719	5.5	14.5	8.0
	Nov	27,902	29,339	2,539	59,780	6.0	16.0	8.5
	Dec	30,098	31,197	2,318	63,613	6.0	17.5	9.0
	Ave	18,422	16,306	2,266	36,994	..	..	..
1946	Jan	34,242	31,405	2,533	68,180	7.0	17.5	10.0
	Feb	36,533	30,709	2,582	69,824	7.0	17.5	10.0
	Mar	38,109	29,125	2,410	69,644	7.5	17.0	10.0
	Apr	39,107	27,487	2,239	68,833	7.5	16.5	9.5
	May	40,414	24,402	2,085	66,901	7.5	15.0	9.0
	June	42,123	21,844	2,349	66,316	7.5	13.5	9.0
	July	39,804	19,445	1,827	61,076	7.0	12.5	8.5
	Aug	40,563	17,688	1,874	60,125	7.5	11.5	8.0
	Sept	39,712	16,058	1,921	57,691	7.0	10.5	8.0
	Oct	38,187	15,951	2,218	56,356	7.0	10.0	8.0
	Nov	36,135	15,781	2,113	54,029	7.0	9.5	7.5
	Dec	36,326	14,898	1,942	53,166	7.0	9.0	7.5
	Ave	38,438	22,066	2,174	62,678	7.2	13.3	8.8

LABOUR 5. Unemployment. Number and Percentage, by sex, each month 1923-75. Wales

Date		Number unemployed				Percent unemployed		
		Men	Women	Juveniles	Total	Men	Women	Total
1947	Jan	37,305	14,114	2,140	53,559	7.0	8.5	7.5
	Feb (15)	60,578	17,906	3,706	82,190	11.5	11.0	11.5
	Mar (15)	64,143	18,067	3,746	85,956	12.0	11.0	12.0
	Apr	37,997	15,203	1,895	55,095	7.0	9.0	7.5
	May	32,288	14,385	1,638	48,311	6.0	8.5	6.5
	June	29,438	13,435	1,303	44,176	5.5	8.0	6.0
	July	27,464	12,864	1,037	41,365	5.0	7.5	5.5
	Aug	26,631	12,088	1,034	39,753	5.0	7.0	5.5
	Sept	24,671	11,285	1,102	37,058	4.5	6.5	5.0
	Oct	25,160	11,471	1,236	37,867	4.5	7.5	5.5
	Nov	26,295	11,934	1,182	39,411	5.0	7.5	5.5
	Dec	27,045	11,041	995	39,081	5.0	7.0	5.5
	Ave	34,918	13,649	1,751	50,319	6.0	8.0	6.9
1948	Jan (16)	29,638	10,723	1,262	41,623	5.5	7.0	5.5
	Feb	29,904	10,826	1,084	41,814	5.5	7.0	5.5
	Mar	28,343	10,954	988	40,285	5.0	7.0	5.5
	Apr	29,084	11,002	1,070	41,156	5.0	7.0	5.5
	May	28,873	11,001	978	40,852	5.0	7.0	5.5
	June	27,807	10,454	898	39,159	5.0	6.5	5.5
	July	27,799	11,020	1,144	39,963	4.1	5.0	4.3
	Aug	28,054	10,618	2,049	40,721	4.2	5.0	4.4
	Sept	27,674	9,393	1,750	38,817	4.1	4.4	4.2
	Oct	27,711	10,183	1,753	39,647	4.1	4.8	4.3
	Nov	28,111	10,250	1,498	39,859	4.1	4.8	4.3
	Dec	27,834	10,010	1,278	39,122	4.1	4.6	4.2
	Ave	28,403	10,536	1,313	40,252	4.6	5.8	4.9

LABOUR 5. Unemployment. Number and Percentage, by sex, each month 1923-75. Wales

Date		Number unemployed				Percent unemployed		
		Men	Women	Juveniles	Total	Men	Women	Total
1949	Jan	29,589	10,358	2,290	42,237	4.4	5.0	4.6
	Feb	27,807	10,504	1,908	40,219	4.2	5.0	4.4
	Mar	26,729	10,194	1,556	38,479	4.0	4.8	4.2
	Apr	25,917	9,508	1,740	37,165	3.9	4.5	4.0
	May	24,820	9,060	1,694	35,574	3.7	4.3	3.9
	June	23,867	8,014	1,223	33,104	3.5	3.7	3.6
	July	23,619	7,375	1,078	32,072	3.5	3.3	3.5
	Aug	23,744	7,706	1,992	33,442	3.6	3.7	3.6
	Sept	23,919	7,617	1,854	33,390	3.6	3.6	3.6
	Oct	25,329	8,970	1,924	36,223	3.8	4.2	3.9
	Nov	26,758	9,664	1,590	38,012	4.0	4.4	4.1
	Dec	26,379	9,465	1,457	37,301	3.9	4.3	4.0
	Ave	25,706	9,036	1,692	36,434	3.8	4.2	3.9
1950	Jan	27,124	10,115	2,622	39,861	4.1	4.8	4.2
	Feb	27,407	9,918	2,140	39,465	4.1	4.7	4.2
	Mar	25,330	9,489	1,672	36,491	3.7	4.4	3.9
	Apr	24,403	8,938	2,395	35,736	3.7	4.3	3.8
	May	23,388	9,350	1,843	34,581	3.5	4.4	3.7
	June	22,160	8,724	1,498	32,382	3.3	4.0	3.4
	July	21,684	8,439	1,453	31,576	3.2	3.9	3.4
	Aug	22,241	8,765	2,779	33,785	3.4	4.3	3.6
	Sept	21,132	8,341	2,583	32,056	3.2	4.0	3.4
	Oct	21,709	9,301	1,922	32,932	3.2	4.3	3.5
	Nov	21,518	9,543	1,479	32,540	3.1	4.2	3.4
	Dec	20,735	9,088	1,327	31,150	3.0	4.0	3.3
	Ave	23,236	9,168	1,976	34,380	3.5	4.3	3.7

LABOUR 5. Unemployment. Number and Percentage, by sex, each month 1923-75. Wales

Date		Number unemployed				Percent unemployed		
		Men	Women	Juveniles	Total	Men	Women	Total
1951	Jan	21,515	9,451	2,354	33,320	3.3	4.4	3.6
	Feb	19,285	8,872	1,507	29,664	2.9	4.0	3.2
	Mar	18,278	8,458	1,189	27,925	2.7	3.8	3.0
	Apr	16,605	7,830	1,255	25,690	2.5	3.5	2.8
	May	15,120	6,723	896	22,739	2.3	3.0	2.4
	June	13,706	6,238	711	20,655	2.0	2.7	2.2
	July	13,430	5,946	1,198	20,574	2.0	2.7	2.2
	Aug	13,874	5,883	1,877	21,634	2.1	2.8	2.3
	Sept	14,123	6,508	1,689	22,320	2.1	3.0	2.4
	Oct	15,051	7,922	1,770	24,743	2.3	3.7	2.6
	Nov	15,219	8,462	1,654	25,335	2.3	3.8	2.7
	Dec	15,422	8,439	1,526	25,387	2.3	3.8	2.7
	Ave	15,969	7,561	1,469	24,999	2.4	3.4	2.7
1952	Jan	17,429	9,981	2,889	30,269	2.7	4.9	3.3
	Feb	16,923	9,503	2,259	28,685	2.6	4.6	3.1
	Mar	16,190	9,547	1,787	27,524	2.5	4.4	3.0
	Apr	16,325	9,314	2,376	28,015	2.5	4.5	3.0
	May	15,350	9,103	1,724	26,177	2.3	4.2	2.8
	June	14,744	8,365	1,296	24,405	2.2	3.8	2.6
	July	14,477	7,463	1,589	23,529	2.2	3.5	2.6
	Aug	14,843	7,422	2,527	24,792	2.3	3.7	2.7
	Sept	14,951	7,722	2,288	24,961	2.3	3.8	2.7
	Oct	16,012	9,002	1,970	26,984	2.5	4.2	2.9
	Nov	16,704	8,981	1,596	27,281	2.5	4.1	3.0
	Dec	17,554	8,333	1,306	27,193	2.7	3.8	3.0
	Ave	15,959	8,726	1,967	26,651	2.4	4.1	2.9

LABOUR 5. Unemployment. Number and Percentage, by sex, each month 1923-75. Wales

Date		Number unemployed				Percent unemployed		
		Men	Women	Juveniles	Total	Men	Women	Total
1953	Jan	20,900	9,186	2,506	32,592	3.3	4.4	3.6
	Feb	21,837	9,702	1,962	33,501	3.4	4.4	3.7
	Mar	20,471	9,290	1,631	31,392	3.1	4.2	3.4
	Apr	21,466	8,648	1,938	32,052	3.3	4.0	3.5
	May	18,950	8,406	1,362	28,718	2.9	3.8	3.1
	June	17,620	6,965	1,097	25,682	2.7	3.1	2.8
	July	15,635	6,367	1,328	23,330	2.4	2.9	2.5
	Aug	16,442	6,480	2,658	25,580	2.6	3.2	2.8
	Sept	15,772	7,116	1,965	24,853	2.5	3.3	2.7
	Oct	16,103	7,711	1,586	25,400	2.5	3.4	2.7
	Nov	15,791	8,065	1,353	25,209	2.4	3.5	2.7
	Dec	16,021	7,942	1,168	25,131	2.5	3.4	2.7
	Ave	18,084	7,990	1,713	27,787	2.8	3.6	3.0
1954	Jan	17,435	8,812	2,703	28,950	2.7	4.1	3.1
	Feb	18,728	8,823	1,921	29,472	2.9	4.0	3.2
	Mar	15,733	8,604	1,654	25,991	2.4	3.9	2.8
	Apr	15,700	8,558	2,184	26,442	2.4	3.9	2.8
	May	14,080	7,353	1,450	22,883	2.2	3.3	2.5
	June	12,624	5,988	970	19,582	1.9	2.6	2.1
	July	12,367	5,693	1,180	19,240	1.9	2.5	2.1
	Aug	12,117	5,534	2,202	19,853	1.9	2.6	2.1
	Sept	11,715	6,126	1,703	19,544	1.8	2.8	2.1
	Oct	12,291	6,885	1,263	20,439	1.9	3.0	2.2
	Nov	12,750	7,227	1,153	21,130	1.9	3.1	2.3
	Dec	12,711	7,138	1,089	20,938	1.9	3.1	2.2
	Ave	14,021	7,228	1,623	22,789	2.2	3.2	2.5

LABOUR 5. Unemployment. Number and Percentage, by sex, each month 1923-75. Wales

Date		Number unemployed				Percent unemployed		
		Men	Women	Juveniles	Total	Men	Women	Total
1955	Jan	14,354	7,604	2,197	24,155	2.2	3.5	2.6
	Feb	12,553	7,509	1,524	21,586	1.9	3.3	2.3
	Mar	12,037	6,802	1,203	20,042	1.8	2.9	2.1
	Apr	10,582	6,032	1,559	18,173	1.7	2.7	1.9
	May	9,344	5,633	914	15,891	1.4	2.4	1.7
	June	9,093	5,032	817	14,942	1.4	2.1	1.6
	July	8,248	4,414	726	13,388	1.3	1.9	1.4
	Aug	8,746	4,443	1,575	14,764	1.4	2.0	1.6
	Sept	8,978	4,694	1,383	15,055	1.4	2.1	1.6
	Oct	9,912	5,433	1,037	16,382	1.5	2.3	1.7
	Nov	..	..	..	..	1.6	2.3	1.8
	Dec	10,457	5,371	763	16,591	1.6	2.2	1.7
	Ave	10,391	5,724	1,245	17,361	1.6	2.5	1.8
1956	Jan	11,483	5,804	1,471	18,758	1.8	2.4	1.9
	Feb	11,791	6,082	1,171	19,044	1.8	2.5	2.0
	Mar	11,936	6,079	1,121	19,136	1.8	2.5	2.0
	Apr	11,599	5,948	1,326	18,873	1.8	2.5	2.0
	May	11,286	5,676	1,015	17,977	1.7	2.4	1.9
	June	11,976	4,999	825	17,800	1.8	2.1	1.9
	July	12,073	5,631	1,586	19,290	1.9	2.5	2.0
	Aug	12,102	5,820	2,004	19,926	1.9	2.6	2.1
	Sept	11,696	5,974	1,682	19,352	1.8	2.6	2.0
	Oct	12,724	6,596	1,358	20,678	1.9	2.8	2.2
	Nov	13,162	7,032	1,210	21,404	2.3	2.5	2.3
	Dec	13,744	6,820	1,111	21,675	2.1	2.8	2.3
	Ave	12,131	6,038	1,323	19,493	1.9	2.5	2.1

LABOUR 5. Unemployment. Number and Percentage, by sex, each month 1923-75. Wales

Date		Number unemployed				Percent unemployed		
		Men	Women	Juveniles	Total	Men	Women	Total
1957	Jan	17,062	7,910	2,350	27,322	2.6	3.4	2.9
	Feb	18,335	8,133	1,933	28,401	2.8	3.5	3.0
	Mar	17,873	7,950	1,601	27,424	2.7	3.3	2.9
	Apr	17,142	7,269	1,777	26,188	2.6	3.1	2.7
	May	15,293	7,179	1,450	23,922	2.3	3.0	2.5
	June	13,217	6,188	1,021	20,426	2.0	2.5	2.1
	July	13,043	5,804	1,229	20,076	2.0	2.4	2.1
	Aug	13,903	5,797	2,253	21,953	2.2	2.5	2.3
	Sept	13,990	6,224	1,771	21,985	2.2	2.6	2.3
	Oct	15,249	6,929	1,454	23,632	2.3	2.8	2.5
	Nov	18,791	7,842	1,507	28,140	2.8	3.2	2.9
	Dec	19,126	7,890	1,405	28,421	2.9	3.2	3.0
	Ave	16,085	7,093	1,646	24,824	2.5	3.0	2.6
1958	Jan	22,176	8,653	2,971	33,800	3.4	3.8	3.5
	Feb	24,741	9,012	2,600	36,353	3.8	3.9	3.8
	Mar	23,462	9,178	2,175	34,815	3.6	3.9	3.7
	Apr	24,647	8,968	3,200	36,815	3.8	4.0	3.9
	May	24,893	9,272	2,738	36,903	3.8	4.1	3.9
	June	24,450	8,438	2,056	34,944	3.7	3.6	3.7
	July	23,039	8,223	2,616	33,878	3.5	3.6	3.6
	Aug	22,652	8,022	4,146	34,820	3.6	3.8	3.7
	Sept	22,854	8,623	3,950	35,427	3.6	4.0	3.7
	Oct	25,644	9,902	3,396	38,942	4.0	4.4	4.1
	Nov	26,034	10,373	2,850	39,257	4.0	4.4	4.1
	Dec	25,952	10,774	2,737	39,643	4.0	4.5	4.1
	Ave	24,212	9,120	2,953	36,300	3.7	4.0	3.8

LABOUR 5. Unemployment. Number and Percentage, by sex, each month 1923-75. Wales

Date	Number unemployed				Percent unemployed		
	Men	Women	Juveniles	Total	Men	Women	Total
1959 Jan	28,040	11,001	4,815	43,856	4.4	4.9	4.6
Feb	29,564	11,316	4,328	45,208	4.6	5.0	4.7
Mar	28,892	11,342	3,619	43,853	4.5	5.0	4.6
Apr	27,276	10,473	3,970	41,719	4.3	4.6	4.4
May	24,434	9,944	3,046	37,424	3.8	4.3	4.0
June	21,931	8,440	1,996	32,367	3.4	3.5	3.4
July	21,385	7,912	2,067	31,364	3.3	3.4	3.3
Aug	20,100	7,612	4,421	32,133	3.3	3.5	3.4
Sept	19,396	8,082	3,455	30,933	3.1	3.6	3.2
Oct	21,316	8,593	2,688	32,597	3.3	3.6	3.4
Nov	21,743	8,629	2,138	32,510	3.3	3.5	3.4
Dec	20,731	8,657	1,865	31,253	3.1	3.5	3.3
Ave	23,734	9,333	3,201	36,268	3.7	4.0	3.8
1960 Jan	21,290	8,876	3,411	33,577	3.4	3.9	3.5
Feb	20,486	9,095	2,483	32,064	3.2	3.7	3.3
Mar	18,256	8,700	1,812	28,768	2.8	3.5	3.0
Apr	17,390	8,064	2,247	27,701	2.7	3.3	2.9
May	15,164	7,355	1,547	24,065	2.3	2.9	2.5
June	14,253	6,342	1,058	21,653	2.2	2.4	2.3
July	14,031	5,703	958	20,692	2.1	2.2	2.1
Aug	14,964	5,907	3,172	24,043	2.4	2.6	2.5
Sept	15,050	6,051	2,331	23,432	2.4	2.5	2.4
Oct	15,202	6,509	1,721	23,432	2.3	2.6	2.4
Nov	16,436	7,368	1,437	25,241	2.5	2.9	2.6
Dec	18,010	7,472	1,501	26,983	2.7	2.9	2.8
Ave	16,711	7,287	1,973	25,971	2.6	3.2	2.7

LABOUR 5. Unemployment. Number and Percentage, by sex, each month 1923-75. Wales

Date	Number unemployed				Percent unemployed		
	Men	Women	Juveniles	Total	Men	Women	Total
1961 Jan	19,483	8,147	2,708	30,338	3.0	3.4	3.1
Feb	17,793	7,880	2,002	27,765	2.7	3.2	2.9
Mar	15,860	7,665	1,540	25,065	2.4	3.1	2.6
Apr	15,212	7,023	1,884	24,119	2.4	2.9	2.5
May	14,258	6,116	1,251	21,625	2.2	2.4	2.2
June	13,922	5,171	930	20,023	2.1	2.0	2.1
July	13,335	4,586	840	18,761	2.0	1.8	1.9
Aug	13,099	4,644	2,927	20,670	2.2	2.1	2.1
Sept	14,653	4,824	2,339	21,816	2.3	2.0	2.2
Oct	26,555	5,910	2,099	34,564	4.0	2.4	3.5
Nov	18,938	6,319	1,855	27,112	2.9	2.5	2.8
Dec	18,886	6,488	1,686	27,060	2.9	2.6	2.8
Ave	16,833	6,231	1,838	24,910	2.6	2.5	2.6
1962 Jan	22,106	6,842	3,174	32,122	3.5	2.9	3.3
Feb	21,484	7,243	2,672	31,399	3.3	3.0	3.2
Mar	21,106	7,489	2,245	30,840	3.2	3.0	3.2
Apr	20,042	6,891	1,950	28,883	3.1	2.8	3.0
May	18,923	6,355	2,489	27,767	2.9	2.7	2.9
June	17,671	5,792	1,939	25,402	2.7	2.4	2.6
July	17,973	5,862	2,701	26,536	2.8	2.5	2.7
Aug	19,090	5,971	4,894	29,955	3.2	2.9	3.1
Sept	20,146	6,310	4,459	30,915	3.3	2.9	3.2
Oct	21,927	7,327	3,657	32,911	3.5	3.2	3.4
Nov	24,209	7,753	3,250	35,212	3.8	3.3	3.6
Dec	25,783	7,769	3,038	36,590	4.0	3.3	3.8
Ave	20,872	6,800	3,039	30,711	3.3	2.9	3.2

LABOUR 5. Unemployment. Number and Percentage, by sex, each month 1923-75. Wales

Date	Number unemployed				Percent unemployed		
	Men	Women	Juveniles	Total	Men	Women	Total
1963 Jan	40,832	8,284	5,748	54,864	6.4	3.9	5.7
Feb	44,279	8,527	5,741	58,547	7.0	3.8	6.0
Mar	31,159	8,328	4,257	43,744	4.9	3.6	4.5
Apr	26,076	7,974	3,886	37,936	4.1	3.4	3.9
May	23,189	7,945	3,821	34,955	3.7	3.4	3.6
June	19,828	6,525	2,658	29,011	3.1	2.7	3.0
July	18,243	6,004	3,277	27,524	2.9	2.6	2.8
Aug	18,124	5,931	5,349	29,404	3.1	2.9	3.0
Sept	18,403	5,941	4,646	28,990	3.0	2.8	3.0
Oct	19,130	6,548	3,283	28,961	3.0	2.8	3.0
Nov	19,671	6,802	2,687	29,160	3.1	2.8	3.0
Dec	19,663	6,674	2,357	28,694	3.1	2.7	2.9
Ave	24,883	7,124	3,976	35,983	4.0	3.1	3.7
1964 Jan	31,011	6,875	2,699	40,585	4.7	2.8	4.1
Feb	19,677	6,691	2,164	28,532	3.0	2.7	2.9
Mar	17,338	6,182	1,765	25,285	2.6	2.4	2.6
Apr	16,820	5,956	2,521	25,297	2.6	2.4	2.6
May	15,250	5,640	1,776	22,666	2.4	2.2	2.3
June	13,940	4,996	1,362	20,298	2.1	1.9	2.1
July	13,554	4,913	2,517	20,984	2.2	2.1	2.1
Aug	14,430	5,039	4,745	24,214	2.5	2.4	2.5
Sept	14,655	5,234	3,632	23,521	2.4	2.4	2.4
Oct	16,699	5,747	2,828	25,274	2.6	2.4	2.6
Nov	17,473	6,074	2,315	25,862	2.7	2.5	2.6
Dec	17,826	6,084	2,178	26,088	2.7	2.4	2.7
Ave	17,389	5,786	2,542	25,717	2.7	2.4	2.6

LABOUR 5. Unemployment. Number and Percentage, by sex, each month 1923-75. Wales

Date	Number unemployed				Percent unemployed		
	Men	Women	Juveniles	Total	Men	Women	Total
1965 Jan	19,279	6,228	2,491	27,998	3.0	2.4	2.8
Feb	18,930	6,452	2,227	27,609	2.9	2.5	2.8
Mar	18,953	6,307	1,887	27,147	2.9	2.4	2.7
Apr	16,882	5,970	2,264	25,116	2.6	2.3	2.5
May	15,952	5,713	1,860	23,525	2.5	2.2	2.4
June	15,197	4,928	1,376	21,501	2.3	1.8	2.2
July	15,358	4,879	2,458	22,695	2.4	2.0	2.3
Aug	16,461	5,151	4,480	26,092	2.8	2.3	2.6
Sept	17,024	5,347	3,428	25,799	2.8	2.3	2.6
Oct	18,302	5,760	2,761	26,823	2.9	2.3	2.7
Nov	19,449	6,039	2,254	27,742	3.0	2.3	2.8
Dec	20,215	6,110	2,088	28,413	3.1	2.3	2.9
Ave	17,667	5,740	2,465	25,872	2.8	2.3	2.6
1966 Jan	22,074	6,025	2,305	30,404	3.4	2.2	3.0
Feb	21,664	5,812	1,961	29,437	3.3	2.1	2.9
Mar	20,677	5,391	1,724	27,792	3.2	1.9	2.8
Apr	20,008	5,228	2,327	27,563	3.1	1.9	2.7
May	17,239	4,901	1,639	23,779	2.7	1.8	2.4
June	15,776	4,601	1,324	21,701	2.4	1.6	2.2
July	15,766	4,567	2,087	22,420	2.5	1.7	2.2
Aug	16,930	4,923	4,654	26,507	2.9	2.1	2.6
Sept	18,974	5,299	4,118	28,391	3.1	2.2	2.8
Oct	24,811	6,903	3,762	35,476	3.9	2.7	3.5
Nov	27,736	8,102	3,524	39,362	4.3	3.0	3.9
Dec	27,988	8,054	3,420	39,462	4.4	3.0	3.9
Ave	20,804	5,817	2,737	29,358	3.3	2.2	2.9

LABOUR 5. Unemployment. Number and Percentage, by sex, each month 1923-75. Wales

Date		Number unemployed				Percent unemployed		
		Men	Women	Juveniles	Total	Men	Women	Total
1967	Jan	31,030	8,024	3,655	42,709	4.9	3.0	4.2
	Feb	30,752	8,392	3,411	42,555	4.8	3.1	4.2
	Mar	29,599	8,050	3,064	40,713	4.6	2.9	4.0
	Apr	29,292	7,964	3,948	41,204	4.6	3.0	4.1
	May	27,945	7,524	3,074	38,543	4.3	2.7	3.8
	June	26,604	6,998	2,557	36,159	4.1	2.5	3.6
	July	62,563	6,967	3,319	36,849	4.2	2.6	3.7
	Aug	27,387	7,145	6,675	41,207	4.6	3.1	4.1
	Sept	27,629	7,040	5,231	39,900	4.5	2.9	4.0
	Oct	28,641	7,366	3,826	39,833	4.5	2.8	4.0
	Nov	30,986	7,481	3,280	41,747	4.8	2.8	4.1
	Dec	31,296	7,632	2,994	41,922	4.8	2.7	4.2
	Ave	31,977	7,549	3,753	40,591	4.6	2.8	4.0
1968	Jan	32,405	7,628	3,193	43,226	5.0	2.8	4.3
	Feb	31,381	7,410	2,813	41,604	4.9	2.7	4.2
	Mar	30,626	7,134	2,321	40,081	4.8	2.6	4.1
	Apr	30,557	6,950	2,331	39,838	4.8	2.5	4.0
	May	28,915	6,463	2,296	37,674	4.5	2.3	3.8
	June	27,946	5,682	1,929	35,557	4.4	2.0	3.6
	July	28,167	5,603	2,125	35,895	4.4	2.0	3.6
	Aug	28,434	5,896	5,538	39,868	4.8	2.5	4.0
	Sept	29,076	5,698	4,420	39,194	4.8	2.3	4.0
	Oct	29,941	5,986	2,945	38,872	4.7	2.3	3.9
	Nov	30,411	6,176	2,497	39,084	4.8	2.3	4.0
	Dec	31,082	6,459	2,245	39,786	4.9	2.3	4.0
	Ave	29,912	6,429	2,888	39,223	4.7	2.4	4.0

LABOUR 5. Unemployment. Number and Percentage, by sex, each month 1923-75. Wales

Date		Number unemployed				Percent unemployed		
		Men	Women	Juveniles	Total	Men	Women	Total
1969	Jan	32,863	6,229	2,520	41,612	5.1	2.3	4.2
	Feb	33,092	6,089	2,307	41,488	5.2	2.2	4.2
	Mar	32,661	5,934	2,165	40,760	5.2	2.1	4.1
	Apr	31,273	5,710	2,562	39,545	5.0	2.1	4.0
	May	29,615	5,396	2,211	37,222	4.7	1.9	3.8
	June	28,262	4,826	1,757	34,845	4.4	1.7	3.5
	July	28,495	5,311	2,813	36,619	4.6	2.0	3.7
	Aug	35,547	5,925	5,480	46,952	5.9	2.5	4.8
	Sept	31,756	5,875	4,326	41,957	5.2	2.3	4.2
	Oct	31,054	6,158	3,166	40,378	5.0	2.3	4.1
	Nov	31,366	6,242	2,641	40,249	5.0	2.2	4.1
	Dec	31,980	6,113	2,420	40,513	5.1	2.2	4.1
	Ave	31,497	5,817	2,864	40,178	5.0	2.2	4.1
1970	Jan	33,427	6,071	2,562	42,060	5.3	2.2	4.3
	Feb	32,759	5,940	2,507	41,206	5.2	2.1	4.2
	Mar	31,822	5,804	2,329	39,955	5.1	2.1	4.1
	Apr	31,316	5,757	2,788	39,861	5.1	2.1	4.1
	May	29,113	5,579	2,261	36,953	4.7	2.0	3.8
	June	26,619	4,597	1,809	33,025	4.2	1.6	3.4
	July	27,602	4,931	2,325	34,858	4.5	1.8	3.6
	Aug	27,662	5,313	4,877	37,852	4.7	2.2	3.9
	Sept	30,622	5,618	3,878	40,118	5.1	2.2	4.1
	Oct	30,552	5,721	2,941	39,214	5.0	2.1	4.0
	Nov	29,272	5,752	2,870	37,894	4.8	2.1	3.9
	Dec	30,234	5,769	2,792	38,795	4.9	2.1	4.0
	Ave	30,083	5,571	2,828	38,483	4.9	2.1	4.0

LABOUR 5. Unemployment. Number and Percentage, by sex, each month 1923-75. Wales

Date		Number unemployed				Percent unemployed		
		Men	Women	Juveniles	Total	Men	Women	Total
1971	Jan	32,991	6,176	3,099	42,266	5.4	2.3	4.3
	Feb	33,199	6,605	3,254	43,058	5.5	2.5	4.4
	Mar	34,249	7,333	3,223	44,805	5.7	2.7	4.6
	Apr	34,640	6,972	3,174	44,786	5.7	2.5	4.6
	May	33,907	6,556	3,309	43,772	5.6	2.4	4.5
	June	31,962	5,783	2,676	40,421	5.3	2.1	4.2
	July	33,972	6,581	3,560	44,113	5.7	2.4	4.6
	Aug	34,479	7,121	7,008	48,608	6.1	3.0	5.0
	Sept	35,427	7,330	6,011	48,768	6.1	3.0	5.0
	Oct	35,941	7,376	4,985	48,302	6.1	2.9	5.0
	Nov	38,046	7,761	4,399	50,206	6.4	2.9	5.2
	Dec	39,448	7,700	3,857	51,035	6.6	2.8	5.3
	Ave	34,855	6,941	4,049	45,845	5.9	2.6	4.7
1972	Jan	43,878	8,100	4,238	56,216	7.3	3.0	5.8
	Feb	58,402	14,195	4,379	76,976	9.6	4.8	7.9
	Mar	43,181	7,872	3,960	55,013	7.1	2.9	5.7
	Apr	42,722	8,275	4,417	55,414	7.1	3.0	5.7
	May	37,637	6,979	3,612	48,228	6.2	2.6	5.0
	June	34,920	6,058	3,004	43,982	5.8	2.2	4.5
	July	40,191	7,442	3,763	51,396	6.7	2.7	5.3
	Aug	36,615	7,827	7,367	51,809	6.4	3.2	5.3
	Sept	37,952	7,900	6,380	52,232	6.6	3.2	5.4
	Oct	35,578	7,195	4,841	47,614	6.0	2.8	4.9
	Nov	35,307	7,109	3,841	46,257	5.9	2.6	4.8
	Dec	35,085	6,887	3,471	45,443	5.8	2.5	4.7
	Ave	40,122	7,987	4,439	52,548	6.7	3.0	5.4

LABOUR 5. Unemployment. Number and Percentage, by sex, each month 1923-75. Wales

Date		Number unemployed				Percent unemployed		
		Men	Women	Juveniles	Total	Men	Women	Total
1973	Jan	36,782	7,531	3,571	47,884	6.1	2.7	4.9
	Feb	32,806	6,388	2,959	42,153	5.4	2.3	4.3
	Mar	31,369	6,290	2,556	40,215	5.1	2.3	4.1
	Apr	32,596	7,608	2,229	42,433	5.3	2.6	4.4
	May	27,940	4,950	1,828	34,718	4.5	1.7	3.6
	June	25,888	4,541	1,527	31,956	4.2	1.6	3.3
	July	26,398	5,155	1,713	33,266	4.3	1.8	3.4
	Aug	26,332	5,380	3,253	34,965	4.4	2.0	3.6
	Sept	26,075	5,501	2,377	33,953	4.3	2.0	3.5
	Oct	25,363	5,049	1,631	32,043	4.1	1.7	3.3
	Nov	25,299	5,073	1,262	31,634	3.9	1.6	3.1
	Dec	25,841	5,009	1,163	32,013	4.0	1.6	3.2
	Ave	28,557	5,706	2,172	36,436	4.6	2.0	3.7
1974	Jan	31,454	5,799	1,748	39,001	4.9	1.9	3.8
	Feb	31,173	5,577	1,674	38,424	4.8	1.8	3.8
	Mar	31,893	5,422	1,642	38,957	4.9	1.8	3.8
	Apr(17)	35,288	8,874	..	44,162	5.3	2.5	4.3
	May	29,492	5,788	..	35,280	4.4	1.7	3.5
	June	..	..	..	..	..	..	3.2
	July	29,844	6,514	..	36,358	4.5	1.8	3.5
	Aug	35,142	9,643	..	44,785	5.8	2.1	4.3
	Sept	34,785	9,671	..	44,456	5.2	2.6	4.3
	Oct	32,525	7,872	..	40,397	4.9	2.1	3.9
	Nov	32,326	7,774	..	40,100	4.9	2.1	3.9
	Dec(18)	..	..	..	..	..	..	..
	Ave	32,392	7,293	..	40,192	..	..	..

LABOUR 5. Unemployment. Number and Percentage, by sex, each month 1923-75. Wales

Date	Number unemployed				Percent unemployed		
	Men	Women	Juveniles	Total	Men	Women	Total
1975 Jan[18]	..	..	..	48,000	..	..	..
Feb	38,913	8,658	..	47,571	..	..	..
Mar	38,952	8,982	..	47,934	..	..	..
Apr	46,154	13,400	..	59,554	..	..	..
May	41,649	9,695	..	51,344	..	..	..
June	41,460	9,357	..	50,817	..	..	..
July	49,789	15,216	..	65,005	..	..	..
Aug	56,713	19,599	..	76,312	8.8	5.2	7.4
Sept	..	..	..	..	..	..	..
Oct	54,553	15,894	..	70,447	8.4	4.2	6.9
Nov	55,031	15,709	..	70,740	8.5	4.2	6.9
Dec	57,609	15,979	..	73,588	8.9	4.2	7.2
Ave	48,082	13,249	..	60,119	..	..	..

General Notes

(i) Sources. British Labour Statistics, Historical Abstracts, 1886-1968; Min. of Labour Gazette, 1924-68 (later, 1968-70, Employment and Productivity Gazette, and then, 1971- , Dept. of Employment Gazette); British Labour Statistics Year Book, 1969- ; 22nd Abstract of Labour Statistics

(ii) The annual averages (both of numbers and percentages) have been obtained from the monthly figures. The average percentages sometimes differ slightly (not usually more than 0.1) from the yearly rates given in some of the sources, because of rounding.

(iii) For 1923-48 the figures derive from counts of unemployed persons, on the registers of Employment Exchanges, Branch Employment Offices and Juvenile or Youth Employment Bureaux. They include, in addition to those wholly unemployed, persons temporalily suspended. They exclude unemployed persons insured under the special schemes for insurance and banking for whom no regional estimates are available and also those who ceased to maintain registration within the two months previous to the date of the count but were not known to have found work. The number of the latter (known as the Two Months File) amounted on average to five per cent of the UK unemployed register.

Notes

1. The figures in May 1926 and subsequent months exclude persons in the coalmining industry who were absent from work because of the dispute which started on 1st May.

2. In January 1928 persons aged 65 and over ceased to be insured under the Unemployment Insurance Acts. This resulted in a reduction of the UK unemployed register by about 25,000 persons.

3. Relaxation of conditions for the receipt of unemployment benefit caused the UK unemployed register to increase by an estimated 40,000 persons in April 1928.

4. The institution of the system of franking the Health Insurance Cards of persons registered as unemployed increased the unemployed register in July 1928 by 25,000 for the UK.

5. The removal of restrictions on the allowance of unemployment benefit resulted in an increase on the UK unemployed register in March 1930 of about 60,000 persons.

6. Between October 1931 and May 1932 restrictions were placed on the receipt of unemployment benefit and transitional payments (principally the Anomalies Regulations and the Transitional Payments Scheme), and alterations were made in the method of reckoning the number of unemployed. The effects began to be felt in October 1931 and it is estimated that, by May 1932, the total reduction for the UK in the number of unemployed persons on the registers, as a result of the changes, amounted to between 180,000 and 190,000. No estimates for later dates have been made.

7. In September 1934 boys and girls aged 14 and 15 became insurable for the first time.

8. The introduction of the Unemployment Assistance Scheme in January 1935 caused the UK unemployed register to be increased by about 20,000 persons.

9. The extension of unemployment insurance payments to agriculture, horticulture etc. in November 1936 and to private gardeners in February 1937 led such workers, who might not otherwise have done so, to register as unemployed. No precise estimates of numbers was possible.

10. Institutional and outdoor domestic workers were included in the scheme in April 1938. No precise estimate of numbers is possible, but it would be small.

11. After the registration of women for war work in September 1939, an estimated additional 50,000 (uninsured) women registered for employment in the UK.

12. Non-manual workers with an annual remuneration of between £250 and £420 became insurable in September 1940.

13. From March 1942 onwards men classified as unsuitable for ordinary industrial employment and women unsuitable for normal full-time employment were excluded from the regional unemployment analysies in GB. An estimate of the total for February for Wales on the new basis is 13,300.

14. The compilation of unemployment statistics on a monthly basis was resumed from October 1945, but from that time no regional breakdown was given for unemployed persons who were uninsured. An estimate of the total for July on this new basis is 21,300.

15. Some of the workpeople who were stood off from employment because of the fuel crisis of 1947 continued to receive wages under guaranteed week and other arrangements and did not register as unemployed. The numbers for Wales were estimated at 4,500 for February and 300 for March.

16. To the end of 1947 the figures exclude persons classified by Interviewing panels as unsuitable for ordinary employment. The panel system ended in January 1948 and from then on the figures include all insured persons on the register except disabled persons who required employment under sheltered conditions. For January 1948 the addition to the total figures for Wales because of this statistical change was about 1,500.

17. From April 1974 no separate figures are given for juveniles who are included in the figures for males and females.

18. The count of numbers unemployed did not take place in December 1974 or January 1975 because of industrial action. An estimate of the total was made for January.

Labour 6 Unemployment Vacancies Unfilled by Sex, Wales, 1949 - 1974

Date		Males 18+	Females 18+	Juveniles	Total
1949	Jan	5,042	3 306	2,739	11,087
	July	5,276	3,143	2,989	11,408
1950	Jan	4,213	1,636	1,680	7,529
	July	5,208	2,198	2,451	9,857
1951	Jan	6,363	1,689	1,915	9,967
	July	8,055	2,459	3,604	14,118
1952	Jan	6,235	963	1,818	9,016
	July	6,177	2,171	2,754	11,102
1953	Jan	4,983	1,207	1,664	7,854
	July	4,685	2,072	2,606	9,363
1954	Jan	4,575	1,177	1,179	6,931
	July(1)	5,955	2,236	2,272	10,463
1955	Jan	6,323	1,490	1,672	9,485
	July(1)	7,995	2,781	3,072	13,848
1956	Jan	7,584	1,595	2,256	11,435
	July(1)	7,678	3,002	3,107	13,787
1957	Jan	5,905	1,131	1,363	8 399
	July	6,081	2,318	2 635	11,034
1958	Jan	5,181	981	1 122	7,284
	July	4,501	1,557	1,679	7,737
1959	Jan	4,406	891	836	6,133
	July	5,549	1,959	2,429	9,937
1960	Jan	6,230	1,059	1,819	9,108
	July	6,590	2,836	3,930	13,356
1961	Jan	7,151	1,431	2,558	11,140
	July	9,578	2,992	4,207	16,777
1962	Jan	7,543	1,274	1,844	10,661
	July	4,542	2,278	2,739	9,559
1963	Jan	2,555	1,327	1,099	4,981
	July	3,319	2,234	2,835	8,388
1964	Jan	4,002	2,317	2,103	8,422
	July	5,203	3,021	3,823	12,047
1965	Jan	4,519	1,954	2,016	8,489
	July	6,660	3,737	4,150	14,547
1966	Jan	4,909	3,508	2,120	10,537
	July	6,589	3,912	3,740	14,241
1967	Jan	4,000	1,864	1,362	7,226
	July	3,945	2,009	2,498	8,452
1968	Jan	2,703	1,917	1,635	6.255
	July	2,863	3,007	3 191	9,061
1969	Jan	2,819	2,258	2,113	7.190
	July	3.407	2,999	3,013	9,419
1970	Jan	3,586	2,077	1,852	7,515
	July	4,321	2,549	2,833	9,703
1971	Jan	3,597	1,777	1,733	7,107
	July	3,080	1,905	2,075	7,060
1972	Jan	2,428	1,386	1,204	5,018
	July	3,128	2,366	1,937	7,431
1973	Jan	3,191	2,126	1,735	7,052
	July	5,712	4,027	3,715	13,454
1974	Jan	4,937	2,884	2,508	10,329
	July(2)	6,076	3,996	..	10,072

General Notes

(i) Sources. Ministry of Labour Gazette; Department of Employment Gazette.

Notes

1. For 1954, 1955 and 1956 the figures relate to 30 June, 29 June and 27 June respectively.

2. From July 1974 figures are also given for vacancies at Careers offices, but these cannot be equated with Juveniles because they include some vacancies suitable for adults.

LABOUR 7. Unemployment by age groups and duration, males and females, Wales, 1935-40; 1946-76

Year	MALES 18-24	MALES 25-44	MALES 45-64	MALES Total	FEMALES 18-24	FEMALES 25-44	FEMALES 45-64	FEMALES Total
1935 May								
Total	33,485	84,562	63,776	181,999	4,765	2,650	774	8,190
1936 May								
Total	26,836	79,527	64,712	171,315	4,838	2,824	838	8,501
1937 May								
Total	16,383	56,813	55,433	128,851	4,529	2,743	905	8,179
1938 Feb								
Less than 3 mos.	12,470	30,412	16,939	59,821	4,256	1,965	351	6,572
3 mos. - 1 year	4,730	14,145	11,777	30,652	1,402	1,001	316	2,719
Over 1 year	1,768	13,968	24,285	40,021	169	333	214	716
Total	18,968	58,425	53,001	130,494	5,827	3,299	881	10,007
1939 May								
Less than 3 mos.	7,987	21,812	13,935	43,734	2,955	1,457	410	4,822
3 mos. - 1 year	4,100	13,654	11,937	29,691	1,370	839	294	2,503
Over 1 year	1,473	11,768	23,080	36,321	194	344	244	782
Total	13,560	47,234	48,952	109,746	4,519	2,640	948	8,107
1940 March								
Total	6,106	28,641(1)	28,505(1)	63,252	..	..	..	..
	14 and under 21	21 and under 41	41 and under 65	Total	14 and under 21	21 and under 41	41 and under 65	Total
9 Dec. 1946								
8 weeks or less	1,214	6,030	4,376	11,620	1,370	3,320	1,052	5,742
Over 8 and up to 26	492	4,043	4,830	9,365	663	3,353	1,321	5,337
Over 26 weeks	232	3,827	11,507	15,566	155	2,595	1,890	4,640
Total	1,938	13,900	20,713	36,551	2,188	9,268	4,263	15,719

LABOUR 7. contd

Year	MALES 14 and under 21	MALES 21 and under 41	MALES 41 and under 65	MALES Total	FEMALES 14 and under 21	FEMALES 21 and under 41	FEMALES 41 and under 65	FEMALES Total
8 Dec. 1947								
8 weeks or less	678	4,338	4,177	9,193	1,039	2,134	855	4,028
Over 8 and up to 26	187	2,028	3,755	5,970	356	1,979	968	3,303
Over 26 weeks	65	2,051	8,805	10,921	120	2,165	1,817	4,102
Total	930	8,417	16,737	26,084	1,515	6,278	3,640	11,433
6 Dec. 1948								
8 weeks or less	936	4,326	3,833	9,095	1,163	2,475	1,213	4,851
Over 8 and up to 26	327	2,480	3,637	6,444	611	1,610	759	2,980
Over 26 weeks	93	2,317	9,424	11,834	130	1,317	1,300	2,747
Total	1,356	9,123	16,894	27,373	1,904	5,402	3,272	10,578
5 Dec. 1949								
8 weeks or less	1,296	4,350	4,288	9,934	1,427	2,555	1,236	5,218
Over 8 and up to 26	472	2,011	3,692	6,175	543	1,592	922	3,057
Over 26 weeks	101	1,771	8,208	10,080	96	717	954	1,767
Total	1,869	8,132	16,188	26,189	2,066	4,864	3,112	10,042
11 Dec. 1950								
8 weeks or less	727	2,748	3,359	6,834	1,270	2,284	1,153	4,707
Over 8 and up to 26	331	1,442	3,122	4,895	597	1,525	1,012	3,134
Over 26 weeks	106	1,314	7,509	8,929	113	713	945	1,771
Total	1,164	5,504	13,990	20,658	1,980	4,522	3,110	9,612
10 Dec. 1951(2)								
8 weeks or less	436	2,383	2,985	5,804	1,220	2,162	1,152	4,534
Over 8 and up to 26	172	908	2,199	3,279	502	1,359	900	2,761
Over 26 weeks	34	675	5,214	5,923	58	473	777	1,308
Total	642	3,966	10,398	15,006	1,780	3,994	2,829	8,603

LABOUR 7. contd

Year	MALES				FEMALES			
	14 and under 21	21 and under 41	41 and under 65	Total	14 and under 21	21 and under 41	41 and under 65	Total
8 Dec. 1952(2)								
8 weeks or less	540	2,941	2,976	6,457	1,133	2,189	1,128	4,450
Over 8 and up to 26	162	1,194	2,583	3,939	526	1,410	956	2,892
Over 26 weeks	43	752	5,082	5,877	109	578	862	1,549
Total	745	4,887	10,641	16,273	1,768	4,177	2,946	8,891
7 Dec. 1953								
8 weeks or less	468	2,789	2,839	6,096	1,044	2,136	1,222	4,402
Over 8 and up to 26	175	1,292	2,504	3,971	425	1,287	967	2,679
Over 26 weeks	57	824	4,320	5,201	73	580	808	1,461
Total	700	4,905	9,663	15,268	1,542	4,003	2,997	8,542
6 Dec. 1954								
8 weeks or less	485	2,157	2,628	5,270	921	1,901	1,029	3,851
Over 8 and up to 26	148	809	2,146	3,103	349	1,205	844	2,398
Over 26 weeks	35	596	3,514	4,145	61	524	778	1,363
Total	668	3,562	8,288	12,518	1,331	3,630	2,651	7,612
12 Dec. 1955								
8 weeks or less	374	1,836	1,988	4,198	600	1,424	883	2,907
Over 8 and up to 26	127	732	1,976	2,835	265	785	674	1,724
Over 26 weeks	31	442	2,839	3,312	30	366	582	978
Total	532	3,010	6,803	10,345	895	2,575	2,139	5,609
10 Dec. 1956								
8 weeks or less	499	2,506	2,551	5,556	894	1,686	990	3,570
Over 8 and up to 26	160	1,151	2,236	3,547	355	1,235	839	2,449
Over 26 weeks	63	716	3,253	4,032	62	547	635	1,244
Total	722	4,373	8,040	13,135	1,311	3,468	2,484	7,263

LABOUR 7. contd

Year	MALES				FEMALES			
	14 and under 21	21 and under 41	41 and under 65	Total	14 and under 21	21 and under 41	41 and under 65	Total
9 Dec. 1957								
8 weeks or less	841	3,721	3,395	7,957	1,119	1,905	1,124	4,148
Over 8 and up to 26	271	1,546	2,587	4,404	375	1,322	973	2,670
Over 26 weeks	84	1,070	3,882	5,036	61	703	836	1,600
Total	1,196	6,337	9,864	17,397	1,555	3,930	2,933	8,418
8 Dec. 1958								
8 weeks or less	1,300	3,822	3,243	8,365	1,441	2,177	1,080	4,698
Over 8 and up to 26	800	2,933	3,639	7,372	1,003	2,128	1,197	4,328
Over 26 weeks	245	2,250	6,017	8,512	223	1,333	1,224	2,780
Total	2,345	9,005	12,899	24,249	2,667	5,638	3,501	11,806
7 Dec. 1959								
8 weeks or less	1,067	3,471	2,847	7,385	1,031	1,723	1,025	3,779
Over 8 and up to 26	543	2,238	2,970	5,751	544	1,569	1,051	3,164
Over 26 weeks	192	2,010	5,551	7,753	166	1,141	1,246	2,553
Total	1,802	7,719	11,368	20,889	1,741	4,433	3,322	9,496
12 Dec. 1960(3)								
8 weeks or less	839	3,038	2,681	6,558	988	1,450	835	3,273
Over 8 and up to 26	288	1,352	2,463	4,103	365	1,143	845	2,353
Over 26 weeks	78	1,049	4,451	5,578	95	718	1,120	1,933
Total	1,205	5,439	9,595	16,239	1,448	3,311	2,800	7,559
11 Dec. 1961(4)								
8 weeks or less	1,069	3,206	2,525	6,800	1,077	1,403	798	3,278
Over 8 and up to 26	349	1,881	2,722	4,952	469	1,020	797	2,286
Over 26 weeks	72	1,074	4,258	5,404	98	513	1,008	1,619
Total	1,490	6,161	9,505	17,156	1,644	2,936	2,603	7,183

LABOUR 7. contd

Year	MALES				FEMALES			
	14 and under 21	21 and under 41	41 and under 65	Total	14 and under 21	21 and under 41	41 and under 65	Total
14 Jan. 1963(5)								
8 weeks or less	3,182	6,894	4,140	14,216	2,621	1,517	759	4,897
Over 8 and up to 26	1,146	4,354	4,303	9,803	1,056	1,581	1,091	3,728
Over 26 weeks	217	2,275	5,606	8,098	225	789	1,205	2,219
Total	4,545	13,253	14,049	32,117	3,902	3,887	3,055	10,844
13 Jan. 1964								
8 weeks or less	1,420	3,650	2,623	7,693	1,401	1,301	718	3,420
Over 8 and up to 26	559	2,410	3,100	6,069	712	1,152	895	2,759
Over 26 weeks	152	1,622	5,407	7,181	209	650	1,110	1,969
Total	2,131	7,652	11,130	20,943	2,322	3,103	2,723	8,148
11 Jan. 1965								
8 weeks or less	1,555	3,784	2,773	8,112	1,345	1,210	595	3,150
Over 8 and up to 26	632	2,295	3,100	6,027	659	1,062	816	2,537
Over 26 weeks	121	963	4,696	5,780	152	584	1,040	1,776
Total	2,308	7,042	10,569	19,919	2,156	2,856	2,451	7,463
10 Jan. 1966								
8 weeks or less	1,807	4,352	3,043	9,202	1,188	1,130	547	2,865
Over 8 and up to 26	826	2,701	3,441	6,968	586	1,004	835	2,425
Over 26 weeks	136	1,153	4,980	6,269	125	509	1,057	1,691
Total	2,769	8,206	11,464	22,439	1,899	2,643	2,439	6,981
9 Jan 1967								
8 weeks or less	2,376	5,913	3,879	12,168	1,662	1,367	698	3,727
Over 8 and up to 26	1,683	4,806	5,027	11,516	1,105	1,421	1,062	3,588
Over 26 weeks	278	1,682	5,739	7,699	229	609	1,099	1,937
Total	4,337	12,401	14,645	31,383	2,996	3,397	2,859	9,252

LABOUR 7. contd

Year	MALES				FEMALES			
	14 and under 21	21 and under 41	41 and under 65	Total	14 and under 21	21 and under 41	41 and under 65	Total
8 Jan 1968								
8 weeks or less	2,089	5,603	3,726	11,418	1,451	1,363	659	3,473
Over 8 and up to 26	1,354	4,748	5,139	11,241	943	1,261	952	3,156
Over 26 weeks	444	3,176	7,454	11,074	338	757	1,248	2,343
Total	3,887	13,527	16,319	33,733	2,732	3,381	2,859	8,972
13 Jan 1969								
8 weeks or less	1,985	5,737	4,053	11,775	1,205	1,291	610	3,106
Over 8 and up to 26	1,170	4,522	4,660	10,352	625	1,004	815	2,444
Over 26 weeks	373	3,146	8,455	11,974	163	498	1,050	1,711
Total	3,528	13,405	17,168	34,101	1,993	2,793	2,475	7,261
12 Jan. 1970								
8 weeks or less	2,031	5,926	3,595	11,552	1,268	1,240	519	3,027
Over 8 and up to 26	1,140	4,958	4,775	10,873	624	994	768	2,386
Over 26 weeks	299	2,988	8,958	12,245	162	518	1,010	1,690
Total	3,470	13,872	17,328	34,670	2,054	2,752	2,297	7,103
11 Jan. 1971								
8 weeks or less	2,413	6,406	3,679	12,498	1,557	1,325	529	3,411
Over 8 and up to 26	1,223	4,642	4,390	10,255	797	976	760	2,533
Over 26 weeks	322	2.517	8,975	11.814	159	406	1,011	1,576
Total	3,958	13,565	17,044	34,567	2,513	2,707	2,300	7,520
10 Jan. 1972								
8 weeks or less	2,677	8,179	4,417	15,291	1,939	1,588	600	4,127
Over 8 and up to 26	2,149	7,165	5,712	15,026	1,331	1,534	881	3,746
Over 26 weeks	658	4,522	10,231	15,411	365	676	1,063	2,104
Total	5,484	19,884	20,360	45,728	3,635	3,798	2,544	9,977

	MALES				FEMALES			
	14 and under 21	21 and under 41	41 and under 65	Total	14 and under 21	21 and under 41	41 and under 65	Total
8 Jan. 1973								
8 weeks or less	2,807	6,609	3,075	12,491	1,905	1,592	524	4,021
Over 8 and up to 26	1,565	5,299	4,421	11,285	1,089	1,264	696	3,049
Over 26 weeks	562	4,579	10,102	15,243	343	651	1,097	2,091
Total	4,934	16,487	17,598	39,019	3,337	3,507	2,317	9,161

	under 20	20 and under 40	40 and over	Total	under 20	20 and under 40	40 and over	Total
8 July 1974(6)								
8 weeks or less	2,249	6,548	2,724	11,521	1,481	1,580	420	3,481
Over 8 and up to 26	620	3,444	2,877	6,941	403	694	421	1,518
Over 26 weeks	207	3,007	8,201	11,415	157	494	861	1,512
Total	3,076	12,999	13,802	29,877	2,041	2,768	1,702	6,511
14 July 1975(7)								
8 weeks or less	6,154	10,467	3,736	20,357	4,687	3,729	630	9,046
Over 8 and up to 26	2,099	7,179	4,277	13,555	1,270	1,521	779	3,570
Over 26 weeks	883	5,982	9,054	15,919	507	912	1,056	2,475
Total	9,136	23,628	17,067	49,831	6,464	6,162	2,465	15,091
8 Jan. 1976								
8 weeks or less	2,753	8,636	4,387	15,776	2,159	2,489	757	5,405
Over 8 and up to 26	3,974	11,580	7,041	22,595	3,047	3,218	1,226	7,491
Over 26 weeks	1,591	9,504	11,000	22,095	1,011	1,524	1,302	3,837
Total	8,318	29,720	22,428	60,466	6,217	7,231	3,285	16,733

LABOUR 7. contd

General Notes

(i) Sources. Min. of Labour Gazette (later Employment and Productivity Gazette and then Department of Employment Gazette).

(ii) The Welsh Digests have published figures twice yearly from June 1946. The Dec. (or from 1963 Jan.) figures which they present do not always fully co-incide with those given here which are taken from Gazette. The later publication of the figures in the Welsh Digest may mean that they are revised figures. There is one large discrepancy: in Dec. 1954 the total figures given in the Welsh Digest are: Males, 12,159; Females 6,946: in the Gazette the corresponding figures are 12,518 and 7,612.

Notes

1. Age groups 25-49 and 50+.

2. For 1951 and 1952 the relevant age group headings, for both males and females, are: 'Under 20'; '20 and under 40'; and '40 and over'.

3. The figures for 1960 have been calculated from a slightly more detailed break-down given for that year only.

4. From 1961 on a more detailed duration break-down is available in the sources.

5. After 1961 the figures are not given for December but shift to January. Thus no figure is given for 1962 because of the jump from December 1961 to January 1963.

6. For 1974 the July figure has been taken because no figure was collected in January because of the energy crisis.

7. For 1975 the July figure is given because no January figure was collected because of industrial action at local offices of the Employment Service Agency.

LABOUR 8. Number of Persons placed in employment by employment exchanges and youth employment services, Wales, 1948-74.

	1948	1949	1950	1951	1952	1953	1954.
Men	136,663	135,177	85,823	70,932	103,632	91,408	84,070
Boys	10,717	12,318	10,923	11,116	12,313	12,703	12,767
Women	48,335	45,446	32,048	28,191	40,515	37,749	34,594
Girls	11,387	14,477	12,124	11,852	13,471	13,865	13,017
Total	207,102	207,418	140,918	122,091	169,931	155,725	144,448

	1955	1956	1957	1958	1959	1960	1961
Men	81,790	58,332	41,605	39 363	46,505	56,756	51,274
Boys	12,429	11,334	10 700	9.229	10.301	11,835	11,364
Women	35,419	26,603	22,208	19,764	21,014	22,863	22,976
Girls	13,298	11,282	10,701	10,135	11,059	11,330	10,554
Total	142,936	107,551	85,214	78,491	88,879	102,784	96,168

	1962	1963	1964	1965	1966	1967	1968
Men	40,681	47,493	50,199	48,485	49,920	51,595	56,766
Boys	10,953	11,026	12,152	11,324	10,232	9,689	9,969
Women	19,740	19,426	21,042	20,913	21,644	20,455	22,785
Girls	11,573	11,622	11,120	10,533	9,683	9,163	9,263
Total	82,947	89,567	94,513	91,255	91,479	90,902	98,783

	1969	1970	1971	1972	1973	1974
Men	58,674	60,281	55,990	61,583	69,399	51,996 (Men and Boys)
Boys	10,469	10,339	8,671	9,592	8,682	
Women	24,098	25,264	23,046	26,216	30,203	25,030 (Women and Girls)
Girls	8,589	8,264	7,511	7,833	5,779	
Total	101,830	104,148	95,218	105,224	114,063	77,026

General Notes

(i) Sources. British Labour Statistics. Historical Abstracts. 1886-1968;

British Labour Statistics. Year Books, 1969-75

(ii) These figures for men and women relate to persons aged 18 years and over.

LABOUR 9. Number of Trades Councils and number of Trade Union Members represented, Wales (and England and Wales), 1894-1924

Date	Number of Trades Councils		Number of Trade Unionists represented (000s)	
	Wales	England and Wales	Wales	England and Wales
1894	6	126	16.4	578.3
1895	7	127	15.4	574.6
1896	7	138	16.9	581.9
1897	6	142	16.7	577.2
1898	7	148	22.0	575.1
1899	7	153	23.4	567.9
1900	11	159	41.3	606.8
1901	11	164	43.8	645.6
1902	12	171	44.7	661.6
1903	14	186	47.8	704.9
1904	17	205	49.0	718.7
1905	18	212	52.4	745.6
1906	20	218	58.2	782.2
1907	20	224	67.7	813.1
1908	19	229	68.3	845.8
1909	20	229	63.0	832.2
1910 (1)	(27) 20	(265) 223	(86.0) 68.3	(1,017.0) 842.7
1911	(27) 20	(271) 219	(84.0) 69.9	(1,161.0) 970.4
1912	(32) 22	(293) 224	(105.0) 83.4	(1,283.0) 1,042.7
1913	(36) 23	(329) 235	(126.0) 97.1	(1,495.0) 1,223.4
1914	40	372	133.0	1,597.0
1915	42	378	139.0	1,666.0
1916	49	397	175.0	1,781.0
1917	64	457	205.0	2,102.0
1918	68	525	229.0	2,602.0
1919	68	550	237.0	3,004.0
1920	71	563	261.0	3,221.0
1921	67	544	227.0	2,889.0
1922	59	516	183.0	2,475.0
1923	54	487	177.0	2,339.0
1924	52	479	171.0	2,241.0

General Notes

(i) Source. Abstracts of Labour Statistics

Notes

1. The figures in brackets for 1910-13 and all those from 1914 on include some 'industrial sections' of local Labour parties, but exclude a few Trades Councils which were stated to exist for purely political purposes.

LABOUR 10. Disputes: Total number of workpeople affected by, and days lost through, industrial disputes, Wales and U.K., 1891-1913

Date	Total number of workpeople affected by disputes (000s)		Number of working days lost through disputes	
	Wales	United Kingdom	Wales	United Kingdom
1891	22.4	267.5		
1892	25.8	356.8		
1893	114.4	636.4		
1894	28.4	324.2		
1895	52.2[1]	263.8		
1896	38.4	198.7		
1897	23.2	230.3	1,216.5	10,345.5
1898	113.8	253.9	11,963.3	15,289.5
1899	37.6	180.2	363.9	2,516.4
1900	48.1	188.5	393.5	3,152.7
1901	36.2	179.5	1,106.4	4,142.3
1902	73.6	256.7	701.6	3,479.3
1903	58.0	116.9	836.3	2,338.7
1904	20.8	87.2	325.8	1,484.2
1905	31.5	93.5	741.6	2,470.2
1906	70.4	217.8	663.9	3,028.8
1907	27.7	147.5	247.5	2,162.2
1908	39.5	295.5	549.6	10,834.2
1909	99.6	300.8	844.5	2,774.0
1910	108.6	515.2	2,274.0	9,894.8
1911	54.9	962.0[2]	3,213.0	10,319.6[2]
1912	46.0	1,463.3[2]	413.4	40,914.7[2]
1913	139.2	688.9[2]	826.0	11,630.7[2]

General Notes

(i) Sources. *Abstracts of Labour Statistics*; *Annual Reports on Strikes and Lock-outs*.

Notes

1. This is a revised figure given in the *5th Abstract*, 1898. The *Annual Report on Strikes and Lock-outs* for 1895 gives 43.2.

2. Excludes figures involving two or more districts. Thus there need to be added on:

1911	(transport strikes)	265.3 workpeople	and 1,509.2	days lost
1912	(national coal strike)	1,000.0 " "	" 30,800.0	" "
1913	(textile strike)	2.0 " "	" 100.0	" "

Of these Additions some in 1911 and a significant part in 1912 would be attributable to Wales.

LABOUR 11. Industrial Disputes by industry, Wales and U.K., various dates, 1897-1974

A. Numbers of workers involved[1]

Year	Mining and Quarrying		Metals, Engineering and Shipbuilding		Employees of Local Authorities		Building		Transport		Miscellaneous		Total	
	Wales	UK	Wales	UK	Wales	UK	Wales	UK	Wales	UK	Wales	UK	Wales	UK
1897	10.80	49.40	8.36	97.19	-	0.37	0.28	15.05	1.16	12.52	2.58	55.75	23.18	230.27
1898	109.35	177.03	3.13	21.43	0.13	0.48	1.20	16.68	-	3.48	0.02	34.80	41.98	253.91
1899	24.84	46.83	9.89	21.12	-	1.16	2.72	30.52	0.04	12.61	0.07	67.97	37.56	180.22
1900	39.54	74.36	6.57	19.81	-	0.90	0.15	19.18	1.49	1.49	0.38	51.27	48.14	188.54
1901	30.81	112.98	3.86	22.49	-	0.36	1.17	9.80	0.02	0.02	0.37	31.23	36.23	179.55
1902	67.06	208.53	6.30	15.91	-	2.11	0.04	5.36	0.05	0.05	0.10	23.18	73.55	256.67
1903	42.07	63.58	15.35	32.38	-	0.71	0.26	3.66	-	2.17	0.30	14.40	57.98	116.90
1904	18.61	45.97	1.91	12.13	-	0.05	0.10	8.70	0.14	1.76	0.04	18.29	20.81	86.89
1905	27.28	44.79	4.10	12.75	0.02	0.73	0.08	6.64	-	2.11	0.04	26.49	31.53	93.50
1906	68.71	83.83	1.61	42.05	-	0.26	0.02	1.44	0.05	1.89	-	88.30	70.40	217.77
1907	26.38	52.57	0.78	19.58	-	0.32	0.19	1.23	0.27	8.71	0.11	65.10	27.72	147.50
1908	36.85	87.02	1.29	58.34	0.05	0.05	0.04	2.89	0.68	4.89	0.63	142.31	39.54	295.51
1909	97.15	272.75	1.77	9.72	-	0.24	0.37	1.59	0.31	4.87	0.05	11.63	99.65	300.82
1910	99.91	296.57	5.84	55.44	0.09	0.22	0.36	0.88	2.02	20.32	0.42	141.74	108.64	515.17
1911	28.16	140.81	15.68	93.78	0.07	5.52	0.13	2.79	9.18	448.62	1.73	270.47	54.95	961.98
1912	38.20	1,106.74	2.03	82.89	0.40	3.89	0.03	5.63	4.58	155.30	0.80	108.84	46.03	1,463.28
1913	122.31	214.08	5.23	132.69	3.04	13.59	2.30	40.00	5.28	86.23	1.00	162.34	139.16	688.93
1934	21.20	59.10	1.90	13.50	-	-	0.10	7.50	1.10	9.00	3.90	24.40	28.20	115.30
1935[2]	76.10	144.40	3.50	17.00	-	-	0.10	3.50	1.90	22.20	3.90	32.40	85.50	219.50

Year	Mining and Quarrying		Metals, Engineering		Shipbuilding and Vehicles		Building & Contracting		Transport & Communications		All other Industries & Services		Total	
	Wales	UK	Wales	UK	Wales	UK	Wales	UK	Wales	UK	Wales	UK	Wales	UK
1955	69.2	353.6	5.0[3]	109.2	-	-	0.2	13.5	7.9	153.6	1.5	41.1	83.8	671.0
1956	69.0	241.4	5.5	191.5	-	-	0.2	13.0	0.9	20.5	3.2	41.5	78.8	507.9
1957	69.7	265.5	9.5	878.1	-	-	0.2	16.5	11.6	167.1	3.4	31.9	94.4	1,359.1
1958	39.5	248.6	7.4	123.0	-	-	0.6	26.9	1.0	100.4	2.0	25.2	50.5	524.1
1959	43.0	192.8	25.1	62.5	1.2	181.7	3.2	21.4	0.4	30.4	4.2	157.1	77.1	645.9
1960	63.3	237.6	9.7	96.3	5.0	253.4	1.6	22.6	8.0	151.3	3.6	57.6	91.2	818.8
1961	44.9	250.0	26.1	112.9	0.3	214.9	5.7	47.9	1.8	58.7	4.3	94.1	83.1	778.5
1962	45.2	154.5	104.4	2,552.1	23.2	1,217.4	14.3	55.1	15.5	307.6	6.8	136.0	209.4	4,422.7
1963	39.8	152.6	20.4	107.3	4.2	183.9	4.5	70.8	3.2	38.8	2.1	39.2	74.2	592.6
1964	31.8	173.4	23.4	180.8	9.1	189.1	4.5	25.8	6.3	250.8	6.0	63.1	81.1	883.0
1965	60.1	118.0	11.8	197.8	3.5	297.4	0.6	27.8	6.7	131.3	5.2	104.0	87.9	876.3
1966	10.8	50.5	9.3	132.3	5.0	166.9	3.1	35.6	2.8	114.5	1.5	44.1	32.5	543.9
1967	9.2	41.6	26.2	207.4	10.7	251.0	3.1	37.0	3.2	112.9	5.3	83.9	57.7	733.8
1968	11.4	30.3	48.3	1,283.8	17.2	628.8	6.2	46.7	3.2	146.0	5.4	121.9	91.7	2,257.5
1969	19.3	145.7	42.5	367.4	9.8	384.8	1.3	44.0	7.5	395.9	28.8	327.3	109.2	1,665.0
1970	30.0	117.7	22.6	370.9	13.3	382.8	7.4	50.8	14.2	347.7	29.0	530.8	116.5	1,800.7
1971	4.3	23.0	28.4	214.9	5.5	437.2	13.1	38.5	10.7	306.3	8.9	158.4	70.9	1,178.3
1972	51.5	342.3	14.6	317.6	5.0	345.2	31.0	208.1	3.7	218.1	18.6	303.1	124.4	1,734.4
1973	10.2	46.7	39.4	281.2	8.2	517.8	5.8	28.5	4.1	147.1	30.7	506.3	98.4	1,527.6
1974	46.2	307.4	40.8	326.8	6.8	382.8	1.5	22.4	6.0	135.1	18.2	452.0	119.5	1,626.5

LABOUR **11. Industrial Disputes by Industry, Wales and U.K., various dates, 1897-1974**

B. Number of working days lost

Year	Mining and Quarrying		Metals, Engineering and shipbuilding		Employees of Local Authorities		Building		Transport		Miscellaneous		Total	
	Wales	UK	Wales	UK	Wales	UK	Wales	UK	Wales	UK	Wales	UK	Wales	UK
1897	780.8	1,445.8	253.1	7,141.3	-	1.4	2.9	353.3	13.5	76.5	166.2	1,372.2	1,216.5	10,345.5
1898	11,887.1	12,876.3	40.6	1,370.8	0.1	5.3	35.4	379.2	-	46.8	0.1	611.2	11,963.3	15,289.5
1899	112.7	504.4	157.5	420.7	-	6.8	92.4	854.2	0.6	62.5	0.8	667.9	363.9	2,516.4
1900	252.6	552.9	93.1	349.1	-	8.5	25.2	726.6	16.7	303.8	5.9	1,211.8	393.5	3,152.7
1901	917.1	2,086.1	145.9	601.6	-	7.8	39.3	574.8	-	38.3	4.1	833.7	1,106.4	4,142.3
1902	605.4	2,550.0	94.2	420.4	-	6.4	0.3	115.9	0.7	10.0	0.9	376.6	701.6	3,479.3
1903	651.5	1,397.9	160.0	481.0	-	0.5	7.1	114.4	-	26.8	17.8	318.1	836.3	2,338.7
1904	300.9	627.3	22.5	185.4	-	0.09	0.2	345.5	1.4	42.3	0.8	253.6	325.8	1,454.2
1905	633.4	1,255.5	106.9	467.6	0.2	5.2	0.5	412.6	-	67.1	0.7	262.2	741.6	2,470.2
1906	644.0	922.1	19.7	1,118.3	-	4.9	0.1	56.2	0.1	10.0	-	917.3	663.9	3,028.8
1907	220.2	569.1	21.6	467.6	-	5.3	2.1	23.1	0.2	85.5	3.3	1,011.5	247.5	2,162.2
1908	500.6	1,351.4	44.0	3,835.7	0.1	0.1	0.4	73.1	1.7	51.6	2.8	5,521.4	549.6	10,834.2
1909	799.5	2,229.5	35.8	179.7	-	0.5	8.3	19.4	0.7	94.7	0.2	250.3	844.5	2,774.0
1910	2,104.8	5,524.2	139.2	3,147.2	0.1	0.7	21.3	35.5	5.1	70.8	3.5	1,116.5	2,274.0	9,894.8
1911	2,923.0	4,101.3	233.9	1,321.9	0.1	18.7	2.7	75.0	23.4	2,729.6	29.9	2,073.2	3,213.0	10,319.6
1912	307.0	31,593.8	46.4	1,369.3	1.3	14.9	0.8	106.6	20.1	2,985.2	37.8	4,844.8	413.4	40,914.7
1913	673.5	1,333.6	53.4	2,987.7	8.0	101.5	62.1	823.3	11.0	1,245.1	17.9	3,117.1	826.0	11,630.7
1934	147.6	373.0	7.4	160.0	-	-	0.2	172.5	4.1	43.5	17.1	210.0	176.4	959.0
1935	645.3	1,349.0	16.8	93.0	-	-	1.5	40.0	42.5	82.0	20.8	360.0	726.8	1,924.0

Year	Mining and Quarrying		Metals, Engineering		Shipbuilding and Vehicles		Building & Contracting		Transport & Communications		All other Industries & Services		Total	
	Wales	UK	Wales	UK	Wales	UK	Wales	UK	Wales	UK	Wales	UK	Wales	UK
1955	139	1,112	16[3]	669	-	-	10	71	75	1,687	6	242	246	3,781
1956	144	503	46	1,017	-	-	-	78	3	35	19	450	212	2,083
1957	125	514	77	6,592	-	-	2	84	77	998	5	224	286	8,412
1958	64	450	24	609	-	-	2	151	1	2,116	4	136	95	3,462
1959	95	370	44	174	9	788	10	138	-	95	71	3,704	229	5,269
1960	137	495	20	368	6	982	5	106	10	640	15	333	193	2,924
1961	97	740	228	592	1	872	24	285	3	230	7	327	360	3,046
1962	92	308	141	2,935	27	1,623	25	222	16	431	11	278	312	5,797
1963	77	326	92	363	17	491	18	356	8	72	9	147	221	1,755
1964	64	309	294	721	18	617	13	125	6	312	25	194	420	2,278
1965	301	413	39	686	16	1,077	2	135	24	305	16	309	398	2,925
1966	23	118	44	449	6	422	20	145	47	1,069	5	195	145	2,398
1967	24	108	80	726	42	696	10	201	10	823	11	233	177	2,787
1968	21	57	152	1,909	47	1,457	25	233	7	559	15	475	267	4,690
1969	83	1,041	437	1,702	57	2,036	5	278	11	787	67	1,002	660	6,846
1970	387	1,092	213	2,289	34	1,957	38	242	62	1,313	193	4,088	927	10,981
1971	15	65	131	1,676	93	4,265	76	255	346	6,539	37	751	698	13,551
1972	1,525	10,800	146	3,446	10	2,882	342	4,188	22	876	78	1,717	2,123	23,909
1973	22	91	136	1,870	39	2,712	25	176	7	331	109	2,019	338	7,199
1974	782	5,628	325	2,897	14	2,726	23	252	14	705	166	2,541	1,324	14,749

General Notes

(i) Sources. Abstracts of Labour Statistics; Annual Reports on Strikes and Lock-outs.

Notes

1. Workers involved in more than one stoppage in any year are counted more than once in the year's total. Workers involved in a stoppage beginning in one year and continuing into another are counted in both years.
2. There is a break in the figures at 1935.
3. Until 1959 these figures include those for shipbuilding and vehicles.

Chapter 3
Wages, earnings and consumer expenditure

Even in the second half of the twentieth century, wage statistics are full of pitfalls for the unwary. The wary, too, can stumble easily enough over the sheer complexity of the figures. An eye has always to be kept on whether the information relates to wage-rates or to earnings; whether they refer to hourly, daily or weekly rates; whether they include or exclude juveniles or women; what precise area the figures relate to; and whether the group referred to is reasonably homogeneous. The National Coal Board figures on average weekly earnings, for example, long included the earnings of managers and officials, a proceeding which was neither made immediately obvious nor was it the natural presumption in the minds of most users of the series.

All these difficulties also exist in any past statistics on wages with the important, and unfortunate, exception that the quantity of available information rapidly dwindles to the merest trickle. At the same time it often becomes even more difficult to determine precisely what the statistics refer to. This emerges particularly starkly in, for example, the first part of table 3 relating to agricultural wages in the nineteenth century (and earlier). The original sources used by Bowley (from whose work the information is mostly drawn) are scattered and were provided by different people for different purposes. Clearly, it is extremely unlikely that they are directly comparable whilst the random years to which they refer also reduces their utility as a series. To varying degrees, however, similar strictures could be directed at most pre-twentieth century wage statistics for Britain.

The figures on wages for Wales are further confined to a small range of groups and trades and places. Additional information is available. A fair amount was found in a wide range of books and theses and occasional reports. But very little of this has been incorporated in the present set of tables, for two main reasons. Most of the information of this kind was of an isolated kind, giving a figure for a particular year for a particular trade, and perhaps relevant only to a particular place. In addition, it was often not at all clear exactly to what any individual figure referred. There is also a great deal of information in newspapers, reports, estate papers, trade papers and business records. All this, however, will require a series of special research projects to collect and categorise. In the meantime it was considered worth-while to bring together such material as was known to be in a, comparatively, usable form. The justification for so doing rested on three main grounds: the intrinsic importance of knowledge of these topics for economic and social history; the judgement that, within the generally-applicable constraints, the material was tolerably reliable and gave a reasonable indication of trends in the particular occupations and for the particular periods which it covered; and from an awareness of the difficulties presently faced by anyone seeking enlightenment in this field. Many of the sources are relatively inaccessible.

The immediate intention, therefore, has been to bring together such material as is relatively easily available. Only for the coal industry (table 1) and agriculture (table 3) does this yield reasonably useful material covering a significant portion of the nineteenth century. It is doubtless fortunate that, especially for Wales, these were extremely important groups but they are probably still inadequate to justify the use of the material upon them to construct a general index of wages for Wales in the second half of the nineteenth century.

The information on miners and agricultural workers remains of fundamental importance and requires a few additional words on each. Tables 1 and 2 indicate that it is possible to obtain continuous and reliable data on wages in coal-mining back to the mid-nineteenth century. In this respect the historian of coal-mining gains from the fact that the industry has been frequently investigated. Even so, in most industries this might not have prevented a general merging of data on Wales with that on England or the United Kingdom. In coal-mining, however, conditions have varied so much from coalfield to coalfield that the largest effective organisational unit was normally the individual coalfield. In particular this has been true over most of its history for the purposes of regulating wages. For South Wales, where there was from the 1870s onwards, a general acceptance that changes in the wage-rates should be determined by centralised agreements between owners and workers, the variations in wage-rates are given in table 1. The general and particular limitations of such figures are indicated above and in the notes to the table; if due note is taken of these then the figures represent a guide of strong reliability. Earnings, especially in coal-mining, are intrinsically more difficult: the public discussions over the miners' claims of the 1970s clearly demonstrated that there was much scope for qualifying and interpreting any figures on average earnings. However, the basis of collection for the figures presented in table 2 is reliable and acceptable from about 1920 onwards. The scattered information for the years up to the first world war is necessarily more suspect. It is difficult to know upon just how representative a sample they are based, and occasional newspaper debates in the 1890s and 1900s indicate how grotesquely estimates of miners' earnings can vary when based on impressionistic accounts or information relating to small groups for a limited period of time. The impression is, however, that the compilation was made with increasing care from the 1890s onwards and called upon a wider range of evidence.

Table 3 gives indicators of wages in agriculture for intermittent dates going back to the eighteenth century. The dates are those in which there were more or less general investigations into agricultural wages, mostly by government commissions; many scattered, isolated figures are encountered in the general literature but these were excluded since they were unlikely to be representative. The figures are given in four separate batches because each of these represents, not a break in a series, but information on different categories: nominal wages; earnings; minimum rates; and earnings again. Any series on agricultural wages necessarily involves substantial difficulties. It is an industry where there has always been a substantial degree of locational variety, and the county is not necessarily the best unit for reflecting these. There are also variations in both levels and regularity of pay between, say, an agricultural labourer and a skilled cowman. Such considerations mean that indications of minimum rates can only be a very rough index, especially as it is an industry with a low level of trade union membership and there are good reasons - such as the agricultural structure in a large number of relatively small and scattered units - for thinking that such membership has been particularly low in Wales. Moreover, this is one of the many areas - the three following tables would be additional examples - where the availability and quality of the data does not necessarily improve over time. No series on actual earnings has been found to cover the half century between 1917 and 1967. Only since 1967 has information on earnings been provided separately from that relating to England and Wales, and even then the information represents only an average for Wales as a whole.

Towards the end of the nineteenth century information of a consecutive kind begins to become available for a wider range of industries and occupations. Much of this is incorporated into tables 4 to 7 dealing respectively with the building trades, the police, engineering and ship-repairing, and printing.

The short-comings of these early years were largely to be expected. What was surprising and disappointing was the relative paucity of material after the first world war. As it turned out the widest range of continuous material before the very recent date of 1960, was found for the decade or so before 1914 in the Abstracts of Labour Statistics. Very little of the great post-1919 boom in British wage statistics was presented in a regional form. As a result coal (tables 1 and 2) is the only industry for which there is a satisfactory continuous series. Even in the case of agriculture (table 3) there is a massive gap of nearly three decades after 1939. Information on the building trades (table 5) virtually peters out in 1914. Engineering and ship-repairing (table 6) and printing (table 7) do yield some indicators for the period beyond 1919 but its sporadic nature necessarily imposes constraints upon its utility.

The severe limitations which have been briefly outlined are applicable even when discussion is confined to wage-rates, the easiest area on which to obtain information. Apart from table 2 (coal) and parts of table 3 (agriculture), all the first seven tables are concerned mainly with wage-rates. The relation between rates and actual income or earnings is, however, by no means simple. Basically it depends on the regularity of working. We have, however, almost no systematic knowledge of the number of hours actually worked, on average, in a week, nor of the average number of weeks worked per year in various industries in Wales. The causes of irregularity of earnings - seasonal and cyclical fluctuations, very short run variations in the level of demand, sickness, age, unemployment etc. - are numerous and pervasive. On the whole they dominate other shortcomings (such as variations in skill and effort as well as the neglect of the increasing extent to which, in the twentieth century, the state had provided some services) involved in using wage-rates to act as indicators of income.

It may seem that the catalogue of inadequacies raises doubts about the validity of collecting material on wages in Wales. So it does, but at least two defensive comments may be made. Many of the strictures detailed above could be aimed at the existing indices for U.K. wages before 1914 compiled by Wood, Bowley, Gilboy, Deane and Cole.(1) In addition, one of the few relatively safe generalisations which can be made about, especially pre-twentieth century wages and earnings is that regional variations were significant. It is thus necessary to struggle towards indices for Wales which are based on separate data for Wales.

An even longer struggle is in prospect before any reasonable Welsh series on money wages can be confronted with a similar series on retail prices; and hence form the basis for the construction of a cost of living index for Wales. Even such constructs for the United Kindgom, mostly based on the work of Wood and Bowley and re-produced in Mitchell(2), are precariously based and, as is emphasised in the originals and re-emphasised by Mitchell, have to be used with extreme care. There are good reasons for thinking, however, that it is better to proceed towards producing even a crudely-based index relating directly to Wales rather than to assume - in the face of much evidence to the contrary - that a U.K. index (even if it were reliable) can be applied in regional contexts.

---

1. These are re-produced in B.R. Mitchell, Abstract of British Historical Statistics, Cambridge, 1962, Ch. XII where the detailed references to these sources are also to be found. The comment applies to the principles behind the difficulties which have been enumerated: an important practical difference between these U.K. indices and the pre-1900 material for Wales is that the latter covers a narrower range of industries and years. Partly for this reason no attempt is made here to supply an index for Wales.

2. Ibid.

Once again, however, it is the period since 1920 which is particularly disappointing. For these years the U.K. indices have been enormously improved whilst the possibilities of constructing such indices for Wales, if anything, receded. Until very recent years published regional information on money wages was, as already indicated, sparser than it had been before 1914 and regional price data had not improved. In each case, however, the potential sources are richer.

During the 1960s a growing interest and concern with regional development and regional economics generated a substantial body of statistics which allowed comparisons to be made between different parts of the United Kingdom. One aspect of this, re-produced in table 8, has been the provision of a reliable measure of average earnings for manual workers in Wales since 1960. In some respects the material in table 9 is even more relevant for issues involving living standards. It relates to households rather than to individual wage-earners, and it takes note of spending as well as income. Starting in the early 1950s the table gives, for the first time, a general indication of consumers' expenditure in Wales. As the comparative basis is especially important here, and as the U.K. figures are not too readily available, the table gives figures for Wales and the U.K. The same is true of table 10 where a more specific aspect of consumers' expenditure is illustrated: namely, the proportion of households having some of major items of consumer durables such as cars, television sets, washing machines and regrigerators.

BOOKS AND THESES

A.L. Bowley — Wages in the United Kingdom in the Nineteenth Century, 1900.

A.L. Bowley — Wages and Income in the United Kingdom since 1860, Cambridge, 1937.

A.L. Bowley — Prices and Wages in the United Kingdom, 1914-20, Oxford, 1921.

A.L. Chapman & R. Knight — Wages and Salaries in the United Kingdom, 1920-38, Cambridge, 1953.

A. Dalziel — The Colliers' Strike in South Wales, Cardiff, 1872.

W.G. Dalziel — The Monmouth and South Wales Coal Owners' Association, Cardiff, 1895.

E.W. Evans — 'A History of Industrial Relations in the South Wales Coal Industry to 1914', Ph.D. thesis, University of Wales, 1955.

F. Gibson — A Compilation of Statistics of the Coal Mining Industry of the United Kingdom, Cardiff, 1922 and annually till 1938.

E.H. Hunt — Regional Wage Variations in Britain, 1850-1914, Oxford, 1973.

H.S. Jevons — The British Coal Trade, 1920.

J.H. Morris & L.J. Williams — The South Wales Coal Industry, 1841-75, Cardiff, 1958.

A.R. Prest & A.A. Adams — Consumers' Expenditure in the United Kingdom, 1900-19, Cambridge, 1954.

G. Routh — Occupation and Pay in Great Britain, 1906-60, 1965.

J.W.E. Rowe — Wages in the Coal Industry, 1923.

R. Stone — Measurement of Consumers' Expenditure and Behaviour in the United Kingdom, 1920-30, Vols. 1 & 2, Cambridge, 1954 and 1966.

ARTICLES

A.W. Ashby & J.H. Smith — 'Agricultural Labour in Wales under Statutory Regulation of Wales, 1924-37', Welsh Journal of Agriculture,

A.L. Bowley & G.H. Wood — A Series of articles (separately and jointly written) published in J.R.S.S. between 1898 and 1910.

A.W. Fox — 'Agricultural wages in England and Wales during the last fifty years', J.R.S.S., 1903.

F. Purdy — 'On the Earnings of Agricultural Labourers in England and Wales', J.R.S.S., 1861.

L.J. Williams and Dot Jones — 'The Wages of Agricultural Labourers in the Nineteenth Century, the evidence from Glamorgan', BBCS., May 1982.

Journal of Ministry of Agriculture, XXVIII-XLVI.

GOVERNMENT AND OFFICIAL PUBLICATIONS

Returns of wages published between 1830 and 1886, P.P., 1887, LXXXIX; and Wage Census, P.P., 1889, LXX; 1890, LXVII; 1891, LXXVIII; 1892, LXVIII; 1893, LXXXIII.

R.C. on Labour, 1892, XXXIV, XXXVI; 1893-4, XXXII, XXXIX; 1894, XXXV.

Board of Trade, Abstract of Labour Statistics, 1894-

Ministry of Labour Gazette (and later titles), 1923-

British Labour Statistics, Historical Abstract, 1886-1968, 1971.

Yearbook of Labour Statistics, annual since 1969.

R.C. on Coal Industry, 1919, XI - XIII.

Reports on the Wages, Earnings and Conditions of Employment in Agriculture, P.P., 1900, LXXXII, 1905, XCVII.

Wages and Conditions of Employment in Agriculture, Vol. ii, P.P., 1919, IX.

Guides to Official Statistics: No. 1. Labour Statistics, 1958.

Annual Report of H.M. Inspector of Mines, 1921-

Quarterly Statistical Statement on Coal, 1944-6, (P.P.)

N.C.B. Annual Report and Accounts, 1945-

Annual Digest of Welsh Agricultural Statistics, 1967-

WAGES 1. Coal. Percentage changes in wage rates, miners, South Wales, 1848 - 1939

Year		Advances	Reductions	Average Position above the 1879 Standard Rate
1848	March		10	
1849	Aug.	10		
1850	Feb.		10	
1852	Feb.		5	
1853	March	10		
	April	5		
	May	5		
	July	10		
1857	Dec.		20	
1863	Nov.	5		
1864	March	10		
1868	Feb.		15	
1870	May	10		
1871	April		5	
	Aug.	2½		
1872	Feb.	10		
	June	10		
	Aug.	10		
1873	May	10		
1874	May		10	
	Aug.		10	
1875	May		12½	
1876	Jan.		7½	
1878	Jan.		5	
1879	June		10	
1880	Feb.	5		4.58
1881	July	2½		
	Nov.	2½		6.66
1882	June	5		12.91
1883	Nov.	2½		15.41
1884				17.50
1885	March		2½	
	July		2½	
	Nov.		2½	13.75
1886	March		2½	
	Nov.		2½	7.50
1887	March		2½	2.91
1888	Nov.	5		3.33
1889	April	7½		
	May	2½		
	Sept.	5		
	Oct.	2½		17.08
1890	Jan.	7½		
	May	13¾		
	Aug.	3¾		
	Nov.	2½		43.64
1891	Feb.	2½		
	May	2½		
	Nov.		3¾	55.83
1892	Jan.		7½	
	Feb.		2½	
	April		3¾	
	June		3¾	
	Aug.		2½	
	Oct.		5	
	Dec.		6¼	36.14
1893	March		2½	
	April		6¼	
	June		3¾	
	Aug.	1¼		
	Oct.	1¼		
	Dec.	7½		15.00
1894	Feb.	6¼		
	April	3¾		
	June		2½	
	Aug.		3¾	
	Oct.		1¼	
	Dec.		1¼	25.10
1895	Feb.		1¼	
	April		1¼	
	June		1¼	
	Aug.		2½	
	Oct.		2½	16.77
1896	Feb.		1¼	
	Oct.		1¼	11.04
1897	April	1¼		10.94

1898	Feb.	1¼		
	Sept.	5		
	Dec.	2½		15.53
1899	Feb.		1¼	
	April	3¾		
	June	1¼		
	Aug.	1¼		
	Oct.	3¾		
	Dec.	1¼		23.95
1900	Feb.	5		
	April	13¾		
	June	5		
	Aug.	5		
	Oct.	12½		
	Dec.	2½		53.23
1901	April	5		
	June		2½	
	Aug.		3¾	
	Oct.		3¾	
	Dec.		2½	73.33
1902	Feb.		2½	
	April		10	
	June		5	
	Aug.		1¼	
	Dec.	1¼		53.12
1903	Dec.		5	48.33
1904	Dec.		5	43.33
1905	June		5	
	Sept.		3¾	34.58
1906	June	2½		
	Sept.	5		33.12
1907	March	3¾		
	June	11¼		
	Sept.	5		
	Dec.	2½		49.06
1909	March		5	1908 60.00
	June		7½	1909 51.45
1910	March	2½		
	Dec.	1¼		49.68
1911	June		1¼	50.52
1912	March	1¼		
	Sept.	6¼		53.12
1913	June	2½		58.95

					Above standard of 1915
1915	May	17½		1914 60.00	
	Aug.	12½			
	Dec.		5	78.05	27.78
1916[1]	June	15		1916 103.75	35.83
	Dec.	15		1917 133.75	55.83
				1918 133.75	55.83
1921	Oct.			1919 133.75	55.83
	Nov.			1920 133.75	55.83
	Dec.			1921 128.48	52.33
1922	Jan.			92.00	28.00
1923				97.93	31.95
1924				106.22	37.48
1925				113.33	42.22
1926				113.33	42.22
1927				100.88	33.93
1928				92.00	28.00
1929				92.00	28.00
1930				92.00	28.00
1931				82.00	21.33
1932				80.00	20.00
1933				80.00	20.00
1934				80.94	20.63
1935				83.75	22.50
1936				87.50	25.00
1937				93.13	28.75
1938				95.00	30.00
1939				95.00	30.00

General Notes

(i) Sources. A. Dalziel, The Colliers' Strike in South Wales, p.8, for 1848-71, W.G. Dalziel, The Monmouthshire and South Wales Coal Owners Association, esp. pp. 104-8, for 1871-94; F.A. Gibson, A compilation of statistics of the coal mining industry, pp. 144-5 for 1880-1938.

(ii) It is important to realize that this table attempts to trace the changes in wage-rates. Thus it gives the percentage change from time to time in the price paid for cutting and loading a ton of (large) steam coal (to take the most basic rate for South Wales), or in the daily rate for other tasks etc. It says nothing about (a) the actual cutting price (which would for a given seam vary from colliery to colliery and valley to valley, depending on a range of factors such as bargaining power, depth and state of the seam etc), nor about (b) actual earnings (which again would depend on a wide range of factors such as individual strength and skill, state of the seam, age,regularity of work, etc). The next table gives some over-lapping information on average earnings (per shift and/or per week).

(iii) From 1848 to 1871 the figures are based on the steam-coal collieries of the Aberdare valley. An extensive reading of other sources suggests that these are reasonably representative at least for miners producing for the export market in steam coal. They reflect less accurately the variations in wage-rates for other groups of coal-miners in South Wales: those producing for the major iron-works; those producing house coal; and those in the anthracite area in the west of the coalfield. These variations tended to be reduced in both size and significance after the formation of the Monmouthshire and South Wales Collieries Association in 1873 and with the increasing predominance of the steam-coal trade.

(iv) There were frequent revisions of the wage agreements. But the extent to which these under-mine the reliability of the variations is greatly reduced because the negotiations revolved around the same base year. Thus all the sliding scale agreements from 1880 on (1880, 1882, 1887, 1890, 1892, 1893, 1895 and 1898) as well as the succeeding conciliation board agreements (1903, 1905 and 1910) took the wage-rates of Dec. 1879 as their starting-point. (1879 was the lowest point reached by rates - and, probably, earnings - in the second half of the nineteenth century). From 1915 to the second world war the rates of July 1915 were taken as the base-rate for negotiations.

Notes

1.From 1916 to 1921 the percentages exclude flat rate increases granted by the government as war bonuses and cost of living increases. These were of 1s 6d per shift in Sept. 1917 and June 1918, 2s in March 1919, 20 per cent in May 1920 and 2s in Oct. 1920. For these years, therefore, the percentage variations do not reflect the true variations in wage-rates.

WAGES 2 etc. Wages. Coal. Average earnings,[1] 1840-1974: earnings per shift, all workers, North Wales, 1888, 1914 and 1918-46 (quarterly), and South Wales, 1840-1914 (occasional dates) and 1918-46 (quarterly); and South Wales (per shift and weekly), 1945-75

Year		North Wales		South Wales	
		s.	d.	s.	d.
1840				4	2
1849				3	0
1860				3	0
1870				3	4
1888[2]		(2	8 to	(2	10 to
		(4	1	(4	10
1891				6	6
1913[3]				7	3
3 month period beginning 1914[4]	June	5	10	6	9
1918	July	11	1¼	14	0
	Oct.	11	6¾	13	11½
1919	Jan.	13	8¼	15	5¼
	Apr.[5]	12	4	15	6½
	July[5]	12	10¾	16	0¾
	Oct.	13	2½	16	3
1920	Jan.	13	5½	16	4¾
	Apr.	15	0	17	9½
	July[6]	15	4	18	2¾
	Oct.[6]	16	7½	19	7¾
1921	Jan.	16	10½	21	6½
	Apr.				
	July				
	Oct.	9	9¾	10	11½
1922	Jan.	8	10¼	9	8½
	Apr.	8	0¼	9	8¼
	July	7	11½	9	7¼
	Oct.	8	0¾	9	6¾
1923	Jan.	8	0¾	9	6½
	Apr.	8	3	9	8½
	July	8	5¼	10	5¾
	Oct.	8	5¾	10	1½
1924	Jan.	8	4¼	9	9¼
	Apr.	9	2	10	5¾
	July	9	5¼	10	10¾
	Oct.	9	4	10	10¼
1925	Jan.	9	4¾	10	8¾
	Apr.	9	4½	10	8½
	July	9	1¼	10	9
	Oct.	9	4¾	10	9
1926	Jan.[7]	9	2½	10	8¾
	Apr.[7]	9	4	10	9
		(8)			
1927	Jan.	9	3½	10	6½
	Apr.	9	1¼	10	2¼
	July	8	10	9	9¼
	Oct.	8	10¾	9	7¾
1928	Jan.	8	9¼	9	6¼
	Apr.	8	8¼	9	6¼
	July	8	8¾	9	7¼
	Oct.	8	8¼	9	6
1929	Jan.	8	7¼	9	4½
	Apr.	8	7¾	9	7¾
	July	8	8	9	6¼
	Oct.	8	7¾	9	5
1930	Jan.	8	8¼	9	5¾
	Apr.	8	9¼	9	6
	July	8	9½	9	6¼
	Oct.	8	9¾	9	6
1931	Jan.	8	9	9	0½
	Apr.	8	9	8	11¼
	July	8	8½	8	11½
	Oct.	8	8¾	8	10¾
1932	Jan.	8	9¼	8	11
	Apr.	8	9½	8	11¼
	July	8	9½	8	11¼
	Oct.	8	9	8	11½
1933	Jan.	8	8	8	11
	Apr.	8	8½	8	11
	July	8	8	8	10¾
	Oct.	8	7¾	8	11
1934	Jan.	8	7¾	8	11¼
	Apr.	8	7½	8	11¼
	July	8	7¾	9	1
	Oct.	8	9	9	2¾
1935	Jan.	8	9¼	9	2¾
	Apr.	8	9¾	9	3¾
	July	8	10½	9	3¾
	Oct.	8	11¼	9	4¼
1936	Jan.	9	6¾	9	7
	Apr.	9	6½	9	8¾
	July	9	7¼	9	8
	Oct.	9	8¼	9	8½
1937	Jan.	9	9½	9	10¾
	Apr.	9	10½	10	6
	July	9	11¾	10	6
	Oct.	10	3¾	10	7
1938	Jan.	10	4½	10	10
	Apr.	10	6	11	0¼
	July	10	8¾	11	0
	Oct.	10	6¾	11	0
1944	1st Qtr.	18	11.71	19	1.61
	2nd Qtr.	20	8.17	20	4.75
	3rd Qtr.	20	11.44	21	3.21
	4th Qtr.	21	1.28	20	10.29
1945	1st Qtr.	21	1.84	20	10.13
	2nd Qtr.	22	0.91	21	7.14
	3rd Qtr.	22	5.14	22	1.88
	4th Qtr.	21	8.25	21	4.79
1946	1st Qtr.	21	9.92	21	5.08
	2nd Qtr.	22	4.60	21	11.24
	3rd Qtr.	22	7.21	22	0.74
	4th Qtr.	23	1.81	22	8.17

WAGES 2 contd.

SOUTH WALES					Year
Earnings (including allowances)					
Per Manshift	Weekly				
All Workers	Face	All Underground	Surface	All Workers	
£	£	£	£	£	
1 2 3.15	..	..	..	5 8 2	1945
1 5 10.27	..	..	..	5 14 7	1946
..	..	..	..	..	1947
1 10 3.29	..	..	..	..	1948
1 11 3.43	..	..	..	..	1949
1 12 5	..	..	..	8 9 11	1950
1 12 9	..	..	..	9 11 9	1951
2 0 1	..	..	..	10 12 8	1952
2 2 2	..	..	..	11 0 7	1953
2 4 8	12 10 5	12 1 4	10 11 2	11 15 8	1954
2 7 11	13 4 1	12 15 6	11 7 9	12 10 3	1955
2 12 6	14 8 7	13 18 11	12 12 9	13 14 1	1956
2 15 11	15 6 9	14 15 6	13 7 9	14 10 3	1957
2 17 6	14 19 11	14 7 8	12 15 1	14 1 6	1958
2 18 9	14 14 11	14 4 2	12 10 1	13 17 8	1959
3 0 2	15 4 4	14 14 7	12 16 6	14 6 11	1960
2 3 11	16 4 11	15 15 4	13 17 4	15 7 5	1961
3 6 9	17 4 1	16 9 6	16 6 11	16 0 2	1962
..	..	..	..	..	1963
3 11 4	18 9 2	17 11 8	15 8 3	17 2 5	1964
3 15 5	18 19 6	18 3 3	16 1 9	17 14 5	1965
3 19 11	19 19 11	19 4 0	17 5 1	18 15 5	1966
4 4 4	21 19 9	20 14 11	18 14 0	20 5 10	1967
East / West		East / West	East / West	East / West	
4 7 6 / 4 8 11	..	21 12 8 / 22 0 1	19 4 6 / 19 16 2	21 1 10 / 21 10 9	1968
4 10 9 / 4 13 11	..	23 12 6 / 23 9 9	21 18 8 / 20 18 8	23 4 11 / 22 18 7	1969
4.86 / 5.16	..	23.64 / 25.88	22.37 / 24.14	23.35 / 25.49	1970
5.52 / 5.69	..	27.03 / 27.90	27.37 / 25.71	24.11 / 27.39	1971
6.36 / 6.55	..	30.95 / 33.67	30.24 / 29.66	30.80 / 32.70	1972
7.78	..	37.71	35.46	37.18	1973
9.16	..	39.09	35.18	38.12	1974
12.50	..	57.04	54.38	56.41	1975

General Notes

(i) Sources. (a) 1840-70, 1891: A.L. Bowley *Wages in the U.K. in the Nineteenth Century*, p.109. (Bowley's sources are: 1840; *Returns of Wages*, 1830-86; 1849, 1860, 1870: Dalziel, *Colliers' Strike in South Wales*; 1891: *R.C. on Labour*, 5th Report, Part II, p.39.)

(b) 1888 and 1914 (note 4) J.W.F. Rowe, *Wages in the Coal Industry*, pp.72-3 (he says 1888 figure is estimated.)

(c) 1913 A.L. Bowley *Prices and Wages in the U.K. 1914-20*, p.154. Bowley's source is Cmd. 361, pp.55-6.

(d) 1914-1938 *Annual Reports of H.M. Chief Inspector of Mines* for 1921 to 1938.

(e) 1944-46 *Quarterly Statistical Statement on Coal* issued as a parliamentary paper for these years, but from 1947 published by the N.C.B.

(f) 1945-75 (South Wales), N.C.B. *Annual Report and Accounts*. The figures relate to the south-western division (see notes to Coal table 3).

Notes

1. The quarterly figures for 1918-46 refer to actual cash earnings, and exclude allowances in kind. Between 1927 and 1938, these varied between 2¼d and 3d per shift for North Wales, and 2½d and 3¼d per shift for South Wales. Between 1944 and 1946, allowances were between 7d and 9d for North Wales, and 8d and 10d for South Wales.

2. The smaller figure is the average earnings of labourers; the larger that of hewers. Detailed figures are also available (Rowe, pp.72-3) for other classes of workers:

	North Wales		South Wales	
	s.	d.	s.	d.
coal getters on day wage	3	6	4	4
putters, etc.	..		3	4
timbermen, storemen, etc.	3	9	4	2
firemen	3	6	4	4

3. Detailed figures for South Wales are available for 1913 from the evidence presented by the Coal Controller to the Royal Commission on the Coal Industry, 1919, pp.55-6.

		s.	d.	
Underground	hewers	8	8	
	putters, hauliers, trimmers, etc.	6	9	
	storemen, brushers, rippers, etc.	8	3	
	deputies, firemen, examiners, etc.	8	6	(day wage)
	mechanical haulage - men	6	1	
	- boys	3	11	
	other underground workers	5	8	
	all underground workers	7	4	
Surface	enginemen	6	6	
	pitheadmen	5	5	
	workers on screens - men	5	3	
	- boys & girls	2	6	
	stokers and boilermen	5	7	
	mechanics, joiners, blacksmiths	5	10	
	other surface workers	5	5	
	all surface workers	5	6	

4. Detailed figures are available (Rowe, pp.72-3) for 1914 from a different source:

	N. Wales	S. Wales
piecework coal getters	8 0	9 4
coal getters on day wage	6 4½	6 5
putters, etc.	5 10	6 7
timbermen, stonemen,etc.	6 2	7 8
firemen	7 3	7 9
labourers	5 5½	5 9

5. The maximum hours of labour below ground were reduced from 8 to 7 per shift on 16 July, 1919.

6. The range of earnings is suggested by the calculation that in November 1920 skilled piece-workers in South Wales received about 26s 1d per shift (compared to about 9s 2d in June 1914) and unskilled men received about 17s 11d (compared to 5s 8d in 1914); in North Wales the comparable figures are 20s 7d (8s 4d) and 17s (5s 8d). See Rowe, pp 95-6.

7. On 1 May 1926, the production of coal at almost all mines stopped, and particulars of earnings for the last eight months of 1926 are not available. The figures given here relate only to the month of April.

8. The figures from January 1927 onwards under North Wales are those given under the heading "Cumberland, North Wales, South Staffordshire, Shropshire, Bristol, Forest of Dean, Somerset, and Kent". They are thus more representative of the smaller coalfields generally than of North Wales in particular.

WAGES 3. Agriculture. Nominal weekly wages, occasional dates, 1788-1882; average weekly earnings, occasional dates, by county, 1867-1917; minimum rates, by county, 1918-39; weekly earnings and hours, Wales, 1967-75

Nominal weekly wages, 1788-1870							
	1788	1789	1795	1811	1813	1821	1824
	s. d.	s. d.	s. d.	s. d.	s. d.	s. d.	s. d.
Wales	6 3	7 0	7 6	..	13 9[1]	..	8 0
Monmouth	..	..	9 0	..	..		10 0
Glamorgan	..	..	..	15 0	..	9 6	..
	1833	1836	1837	1840	1860	1860-1	1867-70
	s. d.	s. d.	s. d.	s. d.	s. d.	s. d.	s. d.
Wales	8 2	10 0	7 6	..	11 3	11 2	..
Monmouth	10 8	..	10 6	13 6	11 8	11 8	12 10 (13 6 actual)
Glamorgan	..	..	..	..	..	..	..
	1882						
	s. d.						
Wales	14 0						
Monmouth	..						
Glamorgan	..						

Average weekly earnings,[2] 1867-1917						
	1867-70	1898	1902	1907	1914	1917
	s. d.	s. d.	s. d.	s. d.	s. d.	s. d.
Anglesey	11 6	15 6	16 7	17 6	..	..
Brecon	13 6	16 8	18 6	18 9	17 11	23 3
Caerns.	13 6	17 2	18 8	18 7	20 0	24 8
Cards.	11 6	14 9	15 8	16 6	16 4	20 0
Carms.	11 6	16 7	17 9	18 1	17 10	23 6
Denbs.	13 6	16 9	17 8	18 1	18 6	25 4
Flint.	13 6	17 3	18 5	18 10	17 9	26 3
Glam.	14 0	19 1	21 3	19 3	20 2	27 10
Merioneth.	13 6	16 5[3]	17 8	18 2	17 9	26 3
Mons.	13 6	16 8	..	18 1	17 0	22 6
Monts.	13 6	15 5	16 0	16 7	16 8	22 9
Pembs.	11 6	15 10	16 7	17 3	16 8	21 0
Radnor.	13 6	15 6	16 10	16 8	15 0	20 1

WAGES 3 contd.

Minimum rates,(4) 1918-39(10)

	1918	1919	1920	1920	1921	1922	1923	1924	1925(9)	1926	1927
		May	May	Aug.	Nov/Dec(5)	April(6)	Nov(7)	April(8)			
	s. d.	s. d.	s. d.	s. d.	s. d.	s. d.	s. d.	s. d.	s. d.	s. d.	s. d.
Monmouth)	36 6	41 6	45 6	50 0	38 0	35 0	..	(32 0)	32 0	32 0	32 0
Glamorgan)					40 0	36 0	..	(32 0)	37 6	36 0	36 0
Carmarthen)	31 0	37 6	42 0	46 0	..	..	..	30 0	31 0	31 0	31 0
Cardigan)						36 0	30 0	(30 0))	31 0	31 0	31 0
Pembroke)						34 0	..	(30 0))	(Jan. 30 0)		
Brecon)					38 0	34 0	30 0	(30 0)	31 0	31 0	31 0
Radnor)											
Montgomery)					35 0	36 0	28 0	28 0	31 6	31 6	31 6
Merioneth)	30 0	36 6	42 0	46 0		33 0					
Flints.)					37 6	31 3	(May 27 0)	27 1	30 6	30 6	30 6
Denbigh)							21 1				
Caerns.)	31 6	36 6	42 0	46 0	..	35 0	30 0	(30 0)	30 0	31 0	31 0
Anglesey)						30 0	..	(28 0)			

	1928	1929	1930	1931	1932	1933	1934	1935	1936	1937	1938	1939
Monmouth	32 0	32 0	32 0	32 0	31 0	31 0	31 0	33 0	32 6	34 0	35 0	35 0
Glamorgan	34 0	34 0	35 0	35 0	31 6	32 6	33 6	33 6	33 6	34 6	36 0	36 0
Carmarthen	31 0	31 0	31 0	31 0	30 6	31 0	31 6	31 6	32 0	33 0	..	..
Cardigan) Pembroke)	31 0	31 0	31 0	31 0	30 0	30 0	30 6	31 0	31 0	33 0	33 0	..
Brecon) Radnor)	31 0	31 0	31 0	31 0	29 6	29 6	29 6	30 0	31 0	32 0	33 0	33 0
Montgomery) Merioneth)	30 0	30 0	30 0	30 0	28 6	27 0	27 0	28 6	28 6	30 0	31 6	32 0
Flintshire) Denbigh)	30 6	30 6	30 6	30 6	30 6	30 6	30 6	30 6	30 6	31 0	32 0	32 0
Caerns.) Anglesey)	31 0	31 0	31 0	31 0	31 0	29 6	30 6	31 0	31 0	32 0	32 0	32 0

Agricultural Earnings for all hired men (aged 20+)

	Average weekly earnings		Net weekly total hours	
	£		£	
1967	14.36		49.1	
1968	15.91	(15.74)[(11)]	50.3	(49.1)
1969	16.54	(17.65)	49.1	(49.7)
1970	18.97	(18.97)	48.5	(48.5)
1971	21.13	(21.13)	47.6	(47.6)
1972	23.47	(23.37)	46.8	(47.8)
1973	26.01	(25.92)	46.9	(46.8)
1974	32.03		44.4	
1975	40.79		44.2	

General Notes

(i) Sources. A.L. Bowley, Wages in the U.K. in the nineteenth century (for 1788-1870); E.H. Hunt, Regional Wage Variations in Britain (for 1867-70) pp.62-3; Board of Trade, Abstracts of Labour Statistics, 6th to 17th (for 1898, 1902 and 1907); A.L. Bowley, Prices and Wages in the U.K., 1914-20, p.176 (for 1914 and 1917; and for 1918-20); Journal of the Min. of Agriculture, XXVIII-XLVI (for 1921-39): figures provided direct by Ministry of Agriculture and from Annual Digest of Welsh Agricultural Statistics (for 1967-75).

Notes

1. South Wales ploughmen only.

2. The figures relate to married labourers, i.e., those not lodging in the farmhouse. The earnings include the estimated value of allowances in kind.

3. Includes labourers lodging in the farmhouse - covers all labourers regularly employed on the farm and in receipt of weekly wages.

4. Relates to wages for ordinary male workers, 21 years or older.

5. From 1921 to 1924 the month given is the terminal month of the wage agreement: from 1925 it is the starting month. The rate for Brecon and Radnor ran to January 1921.

6. The rate ran to November for Anglesey: May for Caernarvonshire; October for Cardiganshire and Pembrokeshire; September for Denbighshire and Flintshire; and January for Glamorganshire.

7. The rate ran to May for Caernarvonshire.

8. The rate ran to May for Carmarthenshire. The rates in brackets are those prevailing before the Agriculture Wages (Regulation) Act, 1924.

9. After 1924 the dates of changes in rates were:

Monmouthshire	- March 1932; March 1935; and Sept. 1936, 1937 and 1938.
Glamorganshire	- in March of the following years: 1925 and 1926; 1928; 1930; 1932, 1933 and 1934; 1937 and 1938.
Carmarthenshire	- from November 1925; February 1932; November 1932; 1934, 1936 and 1937.
Cardiganshire and Pembrokeshire	- From October 1925, 1932, 1934, 1935 and 1937.
Breconshire and Radnorshire	- from February 1925, May 1932, November 1934, May 1936, 1937 and November 1937.
Montgomeryshire and Merionethshire	- from May 1925, 1928 and 1932; March 1933; and May 1935, 1937, 1938 and 1939.
Flintshire and Denbighshire	- from February 1925, 1937 and 1938.
Caernarvonshire and Anglesey	- from June 1926, January 1933, November 1933, December 1935 and December 1937.

10. The rates from 1925 on were related to a standard working week, the hours of which were:

Monmouth

Year	Summer	Winter
1922	54	
1925-7	50	48
1928	52	50
1929-39	54	50

Glamorgan

Year	Summer	Winter
1925-35	54	
1936	52	
1937	54	
1938	52	
1939	50	48

Carmarthen

Year	Summer	Winter
1925-37	54	

Cardigan & Pembroke

Year	Summer	Winter
1925-7	54	50
1928-37	54	52
1938	53	51

Brecon & Radnor

Year	Summer	Winter
1925-30	54	48
1931-7	54	50
1938-9	54	48

Montgomery & Merioneth

Year	Summer	Winter
1925-35	54	
1936	52	
1937	54	
1938	52	
1939	50	48

Flint & Denbigh

Year	Summer	Winter
1925-32	50	
1933-4	54	50
1935-9	50	48

Caernarvon & Anglesey

Year	Summer	Winter
1925-36	50	
1937-9	50	48

11. The figures in brackets are from the Welsh Digest of Agricultural Statistics, the rest were provided direct by the Ministry of Agriculture.

WAGES 4. Police. Maximum and minimum rates of pay of police constables, by county, 1902-14

	At the beginning of:																			
	1902				1903				1905				1907				1908			
	max		min		max		min		max		min		max		min		max		min	
	s.	d.	s.	d.	s.	d.	s.	d.	s.	d.	s.	d.	s.	d.	s.	d.	s.	d.	s.	d.
Anglesey	26	0	22	0	27	0	23	0	27	0	23	0	27	0	23	0	27	0	23	0
Brecon	28	0	23	0	28	0	23	0	30	0	24	0	30	0	24	0	30	0	24	0
Caernarvon	30	0	24	0	30	0	24	0	30	0	24	0	30	0	24	0	30	0	24	0
Cardigan	29	2	22	9	29	2	22	9	29	2	22	9	29	2	22	9	29	2	22	9
Carmarthen	29	9	23	11	29	9	23	11	29	9	23	11	29	9	23	11	29	9	23	11
Denbigh	30	0	24	0	30	0	24	0	30	0	24	0	30	0	24	0	30	0	24	0
Flint	30	7	24	0	30	7	24	0	30	7	24	0	30	0	24	0	30	0	24	0
Glamorgan	31	6	25	1	31	6	25	1	31	6	25	1	31	6	25	1	31	6	25	1
Merioneth	30	0	24	0	30	0	24	0	30	0	24	0	30	0	24	0	30	0	24	0
Monmouth	31	6	25	1	31	6	25	1	31	6	25	1	31	6	25	1	31	6	25	1
Montgomery	30	0	24	0	30	0	24	0	30	0	24	0	30	0	24	0	30	0	24	0
Pembroke	28	0	22	2	28	0	22	2	28	0	22	2	28	0	22	2	28	0	22	2
Radnor	28	0	23	4	28	0	23	4	28	0	23	4	28	7	23	4	28	7	23	4
Cardiff	35	0	26	0	35	0	26	0	35	0	26	0	35	0	26	0	35	0	26	0
Carmarthen	27	0	22	0	27	0	21	0	27	0	21	0	27	0	21	0	27	0	21	0
Neath	31	6	26	6	31	6	26	0	31	6	26	0	31	6	26	0	33	0	26	0
Newport	33	6	26	0	33	6	26	0	33	6	26	0	33	6	26	0	33	6	26	0
Swansea	33	0	26	0	34	0	26	0	34	0	26	0	34	0	26	0	33	0	26	0

	At the beginning of:																			
	1909				1911				1912				1913				1914			
	max		min		max		min		max		min		max		min		max		min	
	s.	d.	s.	d.	s.	d.	s.	d.	s.	d.	s.	d.	s.	d.	s.	d.	s.	d.	s.	d.
Anglesey	27	0	23	0	27	0	23	0	27	0	23	0	30	0	24	0	30	0	24	0
Brecon	30	0	24	0	30	0	24	0	30	0	24	0	31	0	24	0	34	2	26	0
Caernarvon	30	0	24	0	30	0	24	0	30	0	24	0	30	0	24	0	33	3	26	0
Cardigan	29	2	22	9	29	9	23	4	29	9	23	4	29	9	23	4	33	3	26	0
Carmarthen	33	3	25	1	33	3	25	1	33	3	25	1	33	3	25	1	33	3	25	1
Denbigh	30	0	24	0	30	0	24	0	30	0	24	0	30	0	24	0	33	3	26	0
Flint	30	0	24	0	30	0	24	0	30	0	24	0	30	0	24	0	33	3	26	0
Glamorgan	32	8	26	3	32	8	26	3	32	8	26	3	34	5	28	0	34	5	28	0
Merioneth	30	0	24	0	30	0	24	0	30	0	24	0	30	0	24	0	33	3	26	0
Monmouth	31	6	25	1	31	6	25	1	31	6	25	1	34	5	28	0	34	5	28	0
Montgomery	30	0	24	0	30	0	24	0	30	0	24	0	30	0	24	0	33	3	26	0
Pembroke	28	0	22	2	30	0	23	4	30	0	23	4	30	0	25	0	30	0	25	0
Radnor	28	0	23	4	28	0	23	4	29	0	23	4	29	0	23	4	29	0	23	4
Cardiff	35	0	26	0	35	0	26	0	35	0	26	0	37	0	28	0	40	0	30	0
Carmarthen	30	0	23	0	30	0	23	0	32	0	25	0	32	0	25	0	34	0	27	0
Neath	34	6	26	0	34	6	26	0	34	6	26	0	34	6	26	0	35	0	28	0
Newport	34	6	26	0	34	6	26	0	34	6	26	0	38	6	28	0	38	6	28	0
Swansea	33	0	26	0	33	0	26	0	33	0	26	0	37	0	28	0	37	0	28	0

General Notes

(i) Board of Trade, Abstracts of Labour Statistics, no figures for 1904, 1906 and 1910.

WAGES 5. Building. Hours and rates per hour, building trades, main towns, 1886-1914 and 1936

Year	Place	Rates per Hour							
		Brick-layers	Masons	Carpenters and Joiners	House Plumbers	Plasterers	Painters	Labourers	
								Brick-layers	Plasterers
		d.	d.	d.	d.	d.	d.	d.	d.
1886	Newport Cardiff	.. ..	.. ..	$6\frac{1}{2}$ $7\frac{1}{2}$	.. ..	.. ..	.. ..	4 $4\frac{1}{2}$	
1894	Cardiff	$8\frac{1}{2}$	$8\frac{1}{2}$	$8\frac{1}{2}$	$8\frac{1}{2}$	$8\frac{1}{2}$	$7\frac{1}{2}$	..	..
1896	Cardiff	$8\frac{1}{2}$	$8\frac{1}{2}$	$8\frac{1}{2}$	$8\frac{1}{2}$	$8\frac{1}{2}$	$7\frac{1}{2}$	..	..
1897	Cardiff	$8\frac{1}{2}$	$8\frac{1}{2}$	$8\frac{1}{2}$	$8\frac{1}{2}$	$8\frac{1}{2}$	$7\frac{1}{2}$	..	..
end of 1898	Cardiff Swansea	$8\frac{1}{2}$ ..	$8\frac{1}{2}$ $8\frac{1}{2}$	$8\frac{1}{2}$ 8	$8\frac{1}{2}$ 8&9	$8\frac{1}{2}$ 8	$7\frac{1}{2}$ $7\frac{1}{2}$	.. ..	.. ..
Jan 1st 1900	Cardiff Swansea	9 ..	9 $8\frac{1}{2}$	$8\frac{1}{2}$ $8\frac{1}{2}$	$8\frac{1}{2}$ 8&9	9 $8\frac{1}{2}$	$7\frac{1}{2}$ $7\frac{1}{2}$	.. ..	.. ..
Jan 1st 1901	Cardiff Swansea	9 ..	9 $8\frac{1}{2}$	9 $8\frac{1}{2}$	9 (8(S) (1) (9(W)	9 $8\frac{1}{2}$	8 $7\frac{1}{2}$	.. ..	.. ..
Jan 1st 1902	Cardiff Swansea	9 $8\frac{1}{2}$	9 $8\frac{1}{2}$	9 $8\frac{1}{2}$	9 (8(S) (9(W)	9 $8\frac{1}{2}$	8 8	$5\frac{1}{2}$-6 5-$5\frac{1}{2}$	$5\frac{1}{2}$-6 5-$5\frac{1}{2}$
Jan 1st 1903	Cardiff Swansea	9 $8\frac{1}{2}$	9 $8\frac{1}{2}$	9 $8\frac{1}{2}$	9 (8(S) (9(W)	9 $8\frac{1}{2}$	8 8	$5\frac{1}{2}$-6 5-6	$5\frac{1}{2}$-6 5-6
Jan 1st 1905	Cardiff Swansea	9 $8\frac{1}{2}$	9 $8\frac{1}{2}$	9 $8\frac{1}{2}$	9 (8(S) (9(W)	9 $8\frac{1}{2}$	8&$8\frac{1}{2}$ 8	$5\frac{1}{2}$-6 5-6	$5\frac{1}{2}$-6 5-6
1906	Cardiff Newport Abergavenny Caernarvon	.. ..	.. ..	9 $8\frac{1}{2}$ 7 7	.. ..	.. ..	.. ..	$5\frac{1}{2}$d. $5\frac{1}{2}$d. $4\frac{3}{4}$d. 5d.	
July 1907	Cardiff Swansea	9 ..	9 $8\frac{1}{2}$	9 $8\frac{1}{2}$	9 (8(S) (9(W)	9 $8\frac{1}{2}$	$8\frac{1}{2}$ 8	$5\frac{1}{2}$ $5\frac{1}{2}$	
July 1908	Cardiff Swansea	9 ..	9 $8\frac{1}{2}$	9 $8\frac{1}{2}$	(8(S) (9(W) (8(S) (9(W)	9 $8\frac{1}{2}$	$8\frac{1}{2}$ 8	$5\frac{1}{2}$ $5\frac{1}{2}$	
Oct 1909	Cardiff Swansea	9 $8\frac{1}{2}$	9 $8\frac{1}{2}$	9 $8\frac{1}{2}$	9 (8(S) (9(W)	9 $8\frac{3}{4}$	8&$8\frac{1}{2}$ (2) 8	$5\frac{1}{2}$ ..	
Jan 1911	Cardiff Swansea	9 9	9 9	9 9	9 9	9 $8\frac{3}{4}$	8 8	$5\frac{1}{2}$ ..	
March 1912	Cardiff Swansea	9 9	9 9	9 9	9 9	9 9	8 $8\frac{1}{2}$	$5\frac{1}{2}$ $5\frac{1}{2}$-6	
July 1913	Cardiff Swansea	$9\frac{1}{2}$ 9	$9\frac{1}{2}$ 9	$9\frac{1}{2}$ 9	$9\frac{1}{2}$ 9	$9\frac{1}{2}$ 9	$8\frac{1}{2}$ $8\frac{1}{2}$	6 6	
Oct 1914	Cardiff Swansea	$9\frac{1}{2}$ $9\frac{1}{2}$	$9\frac{1}{2}$ $9\frac{1}{2}$	$9\frac{1}{2}$ $9\frac{1}{2}$	$9\frac{1}{2}$ 9	$9\frac{1}{2}$ $9\frac{1}{2}$	$8\frac{1}{2}$ 9	$6\frac{1}{2}$ $6\frac{1}{2}$	
Dec 1936	Cardiff) Swansea) Newport)	$18\frac{1}{2}$	$18\frac{1}{2}$	$18\frac{1}{2}$	$18\frac{1}{2}$	$18\frac{1}{2}$	$18\frac{1}{2}$	14	

General Notes

(i) Sources. Board of Trade, Abstracts of Labour Statistics (for 1894-1905; 1907-14, 1936); E.H. Hunt, Regional Wage Variations in Britain 1850-1914 (for 1886 and 1906). Hunt's sources are: G.H. Wood unpublished wage statistics, library of Royal Statistical Society and Dept. of Employment; Wages of the Manual Labour Classes, P.P. 1893-4, LXXXIII; Earnings and Hours Inquiry, III, P.P. 1910, LXXXIV.

(ii) The summer hours for all craftsmen (except Plasterers), and for Labourers are given for every year from 1894 to 1914 as 54 per week (except for Swansea in 1914 where the hours are 53½). The summer hours for Plasterers are given as 50½ for 1894 to 1898, but thereafter become 54. The summer hours are not as consistently recorded - mostly being given only for 1894 to 1900, when they were 48 for Bricklayers; 47½ (48 in Swansea in 1900) for Masons, Carpenters and Joiners; 54 for 1896-8 for House Plumbers (Cardiff) but 48 for 1898 and 1900 (Swansea); 44½ for Plasterers 1896-8 (Cardiff), 47 in 1894 and 47½ to 51 in 1900 (Cardiff); 48 for Painters (Swansea) in 1900 - the only information recorded. In 1936 the hours for all Craftsmen and Labourers were: 46½ in summer, and 44 in winter.

Notes

1. S = summer; W = winter.

2. Trade union rate.

WAGES 6. Engineering and ship-repairing. Rates for different trades, main ports, 1873-1968[1]

		PATTERN MAKERS		IRON FOUNDERS	ENGINEERS				BOILERMAKERS & IRON SHIPBUILDERS							SHIPWRIGHTS		ENGINEERING LABOURERS	
		weekly rate	weekly hours	weekly rate	weekly rates			weekly hours	weekly rates (new work)						weekly hours	weekly rate (new work)	weekly hours	weekly rate	weekly hours
					turners	fitters	smiths		platers (heavy) boiler shops	platers (heavy) ship yards	platers (light) boiler shops	platers (light) ship yards	rivetters boiler shops	rivetters ship yards					
		s. d.		s. d.	s. d.	s. d.	s. d.		s. d.	s. d.	s. d.	s. d.	s. d.	s. d.		s. d.		s. d.	
1873	Cardiff	..	..	..	..	..	..	..	39 0	39 0	..	..	33 0	33 0	..	..	..	..	..
Jan 1880	Cardiff	..	..	..	36 0	36 0	..	54	..	..	..	..	..	..	..	..	..	..	..
Jan 1886	Cardiff[2]	..	..	..	36 0	36 0	..	54	..	..	..	..	..	..	..	..	..	..	..
Jan 1890	Cardiff	..	..	..	39 0	39 0	..	54	..	..	..	..	..	..	..	..	..	..	..
1894	Cardiff	36 0	54	34 0	36 0	36 0	36 0	54	45 0	42 0	45 0	42 0	42 0	39 0	(S.54 (W.48	..	..	..	..
1896	Cardiff	36 0	54	34 0	36 0	36 0	36 0	54	45 0	42 0	45 0	42 0	42 0	39 0	(S.54 (W.48	39 0	..	..	..
1897	Cardiff	36 0	54	36 0	34 0	34 0	34 0	53	45 0	42 0	45 0	42 0	42 0	39 0	(S.53 (W.47	40 0	..	..	..
1898	Cardiff	36 0	54	36 0	34 0	34 0	34 0	53	45 0	42 0	45 0	42 0	42 0	39 0	(S.53 (W.47	40 0[6]	..	..	..
	Swansea	36 0	54	33 0	30 0	30 0	30 0	54	42 0	39 0	42 0	39 0	42 0	39 0	54	36 0	..	..	..
1900	Cardiff	36 0	53	36 0	39 0[3]	39 0[3]	39 0[3]	53	45 0[4]	42 0[4]	45 0[4]	42 0[4]	42 0[4]	39 0[4]	(S.53 (W.47	40 0[4]	..	..	..
	Swansea	38 3	54	36 0	32 0	32 0	33 0	54	7 6[4][5]	..	..	..	7 0[4][5]	..	48	36 0	..	..	..
1901	Cardiff	36 0	53	36 0	40 0[3]	40 0[3]	40 0[3]	53	42 0	39 0	..	..	39 0	36 0	(S.53 (W.47	40 0[4]	47	..	..
	Swansea	38 3	54	36 0	36 0	36 0	36 0	54	7 6[4][5]	..	..	..	7 0[4][5]	..	48	36 0	54	..	..
1902	Cardiff	38 0	53	36 0	41 0[3]	41 0[3]	41 0[3]	53	42 0	39 0	..	..	39 0	36 0	53, 47	40 0[4]	47	..	..
	Swansea	38 3	54	36 0	36 0	36 0	36 0	54	7 6[4][5]	..	..	..	7 0[4][5]	..	48	(39 0(4) (36 0	53	..	..
1903	Cardiff	38 0	53	36 0	41 0[3]	41 0[3]	41 0[3]	53	42 0	39 0	..	..	39 0	36 0	53, 47	40 0[4]	47	..	..
	Swansea	38 3	54	36 0	36 0	36 0	36 0	54	7 6[4][5]	..	..	..	7 0[4][5]	..	48	39 0(4) 36 0	53	..	..
1905	Cardiff	38 0	53	36 0	41 0[3]	41 0[3]	41 0[3]	53	42 0	39 0	..	..	39 0	36 0	53, 47	40 0[4]	47	..	..
	Swansea	38 3	54	36 0	36 0	36 0	36 0	54	7 6[4][5]	..	..	..	7 0[4][5]	..	48	39 0(4) 36 0	53	..	..
Jan 1906	Cardiff	..	..	..	41 0[3]	41 0[3]	..	53	..	..	..	..	..	..	..	..	..	..	..
Jly 1907	Cardiff	38 0	53	37 6	41 0[3]	41 0[3]	41 0[3]	53	42 0	39 0	..	..	39 0	36 0	53, 47	..	..	..	..
	Swansea	38 3	54	36 0	36 0	36 0	36 0	54	..	..	..	..	..	..	..	..	..	..	..
Jly 1908	Cardiff	38 0	53	37 6	41 0[3]	41 0[3]	41 0[3]	53	42 0	39 0	..	..	39 0	36 0	53, 47	..	..	..	..
	Swansea	38 3	54	37 0	36 0	36 0	36 0	54	..	..	..	..	..	..	..	..	..	..	..
Oct 1909	Cardiff	38 6	53	37 6	41 0[3]	41 0[3]	41 0[3]	53	42 0	42 0	..	..	42 0	42 0	53	..	..	..	..
	Swansea	38 3	54	37 0	36 0	36 0	36 0	54	..	..	..	..	..	..	..	..	..	..	..

WAGES 6. Engineering and ship-repairing. Rates for different trades, main ports, 1873-1968[1] Contd.

Date	Port																		
Jan 1911	Cardiff	38 0	53	37 6	41 0[3]	41 0[3]	41 0[3]	53	45 0	42 0	..	..	42 0	39 0	54	..	..	..	..
	Swansea	38 3	54	37 0	36 0	36 0	36 0	54	..	..	..	..	..	..	..	..	..	..	..
Mar 1912	Cardiff	41 0	53	39 0	45 0[3]	45 0[3]	45 0[3]	(S.53 (W.47	..	..	..	..	..	..	..	..	..	..	..
	Swansea	39 3	54	38 0	37 0	37 0	37 0	54	..	..	..	..	..	..	..	..	..	..	..
Jly 1913	Cardiff	41 0	53	40 0	40 0	40 0	40 0	53	..	..	..	..	..	..	..	..	..	..	..
	Swansea	39 3	54	39 0	37 0	37 0	37 0	54	..	..	..	..	..	..	..	..	..	..	..
Oct 1914	Cardiff	41 0	53	40 0	40 0	40 0	40 0	53	..	..	..	..	..	..	..	..	..	..	..
	Swansea	39 3	54	40 0	40 0	40 0	40 0	54	..	..	..	..	..	..	..	..	..	..	..
Apr 1915	Cardiff	..	..	..	42 0	..	..	..	..	..	..	..	..	..	..	..	..	..	..
Sep 1915	Cardiff	..	..	..	44 0	..	..	..	..	..	..	..	..	..	..	..	..	..	..
Jly 1916	Cardiff	..	..	..	47 0	..	..	..	..	..	..	..	..	..	..	..	..	..	..
Apr 1920	Cardiff	..	..	..	..	..	..	47	..	..	..	..	..	..	..	..	..	..	47
Apr 1924	Cardiff	..	..	..	..	..	..	47	..	..	..	..	..	..	..	..	..	..	47
Apr 1926	Cardiff	..	..	..	..	..	..	47	..	..	..	..	..	..	..	..	..	..	47
Apr 1930	Cardiff	..	..	..	70 0		..	47	..	..	..	..	..	..	..	..	..	49 6	47
Dec 1936[8]	Cardiff	..	..	..	..	..	..	..	..	..	..	..	..	..	..	71 6[4]	..	50 6[7]	..
	Newport	..	..	..	..	..	..	..	..	..	..	..	..	..	..	71 6[4]	..	..[7]	..
	Swansea	..	..	..	..	..	..	..	..	..	..	..	..	..	..	71 6[4]	..	52 6[7]	..
Apr 1938	Cardiff	..	..	..	..	..	..	47	..	..	..	..	..	..	..	..	..	..	47
Apr 1945	Cardiff	..	..	..	..	..	..	47	..	..	..	..	..	..	..	..	..	..	47
Apr 1950	Cardiff	..	..	..	115 1¼		..	44	..	..	..	..	..	..	..	..	..	96 9¾	44
Apr 1955	Cardiff	..	..	..	163 11¼		..	44	..	..	..	..	..	..	..	..	..	137 7¾	44
Apr 1960	Cardiff	..	..	..	191 3¼		..	42	..	..	..	..	..	..	..	..	..	160 5¾	42
Apr 1965	Cardiff	..	..	..	216 3¼		..	41	..	..	..	..	..	..	..	..	..	182 5¾	41
Apr 1968	Cardiff	..	..	..	257 8		..	40	..	..	..	..	..	..	..	..	..	217 4	40

General Notes

(i) Sources. Bowley and Wood, JRSS., 68 (for 1873); Board of Trade, Abstract of Labour Statistics (for 1886, 1894-1905, 1907-14, 1936); British Labour Statistics, Historical Abstract, 1868-1968 (for 1880-1968 (for 1880-90, 1906, 1920-30, 1938-68); Bowley, Prices and Wages in the U.K., 1914-20, (for 1915-16).

Notes

1. Some earlier figures for weekly wages are given in Bowley and Wood, J.R.S.S. vol. 68. The weekly rate for shipwrights in Newport was given as 27s. for 1863-7; 30s. for 1868-75; and 36s. in 1876. The rate for pattern-makers in Cardiff was given as 36s. for every year back to 1874. Bowley and Wood also give figures for 1880-1904 taken from the Reports on changes in Wages and hours of Labour, but the slightly different figures from the Labour Abstracts and the Historical Abstract have been preferred as a more reliable source.

2. Figures are also available for the following shipbuilding workers for 1886, for South Wales:

	s.	d.
fitters	35	8
ships carpenters and joiners	38	10
labourers	23	4

3. Relates to marine shops.

4. Relates to repair work.

5. Rate per day.

6. Rate for piece work.

7. A figure is also available for shipbuilding labourers for 1936:

   Cardiff, Newport and Swansea 55s. 6d.

8. Figures are also given for iron-moulders (sand) for 1936:

	s.	d.
Cardiff	63	0
Newport	66	6
Swansea	70	0

WAGES 7. Rates of pay and hours for Printing trades, main towns, [illegible] 1901-14

	PRINTING TRADES							CABINET MAKERS ETC			
	Litho Printers	COMPOSITORS									
		Min. weekly rate			Max. weekly hours			Hourly Rates			
	weekly rate	book & jobbing	weekly bi-wkly n'papers	daily n'papers	books & jobbing	weekly bi-wkly n'papers	daily n'papers	Cabinet makers	French Polishers	Uphol-sterers	Weekly hours
	s. d.	s. d.	s. d.	s. d.				d.	d.	d.	
Jan 1850 Cardiff	..	21 0	..	..	..	..	..	..	..	..	..
1860 Cardiff	..	21 0	..	..	..	..	..	..	..	..	..
1870 Cardiff	..	24 0	..	..	..	..	..	..	..	..	..
1880 Cardiff	..	29 0	..	..	54	..	..	..	..	..	..
1886 Cardiff	..	29 0	..	..	54	..	..	..	..	..	..
1890 Cardiff	..	30 0	..	..	54	..	..	..	..	..	..
1894 Cardiff	..	30 0	30 0	40 0	54	54	54	..	..	..	..
1896 Cardiff	..	30 0	30 0	40 0	54	54	54	..	..	..	..
1897 Cardiff	..	30 0	30 0	40 0	54	54	54	..	..	..	..
end of 1898 Cardiff	..	30 0	30 0	40 0	54	54	54	..	..	..	..
Swansea	..	28 6	28 6	28 6	54	54	54	..	..	..	..
1 Jan 1900 Cardiff	..	30 0	..	40 0	54	..	52½	..	..	..	..
Swansea	..	28 6	28 6	28 6(1)	54	54	54(1)	..	..	..	..
1901 Cardiff	32 0	32 0	32 0	40 0	52½	52½	52½	7-8	6½-7½	8-9	54
Swansea	..	28 6	28 6	28 6(1)	54	54	54(1)	8	8	8	54
1902 Cardiff	32 0	32 0	32 0	40 0	52½	52½	52½	7½-8	7-7½	8-9	54
Swansea	..	31 0	31 0	31 0(1)	54	54	54(1)	8	8	8	54
1903 Cardiff	32 0	32 0	32 0	40 0	52½	52¼	52½	..	..	..	..
Swansea	..	31 0	31 0	31 0(1)	54	54	54(1)	8	8	8	54
1905 Cardiff	32 0	32 0	32 0	40 0	52½	52½	52½	..	..	..	..
Swansea	37 6	31 0	31 0	31 0(1)	54	54	54(1)	8	8	8	54
1906 Cardiff	..	32 0	..	..	52½	..	..	..	..	..	..
July 1907 Cardiff	33 6	33 6	..	42 0	52½	..	50	..	..	..	..
Swansea	35 0	32 0	..	..	52½	..	..	8	8	8	54
July 1908 Cardiff	32 6	33 6	..	42 0	52½	..	50	..	..	..	..
Swansea	35 0	32 0	..	..	52½	..	..	8	8	8	54
Oct 1909 Cardiff	33 6	33 6	..	42 0	52½	..	50	..	..	..	..
Swansea	36s, 40s	32 6	..	32 6(1)	52½	..	52½(1)	8	8	8	54
Jan 1911 Cardiff	33 6	33 6	..	42 0	52½	..	50	..	..	..	..
Swansea	36s, 40s	32 6	..	32 6(1)	52½	..	52½(1)	8	8	8	54
Mar 1912 Cardiff	34 6	34 6	..	43 0	51½	..	50	..	..	..	..
Swansea	36s, 40s	34 0	..	..	51½	..	..	8	8	8	54
Jly 1913 Cardiff	36 0	36 0	..	43 6	51	..	50	..	..	..	..
Swansea	36 0	34 6	..	..	51	..	..	8	8	8,8½	54
Oct 1914 Cardiff	36 6	36 0	..	..	51	..	..	..	..	..	..
Swansea	38 0	34 6	..	..	51	..	..	8	8	8,8½	54
Jly 1915 Cardiff	..	36 0	..	..	..	..	..	..	..	..	..
1916 Cardiff	..	38 0	..	..	..	..	..	..	..	..	..
1917 Cardiff	..	45 6	..	..	..	..	..	..	..	..	..
1918 Cardiff	..	57 6	..	..	..	..	..	..	..	..	..
1919 Cardiff	..	72 0	..	..	..	..	..	..	..	..	..
Apr 1920 Cardiff	..	79 6	..	..	48	..	..	..	..	..	..
Jly 1920 Cardiff	..	89 6	..	..	..	..	..	..	..	..	..

WAGES 7 cont.

	PRINTING TRADES							CABINET MAKERS ETC			
	Litho Printers	COMPOSITORS						Hourly Rates			
		Min. weekly rate			Max. weekly hours						
	weekly rate	book & jobbing	weekly bi-wkly n'papers	daily n'papers	books & jobbing	weekly bi-wkly n'papers	daily n'papers	Cabinet makers	French Polishers	Uphol-sterers	Weekly hours
Apr 1924 Cardiff	..	75 6	..	..	48	..	..	..	..	..	..
Apr 1926 Cardiff	..	74 6	..	..	48	..	..	..	..	..	..
Apr 1930 Cardiff	..	74 6	..	..	48	..	..	..	..	..	..
Dec 1936[2] Cardiff	..	74 6	..	..	..	..	..	..	..	..	..
Swansea	..	74 6	..	..	..	..	..	18½	..	18½	..
Newport	..	71 6	..	..	..	..	..	..	..	..	..
Apr 1938 Cardiff	..	74 6	..	..	45	..	..	..	..	..	..
Apr 1945 Cardiff	..	93 6	..	..	45	..	..	..	..	..	..
Apr 1950 Cardiff	..	131 0	..	..	43½	..	..	..	..	..	..
Apr 1955 Cardiff	..	174 6	..	..	43½	..	..	..	..	..	..
Apr 1960 Cardiff	..	228 9	..	..	42	..	..	..	..	..	..
Apr 1965 Cardiff	..	281 0	..	..	40	..	..	..	..	..	..
Apr 1968 Cardiff	..	323 6	..	..	40	..	..	..	..	..	..

General Notes

(i) Sources. Board of Trade Abstracts of Labour Statistics (for 1894-1914 and 1936); British Labour Statistics, Historical Abstracts, 1886-1968 (for 1850-86, 1924-30, 1938-68); Bowley, Prices and Wages in the U.K., 1914-20 (for 1915-20).

Notes

1. Relates to evening newspapers.

2. Other figures given for 1936:

	Cardiff s. d.	Swansea s. d.	Newport s. d.
lino-type and mono-type operaters (jobbing work)	74 6	74 6	71 6
general assistants (book and jobbing)	55 6	55 6	53 6

WAGES 8. Earnings. Average weekly and hourly earnings, and average hours for manual workers over 20 in manufacturing, all industries, and selected individual industries, 1960-75

	MANUFACTURING			ALL INDUSTRIES(1)		
	Average weekly earnings	Average weekly hours worked	Average hourly earnings	Average weekly earnings	Average weekly hours worked	Average hourly earnings
	£. s. d.		d.	£. s. d.		d.
pr 1960	15 13 10	46.7	80.6	14 6 0	47.7	71.9
pr 1961	16 11 6	46.1	86.3	15 3 6	47.2	77.2
ct 1961	16 8 9	45.5	86.7	15 5 3	46.5	78.8
pr 1962	16 17 7	45.2	89.6	15 15 8	46.6	81.3
ct 1962	17 8 4	45.2	92.5	16 14 1	46.5	83.6
pr 1963	17 13 5	45.3	93.6	16 9 7	46.5	85.1
ct 1963	18 4 2	45.6	95.8	16 18 7	46.9	86.6
pr 1964	18 19 11	46.1	98.9	17 14 11	47.1	90.4
ct 1964	19 10 3	45.5	102.9	18 0 10	46.5	93.1
pr 1965	20 2 2	45.5	106.1	18 18 6	46.8	97.1
ct 1965	20 14 5	44.5	111.8	19 6 0	45.7	101.4
pr 1966	21 5 6	44.2	115.5	19 13 7	44.7	105.7
ct 1966	21 10 0	43.9	117.5	20 1 10	45.0	107.2
pr 1967	21 11 10	44.1	117.6	20 7 3	45.4	107.7
ct 1967	22 5 9	44.1	121.3	21 2 10	45.2	112.2
pr 1968	23 1 0	44.4	124.7	21 17 9	45.2	116.2
ct 1968	24 1 10	44.6	129.7	22 18 3	45.5	120.9
ct 1969	26 0 11	44.7	139.7	24 9 3	45.7	128.4
	£.	hours	new pence	£.	hours	new pence
ct 1968(a)(2)	24.09	44.6	54.01	22.91	45.5	50.35
ct 1969(a)(2)	26.05	44.7	58.28	24.46	45.7	53.52
(b)(2)	25.97	44.7	58.10	24.46	45.7	53.52
ct 1970	29.65	44.1	67.23	27.93	45.0	62.07
ct 1971	32.25	43.2	74.65	31.10	44.4	70.05
ct 1972	36.99	43.8	84.45	35.61	44.8	79.49
ct 1973	41.76	43.7	95.56	40.52	44.7	90.65
ct 1974	48.58	43.1	112.71	47.55	44.4	107.09
ct 1975	59.52	40.8	145.88	58.19	42.3	137.57

WAGES 8. Earnings. Selected Individual Industries

	INDUSTRIES	Average weekly earnings	Average weekly hours worked	Average hourly earnings
		s. d.		d.
Apr 1960	Construction	261 4(3)	49.3	63.6
	Paper, printing & publishing	288 8	46.3	74.8
	Engineering & electrical goods	298 10	46.3	77.5
	Shipbuilding & marine engineering	294 9	46.4	76.2
Oct 1960	Construction	..	..	..
	Paper, printing & publishing	..	..	..
	Engineering & electrical goods	..	..	..
	Shipbuilding & marine engineering	..	..	..
Apr 1961	Construction	..	..	..
	Paper, printing & publishing	294 3	45.5	77.6
	Engineering & electrical goods	331 1	48.7	81.5
	Shipbuilding & marine engineering	311 3	44.6	83.7
Oct 1961	Construction	..	..	..
	Paper, printing & publishing	303 11	..	..
	Engineering & electrical goods	325 5	..	..
	Shipbuilding & marine engineering	319 10	..	..
Apr 1962	Construction	304 10	49.0	74.7
	Paper, printing & publishing	322 7	45.4	85.3
	Engineering & electrical goods	318 4	46.1	82.9
	Shipbuilding & marine engineering	310 0	44.1	84.4
Oct 1962	Construction	308 3	49.1	75.3
	Paper, printing & publishing	325 3	44.9	86.9
	Engineering & electrical goods	335 2	46.5	86.5
	Shipbuilding & marine engineering	335 10	44.5	90.6
Apr 1963	Construction	308 6	48.4	76.5
	Paper, printing & publishing	342 0	45.9	89.4
	Engineering & electrical goods	330 3	45.2	87.7
	Shipbuilding & marine engineering	368 1	47.3	93.4
Oct 1963	Construction	317 10	49.1	77.7
	Paper, printing & publishing	345 4	46.3	89.5
	Engineering & electrical goods	344 10	46.8	88.4
	Shipbuilding & marine engineering	320 5	43.6	88.2
Apr 1964	Construction	339 7	48.8	83.5
	Paper, printing & publishing	373 9	47.0	95.4
	Engineering & electrical goods	372 0	47.8	93.4
	Shipbuilding & marine engineering	412 4	48.3	102.4
Oct 1964	Construction	333 8	47.8	83.8
	Paper, printing & publishing	368 10	46.3	95.6
	Engineering & electrical goods	370 4	47.2	94.2
	Shipbuilding & marine engineering	459 0	50.7	108.6

	INDUSTRIES	Average weekly earnings	Average weekly hours worked	Average hourly earnings
		s. d.		d.
Apr 1965	Construction	369 6	49.1	90.3
	Paper, printing & publishing	369 2	45.5	97.4
	Engineering & electrical goods	383 6	46.6	98.8
	Shipbuilding & marine engineering	466 5	51.7	103.3
Oct 1965	Construction	366 4	48.1	91.4
	Paper, printing & publishing	396 8	45.7	104.2
	Engineering & electrical goods	381 3	44.9	101.9
	Shipbuilding & marine engineering	412 9	45.7	108.4
Apr 1966	Construction	360 2	45.1	95.8
	Paper, printing & publishing	405 9	45.9	106.1
	Engineering & electrical goods	396 7	45.2	105.3
	Shipbuilding & marine engineering	478 0	49.8	115.2
Oct 1966	Construction	377 4	46.6	97.2
	Paper, printing & publishing	409 10	45.1	109.0
	Engineering & electrical goods	393 6	44.4	106.4
	Shipbuilding & marine engineering	491 7	48.6	121.4
Apr 1967	Construction	390 3	48.2	97.2
	Paper, printing & publishing	424 0	45.3	112.3
	Engineering & electrical goods	408 11	44.8	109.5
	Shipbuilding & marine engineering	389 4	41.2	113.4
Oct 1967	Construction	412 7	47.7	103.8
	Paper, printing & publishing	441 9	45.8	115.7
	Engineering & electrical goods	413 8	44.4	111.7
	Shipbuilding & marine engineering	463 7	46.7	119.1
Apr 1968	Construction	422 4	46.9	108.1
	Paper, printing & publishing	466 8	45.6	122.7
	Engineering & electrical goods	435 11	45.2	115.7
	Shipbuilding & marine engineering	433 0	43.4	119.8
Oct 1968	Construction	443 10	47.5	112.1
	Paper, printing & publishing	475 10	46.2	123.6
	Engineering & electrical goods	459 7	46.0	119.9
	Shipbuilding & marine engineering	591 9	54.2	130.9
Apr 1969	Construction	458 5	47.2	116.5
	Paper, printing & publishing	491 4	46.3	127.3
	Engineering & electrical goods	495 11	46.3	128.5
	Shipbuilding & marine engineering	614 10	54.4	135.8
Oct 1969	Construction	471 5	48.4	116.9
(Sic 1958)	Paper, printing & publishing	510 9	45.9	133.6
	Engineering & electrical goods	509 3	54.9	133.0
	Shipbuilding & marine engineering	584 7	50.7	138.3

	INDUSTRIES	Average weekly earnings	Average weekly hours worked	Averag hourly earnin
		s. d.		d.
Oct 1969	Construction	471 5	48.4	116.9
(Sic 1968)	Paper, printing & publishing	504 2	45.7	132.3
	Mechanical engineering	518 1	46.7	133.3
	Instrument engineering	478 1	42.3	135.7
	Electrical engineering	486 7	44.5	131.4
	Shipbuilding & marine engineering	574 1	50.1	137.4
Oct 1970	Construction	513 11	46.7	132.1
	Paper, printing & publishing	586 2	44.6	157.8
	Mechanical engineering	578 5	45.3	153.2
	Instrument engineering	525 8	40.2	157.1
	Electrical engineering	543 2	44.4	146.7
	Shipbuilding & marine engineering	611 8	47.8	153.6
		£		p.
Oct 1971	Construction	30.23	47.1	64.18
(Sic 1968)	Paper, printing & publishing	33.35	45.5	73.30
	Mechanical engineering	31.60	45.9	68.85
	Instrument engineering	31.34	42.4	73.92
	Electrical engineering	30.81	43.3	71.15
	Shipbuilding & marine engineering	24.97	42.3	59.03
Oct 1972	Construction	34.41	47.0	73.21
	Paper, printing & publishing	36.03	44.8	80.42
	Mechanical engineering	34.25	43.7	78.38
	Instrument engineering	28.62	42.6	67.18
	Electrical engineering	35.89	43.6	82.32
	Shipbuilding & marine engineering	25.65	39.5	64.94
Oct 1973	Construction	40.23	46.5	86.52
	Paper, printing & publishing	40.65	44.2	91.97
	Mechanical engineering	40.40	45.2	89.38
	Instrument engineering	31.96	43.8	72.97
	Electrical engineering	39.57	43.7	90.55
	Shipbuilding & marine engineering	33.80	43.8	77.17
Oct 1974	Construction	46.35	46.6	99.46
	Paper, printing & publishing	47.55	42.2	112.68
	Mechanical engineering	47.81	44.2	108.17
	Instrument engineering	45.98	42.2	108.96
	Electrical engineering	42.92	40.5	105.98
	Shipbuilding & marine engineering	60.96	62.6	97.38
Oct 1975	Construction	54.96	44.8	123.68
	Paper, printing & publishing	55.68	41.7	131.49
	Mechanical engineering	61.15	43.2	141.55
	Instrument engineering	57.88	36.0	160.78
	Electrical engineering	55.24	40.3	137.07
	Shipbuilding & marine engineering	71.04	40.7	174.55

General Notes

(i) Sources. (a) For Manufacturing and All Industries: British Labour Statistics. Historical Abstract, 1886-1968, tables 57-9 (for 1960-68); British Labour Statistics. Yearbooks (for 1969-73); Dept. of Employment Gazette, 1975-6 (for 1974-5).

(b) For Individual Industries: for April 1960, April 1962 - April 1968; Ministry of Labour Gazette, 1963-1968; for April and October 1961, Statistics on Incomes, Prices, Ministry of Labour Gazette, June 1963 Employment and Productivity, Dec. 1962; for October 1968 - October 1975; Employment and Production Gazette, 1969-76

Notes

1. All industries means manufacturing industry plus mining and quarrying (except coal), construction, gas, electricity and water, transport and communications, some miscellaneous services and public administration. From October 1967 postmen and dock workers on daily (or half-daily) engagements are included.

2. a = 1958 S.I.C.
   b = 1968 S.I.C., figures continue on this basis from 1976.

3. This is the figure given in the Gazette. The Statistics on Income and Prices gives 282s. 5d. This latter figure has been used to calculate the earnings for April and October 1961 to keep them on the same basis as for the other industries.

WAGES 9. Income and expenditure. Household income and expenditure, Wales and U.K., 1953-4 and 1961-73

Unweighted average of two years:	Ave weekly h'hold income		Ave weekly income per person		Ave weekly household expenditure		Ave weekly expenditure per person		Ave weekly expenditure on housing	
	Wales	U.K.	Wales	U.K.	Wales	U.K.	Wales	U.K.	Wales	U.K.
	£	£	£	£	£	£	£	£	£	£
1953-4	..	..	..	..	12.03	12.01	3.82	3.77	0.93	1.06
1961-2	18.36	20.62[1]	5.98	6.81[1]	16.27	17.39	5.30	5.74	1.58	1.67
1962-3	18.66	21.33	6.23	7.05	16.54	18.37	5.52	6.07	1.52	1.88
1964-6	22.72	25.17	7.51	8.34	19.13	21.01	6.32	6.96	2.12	2.40
1965-7	23.95	26.72	8.15	8.94	20.38	22.29	6.93	7.45	2.37	2.57
1967-8	26.13	29.12	8.68	9.77	22.64	24.13	7.52	8.10	2.49	2.93
1968-9	27.20	31.22	9.09	10.55	24.24	25.65	7.76	8.67	2.55	3.22
1969-70	30.45	33.87	10.22	11.47	25.42	47.42	8.53	9.28	3.01	3.42
1970-1	33.45	37.04	11.16	12.68	27.85	29.85	9.29	10.22	3.30	3.80
1971-2	37.49	40.63	12.47	13.97	31.55	32.99	10.49	11.35	3.82	4.20
1972-3	42.24	46.16	14.44	16.08	35.21	37.26	12.03	12.98	4.02	4.87

General Notes

(i) Sources. British Labour Statistics, Historical Abstracts, 1886-1968 (for 1953-4, 1962-3 and 1967-8); British Labour Statistics Yearbooks (for 1968-73).

Notes

1. Figure relates to 1962 only. No figure available for 1961.

Wages 10. Household amenities. Proportion of households possessing certain amenities, Wales and U.K., 1964-73

	T.V.		Telephone		Washing Machine		Refrig-erator		Car		Full or Partial Central Heating	
	Wales	U.K.	Wales	U.K.	Wales	U.K.	Wales	U.K.	Wales	U.K.	Wales	U.K.
1964-6	..	..	17	23	58	57	32	40	45	40	5	10
1969	92	91	21	32	64	63	50	60	45	51	17	25
1970	93	91	25	35	71	65	58	66	54	52	20	30
1971	91	91	23	38	67	64	60	69	45	51	28	32
1972	93	93	33	42	75	65	74	74	58	53	36	37
1973	95	93	25	43	66	67	69	78	52	54	27	38

General Notes

(i) Sources. British Labour Statistics, Historical Abstracts, 1886-1968 (for 1964-6); British Labour Statistics Yearbooks (for 1969 73)

Chapter 4
Agriculture

The starting-point for any enquiry into agriculture, and especially into agricultural statistics, for Wales is the work of Ashby and Evans.[1] The present study makes wide use of the material collected by them, but also aims to extend their efforts in two main respects. The obvious extension is chronological and the direction of this is mostly forwards. In general the statistical tables presented by Ashby and Evans have been carried forward for a further three and a half decades. There are also some cases where the tables have been pushed backwards in time. The other major extension has been to include some topics on which Ashby and Evans presented no series specifically relating to Wales. The most obvious examples concern farm machinery and the prices in Wales of some agricultural products.

Whether the purpose has been to check, to supplement or to extend the findings of Ashby and Evans, the major source has been the official annual agricultural statistics. These, after a series of false starts, date from 1867 as a continuous and effective series. Not all the information can be taken back over the whole period since there was a natural tendency to add extra items from time to time. In addition, too, the accuracy of the figures for the earlier years suffers from a combination of initial incompetence, distrust of the objectives of the exercise by many farmers, and a lack of uniformity over the interpretation of the questions. These defects dwindled over time and this process was probably aided by the gradual exclusion of the tiniest holdings[2] where such attitudes and sources

1. A.W. Ashby and I.L. Evans, The Agriculture of Wales and Monmouthshire, Cardiff, 1944.

2. From 1869 information was not required from holdings of less than a quarter-acre, and from 1893 holdings of less than an acre were excluded.

of error were likely to be most persistent. The exclusion of such very small-scale producers would not, moreover, have greatly affected total acreage output figures and hence do not significantly reduce the comparability of the series over time. Such comparability is greatly enhanced by the fact that the questions in the agricultural census relate to the same date, 4th June, in each year.

There are significant differences between agricultural practice and performance in different parts of the country. For this reason, and because they are conveniently available over a long period of time, several of the basic tables give figures (quinquennially, at least) for each county as well as annual for Wales as a whole. This is the case for acreage of crops (Tables 1 and 2);[1] numbers of livestock (Tables 3 and 4); size of holdings (Tables 7 and 8); the number of workers (Tables 9 and 10). The first four tables thus indicate the response of farmers in Wales to changing circumstances by giving the broad shifts in the production mix. Such shifts have to be interpreted with some caution, of course, because of such consideration as changes in quality, and even of function, which can be disguised under unchanging names. Thus, for example, the total number of cattle in Wales in 1939 was almost exactly the same as in 1919, but these years also saw a significant increase in the proportional importance of the breeding and dairy herd. In the case of crops in general an additional indication of these relative shifts is obtained from estimates of the production and yields for the principal crops shown in Tables 5 and 6. These

1. It was hoped to extend the information on crop acreages by including information from the acreage returns which the government attempted to collect in 1800-1 during the Napoleonic wars. In fact, however, the data then collected is far from comprehensive (in the case of most counties only a small number of parishes are included) and is also of dubious reliability. It was considered, therefore, that its inclusion would be more mis-leading than helpful.

estimates, however, mostly derive from the assessments made by local crop reporters whose judgements are, despite their experience and local knowledge, naturally fallible.

The information on agricultural prices (Table 11) is not drawn directly from official sources but comes from the work of David Jones and, especially, the comprehensive thesis of David Howell,[1] who also generously made available his primary notes. Much more work of this careful and painstaking nature is needed before any reliable and comprehensive price indices for Wales can be compiled. Table 12 gives information on agricultural machinery in Wales over the last 30 years or so, and because of their relative importance for Welsh farming in recent generations separate figures are also included (Table 13) for milk producers. Tables 14 and 15 offer some statistics on fishing and forestry, activities normally closely associated with agriculture for census and administrative purposes. The fishing figures, especially in the early years, are not fully reliable. This was partly because they do not alwyas cover the same number of ports, although this was probably not a serious source of error because the bigger ports were always included. Much more significant for the very early years was the clear deficiency in the reporting. The 1887 report, for example, commented that: 'there is no doubt, however, that the collection in 1887 has been rather better than in the former years, the officers having had more experience. But until the system of collection has been longer at work it would be premature to draw conclusions as to the productiveness of the fisheries from year to year'.[2] Similarly, the early figures on forestry are unsatisfactory because they are only available for a few scattered years and even then offer only the barest information.

---

1. D.J.V. Jones, Before Rebecca, 1973; D.W. Howell, 'Welsh Agriculture, 1815-1914', Ph.D. thesis, London, 1970.

2. Sea Fisheries of the U.K. : Statistical Tables and Memorandum for 1887. p.p.1881, xlt.

BOOKS AND THESES

A.W. Ashby and I.L. Evans — The Agriculture of Wales and Monmouthshire, Cardiff, 1944.

D.G. Davies — 'Welsh Agriculture during the Great Depression', M.Sc.(Econ) thesis, Wales, 1973.

Walter Davies — A General View of the Agriculture and Domestic Economy of North Wales, 1810.

Walter Davies — A General View of the Agriculture and Domestic Economy of South Wales, 1814.

D.M. Harding — 'Floods and Droughts in Wales', Ph.D. thesis, Wales, 1972.

Charles Hassall — General View of the Agriculture of Monmouthshire, 1812.

D.W. Howell — 'Welsh Agriculture, 1815-1913', Ph.D. thesis, London, 1970.

D. Jenkins — The Agricultural Community in South-west Wales at the turn of the Twentieth century, Cardiff, 1971.

D.J.V. Jones — Before Rebecca, 1973.

D. Thomas — Agriculture in Wales during the Napoleonic Wars, Cardiff, 1963.

ARTICLES

R.J. Collyer — 'Cattle-price movements in North Wales, 1840-80', Journal Merionethshire Hist. and Rec. Soc., vi, 1971.

J. Davies — The end of the Great Estates and the rise of freehold farming in Wales, W.H.R., 7, 2, 1974.

B.L. James — 'The Great Landowners of Wales in 1873', National Library of Wales Journal, 14, 1966.

W.E. Minchinton — 'The Agricultural returns of 1800 for Wales', B.B.C.S., xxxi.

D. Thomas — 'The Acreage returns of 1801: a test of accuracy', B.B.C.S., xviii, 1960.

D. Thomas — 'The Acreage returns of 1801: an addendum', B.B.C.S., xvii, 1956-7.

D. Williams — 'The Acreage returns of 1801 for Wales', B.B.C.S., xiv, 1950-1.

GOVERNMENT AND OFFICIAL PUBLICATIONS

Agricultural Returns of Great Britain, 1867-1901 (Annual: in Sessional Papers)

Agricultural Statistics (of England and Wales), 1902- (Annual: in Sessional Papers until 1920 and then issued as non-parliamentary papers)

Guides to Official Sources, No.4 Agricultural and Food Statistics, 1958

Digest of Welsh Statistics, Annual since 1954

Census of Woodlands, 1947-49, Report No.1 Woods of Five Acres and Over; Report No.3, Welsh County Details

Annual Reports of the Forestry Commissioners, 1920- (except 1939-44)

Royal Commission on Land in Wales and Monmouth, Appendices, 1896

Tables showing extent in statute acres, and estimated average produce per acre, of principal crops, 1884-8, annually in sessional papers continued as Agricultural Produce Statistics of Great Britain, 1889-93, annually in sessional papers

Ministry of Agriculture, Fisheries and Food, Welsh Department, Annual Digest of Welsh Agricultural Statistics, 1948- (annual)

Agriculture 1 Crops :Acreage, Wales, 1867-1974

(thousand acres)

		TOTAL CULTIVATED AREA																								
		Permanent Grass			ARABLE																					
						Corn and Pulse Crops							Green Crops and Roots						Rotation Grass				Fruit(4)			
	Rough Grazing(3)	total grass(1)	for grazing	for hay	total arable(1)	total(1)	wheat	barley	oats	mixed corn	rye	others(2)	total(1)	pota-toes	turnips and swedes	man-golds	cabbage rape kohl rabi	others(2)	total(1)	for grazing	for hay	bare fallow & others(2)	orchards	small fruit	TOTAL culti-vated area(1)	
1867	..	1,495	..	..	1,130	564	136.6	160.8	255.3	..	3.2	8.1	154	47.2	77.7	4.0	0.8	24.3	319	..	..	93	..	..	2,625	1867
1868	..	1,546	..	..	1,173	592	152.8	163.1	265.0	..	2.1	9.0	143	49.9	80.0	4.6	0.9	7.5	348	..	..	90	..	..	2,719	1868
1869	..	1,668	..	..	1,082	600	157.6	169.6	260.6	..	2.6	9.6	142	51.4	77.0	5.2	0.9	8.0	276	..	..	64	..	..	2,750	1869
1870	..	1,555(5)	1,197	358	1,214(5)	597	148.3	176.2	260.9	..	2.0	9.6	147	51.0	81.8	6.3	0.8	6.8	427(5)	203	223	43	..	..	2,769	1870
1871	..	1,628	1,250	379	1,203	604	147.4	182.0	261.2	..	2.4	11.0	153	54.5	80.1	8.4	1.2	8.4	403	165	238	43	25.7	..	2,831	1871
1872	..	1,666	1,263	403	1,195	604	146.8	180.0	263.3	..	2.4	11.5	152	50.3	78.9	7.5	1.4	13.5	399	165	234	40	13.7	..	2,861	1872
1873	..	1,722	1,321	401	1,151	578	137.0	174.7	252.4	..	1.9	12.0	148	46.8	80.3	8.0	1.4	13.2	384	157	227	41	5.5	..	2,873	1873
1874	..	1,782	1,383	398	1,125	555	138.3	162.0	242.8	..	1.6	10.3	145	47.2	80.0	7.0	1.1	10.0	386	163	223	39	5.5	..	2,907	1874
1875	..	1,816	1,386	430	1,112	552	130.8	165.0	245.3	..	1.6	9.3	145	46.3	79.7	8.1	1.3	9.6	384	153	231	31	5.1	..	2,928	1875
1876	..	1,850	1,420	430	1,095	536	109.9	165.0	251.0	..	1.5	8.6	143	44.3	81.5	8.3	1.3	7.7	384	155	229	32	..	..	2,945	1876
1877	..	1,888	1,439	450	1,079	532	117.9	157.0	247.4	..	1.5	8.2	143	44.6	79.6	8.8	1.4	9.0	375	152	223	29	5.6	..	2,967	1877
1878	..	1,905	1,448	457	1,079	529	120.1	157.7	243.0	..	1.6	6.6	136	42.4	76.2	8.2	1.5	7.6	380	147	233	34	5.7	..	2,984	1878
1879	..	1,937	..	..	1,060	519	111.0	163.2	235.3	..	1.5	8.0	140	44.2	75.5	9.5	1.4	9.2	368	..	..	33	6.2	..	2,997	1879
1880	..	1,974	..	..	1,032	514	105.8	151.8	248.9	..	1.8	5.7	131	40.3	72.7	8.6	1.2	8.6	349	..	..	38	6.5	..	3,006	1880
1881	..	1,989	..	..	1,039	518	106.2	151.1	253.3	..	1.9	5.5	136	44.1	73.9	8.3	1.2	8.8	347	..	..	38	..	..	3,028	1881
1882	..	2,013	..	..	1,023	524	111.5	144.1	259.7	..	2.0	6.7	136	43.5	75.2	7.5	1.4	8.7	329	..	..	34	7.0	..	3,036	1882
1883	..	2,044	..	..	999	507	92.0	142.3	264.2	..	2.3	6.2	136	41.2	77.8	7.7	1.5	7.8	324	..	..	32	7.1	..	3,043	1883
1884	..	2,068	..	..	985	494	90.5	137.6	258.2	..	1.9	5.8	137	42.9	78.4	7.6	1.5	7.1	324	..	..	30	7.2	..	3.053	1884
1885	..	2,073	1,594	479	989	481	85.4	133.1	255.3	..	1.3	5.9	136	42.4	76.9	8.1	1.4	6.5	352	143	209	20	7.3	..	3,062	1885
1886	..	2,098	1,579	519	968	476	78.8	131.9	259.5	..	1.3	4.5	134	42.3	76.6	7.7	1.3	6.0	337	139	198	21	7.4	..	3,066	1886
1887	..	2,115	1,569	546	961	477	80.2	125.3	264.7	..	1.4	5.4	137	42.4	78.1	8.8	1.4	6.4	330	142	187	17	7.4	..	3.076	1887
1888	..	2,125	1,556	570	961	478	88.5	124.2	259.2	..	1.4	4.7	140	43.7	79.5	8.8	1.6	6.1	325	135	190	18	7.3	0.6	3,086	1888
1889	..	2,137	1,560	577	962	471	79.3	128.9	257.8	..	1.3	3.7	135	41.7	79.7	7.8	1.7	4.8	335	136	199	21	7.3	0.7	3,099	1889

(thousand acres)

	Rough Grazing(3)	TOTAL CULTIVATED AREA																								
		Permanent Grass			ARABLE																				TOTAL culti-vated area(1)	
						Corn and Pulse Crops							Green Crops and Roots						Rotation Grass				Fruit(4)			
		total grass(1)	for grazing	for hay	total arable(1)	total(1)	wheat	barley	oats	mixed corn	rye	others(2)	total(1)	pota-toes	turnips and swedes	man-golds	cabbage rape kohl rabi	others(2)	total(1)	for grazing	for hay	bare fallow & others(2)	orchards	small fruit		
1890	..	2,146	1,589	557	964	461	78.7	126.8	249.7	..	1.2	4.6	136	41.7	79.9	8.3	2.2	4.4	347	154	193	20	7.3	0.8	3,110	1890
1891	..	2,203	1,658	545	930	443	70.9	124.4	242.0	..	1.1	4.6	133	40.0	77.6	8.8	2.0	4.8	341	159	182	13	7.5	1.3	3,133	1891
1892	977	2,175	1,621	555	929	431	63.1	121.1	242.2	..	1.4	3.2	131	38.1	78.0	8.9	2.0	4.4	353	163	191	14	7.4	1.3	3,104	1892
1893	1,045	2,193	1,629	564	908	435	62.3	118.4	249.8	..	1.3	3.2	130	36.5	78.4	8.4	1.9	4.3	332	153	180	11	7.3	1.2	3,101	1893
1894	1,082	2,176	1,595	522	925	448	64.3	117.7	260.3	..	1.9	3.8	131	35.5	79.7	9.1	2.4	4.4	336	154	182	10	7.5	1.3	3 101	1894
1895	1,126	2,173	1,601	572	908	424	48.9	118.0	252.0	..	1.4	3.7	129	35.0	78.5	8.7	2.3	3.9	344	157	188	11	7.6	1.4	3,081	1895
1896	1,155	2,172	1,607	566	905	422	52.9	113.4	250.4	..	1.9	3.4	128	35.4	77.3	8.3	3.1	4.0	343	154	189	12	7.7	1.4	3,077	1896
1897	1,183	2,123	1,582	541	953	425	61.3	109.7	247.4	..	2.6	4.0	127	34.0	76.5	8.8	3.4	4.6	390	183	208	11	7.7	1.2	3,076	1897
1898	1,222	2,117	1,575	542	952	419	67.1	107.7	239.2	..	2.2	2.8	124	34.3	73.9	8.9	3.3	4.1	397	185	212	12	7.7	1.2	3,069	1898
1899	1,243	2,115	1,593	522	951	406	61.3	111.0	228.8	..	1.8	3.1	125	34.6	72.7	9.9	3.8	3.6	410	201	209	10	7.7	1.2	3,066	1899
1900	1,258	2,126	1,596	530	941	399	58.5	110.1	225.4	..	1.5	3.5	122	34.7	68.2	11.1	4.1	3.9	411	204	207	9	7.8	1.2	3,067	1900
1901	1,285	2,138	1,611	527	928	381	52.6	106.5	217.3	..	1.5	3.1	119	33.4	67.0	11.0	4.5	3.1	417	204	213	11	7.8	1.2	3,066	1901
1902	1,306	2,121	1,582	539	932	382	53.5	105.5	218.6	..	1.5	2.9	119	32.8	65.7	12.1	4.8	3.6	424	202	221	7	7.8	1.4	3,053	1902
1903	1,321	2,136	1,583	553	907	377	47.8	103.3	221.9	..	1.5	2.5	116	31.4	65.8	11.5	4.7	2.6	404	189	215	10	7.8	1.4	3,043	1903
1904	1,316	2,174	1,604	570	867	364	39.0	100.0	221.4	..	1.3	2.3	115	30.9	65.7	11.4	4.4	2.6	380	165	214	8	7.8	1.4	3,041	1904
1905	1,329	2,191	1,617	574	846	364	49.5	94.4	216.1	..	1.2	2.8	114	30.6	65.0	11.3	4.8	2.3	360	158	202	8	7.8	1.4	3,037	1905
1906	1,325	2,191	1,610	581	845	363	49.5	96.3	213.2	..	1.1	2.9	113	30.4	63.9	11.9	5.5	1.3[6]	360	160	200	9[6]	7.8	1.4	3,035	1906
1907	1,347	2.225	1,637	588	809	354	44.1	94.0	212.5	..	0.8	2.6	112	29.3	63.0	12.5	5.7	1.5	334	141	193	9	7.7	1.4	3,034	1907
1908	1,358	2,246	1,646	600	782	341	38.7	89.8	209.9	..	1.0	1.6	109	28.4	61.8	11.8	5.7	1.4	323	136	187	9	7.5	1.3	3,028	1908
1909	1,362	2,259	1,660	600	764	342	44.9	88.2	205.9	..	0.6	2.4	111	28.1	62.5	12.6	5.7	2.1	303	125	178	8	7.4	1.3	3,023	1909
1910	1,373	2,253	1,636	617	764	352	45.0	90.9	212.7	..	0.6	2.8	109	27.1	62.8	12.5	5.6	1.0	295	118	178	8	7.3	1.1	3,017	1910
1911	1,383	2,250	1,628	621	759	351	43.9	89.8	213.9	..	0.4	3.0	109	27.7	62.3	12.7	5.6	0.7	292	112	180	7	7.1	1.0	3,009	1911
1912	1,376	2,224	1,602	622	774	360	46.9	94.6	214.9	..	1.2	2.4	110	27.0	61.0	14.1	6.3	1.6	296	113	184	8	6.9	1.2	2,998	1912
1913	1,375	2,262	1,621	642	729	347	43.2	92.4	208.9	..	0.5	2.0	106	26.3	60.4	11.7	6.1	1.5	265	91	174	11	6.6	1.1	2,991	1913
1914	1,369	2,257	1,637	620	725	340	43.0	87.2	206.2	..	1.5	2.1	106	26.5	59.4	12.5	6.7	0.9	269	98	171	10	6.5	1.1	2,982	1914

(thousand acres)

	TOTAL CULTIVATED AREA																									
		Permanent Grass			ARABLE																					
						Corn and Pulse Crops							Green Crops and Roots						Rotation Grass				Fruit(4)			
	Rough Grazing(3)	total(1) grass	for grazing	for hay	total(1) arable	total(1)	wheat	barley	oats	mixed corn	rye	others(2)	total(1)	pota-toes	turnips and swedes	man-golds	cabbage rape kohl rabi	others(2)	total(1)	for grazing	for hay	bare fallow & others(2)	orchards	small fruit	TOTAL culti-vated area(1)	
1915	1,342	2,251	1,649	603	727	347	56.0	82.6	205.1	..	0.8	2.5	101	27.6	53.9	12.9	5.6	1.0	261	98	172	9	6.6	0.9	2,978	1915
1916	1,334	2,210	1,581	630	782	377	56.3	89.8	228.4	..	0.7	1.8	107	29.6	56.0	12.7	7.3	1.4	289	101	188	9	6.5	0.8	2,992	1916
1917	1,384	2,167	1,546	622	826	425	70.7	98.1	253.0	..	0.9	2.3	111	36.3	54.2	13.3	5.8	1.4	283	98	185	7	6.6	0.9	2,993	1917
1918	1,403	1,970	1,421	549	988	637	113.0	109.3	381.9	28.2	0.2	4.4	118	39.3	56.0	14.8	6.8	1.1	226	77	150	7	6.7	0.7	2,958	1918
1919	1,432	1,958	1,421	538	949	552	85.0	107.5	327.6	27.3	0.4	4.2	123	30.5	62.0	14.7	15.1	0.7	257	93	164	17	5.4	0.7	2,907	1919
1920	1,463	1,998	1,440	558	888	457	60.8	103.2	262.6	26.3	0.6	3.5	118	29.3	59.8	12.1	15.2	1.6	298	101	196	15	4.8	0.8	2,885	1920
1921	1,549	2,004	1,463	541	819	380	46.9	83.0	225.7	21.2	0.4	2.8	108	27.7	53.8	11.9	13.5	1.1	317	120	198	14	..	1.0	2,822	1921
1922	1,539	2,054	1,467	587	767	340	42.4	63.8	211.3	19.9	0.6	2.0	100	26.5	49.2	13.2	9.7(7)	1.4	315	113	202	12	..	0.9	2,821	1922
1923	1,565	2,085	1,496	589	730	317	36.5	65.3	194.9	18.6	0.4	1.3	99	24.5	49.5	12.5	11.0	1.5	298	108	190	16	5.5	0.8	2,815	1923
1924	1,589	2,104	1,500	604	701	293	26.6	59.6	18.9	0.3	1.5	1.5	97	23.7	49.1	11.6	11.3	1.3	296	109	187	15	5.4	1.1	2 805	1924
1925	1,606	2,108	1,516	592	682	275	23.3	52.8	179.6	17.9	0.2	1.2	94	23.6	47.4	10.8	11.8	0.4	298	113	185	15	5.4	0.9	2,789	1925
1926	1,626	2,105	1,497	608	675	276	26.5	48.3	181.5	18.1	0.2	1.4	91	23.2	45.1	11.2	11.2	0.3	294	113	182	14	5.2	0.8	2,779	1926
1927	1,631	2,122	1,511	612	656	266	25.8	45.6	173.9	19.1	0.2	1.4	91	23.3	43.2	11.0	12.4	1.1	287	107	179	12	5.3	0.8	2,778	1927
1928	1,643	2,131	1,519	611	635	255	20.6	45.2	167.0	20.1	0.2	1.9	87	22.4	41.9	10.7	11.5	0.5	280	109	171	13	5.4	0.8	2,765	1928
1929	1,721	2,117	1,490	627	645	257	20.1	42.9	170.9	21.3	0.2	1.6	86	22.6	42.0	10.6	10.2	0.6	290	114	175	12	5.3	0.8	2,761	1929
1930	1,718	2,104	1,467	637	657	260	20.4	41.5	173.8	22.0	0.3	2.0	86	20.6	41.8	10.6	11.9	1.1	299	120	179	12	5.2	0.8	2,760	1930
1931	1,721	2,127	1,508	619	628	241	15.8	35.7	166.2	21.3	0.2	1.8	83	20.6	39.5	10.1	12.3	0.5	291	114	177	13	5.3	0.8	2,754	1931
1932	1.725	2,133	1,527	606	615	234	17.4	32.6	162.9	19.9	0.2	1.0	83	21.6	40.2	8.4	11.6	1.2	285	114	170	13	5.2	0.7	2,747	1932
1933	1,727	2,124	1,502	622	619	240	21.3	30.5	165.6	20.8	0.1	1.7	83	21.5	38.6	9.7	11.6	1.6	284	116	168	12	4.9	0.6	2,742	1933
1934	1,733	2,112	1,481	631	624	247	24.6	28.9	170.0	21.3	0.1	2.1	84	20.1	35.4	10.5	13.8	4.2	282	111	170	11	5.1	0.6	2,735	1934
1935	1,742	2,101	1,489	611	623	243	25.0	28.0	167.1	21.2	0.2	1.5	82	18.2	33.4	10.3	16.9	3.2	286	119	167	12	5.2	0.6	2,723	1935
1936	1,746	2,133	1,516	617	582	230	20.0	27.6	160.5	20.0	0.1	1.8	78	17.5	31.6	10.6	17.1	1.2	262	102	160	12	5.0	0.6	2,715	1936
1937	1,749	2,142	1,525	618	566	224	18.5	26.4	149.2	18.2	0.1	11.6	74	17.5	29.4	9.5	16.5	1.1	263	101	162	5	4.8	0.6	2,708	1937
1938	1,812	2,159	1,551	608	544	217	19.1	25.1	154.8	16.5	..	1.5	71	17.3	26.6	9.9	15.6	1.6	242	95	148	14	4.7	0.6	2,702	1938
1939	1,813	2,159	1,536	623	538	212	12.9	22.4	160.3	14.2	0.1	2.1	67	16.7	24.1	9.5	15.4	1.3	245	99	147	14	4.6	0.3	2,696	1939

(thousand acres)

	Rough Grazing(3)	TOTAL CULTIVATED AREA																								
		Permanent Grass			ARABLE																				TOTAL cultivated area(1)	
						Corn and Pulse Crops							Green Crops and Roots						Rotation Grass				Fruit(4)			
		total grass(1)	for grazing	for hay	total arable(1)	total(1)	wheat	barley	oats	mixed corn	rye	others(2)	total(1)	potatoes	turnips and swedes	mangolds	cabbage rape kohl rabi	others(2)	total(1)	for grazing	for hay	bare fallow & others(2)	orchards	small fruit		
1940	1,804	1,890	1,327	563	720	389	31.5	34.2	284.6	36.9	0.5	1.5[9]	85	22.1	26.9	9.6	25.0	1.6	231	86	145	14	4.6	0.3	2,609	19
1941	1,853	1,669	1,169	500	903	543	63.7	50.9	354.3	68.2	0.4	5.1	137	48.0	33.8[10]	12.0	40.5	2.3	206	74	133	17	4.7	0.2	2,571	19
1942	1,854	1,512	1,066	446	1,057	638	82.5	62.9	403.3	81.8	0.8	6.7	172	62.7	37.5	12.6	56.8	2.7	224	73	150	22	4.9	0.2	2 569	19
1943	1,868	1,378	983	395	1.176	667	132.8	85.9	369.5	67.3	3.0	8.5	193	66.7	38.3	13.7	70.9	3.6[11]	290[11]	105	185	25	4.8	0.2	2,554	19
1944	1,869	1,316	954	362	1.232	617	113.0	80.4	347.8	65.8	2.0	7.7	207	67.1	38.3	15.5	82.3	3.5	383	165	218	26	4.7	0.2	2 548	19
1945	1,881	1,343	969	374	1,202	541	59.0	67.6	332.5	75.0	1.3	6.0	202	64.1	37.6	15.3	81.5	3.5	432	191	241	27	4.4	0.2	2 545	19
1946	1,885	1,373	1,005	368	1,170	493	42.5	58.2	312.0	74.2	0.9	4.9	197	65.4	34.6	16.6	76.8	3.4	455	208	247	26	5.0	0.2	2,543	19
1947	1,870	1,440	1,025	415	1,100	455	46.7	49.9	278.8	76.2	0.8	3.0	171	60.4	33.1	14.4	59.8	2.8	447	188	259	26	4.6	0.3	2,550	194
1948	1,869	1,449	1,042	408	1,098	458	50.3	41.0	278.1	84.2	0.7	3.8	176	72.9	29.3	15.2	55.9	2.9	441	194	247	23	4.3	0.3	2,548	194
1949	1,856	1,484	1,070	414	1,063	438	37.6	38.0	266.7	91.3	0.8	3.7	172	58.5	28.1	15.2	66.4	3.5	429	180	250	24	4.3	0.4	2,547	194
1950	1,838	1,482	1,059	424	1,077	450	48.6	32.9	259.7	104.0	1.4	3.2	174	52.1	25.0	16.0	75.4	5.0	431	245	186	23	4.3	0.4	2,559	195
1951	1,827	1,545	1,097	448	1,018	390	31.0	31.9	223.0	101.6	0.4[13]	2.0	158	41.1	24.4	14.5	73.2	4.8	448	261	187	23	4.1	0.4	2,563	195
1952	1,820	1,560	1,111	450	1,012	388	33.0	34.8	215.7	101.9	0.7	2.3	162	38.9	25.6	12.3	78.1	7.3	443	263	180	18	3.9	0.4	2,572	195
1953	1,797	1,578	1,132	447	996	369	35.0	33.4	198.9	98.7	0.6	2.4	162	35.0	25.3	12.0	83.0	6.9	447	193	254	17	3.9	0.4	2,574	195
1954	1,777	1,646	1,203	443	945	310	28.6	26.0	172.8	80.0	0.2	1.3	155	31.1	23.5	11.5	83.0	5.7	463	215	248	18	3.6	0.4	2,592	195
1955	1,763	1,690	1,225	465	905	263	17.2	22.7	162.6	59.6	0.3	0.9	143	27.5	24.3	8.8	78.5	4.2	480	220	261	18	3.3	0.3	2,595	195
1956	1,740	1,715	1,234	480	889	274	23.1	25.8	166.3	57.3	0.5	0.8	136	27.8	20.1	8.5	76.0	3.6	462	215	247	16	3.2	0.3	2,603	195
1957	1,729	1,732	1,275	457	874	251	24.1	31.2	145.2	49.4	0.7	0.5	130	23.7	19.1	7.5	76.7	3.0	475	223	253	17	3.1	0.3	2,606	195
1958	1,718	1,756	1,279	477	853	236	21.8	32.0	137.8	43.5	0.7	0.4	126	24.2	18.9	7.2	73.5	2.4	474	219	256	17	2.9	0.3	2,609	195
1959	1,702	1,767	1,304	463	845	213	17.2	34.7	122.3	37.8	0.3	0.2	119	23.6	18.0	6.0	68.7	2.8	498	242	256	15	2.8	0.3	2,612	195
1960	1,692	1,742	1,262	479	867	218	17.6	39.0	126.3	34.7	0.5	0.2	119	24.5	16.2	6.0	70.0	2.5	514	252	262	15	2.6	0.3	2.609	196
1961	1,674	1,746	1,285	461	861	207	15.7	50.3	111.0	29.2	0.3	0.2	113	20.9	15.2	4.6	67.7	5.0[12]	526	263	263	14	2.5	0.4	2.607	196
1962	1,650	1,750	1,292	459	864	207	17.2	61.2	102.1	26.3	0.3	0.2	111	20.4	15.3	4.4	65.5	5.5	534	264	270	12	2.5	0.3	2 614	196
1963	1,646	1,759	1,296	462	860	207	14.3	82.5	88.2	21.1	0.5	0.1	105	22.9	14.7	3.7	58.7	5.2	536	272	263	12	2.2	0.3	2.618	196
1964	1,631	1,776	1,293	483	847	214	18.8	100.5	78.1	16.4	0.3	0.1	102	22.2	15.8	3.0	56.3	4.3	520	258	262	12	1.7	0.3	2.623	196

(thousand acres)

	Rough Grazing(3)	TOTAL CULTIVATED AREA: Permanent Grass: total grass(1)	for grazing	for hay	ARABLE: total arable(1)	Corn and Pulse Crops: total(1)	wheat	barley	oats	mixed corn	rye	others(2)	Green Crops and Roots: total(1)	potatoes	turnips and swedes	mangolds	cabbage rape kohl rab	others(2)	Rotation Grass: total(1)	for grazing	for hay	bare fallow & others(2)	Fruit(4): orchards	small fruit	TOTAL cultivated area(1)	
1965	1,624	1,778	1,312	465	853	224	23.5	117.2	68.2	14.4	0.3	0.2	92	20.6	15.7	2.7	50.1	2.9	526	280	246	11	1.7	0.3	2,631	1965
1966	1,615	1,814	1,352	463	813	224	21.6	132.6	56.7	12.5	0.2	0.2	84	18.3	15.1	2.0	45.2	3.3	493	265	228	13	1.6	0.3	2,628	1966
1967	1,608	1,825	1,364	461	804	225	22.7	126.0	60.5	15.2	0.2	0.3	79	18.5	14.6	1.6	41.7	2.4	487	263	224	12	1.3	0.3	2,628	1967
1968	1,595	1,789	1,354	435	811	219	19.2	124.5	57.6	17.4	0.2	0.5	73	18.9	14.0	1.5	37.0	2.0	506	280	216	12	1.2	0.3	2,600	1968
1969	1,595	1,809	1,370	439	768	208	16.3	112.4	53.7	24.9	0.2	0.4	73	16.8	12.8	1.2	35.3	6.9	472	267	205	14	0.8	0.3	2,577	1969
1970	1,554	1,826	1,373	453	738	204	18.0	104.5	50.9	30.0	0.2	0.4	71	18.4	11.9	1.1	31.3	8.2	451	243	208	12	0.7	0.4	2,564	1970
1971	1,539	1,831	1,370	461	732	211	19.4	120.9	48.3	21.5	0.2	0.4	70	17.8	12.5	1.0	31.5	7.4	440	256	184	11	0.7	0.4	2,563	1971
1972	1,520	1,834	1,390	444	730	206	17.2	120.7	43.6	24.4	0.1	0.4	67	16.2	12.1	0.8	30.2	7.2	446	269	177	11	0.6	0.4	2,564	1972
1973	1,508	1,862	1,419	443	705	205	14.2	127.0	42.7	20.3	0.1	0.6	62	14.2	12.4	0.6	28.7	6.1	427	254	173	11	0.5	0.4	2,567	1973
1974	1,492	1,873	1,434	440	701	210	16.8	137.8	38.2	16.3	0.1	1.0	60	13.4	13.2	0.7	25.5	6.8	426	260	165	10	0.6	0.4	2,575	1974

General Notes.

(i) Sources. Agricultural Statistics; Ashby and Evans, The Agriculture of Wales and Monmouthshire, Cardiff, 1944, Appendix B, Tables 3-7; Annual Digest of Welsh Agricultural Statistics, 1974-5.

(ii) Figures as at June of each year.

Notes.

1. Totals not always exactly the sum of individual items because of rounding. But before 1940 the totals for (a) Corn and Pulse crops and (b) Green Crops and Roots are exactly the sum of the individual crops because the 'others' column was calculated by taking the difference between the overall total and the total of the separately distinguished crops. The figure for 'others' is thus subject to a higher degree of error.

2. 'Others'. The crops covered by this term are :

   (a) for Corn and Pulse crops: peas and beans (after 1940 only peas and beans for stock-feeding), and (from 1970), maize.

   (b) for Green Crops and Roots : sugar beet, vetches or tares, carrots and other root vegetables (before 1906), fodder beet (1952-57), 'other crops for stock-feeding' (since 1961), and lucerne (before 1943 and 1950-72 except 1968 : lucerne included with rotation grass for 1943-49 and 1968).

   (c) for Bare fallows and others: included here are bare fallow only (1867-76); bare fallow and flax (1867-87); bare fallow, flax and small fruit (1888-1905); bare fallow, flax, small fruit, carrots and other vegetables (since 1906). At various times additional vegetables, mustard, flowers and crops grown under grass were also added.

3. From 1892 to 1908 the figure for Rough Grazing is simply an estimate of the area of 'Mountain and Heathland used for grazing.'

4. The figures for 1871 and 1872 are inaccurate. The report for 1873 (p.8) attributes a general decline for England and Wales mainly to 'incorrect returns under this head in previous years in those parts of England where fruit trees are not extensively planted, and in Wales.'
The area of 'orchards' is included twice in the crop figures, once for the area of crops grown below the trees and once for the trees themselves. Thus since the area is already included either (from 1871 - 1922) under the particular crop grown, or (since 1922) under the column 'Bare fallow and others,' the area given in the column for 'orchards' has not been included in the Total Cultivated Area. Until 1964 the area for orchards is obtained by adding 'orchards with crops etc.' to'orchards with small fruit etc.' after 1964 by adding 'orchards grown commercially' to 'orchards not grown commercially.'
Similarly, the acreage for 'small fruit' is already included under 'Bare Fallow and others' and is thus not itself added to the Total Cultivated Area. After 1939 figures for small fruit exclude any grown beneath orchard trees.

5. "A part of the decrease of Pasture and increase of Arable in 1870 was owing to more correct classification on Grass under Rotation and Permanent Pasture." Agricultural Returns, 1878, p.12.

6. From 1906 carrots and other vegetables are excluded and are included under "Bare Fallow and others."

7. From 1922 figures exclude cabbage for human consumption. This is only a small acreage.

8. A revised figure of 1,745.9 is given in Agricultural Statistics, 1939-44.

9. From 1940 figures exclude beans and peas for human consumption, which are included under 'Bare Fallow and others.'
In 1939 the figure for beans and peas, excluding those for human consumption, was 0.4 thousand acres.

10. From 1941 figures exclude turnips and swedes for human consumption which are included under 'Bare Fallow and others.'

11. Lucerne included under 'Rotation Grass' 1943-49 and 1968 instead of Green Crops and roots: others.'

12. From 1961 'Green Crops and Roots: others' includes 'Other crops for stock-feeding.'

Agriculture 2. Acreage, by county, 1867-1972

ANGLESEY

JUNE	TOTAL FARMING AREA	ROUGH GRAZINGS	TOTAL CULTIVATED AREA	CULTIVATED AREA: PERMANENT GRASS: for grazing	for hay	total	ARABLE: TOTAL ARABLE	Rotation Grass: for grazing	for hay	total	Tillage: total	wheat	barley	oats	mixed corn	potatoes	turnips and swedes
	THOUSAND ACRES										ACRES						
1867	..	..	129.5	..	..	54.2	75.3	..	..	26.5	48,789	1,845	5,996	23,584	..	4,583	5,150
1872	..	..	142.8	58.5	7.9	66.4	76.4	10.6	20.0	30.6	45,830	1,952	6,306	25,377	..	5,369	5,096
1877	..	..	146.7	67.8	12.8	80.5	66.2	8.5	20.5	29.0	37,136	874	4,863	20,658	..	4,569	4,974
1882	..	..	147.7	..	..	84.3	63.3	..	..	25.0	38,319	709	3,687	23,461	..	3,944	5,015
1887	..	..	147.9	76.3	18.1	94.4	53.4	2.7	13.0	15.7	37,730	416	2,563	24,499	..	3,668	5,445
1892	154.9	4.8	150.1	67.0	13.3	80.3	69.8	15.9	19.0	34.9	34,885	281	2,340	22,353	..	3,175	5,663
1897	159.8	7.7	152.1	67.4	13.5	80.8	71.3	17.6	20.2	37.8	33,439	330	1,732	21,708	..	2,704	5,607
1902	161.5	9.0	152.5	57.9	13.4	71.3	81.2	26.4	23.1	49.5	31,686	326	1,605	20,362	..	2,662	5,230
1907	161.2	10.1	151.1	73.3	18.2	91.5	59.5	11.9	18.3	30.1	29,379	164	1,468	19,179	..	2,303	5,003
1912	160.7	11.8	148.9	70.1	19.3	89.3	59.5	11.2	18.8	30.0	29,572	346	1,556	19,234	..	1,941	5,132
1917	160.8	12.2	148.6	67.5	18.9	86.4	62.2	9.0	19.8	28.8	33,396	1,344	2,267	21,545	..	2,421	4,452
1922	159.5	17.0	142.4	69.5	19.3	88.8	53.6	9.2	19.3	28.5	25,070	100	1,188	17,120	136	1,621	3,761
1927	161.5	19.7	141.8	75.5	20.6	96.1	45.7	8.7	16.4	25.1	20,611	73	977	13,300	91	1,428	3,640
1932	161.7	21.2	140.5	77.2	19.8	97.0	43.5	9.1	16.0	25.1	18,304	113	718	11,477	160	1,325	3,300
1937	161.0	22.6	138.5	80.7	21.8	102.5	35.9	5.7	14.4	20.1	15,794	83	871	9,886	154	1,038	2,484
1942	157.9	24.3	133.7	51.4	13.9	65.3	68.3	5.0	13.6	18.5	49,791	878	3,219	35,702	1,378	4,066	2,510
1947	157.7	22.7	135.0	55.8	14.7	70.5	63.3	12.3	16.1	28.4	34,907	428	3,592	22,056	879	3,762	1,741
1952	156.9	22.5	134.4	59.3	15.7	75.0	59.4	15.2	16.7	31.8	27,523	598	2,260	15,521	2,263	1,909	1,339
1957	156.1	20.9	135.3	77.6	17.5	95.1	40.2	10.1	11.6	21.6	18,550	816	2,612	8,342	1,625	995	960
1962	154.6	20.1	134.5	75.8	17.5	93.3	41.2	14.4	10.7	25.1	16,020	986	4,056	5,871	997	788	606
1967	151.5	17.6	133.9	78.8	17.4	96.3	37.6	13.6	8.5	22.1	15,474	1,640	7,685	3,335	426	604	415
1972(1)	145.4	17.3	126.8	81.1	14.8	95.9	30.9	10.9	5.1	16.1	14,514	1,073	8,977	2,414	462	605	189

Agriculture 2. Acreage, by county, 1867-1972

BRECONSHIRE

JUNE	TOTAL FARMING AREA	ROUGH GRAZINGS	TOTAL CULTIVATED AREA	CULTIVATED AREA													
				PERMANENT GRASS			ARABLE										
							TOTAL ARABLE	Rotation Grass			Tillage						
				for grazing	for hay	total		for grazing	for hay	total	total	wheat	barley	oats	mixed corn	potatoes	turnips and swedes
	THOUSAND ACRES										ACRES						
1867	..	..	173.8	..	..	109.1	64.7	..	..	17.9	46,789	9,559	8,896	14,356	..	1,799	5,494
1872	..	..	189.9	86.2	28.3	114.5	75.4	12.8	13.0	25.8	49,590	10,504	9,757	15,537	..	1,885	5,806
1877	..	..	196.5	98.5	31.0	129.4	67.0	12.1	11.6	23.8	43,272	8,396	7,850	14,980	..	1,626	5,776
1882	..	..	202.4	..	..	140.4	62.0	..	..	20.0	41,946	8,103	7,210	15,726	..	1,498	4,651
1887	..	..	205.3	107.5	39.1	146.6	58.7	12.4	8.8	21.2	37,528	5,799	6,076	15,508	..	1,430	5,492
1892	400.8	199.2	201.7	113.0	37.4	150.4	51.3	12.0	7.1	19.1	32,174	4,122	5,616	13,878	..	1,199	5,476
1897	407.4	204.1	203.2	115.7	37.3	153.0	50.2	11.3	8.0	19.3	30,943	3,704	4,649	13,976	..	1,090	5,724
1902	409.2	205.2	204.0	118.7	37.0	155.8	48.2	12.4	8.4	20.8	27,406	3,317	4,223	12,256	..	1,027	5,032
1907	418.6	214.5	204.1	123.5	38.3	161.8	42.2	11.1	7.2	18.2	23,978	2,466	3,534	11,098	..	846	4,648
1912	419.1	218.6	200.5	122.6	39.1	161.7	38.8	8.8	6.3	15.1	23,773	2,435	3,415	11,259	..	801	4,479
1917	439.3	243.0	196.3	115.4	40.5	155.9	40.4	7.9	5.9	13.8	26,562	3,840	3,652	12,678	..	1,142	4,055
1922	393.4	213.2	180.2	107.4	35.3	142.7	37.6	9.1	6.4	15.5	22,033	2,244	2,560	10,781	187	807	3,836
1927	394.2	217.7	176.6	105.9	35.6	141.5	35.1	9.6	6.5	16.1	19,058	1,322	1,843	9,565	108	665	3,579
1932	464.9	292.9	172.0	101.2	35.9	137.1	34.9	10.7	6.6	17.3	17,598	807	1,326	9,295	136	594	3,606
1937	464.7	294.8	169.9	101.0	36.0	137.0	33.0	9.9	6.3	16.2	16,762	787	845	9,116	71	542	3,030
1942	410.3	255.6	154.7	69.2	26.6	95.8	58.9	7.5	5.5	13.1	45,888	5,414	4,825	21,295	698	2,727	4,115
1947	403.1	251.7	151.4	59.0	23.1	82.0	69.1	18.8	11.7	30.5	38,545	2,810	3,378	15,770	927	2,722	4,249
1952	430.0	275.3	154.7	65.9	24.6	90.6	64.1	19.5	12.2	31.7	32,449	1,963	2,518	13,061	1,188	1,255	4,003
1957	420.7	259.6	161.1	78.9	24.2	103.1	58.0	21.0	12.2	33.2	24,785	950	1,256	9,935	381	639	3,930
1962	412.6	250.4	162.2	79.0	24.5	103.4	58.8	23.4	13.3	36.7	21,991	800	1,377	8,764	155	579	4,168
1967	409.2	243.3	165.9	84.7	25.0	109.7	56.2	22.0	12.9	34.9	21,239	1,235	3,649	6,572	127	508	4,575
1972(1)	401.7	231.7	165.7	86.3	24.5	110.8	54.9	25.2	10.9	36.1	18,554	1,146	3,723	5,133	206	470	4,080

Agriculture 2. Acreage, by county, 1867-1972

CAERNARVONSHIRE

JUNE	TOTAL FARMING AREA	ROUGH GRAZINGS	TOTAL CULTIVATED AREA	CULTIVATED AREA: PERMANENT GRASS: for grazing	PERMANENT GRASS: for hay	PERMANENT GRASS: total	ARABLE: TOTAL ARABLE	ARABLE: Rotation Grass: for grazing	Rotation Grass: for hay	Rotation Grass: total	Tillage: total	Tillage: wheat	Tillage: barley	Tillage: oats	Tillage: mixed corn	Tillage: potatoes	Tillage: turnips and swedes
	THOUSAND ACRES										ACRES						
1867	..	..	167.7	..	..	93.7	74.0	..	..	30.1	43,897	2,377	8,530	12,963	..	5,119	2,654
1872	..	..	181.4	76.6	32.0	108.6	72.8	11.3	24.2	35.4	37,417	2,033	9,101	13,786	..	5,809	2,371
1877	..	..	186.9	90.3	33.9	124.2	62.7	9.2	22.3	31.5	31,259	1,138	7,807	12,155	..	5,465	2,549
1882	..	..	187.6	..	..	124.5	63.0	..	..	32.4	30,621	982	7,193	12,941	..	5,160	2,618
1887	..	..	188.6	93.0	39.8	132.8	55.8	10.0	16.0	26.0	29,813	555	7,112	12,799	..	5,317	2,877
1892	282.5	89.0	193.6	90.6	43.9	134.6	59.0	11.6	17.5	29.1	29,916	552	6,926	12,402	..	5,381	3,364
1897	300.3	110.9	189.4	82.5	39.7	122.2	67.2	19.3	20.7	40.0	27,192	424	6,163	11,679	..	4,406	3,262
1902	297.6	117.2	180.4	76.3	37.0	113.2	67.2	20.8	21.7	42.4	24,757	367	5,393	10,763	..	4,128	2,822
1907	302.6	131.0	171.6	77.9	44.3	122.2	49.4	10.9	14.5	25.4	24,027	256	5,187	10,721	..	3,638	2,971
1912	305.2	134.6	170.6	74.1	43.6	117.8	52.8	11.9	16.5	28.4	24,413	376	5,241	11,016	..	3,338	3,079
1917	295.6	123.0	172.6	70.4	38.9	109.3	63.3	10.1	20.3	30.4	32,886	1,591	6,552	15,504	..	4,567	3,112
1922	332.2	169.3	163.0	68.3	40.0	108.3	54.7	11.2	20.6	31.8	22,853	193	4,236	10,295	845	3,089	2,538
1927	330.2	172.0	158.2	70.3	38.5	108.8	49.4	11.2	19.2	30.4	18,964	98	2,768	8,621	1,199	2,533	2,270
1932	329.2	173.3	155.9	71.2	35.6	106.8	49.1	11.9	19.4	31.3	17,824	93	1,772	8,315	1,639	2,430	2,130
1937	325.8	174.4	151.4	74.7	37.0	111.7	39.7	9.2	15.4	24.6	15,044	115	1,365	7,293	1,648	1,708	1,462
1942	322.8	197.2	125.6	40.8	26.1	66.9	58.7	5.9	12.5	18.4	40,313	628	2,776	20,590	6,532	5,089	1,750
1947	322.7	197.4	125.2	41.6	22.3	64.0	60.6	11.6	18.0	29.6	30,964	182	1,218	14,825	6,312	3,928	1,526
1952	327.9	199.9	128.0	45.9	23.8	69.7	58.3	13.8	18.6	32.4	25,827	234	658	11,355	6,405	2,534	1,102
1957	321.9	193.2	128.7	58.9	21.4	80.3	48.4	15.0	15.7	30.7	17,713	174	654	7,895	3,958	1,278	766
1962	319.8	190.0	129.8	66.5	20.6	87.1	42.7	14.8	13.3	28.1	14,529	356	1,910	5,614	2,332	866	416
1967	321.7	193.3	128.4	71.1	20.8	91.9	36.5	12.9	10.6	23.5	12,865	363	5,808	2,907	1,084	718	315
1972 (1)	311.3	190.1	119.5	69.5	17.6	87.1	32.5	13.7	7.2	20.9	11,212	333	5,489	2,164	701	715	194

Agriculture 2. Acreage, by county, 1867-1972

CARDIGANSHIRE

JUNE	TOTAL FARMING AREA	ROUGH GRAZINGS	TOTAL CULTIVATED AREA	CULTIVATED AREA: PERMANENT GRASS for grazing	PERMANENT GRASS for hay	PERMANENT GRASS total	ARABLE: TOTAL ARABLE	Rotation Grass for grazing	Rotation Grass for hay	Rotation Grass total	Tillage total	wheat	barley	oats	mixed corn	potatoes	turnips and swedes
	THOUSAND ACRES										ACRES						
1867	..	..	225.1	..	..	110.0	115.1	..	..	33.3	81,844	7,739	21,503	30,461	..	6,799	4,199
1872	..	..	264.9	113.1	27.0	140.2	124.7	21.4	19.1	40.5	84,185	8,430	25,849	31,411	..	8,320	4,902
1877	..	..	262.9	114.0	31.5	145.5	123.8	24.0	19.5	43.6	80,183	8,118	24,128	31,011	..	7,711	5,157
1882	..	..	278.6	..	..	154.2	124.4	..	..	45.1	79,222	7,842	21,503	32,447	..	7,301	4,977
1887	..	..	282.6	125.6	38.0	163.6	119.0	24.9	20.0	44.9	74,173	6,295	19,106	32,621	..	7,090	5,175
1892	381.8	109.1	272.7	121.1	38.4	159.5	113.2	26.4	19.5	45.9	67,334	6,004	17,116	29,422	..	6,342	5,151
1897	399.3	128.3	271.0	122.2	36.4	158.7	112.3	24.8	20.6	45.4	66,891	5,805	15,482	30,905	..	5,936	5,304
1902	404.5	138.8	265.7	122.0	36.4	158.4	107.3	24.7	20.5	45.2	62,088	5,979	15,134	26,729	..	5,818	4,718
1907	407.6	143.7	263.9	126.3	39.4	165.8	98.2	17.7	20.0	37.7	60,409	5,537	14,311	26,972	..	5,439	4,754
1912	404.4	144.7	259.7	124.6	40.4	165.0	94.7	14.2	20.0	34.2	60,488	5,373	14,798	27,239	..	4,940	4,575
1917	413.4	148.9	264.5	115.3	43.5	158.8	105.6	13.4	20.8	34.2	71,406	8,249	16,764	32,265	..	5,929	4,593
1922	400.7	158.0	242.6	108.7	40.8	149.5	93.2	13.5	20.6	34.1	58,989	4,594	10,152	27,175	4,806	4,510	3,869
1927	414.9	172.1	242.8	115.9	42.3	158.2	84.6	12.7	18.8	31.5	53,086	3,032	9,178	24,237	4,609	4,088	3,717
1932	415.3	174.2	241.1	119.1	41.4	160.5	80.6	13.5	18.2	31.7	48,817	1,718	7,471	23,493	4,840	3,741	3,656
1937	410.8	172.6	238.2	122.2	42.2	164.4	73.8	11.0	17.3	28.3	45,493	1,317	6,537	23,272	4,313	2,722	2,540
1942	408.7	171.7	237.0	89.8	33.2	123.0	114.0	10.0	17.3	27.3	86,691	2,571	7,275	47,284	10,770	6,557	2,905
1947	408.2	172.3	235.9	86.4	31.7	118.1	117.0	22.1	24.9	47.0	69,977	2,255	5,511	33,219	9,771	6,587	2,042
1952	405.7	167.0	238.7	94.8	33.7	128.5	110.2	19.1	27.0	46.1	64,083	666	3,906	29,431	12,071	4,486	1,380
1957	400.7	157.3	243.4	111.6	32.1	143.7	99.7	24.0	26.1	50.1	49,492	277	3,615	22,356	7,614	2,243	748
1962	388.9	146.5	242.3	110.6	33.1	143.7	98.6	30.9	29.1	60.0	38,426	177	4,301	16,106	5,755	1,451	390
1967	386.1	141.0	245.1	120.5	37.4	157.9	87.1	32.3	24.9	57.1	29,868	218	11,624	7,986	2,290	1,031	282
1972(1)	373.2	127.9	239.4	121.4	35.8	157.3	82.2	34.3	20.8	55.1	25,783	163	11,565	4,925	4,069	642	210

Agriculture 2. Acreage, by county, 1867-1972

CARMARTHENSHIRE

JUNE	TOTAL FARMING AREA	ROUGH GRAZINGS	TOTAL CULTIVATED AREA	CULTIVATED AREA: PERMANENT GRASS: for grazing	PERMANENT GRASS: for hay	PERMANENT GRASS: total	ARABLE: TOTAL ARABLE	Rotation Grass: for grazing	Rotation Grass: for hay	Rotation Grass: total	Tillage: total	Tillage: wheat	Tillage: barley	Tillage: oats	Tillage: mixed corn	Tillage: potatoes	Tillage: turnips and swedes
	THOUSAND ACRES										ACRES						
1867	..	..	370.9	..	..	232.7	138.3	..	..	37.7	100,535	11.137	18,974	41,097	..	6,430	3,502
1872	..	..	407.6	219.4	54.6	274.0	133.6	20.3	20.7	41.0	92,596	12,432	21,771	41,920	..	4,727	4,759
1877	..	..	423.9	233.7	58.5	292.2	131.7	25.7	23.0	48.7	83,051	11,073	18,781	39,447	..	4,533	5,121
1882	..	..	435.0	..	..	317.2	117.8	..	..	35.8	81,947	11,202	17,561	39,052	..	4,348	4,808
1887	..	..	442.3	261.6	71.3	333.0	109.4	16.3	17.7	34.1	75,311	9,080	14,994	38.120	..	4,386	5,048
1892	472.8	31.0	441.9	267.8	77.4	345.2	92.7	11.7	16.7	28.5	68,192	8,548	13,939	34,174	..	3,784	5,036
1897	486.9	44.8	442.1	265.4	77.4	342.8	99.3	13.7	18.3	32.0	67,310	8,258	13,352	34,297	..	3,677	5,220
1902	505.8	64.3	441.4	266.1	79.1	345.1	96.3	16.5	19.7	36.2	60,137	8,066	14,284	27,005	..	3,603	4,506
1907	507.2	65.2	442.0	271.9	85.7	357.6	84.3	11.2	18.6	29.8	54,486	6,813	12,778	24,313	..	3,360	4,167
1912	506.5	68.0	438.5	265.9	94.6	360.5	77.9	8.2	16.4	24.5	53,397	6.645	11,553	24,900	..	3,204	3,921
1917	511.5	71.5	440.0	248.8	97.0	345.7	94.3	7.7	15.3	23.0	71,282	11,544	15,203	32,980	..	4,769	3,846
1922	507.6	91.8	415.7	246.9	93.8	340.7	75.0	9.0	17.3	26.3	48,703	4,746	5,806	22,591	5,900	3,161	3,175
1927	508.4	98.8	409.7	250.3	103.9	354.2	55.5	5.7	11.4	17.1	38,385	2,475	4,009	18,361	4,627	2,928	2,871
1932	505.6	101.6	404.0	249.0	106.2	355.2	48.8	6.0	9.9	15.9	32,844	1,046	2,465	17,626	3,787	2,646	2,595
1937	502.5	103.8	398.7	248.7	104.7	353.4	45.3	7.1	11.2	18.3	27,054	534	1,653	15,223	2,786	2,034	1,585
1942	500.7	123.8	376.9	166.1	70.5	236.6	140.3	6.0	10.2	16.2	124,042	16,829	7,322	58,177	16,972	7,919	2,299
1947	508.3	133.2	375.1	176.0	76.5	252.4	121.2	22.2	25.8	48.0	73,239	3,718	1,784	31,275	14,811	6,945	2,145
1952	497.5	120.0	377.5	189.4	90.9	280.3	997.2	16.1	23.1	39.2	57,907	1,286	1,309	22,139	13,694	4,788	1,540
1957	496.0	114.3	379.8	215.7	96.1	311.8	68.0	17.7	20.8	38.5	32,740	672	1,214	12,)87	4,853	2,378	792
1962	487.0	110.6	376.5	208.6	91.8	300.3	76.1	25.1	27.0	52.0	23,776	224	3,681	7,462	2,211	1,461	492
1967	484.2	105.0	379.1	218.0	91.4	309.4	69.7	28.2	23.0	51.3	18,355	103	7,792	3,532	1,033	826	443
1972[1]	476.0	98.5	369.3	220.4	90.4	310.8	58.5	28.8	15.3	43.1	15.118	225	7,412	2,008	1,728	546	349

Agriculture 2. Acreage, by county, 1867-1972

DENBIGHSHIRE

JUNE	TOTAL FARMING AREA	ROUGH GRAZINGS	TOTAL CULTIVATED AREA	CULTIVATED AREA: PERMANENT GRASS: for grazing	for hay	total	ARABLE: TOTAL ARABLE	Rotation Grass: for grazing	for hay	total	Tillage: total	wheat	barley	oats	mixed corn	potatoes	turnips and swedes
	THOUSAND ACRES										ACRES						
1867	..	..	238.6	..	..	111.1	127.5	..	..	35.4	92,185	18,804	18,614	28,023	..	4,714	8,713
1872	..	..	251.6	94.6	25.1	119.8	131.9	18.5	25.3	43.8	88,094	19,421	19,785	28,345	..	4,901	8,029
1877	..	..	258.2	113.1	29.7	142.7	115.5	14.8	24.3	39.1	76,359	13,692	18,592	25,945	..	4,090	8,775
1882	..	..	265.6	..	..	152.2	113.4	..	..	37.2	76,218	12,283	17,070	27,982	..	4,350	8,657
1887	..	..	271.5	123.9	38.8	162.7	108.7	16.3	21.5	37.8	70,984	8,932	15,799	29,602	..	4,138	8,933
1892	326.5	53.8	272.6	129.5	38.7	168.2	104.4	17.8	22.1	40.0	64,482	6,477	15,746	26,159	..	3,595	9,358
1897	340.9	70.3	270.6	122.6	32.2	154.8	115.8	25.6	25.2	50.9	64,951	6,128	14,829	27,526	..	3,207	9,590
1902	348.4	81.2	267.2	119.5	33.0	152.5	114.7	28.1	27.2	55.3	59,406	5,854	13,918	24,727	..	3,155	8,317
1907	349.2	83.0	266.1	134.6	37.7	172.2	93.9	15.1	22.8	37.9	55,931	4,856	11,713	24,208	..	2,810	8,131
1912	346.4	84.3	262.1	131.6	41.1	172.7	89.4	12.1	21.4	33.5	55,855	4,933	11,926	24,538	..	2,479	7,997
1917	352.7	90.2	262.5	133.0	39.6	172.6	89.9	9.8	21.7	31.4	58,459	7,448	9,463	27,926	..	3,029	7,094
1922	378.5	120.9	257.6	132.0	39.5	171.5	86.1	13.0	22.4	35.4	50,813	4,206	7,302	24,743	1,752	2,330	6,372
1927	388.1	134.1	254.0	136.9	41.8	178.7	75.2	13.0	20.4	33.4	41,891	2,546	4,762	20,325	2,021	2,024	5,344
1932	385.7	135.9	249.8	140.7	41.6	182.3	67.5	12.6	18.8	31.4	36,031	1,783	3,133	18,244	2,079	1,877	4,849
1937	384.6	138.2	246.4	139.4	43.4	182.8	63.5	12.4	18.4	30.8	32,740	2,156	2,805	15,709	2,238	1,452	3,608
1942	386.1	149.1	237.1	97.0	32.1	129.0	108.0	8.2	15.8	24.0	84,043	8,064	5,391	41,238	9,589	4,509	4,757
1947	386.3	151.9	234.4	89.6	28.7	118.4	115.1	19.9	26.9	46.9	68,251	5,790	5,652	31,371	7,872	4,093	3,790
1952	378.8	140.5	238.3	98.0	30.4	128.4	109.9	18.5	28.6	47.2	62,510	4,093	2,797	24,666	14,546	2,538	2,294
1957	376.7	133.6	243.1	114.6	34.1	148.6	94.5	24.3	28.6	52.9	41,359	3,148	1,973	16,562	7,211	1,391	1,192
1962	372.8	125.7	247.1	121.1	35.5	156.7	90.4	30.0	27.4	57.4	32,844	2,034	4,616	11,573	4,586	855	709
1967	372.0	121.7	250.3	132.1	38.1	170.2	80.1	28.2	21.2	49.4	30,625	2,179	13,155	5,118	2,503	798	788
1972[1]	368.7	119.3	245.8	141.0	36.5	177.5	68.3	25.3	15.5	40.8	27,292	1,925	13,181	2,988	2,221	711	897

Agriculture 2. Acreage, by county, 1867-1972

FLINTSHIRE

JUNE	TOTAL FARMING AREA	ROUGH GRAZINGS	TOTAL CULTIVATED AREA	CULTIVATED AREA: PERMANENT GRASS: for grazing	PERMANENT GRASS: for hay	PERMANENT GRASS: total	ARABLE: TOTAL ARABLE	Rotation Grass: for grazing	Rotation Grass: for hay	Rotation Grass: total	Tillage: total	wheat	barley	oats	mixed corn	potatoes	turnips and swedes
	THOUSAND ACRES										ACRES						
1867	..	..	118.6	..	..	50.7	67.9	..	..	16.4	51,439	14,805	7,329	12,537	..	3,064	5,194
1872	..	..	128.0	44.4	12.8	57.2	68.8	6.4	13.4	19.8	49,033	15,390	7,983	12,042	..	3,352	4,122
1877	..	..	126.3	52.2	14.3	66.5	59.8	4.7	12.2	16.8	42,956	11,055	7,279	11,616	..	2,549	4,314
1882	..	..	129.3	..	..	71.5	57.8	..	..	16.5	41,325	10,487	6,639	11,782	..	3,042	4,188
1887	..	..	128.2	53.8	18.0	71.8	56.4	6.5	12.2	18.6	37,751	7,635	5,944	12,869	..	3,216	4,461
1892	131.7	5.5	126.2	55.8	19.4	75.2	51.0	5.2	11.9	17.2	33,848	5,146	6,247	12,334	..	2,864	4,613
1897	134.2	7.5	126.7	55.3	17.2	72.6	54.2	7.7	14.0	21.7	32,432	4,710	5,563	12,613	..	2,260	4,484
1902	134.4	8.3	126.1	54.6	18.3	72.9	53.2	9.7	15.0	24.7	28,549	3,953	5,394	10,548	..	2,257	3,943
1907	137.5	11.1	126.5	61.8	21.8	83.5	42.9	4.7	12.5	17.2	25,688	3,401	4,469	10,424	..	1,719	3,465
1912	136.7	10.8	125.9	61.1	23.4	84.6	41.3	3.9	12.6	16.5	24,840	3,518	4,148	10,190	..	1,638	3,446
1917	134.1	8.9	125.2	63.7	22.9	86.6	38.6	2.8	10.7	13.5	25,059	3,676	3,420	11,290	..	1,990	2,997
1922	133.4	11.3	122.1	60.8	22.1	82.9	39.2	3.6	13.0	16.6	22,570	2,626	2,434	10,912	302	1,567	2,540
1927	136.0	15.1	120.9	66.1	23.9	90.0	30.9	3.9	11.9	15.8	15,087	1,325	1,090	7,537	374	1,346	1,795
1932	134.9	13.8	121.1	70.6	23.3	93.9	27.2	4.7	9.7	14.4	12,844	867	647	6,642	349	1,196	1,676
1937	134.2	14.0	120.2	72.7	24.2	96.9	23.2	2.9	8.7	11.6	11,716	1,653	510	4,773	345	954	1,140
1942	135.0	18.0	117.1	53.1	17.3	70.4	46.7	2.1	6.9	9.0	37,620	4,694	1,941	16,692	4,484	3,414	1,706
1947	134.2	18.1	116.2	47.0	13.8	60.9	54.8	5.2	13.7	18.9	35,908	3,979	2,617	14,948	4,822	3,572	1,548
1952	131.7	14.6	117.1	49.6	15.5	65.2	51.9	6.0	15.4	21.5	30,267	2,682	1,785	10,132	8,435	1,759	899
1957	130.7	12.8	117.9	55.7	18.5	74.3	43.6	7.4	14.4	21.8	21,618	3,548	1,977	7,006	3,935	1,057	608
1962	127.8	12.1	115.8	55.3	20.5	75.8	40.0	9.8	14.2	24.1	15,866	1,811	4,665	3,778	1,559	808	391
1967	126.5	11.1	115.5	56.0	19.9	75.9	39.6	9.2	11.2	20.5	19.090	2,600	10,623	1,746	909	907	316
1972 (1)	122.3	10.6	110.5	55.1	19.1	74.2	36.3	8.0	9.1	17.0	19,110	1,224	12,018	1,574	1,328	954	192

Agriculture 2. Acreage, by county, 1867-1972

GLAMORGANSHIRE

JUNE	TOTAL FARMING AREA	ROUGH GRAZINGS	TOTAL CULTIVATED AREA	CULTIVATED AREA													
				PERMANENT GRASS			ARABLE										
								Rotation Grass			Tillage						
				for grazing	for hay	total	TOTAL ARABLE	for grazing	for hay	total	total	wheat	barley	oats	mixed corn	potatoes	turnips and swedes
	THOUSAND ACRES										ACRES						
1867	..	..	246.2	..	..	161.9	84.3	..	..	22:0	62,281	13,580	11,996	13,292	..	2,466	10,052
1872	..	..	262.0	114.5	52.0	166.5	95.6	10.3	21.4	31.7	63,915	15,356	14,573	13,176	..	2,614	11,025
1877	..	..	268.3	129.1	58.8	187.9	80.4	7.0	18.9	25.9	54,516	12,086	11,188	12,913	..	2,135	10,449
1882	..	..	275.8	..	..	196.0	79.8	..	..	23.9	55,849	11,769	10,399	14,070	..	2,380	9,950
1887	..	..	280.5	141.0	70.3	211.3	69.2	6.4	17.0	23.3	45,898	7,588	8,738	13,155	..	2,296	9,511
1892	387.3	105.2	282.1	148.9	69.9	218.8	63.3	6.3	15.4	21.7	41,606	5,507	9,064	12,221	..	2,096	8,956
1897	396.8	119.1	277.7	141.4	71.2	212.6	65.1	7.7	16.4	24.1	40,966	5,981	7,673	12,946	..	1,914	8,532
1902	397.0	124.9	272.0	142.1	70.5	212.6	59.4	7.9	16.9	24.8	34,623	4,303	7,112	10,919	..	1,859	6,885
1907	398.2	129.4	268.8	138.9	72.7	211.6	57.2	9.7	15.6	25.3	31,878	3,465	6,015	10,687	..	1,716	6,557
1912	394.2	132.8	261.4	132.0	77.5	209.5	51.8	6.6	13.6	20.2	31,678	4,296	5,576	10,635	..	1,760	5,864
1917	382.3	126.0	256.3	125.5	77.4	202.8	53.4	4.4	11.3	15.6	37,803	5,809	5,746	14,237	..	3,142	5,291
1922	360.4	133.0	227.5	105.6	66.3	171.9	55.5	6.8	14.2	21.0	34,658	5,228	4,418	12,994	488	2,365	5,103
1927	362.9	138.6	224.3	114.6	68.2	182.8	41.6	5.4	11.9	17.3	24,342	2,798	2,655	9,198	491	1,994	3,996
1932	360.4	139.0	221.3	115.6	67.6	183.2	38.1	5.7	10.9	16.6	21,654	1,847	2,084	8,230	481	2,045	3,877
1937	359.7	146.6	213.1	111.1	69.1	180.2	32.9	5.0	9.1	14.1	18,863	2,154	1,355	6,730	410	1,670	2,741
1942	386.4	183.1	203.3	77.2	52.2	129.4	73.9	3.3	9.5	12.8	61,024	10,467	4,486	24,955	3,354	6,568	3,504
1947	389.8	188.9	200.9	75.6	50.1	125.7	74.9	7.1	17.9	24.9	49,948	6,390	3,626	16,465	4,614	6,089	3,380
1952	368.4	164.5	203.9	84.3	52.8	137.1	66.8	8.1	17.5	25.6	41,062	4,434	3,091	10,062	7,132	4,047	2,348
1957	354.5	152.1	202.4	95.7	52.7	148.4	54.0	11.4	16.0	27.4	26,525	2,483	2,446	5,469	2,948	2,584	1,521
1962	342.3	141.0	201.3	96.0	51.5	147.6	53.8	14.0	18.5	32.5	21,170	2,256	5,703	2,402	1,058	1,957	1,098
1967	327.9	132.6	195.2	95.4	44.7	140.2	55.1	14.0	15.4	29.4	25,579	4,018	11,693	2,166	652	1,964	758
1972(1)	308.7	120.9	184.1	91.1	43.5	134.6	49.5	12.7	12.2	24.9	24,497	2,690	12,038	2,667	650	1,845	610

Agriculture 2. Acreage, by county, 1867-1972

MERIONETHSHIRE

				CULTIVATED AREA													
				PERMANENT GRASS			ARABLE										
								Rotation Grass			Tillage						
JUNE	TOTAL FARMING AREA	ROUGH GRAZINGS	TOTAL CULTIVATED AREA	for grazing	for hay	total	TOTAL ARABLE	for grazing	for hay	total	total	wheat	barley	oats	mixed corn	potatoes	turnips and swedes
	THOUSAND ACRES										ACRES						
1867	..	..	123.2	..	..	77.2	46.0	..	..	19.4	26,655	1,647	4,566	10,359	..	2,215	1,171
1872	..	..	125.0	52.0	35.9	87.9	37.1	4.1	8.4	12.5	24,551	1,928	5,539	11,875	..	2,635	1,512
1877	..	..	151.3	78.3	37.1	115.4	35.9	5.2	9.0	14.2	21,678	1,268	5,046	11,018	..	2,431	1,363
1882	..	..	154.4	..	..	119.1	35.3	..	..	13.8	21,518	1,175	4,807	11,232	..	2,392	1,496
1887	..	..	157.7	86.5	37.9	124.4	33.2	3.7	8.6	12.3	20,928	874	4,569	11,437	..	2,249	1,444
1892	296.4	134.2	162.2	89.8	38.4	128.2	33.9	6.6	8.2	14.7	19,207	849	4,226	9,925	..	2,078	1,633
1897	339.2	186.3	152.9	82.9	36.2	119.1	33.8	6.7	8.4	15.0	18,794	863	4,099	10,046	..	1,859	1,614
1902	357.7	205.3	152.5	80.7	35.3	116.0	36.5	9.2	9.9	19.1	17,361	704	4,091	8,841	..	1,793	1,401
1907	341.4	189.4	151.9	85.3	38.1	123.4	28.6	5.2	7.0	12.2	16,345	622	3,693	8,594	..	1,584	1,441
1912	345.7	196.0	149.7	83.1	39.1	122.2	27.5	3.7	6.9	10.5	17,003	519	4,081	8,986	..	1,436	1,530
1917	346.0	196.0	150.0	77.8	38.4	116.2	33.8	5.2	8.4	13.6	20,270	1,516	4,138	10,902	..	1,793	1,396
1922	351.0	206.1	144.9	80.9	35.0	115.9	29.0	5.1	8.8	13.9	15,117	313	2,973	8,248	413	1,273	1,135
1927	362.0	229.8	132.3	69.3	36.0	105.3	27.0	5.1	8.5	13.6	13,340	159	2,056	7,488	509	1,110	1,017
1932	355.6	228.9	126.7	66.9	32.6	99.5	27.1	6.2	8.5	14.7	12,415	86	1,520	7,433	708	1,010	967
1937	354.7	232.9	121.8	64.0	34.4	98.4	23.3	4.6	7.7	12.3	11,005	105	1,161	6,686	684	888	660
1942	358.3	254.4	103.9	42.2	26.5	68.7	35.2	3.7	6.8	10.4	24,783	513	1,799	14,686	2,124	2,273	803
1947	356.8	258.8	98.0	36.1	21.9	58.0	38.9	7.4	11.6	19.1	19,891	218	1,231	11,370	2,365	1,574	527
1952	351.8	254.5	97.3	42.2	22.7	64.9	32.3	5.9	10.2	16.1	16,168	135	452	7,665	3,446	1,034	259
1957	343.1	246.5	96.5	46.8	21.8	68.5	28.0	8.1	9.6	17.7	10,251	77	206	4,746	1,581	565	144
1962	337.1	239.2	97.9	52.3	19.2	71.4	26.5	9.9	8.8	18.8	7,634	4	241	3,150	672	367	129
1967	337.2	240.1	97.0	56.6	18.3	74.9	22.1	9.8	6.8	16.6	5,546	7	1,323	1,363	222	198	74
1972 (1)	317.1	220.4	94.1	61.2	14.4	75.6	18.6	9.9	4.1	14.0	4,482	4	1,095	603	107	130	185

Agriculture 2. Acreage, by county, 1867-1972

MONMOUTHSHIRE

JUNE	TOTAL FARMING AREA	ROUGH GRAZINGS	TOTAL CULTIVATED AREA	CULTIVATED AREA													
				PERMANENT GRASS			ARABLE										
							TOTAL ARABLE	Rotation Grass			Tillage						
				for grazing	for hay	total		for grazing	for hay	total	total	wheat	barley	oats	mixed corn	potatoes	turnips and swedes
	THOUSAND ACRES										ACRES						
1867	..	..	209.7	..	..	126.8	82.9	..	..	18.3	64,544	19,821	12,488	8,297	..	2,141	9,770
1872	..	..	225.6	89.6	44.3	133.8	91.7	8.5	19.8	28.3	63,426	20,473	11,917	7,259	..	1,914	9,714
1877	..	..	235.4	105.8	50.1	155.9	79.5	6.8	16.4	23.2	56,344	17,663	9,765	8,115	..	1,679	8,769
1882	..	..	243.1	..	..	176.1	66.9	..	..	14.7	52,197	16,151	8,596	8,711	..	1,777	7,486
1887	..	..	245.1	123.6	62.3	186.0	59.1	4.9	12.2	17.2	41,976	10,841	6,416	9,222	..	1,836	7,559
1892	268.7	24.0	244.6	129.6	63.0	192.6	52.0	4.0	11.4	15.4	36,620	7,799	6,629	8,803	..	1,557	7,005
1897	271.7	28.9	242.7	125.5	67.2	192.7	50.0	4.8	11.5	16.3	33,682	7,461	5,278	8,925	..	1,422	6,199
1902	277.7	35.3	242.3	131.2	65.2	196.5	45.9	5.7	12.3	18.0	27,886	5,215	4,153	8,482	..	1,319	4,749
1907	278.8	36.9	242.0	132.3	70.4	202.8	39.2	4.1	9.9	13.9	25,313	4,130	3,358	8,601	..	1,188	4,556
1912	274.4	37.0	237.4	127.0	75.0	202.0	35.4	2.6	7.7	10.3	25,091	5,518	3,145	7,994	..	1,086	4,020
1917	266.7	32.0	234.7	127.1	73.6	200.7	34.0	2.1	7.0	9.0	24,946	7,047	2,958	6,834	..	1,608	3,410
1922	265.8	48.7	217.1	110.6	67.1	177.7	39.3	2.9	8.8	11.7	27,633	6,738	2,384	8,772	271	1,518	3,268
1927	265.5	52.1	213.4	117.6	66.6	184.2	29.2	2.4	5.8	8.2	21,104	4,146	1,346	5,792	214	1,216	2,651
1932	270.4	55.5	214.9	123.6	66.7	190.3	24.6	2.2	4.8	7.0	17,577	3,281	838	4,711	212	1,041	2,250
1937	270.1	56.7	213.4	122.1	68.8	190.0	22.5	2.0	4.8	6.8	15,710	3,542	614	3,219	118	908	1,670
1942	269.3	62.4	206.9	86.6	47.5	134.2	72.7	1.2	4.7	5.9	66,785	16,930	3,422	23,620	3,639	6,104	2,842
1947	263.0	55.9	207.1	81.6	42.2	123.8	82.2	10.4	17.0	27.5	54,784	11,920	3,677	15,363	2,450	4,904	3,475
1952	263.0	54.9	208.1	90.1	46.9	137.0	71.1	9.9	16.0	25.9	45,081	8,325	2,483	11,136	4,706	2,939	3,018
1957	258.4	50.0	208.4	104.4	46.1	150.5	57.9	14.4	14.6	29.0	28,709	5,465	2,336	5,117	1,151	1,897	2,278
1962	251.4	46.8	204.6	101.9	48.0	149.9	54.7	15.3	15.9	31.2	23,380	4,166	3,134	3,256	302	1,505	1,836
1967	247.9	44.3	203.6	103.2	45.4	148.6	54.9	14.1	12.8	26.9	27,960	5,656	9,099	2,846	298	1,671	1,881
1972	242.5	43.4	195.4	99.4	43.7	143.1	52.3	15.8	10.7	26.5	25,615	4,880	9,126	3,400	460	1,592	1,432

Agriculture 2. Acreage, by county, 1867-1972

MONTGOMERYSHIRE

JUNE	TOTAL FARMING AREA	ROUGH GRAZINGS	TOTAL CULTIVATED AREA	CULTIVATED AREA: PERMANENT GRASS: for grazing	PERMANENT GRASS: for hay	PERMANENT GRASS: total	ARABLE: TOTAL ARABLE	Rotation Grass: for grazing	Rotation Grass: for hay	Rotation Grass: total	Tillage: total	wheat	barley	oats	mixed corn	potatoes	turnips and swedes
	THOUSAND ACRES										ACRES						
1867	..	..	229.2	..	..	128.7	100.5	..	..	25.7	74,754	20,954	12,087	21,344	..	3,045	8,986
1872	..	..	243.3	96.9	35.5	132.5	110.8	13.7	22.2	35.9	74,903	22,735	12,879	21,785	..	3,208	7,490
1877	..	..	249.2	113.7	39.0	152.7	96.5	10.0	18.2	28.2	68,274	19,242	10,822	21,918	..	2,801	8,119
1882	..	..	256.1	..	..	163.4	92.6	..	..	23.9	68,761	18,655	9,970	23,937	..	2,728	7,761
1887	..	..	259.9	121.4	47.0	168.4	91.5	12.0	17.0	29.0	62,465	14,173	8,647	25,008	..	2,634	8,031
1892	362.9	90.2	272.7	138.4	47.5	185.9	86.8	13.9	17.1	31.0	55,786	11,027	9,075	22,759	..	2,287	7,872
1897	403.8	132.4	271.5	138.9	46.0	184.9	86.5	13.9	17.9	31.8	54,780	10,952	8,359	22,800	..	2,143	7,729
1902	433.0	158.4	274.6	146.5	47.8	194.3	80.3	13.0	18.2	31.2	49,141	9,605	7,798	20,943	..	1,940	6,601
1907	437.8	163.8	274.0	149.5	48.8	198.3	75.8	12.9	17.8	30.7	45,034	8,157	6,758	19,932	..	1,731	6,083
1912	442.1	168.7	273.4	149.7	50.9	200.6	72.8	9.7	16.8	26.5	46,245	8,391	7,234	20,496	..	1,590	5,980
1917	440.5	165.9	274.7	150.6	50.9	201.6	73.1	8.1	16.4	24.6	48,540	10,399	5,620	23,185	..	1,992	4,818
1922	442.9	182.7	260.2	140.0	50.5	190.5	69.8	9.1	17.6	26.7	43,009	8,333	4,363	19,533	1,505	1,420	4,656
1927	446.7	188.4	258.3	144.8	51.0	195.8	62.5	8.7	17.6	26.3	36,219	6,002	2,727	17,511	1,530	1,263	3,978
1932	450.4	192.3	258.1	147.9	51.4	199.3	58.8	9.7	17.8	27.5	31,328	4,385	1,978	15,780	1,326	1,112	3,643
1937	452.0	195.1	256.9	150.3	52.0	202.3	54.7	8.4	17.4	25.8	28,826	3,949	1,658	14,617	1,349	963	2,551
1942	459.0	204.9	254.1	119.1	38.2	157.3	96.8	7.5	18.8	26.3	70,555	9,969	4,694	29,109	8,696	3,498	3,346
1947	462.6	209.1	253.5	113.4	35.2	148.6	103.9	19.3	27.0	46.3	57,608	5,449	4,832	23,055	8,813	3,558	2,653
1952	458.5	206.7	251.8	123.0	35.8	158.7	93.1	14.2	27.2	41.4	51,426	5,237	2,768	16,831	12,989	1,625	1,866
1957	454.7	198.6	256.1	135.0	36.4	171.3	84.7	19.7	29.0	48.7	35,887	3,522	2,060	13,233	6,245	848	1,327
1962	451.0	186.9	264.1	146.4	38.0	184.4	79.7	21.8	28.6	50.3	29,237	2,695	4,399	10,350	3,053	520	1,013
1967	451.1	181.7	269.4	156.4	39.2	195.6	73.8	21.7	25.1	46.9	26,824	2,723	9,565	6,225	1,297	354	1,222
1972 (1)	449.5	173.6	270.6	164.8	38.1	202.9	67.7	25.3	20.1	45.4	21,798	2,190	8,237	3,765	1,797	217	1,032

Agriculture 2. Acreage, by county, 1867-1972

PEMBROKESHIRE

JUNE	TOTAL FARMING AREA	ROUGH GRAZINGS	TOTAL CULTIVATED AREA	CULTIVATED AREA: PERMANENT GRASS: for grazing	for hay	total	ARABLE: TOTAL ARABLE	Rotation Grass: for grazing	for hay	total	Tillage: total	wheat	barley	oats	mixed corn	potatoes	turnips and swedes
	THOUSAND ACRES										ACRES						
1867	..	..	257.2	..	..	148.0	109.2	..	..	26.7	82,484	7,196	24,986	27,230	..	3,417	6,532
1872	..	..	289.2	137.5	29.0	166.4	122.7	21.3	17.4	38.7	84,058	8,497	29,169	28,142	..	4,143	7,339
1877	..	..	299.6	158.9	32.3	191.2	108.3	16.9	16.7	33.6	74,724	6,481	26,181	25,570	..	3,528	7,907
1882	..	..	304.5	..	..	202.5	102.0	..	..	28.0	74,026	5,773	25,258	26,114	..	3,319	8,038
1887	..	..	307.3	163.1	40.8	203.9	103.3	19.5	16.3	35.9	67,489	3,343	21,923	26,996	..	3,063	8,294
1892	341.2	25.1	316.1	166.4	43.2	209.5	106.6	25.4	17.4	42.8	63,794	3,312	20,562	25,523	..	2,736	8,104
1897	345.1	31.8	313.3	166.3	42.5	208.8	104.4	21.5	18.8	40.3	64,116	3,370	19,015	27,507	..	2,503	7,588
1902	344.9	33.4	311.5	169.1	42.7	211.7	99.1	19.4	19.9	39.2	59,880	2,970	18,919	25,494	..	2,346	5,938
1907	349.3	40.2	309.1	165.3	47.2	212.5	96.6	17.3	20.7	38.0	58,584	2,115	17,337	26,413	..	2,261	5,820
1912	350.6	42.8	307.8	163.0	52.3	215.3	92.5	12.9	18.8	31.6	60,920	2,393	18,187	26,834	..	2,140	5,829
1917	351.1	44.6	306.5	154.1	54.5	208.6	97.9	11.0	18.7	29.7	68,163	4,771	19,212	31,809	..	3,031	4,622
1922	365.5	65.3	291.2	142.6	53.3	195.9	95.2	13.8	23.9	37.7	57,568	1,336	13,617	26,443	3,121	2,143	4,258
1927	355.8	65.6	290.2	149.3	58.9	208.2	82.0	13.2	21.6	34.8	47,285	743	10,803	21,282	3,109	2,089	3,833
1932	355.9	67.6	288.3	150.2	59.8	210.0	78.3	13.8	19.9	33.7	44,612	714	7,747	21,044	3,976	2,115	3,375
1937	355.1	68.6	286.5	146.9	59.5	206.4	80.2	13.4	21.2	34.6	45.582	1,330	6,469	22,141	3,892	2,135	2,212
1942	347.0	72.8	274.2	104.0	42.3	146.2	128.0	7.4	19.4	26.8	101.197	2,287	13,179	47,158	12,516	8,265	2,266
1947	346.7	70.1	276.6	101.6	38.4	140.0	135.8	17.6	33.2	50.8	84,984	1,827	9,702	33,128	11,549	10,767	1,899
1952	350.2	70.8	279.3	105.1	41.1	146.2	133.1	18.6	33.9	52.6	80,435	1,657	8,593	29,202	13,248	9,004	1,459
1957	349.6	68.3	281.3	111.5	40.0	151.5	129.8	28.9	36.9	65.8	63,977	1,801	9,505	21,529	7,125	7,267	1,018
1962	347.0	64.3	282.7	107.0	42.2	149.2	133.5	34.5	38.9	73.3	59,862	771	21,876	13,518	3,239	8,795	647
1967	345.0	61.0	284.0	112.6	45.3	158.0	126.0	33.1	32.7	65.8	60,101	1,151	30,596	9,251	4,080	8,641	472
1972 (1)	339.4	57.1	278.1	112.5	46.1	158.5	119.5	35.4	29.8	65.2	53,804	264	24,376	7,024	10,248	7,458	439

Agriculture 2. Acreage, by county, 1867-1972

RADNORSHIRE

JUNE	TOTAL FARMING AREA	ROUGH GRAZINGS	TOTAL CULTIVATED AREA	CULTIVATED AREA: PERMANENT GRASS: for grazing	for hay	total	ARABLE: TOTAL ARABLE	Rotation Grass: for grazing	for hay	total	Tillage: total	wheat	barley	oats	mixed corn	potatoes	turnips and swedes
	THOUSAND ACRES										ACRES						
1867	..	..	135.2	..	..	91.1	44.1	..	..	9.7	34,403	7,090	4,863	11,760	..	1,426	6,280
1872	..	..	150.0	79.3	18.6	97.9	52.0	6.4	8.9	15.3	36,736	7,689	5,302	12,678	..	1,454	6,734
1877	..	..	155.0	83.5	20.5	103.9	51.1	6.6	10.8	17.4	33,669	6,803	4,675	12,067	..	1,504	6,399
1882	..	..	156.4	..	..	111.5	44.9	..	..	12.5	32,333	6,407	4,196	12,289	..	1,212	5,536
1887	..	..	159.4	91.6	24.6	116.2	43.3	6.6	7.1	13.7	29,565	4,717	3,449	12,820	..	1,083	5,776
1892	274.2	106.3	167.9	102.7	24.4	127.0	40.0	6.6	7.1	13.6	26,382	3,453	3,663	12,249	..	973	5,723
1897	273.9	111.1	162.7	95.8	24.2	120.0	42.7	8.1	7.7	15.7	27,006	3,285	3,455	12,507	..	910	5,695
1902	287.4	124.4	163.0	97.1	23.5	120.6	42.4	8.8	8.4	17.2	25,180	2,879	3,455	11,566	..	858	5,535
1907	290.6	128.2	162.4	96.5	25.0	121.5	40.9	8.8	8.3	17.1	23,748	2,078	3,359	11,367	..	734	5,456
1912	287.4	125.6	161.8	97.3	25.2	122.5	39.2	7.0	7.9	14.9	24,307	2,187	3,769	11,583	..	688	5,153
1917	282.8	121.2	161.6	96.5	25.6	122.1	39.4	6.4	8.4	14.8	24,647	3,428	3,129	11,869	..	840	4,545
1922	278.1	121.4	156.7	94.1	24.0	118.1	38.6	6.9	9.2	16.1	22,444	1,737	2,364	11,653	229	647	4,673
1927	283.2	127.5	155.7	94.4	24.2	118.6	37.0	7.7	9.5	17.2	19,760	1,058	1,456	10,659	200	566	4,533
1932	283.1	128.9	154.1	93.4	24.3	117.7	36.5	8.2	9.8	18.0	18,450	690	854	10,656	242	496	4,279
1937	282.1	128.7	153.4	90.9	24.6	115.5	37.8	9.2	10.6	19.8	18,078	732	573	10,553	201	483	3,701
1942	280.7	136.4	144.3	69.5	19.5	89.0	55.2	5.6	9.3	14.9	40,395	3,278	2,617	22,800	1,021	1,754	4,685
1947	280.9	139.8	141.0	61.5	16.4	77.8	62.8	14.4	15.1	29.5	33,361	1.742	3,053	15,958	993	1,895	4,162
1952	272.0	128.7	143.3	63.0	16.0	79.0	64.3	15.1	16.4	31.5	32,770	1,742	2,165	14,452	1,818	1,010	4,067
1957	270.9	121.3	149.7	69.3	16.5	85.8	63.8	20.6	17.2	37.7	26,054	1,160	1,339	10,888	796	577	3,861
1962	271.6	116.0	155.7	71.1	16.3	87.4	68.3	25.7	18.7	44.5	23,683	938	1,278	10,231	416	445	3,396
1967	276.1	115.1	161.1	78.5	17.8	96.3	64.8	23.9	18.9	42.8	21,851	851	3,425	7,502	242	393	3,079
1972 (1)	276.9	108.9	164.6	86.3	19.3	105.5	59.1	25.1	15.8	41.0	17,443	1,124	3,447	4,979	390	357	2,277

General Notes

(i) Sources. Agricultural Returns; Agricultural Statistics; Ashby and Evans, *op.cit.*, tables 22-60.

(ii) Rounding means that the totals do not always exactly equal the sum of the individual items.

(iii) Only selected tillage crops are shown in the county tables. The figure given for total tillage is thus greater than the sum of the individual items. Tillage crops not separately distinguished include: rye, beans and peas, mangold, rape, cabbages, vetches, carrots, other green crops and vegetables, and bare fallow and uncropped arable land.

(iv) In 1896 the county areas of Caernarvonshire and Monmouthshire were increased; and that of Merionethshire reduced.

Notes

1. In 1972 the sum of 'rough grazings' and 'total cultivated area' do not quite equal 'total farming area' because two new categories were introduced: 'woodlands ancillary to farming' and 'other land used for agriculture'. Figures have not been taken for these but they are included in the 'total farming area'.

Agriculture 3. Numbers of Livestock, Wales 1913-1974 a) Poultry

	Fowls	Ducks	Geese	Turkeys	Total
1913	2,763,958	270,869	176,563	99,522	3,310,912
1921	2,338,180	231,022	134,379	67,524	2,771,105
1924	2,702,062	263,687	134,222	74,310	3,174,281
1926	3,192,037	315,063	157,977	96,721	3,761,798
1927	3,307,680	309,455	159,382	93,879	3,870,396
1928	3,289,771	284,679	151,854	85,059	3,811,363
1929	3,469,801	278,873	157,226	100,931	4,006,831
1930	3,602,514	293,100	149,550	93,982	4,139,146
1931	3,804,159	289,698	137,781	79,465	4,311,103
1932	4,061,669	320,409	137,651	79,065	4.598,794
1933	4,490,643	309,269	157,642	113,222	5.070,776
1934	4,461,151	278,056	155,230	105,420	4.999,857
1935	4,366,403	268,576	159.415	106,789	4,901,183
1936	4,406,731	265,192	155.774	105.898	4,933,595
1937	4,109,389	238,886	140.903	101,933	4 591,111
1938	4,120,072	212.611	147,002	107,788	4.587 473
1939	3,966,888	211,451	137,767	90,574	4.406,680
1940	3,486,984	187,424	131,806	78,345	3,884,559
1941	3,339,108	161,418	127,968	65,815	3,694,309
1942	3,002,596	175,779	128,061	63,769	3,370,205
1943	2,657,546	171,140	132,012	58,442	3,019,140
1944	2,910,499	196,941	141,127	65,914	3,314,481
1945	3,349,705	226,213	147,399	76,687	3,800,004
1946	3,513,734	217,571	143,611	77,165	3,952,081
1947	3,448,909	193,859	135,089	72,168	3,850,025
1948	4,212,075	217,027	162,195	92,649	4,683,946
1949	4,910,293	226,178	163,159	88,896	5,388,526
1950	5,072,316	192,847	149,761	72,428	5,487,352
1951	4,985,850	146,376	115,283	62,612	5.310,112
1952	5,066,356	128,924	122,042	82,294	5,399.616
1953	4,896,138	122,969	122,874	86.625	5.228,606
1954	4,471,396	98,787	113.537	77.666	4 761 386
1955	4,528,020	70,408	89,518	90.543	4 778 489
1956	4,844,582	67,609	95.041	142.896	5 150.128
1957	4,849,677	68,477	87,281	130.810	5.136.245
1958	4,684,961	59.378	76,978	131.991	4.953,308
1959	4,574,425	56,979	68,059	170,646	4,870,109
1960	4,155,823	53,078	66,624	146,876	4,422,401
1961	4,133,468	54,697	58,016	196,202	4,442,383
1962	3,927,635	45,939	50,013	169,005	4,192,592
1963	3,831,471	38,222	43,795	215,662	1,129,150
1964	3,939,380	37,350	42,189	184,561	4,203,480
1965	3,689,187	33,582	36,684	183,156	3,942,609
1966	3,783,575	30,464	32,738	162,929	4,009,706
1967	5,040,483	28,408	32,992	143,847	5,245,730
1968	5,311,677	24,648	28,700	162,039	5,527,064
1969	4,406,050	21,674	25,675	101,275	4.554,674
1970	6,280,573	21,091	23,062	137,750	6,462.476
1971	5,558,588	19,219	22,731	141,108	5.741.646
1972	4,761,244	18,726	21,190	93.693	4 894 853
1973	8,238,284	18,960	21,230	84,653	8,363,127
1974(1)	7,769.2	16.7	19.7	76.3	7,881.9

General Notes

(i) Sources. Agricultural Statistics; Ashby and Evans, The Agriculture of Wales and Monmouthshire, 1944, Appendix B, Table 14. Annual Digest of Welsh Agricultural Statistics, 1974/5

(ii) The figures relate to June of each year.

Notes

1. Figures for 1974 are in thousands.

Agriculture 3. Numbers of Livestock, Wales 1867-1974 b) Pigs

	Sows kept for breeding	Boars kept for service(1)	OTHER PIGS 2 months and over(2)	under 2 months	Total
1867	--	--	--	--	249,970
1868	--	--	--	--	202,740
1869	--	--	--	--	185,757
1870	--	--	--	--	214,233
1871	--	--	--	--	242,313
1872	--	--	--	--	257,080
1873	--	--	--	--	227,705
1874	--	--	--	--	230,265
1875	--	--	--	--	217,744
1876	--	--	--	--	230,202
1877	--	--	--	--	246,626
1878	--	--	--	--	234,526
1879	--	--	--	--	205,581
1880	--	--	--	--	194,379
1881	--	--	--	--	205,697
1882	--	--	--	--	251,315
1883	--	--	--	--	247,410
1884	--	--	--	--	233,587
1885	--	--	--	--	232,857
1886	--	--	--	--	220,959
1887	--	--	--	--	238,622
1888	--	--	--	--	247,892
1889	--	--	--	--	257,299
1890	--	--	--	--	275,765
1891	--	--	--	--	289,931
1892	--	--	--	--	210,774
1893	35,818	--	177,874	--	213,692
1894	39,671	--	203,090	--	242,761
1895	44,027	--	234,941	--	278,968
1896	42,690	--	234,018	--	276,708
1897	38,131	--	192,901	--	231,032
1898	42,042	--	213,185	--	255,227
1899	43,818	--	232,091	--	275,909
1900	38,700	--	205,823	--	244,523
1901	38,065	--	189,564	--	227,629
1902	39,788	--	191,696	--	231.484
1903	42,545	--	219 864	--	262,409
1904	39,481	--	219,768	--	259,249
1905	36,239	--	192,205	--	228,444
1906	37,176	--	188,327	--	225.503
1907	42,686	--	207,903	--	250,589
1908	40,308	--	218,521	--	258,829
1909	35,203	--	184,841	--	220,044
1910	35,699	--	174,641	--	210,340
1911	44,629	--	208,728	--	253.357
1912	45,617	--	199,063	--	244.680
1913	35,909	--	168,282	--	204,191
1914	36,193	--	200,779	--	236,972
1915	33,287	--	197,850	--	231,137
1916	31,465	--	173,349	--	204,814
1917	29,856	--	166,455	--	196,311
1918	29,726	--	138,520	--	168,246
1919	27,105	2,616	155,532	--	185,253
1920	29,584	2,175	163,082	--	194,841
1921	32,674	1,658	200,353	--	234,685
1922	29,419	1,631	169,618	--	200,668
1923	35,505	1,584	190,921	--	228,010
1924	38,061	1,820	219,117	--	258,998
1925	27,675	1,484	173,696	--	202,855
1926	28,147	1,224	156,793	--	186,164
1927	37,194	1,418	198,649	--	237,261
1928	34,768	1,556	210,060	--	246,384
1929	28,976	1,272	163,667	--	193,915
1930	32,197	1.458	172,287	--	205.942
1931	38,780	1,510	211,655	--	251,945
1932	36,349	1.536	213,594	--	251,479
1933	32,765	1,480	119,478	69,897	223,620
1934	37,681	1,782	112,546	88,590	240,599

	Sows kept for breeding	Boars kept for service(1)	OTHER PIGS 2 months and over(2)	under 2 months	Total
1935	41,042	2,343	135,153	102,204	280,740
1936	37,276	1,876	124,848	91,247	255,247
1937	34,081	1,871	120,768	82,970	239,690
1938	31,860	1,416	130,694	58,811	222,781
1939	31,100	1,384	116,526	58,769	207,779
1940	28,613	1,219	128,204	46,130	204,166
1941	17,593	800	102,200	31,058	151,651
1942	18,015	800	92,276	33,321	144,412
1943	12,403	648	82,704	25,038	120,793
1944	14,791	718	69,483	24,767	109,759
1945	14,495	730	91,231	25,887	132,793
1946	11,247	623	72,934	17,884	102,688
1947	10,616	644	55,014	12,788	79,062
1948	18,613	968	78,387	25,595	123,563
1949	16,177	869	90,874	24,939	132,859
1950	16,031	657	75,657	22,871	115,472
1951	26,605	934	96,616	36,275	160,958
1952	29,313	1,115	147,678	52,569	231,222
1953	34,260	1,214	142,068	59,610	237,688
1954	41,860	1,736	174,921	72,263	290,780
1955	31,422	1,603	142,358	64,189	239,572
1956	33,454	1,496	132,048	61,012	228,010
1957	36,657	1,816	142,297	66,403	247,173
1958	40,206	1,843	164,028	75,185	281,262
1959	30,790	1,486	136,559	57,038	225,873
1960	30,154	1,339	110,764	55,026	197,283
1961	33,875	1,442	124,039	56,973	216,329
1962	36,944	1,544	133,247	69,680	241,415
1963	38,543	1,640	140,761	64,101	245,045
1964	41,349	1,698	146,011	78,560	267,618
1965	45,730	1,955	157,952	98,164	303,801
1966	37,547	1,804	141,400	86,225	266,976
1967	36,840	1,662	128,004	84,515	251,021
1968	38,008	1,681	115,293	81,169	236,151
1969	36,447	1,686	123,191	83,044	244,368
1970	36,317	1,715	122,122	81,311	241,465
1971	36,129	1,805	156,886	85,491	253,171
1972	31,936	1,677	118,915	75,651	228,179
1973	30,554	1,647	117,300	67,775	217,276
1974(3)	25.4	1.5	107.6	58.4	194.7

General Notes

(i) Sources. Agricultural Statistics; Ashby and Evans, The Agriculture of Wales and Monmouthshire, 1944, Appnedix B, Table 13; Annual Digest of Welsh Agricultural Statistics, 1974/5

(ii) The figures relate to June of each year.

Notes

1. 1947-53 includes "young boars being reared for service".
2. 1940-53, 1956-72 includes "barren sows for fattening".
3. Figures for 1974 are in thousands

Agriculture 3. Numbers of Livestock, Wales 1867-1974. c) Cattle

	Cows in milk and in calf and heifers in milk(1)	Heifers in calf	Bulls used for service	Other cattle under 1 year	Cattle 1-2 years	Cattle 2 years and over	Total
1867	259,931	--	--	200,142		119,633	579,706
1868	270,479	--	--	231,535		129,857	631,871
1869	272,436	--	--	225,086		130,528	628,050
1870	271,816	--	--	240,697		132,440	644,953
1871	265,286	--	--	242,492		127,367	635,145
1872	265,602	--	--	258,137		117,918	641,657
1873	275,167	--	--	293,412		116,593	685,172
1874	280,008	--	--	294,482		136,208	710,698
1875	276,949	--	--	264,900		153,266	695,115
1876	275,010	--	--	256,682		147,174	678,866
1877	269,412	--	--	256,612		130,563	656,587
1878	267,582	--	--	259,081		121,126	647,789
1879	277,379	--	--	286,770		121,312	685,461
1880	277,062	--	--	283,484		136,090	696,636
1881	276,697	--	--	278,634		143,525	698,856
1882	276,348	--	--	285,732		126,598	688,678
1883	276,833	--	--	303,333		116,903	679,069
1884	284,049	--	--	321,710		122,544	728,303
1885	298,547	--	--	327,354		133,512	759,413
1886	302,594	--	--	317,099		151,722	771,415
1887	301,571	--	--	301,423		143,245	746,239
1888	293,112	--	--	288,778		129,741	711,631
1889	289,612	--	--	297,076		123,933	710,621
1890	300,768	--	--	336,364		114,876	752,008
1891	314,303	--	--	358,680		136,805	809,788
1892	311,333	--	--	338,671		157,135	807,139
1893	299,827,	--	--	165,927	171,485	150,645	787,884
1894	290,064	--	--	163,663	156,494	130,212	740,433
1895	293,246	--	--	183,055	159,366	113,699	749,366
1896	292,291	--	--	188,366	175,096	103,276	759,029
1897	289,943	--	--	180,933	179,612	103,915	754,403
1898	291,726	--	--	186,360	168,928	100,585	747,599
1899	304,311	--	--	206,263	179,458	95,274	785,306
1900	305,022	--	--	203,912	196,444	102,807	808,185
1901	298,925	--	--	197,912	190,272	104,239	791,348
1902	293,442	--	--	188,713	183,932	102,682	768,769
1903	292,282	--	--	196,605	173,723	95,554	758,164
1904	296,327	--	--	201,112	187,455	93,032	777,926
1905	299,316	--	--	200,820	189,486	100,026	789,648
1906	302,761	--	--	198,478	192,520	104,663	798,422
1907	306,985	--	--	191,044	184,731	106,016	788,776
1908	304,163	--	--	199,904	183,387	94,715	782,169
1909	304,646	--	--	206,150	192,377	91,357	794,530
1910	300,690	--	--	200,383	193,977	94,746	789,796
1911	302,889	--	--	202,558	185,287	98,698	789,432
1912	304,249	--	--	197,224	197,396	104,435	803,304
1913	283,040	--	--	199,611	182,055	109,840	774,546
1914	290,314	28,841	--	217,060	190,442	81,246	807,903
1915	292,431	28,858	--	227,379	207,573	80,963	837,204
1916	293,226	33,243	--	231,618	215,960	94,601	868,648
1917	286,922	36,102	--	224,000	218,910	92,767	858,701
1918	288,679	31,339	--	217,860	212,351	80,344	830,573
1919	296,876	29,025	13,655	205,721	211,997	102,065	859,339
1920	280,399	25,095	13,010	163,460	184,975	107,368	774,307
1921	288,597	31,773	13,125	188,665	157,299	90,531	769,990
1922	299,355	30,980	12,696	183,578	190,102	82,929	799,640
1923	298,108	30,189	11,875	186,243	180,788	82,938	790,141
1924	298,547	33,072	11,972	192,898	180,654	81,505	798,648
1925	300,556	32,143	12,136	199,848	184,666	88,716	818,065
1926	300,137	34,212	12,010	196,212	189,600	84,411	816,582
1927	308,288	35,585	11,891	204,276	186,683	81,974	828,797
1928	302,921	30,000	11,253	195,390	195,220	83,273	818,057
1929	296,911	33,787	10,848	183,572	185,628	82,950	793,696
1930	299,532	37,601	11,395	189,039	170,315	76,868	784,750
1931	305,303	39,118	11,999	207,219	182,559	73,689	819,887
1932	314,078	36,368	11,707	211,442	199,265	84,982	857,842
1933	315,916	38,593	12,112	201,087	200,765	88,384	856,857
1934	317,226	36,780	12,093	194,636	199,868	92,417	853,020

Agriculture 3. Cattle (cont)

	Cows in milk and in calf and heifers in milk(1)	Heifers in calf	Bulls used for service	Other cattle under 1 year(2)	Cattle 1-2 years	Cattle 2 years and over	Total
1935	318,462	41,753	9,645(2)	184,747	191,487	85,484	831,578
1936	322,142	41,967	9,208	201,202	185,404	82,403	842,326
1937	320,257	43,820	9,535	202,367	192,837	75,252	844,068
1938	318,101	43,363	9,634	212,332	196,334	78,879	858,643
1939	321,534	45,015	9,868	192,186	201,928	88,066	858,597
1940	320,855	46,722	9,852	195,253	187.041	83 830	843.553
1941	335,332	44,414	10,238	192,670	195 039	91.665	869,358
1942	332,186	60,796	11.014	190.450	175 087	90,092	859.625
1943	352,717	67,615	11,852	199,418	179,183	94,670	905.455
1944	366,551	67.495	12,292	199,541	187,072	104,922	937,873
1945	365,851	67,034	12,408	187,054	192,902	120,712	945,961
1946	368,986	75,745	12,622	172,890	177,322	120,128	927,693
1947	368,316	67,189	12,422	165,988	167,736	117,095	898,746
1948	377,346	78,897	12,132	205,560	152,367	114,306	940,608
1949	391,839	73,211	11,293	216,897	184,464	107,677	985,381
1950	396,281	71,393	10,536	215,067	196,893	121,048	1,011,218
1951	379,013	67,985	9,722	188,760	188,984	126,664	961,128
1952	380,995	81,014	8,773	196,310	170,933	120,402	958,427
1953	396,975	73,759	8,365	230,237	189,200	117,051	1,016,587
1954	408,094	78,788	7,801	236,329	213,338	118,645	1,062,995
1955	399,875	69,875	6,526	219,790	213,634	121,127	1,030,827
1956	407,483	85,962	6,220	226,861	208,840	119,605	1,054,971
1957	430,509	79,637	5,836	246,163	208,121	101,710	1,071,976
1958	433,060	72,196	5,511	266,861	227,350	94 020	1 098,998
1959	427,491	73,122	5,233	275,823	245.874	98,052	1 125 595
1960	440,393	76,413	5,337	281.531	260.387	103.914	1.167,975
1961	454,564	78,200	5,384	280,595	252.120	100,302	1 171,165
1962	469,127	79.537	5.225	291.689	242,175	86.375	1,174,128
1963	473,535	74,610	5,197	197,214	247,593	85,219	1,183,368
1964	463,002	79,408	5,025	303,720	246,338	83,964	1,181,457
1965	475,102	71,110	5,383	360,928	246,402	77,528	1,236,453
1966	486,333	73,706	5,845	378,602	267,947	75,953	1,288,386
1967	503,827	80,732	6,173	378,903	271,050	78,853	1,319,538
1968	510,711	77,505	6,255	380,319	263,194	77,673	1,315,657
1969	524,971	77,248	6,568	394,348	264,650	75,759	1,343,544
1970	528,420	81,525	6,800	392,592	265,345	75,417	1,349,919
1971	535,472	77,906	7,053	403,513	265,896	78,435	1,368,275
1972	552,978	85,300	7,509	428,006	276,235	73,800	1,423,828
1973	577,848	85,769	8,190	449,629	301,694	81,166	1,504,296
1974(3)	587.7	99.8	7.3	459.2	330.5	87.1	1,578.2

General Notes

i) Sources. Agricultural Statistics; Ashby and Evans, The Agriculture of Wales and Monmouthshire, 1944, Appendix B, Table 10; Annual Digest of Welsh Agricultural Statistics, 1974/5.

ii) The figures relate to June of each year.

Notes

(1) Cows and heifers in milk and in calf down to 1913; cows in milk and in calf thereafter, the heifers being shown separately.

(2) The returns from 1935 on distinguish an additional category of 'Bulls reared for service'. These have been included in 'Other Cattle under 1 year'. The figures below indicate the order of magnitude involved in this change:

No. of bulls reared for service:

1935	4,848	1937	4,527
1936	5,265	1938	5,131

(3) Figures for 1974 are in thousands.

Agriculture 3. Numbers of Livestock, Wales 1867-1974. d) Sheep

	Ewes for Breeding(1)	Other Sheep 1 year and above	Rams for service(2)	Other Sheep under 1 year	Total
1867	1,635,883		..	774,263	2,410,146
1868	1,955,150		..	918,937	2,874,087
1869	2,004,524		..	918,290	2,922,814
1870	2,023,788		..	878,659	2,902,447
1871	2,007,456		..	877,663	2,885,119
1872	2,089,027		..	962,604	3,051,631
1873	2,188,044		..	986,101	3,174,145
1874	2,254,009		..	1,024,379	3,278,388
1875	2,225,111		..	938,282	3,163,393
1876	2,133,163		..	934,433	3,067,596
1877	2,097,475		..	953,572	3,051,047
1878	2,124,408		..	998,071	3,122.479
1879	2,121,578		..	919,383	3 040.961
1880	1,992,401		..	852 667	2,845,068
1881	1,851,997		..	732,350	2,584,347
1882	1,833,747		..	819,009	2,652,756
1883	1,860,190		..	866,368	2,726,558
1884	1,888,944		..	932,493	2,821,437
1885	1,960,964		..	991,650	2,952,614
1886	1,882,051		..	811,544	2,693,595
1887	1,915,266		..	1,006,636	2,921,902
1888	1,950,216		..	966,451	2,916,667
1889	1,992,020		..	1,028,240	3,020,260
1890	2,107,416		..	1,162,605	3,270,021
1891	2,278,491		..	1,181,739	3,460,230
1892	2,302,710		..	1,129,853	3,432,563
1893	1,220,909	988,402	..	1,105,174	3,314,485
1894	1,205,594	956,297	..	1,109,755	3,271,646
1895	1,215,855	938,233	..	1,049,027	3,201,115
1896	1,301,368	909,658	..	1,209,763	3,420,789
1897	1,323,837	904,729	..	1,171,143	3,399,709
1898	1,359,764	869,922	..	1,252,260	3,481,946
1899	1,424,257	898,770	..	1,316,516	3,639,543
1900	1,454,437	918,735	..	1,286,486	3,659,658
1901	1,459,016	888,657	..	1,307,993	3,655,666
1902	1,469,158	878,970	..	1,347,673	3,695,801
1903	1,498,202	871,277	..	1,379,119	3,748,598
1904	1,516,073	869,406	..	1,342,768	3,728,247
1905	1,534,296	852,767	..	1,380,857	3,767,920
1906	1,561,923	859,638	..	1,400,368	3,821.929
1907	1,616,385	860,864	..	1,466,612	3,943,861
1908	1,653,215	856,673	..	1.462.681	3,972.569
1909	1,693,567	874,813	..	1.486,186	4.054,566
1910	1,646,722	855,043	..	1.435,855	3,937,620
1911	1,613,157	835,412	..	1,380,823	3,829,392
1912	1,594,071	801,127	..	1,382,414	3,777,612
1913	1,512,462	802,091	..	1,285,332	3,599,885
1914	1,609,919	768,273	..	1,440,070	3,818,262
1915	1,668,594	756,352	..	1,501,394	3,926,340
1916	1,769,620	815,003	..	1,532,325	4,116,948
1917	1,727,772	761,671	..	1,408,455	3,897,898
1918	1,616,046	660,501	..	1,427,703	3,704,250
1919	1,478,458	661,486	50,513	1,224,673	3,415,130
1920	1,402,881	626,012	46.948	1,255,282	3,331,123
1921	1,433,351	607,623	46,688	1,304,509	3,392,171
1922	1,486,345	587,419	44,958	1,321,794	3,440,516
1923	1,513,736	599,487	45,484	1.360,473	3.519.180
1924	1,639,535	586,109	49,926	1.465.610	3,741,180
1925	1,712,540	581,182	50,177	1.547,141	3,891,040
1926	1,819,285	596,760	53,300	1,667,848	4,137,193
1927	1,885,705	591,500	53,722	1,700,704	4,231,031
1928	1,825,105	575,907	52,278	1,547,194	4,000,484
1929	1,812,033	519,771	51,900	1,561,662	3,945,366
1930	1,877,364	513,468	54,304	1,657,269	4,102,405
1931	1,967,379	530,575	58,070	1,765,684	4,321,708
1932	2,012,022	546,855	59,088	1,743,588	4,361,553
1933	2,030,815	490,892	61,220	1,734,543	4,317,470
1934	1,982,467	359,413	58,116	1,773,560	4,173,556

	Ewes for Breeding(1)	Other Sheep 1 year and above	Rams for service(2)	Other Sheep under 1 year	Total
1935	2,003,834	372,334	62,334	1,839,107	4,277,609
1936	2,057,294	364,701	63,266	1,862,470	4,347,731
1937	2,070,173	253,312	66,540	2,073,322	4,463,347
1938	2,407,008	237,818	108,719	1,814,196	4,567,741
1939	2,464,873	226,129	103,540	1,853,886	4,648,428
1940	2,340,981	275,856	87,273	1,808,713	4,512,823
1941	2,136,847	259,973	68,462	1,443,824	3,909,106
1942	2,050,829	195,697	64,615	1,537,905	3 849,046
1943	2,067,694	207,917	62,231	1,526,361	3,864,203
1944	2,128,554	210,837	61,231	1,546,873	3,947,495
1945	2,160,151	232,916	63,606	1 523,351	3,980,024
1946	2,193,587	243,268	65,204	1,547,642	4,049,701
1947	1,613,092	224,353	58,826	919,437	2,815,708
1948	1,714,227	189,365	62,931	1,319,749	3,286,272
1949	1,884,859	229,790	66,547	1,460,866	3,642,062
1950	2,028,945	245,264	69,304	1,526,449	3,869,962
1951	2,085,691	276,833	68,443	1,404,081	3,835,048
1952	2,197,074	272,702	68,110	1,697,295	4,235,181
1953	2,310,799	298,923	72,499	1,744,393	4,426,614
1954	2,333,078	287,782	67,637	1,808,689	4,497,186
1955	2,322,799	276,484	69,632	1,701,865	4,370,780
1956	2,380,772	219,977	70,957	1,820,958	4,492,666
1957	2,434,886	271,362	54,054	1,985,412	4,745,714
1958	2,559,848	271,435	58,450	2,138,633	5,028,366
1959	2,630,185	311,972	59,775	2,185,942	5,187,874
1960	2,751,912	310,372	60,817	2,210,239	5,333,340
1961	2,801,446	300,968	63,015	2,360,640	5,526,069
1962	2,898,100	298,316	65,866	2,441,678	5,703,960
1963	2,914,931	294,907	66,269	2,359,464	5,635,571
1964	2,983,344	284,826	65,747	2,549,190	5,883,107
1965	3,083,020	299,626	68,688	2,587,641	6,038,975
1966	3,189,328	299,768	71,749	2,723,555	6,284,400
1967	3,231,961	316,251	72,131	2,618,540	6,238,883
1968	3,275,075	304,738	73,772	2,646,513	6,300,098
1969	3,180,930	274,750	71,418	2,524,439	6,051,537
1970	3,066,885	310,947	69,830	2,544,656	5,992,318
1971	3,085,676	303,448	70,234	2,593,543	6,052,901
1972	3,195,544	304,775	72,633	2,710,125	6,283,077
1973	3,309,400	311,827	74,658	2,855,798	6,551,683
1974[3]	3,401.2	320.3	77.0	2,938.3	6,736.8

General Notes

(i) Sources. Agricultural Statistics; Ashby and Evans, The Agriculture of Wales and Monmouthshire, 1944, Appendix B, Table 11.; Annual Digest of Welsh Agricultural Statistics 1974/5.

(ii) The figures relate to June of each year.

Notes

1. From 1938 includes two-tooth ewes.

2. Until 1956 includes ram lambs intended for service. In 1956 numbers were:

Rams	51,445
Ram lambs for service	19,512

3. Figures for 1974 are in thousands.

Agriculture 3. Numbers of Livestock, Wales 1870-1958. (f) Horses

	Used solely for purposes of Agriculture	Unbroken Horses of any age and Mares for breeding	Total
1870	77,278	48,702	125,980
1871	74,671	52,232	126,903
1872	75,408	52,600	128,008
1873	75,730	54,562	130,292
1874	75,194	58,748	133.942
1875	75,725	59,445	135,170
1876	77,505	61,455	138.960
1877	77,275	63,093	140,368
1878	78,426	64.433	142,859
1879	79,232	67,724	146,956
1880	78,602	67,169	145,771
1881	78,519	70,838	149,357
1882	79,634	70,485	150,119
1883	79,901	70,687	150,588
1884	79,135	72,694	151,829
1885	77,847	73,642	151,489
1886	78,916	73,398	152,314
1887	78,835	73,547	152,382
1888	79,355	71,755	151,110
1889	81,788	71,356	153,144
1890	81,119	74,216	155,335
1891	87,440	75,235	162,675
1892	85,495	76,630	162,125
1893	83,898	77,000	160,898
1894	83,358	77,773	161,131

	Horses for Agriculture and Mares for Breeding	Stallions over 2 years to be used for service	Unbroken Horses		Other Horses	Total
			under 1 year	1 year and over		
1895	99,569	..	21,881	45.654	..	167,104
1896	100,614	..	23,668	46,187	..	170,469
1897	96,000	..	23,138	48,088	..	167,226
1898	97,551	..	22,252	46,027	..	165,830
1899	99,048	..	23,008	45,369	..	167,425
1900	98,747	..	23,176	44.570	..	166,493
1901	99,747	..	22,927	45,303	..	167,977
1902	99,110	..	22,746	45,565	..	167,421
1903	102,594	..	23,562	44,955	..	171,111
1904	102,745	..	25,267	46,107	..	174,119
1905	103,453	..	25,187	47,592	..	176,232
1906	103,399	..	24,501	48,689	..	176,589
1907	105,042	..	23,872	48,033	..	176,947
1908	105,421	..	23,795	46,220	..	175,436
1909	105,507	..	23,699	45,636	..	174,842
1910	105,315	..	22,882	43,599	..	171,796
1911	101,204	1,598	21,947	39,790	12,757	177,296
1912	97,498	1,796	23,080	39,075	13.967	175,416
1913	87,831	1,569	23.236	38.260	24.050	174,946
1914	85,625	1,435	21,390	37,759	27,758	173,967
1915	79,520	1,413	20,333	36,074	24,719	162,059
1916	87,951	1,554	23,001	38,102	25,454	176,062
1917	90,316	1,556	21,982	38,478	24,578	176,910
1918	95,803	1,299	21,080	35,606	24,742	178,530
1919	93,276	1,205	21,525	37,082	25,212	178,300
1920	89,474	1,218	20,574	38,498	25,925	175,689
1921	94,168	1,354	19,087	38,181	30,845	183,635
1922	91,235	1,195	18,461	38,272	25,686	174,849
1923	90,153	1,217	14,696	33,458	24,483	164,007
1924	87,378	1,181	12,586	29,452	26,241	156,838
1925	86,285	1,147	10,459	24,441	25,082	147,414
1926	83,536	842	9,317	21,456	27,499	142,650
1927	82,479	898	9,073	18,229	24,495	135,624
1928	80,890	772	9,067	17,178	23,540	131,447
1929	78,934	660	8,961	17,110	21,331	126,996
1930	78,534	675	8,954	16,484	20,163	124,810
1931	78,378	567	9,193	16,199	19,054	123,591
1932	78,135	519	9,469	16,221	17.928	122,272
1933	76,955	651	9,636	15,979	16,107	119,328
1934	73,013	681	10,035	15.663	17,710	117,102

Agriculture 3. Horses (cont)

	Horses for Agriculture and Mares for Breeding	Stallions over 2 years to be used for service	Unbroken Horses under 1 year	Unbroken Horses 1 year and over	Other Horses	Total
1935	73,174	1,134	10,912	15,946	16,122	117,288
1936	71,386	712	11,614	16,999	18,379	119,090
1937	71,807	639	12,479	18,118	17,562	120,605
1938	72,203	760	13,005	20,305	18,449	124,772
1939	72,773	1,006	11,915	22,281	17,396	125,371
1940	72,033	560	10,579	20,059	17,396	121,554
1941	73,558	467	8,290	17,542	18,323	117,809
1942	66,256	477	7,449	14,865	17,952	114,017
1943	70,728	440	7,190	12,103	24,970	108,160
1944	67,206	483	7,381	13,066	17,699	105,798
1945	63,644	415	7,054	13.619	17,643	102,375
1946	61,516	394	5,810	13,156	16.191	97,067
1947	59,726	378	4,436	11.362	14,160	90.062
1948	56,703	381	3,467	9,437	11,474	81 462
1949	48,429	348	3,026	7,595	11.185	70,583
1950	41,036	303	2,314	6,719	10,753	61,125
1951	34,567	305	1,692	5,327	9,965	51,856
1952	29,675	270	1,747	4,355	8,952	44,999
1953	25,602	286	1,899	4,368	8,818	40,973
1954[1]	20,418	96	380	971	14,914	36,779
1955	17,298	51	239	814	14,328	32,730
1956	13,070	..	..	..	14,797	27,867
1957	10,959	..	..	..	14,586	25,545
1958	9,225	..	..	..	14,257	23,482

General Notes

(i) Sources. Agricultural Statistics; Ashby and Evans, The Agriculture of Wales and Monmouthshire, 1944, Appendix B, Table 12.

(ii) The figures relate June of each year.

Notes

1. Headings for columns 2-4 change to 'Heavy horses over one year'; 'Heavy horses under one year'; and 'Heavy stallions for service'.

Agriculture 4. Number of Livestock. By County. 1867 - 1972

Anglesey

	Cows and Heifers in milk & in calf	Other Cattle	Sheep	Horses	Pigs (1)	Poultry (1)
1867	13,608	20,227	49,702	..	17,631	..
1872	13,610	24,100	52,132	6,560	17,639	..
1877	14,190	25,943	57,945	6,824	19,418	..
1882	15,067	28,843	37,246	7,312	18,236	..
1887	16,111	30,753	47,521	7,224	16,317	..
1892	16,833	35,791	74,602	7,135	13,646	..
1897	16,303	34,957	71,129	8,029	15,499	..
1902	16,425	37,994	75,441	8,286	14,662	..
1907	16,149	38,007	113,845	8,721	15,317	..
1912	16,131	41,108	94,580	8,461	12,107	..
1917	16,183	38,723	125,246	8,390	9,922	..
1922	16,070	37,460	78,188	8,031	9,427	..
1927	16,749	36,605	145,857	6,348	11,990	210,384
1932	16,654	36,881	166,419	5,470	12,995	236,778
1937	15,158	36,093	173,177	5,274	13,608	189,158
1942	15,573	32,466	85,310	5,268	9,093	183,571
1947	18,764	35,002	85,237	3,990	3,683	219,161
1952	19,150	34,970	137,262	1,465	16,000	328,808
1957	20,039	42,774	185,226	785	15,315	284,506
1962	19,998	46,905	217,957	..	12,340	186,710
1967	19,319	53,782	196,175	..	17,509	96,657
1972	19,214	52,827	182,190	..	14,936	215,910

Breconshire

	Cows and Heifers in milk & in calf	Other Cattle	Sheep	Horses	Pigs (1)	Poultry (1)
1867	12,774	18,412	300,107	..	11,991	..
1872	13,521	20,548	430,237	10,365	11,921	..
1877	13,250	20,800	420,583	10,483	9,899	..
1882	13,878	21,485	340,382	11,655	10,245	..
1887	15,383	23,764	394,542	12,348	8,864	..
1892	15,739	25,986	460,888	12,534	6,935	..
1897	14,663	24,590	475,868	12,339	8,213	..
1902	15,394	24,646	498,612	11,865	7,711	..
1907	15,956	24,163	534,819	12,992	8,104	..
1912	15,900	25,051	491,134	12,807	8,510	..
1917	16,655	25,545	509,422	12,588	5,294	..
1922	16,426	21,293	482,450	12,612	7,011	..
1927	17,143	22,494	539,312	10,709	7,567	196,103
1932	17,566	23,395	504,542	8,887	7,487	203,357
1937	17,809	22,717	536,726	9,267	8,153	199,208
1942	17,851	24,099	508,863	8,494	5,726	153,075
1947	18,596	24,767	358,776	6,854	3,625	166,756
1952	20,178	26,277	599,394	4,665	5,594	205,607
1957	24,590	30,022	622,850	3,585	6,080	170,450
1962	27,431	32,857	707,825	..	5,820	108,536
1967	29,802	40,094	765,860	..	5,931	88,293
1972	31,667	42,115	790,957	..	5,971	68,213

Agriculture 4. Number of Livestock. By County. 1867 - 1972

Caernarvonshire

	Cows and Heifers in milk & in calf	Other Cattle	Sheep	Horses	Pigs(1)	Poultry(1)
1867	19,894	22,520	164,180	..	20,272	..
1872	19,966	27,015	218,881	7,064	21,002	..
1877	21,013	28,001	219,298	7,840	20,799	..
1882	21,140	29,399	198,685	8,626	21,069	..
1887	22,483	31,919	204,019	8,209	22,236	..
1892	24,288	35,327	250,392	8,493	22,552	..
1897	23,129	32,600	256,395	9,326	21,437	..
1902	22,401	33,252	268,852	9,091	18,803	..
1907	23,749	29,908	288,527	9,470	18,433	..
1912	22,905	31,220	280,660	9,357	16,391	..
1917	23,247	32,920	289,465	8,841	13,280	..
1922	24,192	30,974	255,897	8,409	12,130	..
1927	24,567	28,667	320,649	7,215	11,196	217,702
1932	24,313	29,903	320,039	6,085	11,352	262,241
1937	22,210	27,115	326,153	5,808	14,417	251,490
1942	26.165	29,558	314,876	5,691	8,422	219,446
1947	29,608	28,827	270,411	4,341	4,174	300,512
1952	27,876	30,892	376,165	1,869	14,792	412,224
1957	27,621	37,352	397,005	861	12,294	415,228
1962	27,969	40,831	452,247	..	11,147	305,444
1967	29,074	46,775	495,434	..	13,738	238,076
1972	31,860	47,417	499,851	..	14,065	243,628

Cardiganshire

	Cows and Heifers in milk & in calf	Other Cattle	Sheep	Horses	Pigs(1)	Poultry(1)
1867	23,007	25,544	138,028	..	19,678	..
1872	24,735	31,830	203,619	11,762	23,739	..
1877	25,602	33,940	201,545	13,428	24,085	..
1882	25,260	35,442	192,649	14,063	23,364	..
1887	27,360	38,562	208,308	13,954	23,512	..
1892	27,222	43,203	227,918	15,400	19,293	..
1897	24,952	40,821	253,792	16,533	21,722	..
1902	25,619	42,442	270,494	17,881	21,131	..
1907	26,530	42,403	276,369	18,906	21,665	..
1912	25,839	43,885	263,104	18,107	22,096	..
1917	26,791	46,771	268,787	18,285	17,987	..
1922	26,616	40,778	248,797	17,360	17,486	..
1927	27,236	42,659	305,644	13,362	20,320	379,735
1932	26,992	43,328	327,850	12,715	22,336	462,241
1937	27,797	38,159	308,706	13,281	20,082	429,479
1942	32,380	37,151	295,023	12,332	12,376	331,290
1947	37,942	32,757	189,311	9,960	5,663	357,411
1952	43,096	36,614	287,304	4,987	13,696	433,547
1957	48,729	41,685	340,270	2,870	13,143	345,687
1962	51,897	46,097	439,225	..	12,268	215,079
1967	56,560	56,612	498,127	..	17,620	133,052
1972	62,516	62,780	509,686	..	16,977	110,937

Agriculture 4. Number of Livestock. By County. 1867 - 1972

Carmarthenshire

	Cows and Heifers in milk & in calf	Other Cattle	Sheep	Horses	Pigs(1)	Poultry(1)
1867	45,238	42,591	158,750	..	27,078	..
1872	47,016	51,006	212,236	16,837	30,201	..
1877	47,902	52,987	211,266	18,694	30,872	..
1882	48,567	56,148	179,756	19,353	31,836	..
1887	53,222	61,681	217,322	19,445	31,746	..
1892	52,814	67,989	248,722	20,938	28,614	..
1897	50,455	65,345	253,397	22,049	33,570	..
1902	50,684	67,827	279,729	22,947	34,800	..
1907	52,930	68,199	294,416	25,115	37,778	..
1912	52,748	68,422	273,543	23,836	37,688	..
1917	56,229	75,530	299,538	24,989	28,474	..
1922	57,015	60,347	255,188	24,033	28,645	441,974
1927	59,199	61,271	308,631	17,833	33,586	613,505
1932	60,342	62,656	324,111	17,732	30,371	708,943
1937	67,297	57,669	330,897	18,199	22,215	697,176
1942	70,348	50,305	240,481	16,634	14,655	497,940
1947	73,408	51,434	165,917	13,410	7,658	500,997
1952	82,421	57,146	221,895	6,044	16,444	689,205
1957	95,046	61,696	264,955	3,053	17,574	488,214
1962	100,018	74,018	357,621	..	17,569	322,935
1967	104,173	86,695	431,121	..	18,734	1,138,750
1972	113,811	95,216	434,308	..	14,634	224,009

Denbighshire

	Cows and Heifers in milk & in calf	Other Cattle	Sheep	Horses	Pigs(1)	Poultry(1)
1867	22,131	24,307	212,398	..	27,115	..
1872	23,113	31,251	261,061	10,959	26,822	..
1877	22,820	31,966	261,804	11,919	25,495	..
1882	22,882	33,691	243,823	12,484	26,832	..
1887	25,532	36,400	253,695	12,818	25,238	..
1892	27,752	43,192	323,797	14,050	22,922	..
1897	25,208	40,804	303,676	14,291	25,642	..
1902	25,526	41,040	344,801	13,783	24,566	..
1907	26,752	42,057	383,102	14,021	28,727	..
1912	27,100	45,466	389,324	14,264	27,156	..
1917	30,170	52,046	422,253	14,936	22,824	..
1922	31,045	47,296	364,155	14,384	22,809	230,096
1927	32,091	48,984	482,448	10,821	28,751	313,170
1932	32,735	51,093	511,488	9,506	28,972	374,056
1937	34,800	50,735	503,836	8,851	28,561	369,827
1942	39,978	49,311	373,971	8,712	14,457	275,284
1947	47,585	47,755	272,302	6,767	8,414	318,291
1952	49,448	52,288	390,675	2,549	30,566	512,423
1957	50,984	57,706	482,066	1,101	35,601	586,040
1962	54,616	64,543	603,520	..	36,941	514,960
1967	57,658	72,299	701,642	..	36,535	599,915
1972	62,159	76,713	718,299	..	33,587	638,002

Agriculture 4. Number of Livestock. By County. 1867 - 1972

Flintshire

	Cows and Heifers in milk & in calf	Other Cattle	Sheep	Horses	Pigs[1]	Poultry[1]
1867	12,110	9,043	64,580	..	17,268	..
1872	13,578	13,773	62,077	5,254	16,956	..
1877	13,122	13,651	63,750	5,591	14,862	..
1882	12,998	14,457	50,484	5,720	15,359	..
1887	15,013	16,175	58,920	5,803	15,164	..
1892	16,553	19,549	80,167	6,539	13,792	..
1897	15,958	19,104	72,767	6,989	16,175	..
1902	16,656	19,159	84,343	6,773	16,387	
1907	18,001	19,630	98,831	6,795	19,389	..
1912	18,951	20,778	93,919	7,034	18,540	..
1917	20,614	24,090	113,372	7,513	15,235	..
1922	22,629	21,097	69,879	7,755	15,084	..
1927	23,728	21,690	128,475	5,091	19,997	237,764
1932	24,637	23,433	153,352	4,439	19,358	295,097
1937	27,220	23,563	154,795	4,149	20,058	286,165
1942	29,878	24,857	87,640	4,397	10,569	200,460
1947	33,565	24,332	49,982	3,484	7,793	240,962
1952	33,931	26,983	73,778	1,399	26,043	368,570
1957	32,264	29,969	90,989	785	34,723	405,201
1962	34,724	32,505	128,958	..	34,382	418,790
1967	35,536	38,122	131,150	..	33,121	551,572
1972	37,092	39,056	108,225	..	29,731	777,001

Glamorganshire

	Cows and Heifers in milk & in calf	Other Cattle	Sheep	Horses	Pigs[1]	Poultry[1]
1867	20,599	24,500	229,547	..	19,462	..
1872	19,247	27,830	285,267	12,016	18,324	..
1877	20,332	26,145	274,798	13,365	16,595	..
1882	21,981	29,668	258,360	15,746	17,360	..
1887	24,668	30,888	283,080	15,860	15,396	..
1892	26,359	33,223	305,223	16,947	13,719	..
1897	24,133	27,535	304,359	17,156	15,298	..
1902	25,299	30,384	343,071	16,639	15,933	..
1907	26,537	31,334	347,913	17,372	17,217	..
1912	25,630	30,441	319,607	17,806	17,915	..
1917	27,382	35,240	312,057	17,753	14,444	..
1922	27,906	26,798	259,373	17,425	15,185	..
1927	29,555	29,233	319,728	13,730	20,195	358,726
1932	32,347	33,766	335,194	12,201	21,729	418,737
1937	33,605	33,308	346,133	11,419	20,594	351,319
1942	35,023	32,569	296,206	11,311	15,767	238,697
1947	37,232	33,472	210,075	9,597	8,967	231,346
1952	36,334	37,119	290,618	5,804	26,167	339,431
1957	37,435	41,604	288,800	3,725	25,742	341,745
1962	39,287	47,066	347,750	..	23,313	352,372
1967	39,805	54,871	372,854	..	23,545	424,255
1972	41,790	58,182	350,550	..	22,494	587,219

Agriculture 4. Number of Livestock. By County. 1867 - 1972

Merionethshire

	Cows and Heifers in milk & in calf	Other Cattle	Sheep	Horses	Pigs(1)	Poultry(1)
1867	13,808	19,476	293,697	..	8,621	..
1872	14,742	23,537	401,565	5,227	9,968	..
1877	14,442	23,198	396,990	5,866	10,042	..
1882	14,306	23,337	400,553	6,088	10,205	..
1887	14,639	23,703	375,971	5,211	9,524	..
1892	14,708	25,662	406,310	5,238	7,961	..
1897	13,634	24,251	411,570	5,386	7,957	..
1902	13,062	23,323	433,278	5,124	7,338	..
1907	13,780	23,274	441,803	5,204	7,832	..
1912	13,060	23,877	455,789	5,084	7,356	..
1917	13,726	25,344	414,934	5,086	6,132	..
1922	13,428	23,519	423,311	4,911	5,718	..
1927	13,910	23,489	461,810	4,091	6,378	97,994
1932	13,341	23,856	431,865	3,679	6,412	113,060
1937	12,591	22,935	425,978	3,604	6,188	112,112
1942	14,662	23,705	467,402	3,564	4,259	90,734
1947	14,721	24,130	335,737	2,881	2,392	100,234
1952	15,137	24,946	510,571	1,192	4,793	160,409
1957	15,066	25,023	542,932	613	4,244	150,264
1962	15,988	24,774	589,162	..	2,747	101,757
1967	18,141	26,812	622,804	..	3,233	70,680
1972	20,014	26,824	636,597	..	2,229	41,114

Monmouthshire

	Cows and Heifers in milk & in calf	Other Cattle	Sheep	Horses	Pigs(1)	Poultry(1)
1867	15,390	19,778	182,985	..	20,053	..
1872	14,939	23,980	184,487	9,742	18,763	..
1877	15,020	25,358	189,034	10,730	15,906	..
1882	16,500	27,668	134,842	11,631	17,621	..
1887	18,885	30,117	181,543	12,254	15,452	..
1892	20,298	32,374	235,062	13,298	13,472	..
1897	17,316	27,967	204,350	13,944	14,585	..
1902	17,562	29,333	233,103	13,307	16,201	..
1907	18,978	30,914	240,489	14,449	17,593	..
1912	18,537	30,502	228,736	14,657	18,164	..
1917	20,136	35,898	230,385	14,633	14,292	..
1922	20,071	27,797	174,890	15,056	16,577	..
1927	22,055	30,112	222,452	11,090	16,876	335,935
1932	23,508	33,837	250,890	9,772	21,504	444,245
1937	25,172	34,617	267,783	9,223	22,089	491,874
1942	25,360	33,028	223,446	9,117	12,104	265,164
1947	29,391	34,558	156,006	6,886	7,514	284,932
1952	30,680	37,298	251,945	4,097	19,705	404,572
1957	33,709	41,743	279,069	2,528	21,163	494,562
1962	36,723	45,623	330,605	..	17,607	472,368
1967	37,805	54,388	341,571	..	14,828	867,964
1972	41,934	62,794	292,839	..	19,439	1,144,794

Agriculture 4. Number of Livestock. By County. 1867 - 1972

Montgomeryshire

	Cows and Heifers & in calf	Other Cattle	Sheep	Horses	Pigs[1]	Poultry[1]
1867	23,374	36,136	277,059	..	28,564	..
1872	23,266	39,088	356,265	12,138	27,185	..
1877	21,977	39,218	355,645	13,631	24,368	..
1882	21,912	40,121	305,641	13,985	24,512	..
1887	23,916	44,159	339,365	14,899	22,626	..
1892	24,042	48,539	403,200	15,522	19,299	..
1897	22,585	48,181	389,473	15,555	20,299	..
1902	22,302	47,950	438,023	16,019	20,918	..
1907	23,307	49,117	470,425	16,356	21,903	..
1912	23,365	52,961	456,826	16,147	22,196	..
1917	26,487	54,088	482,427	16,439	18,648	..
1922	27,373	50,896	436,280	16,468	19,728	..
1927	27,744	52,934	519,419	12,840	22,668	395,774
1932	28,341	54,568	535,092	11,329	25,310	473,538
1937	30,160	52,493	576,075	11,608	25,619	569,349
1942	33,021	55,299	538,964	11,059	15,952	419,491
1947	35,668	54,947	397,906	8,615	10,091	559,071
1952	39,762	56,487	603,972	3,710	27,935	805,642
1957	47,145	61,822	671,325	1,708	29,144	800,237
1962	52,730	68,573	805,534	..	31,280	691,261
1967	58,967	79,968	868,107	..	30,199	601,579
1972	65,055	81,779	931,898	..	24,824	559,955

Pembrokeshire

	Cows and Heifers in milk & in calf	Other Cattle	Sheep	Horses	Pigs[1]	Poultry[1]
1867	28,851	38,232	95,166	..	23,758	..
1872	28,826	43,316	103,818	12,864	26,739	..
1877	30,414	46.117	110,708	13,869	26,740	..
1882	32,297	52,213	86,341	14,502	28,076	..
1887	33,677	55,168	99,655	14,756	26,763	..
1892	33,949	61,786	135,048	15,966	24,222	..
1897	31,725	56,821	130,064	16,099	25,845	..
1902	32,037	58,176	139,772	16,362	28,208	..
1907	33,352	60,849	150,312	17,526	31,822	..
1912	33,191	62,466	149,116	17,563	31,478	..
1917	34,636	67,045	142,860	17,467	25,605	..
1922	36,153	59,987	112,556	17,841	26,479	..
1927	37,722	63,916	145,790	13,564	33,033	350,969
1932	37,219	67,489	173,981	12,908	39,103	437,329
1937	38,533	57,991	161,869	12,331	33,340	453,952
1942	41,341	47,570	99,158	10,757	17,493	342,335
1947	47,694	47,432	71,133	8,207	6,701	382,123
1952	51,861	51,437	101,365	4,032	25,194	514,993
1957	60,846	62,423	129,371	2,035	27,819	450,528
1962	66,207	69,641	166,029	..	32,975	363,029
1967	72,595	84,870	172,311	..	32,536	348,254
1972	82,753	97,985	136,340	..	24,797	223,083

Agriculture 4. Number of Livestock. By County. 1867 - 1972

Radnorshire

	Cows and Heifers in milk & in calf	Other Cattle	Sheep	Horses	Pigs(1)	Poultry(1)
1867	9,147	19,009	243,947	..	8,479	..
1872	9,043	18,781	279,986	7,220	7,821	..
1877	9,328	19,851	287,681	8,128	7,545	..
1882	9,560	19,858	223,994	8,954	6,600	..
1887	10,682	21,379	257,961	9,601	5,784	..
1892	10,776	23,185	281,234	10,065	4,347	..
1897	9,882	21,484	272,869	9,530	4,790	..
1902	10,475	22,001	286,282	9,867	4,826	..
1907	10,964	21,936	303,010	10,020	4,809	..
1912	10,892	22,878	281,274	10,284	5,083	..
1917	10,766	22,437	287,152	9,990	4,174	..
1922	11,411	21,063	279,552	10,564	4,389	..
1927	12,174	22,870	331,394	8,930	4,704	162,755
1932	12,451	23,191	326,730	7,549	4,550	169,182
1937	11,725	22,596	351,219	7,519	4,766	190,002
1942	11,402	23,725	317,886	6,681	3,539	152,718
1947	11,331	23,828	252,915	5,070	2,387	188,229
1952	12,135	23,961	390,237	3,186	4,303	224,185
1957	16,672	28,011	450,856	1,896	4,331	203,583
1962	21,076	32,031	557,527	..	3,026	139,352
1967	25,124	39,691	641,727	..	3,492	86,683
1972	29,035	40,790	691,337	..	4,495	60,988

General Notes

(i) Sources. Agricultural Statistics; Ashby and Evans, The Agriculture of Wales and Monmouthshire, 1944, Tables 74-112.

Notes

1. From 1869 returns were only collected from holdings over one quarter of an acre, and in 1893 this was raised to one acre. Pigs and poultry were most affected by these changes.

AGRICULTURE 5. Estimated Production of principal crops, Wales, 1885-1974

Year	Wheat	Barley	Oats	Potatoes(1)	Turnips & Swedes(2)	Mangolds	Seeds Hay(3)	Meadow Hay
	Thousand bushels	Thousand bushels	Thousand bushels	Thousand tons	Thousand tons	Thousand tons	Thousand tons	Thousand tons
1885	1,959.1	3,689.2	8,276.5	220.7	892.9	124.3	782.0	
1886	1,708.0	3,453.8	8,276.2	224.0	1,105.5	131.8	249.0	484.3
1887	1,904.4	3,312.4	8,163.9	292.3	801.0	124.3	202.7	410.5
1888	1,866.3	3,259.2	7,759.8	196.9	1,001.6	130.0	233.6	591.3
1889	1,924.2	3,701.0	8,440.0	246.0	1,814.1	136.8	254.8	623.3
1890	2,001.9	3,842.2	8,395.5	185.7	1,248.2	142.7	240.0	579.2
1891	1,714.9	3,630.4	7,941.4	216.1	1,079.3	144.5	211.5	512.2
1892	1,523.9	3,550.0	8,272.9	214.6	1,232.0	158.9	199.6	459.8
1893	1,388.4	2,981.0	7,710.2	239.1	1,159.9	139.8	135.3	292.0
1894	1,614.0	3,517.5	9,334.5	191.5	1,247.7	158.8	251.6	660.9
1895	1,040.1	3,135.9	7,935.7	233.4	1,182.5	133.5	200.0	452.5
1896	1,238.9	2,948.2	7,419.8	224.0	1,028.0	114.3	171.4	357.4
1897	1,520.5	3,257.6	8,051.8	172.9	1,217.5	146.9	264.5	550.7
1898	1,792.1	3,514.4	8,680.3	191.6	1,080.6	146.0	302.8	628.6
1899	1,565.5	3,460.5	7,801.8	178.2	784.6	151.1	256.1	476.5
1900	1,487.5	3,484.8	7,519.6	157.2	1,031.6	195.5	258.5	531.7
1901	1,302.0	3,133.6	6,738.7	187.4	994.8	200.5	217.2	374.1
1902	1,483.5	3,521.6	7,960.8	159.5	1,072.3	228.0	315.0	569.5
1903	1,157.2	2,984.3	6,868.2	134.8	926.5	176.5	245.2	500.0
1904	989.1	3,037.9	7,709.3	148.0	1,063.8	205.5	269.2	581.7
1905	1,307.8	2,907.3	7,303.1	167.9	840.3	192.9	247.0	547.3
1906	1,405.8	3,122.6	8,087.4	147.2	998.1	230.2	272.8	622.1
1907	1,215.9	2,8887.8	7,891.0	118.6	962.9	241.1	267.7	640.5
1908	1,046.9	2,681.0	7,175.7	155.7	1,005.9	229.4	241.1	627.7
1909	1,257.4	2,800.2	7,234.2	153.9	1,039.1	250.2	204.1	553.1
1910	1,237.9	2,899.8	8,008.3	135.3	1,076.6	242.7	247.1	663.6
1911	1,260.0	2,733.3	7,152.9	181.5	881.5	223.0	195.1	503.6
1912	1,230.4	2,838.6	7,049.7	130.6	847.6	249.6	241.1	661.8
1913	1,170.9	2,773.4	6,923.2	144.5	907.1	202.7	247.9	721.1
1914	1,243.9	2,748.0	7,453.0	153.2	938.0	248.2	224.2	634.0
1915	1,600.4	2,471.0	7,309.5	163.0	799.4	247.6	222.3	566.6
1916	1,630.0	2,722.9	8,227.6	141.8	891.0	242.1	265.4	706.3
1917	1,905.8	2,788.6	8,680.7	206.4	814.7	265.2	234.2	625.1
1918	3,360	3,408	14,056	234	847	286	188.6	534
1919	2,408	3,288	11,416	169.8	815	223	175.8	439
1920	1,488	2,928	7,608	103.9	770	167	272	661
1921	1,344	2,000	6,400	153.7	675	210	201	394
	Thousand tons	Thousand tons	Thousand tons					
1922	32	40	102	175	557	210	224	524
1923	28	41	99	116	653	201	248	596
1924	19	37	98	106	600	173	245	620
1925	17	35	101	136	612	190	221	539
1926	20	34	114	122	622	201	224	586
1927	19	30	110	117	532	172	221	573
1928	16	33	117	127	609	185	195	534
1929	16	32	123	142	599	195	194	540
1930	15	28	115	118	526	179	2 16	610
1931	12	24	105	95	475	157	218	606
1932	13	23	113	125	538	139	200	552
1933	16	21	115	130	426	155	185	547
1934	20.1	19.0	115.6	117.6	310.2	169.3	187.3	549.8
1935	19.8	19.5	116.9	93.2	382.2	171.6	197.3	579.8
1936	14.9	18.7	106.1	94.2	360.7	174.1	181.9	583.2
1937	14.7	18.3	101.1	98.5	335.1	160.7	189.0	595.0
1938	16.0	17.4	106.3	99.1	321.2	166.4	154.3	512.1
1939	11	16	112	98	296.9	157	153	558
1940	27	26	217	138	322.4	165	158	501
1941	52	37	258	301	375	198	138	429
1942	74	47	301	388	474	218	162	392
1943	111	60	246	372	492	249	218	366
1944	100	61	259	390	469	260	247	314

Agriculture 5 contd

1945	52	51	244		377	492	285	284	341
1946	34	41	209		361	415	289	264	287
1947	35	35	194		296	363	228	288	363
1948	43	30	198		453	335	251	277	350
1949	35	33	214		313	333	291	293	369
1950	40	24	174	54	245	290	295	238	295
1951	30	29	190	53	189	359	305	305	435
1952	33	33	189	59	178	399	249	321	433
1953	36	34	186	50	184	439	264	293	428
1954	27	23	137	52	130	352	209	252	338
1955	18	23	151	49	110	307	161	337	483
1956	23	24	137	59	140	303	183	278	437
1957	25	30	121	47	106	301	155	291	401
1958	22	30	111	53	90	300	153	306	453
1959	21	40	113	51	104	254	118	320	468
1960	22	45	114	64	101	267	142	335	474
1961	21	63	113	55	81	269	102	357	494
1962	25	82	110	58	81	242	99	358	493
1963	20	110	93	84	90	255	80	365	550
1964	28	142	87	80	90	286	69	404	614
1965	35	164	73	70	86	295	70	391	619
1966	28	182	64	63	69	274	48	357	598
1967	36	181	74	58	81	259	37	364	599
1968	30	182	68	74	88	234	34	369	603
1969	26	164	68	63	94	216	33	330	593
1970	29	135	51	53	118	212	27	305	597
1971	32	190	66	59	110	228	25	315	706
1972	26	185	61	57	90	189	18	294	697
1973	26	201	56	43	100	226	18	301	718
1974	27	205	44	41	88	274	19	261	622

General Notes

(i) Sources. Agricultural Produce. Statistics of Great Britain, for 1885-93; Agricultural Returns for 1894-1901; and then Agricultural Statistics

Notes

1. From 1950 two figures are given for potatoes: the left hand figure relates to first earlies, and the right hand figure to second earlies and main crops.

2. From 1941 the figures for turnips and swedes relate to production for stock-feeding only, and from 1952 they include fodder beet.

3. For 1943-49 and after 1966, these figures include lucerne. From 1950-66 lucerne is excluded. There is no indication of whether lucerne is included or not before 1943.

AGRICULTURE 6. Estimated yields of principal crops, Wales, 1885-1974

(per acre)

Year	Wheat	Barley	Oats	Potatoes(1)	Turnips(2) & Swedes	Mangolds	Seeds(3) Hay	Meadow Hay
	Bushels	Bushels	Bushels	Tons	Tons	Tons	Cwt	Cwt
1885	22.9	27.7	32.4	5.2	11.6	15.3	22.73	
1886	21.7	26.2	31.9	5.3	14.4	17.1	18.7	25.2
1887	23.8	26.4	30.8	6.9	10.3	14.1	21.7	15.0
1888	21.1	26.2	29.9	4.5	12.6	14.8	24.6	20.8
1889	24.3	28.7	32.7	5.9	14.9	17.5	25.6	21.6
1890	25.4	30.3	33.6	4.5	15.6	17.2	24.9	20.8
1891	24.1	29.2	32.8	5.4	13.9	16.4	23.2	18.8
1892	24.2	29.3	34.2	5.6	15.8	17.9	20.9	16.6
1893	22.3	25.2	30.9	6.6	14.8	16.6	15.0	10.4
1894	25.1	29.9	35.9	5.4	15.7	17.5	27.7	25.3
1895	21.3	26.6	31.5	6.7	15.1	15.4	21.3	15.8
1896	23.4	26.0	29.6	6.3	13.3	13.8	18.1	12.6
1897	24.8	29.7	32.6	5.1	15.9	16.7	25.4	20.4
1898	26.7	32.6	36.3	5.6	14.6	16.4	28.6	23.2
1899	25.5	31.2	34.1	5.2	10.8	15.3	24.5	18.3
1900	25.4	31.7	33.4	4.5	15.1	17.6	25.0	20.1
1901	24.8	29.4	31.0	5.6	14.9	18.2	20.4	14.2
1902	27.7	33.4	36.4	4.9	16.3	18.8	28.5	21.1
1903	24.2	28.9	31.0	4.3	14.1	15.4	22.8	18.1
1904	25.4	30.4	34.8	4.8	16.2	18.0	25.2	20.4
1905	26.4	30.8	33.8	5.5	12.9	17.1	24.5	19.1
1906	28.4	32.4	37.9	4.8	15.6	19.3	27.3	21.4
1907	27.6	30.7	37.1	4.1	15.3	19.3	27.7	21.8
1908	27.1	29.9	34.2	5.5	16.3	19.4	25.8	20.9
1909	28.0	31.7	35.1	5.5	16.6	19.9	22.9	18.4
1910	27.5	31.9	37.7	5.0	17.1	19.4	27.8	21.5
1911	29.0	30.4	33.4	6.6	14.2	17.6	21.7	16.2
1912	26.2	30.0	32.8	4.8	13.9	17.7	26.2	21.3
1913	27.1	30.0	33.1	5.5	15.0	17.3	28.5	22.5
1914	28.9	31.5	36.1	5.8	15.8	19.9	26.2	20.5
1915	28.6	29.9	35.6	6.0	14.8	19.2	25.9	18.8
1916	29.0	30.3	36.0	4.8	15.9	19.1	28.2	22.4
1917	27.0	28.4	34.3	5.7	15.0	19.9	25.3	20.1
1918	29.7	31.2	36.8	6.0	15.1	19.3	25.2	19.5
1919	28.3	30.6	34.8	5.6	13.2	15.2	21.4	16.3
1920	24.5	28.4	29.0	3.6	12.9	13.8	27.8	23.7
1921	28.7	24.1	28.4	5.6	12.6	17.7	20.3	14.6
	Cwt	Cwt	Cwt					
1922	14.9	12.6	9.6	6.6	11.7	15.9	22.2	17.9
1923	15.0	12.6	10.2	4.7	13.2	16.1	26.1	20.2
1924	14.3	12.3	10.5	4.5	12.2	14.9	26.2	20.5
1925	15.1	13.2	11.2	5.8	12.9	17.7	24.0	18.2
1926	15.4	13.9	12.6	5.3	13.8	17.9	24.7	19.3
1927	14.9	13.3	12.7	5.0	12.3	15.7	24.7	18.7
1928	15.4	14.6	14.0	5.7	14.5	17.3	22.7	17.5
1929	15.7	14.9	14.5	6.3	14.3	18.3	22.1	17.2
1930	14.6	13.5	13.2	5.7	12.6	16.9	24.1	19.1
1931	14.6	13.3	12.7	4.6	12.0	15.6	24.7	19.6
1932	15.3	14.0	13.9	5.8	13.4	16.5	23.5	18.2
1933	15.5	13.9	13.8	6.0	11.0	16.0	22.0	17.6
1934	16.3	13.2	13.6	5.9	8.8	16.1	22.0	17.4
1935	15.8	14.0	14.0	5.1	11.5	16.7	23.6	19.0
1936	14.9	13.6	13.2	5.4	11.4	16.4	22.7	18.9
1937	15.9	13.9	13.6	5.6	11.4	16.9	23.3	19.3
1938	16.8	13.9	13.7	5.7	12.1	16.7	21.0	16.8
1939	16.6	14.2	14.0	5.9	12.3	16.5	20.8	17.9
1940	17.4	15.1	15.3	6.2	12.0	17.2	21.8	17.8
1941	16.4	14.5	14.6	6.3	11.1	16.4	20.8	17.2
1942	18.0	14.8	15.0	6.2	12.6	17.3	21.7	17.6
1943	16.6	14.1	13.3	5.6	12.8	18.1	23.6	18.5
1944	17.6	15.1	14.9	5.8	12.2	16.8	22.6	17.3
1945	17.7	15.1	14.7	5.9	13.1	18.6	23.5	18.2
1946	16.2	14.0	13.4	5.5	12.0	17.4	21.4	15.6
1947	15.1	14.2	14.0	4.9	11.0	15.8	22.2	17.5
1948	17.0	14.6	14.3	6.2	11.4	16.5	22.4	17.2
1949	18.8	17.4	16.0	5.4	11.8	19.2	23.5	18.8

1950	16.6	14.5	13.5	3.8	6.5	11.6	18.5	21.8	16.9
1951	19.5	17.9	17.1	4.2	6.6	14.7	21.1	24.8	20.3
1952	19.8	19.2	17.6	5.0	6.5	13.8	20.3	26.1	20.5
1953	20.8	20.2	18.7	4.9	7.4	15.4	21.9	26.5	20.8
1954	18.7	17.3	15.8	4.9	6.3	13.8	18.2	24.2	19.6
1955	21.2	20.5	19.2	4.8	6.4	12.1	18.3	26.9	21.5
1956	20.0	18.5	16.5	5.6	8.1	14.5	21.4	24.5	20.1
1957	20.4	19.5	16.9	5.3	7.2	15.2	20.6	24.9	19.5
1958	20.2	19.0	16.3	5.6	6.1	15.9	21.2	27.1	22.6
1959	24.4	23.1	19.7	5.2	7.6	14.1	19.5	26.5	21.1
1960	25.2	23.0	18.6	5.7	7.6	16.5	23.5	28.2	22.4
1961	26.5	24.9	20.9	5.3	7.6	17.7	22.3	29.7	22.9
1962	29.6	26.7	22.3	5.8	7.8	15.8	22.6	29.6	23.2
1963	28.3	26.8	22.0	7.1	8.1	17.4	21.8	30.5	25.7
1964	30.4	28.4	22.9	6.8	8.5	18.0	23.4	33.0	26.6
1965	29.7	28.1	22.9	6.3	9.0	18.7	26.4	34.4	28.4
1966	26.4	27.5	23.7	6½3	8.3	18.2	24.2	33.1	27.5
1967	31.6	28.8	25.3	5.9	9.3	17.7	23.9	33.8	27.6
1968	30.7	29.2	25.5	7.5	9.8	16.7	23.6	35.1	28.9
1969	31.6	29.3	26.8	8.0	10.5	16.8	26.6	33.5	28.2
1970	31.9	25.9	21.4	7.0	10.9	17.8	25.1	32.2	28.9
1971	32.7	31.4	28.1	7.3	11.4	18.1	24.2	36.6	31.7
1972	30.1	30.7	28.0	7.6	10.3	15.6	23.1	37.5	33.3
1973	35.9	31.7	28.0	7.1	12.4	18.2	28.1	35.6	33.2
1974	32.5	29.8	23.2	7.0	11.8	20.7	26.3	34.1	31.6

General Notes

(i) Sources. Agricultural Produce. Statistics of Great Britain, for 1885-93: Agricultural Returns for 1894-1901: and then Agricultural Statistics

Notes

1. From 1950 two figures are given for potatoes: the left hand figure relates to first earlies, and the right hand figure to second earlies and main crops.

2. From 1941 the figures for turnips and swedes relate to production for stock-feeding only, and from 1952 they include fodder beet.

3. For 1943-49 and after 1966, these figures include lucerne. From 1950-66 lucerne is excluded. There is no indication of whether lucerne is included or not before 1943.

AGRICULTURE 7. Size of Agricultural Holdings,[1] Wales, 1875-1974 and percentage of holding and acreage owned by occupiers, Wales and each county, various dates, 1887-1970

Year	Number of Agricultural Holdings of the following sizes (acres)								TOTAL
	1-5	5-20	20-50	50-100	100-150	150-300	300-500	500+	
1875		43,403		10,375	7,975		486	102	62,341
1880		44,497		10,554	8,430		502	92	64,075
1885	12,130	18,787	13,251	10,772	8,558		432	82	64,012
1890	..	..	..	..	..	..	..	..	..
1895	11,749	20,043	13,338	10,980	8,583		438	67	65,198
1900	..	..	..	..	..	..	..	..	..
1901	..	..	..	..	..	..	..	..	..
1902	..	..	..	..	..	..	..	..	..
1903	11,226	33,801			19,429		485		64,941
1904	11,154	33,976			19,411		475		65,016
1905	11,276	34,027			19,468		467		65,238
1906	11,173	34,047			19,472		470		65,162
1907	11,086	34,284			19,507		453		65,330
1908	10,913	34,239			19,493		447		65,092
1909	11,007	34,249			19,458		443		65,157
1910	11,031	34,307			19,434		420		65,192
1911	11,052	34,437			19,412		424		65,325
1912	11,155	34,806			19,393		390		65,744
1913	11,028	20,617	14,154	11,066	4,819	3,471	392		65,547
1914	10,897	20,546	14,275	11,085	4,759	3,442	387		65,391
1915	10,792	20,567	14,213	11,150	4,736	3,437	391		65,286
1916	10,524	20,305	14,146	11,267	4,792	3,446	375		64,855
1917	10,233	19,991	14,127	11,280	4,859	3,450	390		64,330
1918	10,145	19,663	13,956	11,256	4,807	3,386	381		63,594
1919	10,074	19,615	14,096	11,097	4,723	3,257	373		63,235
1920	9,897	19,663	14,215	11,059	4,721	3,190	376		63,121
1921	9,927	20,028	14,525	11,095	4,558	2,973	327		63,433
1922	9,359	19,446	14,414	11,009	4,562	3,023	320		62,133
1923	9,136	19,309	14,356	11,037	4,579	2,972	335		61,724
1924	8,966	19,135	14,423	11,005	4,572	2,966	326		61,393
1925	8,960	19,044	14,364	11,084	4,566	2,918	309		61,245
1926	8,890	19,076	14,355	11,077	4,550	2,881	305		61,134
1927	8,891	19,094	14,375	11,170	4,558	2,882	298		61,208
1928	8,858	19,103	14,378	11,128	4,547	2,800	290		61,104
1929	8,892	19,053	14,391	11,149	4,555	2,785	284		61,109
1930	8,820	18,858	14,433	11,155	4,546	2,762	294		60,868
1931	8,589	18,590	14,445	11,219	4,500	2,780	287		60,410
1932	8,482	18,506	14,424	11,252	4,472	2,787	269		60,192
1933	8,420	18,469	14,414	11,256	4,456	2,793	260		60,068
1934	8,253	18,379	14,328	11,274	4,478	2,772	259		59,743
1935	8,233	18,167	14,201	11,260	4,462	2,761	238	24	59,34
1936	8,029	17,924	14,179	11,245	4,448	2,754	240	23	58,84
1937	8,008	17,628	14,137	11,219	4,449	2,745	244	26	58,45
1938	7,833	17,566	14,151	11,187	4,460	2,723	248	20	58,18
1939	7,800	17,525	14,040	11,231	4,451	2,712	242	23	58,02
1940	7,398	16,996	14,067	11,159	4,250	2,494	218	18	56,60
1941	8,268	17,322	14,047	11,045	4,217	2,389	210	17	57,52
1942	7,016	17,470	14,074	11,175	4,419	2,544	224	26	56,94
1943	7,072	17,124	13,992	11,089	4,454	2,478	223	22	56,45
1944	6,853	16,886	13,863	11,053	4,435	2,509	229	21	55,84
1945	6,836	16,720	13,791	11,026	4,429	2,524	227	20	55,57
1946	6,737	16,648	13,696	10,996	4,367	2,549	232	26	55,25
1947	6,533	16,347	13,686	10,940	4,424	2,576	233	28	54,76
1948	6,517	16,274	13,654	11,012	4,420	2,565	231	26	54,69
1949	6,715	16,215	13,711	11,003	4,414	2,570	225	25	54,87
1950	7,015	16,072	13,699	11,056	4,452	2,588	230	22	55,13
1951	7,260	16,084	13,669	11,061	4,476	2,596	233	23	55,40
1952	7,370	16,009	13,688	11,068	4,477	2,619	234	20	55,48
1953	7,407	15,914	13,552	11,152	4,529	2,638	239	20	55,45
1954	7,230	15,659	13,472	11,167	4,536	2,688	241	20	55,01
1955	7,063	15,426	13,365	11,135	4,549	2,704	253	22	54,51
1956	6,963	15,167	13,288	11,040	4,616	2,729	259	26	54,08
1957	6,796	14,931	13,119	10,989	4,564	2,792	271	32	53,49
1958	6,610	14,577	12,919	10,975	4,588	2,840	271	36	52,81
1959	6,313	14,149	12,875	11,051	4,475	2,882	282	39	52,06
1960[1]	6,235	13,685	12,646	11,026	4,490	2,919	285	42	51,32
1960[1]	5,912	12,877	10,860	10,710	5,419	4,845	1,046	572	51,32
1961	5,825	12,543	10,663	10,587	5,343	4,837	1,071	560	51,42
1962	5,743	12,259	10,451	10,539	5,274	4,817	1,081	572	50,73
1963	5,698	12,023	10,314	10,393	5,212	4,826	1,107	586	50,15
1964	5,538	11,826	10,082	10,296	5,160	4,824	1,123	595	49,44
1965	5,447	11,623	9,841	10,172	5,128	4,816	1,141	612	48,78
1966	5,346	11,443	9,585	9,916	5,133	4,799	1,161	626	48,00
1967[2]	4,968	11,097	9,359	9,720	5,075	4,813	1,165	652	46,84
1968	1,301	8,224	9,060	9,517	5,023	4,854	1,193	653	39,82
1969	1,415	7,657	8,636	9,304	4,979	4,852	1,199	680	38,72
1970	1,201	6,661	7,860	8,704	4,844	4,896	1,310	708	36,18
1971	1,096	6,350	7,578	8,515	4,843	4,879	1,308	728	35,29
1972	848	5,817	7,323	8,267	4,777	4,939	1,324	726	34,02
1973	663	5,240	7,126	8,137	4,705	4,930	1,334	753	32,88
1974									

	PERCENTAGE OF HOLDINGS OWNED BY OCCUPIER					PERCENTAGE OF ACREAGE OWNED BY OCCUPIER				
	1887	1909	1941-43	1960	1970	1887	1909	1941-43	1960	1970
Anglesey	5.1	12.08	30	48.2	54.5	5.8	12.9	34	47.2	54.0
Breconshire	9.4	9.37	44	60.0	64.2	9.8	9.7	46	60.5	60.7
Cardiganshire	21.6	18.53	48	71.4	72.0	19.3	15.9	48	69.4	69.6
Carmarthenshire	11.3	11.57	42	53.4	68.2	12.6	11.6	42	59.9	67.0
Caernarfonshire	4.2	11.66	30	48.8	58.4	4.6	11.5	32	44.7	49.9
Denbighshire	12.2	7.3	34	56.0	60.6	11.0	7.3	38	56.7	57.0
Flintshire	10.0	8.3	36	54.9	58.3	9.4	9.1	36	52.0	52.7
Glamorgan	9.1	6.02	24	52.9	57.6	8.6	6.5	22	47.4	53.9
Merioneth	7.5	7.09	25	48.3	58.6	7.6	6.9	26	49.7	62.1
Monmouthshire	13.8	12.84	33	61.0	64.2	11.4	9.9	34	57.5	60.1
Montgomeryshire	6.8	8.47	48	64.5	66.8	6.7	8.0	49	66.7	67.6
Pembrokeshire	10.3	10.53	36	57.7	64.2	14.0	11.2	40	56.8	62.3
Radnorshire	15.7	13.49	40	62.3	67.5	14.3	11.3	41	63.0	67.7
Wales	10.5	10.58	37	58.4	63.7	10.2	10.2	39	57.5	61.7
England	16.1	13.37	34	56.4	59.6	15.5	12.4	33	47.8	51.7

General Notes

(i) Sources. Agricultural Returns (for 1875, 1880 and 1885); Returns as to the Number and Size of Agricultural Holdings in G.B. (for 1895); and Agricultural Statistics (for 1903-); John Davies, 'The end of the Great Estates and the Rise of freehold farming in Wales', Welsh Hist. Rev. 7, 2, 1974, p.212 (for percentages owned by occupier).

Notes

1. For all crops before 1960 the statistics relate only to the acreage under crops and grass, excluding any acreage of rough grazings. Holdings consisting solely of rough grazings are excluded. From 1960 onwards the term 'agricultural holding' comprises crops and grass, rough grazing (sole rights), woodland, and other land (roads, yards, farm buildings etc.). Two figures are given for 1960 one on the pre-1960 basis and one on the post-1960 basis.

2. There is a sharp fall in the number of holdings in 1968. Although this is not directly explained, the following footnote appears to Table 63A, 1968/9: 'In June 1968 about 47,000 holdings with less than 10 acres of crops and grass and a negligible agricultural output were excluded from the census'.

AGRICULTURE 8. Size of Agricultural Holdings,[1] each county, 1875-1974

ANGLESEY

Year	Number of Agricultural Holdings of the following sizes (acres)								TOTAL
	1-5	5-20	20-50	50-100	100-150	150-300	300-500	500+	
1875		2,757		417	374		23	5	3,576
1880		2,784		432	382		23	3	3,624
1885		1,351	735	432	389		17	3	3,752
1890	..	..	..	..	..		..	..	..
1895	853	1,530	797	455	382		22	1	4,040
1900	..	..	..	..	..		..	..	..
1901	..	..	..	..	..		..	..	..
1902	..	..	..	..	..		..	..	..
1903	862	2,428			833		25		4,148
1904	867	2,424			830		23		4,144
1905	893	2,433			836		20		4,182
1906	858	2,473			829		19		4,179
1907	895	2,508			817		18		4,238
1908	901	2,497			827		19		4,244
1909	932	2,543			809		22		4,306
1910	949	2,561			804		18		4,332
1911	988	2,556			813		16		4,373
1912	990	2,598			811		16		4,415
1913	1,004	1,705	927	437	185	178	15		4,435
1914	981	1,729	908	443	177	182	15		4,435
							300+		
1915	963	1,737	925	460	172	176	16		4,449
1916	961	1,711	917	452	179	178	15		4,413
1917	919	1,726	925	460	171	178	14		4,393
1918	921	1,658	894	466	175	174	15		4,303
1919	921	1,675	888	456	180	168	15		4,303
1920	913	1,676	948	462	184	148	27		4,358
1921	939	1,727	930	449	175	146	16		4,382
1922	914	1,679	933	468	167	153	13		4,327
1923	900	1,701	940	463	164	151	12		4,331
1924	871	1,708	940	468	172	148	11		4,318
1925	885	1,732	957	460	171	148	11		4,364
1926	869	1,743	960	461	171	146	16		4,366
1927	867	1,766	936	475	172	148	13		4,377
1928	865	1,776	947	468	166	141	14		4,377
1929	861	1,780	950	467	168	137	13		4,376
1930	870	1,763	973	458	170	138	12		4,384
1931	859	1,755	974	460	167	139	13		4,367
1932	851	1,751	978	477	165	139	14		4,375
1933	864	1,762	968	462	163	141	9		4,369
1934	842	1,784	974	463	166	137	10		4,376

Year	Number of Agricultural Holdings of the following sizes (acres)								TOTAL
	1-5	5-20	20-50	50-100	100-150	150-300	300-500	500+	
1935	837	1,795	964	477	168	136	8	-	4,385
1936	824	1,754	985	466	164	138	8	-	4,339
1937	818	1,693	986	480	164	133	9	-	4,283
1938	792	1,692	980	468	166	135	9	-	4,242
1939	802	1,748	955	467	166	128	10	-	4,276
1940	743	1,570	938	490	175	128	8	-	4,052
1941	759	1,577	896	505	169	120	9	-	4,035
1942	634	1,580	898	503	186	126	8	2	3,937
1943	635	1,555	887	485	200	125	10	1	3,898
1944	599	1,525	886	494	197	126	10	-	3,837
1945	590	1,507	877	494	189	133	9	1	3,800
1946	578	1,482	882	487	191	138	7	3	3,768
1947	574	1,458	882	485	195	139	9	3	3,745
1948	565	1,446	895	483	185	135	10	3	3,722
1949	579	1,453	901	484	187	131	10	4	3,749
1950	598	1,444	885	484	191	131	13	4	3,750
1951	610	1,474	870	480	187	132	13	4	3,770
1952	650	1,439	870	484	182	138	12	2	3,777
1953	658	1,431	870	480	186	137	12	3	3,77[illegible]
1954	654	1,413	867	483	178	138	13	3	3,74[illegible]
1955	646	1,393	851	489	179	142	13	3	3,716
1956	649	1,369	844	484	193	136	11	4	3,690
1957	635	1,349	848	476	190	140	12	4	3,65[illegible]
1958	628	1,314	845	476	192	137	14	4	3,610
1959	584	1,271	850	485	183	143	15	4	3,535
1960[1]	564	1,225	835	508	173	140	15	4	3,46[illegible]
1960[1]	520	1,216	813	536	216	169	22	9	3,50[illegible]
1961	507	1,181	790	526	210	175	28	8	3,425
1962	499	1,152	774	535	211	169	29	9	3,378
1963	496	1,141	753	538	211	164	31	9	3,34[illegible]
1964	492	1,132	732	539	206	165	31	10	3,30[illegible]
1965	497	1,122	708	540	211	161	29	11	3,27[illegible]
1966	497	1,114	705	529	211	161	30	11	3,258
1967	468	1,075	692	515	208	161	31	12	3,16[illegible]
1968[2]	88	812	674	498	205	162	31	14	2,48[illegible]
1969	103	742	662	478	201	157	35	17	2,39[illegible]
1970	75	611	598	439	200	160	44	19	2,14[illegible]
1971	71	580	577	432	204	157	48	20	2,08[illegible]
1972	51	532	551	430	199	156	52	19	1,99[illegible]
1973	36	487	519	420	204	156	59	16	1,89[illegible]
1974									

AGRICULTURE 8. Size of Agricultural Holdings,(1) each county, 1875-1974

BRECONSHIRE

Year	Number of Agricultural Holdings of the following sizes (acres)								TOTAL
	1-5	5-20	20-50	50-100	100-150	150-300	300-500	500+	
1875		1,927		735	539		27	10	3,238
1880		1,904		758	622		27	5	3,316
1885	512	638	716	799	634		22	4	3,325
1890	..	..	..	..	..		..	..	..
1895	417	627	687	816	644		24	5	3,220
1900	..	..	..	..	..		..	..	..
1901	..	..	..	..	..		..	..	..
1902	..	..	..	..	..		..	..	..
1903	411	1,335			1,494		29		3,269
1904	401	1,334			1,495		30		3,260
1905	399	1,319			1,505		29		3,252
1906	395	1,325			1,509		26		3,255
1907	396	1,353			1,489		26		3,264
1908	401	1,362			1,473		27		3,263
1909	416	1,353			1,473		25		3,267
1910	404	1,373			1,473		23		3,273
1911	405	1,355			1,476		23		3,259
1912	396	1,383			1,462		22		3,263
1913	383	681	692	817	391	247	24		3,235
1914	374	679	706	810	389	246	25		3,229
1915	385	711	697	820	372	236	24		3,245
1916	364	687	710	816	377	239	26		3,219
1917	366	666	706	804	384	238	25		3,189
1918	355	635	696	790	383	230	26		3,115
1919	286	531	644	729	360	219	26		2,795
1920	252	473	586	713	376	235	30		2,665
1921	248	494	611	751	338	211	27		2,680
1922	222	469	616	701	333	223	35		2,599
1923	203	441	596	718	335	229	39		2,561
1924	197	422	594	695	348	227	39		2,522
1925	202	411	589	703	337	2 24	35		2,501
1926	194	422	605	710	316	223	34		2,504
1927	206	404	596	733	311	212	36		2,498
1928	206	398	604	728	329	202	34		2,501
1929	202	394	624	703	330	208	32		2,493
1930	200	375	621	697	338	206	32		2,469
1931	180	386	610	711	331	204	30		2,452
1932	177	381	618	703	322	212	27		2,440
1933	182	371	592	703	335	212	26		2,421
1934	175	366	597	695	345	206	24	1	2,409

Year	Number of Agricultural Holdings of the following sizes (acres)								TOTAL
	1-5	5-20	20-50	50-100	100-150	150-300	300-500	500+	
1935	178	355	586	697	335	209	27	1	2,388
1936	169	355	567	698	335	210	25	2	2,361
1937	167	349	584	684	338	205	26	3	2,356
1938	168	356	571	678	342	203	28	3	2,349
1939	167	364	557	678	348	204	26	4	2,348
1940	148	373	580	652	317	202	25	4	2,301
1941	236	451	582	644	301	177	22	1	2,414
1942	207	454	604	658	306	191	22	1	2,443
1943	213	476	624	612	303	184	22	1	2,435
1944	218	477	606	629	288	196	21	1	2,436
1945	229	457	615	619	301	186	21	2	2,430
1946	222	468	618	592	303	186	21	1	2,411
1947	214	466	615	595	303	191	20	1	2,405
1948	206	460	608	602	315	189	20	-	2,400
1949	206	454	615	581	310	200	16	-	2,382
1950	200	459	601	595	306	206	18	-	2,385
1951	198	450	608	588	314	206	19	-	2,383
1952	198	446	611	582	326	207	19	-	2,389
1953	189	441	599	592	322	207	22	-	2,372
1954	179	438	596	581	330	215	22	-	2,361
1955	182	410	584	579	339	219	21	1	2,335
1956	180	390	564	564	343	227	25	-	2,293
1957	171	398	549	561	351	225	27	1	2,283
1958	170	369	529	559	350	232	27	2	2,237
1959	171	352	529	578	334	230	29	2	2,225
1960(1)	165	351	525	562	341	229	30	2	2,205
1960(1)	145	314	319	514	408	426	74	31	2,231
1961	141	311	318	503	408	423	75	26	2,205
1962	141	302	314	502	403	411	79	29	2,181
1963	144	304	302	493	401	415	79	31	2,169
1964	141	317	290	479	388	423	82	30	2,150
1965	136	312	280	480	381	426	84	30	2,129
1966	137	302	277	466	379	419	89	29	2,098
1967	130	278	276	458	355	424	91	32	2,044
1968(2)	38	211	263	451	362	423	95	29	1,872
1969	33	204	261	436	362	412	90	33	1,831
1970	31	155	248	392	336	410	100	35	1,707
1971	27	149	240	380	336	403	100	40	1,675
1972	23	132	233	364	331	406	98	42	1,629
1973	16	118	240	362	315	403	101	44	1,599
1974									

AGRICULTURE 8. Size of Agricultural Holdings,[1] each county, 1875-1974

CAERNARVONSHIRE

Year	Number of Agricultural Holdings of the following sizes (acres)								TOTAL
	1-5	5-20	20-50	50-100	100-150	150-300	300-500	500+	
1875	4,430			583	390		32	11	5,446
1880	4,550			572	416		25	10	5,573
1885	1,320	2,330	1,085	611	396		25	5	5,742
1890	..	..	..	..	..		..	..	..
1895	1,739	2,459	1,126	630	395		30	3	6,382
1900	..	..	..	..	..		..	..	..
1901	..	..	..	..	..		..	..	..
1902	..	..	..	..	..		..	..	..
1903	1,523	3,789		937			27		6,276
1904	1,535	3,796		913			26		6,270
1905	1,578	3,817		910			21		6,326
1906	1,557	3,827		904			20		6,308
1907	1,531	3,861		906			21		6,319
1908	1,515	3,899		894			22		6,330
1909	1,508	3,924		905			19		6,356
1910	1,553	3,912		905			20		6,390
1911	1,535	3,932		895			22		6,384
1912	1,564	3,977		912			15		6,468
1913	1,543	2,743	1,222	599	182	135	16		6,440
1914	1,549	2,712	1,236	607	180	127	16		6,427
1915	1,560	2,680	1,241	607	184	130	17		6,419
1916	1,502	2,676	1,241	609	182	130	15		6,355
1917	1,457	2,666	1,239	607	186	139	33		6,327
1918	1,478	2,582	1,210	594	201	129	19		6,213
1919	1,499	2,564	1,214	600	186	135	20		6,218
1920	1,500	2,602	1,204	580	187	128	21		6,222
1921	1,556	2,610	1,218	568	169	118	20		6,259
1922	1,400	2,475	1,225	560	169	123	19		5,971
1923	1,373	2,466	1,214	567	168	131	18		5,937
1924	1,346	2,445	1,210	561	180	117	18		5,877
1925	1,339	2,450	1,195	562	175	122	18		5,861
1926	1,344	2,454	1,190	554	178	118	19		5,857
1927	1,395	2,466	1,176	554	178	111	17		5,897
1928	1,396	2,448	1,193	547	173	104	16		5,877
1929	1,445	2,422	1,175	571	167	108	17		5,905
1930	1,427	2,424	1,201	564	159	108	18		5,901
1931	1,387	2,402	1,196	567	165	107	17		5,841
1932	1,396	2,376	1,201	571	158	109	15		5,826
1933	1,379	2,375	1,201	563	155	112	15		5,800
1934	1,358	2,384	1,187	564	152	111	10	4	5,770

Year	Number of Agricultural Holdings of the following sizes (acres)								TOTAL
	1-5	5-20	20-50	50-100	100-150	150-300	300-500	500+	
1935	1,380	2,371	1,177	556	158	111	10	4	5,76
1936	1,355	2,335	1,184	554	149	106	11	4	5,69
1937	1,383	2,334	1,166	540	153	105	13	3	5,69
1938	1,356	2,347	1,186	538	152	102	13	1	5,69
1939	1,368	2,326	1,176	540	145	103	12	3	5,67
1940	1,260	2,275	1,189	509	120	73	8	1	5,43
1941	1,258	2,237	1,148	489	111	55	8	2	5,30
1942	2,098	2,246	1,148	505	118	57	7	2	5,18
1943	1,076	2,186	1,157	504	114	55	8	1	5,10
1944	1,028	2,160	1,141	507	109	61	9	1	5,01
1945	1,054	2,102	1,139	501	111	60	9	1	4,97
1946	1,026	2,108	1,122	493	114	61	10	1	4,93
1947	1,002	1,999	1,143	505	110	71	10	1	4,84
1948	949	2,010	1,162	506	120	64	9	1	4,82
1949	932	2,024	1,149	515	119	70	9	1	4,81
1950	946	2,013	1,133	524	121	72	10	1	4,82
1951	984	2,005	1,140	516	132	68	10	1	4,85
1952	1,001	2,003	1,142	527	125	71	9	-	4,87
1953	981	2,002	1,146	535	135	71	11	-	4,88
1954	966	1,996	1,131	542	133	74	11	-	4,85
1955	984	2,006	1,114	518	131	69	12	1	4,83
1956	956	1,984	1,124	534	129	71	12	1	4,81
1957	909	1,931	1,108	519	128	80	11	2	4,68
1958	888	1,885	1,095	521	133	79	12	2	4,61
1959	808	1,850	1,102	531	125	83	11	2	4,51
1960[1]	807	1,759	1,094	527	127	88	12	2	4,41
1960[1]	670	1,603	982	676	239	245	70	77	4,56
1961	659	1,550	952	663	227	245	72	77	4,44
1962	655	1,455	915	658	227	240	73	80	4,30
1963	646	1,410	897	636	229	243	77	83	4,221
1964	636	1,376	868	623	232	246	76	83	4,14
1965	627	1,322	844	625	225	245	79	84	4,051
1966	608	1,290	816	615	223	253	78	82	3,965
1967	554	1,204	799	602	220	252	80	85	3,796
1968[2]	141	872	767	581	227	252	81	86	3,007
1969	148	807	726	569	231	252	82	87	2,902
1970	126	676	653	527	222	243	96	84	2,553
1971	107	651	623	528	216	249	94	85	2,553
1972	84	567	610	516	202	256	97	86	2,418
1973	64	486	594	502	197	264	95	92	2,284
1974									

AGRICULTURE 8. Size of Agricultural Holdings,[1] each county, 1875-1974

CARDIGANSHIRE

Year	Number of Agricultural Holdings of the following sizes (acres)								TOTAL
	1-5	5-20	20-50	50-100	100-150	150-300	300-500	500+	
1875		3,700		1,013	822		32	5	5,572
1880		3,973		1,038	864		21	1	5,897
1885	1,114	2,070	1,088	1,054	863		15	1	6,205
1890	..	..	..	..	..		..	..	..
1895	1,091	2,142	1,138	1,025	805		15	1	6,217
1900	..	..	..	..	..		..	..	..
1901	..	..	..	..	..		..	..	..
1902	..	..	..	..	..		..	..	..
1903	1,179	3,392			1,762		15		6,348
1904	1,155	3,426			1,746		14		6,341
1905	1,204	3,413			1,785		12		6,414
1906	1,169	3,395			1,806		12		6,382
1907	1,154	3,469			1,819		12		6,454
1908	1,091	3,435			1,829		11		6,366
1909	1,117	3,400			1,836		11		6,364
1910	1,142	3,406			1,822		13		6,383
1911	1,163	3,440			1,804		11		6,418
1912	1,177	3,545			1,799		9		6,530
1913	1,185	2,234	1,238	1,066	493	249	9		6,474
1914	1,159	2,255	1,219	1,074	484	245	9		6,445
1915	1,140	2,248	1,257	1,044	487	245	10		6,431
1916	1,101	2,215	1,252	1,086	489	254	9		6,406
1917	1,099	2,167	1,241	1,097	498	260	11		6,373
1918	1,134	2,192	1,208	1,078	484	243	12		6,351
1919	1,128	2,231	1,235	1,081	487	227	9		6,398
1920	1,096	2,201	1,224	1,061	480	218	9		6,289
1921	1,068	2,166	1,269	1,067	472	188	9		6,239
1922	1,016	2,135	1,213	1,120	449	192	8		6,133
1923	981	2,135	1,196	1,105	457	196	9		6,079
1924	934	2,099	1,206	1,108	452	211	8		6,018
1925	919	2,041	1,222	1,127	451	202	5		5,967
1926	923	2,034	1,244	1,118	449	204	3		5,975
1927	926	2,011	1,248	1,138	448	194	5		5,970
1928	915	2,012	1,247	1,132	443	193	5		5,947
1929	907	1,990	1,229	1,161	447	181	4		5,919
1930	893	1,992	1,225	1,161	445	183	4		5,903
1931	875	1,976	1,208	1,164	448	184	4		5,859
1932	838	1,975	1,196	1,181	430	188	5		5,813
1933	836	1,955	1,205	1,180	433	183	3		5,795
1934	802	1,939	1,199	1,182	424	188	2	1	5,737
1935	782	1,907	1,170	1,175	439	181	3	1	5,658
1936	772	1,883	1,161	1,161	446	184	3	1	5,611
1937	760	1,846	1,146	1,171	442	187	3	1	5,556
1938	723	1,789	1,169	1,154	438	191	4	-	5,468
1939	696	1,763	1,162	1,163	439	189	4	-	5,416
1940	664	1,758	1,126	1,156	445	174	6	-	5,329
1941	762	1,774	1,124	1,147	448	174	8	-	5,437
1942	608	1,852	1,122	1,155	470	201	8	-	5,416
1943	600	1,817	1,218	1,150	491	191	8	-	5,385
1944	580	1,792	1,132	1,128	499	188	9	-	5,328
1945	581	1,754	1,130	1,138	498	191	10	-	5,302
1946	561	1,768	1,130	1,133	472	203	10	-	5,277
1947	543	1,737	1,117	1,146	476	197	14	-	5,230
1948	533	1,751	1,099	1,148	474	200	11	1	5,217
1949	527	1,735	1,112	1,154	485	191	10	1	5,215
1950	534	1,721	1,137	1,142	495	195	10	1	5,235
1951	524	1,737	1,135	1,136	499	194	9	1	5,235
1952	539	1,715	1,157	1,130	496	201	9	1	5,248
1953	542	1,712	1,150	1,146	486	208	11	1	5,256
1954	535	1,671	1,171	1,148	489	210	10	1	5,235
1955	513	1,653	1,166	1,166	474	229	9	1	5,211
1956	523	1,625	1,168	1,148	486	229	12	1	5,192
1957	504	1,605	1,142	1,161	481	221	13	1	5,128
1958	494	1,584	1,136	1,142	489	234	12	1	5,092
1959	479	1,541	1,153	1,148	454	239	14	1	5,029
1960[1]	487	1,465	1,122	1,153	451	245	16	1	4,940
1960[1]	459	1,394	943	1,088	555	426	82	71	5,018
1961	453	1,381	931	1,097	546	426	77	73	4,984
1962	445	1,372	914	1,097	542	430	80	69	4,949
1963	442	1,353	920	1,090	532	427	85	70	4,919
1964	443	1,348	894	1,094	522	434	82	70	4,887
1965	415	1,324	885	1,070	525	431	83	71	4,804
1966	408	1,321	864	1,064	520	430	87	72	4,766
1967	377	1,278	841	1,047	523	434	89	72	4,661
1968[2]	87	910	818	1,033	518	442	91	72	3,971
1969	115	840	765	1,019	522	442	86	72	3,861
1970	83	742	696	938	502	439	99	78	3,577
1971	87	716	667	909	507	449	99	80	3,514
1972	58	696	660	890	512	451	99	78	3,444
1973	46	638	595	877	503	459	99	77	3,344
1974									

Note: In 1875–1902 the figure shown under 5-20 covers 1-50 acres (where no separate 1-5 and 20-50 figures are given) and the figure under 100-150 covers 100-300 acres; in 1903–1912 the figure under 5-20 covers 5-50 acres, the figure under 100-150 covers 50-300 acres, and the figure under 300-500 covers 300+ acres; in 1913–1933 the figure under 300-500 covers 300+ acres.

AGRICULTURE 8. Size of Agricultural Holdings,[1] each county, 1875-1974

CARMARTHENSHIRE

Year	Number of Agricultural Holdings of the following sizes (acres)								TOTAL
	1-5	5-20	20-50	50-100	100-150	150-300	300-500	500+	
1875		5,071		1,785	1,214		37	2	8,109
1880		5,120		1,747	1,363		30	4	8,264
1885	1,106	2,137	1,852	1,806	1,335		29	4	8,269
1890	..	..	..	..	..		..	..	..
1895	937	2,340	1,918	1,865	1,295		20	5	8,380
1900	..	..	..	..	..		..	..	..
1901	..	..	..	..	..		..	..	..
1902	..	..	..	..	..		..	..	..
1903	927	4,366			3,166		26		8,485
1904	1,001	4,456			3,183		26		8,666
1905	1,038	4,486			3,160		26		8,710
1906	1,029	4,529			3,154		27		8,739
1907	1,005	4,567			3,173		25		8,770
1908	1,022	4,556			3,171		27		8,776
1909	1,029	4,551			3,155		29		8,764
1910	1,012	4,581			3,153		26		8,772
1911	1,039	4,578			3,155		29		8,801
1912	1,044	4,584			3,151		29		8,808
1913	1,012	2,454	2,099	1,905	815	433	28		8,746
1914	977	2,421	2,122	1,918	813	422	27		8,700
1915	969	2,419	2,115	1,954	778	426	35		8,696
1916	982	2,407	2,103	1,962	819	422	25		8,720
1917	976	2,373	2,114	1,978	812	415	25		8,693
1918	930	2,389	2,139	1,975	799	410	22		8,664
1919	959	2,406	2,177	1,966	802	374	21		8,705
1920	931	2,404	2,188	1,949	809	358	19		8,658
1921	909	2,487	2,256	1,989	776	331	18		8,766
1922	861	2,439	2,201	1,996	804	316	17		8,634
1923	867	2,369	2,203	1,999	789	312	17		8,556
1924	824	2,343	2,206	2,017	771	322	18		8,501
1925	835	2,365	2,191	2,023	771	306	16		8,507
1926	817	2,391	2,171	2,030	780	300	16		8,505
1927	814	2,404	2,194	2,036	783	288	14		8,533
1928	800	2,386	2,196	2,040	784	285	14		8,505
1929	783	2,358	2,208	2,040	773	281	12		8,455
1930	755	2,315	2,209	2,047	772	274	14		8,386
1931	747	2,266	2,216	2,068	755	270	14		8,336
1932	754	2,243	2,211	2,066	760	263	13		8,310
1933	779	2,322	2,221	2,060	751	263	10		8,406
1934	770	2,297	2,207	2,059	749	259	11	1	8,353
1935	788	2,250	2,186	2,069	740	267	8	1	8,309
1936	754	2,186	2,167	2,076	751	262	9	-	8,205
1937	737	2,171	2,166	2,062	745	272	10	-	8,16[illegible]
1938	725	2,215	2,190	2,058	753	2 69	7	-	8,21[illegible]
1939	732	2,209	2,197	2,069	736	269	9	1	8,22[illegible]
1940	771	2,188	2,287	2,029	644	206	3	-	8,12[illegible]
1941	910	2,279	2,303	2,060	648	206	2	-	8,408
1942	763	2,255	2,250	2,086	728	241	5	-	8,32[illegible]
1943	754	2,102	2,237	2,073	733	221	6	-	8,12[illegible]
1944	714	2,073	2,188	2,058	742	232	7	-	8,01[illegible]
1945	665	2,045	2,189	2,044	733	237	7	-	7,92[illegible]
1946	658	1,998	2,159	2,073	725	235	10	-	7,858
1947	618	1,953	2,150	2,050	736	244	9	-	7,76[illegible]
1948	613	1,951	2,128	2,062	743	237	7	-	7,74[illegible]
1949	618	1,955	2,141	2,072	715	239	8	-	7,74[illegible]
1950	592	1,905	2,197	2,063	722	241	7	-	7,72[illegible]
1951	591	1,895	2,174	2,088	721	248	6	-	7,72[illegible]
1952	603	1,898	2,192	2,097	719	237	6	-	7,752
1953	634	1,890	2,183	2,113	727	241	8	-	7,796
1954	620	1,851	2,144	2,130	749	245	8	1	7,74[illegible]
1955	608	1,824	2,129	2,138	753	250	8	1	7,71[illegible]
1956	628	1,800	2,141	2,107	759	261	9	1	7,706
1957	602	1,810	2,116	2,095	753	260	7	1	7,644
1958	550	1,792	2,058	2,087	745	275	6	1	7,514
1959	544	1,711	2,041	2,106	710	275	9	-	7,396
1960[1]	541	1,683	2,003	2,105	708	289	10	-	7,339
1960[1]	534	1,588	1,791	1,996	911	519	51	12	7,402
1961	526	1,538	1,762	2,014	902	514	51	13	7,320
1962	513	1,513	1,743	2,015	902	505	51	15	7,257
1963	513	1,482	1,743	1,986	888	520	50	16	7,198
1964	518	1,488	1,740	1,971	881	525	51	16	7,190
1965	506	1,465	1,710	1,955	876	531	49	17	7,109
1966	490	1,432	1,691	1,921	899	525	54	17	7,029
1967	456	1,399	1,658	1,897	887	536	58	18	6,909
1968[2]	95	1,068	1,626	1,868	896	538	60	18	6,169
1969	115	1,019	1,540	1,829	909	549	62	18	6,04[illegible]
1970	110	901	1,393	1,741	895	595	80	18	5,733
1971	95	837	1,361	1,692	901	606	76	22	5,590
1972	67	779	1,329	1,635	905	629	76	20	5,440
1973	60	710	1,294	1,608	887	647	76	21	5,303
1974									

AGRICULTURE 8. Size of Agricultural Holdings,[1] each county, 1875-1974

DENBIGHSHIRE

Year	Number of Agricultural Holdings of the following sizes (acres)								TOTAL
	1-5	5-20	20-50	50-100	100-150	150-300	300-500	500+	
1875		4,016		940	687		38	4	5,685
1880		4,017		980	681		41	7	5,726
1885	1,153	1,566	1,278	993	719		41	7	5,757
1890	..	..	..	..	..		..	..	..
1895	992	1,764	1,236	1,051	717		38	6	5,804
1900	..	..	..	..	..		..	..	..
1901	..	..	..	..	..		..	..	..
1902	..	..	..	..	..		..	..	..
1903	961	2,909			1,722		36		5,628
1904	938	2,932			1,723		37		5,630
1905	935	2,933			1,726		41		5,635
1906	949	2,952			1,716		44		5,661
1907	968	2,953			1,741		37		5,699
1908	969	2,935			1,744		39		5,687
1909	980	2,954			1,724		42		5,700
1910	970	2,968			1,724		35		5,697
1911	953	2,994			1,714		33		5,694
1912	962	3,054			1,701		32		5,749
1913	986	1,774	1,325	989	400	300	29		5,803
1914	982	1,774	1,344	1,000	392	290	32		5,814
1915	971	1,752	1,324	993	397	295	30		5,762
1916	934	1,747	1,335	1,002	414	282	29		5,743
1917	910	1,710	1,315	1,002	417	299	28		5,681
1918	874	1,674	1,308	1,005	421	292	29		5,603
1919	875	1,653	1,330	1,028	408	285	34		5,613
1920	891	1,657	1,343	1,025	407	284	31		5,638
1921	873	1,748	1,364	1,017	402	272	22		5,698
1922	842	1,699	1,353	1,018	402	279	22		5,615
1923	840	1,713	1,355	1,009	403	274	25		5,619
1924	882	1,730	1,389	1,005	411	263	23		5,703
1925	873	1,699	1,373	999	418	257	23		5,642
1926	875	1,739	1,353	1,006	407	258	25		5,663
1927	865	1m743	1,363	1,030	402	254	25		5,682
1928	839	1,764	1,347	1,019	401	255	22		5,647
1929	837	1,761	1,350	1,019	401	256	20		5,644
1930	850	1,758	1,348	1,033	401	245	21		5,656
1931	837	1,750	1,354	1,023	403	253	20		5,640
1932	850	1,726	1,353	1,031	396	251	21		5,628
1933	856	1,742	1,353	1,033	380	255	20		5,639
1934	852	1,724	1,317	1,054	392	252	15	4	5,610

Year	Number of Agricultural Holdings of the following sizes (acres)								TOTAL
	1-5	5-20	20-50	50-100	100-150	150-300	300-500	500+	
1935	845	1,725	1,314	1,041	396	244	16	3	5,584
1936	829	1,697	1,329	1,037	390	245	16	3	5,546
1937	815	1,670	1,316	1,044	392	247	17	3	5,504
1938	824	1,642	1,307	1,042	392	248	18	3	5,476
1939	796	1,633	1,312	1,045	384	250	17	3	5,440
1940	770	1,564	1,307	1,018	382	230	16	2	5,289
1941	808	1,552	1,301	1,014	375	228	17	2	5,297
1942	736	1,544	1,307	1,038	400	241	17	4	5,287
1943	710	1,525	1,264	1,068	399	230	19	3	5,218
1944	696	1,482	1,253	1,060	397	237	18	4	5,147
1945	686	1,470	1,256	1,063	394	240	17	3	5,129
1946	667	1,476	1,255	1,058	395	234	20	2	5,107
1947	653	1,461	1,253	1,048	396	236	20	2	5,069
1948	643	1,450	1,256	1,058	394	223	20	2	5,046
1949	673	1,442	1,258	1,059	391	236	18	2	5,079
1950	684	1,410	1,246	1,072	398	240	16	3	5,069
1951	691	1,401	1,264	1,068	400	239	16	3	5,082
1952	687	1,396	1,266	1,053	405	252	15	4	5,078
1953	714	1,389	1,249	1,066	411	243	17	4	5,093
1954	714	1,378	1,251	1,063	400	248	19	4	5,077
1955	726	1,364	1,260	1,053	403	239	22	5	5,072
1956	708	1,339	1,239	1,051	410	243	19	7	5,016
1957	689	1,302	1,221	1,066	403	253	22	6	4,962
1958	677	1,243	1,213	1,041	416	267	21	7	4,885
1959	646	1,202	1,202	1,066	402	266	21	9	4,814
1960[1]	645	1,149	1,190	1,048	418	267	19	9	4,745
1960[1]	625	1,109	1,040	1,002	483	422	79	49	4,809
1961	623	1,077	1,030	973	495	411	88	49	4,746
1962	605	1,032	1,022	965	490	413	86	48	4,661
1963	606	1,002	994	963	486	414	92	44	4,601
1964	538	976	975	955	483	414	92	46	4,479
1965	520	975	953	937	479	413	96	46	4,419
1966	512	955	921	915	483	413	98	48	4,345
1967	487	932	894	906	472	423	104	46	4,264
1968[2]	160	710	867	884	469	435	105	44	3,674
1969	152	663	834	851	451	440	103	50	3,544
1970	131	439	718	807	431	453	110	57	3,286
1971	128	547	700	780	448	430	105	62	3,200
1972	95	490	670	749	436	442	108	62	3,052
1973	86	429	643	738	422	443	103	68	2,932
1974									

AGRICULTURE 8. Size of Agricultural Holdings,[1] each county, 1875-1974

FLINTSHIRE

Year	1-5	5-20	20-50	50-100	100-150	150-300	300-500	500+	TOTAL
	Number of Agricultural Holdings of the following sizes (acres)								
1875		3,356		427	318		20	4	4,125
1880		3,316		414	321		26	3	4,080
1885	1,169	1,162	589	406	322		26	4	3,678
1890	..	..	..	..	..		..	..	..
1895	1,061	1,266	611	406	328		19	4	3,695
1900	..	..	..	..	..		..	..	..
1901	..	..	..	..	..		..	..	..
1902	..	..	..	..	..		..	..	..
1903	971	1,815			745		19		3,550
1904	951	1,831			733		20		3,535
1905	935	1,850			743		18		3,546
1906	933	1,845			749		17		3,544
1907	915	1,837			740		19		3,511
1908	890	1,851			750		14		3,505
1909	892	1,832			744		16		3,484
1910	884	1,804			761		13		3,462
1911	866	1,826			756		14		3,462
1912	896	1,841			750		13		3,500
1913	871	1,180	645	423	181	145	14		3,459
1914	865	1,171	649	428	184	141	15		3,453
1915	850	1,161	646	434	183	138	16		3,428
1916	822	1,142	649	432	188	137	17		3,387
1917	777	1,136	632	439	190	137	15		3,326
1918	770	1,115	627	441	187	135	17		3,292
1919	757	1,142	625	446	181	129	18		3,298
1920	746	1,168	675	426	186	122	14		3,337
1921	777	1,200	690	425	186	119	13		3,410
1922	744	1,175	700	433	182	120	14		3,368
1923	738	1,178	694	429	176	125	19		3,359
1924	737	1,165	704	426	185	120	13		3,350
1925	745	1,157	709	428	186	117	13		3,355
1926	760	1,133	706	432	185	116	12		3,344
1927	747	1,137	700	440	184	118	12		3,338
1928	742	1,140	704	433	190	113	12		3,334
1929	746	1,131	711	425	198	109	14		3,334
1930	734	1,098	716	429	189	115	12		3,293
1931	721	1,083	717	432	191	114	12		3,270
1932	696	1,083	735	430	182	118	12		3,256
1933	679	1,089	751	430	182	120	10		3,261
1934	677	1,077	743	437	179	118	9	3	3,243
1935	669	1,071	751	431	177	117	8	3	3,227
1936	654	1,076	742	430	177	117	7	5	3,208
1937	665	1,039	734	447	176	114	7	6	3,188
1938	641	1,041	729	446	174	113	8	5	3,157
1939	628	1,038	720	450	172	110	7	4	3,129
1940	576	999	712	449	173	110	8	3	3,030
1941	667	1,035	713	436	174	107	9	3	3,144
1942	577	1,061	719	445	181	109	10	3	3,105
1943	569	1,033	702	449	186	104	9	3	3,055
1944	557	1,033	679	448	188	105	11	3	3,024
1945	561	1,035	676	461	178	109	10	3	3,033
1946	554	1,047	672	460	175	110	10	3	3,031
1947	544	1,031	668	464	182	105	10	3	3,007
1948	545	1,028	660	471	173	111	9	4	3,001
1949	583	1,031	665	461	179	111	8	4	3,042
1950	642	1,017	668	458	180	106	11	5	3,087
1951	667	1,009	652	467	190	105	10	6	3,106
1952	661	992	663	457	191	105	12	4	3,085
1953	660	991	651	466	195	107	11	4	3,085
1954	639	973	647	475	196	107	12	4	3,053
1955	613	954	648	467	197	108	12	4	3,003
1956	583	938	650	463	198	112	11	4	2,959
1957	580	927	646	450	208	108	13	5	2,937
1958	571	904	650	444	209	106	12	4	2,900
1959	553	890	631	453	209	111	10	4	2,861
1960[1]	516	853	641	448	205	114	11	3	2,791
1960[1]	514	845	631	466	213	139	16	5	2,829
1961	526	837	614	477	211	141	14	5	2,825
1962	519	819	609	465	206	144	15	5	2,782
1963	518	806	604	455	203	151	14	5	2,756
1964	489	780	589	437	205	156	15	5	2,676
1965	502	760	563	450	206	153	15	5	2,654
1966	497	739	553	437	203	159	17	4	2,609
1967	474	724	548	432	202	161	19	4	2,564
1968[2]	158	553	541	425	194	170	19	4	2,064
1969	158	509	511	425	187	173	20	4	1,987
1970	145	462	477	413	194	174	23	4	1,892
1971	131	442	459	403	185	175	27	5	1,827
1972	105	407	443	393	180	178	29	5	1,740
1973	83	362	430	379	178	179	27	7	1,645
1974									

AGRICULTURE 8. Size of Agricultural Holdings,(1) each county, 1875-1974

GLAMORGANSHIRE

Year	Number of Agricultural Holdings of the following sizes (acres)								TOTAL
	1-5	5-20	20-50	50-100	100-150	150-300	300-500	500+	
1875		3,483		989	687		45	17	5,221
1880		3,861		1,012	671		76	15	5,635
1885	1,179	1,547	1,327	1,061	742		43	11	5,910
1890	..	..	..	..	..		..	..	..
1895	1,080	1,633	1,262	999	752		44	8	5,778
1900	..	..	..	..	..		..	..	..
1901	..	..	..	..	..		..	..	..
1902	..	..	..	..	..		..	..	..
1903	1,082	2,941			1,725		45		5,793
1904	1,061	2,930			1,720		44		5,755
1905	1,010	2,916			1,719		46		5,691
1906	1,042	2,901			1,710		49		5,702
1907	1,057	2,896			1,712		47		5,712
1908	1,026	2,855			1,719		46		5,646
1909	1,032	2,818			1,716		44		5,610
1910	1,004	2,820			1,710		41		5,575
1911	976	2,844			1,704		47		5,571
1912	949	2,835			1,702		44		5,530
1913	944	1,558	1,275	1,031	392	290	40		5,530
1914	917	1,541	1,291	1,010	393	291	36		5,479
1915	915	1,555	1,298	999	402	286	34		5,489
1916	908	1,526	1,279	1,033	400	281	32		5,459
1917	894	1,501	1,288	1,018	397	277	35		5,410
1918	859	1,478	1,262	1,027	403	262	42		5,333
1919	820	1,457	1,284	989	376	252	35		5,213
1920	773	1,453	1,276	993	352	251	36		5,134
1921	734	1,447	1,300	954	327	212	38		5,012
1922	680	1,409	1,278	931	327	223	35		4,883
1923	655	1,408	1,287	928	338	211	35		4,862
1924	634	1,385	1,283	935	324	211	34		4,806
1925	634	1,335	1,301	934	339	209	32		4,784
1926	621	1,332	1,286	951	334	211	27		4,762
1927	617	1,316	1,299	931	344	209	26		4,742
1928	602	1,298	1,296	942	343	211	26		4,718
1929	605	1,289	1,297	936	347	206	26		4,706
1930	587	1,260	1,286	943	349	207	27		4,659
1931	575	1,230	1,293	947	345	203	29		4,622
1932	577	1,212	1,271	944	351	207	25		4,587
1933	556	1,166	1,250	965	334	211	23		4,505
1934	529	1,138	1,248	960	339	216	18	3	4,451

Year	Number of Agricultural Holdings of the following sizes (acres)								TOTAL
	1-5	5-20	20-50	50-100	100-150	150-300	300-500	500+	
1935	537	1,104	1,241	965	328	206	18	4	4,403
1936	514	1,107	1,220	954	324	208	20	2	4,349
1937	503	1,096	1,198	954	325	209	18	4	4,307
1938	506	1,090	1,208	963	325	202	16	3	4,313
1939	522	1,059	1,218	978	338	195	15	3	4,328
1940	499	1,051	1,207	980	332	190	15	3	4,277
1941	564	1,082	1,227	947	315	183	20	3	4,341
1942	488	1,109	1,240	987	307	173	19	5	4,328
1943	626	1,150	1,221	975	315	183	19	3	4,492
1944	610	1,129	1,229	959	320	182	16	3	4,448
1945	610	1,142	1,205	956	330	182	15	3	4,443
1946	621	1,129	1,170	973	310	186	14	3	4,406
1947	611	1,091	1,187	934	327	179	17	3	4,349
1948	635	1,108	1,174	943	317	190	19	3	4,389
1949	685	1,110	1,187	923	332	185	21	2	4,445
1950	761	1,114	1,166	937	339	184	18	2	4,521
1951	813	1,121	1,154	927	343	181	22	2	4,563
1952	811	1,110	1,158	926	336	188	23	2	4,554
1953	833	1,101	1,123	942	343	195	18	2	4,557
1954	780	1,063	1,107	923	354	208	17	2	4,454
1955	733	1,026	1,079	920	362	200	18	2	4,340
1956	713	1,011	1,073	903	363	205	17	2	4,287
1957	710	1,002	1,098	877	343	212	18	3	4,263
1958	685	996	1,066	902	345	213	16	2	4,225
1959	665	966	1,061	896	347	211	17	4	4,167
1960(1)	655	936	1,037	881	352	218	17	4	4,100
1960(1)	660	888	846	876	467	405	83	48	4,273
1961	643	837	819	849	447	404	90	46	4,135
1962	649	854	787	854	430	400	91	46	4,111
1963	636	833	810	830	419	393	93	48	4,062
1964	612	784	798	821	407	381	94	48	3,945
1965	607	762	789	801	391	386	97	50	3,883
1966	600	749	750	785	388	382	95	50	3,799
1967	549	736	731	768	384	374	93	54	3,689
1968(2)	160	513	686	746	372	372	94	56	2,999
1969	154	480	511	717	359	368	96	59	2,902
1970	157	441	627	660	354	371	102	61	2,773
1971	141	419	596	643	347	358	103	62	2,669
1972	117	375	555	628	339	352	106	63	2,535
1973	95	3[illegible]3	534	612	341	350	107	62	2,434
1974									

AGRICULTURE 8. Size of Agricultural Holdings,[1] each county, 1875-1974

MERIONETHSHIRE

Year	1-5	5-20	20-50	50-100	100-150	150-300	300-500	500+	TOTAL
	Number of Agricultural Holdings of the following sizes (acres)								
1875		2,233		580	341		18	10	3,182
1880		2,283		608	344		21	9	3,265
1885	397	836	931	638	355		18	9	3,184
1890	..	..	..	..	..		..	..	..
1895	394	794	864	644	368		18	4	3,086
1900	..	..	..	..	..		..	..	..
1901	..	..	..	..	..		..	..	..
1902	..	..	..	..	..		..	..	..
1903	334	1,631			1,004		25		2,994
1904	335	1,623			1,020		24		3,002
1905	342	1,642			1,016		23		3,023
1906	340	1,626			1,023		24		3,013
1907	361	1,604			1,014		24		3,003
1908	357	1,622			1,004		26		3,009
1909	336	1,623			1,006		25		2,990
1910	338	1,638			994		25		2,995
1911	338	1,649			1,000		23		3,010
1912	352	1,659			988		20		3,019
1913	342	779	866	626	221	142	24		3,000
1914	337	796	863	620	222	142	19		2,999
1915	332	817	846	618	225	150	19		3,007
1916	321	795	846	625	224	150	18		2,979
1917	319	779	841	631	220	145	20		2,955
1918	318	757	819	647	214	146	18		2,919
1919	318	775	811	640	220	141	14		2,919
1920	318	778	847	628	212	137	15		2,935
1921	325	779	856	638	222	131	16		2,967
1922	324	764	853	639	215	140	13		2,948
1923	318	772	865	624	201	123	14		2,917
1924	307	779	868	609	204	119	15		2,901
1925	307	783	852	612	195	116	16		2,881
1926	303	771	851	604	188	105	15		2,837
1927	287	778	860	596	179	102	17		2,819
1928	271	780	877	591	169	98	17		2,803
1929	262	785	867	579	170	99	18		2,780
1930	270	753	868	579	171	96	20		2,757
1931	256	737	867	583	172	98	17		2,730
1932	245	750	866	580	171	98	13		2,723
1933	225	743	872	584	168	99	15		2,706
1934	210	742	864	571	176	95	14	2	2,674

Year	1-5	5-20	20-50	50-100	100-150	150-300	300-500	500+	TOTAL
	Number of Agricultural Holdings of the following sizes (acres)								
1935	208	738	837	579	175	92	14	2	2,645
1936	201	733	854	572	175	87	10	1	2,633
1937	198	722	869	557	177	84	12	1	2,620
1938	202	720	876	556	168	88	13	1	2,624
1939	203	715	872	552	172	81	14	1	2,610
1940	202	744	884	536	132	68	5	-	2,571
1941	233	757	886	478	131	69	6	-	2,560
1942	179	744	907	504	137	70	5	-	2,546
1943	164	739	912	483	132	59	4	-	2,493
1944	166	725	880	493	130	57	3	-	2,454
1945	181	727	876	483	129	51	3	-	2,450
1946	162	741	880	473	122	54	5	-	2,437
1947	151	731	866	471	130	58	5	1	2,413
1948	155	710	865	487	130	54	4	-	2,405
1949	153	684	872	482	131	53	5	-	2,380
1950	151	677	870	489	118	60	7	-	2,372
1951	149	669	868	482	128	59	7	-	2,362
1952	137	672	864	479	128	58	7	-	2,345
1953	135	643	866	481	129	57	4	-	2,315
1954	142	626	877	472	121	60	4	-	2,302
1955	130	623	868	473	117	61	4	-	2,276
1956	118	624	838	465	127	62	5	1	2,240
1957	122	598	808	475	132	61	7	2	2,205
1958	121	575	799	481	126	63	8	3	2,176
1959	101	565	791	476	131	62	9	3	2,138
1960[1]	101	552	774	470	139	61	9	3	2,109
1960[1]	81	363	424	422	239	330	160	125	2,144
1961	80	354	413	393	220	339	162	119	2,080
1962	80	347	407	383	216	327	166	120	2,046
1963	84	348	387	389	207	325	167	120	2,027
1964	80	338	378	379	209	328	163	121	1,996
1965	81	334	361	377	204	323	165	124	1,969
1966	74	338	346	344	205	313	162	130	1,912
1967	69	318	343	332	201	295	159	139	1,856
1968[2]	11	236	324	335	193	294	161	138	1,692
1969	21	214	294	329	188	286	165	140	1,637
1970	11	168	246	283	172	281	168	137	1,466
1971	10	162	237	284	175	266	164	137	1,435
1972	9	130	232	273	169	266	164	129	1,372
1973	5	115	220	264	162	265	164	138	1,333
1974									

AGRICULTURE 8. Size of Agricultural Holdings,[1] each county, 1875-1974

MONMOUTHSHIRE

ar	Number of Agricultural Holdings of the following sizes (acres) 1-5	5-20	20-50	50-100	100-150	150-300	300-500	500+	TOTAL
5		3,242		719	659		53	8	4,681
0		3,661		787	734		48	11	5,241
5	1,086	1,398	925	728	714		43	11	4,905
0	..	..	..	..	..		..	..	..
5	986	1,474	938	763	687		52	10	4,910
0	..	..	..	..	..		..	..	..
1	..	..	..	..	..		..	..	..
2	..	..	..	..	..		..	..	..
3	931	2,361			1,434		62		4,788
4	885	2,350			1,456		58		4,749
5	934	2,356			1,460		59		4,809
6	894	2,334			1,450		59		4,737
7	831	2,342			1,465		56		4,694
8	792	2,286			1,459		57		4,594
9	797	2,304			1,454		56		4,611
0	797	2,323			1,438		56		4,614
1	842	2,325			1,447		54		4,668
2	841	2,322			1,456		48		4,667
3	809	1,331	986	759	369	327	48		4,629
4	807	1,322	991	769	363	326	45		4,623
5	795	1,315	954	779	352	326	49		4,570
6	775	1,276	925	791	352	330	49		4,498
7	731	1,231	928	802	359	326	45		4,422
8	723	1,207	925	790	349	324	48		4,366
9	718	1,197	925	755	343	318	51		4,307
0	707	1,174	943	752	343	310	58		4,287
1	738	1,219	942	751	328	308	43		4,329
2	677	1,158	962	716	326	307	45		4,191
3	656	1,139	950	729	339	297	45		4,155
4	663	1,121	933	730	323	302	44		4,116
5	667	1,103	912	745	326	301	40		4,094
6	647	1,114	900	742	339	281	41		4,064
7	646	1,109	914	740	343	277	42		4,071
8	705	1,116	927	720	344	286	40		4,138
9	777	1,183	937	740	351	284	37		4,309
0	770	1,162	923	748	342	283	38		4,266
1	754	1,121	931	750	340	288	37		4,221
2	729	1,141	915	745	358	279	38		4,205
3	715	1,128	920	744	360	278	38		4,183
4	708	1,110	918	740	364	278	35	3	4,156

Year	Number of Agricultural Holdings of the following sizes (acres) 1-5	5-20	20-50	50-100	100-150	150-300	300-500	500+	TOTAL
1935	702	1,092	898	751	363	273	41	2	4,122
1936	679	1,069	902	761	355	273	42	2	4,083
1937	663	1,043	893	750	353	279	39	2	4,022
1938	646	1,021	868	754	363	274	40	2	3,968
1939	623	1,042	831	744	373	272	39	2	3,926
1940	595	1,023	849	742	356	269	36	3	3,873
1941	756	1,085	854	751	359	250	33	5	4,093
1942	719	1,084	859	739	354	277	38	5	4,075
1943	726	1,055	870	720	361	280	38	4	4,054
1944	715	1,051	860	728	367	272	42	2	4,037
1945	723	1,049	859	718	360	285	41	1	4,036
1946	717	1,049	855	694	364	288	39	3	4,009
1947	685	1,057	868	689	359	299	35	3	3,995
1948	741	1,035	878	689	358	302	37	3	4,043
1949	768	1,016	871	710	350	304	36	2	4,057
1950	876	1,016	884	691	363	298	36	2	4,166
1951	889	1,015	872	695	366	299	34	2	4,172
1952	901	1,013	853	709	368	294	34	2	4,174
1953	886	998	840	709	370	294	34	2	4,133
1954	855	990	828	710	367	299	33	2	4,084
1955	829	973	819	711	376	293	38	1	4,040
1956	815	964	824	711	376	294	34	2	4,020
1957	801	957	815	704	378	294	37	2	3,988
1958	780	947	795	704	376	297	39	2	3,940
1959	749	907	802	711	361	303	37	3	3,873
1960[1]	744	886	765	713	363	300	36	3	3,810
1960[1]	745	895	755	761	388	358	47	6	3,955
1961	738	868	747	743	393	354	48	5	3,896
1962	711	871	709	746	384	360	50	4	3,835
1963	698	853	706	741	377	356	50	6	3,787
1964	682	841	692	717	386	347	57	5	3,727
1965	660	843	678	687	394	343	62	5	3,672
1966	644	855	661	661	393	341	64	6	3,625
1967	573	843	649	658	379	346	63	8	3,519
1968[2]	159	575	626	638	378	348	64	9	2,797
1969	165	531	614	622	378	349	63	10	2,732
1970	130	469	613	591	376	341	73	13	2,606
1971	116	474	585	594	360	350	74	15	2,568
1972	98	440	574	571	358	351	74	14	2,480
1973	74	420	558	573	362	346	74	15	2,422
1974									

AGRICULTURE 8. Size of Agricultural Holdings,[1] each county, 1875-1974

MONTGOMERYSHIRE

Year	Number of Agricultural Holdings of the following sizes (acres)								TOTAL
	1-5	5-20	20-50	50-100	100-150	150-300	300-500	500+	
1875		3,731		910	663		44	6	5,354
1880		3,572		958	692		38	7	5,267
1885	974	1,505	1,094	950	717		36	8	5,284
1890	..	..	..	..	..		..	..	..
1895	1,001	1,626	1,073	1,019	764		37	7	5,527
1900	..	..	..	..	..		..	..	..
1901	..	..	..	..	..		..	..	..
1902	..	..	..	..	..		..	..	..
1903	928	2,731			1,826		46		5,531
1904	936	2,745			1,812		47		5,540
1905	911	2,755			1,822		44		5,532
1906	933	2,770			1,821		44		5,568
1907	920	2,780			1,826		43		5,569
1908	929	2,787			1,830		37		5,583
1909	901	2,759			1,838		37		5,535
1910	910	2,770			1,841		34		5,555
1911	904	2,773			1,848		38		5,563
1912	947	2,830			1,848		33		5,658
1913	946	1,731	1,141	1,043	459	321	36		5,677
1914	953	1,714	1,191	1,022	445	323	39		5,687
1915	936	1,724	1,165	1,043	448	321	39		5,676
1916	930	1,697	1,158	1,058	429	331	39		5,642
1917	909	1,669	1,150	1,030	466	335	37		5,596
1918	929	1,649	1,135	1,038	449	336	39		5,575
1919	918	1,632	1,185	1,033	440	314	41		5,563
1920	905	1,695	1,186	1,042	436	317	33		5,614
1921	883	1,703	1,255	1,036	423	292	30		5,622
1922	823	1,606	1,225	1,016	436	291	33		5,430
1923	792	1,576	1,187	1,042	451	285	30		5,363
1924	763	1,547	1,197	1,040	440	295	27		5,309
1925	737	1,558	1,169	1,067	436	294	26		5,287
1926	718	1,555	1,166	1,058	442	294	28		5,261
1927	697	1,548	1,163	1,056	448	296	23		5,231
1928	687	1,553	1,122	1,077	445	296	24		5,204
1929	676	1,546	1,137	1,053	456	294	24		5,186
1930	669	1,551	1,151	1,053	453	291	27		5,195
1931	654	1,544	1,163	1,062	443	296	24		5,186
1932	647	1,533	1,173	1,065	440	295	23		5,176
1933	645	1,506	1,166	1,074	444	299	25		5,159
1934	632	1,506	1,153	1,079	440	298	26	1	5,135

Year	Number of Agricultural Holdings of the following sizes (acres)								TOTA
	1-5	5-20	20-50	50-100	100-150	150-300	300-500	500+	
1935	613	1,499	1,173	1,052	450	290	26	1	5,10
1936	595	1,513	1,181	1,062	450	288	26	1	5,11
1937	592	1,502	1,182	1,050	455	286	25	1	5,09
1938	584	1,484	1,170	1,050	450	285	25	1	5,04
1939	573	1,468	1,158	1,061	449	292	25	1	5,02
1940	544	1,457	1,137	1,078	440	277	27	1	4,96
1941	631	1,491	1,149	1,078	450	266	24	-	5,08
1942	494	1,573	1,147	1,060	470	279	29	2	5,05
1943	494	1,570	1,135	1,075	456	279	30	3	5,04
1944	485	1,556	1,152	1,060	452	285	29	4	5,02
1945	487	1,542	1,136	1,069	457	279	30	4	5,00
1946	491	1,559	1,125	1,062	454	281	26	6	5,00
1947	479	1,562	1,114	1,053	455	286	26	6	4,98
1948	473	1,551	1,112	1,058	457	289	25	5	4,97
1949	511	1,542	1,117	1,062	452	291	26	4	5,00
1950	542	1,548	1,117	1,059	448	297	27	1	5,03
1951	592	1,549	1,113	1,061	445	295	28	1	5,08
1952	627	1,554	1,099	1,076	440	293	29	1	5,11
1953	633	1,535	1,089	1,074	448	295	28	1	5,10
1954	606	1,514	1,089	1,061	449	298	28	1	5,04
1955	583	1,485	1,080	1,058	449	305	28	1	4,98
1956	561	1,440	1,079	1,041	460	309	28	1	4,91
1957	552	1,407	1,054	1,047	454	326	27	2	4,86
1958	530	1,368	1,041	1,050	465	324	28	4	4,81
1959	514	1,339	1,036	1,048	473	323	29	3	4,76
1960[1]	510	1,300	1,018	1,045	471	337	31	3	4,71
1960[1]	490	1,235	828	865	501	576	160	101	4,75
1961	477	1,201	835	854	500	578	158	94	4,69
1962	469	1,174	818	853	488	580	154	97	4,63
1963	465	1,172	790	827	496	573	160	99	4,58
1964	447	1,151	764	824	484	570	167	102	4,50
1965	440	1,136	753	808	485	568	168	106	4,46
1966	428	1,111	723	787	481	563	168	110	4,37
1967	403	1,102	697	757	484	567	161	112	4,28
1968[2]	109	809	687	741	473	569	167	111	3,72
1969	125	800	654	729	457	580	167	113	3,62
1970	90	702	606	677	434	577	185	115	3,38
1971	81	644	584	671	437	577	182	116	3,29
1972	67	591	555	651	436	582	179	119	3,18
1973	45	513	559	647	419	571	185	121	3,06
1974									

AGRICULTURE 8. Size of Agricultural Holdings,[1] each county, 1875-1974

PEMBROKESHIRE

Year	Number of Agricultural Holdings of the following sizes (acres)								TOTAL
	1-5	5-20	20-50	50-100	100-150	150-300	300-500	500+	
1875	4,190			857	806		71	11	5,935
1880	4,222			837	853		79	8	5,999
1885	1,023	1,837	1,225	871	876		76	8	5,916
1890	..	..	..	..	..		..	..	..
1895	908	1,869	1,317	865	908		77	7	5,951
1900	..	..	..	..	..		..	..	..
1901	..	..	..	..	..		..	..	..
1902	..	..	..	..	..		..	..	..
1903	843	3,221			1,785		80		5,929
1904	809	3,249			1,785		77		5,920
1905	823	3,223			1,785		79		5,910
1906	797	3,184			1,796		80		5,857
1907	772	3,229			1,796		78		5,875
1908	762	3,254			1,791		74		5,881
1909	808	3,277			1,790		71		5,946
1910	810	3,237			1,805		69		5,921
1911	785	3,255			1,798		70		5,908
1912	766	3,241			1,812		67		5,886
1913	745	1,902	1,345	901	477	425	64		5,859
1914	734	1,899	1,355	902	472	423	66		5,851
1915	722	1,885	1,344	917	475	425	65		5,833
1916	676	1,856	1,335	932	470	425	66		5,760
1917	634	1,806	1,350	951	474	423	71		5,709
1918	618	1,763	1,341	946	460	427	61		5,616
1919	638	1,777	1,357	928	460	414	56		5,630
1920	623	1,801	1,374	956	475	407	50		5,686
1921	624	1,832	1,397	976	465	386	40		5,720
1922	635	1,865	1,430	942	487	384	34		5,777
1923	594	1,848	1,463	948	491	376	38		5,758
1924	593	1,847	1,480	939	491	376	38		5,764
1925	600	1,869	1,482	955	488	363	37		5,794
1926	606	1,858	1,500	942	489	367	33		5,795
1927	630	1,861	1,516	978	482	360	33		5,860
1928	640	1,889	1,511	973	482	358	30		5,883
1929	603	1,898	1,504	996	473	357	33		5,864
1930	614	1,901	1,501	992	480	356	33		5,877
1931	580	1,847	1,506	1,002	471	353	34		5,793
1932	560	1,844	1,501	1,005	466	360	30		5,766
1933	552	1,826	1,512	1,009	475	353	31		5,758
1934	542	1,837	1,521	1,017	476	351	26	1	5,771
1935	543	1,781	1,510	1,014	458	369	25	1	5,701
1936	536	1,745	1,489	1,029	461	370	25	1	5,656
1937	558	1,695	1,498	1,028	461	365	24	1	5,630
1938	516	1,697	1,501	1,031	465	358	26	1	5,595
1939	540	1,695	1,480	1,032	459	362	26	1	5,595
1940	482	1,543	1,446	1,067	456	349	28	1	5,372
1941	512	1,548	1,454	1,044	464	326	22	1	5,371
1942	379	1,496	1,460	1,043	473	351	22	2	5,226
1943	372	1,450	1,438	1,043	488	332	25	2	5,150
1944	354	1,424	1,438	1,037	469	344	25	2	5,093
1945	343	1,433	1,407	1,045	466	344	27	2	5,067
1946	346	1,373	1,409	1,054	462	348	29	4	5,025
1947	332	1,347	1,407	1,063	468	347	28	5	4,997
1948	324	1,329	1,401	1,066	471	349	29	4	4,973
1949	338	1,328	1,415	1,061	477	335	28	4	4,986
1950	357	1,316	1,384	1,097	484	338	25	2	5,003
1951	418	1,328	1,412	1,098	468	343	28	2	5,097
1952	419	1,351	1,413	1,097	469	346	25	3	5,123
1953	405	1,368	1,383	1,097	486	350	27	2	5,118
1954	399	1,341	1,368	1,123	477	350	28	2	5,088
1955	379	1,317	1,362	1,115	480	350	30	3	5,036
1956	385	1,294	1,342	1,123	481	343	34	2	5,004
1957	382	1,256	1,323	1,116	458	365	34	3	4,937
1958	379	1,221	1,315	1,119	467	363	33	3	4,900
1959	367	1,189	1,305	1,109	471	375	33	3	4,852
1960[1]	373	1,175	1,283	1,109	468	374	31	5	4,818
1960[1]	348	1,090	1,198	1,147	512	477	79	10	4,861
1961	332	1,069	1,170	1,134	511	473	83	12	4,784
1962	332	1,040	1,162	1,105	515	476	84	14	4,728
1963	324	1,005	1,135	1,093	506	480	85	17	4,645
1964	336	987	1,106	1,100	500	471	86	20	4,606
1965	334	975	1,062	1,087	501	474	89	20	4,542
1966	331	953	1,027	1,063	499	479	90	21	4,463
1967	314	929	987	1,033	512	473	94	23	4,365
1968[2]	66	688	948	1,012	503	476	100	26	3,819
1969	94	651	890	1,001	500	479	102	26	3,743
1970	90	587	798	961	495	481	105	33	3,550
1971	79	575	764	939	493	497	104	31	3,482
1972	54	545	730	906	496	504	112	31	3,378
1973	44	508	704	896	500	497	114	33	3,296
1974									

AGRICULTURE 8. Size of Agricultural Holdings,[1] each county, 1875-1974

RADNORSHIRE

Year	Number of Agricultural Holdings of the following sizes (acres)								TOTAL
	1-5	5-20	20-50	50-100	100-150	150-300	300-500	500+	
1875		1,267		420	475		46	9	2,217
1880		1,234		411	487		47	9	2,188
1885	272	440	406	423	496		41	7	2,085
1890	..	..	..	..	..		..	..	..
1895	290	519	371	442	538		42	6	2,208
1900	..	..	..	..	..		..	..	..
1901	..	..	..	..	..		..	..	..
1902	..	..	..	..	..		..	..	..
1903	274	882			996		50		2,202
1904	280	880			995		49		2,204
1905	274	884			1,001		49		2,208
1906	277	886			1,005		49		2,217
1907	281	885			1,009		47		2,222
1908	258	900			1,002		48		2,208
1909	259	911			1,008		46		2,224
1910	258	914			1,004		47		2,223
1911	258	910			1,002		44		2,214
1912	271	937			1,001		42		2,251
1913	258	545	393	470	254	279	45		2,244
1914	262	533	400	482	245	284	43		2,249
1915	254	563	401	482	261	283	37		2,281
1916	248	570	396	469	269	287	35		2,274
1917	242	561	398	461	285	278	31		2,256
1918	236	564	392	459	282	278	33		2,244
1919	237	575	421	446	280	281	33		2,273
1920	242	581	421	472	274	275	33		2,298
1921	253	616	437	474	275	259	35		2,349
1922	221	573	425	469	265	272	32		2,257
1923	219	563	406	476	267	262	34		2,227
1924	215	544	413	472	271	255	38		2,208
1925	217	541	412	469	273	259	37		2,208
1926	213	530	423	469	272	258	36		2,201
1927	194	551	410	463	284	253	35		2,190
1928	190	543	407	458	278	258	36		2,170
1929	188	516	402	459	274	265	34		2,138
1930	181	506	411	451	277	260	36		2,122
1931	164	493	410	450	269	271	36		2,093
1932	162	491	406	454	273	268	33		2,087
1933	152	484	403	449	276	267	35		2,066
1934	156	475	400	453	276	263	34	1	2,058

Year	Number of Agricultural Holdings of the following sizes (acres)								TOTAL
	1-5	5-20	20-50	50-100	100-150	150-300	300-500	500+	
1935	151	479	394	453	275	266	34	1	2,053
1936	147	471	398	445	271	266	38	1	2,037
1937	149	468	399	452	268	259	41	1	2,037
1938	150	472	396	449	272	255	41	-	2,035
1939	150	465	402	452	270	257	38	-	2,034
1940	144	451	405	453	278	218	33	-	1,982
1941	172	464	410	452	272	228	30	-	2,028
1942	134	472	413	452	289	228	34	-	2,022
1943	133	456	427	452	276	235	25	1	2,005
1944	131	459	419	452	277	224	29	1	1,992
1945	126	457	426	435	283	227	28	-	1,982
1946	134	450	419	444	280	225	31	-	1,983
1947	127	454	416	437	287	224	30	-	1,975
1948	135	445	416	439	283	222	31	-	1,971
1949	142	441	408	439	286	224	30	1	1,971
1950	132	432	411	445	287	220	32	1	1,960
1951	134	431	407	455	283	227	31	1	1,969
1952	136	420	400	451	292	229	34	1	1,963
1953	137	413	403	451	291	233	36	1	1,965
1954	141	405	396	456	293	236	36	-	1,963
1955	137	398	405	448	289	239	38	-	1,954
1956	144	389	402	446	291	237	42	-	1,951
1957	139	389	391	442	285	247	43	-	1,936
1958	137	379	377	450	275	250	43	1	1,912
1959	132	366	372	444	275	261	48	1	1,899
1960[1]	127	351	359	457	274	257	48	3	1,876
1960[1]	121	337	290	361	287	353	123	28	1,900
1961	120	339	282	361	273	354	125	33	1,887
1962	125	328	277	361	260	362	123	36	1,872
1963	126	314	273	352	257	365	124	38	1,849
1964	124	308	256	357	257	364	127	39	1,832
1965	122	293	265	355	250	362	125	43	1,815
1966	120	284	251	329	249	361	129	46	1,769
1967	114	279	244	315	248	367	123	47	1,737
1968[2]	29	207	233	305	233	373	125	46	1,551
1969	32	197	216	299	234	365	128	51	1,522
1970	22	168	187	275	233	371	125	54	1,435
1971	23	154	185	260	234	362	132	53	1,403
1972	20	133	181	261	214	366	130	58	1,363
1973	9	121	186	259	215	360	130	59	1,339
1974									

Notes See notes to Table 7.

AGRICULTURE 9. Workers employed on agricultural holdings,[1] Wales, 1921 - 1974

	REGULAR WORKERS[2]						SEASONAL OR CASUAL			
	Whole Time			Part Time						
	Males 20 yrs. old & over[3]	Males under 20[3]	Females	Males 20+[3]	Males under 20[3]	Females	Males 20+[3]	Males under 20[3]	Females	TOTAL WORKERS
1921	29,003	12,378	12,089				9,371	2,593	2,705	68,139
1922	..	..	..				..	..	..	..
1923	26,475	11,266	10,293				6,979	2,040	2,205	59,258
1924	27,591	12,066	10,973				7,724	2,374	2,362	63,090
1925	26,928	11,900	10,175				7,845	1,841	2,493	61,182
1926	28,869	12,152	10,315				6,750	2,104	2,354	62,364
1927	28,677	12,157	11,565				5,856	1,988	2,602	62,845
1928	28,881	12,006	13,266				7,013	1,079	1,716	63,961
1929	29,429	12,014	13,536				6,832	1,034	1,676	64,521
1930	29,969	11,637	12,821				5,559	1,160	1,909	63,055
1931	30,027	11,713	12,793				5,223	916	1,815	62,487
1932	29,067	11,438	12,623				5,287	921	1,784	61,120
1933	27,900	10,740	10,821				5,016	946	1,667	57,090
1934	26,339	10,274	9,595				4,964	859	1,495	53,526
1935	25,853	10,100	9,312				5,053	998	1,570	52,886
1936	24,058	9,445	7,813				4,074	829	1,544	47,763
1937	23,873	8,846	7,648				4,141	820	1,360	46,688
1938	22,654	8,432	6,835				3,879	726	1,419	43,945
1939	21,151	9,113	6,384				4,130	598	1,267	42,643
1940	20,820	8,634	4,161				3,587	1,038	1,238	39,478
1941	21,585	8,578	4,883				5,226	840	1,346	42,458
1942	21,863	8,608	7,216				6,007	1,016	2,294	47,004
1943	20,986	8,126	7,591				6,703	1,115	2,402	46,923
1944	21,878	8,378	7,129				6,897	1,226	2,172	52,305[5]
1945	21,569	8,638	6,799				7,177	1,041	2,073	53,532
1946	22,341	8,853	6,679				6,722	786	1,593	52,059
1947	23,484	8,087	5,774				7,177	674	1,586	51,670
1948	24,576	7,523	5,795				8,318	853	2,018	50,625
1949[4]	25,784	7,601	5,699				9,002	949	1,896	51,605
1950	25,010	7,622	5,225				8,586	902	1,918	49,705
1951	23,861	7,440	4,339				7,976	924	1,969	46,509
1952	23,176	7,021	4,553				8,763	1,039	2,524	47,076
1953	22,911	6,805	4,498				8,552	1,017	2,724	46,507
1954	22,119	6,830	4,031				7,965	1,023	2,281	44,249
1955	20,679	6,639	3,744	3,996	672	1,385	4,259	478	1,014	42,866
1956	20,297	5.427	3,793	3.797	496	1,129	3,929	445	1,120	40,433
1957	19,945	5 470	3,582	4.040	621	1.117	4,386	496	1,544	41,201
1958	19,251	5,354	3,352	3,608	682	1.101	4,393	547	1,035	39,323
1959	18,648	5,346	3,188	3,790	681	1,201	4,485	536	1,671	39,546
1960	18,033	5,234	2,995	3,812	660	1,344	4,148	704	1,742	38,672
1961	16,595	4,863	2,417	2,577	623	1,015	5,399	721	1,953	36,163
1962	15,532	4,744	2,123	2,391	580	912	5,396	641	1,740	34,059
1963	15,055	4,661	2,107	2,409	550	913	4,573	561	1,381	32,210
1964	14,152	4,269	1,823	2,850	550	954	4,687	651	1,711	31,647

1965	13,269	3,867	2,064	2,586	457	745	4,028	615	1,437	29,068
1966	12,547	3,488	1,949	2,422	456	768	3,886	674	1,505	27,695
1967	11,964	3,061	1,685	2,011	298	605	3,313	477	1,340	24,754
1968	11,418	2,819	1,483	1,828	297	575	2,947	518	1,239	23,124
1969	11,022	2,531	1,428	1,805	280	510	2,996	479	1,223	22,274
1970(6)	11,075		2,471	2,412		1,363	4,250		1,538	23,109
1971	11,431		3,264(7)	2,654		1,838(7)	4,530		1,836(7)	25,553
1972	10,908(8)		2,962	3,009		1,825	4,202		1,444	24,350
1973	11,292		3,322	3,092		1,932	4,635		1,531	25,804
1974	10,582		3,263	2,901		2,105	4,717		1,563	25,131

General Notes

(i) Sources. Agricultural Statistics; Ashby and Evans, 1944, Appendix A, Table 21.

(ii) Figures relate to June of each year.

Notes

1. Figures exclude the occupier, his wife, domestic servants and children still at school. But see note 6(c) below.

2. Up to, and including, 1954 'regular whole-time workers' includes 'part-time workers'.

3. Up to, and including, 1955 categories are 'males under 21' and 'males 21 and over'.

4. 'Revised and more comprehensive instructions on the labour section of the census returns, introduced for the first time at the September 1948 census, resulted in the return of additional workers. Figures ..... for subsequent censuses are not therefore comparable with those for censuses taken earlier'. Note to Table 156, 1945/9 statistics.

5. From 1944-50 separate figures are available for the number of prisoners of war and Land Army workers. Before 1944, these workers were included under other headings. The figures are:

	P.O.W.'s	Land Army
1944	2,198	2,427
1945	3 696	2,539
1946	3 657	1,428
1947	3,715	1,173
1948	531	1,011
1949	-	674
1950	-	442

6. 'The numbers of workers returned from June 1970 onwards are not comparable with those returned in previous years because of changes in the coverage of labour. These changes comprised

(a) extending the concept of farmwork to include managerial and secretarial work,

(b) defining "regular whole-time workers" as those engaged in work on the holding for 40 hours or more per week and "regular part-time" as those engaged for less than 40 hours per week, and

(c) requesting for the first time the separate return of farmers, partners and directors.' Note to Table 103, Agricultural Statistics, 1970-1.
The returns under (c) are as follows (they exclude the wives of farmers, partners and directors, even though the wives themselves may be partners and directors):

	Farmers, partners and directors		Salaried Managers
	Whole time	Part time	
1970	18,734	4,580	-
1971	22,565(7)	5,273(7)	-
1972	23,580	5,084	230
1973	23,363	4,920	252
1974	22,365	4,735	252

7. The increase in female workers (and in farmers, partners and directors) since June 1970 'is probably due to an under-statement of these categories in June 1970 when clerical workers and farmers etc. were included in the census for the first time.' Note to Table 105, Agricultural Statistics, 1970-1.

8. Most of fall was thought to be explained by the separate return of salaried managers, most of whom had previously been recorded as employees. Note to Table 91, Agricultural Statistics, 1972.

AGRICULTURE 10. Workers employed on agricultural holdings[1] by County, 1921 - 1974

Anglesey

	REGULAR WORKERS[2]						SEASONAL OR CASUAL			TOTAL
	Whole Time			Part Time						
	Males 20 & over[3]	Males under 20[3]	Females	Males 20 & over[3]	Males under 20[3]	Females	Males 20 & over[3]	Males under 20[3]	Females	
1921	1,771	634	490				704	186	142	3,927
1922	..	..	..				..	..	..	..
1923	1,630	600	422				572	181	113	3,518
1924	1,669	605	453				593	196	110	3,626
1925	1,697	625	460				587	125	151	3,645
1926	1,674	652	477				483	138	174	3,598
1927	1,710	621	551				455	145	170	3,652
1928	1,754	626	649				620	55	144	3,848
1929	1,736	588	580				591	46	124	3,665
1930	1,808	532	548				408	47	114	3,457
1931	1,788	552	571				397	52	99	3,459
1932	1,714	506	532				362	47	105	3,266
1933	1,699	425	376				376	39	79	2,994
1934	1,544	464	321				333	47	56	2,765
1935	1,504	485	272				335	41	68	2,705
1936	1,347	456	253				257	44	66	2,423
1937	1,325	377	261				248	44	70	2,325
1938	1,235	360	282				242	28	51	2,198
1939	1,111	427	240				280	30	50	2,138
1940	1,190	452	172				287	79	55	2,235
1941	1,320	431	191				421	61	74	2,498
1942	1,264	398	147				297	30	68	2,204
1943	1,205	382	261				460	59	100	2,467
1944	1,319	394	320				458	43	81[5]	2,883
1945	1,302	424	277				484	46	71	2,927
1946	1,311	476	281				437	55	66	2,857
1947	1,400	384	242				447	47	67	2,775
1948	1,429	353	246				469	49	63	2,706
1949[4]	1,505	362	252				532	44	81	2,827
1950	1,465	356	213				493	43	73	2,666
1951	1,324	320	167				465	56	71	2,403
1952	1,307	318	174				567	65	122	2,553
1953	1,276	367	171				484	53	87	2,438
1954	1,208	344	125				460	41	48	2,226
1955[1]	1,161	304	111	278	26	52	271	15	22	2,240
1956	1,100	249	118	252	18	33	243	21	12	2,046
1957	1,125	272	163	252	18	43	311	22	92[9]	2,298
1958	1,097	238	135	257	38	53	296	29	47	2,190
1959	1,060	244	127	265	34	57	284	26	60	2,157

1960	1,001	220	119	264	40	55	257	29	48	2,033
1961	877	226	93	159	22	39	388	35	89	1,928
1962	841	198	66	157	24	37	364	23	106	1,816
1963	803	180	70	173	25	37	277	32	31	1,128
1964	729	167	58	192	15	46	286	30	84	1,607
1965	619	161	67	177	15	21	205	24	110	1,399
1966	578	116	72	133	19	30	213	30	45	1,236
1967	547	114	57	111	11	18	164	11	38	1,071
1968	509	106	41	101	8	16	139	19	17	956
1969	475	97	54	82	7	16	145	20	25	921
1970 (6)	483		86	101		47	155		36	908
1971	504		108 (7)	103		65 (7)	207		49 (7)	1,036
1972	451 (8)		84	145		67	174		55	976
1973	477		98	157		94	180		53	1,059
1974										

General Notes

(i) Sources. Agricultural Statistics;Table 114-26.

(ii) Figures relate to June of each year.

Notes

1. - 8. As for Table 9.

The comparable county figures for notes 5 and 6 are:

	P.O.W.'s	Land Army
1944	121	147
1945	140	183
1946	115	116
1947	111	77
1948	11	86
1949		51
1950		23

	Farmers, partners and directors		Salaried managers
	Whole Time	Part Time	
1970	865	254	
1971	1,051	269	
1972	1,106	254	13
1973	1,051	245	29
1974			

9. No explanation suggested in source.

AGRICULTURE 10. Workers employed on agricultural holdings[1] by County, 1921 - 1974

Breconshire

	REGULAR WORKERS[2]						SEASONAL OR CASUAL			TOTAL
	Whole Time			Part Time						
	Males 20 & over[3]	Males under 20[3]	Females	Males 20 & over[3]	Males under 20[3]	Females	Males 20 & over[3]	Males under 20[3]	Females	
1921	1,584	660	763				388	101	150	3,646
1922	..	..	..				..	..	..	..
1923	1,377	599	645				284	103	111	3,119
1924	1,462	678	718				326	101	150	3,435
1925	1,449	638	680				334	76	153	3,330
1926	1,581	646	741				337	104	113	3,522
1927	1,622	678	760				274	82	144	3,560
1928	1,646	654	846				306	49	84	3,585
1929	1,655	649	801				315	50	97	3,567
1930	1,611	603	677				210	57	74	3,232
1931	1,660	629	782				230	33	97	3,431
1932	1,684	609	743				214	36	77	3,363
1933	1,626	535	653				230	40	76	3,160
1934	1,504	519	581				197	37	55	2,893
1935	1,468	510	562				241	40	59	2,880
1936	1,302	453	414				201	42	81	2,494
1937	1,293	480	381				197	37	85	2,473
1938	1,248	442	375				158	38	68	2,329
1939	1,158	441	345				203	31	55	2,233
1940	1,081	406	205				153	36	51	1,932
1941	1,089	384	210				213	36	43	1,975
1942	1,111	375	317				246	59	99	2,207
1943	996	346	328				285	46	115	2,116
1944	1,061	401	314				318	57	130[5]	2,415
1945	1,073	401	314				328	35	89	2,396
1946	1,108	434	325				277	34	70	2,389
1947	1,077	382	274				280	22	70	2,293
1948	1,101	350	252				308	32	53	2,130
1949[4]	1,189	379	290				327	25	56	2,275
1950	1,141	373	255				332	28	68	2,216
1951	1,143	338	188				334	39	72	2,114
1952	1,099	323	197				331	41	77	2,068
1953	1,087	305	205				352	44	62	2,055
1954	1,065	316	169				301	39	70	1,960
1955	1,030	308	170	156	28	43	163	20	28	1,946
1956	1,003	269	189	176	16	37	138	16	29	1,873
1957	998	249	139	159	26	43	157	15	50	1,836
1958	970	243	128	122	31	44	201	7	15	1,761
1959	926	255	129	156	41	50	147	15	44	1,763

1960	901	273	129	157	33	54	147	24	31	1,749
1961	828	236	101	107	26	36	208	38	36	1,616
1962	747	264	79	100	18	46	225	24	48	1,551
1963	730	239	71	94	13	31	189	21	64	1,452
1964	704	191	73	109	17	34	188	29	35	1,380
1965	667	208	89	92	15	27	230	30	18	1,376
1966	647	172	69	104	25	29	177	19	38	1,280
1967	547	126	59	77	13	27	134	16	52	1,121*
1968	566	128	47	94	14	27	121	7	51	1,055
1969	546	107	56	76	6	20	124	16	48	999
1970 (6)	500		96 (7)	102		51 (7)	207		49 (7)	1,005
1971	526		141	123		74	191		51	1,106
1972	546		143	143		81	199		21	1,133
1973	555		142	133		84	200		47	1,059
1974										

* Total given in source 1,121. In fact, total is 1,051. In source, total figure for male whole time regular workers is 743 instead of 673; this accounts for the difference in total.

General Notes

(i) Sources. Agricultural Statistics; Table 114-26.

(ii) Figures relate to June of each year.

Notes

1. - 8. As for Table 9.

The comparable county figures for notes 5 and 6 are:

	P.O.W.'s	Land Army
1944	60	74
1945	86	70
1946	102	39
1947	156	32
1948	16	18
1949		9
1950		19

	Farmers, partners and directors		Salaried managers
	Whole Time	Part Time	
1970	996	171	
1971	1,233	224	
1972	1,268	211	7
1973	1,051	245	29
1974			

AGRICULTURE 10. Workers employed on agricultural holdings[1] by County, 1921 - 1974

Caernarvonshire

	REGULAR WORKERS[2]						SEASONAL OR CASUAL			TOTAL
	Whole Time			Part Time						
	Males 20 & over[3]	Males under 20[3]	Females	Males 20 & over[3]	Males under 20[3]	Females	Males 20 & over[3]	Males under 20[3]	Females	
1921	2,281	910	594				689	210	179	4,863
1922	..	..	..				..	..	..	..
1923	2,002	715	523				540	151	157	4,088
1924	2,127	806	565				634	172	129	4,433
1925	2,058	723	422				635	113	151	4,102
1926	2,119	714	396				474	143	118	3,964
1927	2,158	733	394				425	145	161	4,016
1928	2,184	670	500				551	65	104	4,074
1929	2,218	651	495				578	66	92	4,100
1930	2,248	624	485				434	57	117	3,965
1931	2,334	618	476				387	54	111	2,980
1932	2,196	576	443				373	43	89	3,720
1933	2,159	579	447				365	43	97	3,690
1934	2,072	551	394				369	37	77	3,500
1935	2,010	559	383				354	66	86	3,458
1936	1,868	500	352				263	34	86	3,103
1937	1,825	439	264				236	38	57	2,859
1938	1,734	450	228				253	43	85	2,793
1939	1,667	487	282				273	30	69	2,808
1940	1,766	511	185				304	70	64	2,900
1941	1,810	531	263				435	77	75	3,191
1942	1,825	474	350				532	58	95	3,334
1943	1,777	478	405				541	56	117	3,374
1944	1,836	486	440				551	71	104[5]	3,777
1945	1,716	610	390				523	94	103	3,788
1946	1,697	576	382				498	53	92	3,653
1947	1,831	475	304				458	55	90	3,505
1948	1,848	452	342				526	56	83	3,380
1949[4]	1,886	484	331				556	65	108	3,459
1950	1,800	478	285				526	56	85	3,248
1951	1,740	451	250				550	73	125	3,189
1952	1,742	414	284				602	53	109	3,204
1953	1,739	396	280				607	44	114	3,180
1954	1,691	402	256				562	62	107	3,080
1955	1,504	420	214	321	41	72	277	12	33	2,894
1956	1,476	341	214	310	36	63	282	14	48	2,784
1957	1,456	345	207	292	37	77	288	17	50	2,769
1958	1,372	317	198	253	33	53	286	18	41	2,571
1959	1,311	316	192	265	35	74	276	36	32	2,537

1960	1,290	279	187	267	32	104	234	18	46	2,457
1961	1,157	257	127	181	34	47	328	36	39	2,206
1962	1,045	263	120	152	35	53	340	20	40	2,068
1963	997	255	125	157	31	38	272	13	32	1,920
1964	941	210	84	201	24	54	217	20	37	1,788
1965	857	177	90	159	23	38	207	17	40	1,608
1966	831	186	105	164	23	38	215	26	30	1,618
1967	779	153	90	138	16	29	139	8	31	1,383
1968	715	143	79	117	9	37	135	11	22	1,268
1969	702	142	63	111	18	19	141	16	17	1,229
1970(6)	649		107	165		79	197		26	1,223
1971	703		133(7)	159		90(7)	206		22(7)	1,313
1972	647(8)		120	189		99	179		26	1,260
1973	626		109	161		82	213		30	1,221
1974										

General Notes

(i) Sources. Agricultural Statistics; Table 114-26.

(ii) Figures relate to June of each year.

Notes

1. - 8. As for Table 9.

The comparable county figures for notes 5 and 6 are:

	P.O.W.'s	Land Army
1944	182	107
1945	242	110
1946	298	57
1947	240	52
1948	35	38
1949		29
1950		18

	Farmers, partners and directors		Salaried managers
	Whole Time	Part Time	
1970	1,127	340	
1971	1,299	384	
1972	1,358	368	14
1973	1,317	329	11
1974			

AGRICULTURE 10. Workers employed on agricultural holdings[1] by County, 1921 - 1974

Cardiganshire

	REGULAR WORKERS[2]						SEASONAL OR CASUAL			TOTAL
	Whole Time			Part Time						
	Males 20 & over[3]	Males under 20[3]	Females	Males 20 & over[3]	Males under 20[3]	Females	Males 20 & over[3]	Males under 20[3]	Females	
1921	2,340	1,126	1,418				766	143	325	6,118
1922	..	..	..				..	..	..	..
1923	2,111	1,044	1,208				523	163	244	5,293
1924	2,281	1,107	1,384				601	150	247	5,770
1925	2,095	1,023	1,034				520	114	228	5,014
1926	2,269	1,019	954				525	145	249	5,161
1927	2,414	1,027	1,366				478	135	284	5,704
1928	2,447	1,015	1,600				506	69	177	5,814
1929	2,431	1,049	1,604				478	71	178	5,811
1930	2,894	1,022	2,050				457	171	211	6,805
1931	2,525	1,010	1,540				423	57	171	5,726
1932	2,696	972	1,798				384	62	177	6,089
1933	2,304	975	1,281				358	63	192	5,173
1934	2,131	899	1,164				344	58	173	4,769
1935	2,078	863	1,155				338	75	164	4,673
1936	1,856	777	951				324	76	151	4,135
1937	1,943	769	907				292	56	112	4,079
1938	1,854	763	820				293	39	110	3,879
1939	1,738	795	814				326	41	116	3,830
1940	1,683	728	420				266	59	93	3,249
1941	1,821	742	553				346	46	112	3,620
1942	1,892	737	829				386	36	170	4,050
1943	1,814	653	739				443	43	145	3,837
1944	1,893	647	851				402	68	166[5]	4,301
1945	1,801	702	740				422	54	164	4,284
1946	1,820	719	807				394	34	113	4,080
1947	2,012	680	681				424	44	110	4,282
1948	2,060	602	658				424	49	117	3,990
1949[4]	2,141	615	673				495	60	140	4,163
1950	2,059	616	628				474	50	128	3,978
1951	1,959	656	568				555	57	156	3,951
1952	1,910	634	589				553	60	142	3,888
1953	1,921	594	555				535	60	148	3,813
1954	1,866	556	495				532	85	140	3,674
1955	1,775	555	452	286	54	95	253	29	45	3,544
1956	1,715	444	424	270	35	97	229	9	40	3,263
1957	1,704	441	442	294	43	100	209	16	32	3,281
1958	1,650	421	394	233	40	85	238	17	47	3,125
1959	1,552	385	350	273	34	65	222	22	29	2,932

1960	1,509	396	339	271	44	93	237	27	47	2,963
1961	1,399	387	284	213	52	70	319	33	61	2,818
1962	1,323	336	277	189	51	59	326	24	50	2,635
1963	1,297	361	272	192	43	58	285	21	41	2,570
1964	1,189	341	229	199	39	72	282	35	53	2,439
1965	1,150	291	266	191	26	42	243	20	30	2,259
1966	1,123	279	257	182	36	63	225	26	19	2,210
1967	1,079	256	207	155	30	44	186	16	32	2,005
1968	1,065	217	175	136	18	47	186	18	27	1,889
1969	1,034	210	171	144	28	42	180	15	25	1,849
1970(6)	963		270	216		95	261		45	1,850
1971	1,072		385(7)	223		146(7)	285		45(7)	2,156
1972	1,027(8)		356	212		148	292		47	2,082
1973	1,085		374	252		163	342		46	2,262
1974										

General Notes

(i) Sources. Agricultural Statistics; Table 114-26.

(ii) Figures relate to June of each year.

Notes

1\. - 8. As for Table 9.

The comparable county figures for notes 5 and 6 are:

	P.O.W.'s	Land Army
1944	185	89
1945	316	85
1946	165	28
1947	292	39
1948	34	46
1949		39
1950		23

	Farmers, partners and directors		Salaried managers
	Whole Time	Part Time	
1970	1,739	443	
1971	2,131	481	
1972	2,255	427	26
1973	2,204	447	25
1974			

AGRICULTURE 10. Workers employed on agricultural holdings[1] by County, 1921 - 1974

Carmarthenshire

	REGULAR WORKERS[2]						SEASONAL OR CASUAL			TOTAL
	Whole Time			Part Time						
	Males 20 & over[3]	Males under 20[3]	Females	Males 20 & over[3]	Males under 20[3]	Females	Males 20 & over[3]	Males under 20[3]	Females	
1921	2,805	1,464	2,059				925	289	387	7,929
1922	...	..	..				..	..	..	..
1923	2,581	1,334	1,722				685	195	343	6,860
1924	2,653	1,487	1,938				747	230	396	7,451
1925	2,546	1,487	1,661				716	172	419	7,001
1926	2,971	1,526	1,735				733	222	404	7,591
1927	2,966	1,508	2,230				646	230	479	8,059
1928	3,094	1,560	2,795				676	119	298	8,542
1929	3,112	1,619	2,765				687	123	259	8,565
1930	3,154	1,688	2,669				598	124	263	8,496
1931	3,247	1,684	2,619				528	134	306	8,518
1932	3,229	1,612	2,512				604	142	308	8,407
1933	2,658	1,361	1,873				552	131	314	6,889
1934	2,851	1,474	1,866				532	116	296	7,135
1935	2,877	1,360	1,943				571	131	288	7,170
1936	2,501	1,278	1,675				443	115	245	6,257
1937	2,511	1,222	1,586				462	100	226	6,107
1938	2,335	1,085	1,391				404	108	236	5,559
1939	2,129	1,214	1,316				407	59	220	5,345
1940	2,099	1,117	834				390	116	165	4,721
1941	2,234	1,167	967				529	85	188	5,170
1942	2,316	1,186	1,375				654	126	331	5,988
1943	2,251	1,100	1,267				768	118	346	5,850
1944	2,312	1,128	1,326				781	140	346[5]	6,397
1945	2,332	1,093	1,319				752	125	325	6,640
1946	2,406	1,098	1,286				683	120	218	6,226
1947	2,434	1,009	1,089				763	87	251	6,089
1948	2,540	903	1,069				817	81	289	5,863
1949[4]	2,677	940	1,081				934	101	288	6,071
1950	2,523	902	988				857	87	255	5,647
1951	2,461	926	838				883	122	323	5,553
1952	2,391	921	829				889	132	261	5,423
1953	2,345	897	836				896	120	288	5,382
1954	2,249	886	740				832	114	284	5,105
1955	2,132	904	721	406	84	193	412	62	104	5,018
1956	2,125	724	733	379	69	160	395	60	93	4,738
1957	2,127	744	659	432	77	148	378	57	78	4,700
1958	2,034	724	614	423	80	140	436	50	81	4,582
1959	1,986	737	596	400	71	152	494	58	92	4,586

1960	1,938	669	525	416	77	166	444	67	97	4,399
1961	1,801	632	433	297	90	153	528	70	101	4,105
1962	1,703	604	351	307	77	138	543	88	127	3,938
1963	1,604	600	371	283	77	115	492	82	89	3,713
1964	1,545	524	292	310	65	136	470	85	69	3,496
1965	1,459	472	361	274	47	103	451	70	66	3,303
1966	1,337	441	343	231	62	86	462	76	76	3,114
1967	1,267	356	276	209	25	69	401	77	94	2,774
1968	1,251	360	275	204	43	51	330	77	70	2,661
1969	1,224	309	259	194	24	47	367	63	72	2,559
1970(6)	1,385		530	279		179	492		91	2,956
1971	1,521		765(7)	340		242(7)	564		100(7)	3,532
1972	1,314(8)		616	374		259	589		89	3,241
1973	1,525		809	381		244	712		103	3,774
1974										

General Notes

(i) Sources. Agricultural Statistics; Table 114-26.

(ii) Figures relate to June of each year.

Notes

1. - 8. As for Table 9.

The comparable county figures for notes 5 and 6 are:

	P.O.W.'s	Land Army
1944	285	79
1945	585	109
1946	357	58
1947	387	69
1948	97	67
1949		50
1950		35

	Farmers, partners and directors		Salaried managers
	Whole Time	Part Time	
1970	2,682	601	
1971	3,403	715	
1972	3,693	729	25
1973	3,716	677	25
1974			

AGRICULTURE 1Q. Workers employed on agricultural holdings[1] by County, 1921 - 1974

Denbighshire

	REGULAR WORKERS[2]						SEASONAL OR CASUAL			TOTAL
	Whole Time			Part Time						
	Males 20 & over[3]	Males under 20[3]	Females	Males 20 & over[3]	Males under 20[3]	Females	Males 20 & over[3]	Males under 20[3]	Females	
1921	3,221	1,273	828				1,342	306	257	7,227
1922	..	..	..				..	..	..	..
1923	2,878	1,147	784				753	184	195	5,941
1924	3,017	1,211	859				902	302	274	6,565
1925	2,968	1,195	919				924	208	277	6,491
1926	3,078	1,227	881				787	231	250	6,454
1927	3,177	1,266	961				707	256	315	6,682
1928	3,165	1,183	1,191				918	124	159	6,740
1929	3,173	1,223	1,210				825	101	180	6,712
1930	3,208	1,084	1,049				573	112	209	6,235
1931	3,176	1,131	1,008				601	104	242	6,262
1932	3,070	1,166	1,044				586	96	199	6,161
1933	3,063	1,083	927				546	102	192	5,913
1934	2,848	1,012	807				499	80	177	5,423
1935	2,738	990	722				570	98	168	5,286
1936	2,614	957	590				464	87	191	4,903
1937	2,605	851	555				513	89	183	4,796
1938	2,478	847	522				436	62	192	4,537
1939	2,327	956	491				451	52	146	4,423
1940	2,302	902	314				384	109	192	4,203
1941	2,415	870	406				566	59	152	4,468
1942	2,387	887	586				690	99	231	4,880
1943	2,403	845	651				741	88	205	4,933
1944	2,399	842	590				696	110	171[5]	5,440
1945	2,362	926	589				716	95	163	5,549
1946	2,416	967	548				682	78	126	5,332
1947	2,673	913	513				687	53	127	5,531
1948	2,863	816	525				749	71	143	5,338
1949[4]	2,893	828	513				852	87	138	5,407
1950	2,815	826	458				867	88	136	5,230
1951	2,682	795	383				773	81	179	4,893
1952	2,620	755	418				811	96	163	4,863
1953	2,523	725	417				789	74	166	4,694
1954	2,393	760	348				695	91	192	4,479
1955	2,326	695	351	387	68	123	384	34	71	4,439
1956	2,250	574	348	379	37	131	297	34	51	4,101
1957	2,213	561	327	382	52	80	362	32	70	4,079
1958	2,096	558	296	371	71	90	379	54	56	3,971
1959	2,046	574	282	377	49	99	364	43	67	3,901

1960	1,975	601	263	391	66	105	337	44	[illegible]	3,8[illegible]
1961	1,802	524	248	245	59	70	468	63	73	3,552
1962	1,640	558	172	234	51	100	445	49	71	3,320
1963	1,567	534	215	237	56	72	399	48	62	3,190
1964	1,498	531	175	274	52	79	406	46	66	3,127
1965	1,390	468	164	241	38	72	277	52	67	2,769
1966	1,295	394	165	249	43	61	311	60	62	2,640
1967	1,239	349	149	174	33	56	274	44	45	2,363
1968	1,156	306	116	168	36	42	234	57	44	2,159
1969	1,093	267	89	179	31	40	228	37	32	1,996
1970(6)	1,150		170	247		101	345		66	2,079
1971	1,101		228(7)	274		150(7)	349		58(7)	2,160
1972	1,125		214	291		148	318		42	2,138
1973	1,094		228	319		163	389		46	2,239
1974										

General Notes

(i) Sources. Agricultural Statistics; Table 114-26.

(ii) Figures relate to June of each year.

Notes

1. - 8. As for Table 9.

The comparable county figures for notes 5 and 6 are:

	P.O.W.'s	Land Army
1944	249	383
1945	336	362
1946	277	238
1947	387	178
1948	69	102
1949		96
1950		40

	Farmers, partners and directors		Salaried managers
	Whole Time	Part Time	
1970	1,626	467	
1971	2,005	507	
1972	2,077	485	22
1973	2,107	459	22
1974			

AGRICULTURE 10 Workers employed on agricultural holdings[1] by County, 1921 - 1974

Flintshire

	REGULAR WORKERS[2]						SEASONAL OR CASUAL			TOTAL
	Whole Time			Part Time						
	Males 20 & over[3]	Males under 20[3]	Females	Males 20 & over[3]	Males under 20[3]	Females	Males 20 & over[3]	Males under 20[3]	Females	
1921	1,777	725	549				486	153	126	3,816
1922	..	..	..				..	..	..	..
1923	1,543	657	464				352	99	105	3,220
1924	1,653	663	411				376	194	91	3,388
1925	1,628	677	531				422	98	133	3,489
1926	1,800	649	426				344	111	125	3,455
1927	1,693	659	554				278	103	113	3,400
1928	1,723	690	553				322	42	104	3,434
1929	1,814	613	594				318	42	81	3,462
1930	1,754	636	517				284	65	82	3,338
1931	1,799	586	560				275	44	92	3,356
1932	1,700	657	508				277	58	77	3,277
1933	1,644	606	454				303	54	75	3,136
1934	1,631	538	423				251	44	72	2,959
1935	1,573	580	446				274	50	85	3,008
1936	1,616	540	357				232	39	79	2,863
1937	1,550	598	399				247	39	75	2,908
1938	1,670	538	421				223	58	76	2,986
1939	1,527	544	413				252	57	72	2,865
1940	1,432	470	352				203	52	90	2,599
1941	1,450	478	394				315	38	119	2,794
1942	1,458	506	487				382	73	178	3,084
1943	1,436	466	587				399	82	167	3,137
1944	1,512	531	360				395	72	143[5]	3,507
1945	1,528	546	383				455	65	151	3,706
1946	1,614	564	365				442	40	144	3,624
1947	1,666	541	368				446	36	150	3,638
1948	1,817	526	359				429	38	135	3,490
1949[4]	1,895	508	366				523	74	107	3,560
1950	1,913	525	369				527	52	93	3,541
1951	1,761	511	316				487	51	105	3,231
1952	1,666	476	369				514	48	101	3,174
1953	1,647	480	354				474	55	110	3,120
1954	1,616	491	306				423	68	105	3,009
1955	1,470	477	269	226	40	94	235	36	25	2,872
1956	1,415	393	264	202	31	77	197	29	19	2,627
1957	1,362	400	245	228	50	61	212	22	36	2,616
1958	1,336	384	265	221	45	102	225	31	19	2,628
1959	1,295	344	223	247	48	83	212	23	31	2,506

1960	1,261	365	206	219	39	92	210	34	34	2,460
1961	1,130	320	163	181	50	83	260	34	31	2,252
1962	1,033	324	156	144	37	63	269	41	32	2,099
1963	1,049	322	121	127	44	76	238	38	37	2,052
1964	953	313	133	157	37	88	204	78	42	2,005
1965	927	278	153	170	33	70	205	42	12	1,890
1966	876	256	110	144	38	69	209	41	21	1,764
1967	878	223	116	120	35	67	171	42	17	1,669
1968	808	215	114	111	25	70	155	29	21	1,548
1969	791	196	154	112	25	52	138	38	40	1,546
1970 (6)	847		178	143		114	252		20	1,554
1971	811		221 (7)	168		165 (7)	295		42 (7)	1,702
1972	667 (8)		257	296		131	255		34	1,640
1973	815		251	277		159	278		48	1,828
1974										

General Notes

(i) Sources. Agricultural Statistics; Table 114-26.

(ii) Figures relate to June of each year.

Notes

1. - 8. As for Table 9.

The comparable county figures for notes 5 and 6 are:

	P.O.W.'s	Land Army
1944	140	354
1945	226	352
1946	215	213
1947	233	198
1948	32	154
1949		87
1950		62

	Farmers, partners and directors		Salaried managers
	Whole Time	Part Time	
1970	1,100	286	
1971	1,244	325	
1972	1,265	301	10
1973	1,273	295	21
1974			

AGRICULTURE 10. Workers employed on agricultural holdings[1] by County, 1921 - 1974

Glamorgan

	REGULAR WORKERS[2]						SEASONAL OR CASUAL			TOTAL
	Whole Time			Part Time						
	Males 20 & over[3]	Males under 20[3]	Females	Males 20 & over[3]	Males under 20[3]	Females	Males 20 & over[3]	Males under 20[3]	Females	
1921	2,902	965	906				1,030	319	252	6,374
1922	..	..	..				..	..	..	..
1923	2,450	849	658				615	201	195	4,968
1924	2,713	976	809				711	223	198	5,630
1925	2,570	1,069	757				772	204	161	5,533
1926	2,767	1,181	820				582	291	199	5,840
1927	2,661	1,206	852				488	200	189	5,596
1928	2,539	1,218	978				620	167	145	5,667
1929	2,605	1,192	1,058				569	132	142	5,698
1930	2,690	1,189	876				603	151	191	5,698
1931	2,741	1,188	1,038				635	97	166	5,865
1932	2,596	1,180	928				744	115	178	5,741
1933	2,689	1,128	886				553	120	160	5,536
1934	2,441	1,041	753				514	102	138	4,989
1935	2,491	1,059	712				510	100	132	5,004
1936	2,410	993	547				389	75	128	4,542
1937	2,430	881	553				386	97	122	4,469
1938	2,322	831	476				430	96	119	4,274
1939	2,203	936	425				447	72	120	4,203
1940	2,239	925	317				340	142	143	4,106
1941	2,338	914	419				606	125	138	4,540
1942	2,410	937	705				675	148	285	5,160
1943	2,251	918	773				781	159	327	5,209
1944	2,349	988	714				960	212	284[5]	5,947
1945	2,367	991	618				1,032	150	229	5,914
1946	2,747	1,041	573				1,010	102	206	5,787
1947	2,493	1,006	471				1,163	87	170	5,754
1948	2,546	944	463				1,213	139	188	5,599
1949[4]	2,625	936	442				1,314	148	173	5,710
1950	2,604	921	391				1,283	140	170	5,548
1951	2,383	866	311				1,068	127	190	4,945
1952	2,333	721	334				1,091	165	196	4,840
1953	2,304	672	312				1,089	148	224	4,749
1954	2,177	666	277				1,114	164	217	4,615
1955	1,914	662	251	422	99	153	574	94	72	4,241
1956	1,833	536	272	443	98	96	515	110	81	3,984
1957	1,751	538	249	456	105	119	523	112	71	3,924
1958	1,697	543	224	409	113	88	497	97	65	3,733
1959	1,570	565	211	412	131	110	486	116	80	3,681

1960	1,552	559	215	380	106	141	514	151	94	3,712
1961	1,406	514	161	232	74	121	605	117	94	3,324
1962	1,326	478	128	202	78	59	684	126	106	3,187
1963	1,271	489	120	212	74	85	597	130	105	3,083
1964	1,219	446	104	297	87	91	634	139	86	3,103
1965	1,144	421	124	304	58	82	490	151	64	2,838
1966	1,078	372	124	245	61	94	517	143	107	2,741
1967	1,004	336	105	190	34	73	476	103	88	2,409
1968	947	312	102	193	35	69	436	96	94	2,284
1969	910	309	86	201	33	59	372	105	87	2,162
1970(6)	944		174	225		157	630		122	2,252
1971	917		207(7)	242		189(7)	583		129(7)	2,267
1972	885(8)		195	276		218	539		124	2,237
1973	851		222	289		235	565		132	2,294
1974										

General Notes

(i) Sources. Agricultural Statistics; Table 114-26.

(ii) Figures relate to June of each year.

Notes

1. - 8. As for Table 9.

The comparable county figures for notes 5 and 6 are:

	P.O.W.'s	Land Army
1944	53	387
1945	123	404
1946	191	190
1947	260	104
1948	29	77
1949		72
1950		39

	Farmers, partners and directors		Salaried managers
	Whole Time	Part Time	
1970	1,713	401	
1971	1,942	511	
1972	1,971	553	19
1973	1,907	633	22
1974			

AGRICULTURE 10. Workers employed on agricultural holdings[1] by County, 1921 - 1974

Merioneth

	REGULAR WORKERS[2]						SEASONAL OR CASUAL			TOTAL
	Whole Time			Part Time						
	Males 20 & over[3]	Males under 20[3]	Females	Males 20 & over[3]	Males under 20[3]	Females	Males 20 & over[3]	Males under 20[3]	Females	
1921	1,247	552	485				418	133	103	2,938
1922	..	..	..				..	..	..	..
1923	1,130	526	361				359	93	104	2,573
1924	1,255	543	409				363	111	96	2,777
1925	1,272	497	404				369	105	131	2,778
1926	1,345	517	392				307	120	119	2,800
1927	1,342	532	497				254	124	140	2,889
1928	1,346	484	574				361	54	85	2,904
1929	1,336	490	619				331	53	89	2,918
1930	1,419	463	509				259	54	113	2,817
1931	1,399	476	546				236	46	109	2,812
1932	1,348	449	496				240	41	104	2,678
1933	1,354	462	470				192	43	96	2,617
1934	1,273	412	465				187	40	67	2,444
1935	1,243	385	411				211	31	79	2,360
1936	1,134	331	353				145	51	73	2,087
1937	1,079	338	338				167	38	57	2,017
1938	1,027	346	307				171	35	73	1,959
1939	938	415	293				187	30	44	1,907
1940	948	402	166				163	44	57	1,780
1941	960	387	177				238	51	41	1,854
1942	935	380	218				310	45	68	1,956
1943	852	348	210				281	47	68	1,806
1944	923	318	295				292	37	77[5]	2,110
1945	833	403	284				269	47	59	2,093
1946	860	385	292				283	28	62	2,085
1947	930	313	243				278	29	67	2,044
1948	980	293	241				295	28	65	1,971
1949[4]	1,017	310	265				325	32	62	2,017
1950	989	305	237				291	38	53	1,915
1951	925	307	208				279	42	88	1,849
1952	917	293	209				319	28	56	1,822
1953	908	260	212				323	41	65	1,809
1954	907	247	174				293	41	90	1,752
1955	843	229	162	161	29	59	153	19	14	1,669
1956	836	187	165	147	11	38	156	10	17	1,567
1957	810	177	156	187	31	39	131	17	14	1,562
1958	751	169	133	147	25	34	138	10	22	1,429
1959	738	169	138	166	22	52	141	10	23	1,459

1960	691	130	118	157	16	39	148	12	15	1,346
1961	650	124	92	106	20	33	203	21	20	1,269
1962	586	136	72	84	24	45	215	25	21	1,208
1963	586	150	78	95	18	26	186	14	12	1,165
1964	526	129	67	119	21	26	173	16	17	1,094
1965	478	117	92	94	21	19	141	21	6	989
1966	445	107	82	105	11	26	139	14	6	935
1967	425	79	62	94	13	15	116	16	8	828
1968	415	75	49	73	14	15	105	15	12	773
1969	410	58	51	74	7	14	102	15	7	738
1970[6]	365		88	117		30	125		14	739
1971	390		102[7]	126		50[7]	128		26[7]	822
1972	367[8]		103	140		45	143		19	817
1973	406		116	151		60	139		15	887
1974										

General Notes

(i) Sources. Agricultural Statistics; Table 114-26.

(ii) Figures relate to June of each year.

Notes

1. - 8. As for Table 9.

The comparable county figures for notes 5 and 6 are:

	P.O.W.'s	Land Army
1944	143	25
1945	174	24
1946	151	24
1947	137	47
1948	22	47
1949		6
1950		2

	Farmers, partners and directors		Salaried managers
	Whole Time	Part Time	
1970	690	182	
1971	804	218	
1972	862	213	7
1973	873	182	4
1974			

AGRICULTURE 10. Workers employed on agricultural holdings[1] by County, 1921 - 1974

Monmouthshire

	REGULAR WORKERS[2]						SEASONAL OR CASUAL			TOTAL
	Whole Time			Part Time						
	Males 20 & over[3]	Males under 20[3]	Females	Males 20 & over[3]	Males under 20[3]	Females	Males 20 & over[3]	Males under 20[3]	Females	
1921	2,538	1,121	743				879	272	151	5,704
1922	..	..	..				..	..	..	..
1923	2,406	967	614				784	238	138	5,147
1924	2,345	1,047	669				743	237	174	5,215
1925	2,353	999	585				820	268	168	5,193
1926	2,446	1,030	628				693	211	132	5,140
1927	2,339	1,025	592				571	192	144	4,863
1928	2,413	1,061	678				637	115	110	5,014
1929	2,442	1,034	652				649	123	120	5,020
1930	2,236	963	564				525	97	125	4,600
1931	2,361	1,035	646				463	101	96	4,702
1932	2,268	1,019	625				497	99	102	4,610
1933	2,240	952	543				470	105	86	4,396
1934	2,135	924	471				468	104	82	4,184
1935	2,088	892	414				436	127	87	4,044
1936	1,995	866	327				408	62	115	3,773
1937	1,983	742	344				399	91	99	3,658
1938	1,815	725	272				289	47	87	3,235
1939	1,746	743	241				304	60	68	3,162
1940	1,678	690	234				292	89	87	3,070
1941	1,727	698	346				465	118	127	3,481
1942	1,683	664	638				623	137	225	3,970
1943	1,668	695	767				675	154	251	4,210
1944	1,675	734	405				733	154	233[5]	4,471
1945	1,680	740	370				790	130	210	4,610
1946	1,781	769	399				682	101	157	4,694
1947	1,883	697	375				816	103	160	4,768
1948	1,958	683	384				805	108	153	4,293
1949[4]	2,227	717	305				818	143	119	4,427
1950	2,171	761	274				870	120	116	4,392
1951	2,105	699	226				838	110	139	4,117
1952	1,985	620	248				955	121	168	4,097
1953	1,968	567	237				918	124	235	4,049
1954	1,859	550	252				861	116	173	3,811
1955	1,722	519	193	416	60	167	438	41	98	3,654
1956	1,686	399	206	355	45	153	456	33	115	3,448
1957	1,611	421	196	411	62	144	430	46	100	3,421
1958	1,600	400	208	349	59	149	412	63	137	3,377
1959	1,525	454	170	336	52	157	435	32	120	3,281

1960	1,421	433	143	348	60	153	381	92	94	3,125
1961	1,332	404	138	215	43	90	430	70	158	2,880
1962	1,249	381	117	223	49	91	415	52	141	2,718
1963	1,190	377	129	255	49	100	356	39	104	2,599
1964	1,102	346	142	236	65	103	316	42	141	2,493
1965	1,045	317	130	211	60	101	358	52	141	2,415
1966	977	303	142	214	43	77	329	81	148	2,314
1967	918	291	130	177	23	74	279	53	169	2,114
1968	919	261	105	159	22	78	249	58	134	1,985
1969	871	224	85	171	22	68	270	46	157	1,914
1970 (6)	891		159	221		169	394		166	2,000
1971	909		194 (7)	248		219 (7)	436		161 (7)	2,167
1972	906 (8)		167	274		225	353		161	2,086
1973	856		187	267		248	407		147	2,112
1974										

General Notes

(i) Sources. Agricultural Statistics; Table 114-26.

(ii) Figures relate to June of each year.

Notes

1. - 8. As for Table 9.

The comparable county figures for notes 5 and 6 are:

	P.O.W.'s	Land Army
1944	153	384
1945	290	400
1946	575	230
1947	545	189
1948	40	162
1949		98
1950		80

	Farmers, partners and directors		Salaried managers
	Whole Time	Part Time	
1970	1,504	399	
1971	1,754	491	
1972	1,815	497	25
1973	1,791	457	30
1974			

AGRICULTURE 10. Workers employed on agricultural holdings[1] by County, 1921 - 1974

Montgomeryshire

	REGULAR WORKERS[2]						SEASONAL OR CASUAL			TOTAL
	Whole Time			Part Time						
	Males 20 & over[3]	Males under 20[3]	Females	Males 20 & over[3]	Males under 20[3]	Females	Males 20 & over[3]	Males under 20[3]	Females	
1921	2,597	1,074	1,034				659	206	219	5,789
1922	..	..	..				..	..	..	..
1923	2,512	1,033	934				602	179	157	5,417
1924	2,544	1,111	808				717	198	138	5,516
1925	2,515	1,128	913				718	145	189	5,608
1926	2,549	1,157	877				612	164	156	5,515
1927	2,588	1,113	774				498	183	179	5,335
1928	2,617	1,088	768				617	85	96	5,271
1929	2,733	1,142	859				595	94	104	5,527
1930	2,718	1,065	751				471	83	109	5,197
1931	2,797	1,012	921				413	65	122	5,330
1932	2,686	1,007	921				385	86	116	5,201
1933	2,653	998	933				373	75	99	5,131
1934	2,377	907	714				410	52	114	4,574
1935	2,406	899	708				433	80	119	4,645
1936	2,271	855	664				379	95	118	4,382
1937	2,248	838	689				391	77	116	4,359
1938	2,084	786	568				330	73	120	3,961
1939	1,925	872	509				377	56	132	3,871
1940	1,842	842	304				319	90	85	3,482
1941	1,870	886	330				474	62	97	3,719
1942	1,969	893	553				552	80	185	4,232
1943	1,801	843	579				536	87	138	3,984
1944	1,915	803	530				529	71	142[5]	4,420
1945	1,921	728	499				574	61	155	4,464
1946	1,997	768	496				601	43	87	4,304
1947	2,105	657	408				622	42	104	4,272
1948	2,161	619	431				621	49	88	4,058
1949[4]	2,241	575	398				687	40	102	4,068
1950	2,165	606	386				666	47	95	3,978
1951	2,027	619	295				645	59	93	3,738
1952	1,974	623	321				688	54	125	3,785
1953	1,979	605	325				708	65	131	3,813
1954	1,924	635	306				691	62	111	3,729
1955	1,824	605	312	368	56	92	298	31	41	3,627
1956	1,847	494	327	342	28	72	316	14	39	3,479
1957	1,827	490	272	369	40	86	316	25	29	3,454
1958	1,773	497	274	331	52	103	328	24	30	3,412
1959	1,745	475	281	348	60	77	328	30	24	3,368

1960	1,672	514	271	370	53	103	290	26	22	3,321
1961	1,558	476	228	238	51	81	419	36	42	3,129
1962	1,474	443	208	242	44	53	456	36	50	3,006
1963	1,402	428	202	235	46	74	390	27	38	2,842
1964	1,356	379	166	297	43	55	358	25	37	2,716
1965	1,284	340	205	264	49	58	336	29	20	2,585
1966	1,221	306	177	239	30	70	318	53	25	2,439
1967	1,157	283	175	223	21	36	283	23	28	2,229
1968	1,099	238	140	179	33	42	256	17	25	2,029
1969	1,038	209	135	185	27	31	238	19	26	1,908
1970[6]	936		216	222		104	347		38	1,863
1971	1,002		263[7]	248		154[7]	380		37[7]	2,084
1972	1,056		265	259		141	334		44	2,099
1973	1,082		290	266		152	350		32	2,172
1974										

General Notes

(i) Sources. Agricultural Statistics; Table 114-26.

(ii) Figures relate to June of each year.

Notes

1. - 8. As for Table 9.

The comparable county figures for notes 5 and 6 are:

	P.O.W.'s	Land Army
1944	308	122
1945	399	127
1946	234	78
1947	271	63
1948	40	49
1949		25
1950		13

	Farmers, partners and directors		Salaried managers
	Whole Time	Part Time	
1970	1,933	441	
1971	2,290	504	
1972	2,335	442	13
1973	2,302	414	18
1974			

AGRICULTURE 10. **Workers employed on agricultural holdings[1] by County, 1921 - 1974**

Pembrokeshire

	REGULAR WORKERS[2]						SEASONAL OR CASUAL			TOTAL
	Whole Time			Part Time						
	Males 20 & over[3]	Males under 20[3]	Females	Males 20 & over[3]	Males under 20[3]	Females	Males 20 & over[3]	Males under 20[3]	Females	
1921	2,805	1,234	1,793				808	229	358	7,227
1922	..	..	..				..	..	..	..
1923	2,661	1,196	1,722				659	181	246	6,665
1924	2,694	1,220	1,752				718	206	283	6,873
1925	2,595	1,205	1,584				722	163	262	6,531
1926	2,850	1,227	1,764				627	159	275	6,902
1927	2,801	1,189	1,818				585	156	245	6,794
1928	2,748	1,173	1,897				663	102	176	6,759
1929	2,946	1,186	2,035				670	104	186	7,127
1930	2,957	1,198	1,848				585	114	247	6,949
1931	2,986	1,188	1,896				489	100	187	6,846
1932	2,730	1,151	1,829				493	85	224	6,512
1933	2,759	1,092	1,766				560	111	174	6,462
1934	2,520	1,029	1,409				704	115	165	5,942
1935	2,374	1,042	1,317				604	123	195	5,655
1936	2,190	976	1,094				422	83	175	4,940
1937	2,170	890	1,068				437	82	132	4,779
1938	1,968	843	951				492	81	167	4,502
1939	1,842	861	812				464	60	143	4,182
1940	1,791	792	531				353	110	132	3,709
1941	1,799	718	487				449	47	139	3,639
1942	1,866	777	791				463	80	293	4,270
1943	1,843	718	818				583	110	356	4,428
1944	1,957	761	794				573	126	234[5]	4,927
1945	1,923	740	829				609	88	291	5,390
1946	2,045	738	758				508	62	209	5,328
1947	2,166	712	654				574	50	178	5,043
1948	2,415	697	654				1,383	138	597	6,135
1949[4]	2,585	672	616				1,381	108	481	5.945
1950	2,491	681	588				1,144	124	588	5,701
1951	2,478	694	469				851	68	379	4,939
1952	2,365	658	473				1,175	144	953	5,768
1953	2,354	687	468				1,075	150	1,054	5,788
1954	2,331	710	463				919	105	695	5,223
1955	2,197	703	424	398	59	195	697	78	439	5,190
1956	2,222	598	428	358	42	123	596	87	553	5,007
1957	2,201	612	421	406	53	143	946	104	899	5,785
1958	2,112	637	378	339	55	136	809	134	456	5,054
1959	2,143	608	383	370	72	167	977	103	1,053	5,876

1960	2,045	565	381	415	59	186	825	164	1,139	5,779
1961	1,936	559	280	296	71	147	1,065	130	1,165	5,649
1962	1,873	561	300	252	57	112	931	108	923	5,117
1963	1,889	533	248	228	48	160	710	73	749	4,638
1964	1,746	492	222	315	56	123	990	82	1,033	5,059
1965	1,657	449	234	273	43	76	722	90	853	4,397
1966	1,547	404	222	292	31	82	610	85	908	4,181
1967	1,487	357	190	238	25	67	566	56	716	3,702
1968	1,427	350	179	191	30	49	469	98	696	3,489
1969	1,373	314	171	190	36	83	544	77	659	3,447
1970 (6)	1,476		306	264		178	680		828	3,732
1971	1,501		402 (7)	279		225 (7)	725		1,078 (7)	4,210
1972	1,450 (8)		333	275		198	655		745	3,656
1973	1,448		392	297		179	706		792	3,814
1974										

General Notes

(i) Sources. Agricultural Statistics; Table 114-26.

(ii) Figures relate to June of each year.

Notes

1. - 8. As for Table 9.

The comparable county figures for notes 5 and 6 are:

	P.O.W.'s	Land Army
1944	245	237
1945	638	272
1946	875	133
1947	601	108
1948	96	155
1949		102
1950		85

	Farmers, partners and directors		Salaried managers
	Whole Time	Part Time	
1970	1,863	420	
1971	2,327	457	
1972	2,435	418	38
1973	2,399	431	28
1974			

AGRICULTURE 10. Workers employed on agricultural holdings[1] by County, 1921 - 1974

Radnorshire

	REGULAR WORKERS[2]						SEASONAL OR CASUAL			TOTAL
	Whole Time			Part Time						
	Males 20 & over[3]	Males under 20[3]	Females	Males 20 & over[3]	Males under 20[3]	Females	Males 20 & over[3]	Males under 20[3]	Females	
1921	1,135	640	427				277	46	56	2,581
1922	..	..	..				..	..	..	..
1923	1,194	599	236				251	72	97	2,449
1924	1,178	612	198				293	54	76	2,411
1925	1,182	634	225				306	50	70	2,467
1926	1,240	607	224				246	65	40	2,422
1927	1,206	600	216				197	37	39	2,295
1928	1,205	584	237				216	33	34	2,309
1929	1,228	578	264				226	29	24	2,349
1930	1,182	572	278				152	28	54	2,266
1931	1,214	604	190				146	29	17	2,200
1932	1,150	534	244				128	11	28	2,095
1933	1,052	544	212				138	20	27	1,993
1934	1,012	504	227				156	27	23	1,949
1935	1,003	476	267				176	36	40	1,998
1936	954	463	236				147	26	35	1,861
1937	911	421	303				166	32	26	1,859
1938	884	416	222				158	18	35	1,733
1939	840	422	203				159	20	32	1,676
1940	769	397	127				133	42	24	1,492
1941	752	372	140				169	35	41	1,509
1942	747	394	220				197	45	66	1,669
1943	689	334	206				210	66	67	1,572
1944	727	345	190				209	65	61[5]	1,710
1945	731	334	187				223	51	63	1,771
1946	785	318	167				225	36	43	1,700
1947	814	318	152				219	19	42	1,676
1948	858	285	171				279	15	44	1,672
1949[4]	903	275	167				258	22	41	1,676
1950	874	272	153				256	29	58	1,645
1951	873	258	120				248	39	49	1,587
1952	867	265	108				268	32	51	1,591
1953	860	250	126				302	39	40	1,617
1954	833	267	120				282	35	49	1,586
1955	781	258	114	171	28	47	104	7	22	1,532
1956	789	219	105	184	30	49	109	8	23	1,516
1957	760	220	106	172	27	34	123	11	23	1,476
1958	763	223	105	153	40	24	150	13	19	1,490
1959	751	220	106	175	32	58	119	22	16	1,499

1960	777	210	99	157	35	53	124	16	22	1,493
1961	719	204	69	107	31	45	178	38	44	1,435
1962	692	198	77	105	35	56	183	25	25	1,396
1963	670	193	85	121	26	41	182	23	17	1,358
1964	644	200	78	144	29	47	163	24	11	1,340
1965	592	168	89	136	29	36	163	17	10	1,240
1966	592	152	81	120	34	43	161	20	20	1,223
1967	567	138	69	105	19	30	124	12	22	1,086
1968	541	108	61	102	10	32	132	16	26	1,028
1969	555	89	54	86	16	19	147	12	28	1,006
1970[6]	486		91	110		59	165		37	948
1971	474		115[7]	121		69[7]	181		38[7]	998
1972	467[8]		109	135		65	172		37	985
1973	472		142	142		69	154		40	981
1974										

General Notes

(i) Sources. Agricultural Statistics; Table 114-26.

(ii) Figures relate to June of each year.

Notes

1. - 8. As for Table 9.

The comparable county figures for notes 5 and 6 are:

	P.O.W.'s	Land Army
1944	74	39
1945	141	41
1946	102	24
1947	95	17
1948	10	10
1949		10
1950		3

	Farmers, partners and directors		Salaried managers
	Whole Time	Part Time	
1970	896	175	
1971	1,082	187	
1972	1,140	186	11
1973	1,155	157	9
1974			

AGRICULTURE 11. Prices. Wheat, barley and oats in selected markets 1794-1920; Meat prices at Bangor, 1828-1907; salt butter at Carmarthen, 1811-1913. Annual averages[1]

A. WHEAT, BARLEY AND OATS

Year	WHEAT			BARLEY			OATS		
	Carms.	Caerns.	Denbs.	Carms.	Caerns.	Denbs.	Carms.	Caerns.	Denbs.
	s. d.	s. d.	s. d.	s. d.	s. d.	s. d.	s. d.	s. d.	s. d.
1794(Sept)	6 1	6 2	6 10	3 6	3 11	4 7	1 9	2 1	2 4
1795(Aug)	11 2	13 0	14 5	7 2	6 11	8 9	-	3 1	4 4
1796(March)	10 6	11 3	13 0	4 4	5 1	5 0	2 3	2 9	3 7
1799(Sept)	9 7	16 1	10 1	4 10	5 3	6 2	6 0	2 5	3 5
1800(Aug)	17 11	15 11	17 7	10 1	10 3	11 1	4 4	4 6	7 5
1801(March)	16 10	17 2	19 5	12 11	11 8	13 8	4 7	5 11	7 1
1813	108 8	121 7	133 6	61 4	62 0	79 0	31 9	40 10	43 11
1814	82 0	93 5	92 10	46 1	49 1	52 9	18 2	29 4	30 9
1815	69 11	73 10	74 1	34 10	34 10	39 3	19 1	24 7	29 1
1816	55 10	67 0	59 5	24 7	27 5	30 0	13 9	20 6	19 2
1817	115 6	105 7	96 0	54 10	59 3	60 10	22 1	33 9	37 8
1818	104 10	89 4	81 2	57 0	48 7	52 2	21 2	34 4	30 0
1819	84 11	83 0	80 7	52 1	48 10	60 10	23 2	31 8	29 3
1820	68 6	74 4	65 11	39 6	38 4	41 1	18 4	25 9	24 8
1821	45 7	58 6	47 5	22 9	27 7	28 4	14 0	-	17 11
1822	50 11	61 6	46 5	22 2	27 9	27 8	11 11	-	17 9
1823	40 8	53 9	47 2	26 2	26 10	30 1	14 4	16 2	17 3
1824	52 4	66 2	64 1	-	39 5	41 1	17 4	22 10	23 6
1825	56 6	65 8	61 1	-	38 0	40 6	18 2	19 10	-
1826	57 6	67 8	57 11	32 6	36 8	39 10	18 7	20 6	-
1827	57 2	69 9	58 10	38 7	44 6	44 8	23 9	28 1	-
1828	48 4	53 8	50 7	31 10½	31 0½	34 10	15 6	18 4½	-
1829	60 0	69 6½	63 9	33 1	34 9	38 7	18 2½	20 8	20 9
1830	59 6	61 0	57 4½	32 5	32 11½	37 5	16 5	20 3½	23 8½
1831	60 11	67 10	62 10	34 4	36 7	39 0½	18 1	23 4½	24 1½
1832	50 1½	57 10½	53 1½	30 1	30 6	34 1	14 11	18 3½	16 10½
1833	44 2	55 8½	49 6½	23 7	26 2½	27 11½	12 1	14 4½	15 6
1834	43 3	49 2½	44 2½	21 6½	24 11½	22 7½	14 8	16 11	-
1835	43 7	48 1	42 6	28 4½	29 7½	30 1	16 9	18 10	-
1836	42 0	47 2½	39 9½	23 4	26 6	28 1	15 9	18 8½	-
1837	56 5	60 0	55 6½	29 8	34 7½	38 0	17 5	20 8½	21 11
1838	58 5	61 9	56 5	31 6	32 6	36 11	15 6	19 0½	21 6½
1839	72 6	68 2½	72 2½	38 5	42 0	41 7½	18 5½	23 11½	27 0½
1840	76 1	67 9	67 5½	42 3½	40 4½	42 2½	18 11	26 1	28 0½
1841	59 5½	62 9	59 9½	30 1	34 5½	32 4	16 7½	20 3	21 8½
1842	55 8	65 4½	58 8	32 11	33 7	33 7	14 8½	19 11½	20 6½
1843	46 6	51 10½	46 5½	23 8½	25 10	25 3½	12 1	15 4	17 1½
1844	48 2½	55 6	49 5½	29 0	28 10	29 4	15 8	16 3	18 1
1845	43 1	49 10	44 1½	30 4	30 7	32 7	17 5	19 4	20 9½
1846	47 5	58 4½	53 4	29 7½	32 5	27 8	17 3½	21 3	20 4½
1847	68 5½	-	68 6½	39 9½	-	45 7	22 8	-	-
1848	55 3	57 11	52 8	34 4½	32 8	33 0½	17 6	19 5	-
1849	44 2	5 2 6	46 8	-	29 3	28 5	15 9½	18 2	19 4
1850	37 0	40 6½	37 3½	24 2	20 8	21 10	14 4	15 4	-
1851	38 3	42 4	39 6½	22 11	25 4	24 1	15 6	17 1	-
1852	38 9½	40 2	36 7	28 2½	27 0	24 11	16 2	18 2	18 7
1853	44 5	48 0	46 4	29 0½	26 4	27 0½	16 6	16 8	19 11½
1854	66 6½	-	67 1½	40 3	-	41 1½	23 0	-	-
1855	61 6	-	65 0	-	-	34 8	23 5	-	29 7½
1856	70 0	74 4	68 6½	-	39 8	39 9	24 6	-	29 7½
1857	58 2	60 0	59 6½	38 11	38 0	40 1	22 1½	21 4	29 1½
1858	46 11½	56 8	46 11½	-	33 8	31 1	22 2	21 8	25 2
1859	39 5	-	38 8	28 2½	-	25 5	21 2½	-	22 6
1860	46 0	-	47 5	33 11½	-	31 2½	21 7	-	23 10½
1861	57 10½	-	52 7½	39 1	-	39 0	21 4½	23 9	27 6½
1862	48 11	-	56 3	34 2½	35 6	33 11½	20 1	22 3	22 8½
1863	48 6	-	41 8	32 9	-	33 6	18 10	21 9	-
1864	40 6	-	38 1	30 0	27 9½	29 2½	17 1	19 3	-
1865	39 9	39 8	43 2½	27 0	25 8	28 11	17 9	19 0	25 1
1866	48 0	48 3	50 7	33 3	32 9	36 4	21 0	25 2	27 2
1867	59 8	58 2	64 4	41 3	39 3	43 0	24 6	26 6	28 8
1868	65 9	71 6	75 0	40 11	38 6	45 0	24 9	27 4	30 4
1869	55 10	51 0¾	54 2	35 9	37 7½	47 10	22 6	25 3	32 2

1870	46 1	42 0	48 8	32 8	29 4	41 6	21 0	21 4	25 4
1871	53 2	-	-	34 0	-	-	23 6	-	-
1872	57 0	-	61 9	32 6	-	38 11	22 0	-	29 1
1873	59 0	-	-	36 4	-	-	20 8	-	-
1874	60 3	-	65 4	41 2	-	48 11	25 8	-	30 8
1875	45 6	-	48 4	39 0	-	44 2	25 6	-	30 8
1876	46 0	-	51 6	34 0	-	40 10	23 8	-	28 2
1877	53 0	-	56 0	35 C	-	41 6	24 2	-	30 4
1878	52 4	-	-	38 6	-	-	23 10	-	-
1879	-	-	-	-	-	-	-	-	-
1880	-	-	-	-	-	-	-	-	-
1881	44 0	-	-	-	-	-	19 2	-	-
1882	48 2	-	-	32 0	-	-	19 5	-	-
1883	-	-	-	-	-	-	-	-	-
1884	-	-	-	-	27 11	-	-	17 9½	-
1885	35 6	-	-	31 9	-	-	20 10½	-	-
1886	37 6	32 9	28 1	29 11	25 0	24 10	17 2	16 2	-
1887	37 6	-	28 0	22 3	24 0	24 1	16 11	14 9	-
1888	35 6	34 0	30 2	28 9	24 11	26 7	16 2	15 4	16 7
1889	37 6	-	29 4	24 0	23 10	24 11	18 1	15 8	18 5
1890	37 6	-	30 0	24 1	25 3	26 8	18 11	16 6	18 8
1891	37 6	-	34 4	-	26 9	26 1	-	18 7	20 6
1892	-	-	29 8	-	23 4	25 0	-	17 1	21 1
1893	-	-	25 7	-	22 8	22 0	15 1	15 8	21 3
1894	-	-	24 5	-	19 7	24 9	15 1	14 6	17 2
1895	38 7	-	23 7	25 6	17 4	20 1	16 0	12 8	16 1
1896	26 3	-	27 11	23 6	19 4	21 2	17 9	13 2	15 7
1897	38 7	-	29 7	27 5	20 0	23 10	16 8	14 4	19 9
1898	26 3	-	31 11	-	20 10	25 4	14 8	14 8	20 4
1899	34 11	-	25 9	-	19 11	25 9	18 4	14 1	-
1900	34 11	-	26 5	-	20 9	25 2	18 4	14 11	-
1901	-	-	26 11	-	20 11	25 8	-	15 10	21 6
1902	-	-	27 6	-	22 8	26 8	-	17 10	-
1903	-	-	-	-	22 2	24 4	-	15 1	19 1
1904	-	-	28 9	-	23 4	23 6	-	15 8	14 11
1905	-	-	29 1	-	22 5	23 2	-	16 2	-
1906	-	-	25 11	-	21 4	22 11	-	15 8	-
1907	-	-	30 11	-	23 5	24 9	-	16 10	21 7
1908	-	-	30 8	-	22 10	26 5	-	15 8	-
1909	-	-	31 3	-	23 0	26 11	-	16 4	24 7
1910	-	-	-	-	21 6	24 9	-	14 8	-
1911	-	-	30 0	-	24 6	28 3	-	16 11	-
1912	-	33 3	34 1	-	24 7	31 5	-	18 9	21 11
1913	-	-	32 4	-	26 4	27 2	-	18 2	20 5
1914	-	38 2	35 5	-	26 1	25 8	-	19 2	21 7
1915	-	49 9	52 10	-	34 6	35 10	-	27 5	30 1
1916	-	60 3	57 4	-	44 6	54 3	-	32 11	35 8
1917	-	70 0	72 3	-	56 0	59 9	-	39 1	46 9
1918	-	-	72 7	-	55 3	57 10	-	48 2	46 11
1919	-	70 11	71 7	-	71 2	70 9	-	48 2	48 9
1920	-	-	75 6	-	66 5	92 8	-	45 5	59 0

Agriculture 11. Prices.

B. MEAT AND SALT BUTTER

Year	MEAT (Bangor market)				SALT BUTTER (Carmarthen)		
	Beef		Mutton		Price/lb.		Index(2)
	Price/lb. d.	Index(2)	Price/lb. d.	Index(2)	s.	d.	
1811						11½	131
1828	5	100	5¼	91		8	91
1829	6	120	5¼	91		6¾	77
1830	-	-	-	-		6	69
1831	4¾	95	4¾	83		8¾	100
1832	5¼	105	5¾	100		8	91
1833	5½	110	6¼	109		7¼	83
1834	5¼	105	6½	113		7¼	83
1835	5	100	5¾	100		6¾	77
1836	5¼	105	6¼	109		7	80
1837	-	-	-	-		9½	109
1838	5¾	115	5¾	100		9¼	106
1839	5½	110	6¼	109		9¼	106
1840	5¼	105	6	104		10¼	117
1841	5	100	6	104		9¾	111
1842	5½	110	6¼	109		8¼	94
1843	4½	90	5¾	100		7¼	83
1844	4¼	85	5½	96		7	80
1845	4½	90	5¼	91		9	103
1846	-	-	-	-		8¾	100
1847	-	-	-	-		9½	109
1848	6½	130	6½	113		9¾	111
1849	5½	110	6½	113		7¾	89
1850	-	-	-	-		7½	86
1851	-	-	-	-		7¾	89
1852	-	-	-	-		8¼	94
1853	-	-	-	-		9	103
1854	-	-	-	-		10½	120
1855	6¼	125	6¾	117		10½	120
1856	6¼	125	6½	113		11½	131
1857	6	120	6¼	109		11½	131
1858	6½	130	6½	113		10¾	123
1859	6½	130	7¼	126		10¾	123
1860	7	140	7¼	126		11¾	134
1861	6¾	135	7¾	135		10¾	123
1862	7¼	145	8½	148		10½	120
1863	7	140	7¾	135		9½	109
1864	7	140	7¾	135		10¾	123
1865	7¼	145	8¾	152	1	0¾	140
1866	8	160	9¼	161	1	0¾	146
1867	8	160	9½	165		11½	131
1868	7	140	7¼	126		10¼	117
1869	7¾	155	8¼	143	1	2	160
1870	7¾	155	8½	148	-	-	-
1871	-	-	-	-	1	1½	154
1872	9¾	195	9	157	1	0½	143
1873	10¼	205	9½	165	1	1½	154
1874	-	-	-	-	1	2	160
1875	-	-	-	-	1	2¼	163
1876	-	-	-	-	1	2	160
1877	-	-	-	-	1	2½	166
1878	-	-	-	-	1	1	149
1879	-	-	-	-		11	126
1880	-	-	-	-	1	1¼	151
1881	-	-	-	-	1	1	149
1882	10¾	215	10¾	187	1	1¼	151
1883	9¾	195	10¾	187	1	1	149
1884	9	180	9½	165	1	0¾	146
1885	9¾	195	10½	183	1	0	137
1886	8¼	165	9¼	161		11	126
1887	7½	150	9¼	161		11	126
1888	7½	150	9¼	161		11¼	131
1889	8	160	9	157	1	0	137

1890	$8\frac{1}{4}$	165	$8\frac{3}{4}$	152		11	126
1891	$8\frac{1}{4}$	165	$8\frac{3}{4}$	152	1	0	137
1892	$7\frac{3}{4}$	155	9	157	1	$0\frac{3}{4}$	146
1893	$7\frac{3}{4}$	155	$8\frac{1}{2}$	148	1	$0\frac{1}{2}$	143
1894	$7\frac{1}{2}$	150	$8\frac{1}{4}$	143		11	126
1895	-	-	-	-		$10\frac{3}{4}$	123
1896	-	-	-	-		$10\frac{1}{2}$	120
1897	-	-	-	-		11	126
1898	-	-	-	-		$9\frac{3}{4}$	111
1899	$8\frac{3}{4}$	175	$8\frac{3}{4}$	152		$11\frac{1}{4}$	129
1900	8	160	$8\frac{3}{4}$	152	1	0	137
1901	-	-	-	-	1	$0\frac{1}{4}$	140
1902	$8\frac{1}{4}$	165	$8\frac{3}{4}$	152		$11\frac{1}{2}$	131
1903	$8\frac{1}{2}$	170	$8\frac{1}{2}$	148		$11\frac{1}{2}$	131
1904	8	160	$8\frac{1}{2}$	148	1	$0\frac{1}{4}$	140
1905	$7\frac{1}{2}$	150	$8\frac{1}{4}$	143		$11\frac{3}{4}$	134
1906	$7\frac{1}{2}$	150	$8\frac{1}{4}$	143	-	-	-
1907	$7\frac{3}{4}$	155	$8\frac{3}{4}$	152	-	-	-
1908	-	-	-	-	1	$0\frac{3}{4}$	146
1909	-	-	-	-	1	$0\frac{1}{2}$	143
1910	-	-	-	-	1	$0\frac{1}{2}$	143
1911	-	-	-	-	1	0	137
1912	-	-	-	-	1	$1\frac{1}{4}$	151
1913	-	-	-	-	1	$1\frac{1}{2}$	154

Agriculture 11. Prices. contd

General Notes

(i) Sources. 1794-1801 from D.J.V. Jones, Before Rebecca, pp. 180-19 which gives figures for all Welsh counties for these years drawn from Annuals of Agriculture, XXIII, XXV and XXVI: 1813- from David Howells 'Welsh Agriculture, 1815-1913', Ph.D. thesis. For years up to 1914 where two figures are given the second is calculated from Agricultural Statistics which is the source for all figures for 1915-20.

Notes

1. The prices are yearly averages except for wheat, barley and oats 1794-1801 which are for one month as indicated. They are for quarters except for 1794-1801 which are the prices for a Winchester bushel of 8 gallons.

2. The index is based on average of 1839-45 = 100

AGRICULTURE 12. Agricultural Machinery, Wales, 1942-72

	TRACTORS									
	Agri. types (1)	Market garden types (2)	TOTAL TRACTORS	PICK-UP BALERS	FARM-YARD MANURE SPREADERS	CHEMICAL FERTILISER DISTRIBUTORS	CORN DRILLS	MOWING MACHINES over 3' wide	COMBINED HARVESTER THRESHERS	MILKING MACHINES (3)
1937	..	..	1,932	..	..	..	..	..	..	..
1942	6,511	199	6,710	--	--	..	6,086	29,399	64	1,753
1944	..	..	11,305	..	..	..	..	27,488	..	2,616
1946	12,827	825	13,652	..	..	..	7,468	31,836	112	3,649
1948	17,528	1,424	18,952	70	..	..	7,771	32,161	118	4,441
1950	25,113	1,934	27,047	140	..	..	8,411	34,305	97	7,842
1952	28,132	2,108	30,240	580	..	..	8,817	35,422	200	9,652
1954 (4)	35,990	2,550	38,540	1,540	5,531	..	9,420	35,160	380	11,740
1956	39,440	2,470	41,900	3,960	8,820	..	9,260 (5)	30,910	900	35,810
1957	40,170	2,345	42,515	4,865	9,795	..	11,625	30,295	1,150	39,905
1958	42,175	2,165	44,800	6,130	10,380	..	11,810	30,000	1,375	40,215
1959	41,240	2,165	43,405	7,640	11,295	..	15,130	30,545	1,435	42,155
1960	41,265	2,055	43,320	8,465	12,035	..	11,505	28,295	1,395	43,885
1961	41,485	2,165	43,650	9,035	13,285	..	14,240	28,360	1,380	17,715
1962	41,940	1,910	43,850	10,210	14,110	..	8,520	27,960	1,610	17,920
1963	41,580	2,030	43,610	10,820	..	..	..	29,240	1,750	17,830
1964	44,520	1,960	46,480	..	..	..	..	..	..	..
1965	41,997	2,509	44,506	11,598	15,877	..	7,674	..	..	46,258
1966	42,000	2,320	44,320	..	..	..	..	27,940	..	43,500
1967	..	..	45,230	..	..	..	..	..	..	..
1968	38,170	7,740	45,910	11,050	15,060	14,170	8,300	..	2,770	44,420
1969	38,680	7,910	46,590	..	..	..	..	..	..	..
1970	38,540	1,760	45,700	11,469	..	..	..	25,790	2,864	19,700
1971	41,650	4,950	46,600	..	15,050	14,370	6,700	23,180	2,840	..
1972	43,150	3,920	47,070	10,740	..	..	..	..	2,490	..

Notes

1. 10 h.p. and over
2. under 10 h.p.
3. 1942 - 1954) "number of installations"
   1961 - 1963)
   1956 - 1960 "number of units"
   1965 - 1972 "number of teat-cup clusters"
4. Biennial censuses until 1954. From 1956 the statistics are based on sample censuses and therefore liable to a degree of sampling error.
5. The figures for 1957-62 are stated to include combined seed and fertilis drills. It is not clear if this was true after 1962.

General Notes

(i) Source. Digest of Welsh Statistics (for figures for 1942 and 1946 onwards); Agricultural Statistics (give figures for 1944)

(ii) The figures relate to January of each year except for 1942 where they relate to May.

AGRICULTURE 13. Number of Producers and Sales through marketing scheme. Wales, 1934-74

Year	Fresh for liquid Consumption	For Manufacture	Total	No. of Registered milk Producers (1)
	MILLION GALLONS			
1934	-	-	-	9,350 (2)
1938	52.27	29.83	82.10	18,130 (2)
1939	-	-	-	18,660 (2)
1945	105.09	20.01	125.10	27,109
1946	107.47	23.93	131.40	27,670
1947	116.95	17.60	134.55	28,131
1948	129.14	25.76	154.90	28,759
1949	137.30	26.81	164.11	29,252
1950	142.27	37.90	180.17	29,438
1951	143.09	28.29	171.38	28,530
1952	146.76	34.06	180.82	28,336
1953	143.52	50.93	194.45	28,054
1954	146.27	51.31	197.58	27,923
1955	145.22	47.75	192.97	27,503
1956	143.07	76.97	220.04	27,270
1957	141.55	92.48	234.03	26,606
1958	149.42	79.12	228.54	25,638
1959	146.49	70.03	216.52	25,065
1960	122.42	119.00	241.42	24,225
1961	125.98	128.77	254.75	23,538
1962	124.60	136.37	260.97	22,493
1963	132.70	117.45	250.15	21,689
1964	148.36	99.51	247.87	20,711
1965	128.67	129.64	258.31	19,808
1966	144.27	112.20	256.47	18,849
1967	134.07	132.51	266.58	18,201
1968	132.51	140.57	273.08	17,178
1969	127.96	147.15	275.11	16,447
1970	124.62	153.33	277.95	15,433
1971	103.85	177.64	281.49	14,616
1972	84.33	213.50	297.83	13,857
1973	78.35	218.30	296.65	13,172
1974	81.35	199.53	280.88	12,735

General Notes

(i) Sources. Digests of Welsh Statistics for 1938, 1945-74 (except number of producers); for 1934, M.M.B. The Work of the Milk Marketing Board, 1961; for 1939 and for producers for 1974, M.M.B., Dairy Facts and Figures, 1957 and 1974.

Notes

1. In December each year except for 1934 when the figures relate to September.

2. Figures for 1934 and 1939 exclude Monmouthshire.

AGRICULTURE 14. Fishing. Landings at Welsh ports.[1] Quantity and value, 1886-1974

Year	WET FISH		SHELLFISH		TOTAL VALUE Wet & Shell	Fishing vessels based in Wales[8]
	Amount	Value	Crabs, oysters lobsters, crawfish[2]	Others		
	cwt.	£	number	cwt.	£	
1886	17,958	15,390			17,476	
1887	22,799	27,725			29,602	
1888	194,752	185,779			187,413	
1889	304,756	300,611			303,202	
1890	520,196	485,249			492,282	
1891	440,221	416,938			425,428	
1892	422,749	399,985			407,004	
1893	350,885	316,506			327,918	
1894	334,570	322,536			335,372	
1895	295,603	298,805			310,973	
1896	347,606	350,792			373,692	
1897	400,515	364,315			374,612	
1898	513,773	463,480			475,462	
1899	501,306	433,479			443,738	
1900	448,994	431,216			439,905	
1901	541,627	458,288			467,754	
1902	593,650	516,294			525,858	
1903	588,481	495,087			503,323	
1904	658,091	476,403			479,119	
1905	641,617	502,429			506,315	
1906	722,096	585,849			594,730	
1907	871,241	632,927			640,337	
1908	902,679	626,474			635,804	
1909	917,072	640,932			647,533	
1910	909,373	698,013			703,161	
1911	969,081		776,734	16,867		
1912[3]	954,180		1,117,458	57,801		
1913	843,844		1,340,515	70,350		
1914[4]	768,969		805,051	53,805		
1915						
1916						
1917						
1918						
1919	519,755		1,583,969	67,214		
1920	1,047,589		1,256,624	66,694		
1921	831,309		912,150	61,202		
1922	1,014,533	1,373,166	82,016	51,283	1,387,154	
1923[5]	925,990	1,459,262	38,300	34,500	1,472,365	
1924[6]	1,062,753	1,533,092	22,100	61,102[5]	1,548,286	

Agriculture 14 Fishing contd.

1925	1,187,623	1,522,526	11,600		75,791	1,542,015	
1926	1,029,121	1,348,869	56,100		75,847	1,369,781	
1927	1,052,538	1,402,708	154,100		78,946	1,423,929	
1928	1,014,804	1,433,447	1,145,000		78,613	1,455,625	
1929	1,039,652	1,626,950	114,200		68,628	1,646,467	
1930	1,062,898	1,643,100	72,800		72,417	1,662,860	
1931	1,069,454	1,558,780	95,400		66,514	1,577,574	
1932	931,263	1,273,390	74,600		86,209	1,296,773	
1933	947,745	1,225,218	82,900		81,207	1,247,948	
1934	911,049	1,232,457	52,900		80,805	1,253,649	
1935	903,928	1,248,880	69,300		79,559	1,270,345	
1936	956,664	1,143,296	58,906		77,739	1,165,524	
1937	1,011,610	1,210,367	63,400		70,085	1,233,189	
1938	1,028,892	1,298,428	58,200		62,400	1,318,265	
1945	830,701	2,228,996 (7)	12,042		28,469	2,242,026	
1946	1,157,634	2,937,442	20,321		61,166	2,964,981	
1947	1,070,651	2,746,364	35,079		55,929	2,777,749	
1948	936,956	3,060,510	35,735		57,263	3,093,840	
1949	782,013	2,427,649	35,728		44,695	2,455,867	
1950	687,962	2,259,981	36,536		37,574	2,284,798	
1951	661,207	2,652,546	32,969		33,844	2,679,803	
1952	627,641	2,407,254	39,304		37,856	2,435,668	
1953	610,784	2,250,940	37,005		54,712	2,283,272	
				cwt			
1954	564,042	2,194,438		59,206		2,229,430	
1955	561,336	2,054,620		52,037		2,103,906	
1956	426,801	1,642,619		45,224		1,692,165	
1957	379,570	1,375,476		43,150		1,434,262	
1958	370,955	1,381,070		28,721		1,447,402	
1959	254,043	1,087,427		30,383		1,161,556	
1960	194,629	910,309		50,728		997,074	513
1961	195,127	886,323		48,319		967,689	524
1962	177,398	831,940		52,123		918,223	525
1963	197,890	842,448		45,164		939,449	483
1964	183,571	855,278		56,788		972,549	507
1965	185,712	869,587		74,936		1,012,227	527
1966	163,252	800,209		95,137		968,849	408
1967	145,226	761,046		173,607		987,760	310
1968	134,972	704,840		117,131		907,879	323
1969	111,489	672,157		125,754		940,839	346
1970	92,683	657,194		142,582		991,703	365
1971	95,837	746,938		99,907		1,084,433	378
1972	78,928	722,728		145,689		1,174,028	397
1973	75,316	893,753		114,638		1,421,540	413
1974	85,727	1,176,871		144,976		1,568,360	405

General Notes

(i) Sources. (for 1886-1902), Statistical tables and Memorandum Relating to the Sea Fisheries of the U.K. (published annually as a parliamentary paper); (for 1903-14), Ministry of Agriculture and Fisheries, Annual report of proceedings under Acts relating to Sea Fisheries (parliamentary papers); (for 1915-18), there are no separate figures for Wales given in the single report covering these years published in 1920; (for 1919-38) Min. of Agric. and Fisheries, Sea Fisheries Statistics (an annual non-parliamentary publication); (for 1945-73) Digest of Welsh Statistics.

(ii) The figures have perhaps a slightly specious air of accuracy since their nature and their scattered collection (making complete uniformity difficult) necessarily introducés sources of error. Except for the early years (until the early 1890s) the unreliability is probably not serious. For the early years there is a variation in the ports included (see notes 1-3 below) and, as the 1887 report observed, the figures were gaining in reliability as the collecting officers accumulated more experience 'but until the system of collection has been longer at work it would be premature to draw conclusions as to changes in the productiveness of the fisheries from year to year'.

Notes

1. The ports included are:

   in 1886, Mumbles, Tenby, St. Dogmaels, Caernarvon, Holyhead, Bangor and Rhyl;

   in 1887, Neyland (Milford) added;

   in 1888, Cardiff, Swansea, Llanelli added;

   in 1889, Milford appears separately, and New Quay (Cardigan), Aberaeron and Aberystwyth added;

   in 1890, Pwllheli, Borth, Aberdovey and Barmouth added, and landings at Llanfairfechan, Aber, Beaumaris and Menai are included with Bangor;

   in 1895, the collection of figures at St. Dogmaels was discontinued.

2. Crabs, lobsters and oysters until 1913. From 1914 crawfish transferred to this category from 'others', but only accounted for 392 fish in 1914. From 1945 oysters are excluded altogether.

3. Ferryside included from 1912 and accounts in 1912 for 41,160 cwts. of the shellfish figure.

4. Neyland and New Quay ommitted after 1914.

5. Newport was included for 1923 only and accounted for 5,146 cwts. of wet fish valued at £10,711.

6. From 1924 on Penclawdd, Laugharne and Portmadoc are included and in that year accounted for £5,647 of 'other shellfish' only.

7. From 1945 on this is wholesale value obtained at landing ports.

8. Figures include estimates for non-response. 1966 was a sample census and from 1966 on the figures exclude vessels not used for commercial fishing (there were 100 of these in 1966).

AGRICULTURE 15. Forestry. Woodland area, Wales, 1924 and 1938-75 (and figures for 'woods' for various dates, 1871-1905).

WOODS[1] ('000s of acres)

1871	1881	1888	1891	1895	1905
155	193	197	208	214	217

WOODLAND AREA[2] ('000s of acres)

Year	Total	Forestry Commission[5]	Privately Owned		
			Total	Productive[3]	Other[4]
1924	253	4	249	144	105
1938	315	65	250	175	75
1947[6]	346	94	252	138	114
1948	350	100	250	138	112
1949	359	110	249	138	111
1950	370	125	245	137	108
1951	380	138	242	137	105
1952	388	151	237	136	101
1953	399	167	232	136	96
1954	407	185	222	135	87
1955	414	198	216	134	82
1956	421	208	213	133	80
1957	428	218	210	133	77
1958	434	227	207	133	74
1959	439	238	201	126	75
1960	450	250	200	129	71
1961	458	260	198	132	66
1962	466	269	197	134	63
1963	472	277	195	136	59
1964	479	284	195	139	56
1965	487	292	195	141	54
1966	496	300	196	142	54
1967[6]	509	303	206	130[7]	76[8]
1 Oct 1967 – 31 Mar 1969	520	310	210	135	75
1970	527	314	213	138	75
1971	535	320	215	141	74
1972	542	324	218	144	74
1973	550	328	222	148	74
1974	556	331	225	151	74
1975	563	335	228	154	74

General Notes

(i) Sources. For Woods: Agricultural Returns (special surveys carried out 1871/2, 1880/81, 1888, 1891, 1895, 1905).

For Woodland Areas: Provided by Forestry Commission (for 1924); Welsh Digests (for 1938 onwards).

Notes

1. The surveys give an impression of increasing accuracy, but all need to be treated with caution as the following excerpts indicate.

> 'The acreage of woodland was ascertained by the officers of Inland Revenue. A column for this information could not have been usefully added to the form issued to Occupiers of Land, as Woods are not often held by farmers'. (1871 Report, p.7)

The 1871 figures were re-examined in 1872 for general accuracy, producing a slight increase (from 155,100 acres to 155,407 acres) (1872 Report, p.10). In 1873 it was stated that the area 'was not considered to vary sufficiently to require a new Return to be taken annually'. (1873 Report, p.8).

In 1888 it was stated that 'considerable difficulties are met with in obtaining the information ..... great pains have been taken in every district by the Officers to render the Return as complete and accurate as possible (1888 Report, p.11).

In 1891 it was said that previous figures were 'confessedly defective ...... Greater accuracy is believed to be secured in the new Returns obtained by direct personal application to the holders of wooded land, and in many instances corrected measurements are now obtainable from the Ordnance Survey maps .....' (1891 Report, p.viii). The 1895 repeats cautions about accuracy and belief that this had been improved. By 1905 it was thought that the figures were 'substantially accurate..... It is to be observed, however, that in some instances the inclusion of woodland areas, which were formerly overlooked, may tend to vitiate comparisons with previous figures for particular counties or districts, and may account to some extent for apparent increases in the areas returned'. (1905 Report, p.xiii).

2. For 1924-67 the year refers to year ending 30th September: for 1970 onwards it refers to the year ending 31st March.

The figures for 1938 for privately owned woodland were estimated, while those for 1948 to 1966 were calculated by adjusting the 1947-1949 census of woodlands results on the basis of records of planting, felling, etc. The figures for 1967 for privately owned woodland were based on estimates derived from a sample survey of private woodlands carried out in 1965 and not directly comparable with those for preceding years owing to changes in the area regarded as woodlands. The figures for subsequent years are again based on the 1965 survey figures and estimated planting, felling, deforestation, etc., since the survey was carried out.

3. Includes high forest, productive coppice, coppice with standards and utilisable scrub.

4. Includes amenity woods, scrub, devastated and felled woodland.

5. Productive forest only.

Notes contd

6. Slightly different figures are available for 1947 and 1968, obtained directly from the Forestry Commission:

Productive ('000s of acres)

	1947	1967
Forestry Commission	86	295
Private Woodlands	121	130
Total	207	425

Unproductive ('000s of acres)

Scrub, devasted or felled	111	76
Total	318	501

7. The apparent fall in the area of productive woodland between 1966 and 1967 results from the use of different definitions of productive woodland in the 1947-9 and the 1965 Censuses of Private Woodlands, and the figures are therefore not directly comparable.

8. The figures for 1966 and 1967 are not directly comparable owing to the use of different definitions of scrub and changes in the area recognised as unproductive woodland.

Chapter 5
Coal

In looking at the industries of Wales, it is natural to take agriculture first and equally natural then to turn immediately to coal. These two extractive industries have until very recent times dominated the economic development of Wales. In the pre-statistical era (which for Wales for most purposes means at least until 1800) it is tolerably certain that agriculture was overwhelmingly the major source of employment. With the onset of industrialisation, mining became increasingly important. Certainly, by the time that reasonably reliable figures on occupational distribution became available in 1851 (see above, Ch. 2. Labour, Table 1) agriculture and mining already dominated the occupational structure for men in Wales. And this dominance, although fluctuating in its degree, lasted essentially for a full century, despite the fact that the number of men occupied in agriculture was already declining in 1851 and the number occupied in mining began to fall after 1921.

In many respects, indeed, mining has been of more importance than agriculture. In particular, mining has played a central role in the changes which have occurred in the economy of Wales over the last century and a half. It was mining which was the main vehicle by which industrialism was introduced to Wales, and the rapid development of mining - especially of coal mining in South Wales - dictated the course of such crucial variables as the pattern of migration. Equally the decline of mining over the last half century has strongly coloured the economic experience of Wales. Much is rightly made of the impact upon economic, social and cultural values because of the absolute and relative decline in agriculture, but in modern times many more Welshmen have been much more dramatically affected by the eclipse of mining: in the 120 years after 1851 agriculture shed 90,000 men from its occupational work-force; in the 50 years after 1921 mining shed almost a quarter of a million.

There are no reasonably reliable figures for the numbers occupied in mining before the census of 1851. Similarly, basic output figures date from about the same time with the publication in 1854 of the first edition of Mineral Statistics compiled by Robert Hunt and published by the Geological Survey. Table 1 is based on Hunt's figures, either directly or as presented to the Royal Commission on Coal in 1871. The results must necessarily be treated with some caution because they were derived from voluntary returns from the collieries, and there is also some doubt as to whether they included coal used at the collieries themselves or provided (cheap or free) to mine-workers. However, a substantial number of colliery firms did take part and there is little doubt that the series faithfully reflects the general trends. Moreover, confidence in them is further increased because of their close agreement (where they overlap) with the figures later obtained through compulsory returns. These returns - obtained first through the Inspectors of Mines and later from the Department of Mines and the Ministry of Fuel and Power - form the basis of Table 2. Besides the overall output this table also gives information on the numbers employed and on output per head. This last statistic is, it should be noted, only a fairly crude indicator of productivity because it is based on annual averages which conceal many variations in the number working and in the regularity of employment; the material is not, however, available to compile a more reliable indicator based on output per man shift. For South Wales, the information in Table 2 is also (up to 1938) given on a county basis.

Table 3 is essentially a continuation of Table 2 for the period since 1945. It is presented as a separate table partly because the basis of some of the figures changes (output is of 'saleable' coal and there is a much more reliable indicator of productivity in the form of output per man-shift), and also partly because - perhaps surprisingly - the information available in recent years is often much less full than it was in the past. It is, for example, not possible to give information on a county basis after 1945 but, with the over-all decline in the size of the coal-mining industry, this break-down perhaps becomes less necessary.

One of the most important characteristics of the South Wales coalfield is that it contains virtually the full range of qualities of coal, from highly bituminous to almost pure anthracite. Most of these qualities are, of course, available in one or more of the other British coalfields but in the case of anthracite South Wales has long been the dominant source of supply. Table 4 attempts to indicate this and it can also be used as a measure of the increasing relative importance of anthracite production to the total production of South Wales. The more recent emergence of open-cast working is traced in Table 5 and, comparison with Table 3 makes it clear that this, often controversial, type of production has at times represented a significant proportion of the output of the coalfield.

For many purposes, it is helpful to see the trends in the Welsh coal industry in relation to those for the British coal industry as a whole. Table 6 does this for South Wales for the major variables of output and man-power. In the case of coal coke and patent fuel shipments the figure indicating the relative size of the South Wales trade is included in the tables (Tables 8 and 9) dealing with that topic.

The shipment of coal was, until recently, an especially important feature of the Welsh coal industry. Tables 7 to 10 record various aspects of trade from South Wales. In addition to the overall figures, the trade has been considered to be sufficiently central to the economy and development of the region to justify giving separate figures for the coal trade of each of the main ports. (Table 10)

The coal miners' craft is invariably dangerous: and in South Wales these dangers have tended to be especially marked. Table 11 gives some indication of both these aspects. Public imagination and concern is naturally most aroused by dramatic pit explosions, floodings etc., but most of the deaths recorded in the table resulted from isolated incidents, a roof fall or a waggon accident crushing out a life here and another there. South Wales miners were heavily at risk from each of these broad types of accident: the mines, especially those working steam coal, were fiery and the roofs and floors unstable. The table much under-estimates the danger as it does not give, because the information is only available for very recent years, any indication of the non-fatal accidents and of the illnesses attributable to such mining diseases as pneumoconiosis.

Some measure of the spread of mechanisation in coal-mining since 1900 is given in Tables 12 and 13. These should not, however, be taken as a general measure of innovation in the industry. Some important improvements, like the use of compressed air for underground haulage, largely preceded 1900, and the range of innovation was not limited to increased mechanisation. Innovation was one of the factors influencing, and influenced by, the trend of prices. (Table 14) Besides the pit-head price information is also given on the f.o.b. prices since, especially for the important steam-coal trade, a high proportion of Welsh coal was sold in this way (i.e. with the coal loaded in ships at the South Wales ports), whilst it was the f.o.b. price which, formally or informally, was the main determinant of colliery wage rates. Since the first world war it is possible to bring together the average costs and proceeds in the industry. (Table 15)

The last three tables in this section deal with a diversity of less central topics: the development of the Coal Owners' Association (Table 16); the earliest continuous, and reasonably reliable, output series for the parish of Aberdare, and the quantity of coal carried on the oldest and the most important of the railway lines primarily built to serve the coalfield (Table 17); and the output of coke (Table 18).

BOOKS AND THESES

T. Boyns — 'Labour Productivity in the British Coal Industry, 1874-1913', University of Wales Ph.D. Thesis, 1982

W.G. Dalziel — The Monmouthshire and South Wales Coal Owners' Association, Cardiff, 1895

F.A. Gibson — A Compilation of Statistics of the Coal Mining Industry

R. Meade — Coal and Iron Industries of the United Kingdom, 1882

J.H. Morris and L.J. Williams — The South Wales Coal Industry, 1841-1875, Cardiff, 1958

R.H. Walters — 'Economic and Business History of the South Wales Wales Steam Coal Industry, 1840-1914', Ph.D. thesis (Oxon.), 1975

C. Wilkins — The South Wales Coal Trade, Cardiff, 1888

ARTICLES

D.A. Thomas — 'The Growth and Direction of our Foreign Trade in Coal', J.R.S.S., vol. lxvi (1903)

GOVERNMENT AND OFFICIAL PUBLICATIONS

Royal Commission on Coal Supplies, P.P. 1871 XVIII (Cd. 435).

Hunt. Mineral Statistics.

Mines Inspectors' Reports.

Mines and Quarries General Reports.

Annual Reports of H.M. Chief Inspector of Mines.

Report of Select Committee on Coal, 1873 X (313)

Ministry of Fuel and Power, Statistical Digest, 1938-55 (published as sessional papers till 1947), continued as Min. of Power, Statistical Digest, 1956-67; Min. of Power, Digest of Energy Statistics, 1968-9; same title published by Min. of Technology, 1970, and Dept. of Trade and Industry, 1971; Dept. of Trade and Industry, Digest of U.K. Energy Statistics, 1972-3; and same title published by Dept. of Energy, 1974-5.

N.C.B. Annual Reports and Accounts.

Reports on Government Action in Wales and Monmouthshire

Select Comm. of House of Lords on the State of the Coal Trade, 1830 (9).

Royal Commission on Coal Industry, 1919 XI-XIII (Cd. 361)

Royal Commission on Coal Industry, 1926 XIV (Cd. 2600)

Royal Commission on Coal Supplies, 1905 XVI (Cd. 2363)

COAL 1. Output and number of collieries, North Wales and South Wales, 1854-78.

	North Wales				South Wales						
	Output	Number of Collieries			Output			Number of Collieries[9]			
	('000s of tons)	Anglesey	Denbs	Flints	('000s of tons)			Carms	Glam	Mon	Pemb
					S.Wales	Mon	Total				
1854	1,143[1]	5[3]	25	30	..	..	8,500	42	138	60	19
1855	1,125	5	29	31	..	..	8,550[8]	47	147	63	18
1856	1,047	5	34	42	5,400	..	8,919	57	165	65	17
1857	1,047	5	39	40	5,200	..	7,132	67	171	69	18
1858	1,023	5	38	38	5,700	..	7,495	87	175	73	17
1859	1,662	5	39	37	6,000[5]	..	9,600	87	181	74	20
1860	1,751	5	39	40	6,255	4,001	10,256	86	193	79	20
1861	1,870	5	35	38	6,691[6]	4,975	11,666	88	204	90	21
1862	1,660	5	31	41	6,749[6]	3,750	10,499	87	222	86	21
1863	1,728	5	35	41	6,917[6]	4,075	10,992	92	233	90	21
1864	1,987	5	35	41	6,948	4,029	10,977	80	233	85	20
1865	1,983	5	36	43	8,531[7]	4,125	12,656	80	222	83	20
1866	2,082	5	35	40	9,376	4,445	13,821	80	254	78	20
1867	2,371	4	34	37	9,092	4,570	13,662	78	252	73	19
1868	2,385	3[4]	29	34	8,960	4,251	13,211	67	214	92	17
1869	2,155	2	31	32	9,180	4,275	13,455	60	239	73	16
1870	2,329	2	23	28	9,300	4,364	13,664	65	247	75	16
1871	2,500	2	24	32	9,120	4,916	14,036	44	246	74	9
1872	2,600[2]	[2]	..	..	10,132	4,750	14,882	..	..	..	..
1873	2,450	3	50	62	9,842	4,500	14,342	65	347	119	11
1874	2,425	[2]	..	..	..	..	..	..	..	119	..
1875	..	..	..	..	..	..	..	..	..	..	..
1876	2,207	3	61	64	11,973	4,500	16,473	..	..	134	..
1877	2,480	2	59	51	12,634	4,351	16,985	44	268	116	10
1878	2,223	2	54	51	12,926	4,490	17,416	41	277	131	8

General Notes

(i) Sources. R.Hunt, Mineral Statistics, Report of R.C. on Coal, 1871, vol.iii; Mines Inspectors Reports, Thomas Evans's report for 1861 (for South Wales figures 1856-9); W.G. Dalziel, The Monmouthshire and South Wales Coalowners' Association, 1895, p.610 (for Mon. figure for 1872).

(ii) The output figures for South Wales and for Monmouthshire relate to the relevant inspection districts. Thus South Wales covers Pembrokeshire, Carmarthenshire and most of Glamorgan and Brecon; Monmouthshire relates, in addition to that county to parts of Glamorgan (the western side of the Rhymney valley) and Brecon.

Notes

1. This is figure given by Hunt. The Royal Commission of 1871 gives 1,430, but this seems likely to be a copying error.

2. R. Meade, Coal and Iron Industries of the United Kingdom, gives this as an estimated figure for North Wales. The only figure in Hunt for 1872 is of 9 m.tons for North Wales and West Lancashire together. There are no separate figures for the number of collieries in North Wales for 1872 and 1874.

3. Hunt gives 61 collieries and 200 pits in the three counties.

4. Hunt only gives the total for 1868 of 66 collieries.

5. The South Wales figures for the 1850s are taken from the Mines Inspectors' Reports, and the same figures are given in the Report of the Select Committee on Coal, 1873, Appendix 3. The size of possible differences in these early years is, however, indicated from Hunt which gives figures for 1859 as 5,050,350 tons for the South Wales inspection district (made up of 800,000 tons of anthracite and 4,250,000 tons of bituminous). Just below this Hunt himself gives yet another figure of 4,750,350 for the South Wales inspection district. It is this reduced figure which he used to get the total for South Wales and Mon. which is given here and was taken by the 1871 Commission (Appendix 62). Presumably Hunt either shifted the missing 300,000 tons to the Monmouthshire district or the total is that much too low. In any event Hunt arrives at 9,600 by an error in addition - the figures given actually add up to 9,700.

6. The table follows the 1871 report which reduced, without explanation, the figures given for these years for the South Wales inspection district as respectively 6.8, 6.9 and 7.2 m.tons.

7. The 1871 Commission gives 7,911 but this is the figure given by Hunt excluding anthracite.

8. The 1871 Commission gives 8,552.

9. The number of collieries for 1854-69 is taken from the 1871 Commission, which bases itself on Hunt's Mineral Statistics. There are departures from Hunt, as follows:

1854 Hunt gives no figures for collieries in the statistics for this year.

1855 Hunt gives 117 collieries for Glamorgan.

1859 Hunt gives Glam, 181: Mon and edge of Glam, 100. The 1871 report seems to have taken collieries in edge of Glam. (Rhymney valley) out of Mon figures but not added them to Glam figure.

1860 Hunt gives Glam, 186; Mon, 79; Eastern edge of Glam, 7. The 7 have been added to figure for Glam.

1864 Hunt gives Glam, 216; Mon and edge of Glam, 102. 17 have been added to Glam, and taken from Mon.

1865 Hunt gives Glam, 222; Mon, 194. 21 seem to have been removed from Mon but not added to Glam.

1866 Hunt gives Glam, 232; Mon, 100. 22 been added to Glam and taken from Mon.

1867 Hunt gives Glam, 232; Mon, 92. Seem to have added 20 to Glam figure and taken 19 from Mon.

In 1872 Hunt only gives a total for South Wales inspection district (284), and a further total for Mon etc including Gloucester & Somerset (215).

COAL 2. Output, numbers employed and output per head, by region and county, 1874 - 1945

NORTH WALES

Year	Output (000s tons)	Number Employed: Under Ground	Number Employed: Above Ground	Number Employed: Total Under and Above Ground	Output per Head: Under Ground	Output per Head: Total Under and Above Ground
					Tons	Tons
1874	2,429	11,087	3,049	14,136	219	171
1875	2,349	10,700	2,898	13,598	219	172
1876	2,418	9,431	2,550	11,981	256	201
1877	2,474	8,316	2,480	10,796	297	229
1878	2,224	7,640	2,004	9,644	291	230
1879	2,227	8,110	2,032	10,142	273	219
1880	2,429	8,322	1,886	10,208	291	231
1881	2,671	8,251	1,925	10,176	323	262
1882	2,421	8,332	1,766	10,098	290	239
1883	2,751	8,289	1,806	10,095	331	272
1884	2,600	8,425	1,750	10,175	308	255
1885	2,312	7,691	1,623	9,314	300	248
1886	2,557	7,692	1,613	9,305	332	274
1887	2,712	8,114	1,666	9,780	334	277
1888	2,741	8,403	1,748	10,151	326	269
1889	2,895	8,939	1,820	10,759	323	269
1890	2,976	10,142	2,132	12,274	293	242
1891	3,152	10,634	2,155	12,789	296	246
1892	2,960	10,568	2,160	12,728	280	232
1893	2,206	10,368	2,281	12,649	212	174
1894	3,151	..(1)	..	..	..	..
1895	2,848	..	..	..	..	..
1896	2,893	9,488	2,048	11,536	304	250
1897	2,925	9,595	2,069	11,664	304	250
1898	3,199	9,470	2,063	11,533	337	277
1899	3,195	9,804	2,204	12,008	325	266
1900	3,110	10,295	2,334	12,629	302	246
1901	3,076	10,899	2,478	13,377	282	229
1902	3,173	10,871	2,471	13,342	291	237
1903	3,184	10,876	2,372	13,248	292	240
1904	2,993	10,624	2,325	12,949	281	231
1905	2,902	10,398	2,345	12,743	279	227
1906	3,170	10,593	2,377	12,970	299	244
1907	3,470	11,759	2,611	14,370	295	241
1908	3,366	12,204	2,659	14,863	275	226
1909	3,281	12,119	2,789	14,908	270	220
1910	3,411	12,424	2,747	15,171	274	224
1911	3,443	12,688	2,736	15,424	271	223
1912	3,251	12,884	2,815	15,699	252	207
1913	3,506	13,073	2,875	15,948	268	219
1914	3,315	13,270	2,987	16,257	249	203
1915	3,241	..	..	..	..	..
1916	3,179	..	..	..	..	..
1917	3,147	..	..	..	..	..
1918	2,809	..	..	..	..	..
1919	2,780	..	..	..	..	..
1920	2,670	15,339	3,734	19,073	174	140
1921	1,817	13,427	3,322	16,749	135	108
1922	2,763	13,689	3,405	17,094	202	162
1923	3,380	14,767	3,531	18,298	229	185
1924	3,446	15,404	3,785	19,189	224	179
1925	3,099	14,210	3,401	17,611	218	176
1926	1,761	14,397	3,432	17,829	..	..
1927	3,446	12,405	3,270	15,675	278	220
1928	3,328	11,814	3,036	14,850	282	224
1929	3,456	12,338	2,988	15,326	280	225
1930	3,295	11,537	2,934	14,471	286	228
1931	3,117	11,039	2,804	13,843	282	225
1932	2,902	10,471	2,653	13,124	277	221
1933	2,853	9,112	2,432	11,544	313	247
1934	2,786	8,213	2,407	10,620	339	262
1935	2,487	6.680	2,120	8,800	372	283
1936	2,839	7,549	2,273	9,822	376	289
1937	2,772	7,740	2,344	10,084	358	275
1938(2)	2,712)	7,618	2,340	9,958)	356	272
	2,712)			9,744)		
1939	2,666	..	..	9,347	..	..
1940	2,408	..	..	8,694	..	..
1941	2,126	..	..	8,122	..	..
1942	2,096	..	..	8,423	..	..
1943	1,986	..	..	8,487	..	..
1944	1,974	..	..	8,760	..	..
1945	1,902	..	..	8,842	..	..

COAL 2. Output, numbers employed and output per head, by region and county, 1874 - 1945

SOUTH WALES

Year	Output (000s tons)	Number Employed: Under Ground	Number Employed: Above Ground	Number Employed: Total Under and Above Ground	Output per Head: Under Ground	Output per Head: Total Under and Above Ground
					Tons	Tons
1874	16,491	59,463	13,865	73,328	277	224
1875	14,173	60,750	11,893	72,643	233	195
1876	16,972	56,647	10,836	67,483	299	251
1877	16,911	55,126	10,180	65,306	306	258
1878	17,417	54,146	9,590	63,736	321	273
1879	17,819	56,308	10,187	66,495	316	267
1880	21,166	58,238	10,920	69,158	363	306
1881	22,234	61,546	11,346	72,892	361	305
1882	22,817	63,631	11,323	74,954	358	304
1883	24,975	68,622	12,075	80,697	363	309
1884	25,552	71,402	12,492	83,894	357	304
1885	24,343	73,050	12,167	85,217	333	285
1886	24,204	73,090	12,040	85,130	331	284
1887	26,046	74,381	12,534	86,915	350	299
1888	27,355	78,213	13,210	91,423	349	299
1889	28,064	84,928	14,498	99,426	330	282
1890	29,415	94,071	15,864	109,935	312	267
1891	29,993	100,148	16,476	116,624	299	257
1892	31,207	101,118	16,595	117,713	308	265
1893	30,155	99,897	18,092	117,989	301	255
1894	33,418	106,240	18,415	124,655	314	268
1895	33,040	107,554	18,645	126,199	307	261
1896	33,868	106,766	18,439	125,205	317	270
1897	35,806	107,929	18,873	126,802	331	282
1898	26,724	109,088	19,725	128,813	245	207
1899	39,870	111,981	20,701	132,682	356	300
1900	39,328	124,441	23,211	147,652	316	266
1901	39,209	127,339	23,073	150,412	307	260
1902	41,306	131,062	23,509	154,571	315	267
1903	42,154	135,317	23,844	159,161	311	264
1904	43,730	138,624	24,410	163,034	315	268
1905	43,203	140,860	24,749	165,609	306	260
1906	47,056	148,433	26,227	174,660	317	269
1907	49,978	161,576	28,687	190,263	309	262
1908	50,227	171,318	30,434	201,752	293	248
1909	50,364	174,262	30,722	204,984	289	245
1910	48,700	181,261	31,991	213,252	268	228
1911	50,201	188,349	32,538	220,887	266	227
1912 (3)	50,116	191,581	33,954	225,535	261	222
1913	56,830	198,123	35,011	233,134	286	243
1914	53,880	199,324	34,793	234,117	270	230
1915	50,453	169,779	32,876	202,655	297	248
1916	52,081	179,245	34,855	214,100	290	243
1917	48,508	184,633	35,085	219,718	262	220
1918	46,717	182,912	35,941	218,852	255	213
1919	47,522	216,113	41,500	257,613	219	184
1920	46,249	226,214	45,302	271,516	204	170
1921	30,572	194,924	37,291	232,215	157	132
1922	50,325	204,754	38,549	243,303	246	207
1923	54,252	212,824	40,085	252,909	255	214
1924	51,085	209,480	40,891	250,371	244	204
1925	44,630	177,151	34,103	211,254	252	211
1926	20,273	183,150	34,839	217,989	..	..
1927	46,256	162,693	31,567	194,260	284	238
1928	43,312	141,246	27,219	168,465	307	257
1929	48,141	150,975	27,555	178,530	319	270
1930	45,108	145,723	27,268	172,991	310	261
1931	37,085	132,823	25,448	158,271	279	234
1932	34,874	121,711	24,099	145,810	286	239
1933	34,355	119,115	23,899	143,014	288	240
1934	35,173	116,611	23,324	139,935	302	251
1935	35,025	109,687	22,168	131,855	319	266
1936	33,886	104,595	21,817	126,412	324	268
1937	37,773	113,210	22,878	136,088	334	277
1938 (2)	38,185	112,800	23,316	136,116	..	..
	35,293	..	..	134,824	..	..
1939	35,269	..	..	128,774	..	..
1940	32,352	..	..	128,470	..	..
1941	27,426	..	..	111,649	..	..
1942	26,723	..	..	114,181	..	..
1943	25,116	..	..	114,274	..	..
1944	22,393	..	..	112,344	..	..
1945	20,470	..	..	110,057	..	..

COAL 2. Output, numbers employed and output per head, by region and county, 1874 - 1945

BRECKNOCK

Year	Output (000s tons)	Number Employed: Under Ground	Number Employed: Above Ground	Number Employed: Total Under and Above Ground	Output per Head: Under Ground	Output per Head: Total Under and Above Ground
					Tons	Tons
1874	..	..	..	..	..	..
1875	..	..	..	..	..	..
1876	130	1,108	188	1,296	117	100
1877	114	510	79	589	222	192
1878	121	395	63	458	305	263
1879	84	438	65	503	190	166
1880	101	438	96	534	229	188
1881	103	423	86	509	242	201
1882	144	504	98	602	295	238
1883	164	604	116	720	272	228
1884	160	551	92	643	290	249
1885	105	487	78	565	215	186
1886	159	600	98	698	264	227
1887	188	699	105	804	268	233
1888	207	795	142	937	260	220
1889	234	895	127	1,022	261	228
1890	259	1,006	146	1,152	257	225
1891	272	979	163	1,142	277	237
1892	214	735	150	885	290	241
1893	194	783	160	943	248	205
1894	241	868	153	1,021	277	235
1895	266	923	185	1,108	288	240
1896	273	1,073	177	1,250	254	218
1897	299	977	157	1,134	305	263
1898	317	1,116	198	1,316	283	240
1899	383	1,222	222	1,444	313	265
1900	441	1,414	239	1,653	311	266
1901	442	1,380	269	1,649	320	268
1902	432	1,542	284	1,826	280	236
1903	414	1,536	306	1,842	269	224
1904	430	1,495	289	1,784	287	241
1905	455	1,573	310	1,883	291	241
1906	531	1,759	362	2,121	301	250
1907	623	2,185	416	2,601	285	239
1908	664	2,341	464	2,805	283	236
1909	698	2,543	482	3,025	274	230
1910	739	2,941	585	3,526	251	209
1911	776	2,945	618	3,563	263	217
1912	736	2,942	607	3,549	250	207
1913	778	3,053	658	3,711	254	209
1914	651	2,710	598	3,308	240	196
1915	655	..	..	..	..	..
1916	580	..	..	..	..	..
1917	385	..	..	..	..	..
1918	415	..	..	..	..	..
1919	481	..	..	..	..	..
1920	502	2,228	566	2,794	225	179
1921	429	2,377	543	2,920	180	147
1922	562	2,394	590	2,984	235	188
1923	586	2,472	603	3,075	237	191
1924	638	2,546	626	3,172	251	201
1925	574	2,670	676	3,346	215	171
1926	259	2,662	681	3,343	..	..
1927	552	2,486	630	3,116	222	177
1928	535	2,038	577	2,615	263	205
1929	711	2,328	617	2,945	305	241
1930	689	2,361	588	2,949	292	234
1931	624	2,338	588	2,926	267	213
1932	658	2,312	560	2,872	285	229
1933	659	2,463	614	3,077	268	214
1934	624	2,376	558	2,934	262	213
1935	527	1,860	493	2,353	283	224
1936	511	1,701	472	2,173	300	235
1937	517	1,781	485	2,266	290	228
1938	465	1,672	453	2,125	278	219

COAL 2. Output, numbers employed and output per head, by region and county, 1874 - 1945

CARMARTHENSHIRE

Year	Output (000s tons)	Number Employed			Output per Head	
		Under Ground	Above Ground	Total Under and Above Ground	Under Ground	Total Under and Above Ground
					Tons	Tons
1874	..	..	..	..	..	..
1875	..	..	..	..	..	..
1876	555	2,389	717	3,106	232	178
1877	525	1,887	453	2,340	278	224
1878	624	1,917	509	2,426	325	257
1879	632	1,964	542	2,506	321	252
1880	626	1,899	547	2,446	329	255
1881	652	1,987	516	2,503	328	260
1882	487	1,665	458	2,123	292	229
1883	664	1,918	519	2,437	346	272
1884	599	1,705	486	2,191	351	273
1885	591	1,832	469	2,301	322	257
1886	540	1,803	471	2,274	299	237
1887	557	1,674	526	2,200	332	253
1888	649	2,040	621	2,661	317	243
1889	711	2,064	551	2,615	344	271
1890	762	2,364	694	3,058	322	249
1891	725	2,683	697	3,380	270	214
1892	697	2,789	802	3,591	249	194
1893	727	2,721	842	3,563	267	204
1894	889	3,003	979	3,982	295	223
1895	1,015	3,404	980	4,384	298	231
1896	1,043	3,475	946	4,421	300	235
1897	1,006	3,248	857	4,105	309	244
1898	1,124	3,653	975	4,628	307	242
1899	1,207	3,880	1,004	4,884	311	247
1900	1,334	4,518	1,141	5,659	295	235
1901	1,417	4,816	1,295	6,111	294	231
1902	1,572	5,458	1,492	6,950	287	226
1903	1,632	5,727	1,574	7,301	284	223
1904	1,693	5,981	1,555	7,536	283	224
1905	1,734	5,915	1,496	7,411	293	233
1906	1,927	6,518	1,639	8,157	295	236
1907	1,972	6,936	1,861	8,797	284	224
1908	1,937	7,340	1,964	9,304	263	208
1909	1,950	7,732	2,025	9,757	252	199
1910	2,035	8,522	2,227	10,749	238	189
1911	2,115	8,088	2,181	10,269	261	205
1912	2,218	9,539	2,501	12,040	232	184
1913	2,589	9,454	2,527	11,981	273	216
1914	2,311	9,242	2,434	11,676	250	197
1915	2,406	..	..	..	..	..
1916	2,469	..	..	..	..	..
1917	2,260	..	..	..	..	..
1918	2,211	..	..	..	..	..
1919	2,337	..	..	..	..	..
1920	2,328	11,766	3,247	15,013	198	155
1921	1,776	11,463	3,136	14,599	155	122
1922	2,532	11,733	3,120	14,853	216	170
1923	2,616	11,949	3,332	15,281	219	171
1924	2,671	12,028	3,400	15,428	222	173
1925	2,407	11,967	3,356	15,323	201	157
1926	1,116	12,062	3,337	15,399	..	..
1927	2,357	10,892	3,098	13,990	216	168
1928	2,184	8,223	2,400	10,623	266	206
1929	2,690	9,190	2,409	11,599	293	232
1930	2,653	9,323	2,464	11,787	285	225
1931	2,440	9,197	2,470	11,667	265	209
1932	2,506	9,456	2,482	11,938	265	210
1933	2,525	9,564	2,520	12,084	264	209
1934	2,389	9,140	2,400	11,540	261	207
1935	2,186	8,505	2,290	10,795	257	202
1936	2,038	8,086	2,201	10,287	252	198
1937	1,841	7,508	2,106	9,614	245	191
1938	1,835	7,556	2,088	9,644	243	190

COAL 2. Output, numbers employed and output per head, by region and county, 1874 - 1945

GLAMORGAN

Year	Output (000s tons)	Number Employed: Under Ground	Number Employed: Above Ground	Number Employed: Total Under and Above Ground	Output per Head: Under Ground	Output per Head: Total Under and Above Ground
					Tons	Tons
1874(4)	12,264	44,390	10,510	54,900	276	223
1875(4)	10,639	45,617	9,025	54,642	233	194
1876	11,709	37,216	6,818	44,034	314	265
1877	11,845	37,019	6,839	43,858	317	270
1878	12,145	36,892	6,561	43,453	329	279
1879	12,358	39,843	7,238	47,081	310	262
1880	15,320	41,762	7,746	49,508	366	309
1881	15,988	44,264	8,132	52,396	361	305
1882	16,393	45,847	7,998	53,845	357	304
1883	17,709	48,815	8,429	57,244	362	309
1884	18,218	51,022	8,982	60,004	357	303
1885	17,209	52,165	8,698	60,863	349	282
1886	17,041	52,206	8,726	60,932	326	279
1887	18,411	53,139	8,920	62,059	346	296
1888	19,595	56,192	9,585	65,777	348	297
1889	20,297	61,535	10,622	72,157	329	281
1890	21,426	68,714	11,650	80,364	311	266
1891	21,762	72,481	11,925	84,406	300	257
1892	22,808	73,290	11,989	85,279	311	267
1893	21,835	71,300	12,675	83,975	306	260
1894	23,994	76,588	12,728	89,316	313	268
1895	23,760	77,398	12,995	90,393	306	260
1896	23,630	76,284	12,729	89,013	309	265
1897	25,113	77,052	13,079	90,131	325	278
1898	19,141	78,184	13,762	91,946	244	208
1899	28,117	79,613	14,495	94,108	353	298
1900	27,687	89,040	16,234	105,274	310	262
1901	27,709	91,099	16,084	107,183	304	258
1902	29,077	92,236	16,193	108,429	315	268
1903	29,376	93,944	16,298	110,242	301	266
1904	30,340	96,071	16,742	112,813	315	268
1905	30,076	97,535	17,033	114,568	308	262
1906	32,313	102,370	17,971	120,341	315	268
1907	34,138	111,889	19,690	131,579	305	259
1908	34,540	118,500	20,772	139,272	291	248
1909	34,462	119,345	20,935	140,280	288	238
1910	32,879	123,339	21,594	144,933	266	226
1911	33,464	128,368	21,717	150,085	260	222
1912	33,727	129,311	22,465	151,776	260	222
1913	38,033	133,371	23,304	156,675	285	241
1914	35,847	133,924	23,014	156,938	267	228
1915	33,110	112,170	21,834	134,004	295	247
1916	34,151	118,154	23,156	141,310	289	241
1917	32,133	121,306	23,225	144,531	264	222
1918	30,865	120,597	23,592	144,189	255	214
1919	31,058	142,196	27,641	169,837	218	182
1920	30,252	149,339	30,644	179,983	202	168
1921	19,772	128,631	25,014	153,645	154	129
1922	32,858	135,370	25,962	161,332	243	204
1923	35,530	140,605	26,967	167,572	253	212
1924	33,376	136,862	26,939	163,801	244	204
1925	28,839	114,412	21,934	136,346	252	211
1926	13,121	118,335	22,555	140,890	..	..
1927	30,503	104,840	20,505	125,345	291	243
1928	28,299	92,229	17,717	109,946	307	257
1929	31,308	97,792	17,858	115,650	320	271
1930	28,631	92,763	17,290	110,053	309	260
1931	23,292	84,847	16,027	100,874	275	231
1932	22,344	78,652	15,298	93,950	284	238
1933	22,143	76,677	15,254	91,931	289	241
1934	22,399	73,835	14,802	88,637	303	253
1935	22,191	68,481	13,857	82,338	324	269
1936	21,244	65,684	13,663	79,347	323	268
1937	24,326	71,711	14,339	86,050	339	283
1938	22,347	71,216	14,520	85,736	314	261

COAL 2. Output, numbers employed and output per head, by region and county, 1874 - 1945

MONMOUTHSHIRE

Year	Output (000s tons)	Number Employed			Output per Head	
		Under Ground	Above Ground	Total Under and Above Ground	Under Ground	Total Under and Above Ground
					Tons	Tons
1874	4,227	15,073	3,355	18,428	280	229
1875	3,534	15,133	2,868	18,001	233	196
1876	4,499	15,284	2,842	18,126	294	248
1877	4,352	15,193	2,618	17,811	286	244
1878	4,491	14,750	2,367	17,117	304	262
1879	4,661	13,639	2,160	15,799	340	295
1880	5,040	13,789	2,334	16,123	365	312
1881	5,413	14,486	2,465	16,951	373	319
1882	5,722	15,219	2,568	17,787	375	321
1883	6,346	16,828	2,835	19,663	377	322
1884	6,480	17,684	2,777	20,461	366	316
1885	6,384	18,253	2,785	21,038	349	303
1886	6,368	18,059	2,577	20,636	352	308
1887	6,796	18,495	2,834	21,329	367	318
1888	6,831	18,853	2,708	21,561	362	316
1889	6,751	20,078	3,052	23,130	336	291
1890	6,895	21,674	3,227	24,901	318	276
1891	7,159	23,644	3,551	27,195	302	263
1892	7,408	23,922	3,495	27,417	309	270
1893	7,309	24,664	4,237	28,901	296	252
1894	8,213	25,345	4,390	29,735	324	276
1895	7,915	25,469	4,323	29,792	310	265
1896	8,841	25,542	4,433	29,975	346	295
1897	9,307	26,267	4,626	30,893	354	301
1898	6,060	25,743	4,622	30,365	235	199
1899	10,103	26,973	4,871	31,844	374	317
1900	9,819	29,158	5,465	34,623	336	283
1901	9,598	29,689	5,317	35,006	323	274
1902	10,175	31,447	5,390	36,837	323	276
1903	10,671	33,721	5,514	39,235	316	271
1904	11,210	34,736	5,688	40,424	293	277
1905	10,886	35,449	5,779	41,228	307	264
1906	12,238	37,454	6,134	43,588	326	280
1907	13,196	40,225	6,594	46,819	328	281
1908	13,035	42,791	7,119	49,910	304	261
1909	13,204	44,298	7,175	51,473	298	256
1910	13,006	46,142	7,470	53,612	281	242
1911	13,799	48,635	7,917	56,552	283	244
1912	13,392	49,450	8,268	57,718	270	232
1913	15,374	51,843	8,388	60,231	296	255
1914	15,016	53,072	8,615	61,687	282	243
1915	14,225	46,740	8,010	54,750	304	259
1916	14,823	49,408	8,514	57,922	300	255
1917	13,683	51,890	8,693	60,583	263	225
1918	13,179	50,755	9,011	59,766	259	220
1919	13,583	60,131	10,168	70,299	225	193
1920	13,113	62,373	10,696	73,069	210	179
1921	8,556	52,096	8,475	60,571	164	141
1922	14,321	54,893	8,745	63,638	261	225
1923	15,470	57,433	9,042	66,475	269	233
1924	14,348	57,663	9,770	67,433	249	213
1925	12,762	47,760	8,015	55,775	267	229
1926	5,748	49,729	8,145	57,874	..	..
1927	12,802	44,138	7,207	51,345	290	249
1928	12,243	38,412	6,381	44,793	319	273
1929	13,403	41,372	6,566	47,938	324	280
1930	13,107	41,052	6,817	47,869	319	274
1931	10,695	36,290	6,303	42,593	295	251
1932	9,326	31,065	5,686	36,751	300	254
1933	8,992	30,194	5,437	35,631	298	252
1934	9,712	31,008	5,460	36,468	313	266
1935	10,070	30,564	5,411	35,975	329	280
1936	10,053	28,931	5,338	34,269	347	293
1937	11,045	31,995	5,811	37,806	345	292
1938	10,574	32,109	6,116	38,225	329	277

COAL 2. Output, numbers employed and output per head, by region and county, 1874 - 1945

PEMBROKESHIRE

Year	Output (000s tons)	Number Employed			Output per Head	
		Under Ground	Above Ground	Total Under and Above Ground	Under Ground	Total Under and Above Ground
					Tons	Tons
1874	..	..	..	..	..	..
1875	..	..	..	..	..	..
1876	80	650	271	921	122	86
1877	75	517	191	708	145	106
1878	36	192	90	282	189	129
1879	85	424	182	606	199	139
1880	79	350	197	547	226	145
1881	79	386	147	533	205	148
1882	72	396	201	597	180	119
1883	93	457	176	633	202	146
1884	95	440	155	595	215	159
1885	53	313	137	450	168	117
1886	96	422	168	590	227	163
1887	95	374	149	523	254	181
1888	74	333	154	487	223	152
1889	71	356	146	502	200	141
1890	72	313	147	460	229	156
1891	75	361	140	501	207	149
1892	81	382	159	541	211	149
1893	89	429	178	607	207	146
1894	82	436	165	601	189	137
1895	85	360	162	522	236	162
1896	81	392	154	546	206	148
1897	82	385	154	539	213	152
1898	82	390	168	558	211	147
1899	59	293	109	402	202	147
1900	48	311	132	443	154	108
1901	42	355	108	463	118	91
1902	49	379	150	529	130	93
1903	61	389	152	541	156	112
1904	58	341	136	477	169	121
1905	52	388	131	519	134	100
1906	47	332	121	453	141	103
1907	50	341	126	467	145	106
1908	51	346	115	461	147	110
1909	50	344	105	449	145	111
1910	41	317	115	432	128	94
1911	46	313	105	418	147	110
1912	43	339	113	452	127	95
1913	55	396	132	528	139	104
1914	54	374	131	505	145	107
1915	56	..	..	..	..	..
1916	58	..	..	..	..	..
1917	47	..	..	..	..	..
1918	46	..	..	..	..	..
1919	63	..	..	..	..	..
1920	53	442	141	583	121	91
1921	39	357	123	480	109	81
1922	52	364	132	496	144	106
1923	49	365	141	506	134	82
1924	52	381	156	537	135	96
1925	48	342	122	464	140	103
1926	28	362	121	483	..	..
1927	42	337	127	464	125	91
1928	51	344	144	488	147	104
1929	38	293	105	398	130	96
1930	28	224	109	333	127	85
1931	34	151	60	211	228	163
1932	39	226	73	299	173	130
1933	36	217	74	291	164	122
1934	50	252	104	356	198	140
1935	52	277	117	394	186	131
1936	40	193	143	336	207	119
1937	43	215	137	352	202	123
1938	71	247	139	386	287	184

General Notes

(i) Sources. Mines Inspectors' Reports 1874-1914 (Sessional Papers); F.A. Gibson, A Compilation of Statistics of the coal mining industry, 1922 and (to 1938); Ministry of Fuel and Power, Supplement to the Statistical Digest, 1945 (for 1939-45).

(ii) The annual output figures were occasionally affected by major stoppages. In South Wales, this occurred in 1875, 1893, 1898, 1910, 1921 and 1926. North Wales was most clearly affected in 1893, 1921 and 1926. The national coal strike of 1912 also had some impact on output.

(iii) There are no separate figures for the individual counties after 1938.

Notes

1. For 1894 and 1895 it is only possible to obtain a separate figure for North Wales for output. The other information is included with the Lancashire coalfield for these years.

2. Two figures are included for 1938. The top figure is from Gibson and the bottom figure from the Ministry of Fuel and Power's Statistical Digest. The number employed is smaller in the Digest because it refers only to wage-earners (i.e. excludes salaried staff). This is the basis for all the 1939-45 figures. The output figures given are for 'saleable coal'. The Digest also gives from 1958 a figure for 'coal raised and weighed'.

3. Before 1912 some collieries returned gross weight, including dirt. From 1912 the net output is given. The gross output figure for 1912 would be 50,268.

4. Includes Carmarthen, Brecon and Pembroke.

COAL 3. **Output, number employed and productivity, North Wales and South Wales, deep-mined coal, 1945-74**

NORTH WALES

	Saleable mined coal	Ave. no. of wage-earners on colliery books[1]	Output per wage-earner		Output per manshift	
			coalface	overall	coalface	overall
	(a)	(b)	(c)	(d)	(e)	(f)
	million tons		tons	tons	tons	tons
1945	1.90	8,842	6,671	215.1		
1946	2.00	8,808	718.3	229.1		
1947	2.05	8,996	705.1	227.5		
1948	2.17	8,919	736.2	241.6	3.28[2]	1.04[2]
1949	2.13	8,616	..	248.7	3.19[2]	1.10[2]
1950	2.20	8,431	..	260.9	3.25	1.08
1951	2.35	8,932	..	263.1	3.25	1.05
1952	2.23	9,255	..	242.4	3.01	0.97
1953	2.19	..	..	..	..	..
1954	2.17	..	..	..	..	..
1955	2.35	..	..	..	..	..
1956	2.30	..	..	..	..	..
1957	2.26	..	..	..	..	..
1958	2.14	..	..	..	..	..
1959	2.07	..	..	..	..	..
1960	1.92	6,684	..	287.3	..	1.20
1961	1.81	6,938	..	260.9	..	1.19
1962	1.88	6,614	..	284.2	..	1.28
1963	1.85	6,273	..	294.9	..	1.34
1964	1.87	6,084	..	307.4	..	1.39
1965	1.54	5,810	..	265.1	..	1.24
1966	1.37	5,180	..	264.5	..	1.23
1967	1.50	4,830	..	310.6	..	1.34
1968	1.18	2,919	..	404.2	..	1.31
1969	0.92	2,513	..	366.1	..	1.57
1970	1.01	..	..	..	..	..
1971	0.80	..	..	..	..	..
1972	0.68	..	..	..	..	..
1973	0.61	..	..	..	..	..
1974	0.46	..	..	..	..	..

COAL 3. Output, number employed and productivity, North Wales and South Wales, deep-mined coal, 1945-75

SOUTH WALES

	No. of collieries	Saleable output	No. of wage-earners on colliery books: Face	All U/G	All Workers	Output per Manshift: Face: cwts.		Face: S.W. as % of U.K.	Overall: cwts.		Overall: S.W. as % of U.K.	Estimated saleable output lost through disputes: '000s tons	S.W. as % of U.K.
	1st Jan	m. tons	Annual Average ('000)										
1945		20.47											
1946		19.09	48.4	..	114.9	39.0		70.7	15.2		73.8	88.0	11.4
1947		21.20	49.7	..	115.5	39.6		69.2	15.8		73.8	109.4	6.7
1948		22.49	50.7	..	115.5	40.2		68.8	16.6		74.8	79	8.8
1949		22.77	50.7	..	113.0	41.8		69.2	17.6		75.9	84	6.6
1950		23.03	48.2	86.0	107.8	43.4		69.8	18.2		76.5	63	7.4
1951		23.43	47.8	85.6	108.0	43.6		68.8	18.2		75.2	151	18.8
1952		23.6(4)	49.3	87.6	110.0	42.8		67.9	18.0		75.6	224	16.2
1953	155	23.4	50.6	88.6	110.1	42.2		67.2	18.2		75.2	142	15.1
1954	151	23.6	50.4	87.9	109.1	42.3		65.0	18.5		75.2	156	12.8
1955	149	22.7	49.5	86.5	107.1	42.5		64.9	18.5		75.5	310	11.5
1956	143	22.4	46.4	84.0	103.8(4)	44.2		66.3	18.7		76.0	467	21.8
1957	136	22.5	43.4	84.2	104.6	45.6		67.8	18.8		76.4	325	17.8
1958	136	21.0	42.6	82.3	102.1	48.3		68.6	19.4		76.7	184	12.7
1959	130	19.4	39.3	76.3	94.9	51.5(4)		68.7	20.3(4)		75.5	182	18.7
1960	121	18.5	35.3	69.1	87.0	53.5		67.3	20.6		73.6	343	22.0
1961	111	17.4	32.1	64.2	81.6	55.4		66.3	20.5		70.9	283	13.7
1962	107	18.2	30.8	62.3	79.6	60.0		65.9	22.1		70.8	264	23.5
Years ending March	End of March												
1964	97	18.9	29.3	59.9	76.5	65.9		66.5	23.9		71.6	226	16.7
1965	86	18.4	27.4	56.4	72.0	68.7		66.3	24.7		71.0	297	22.8
1966	77	16.6	24.2	50.5	64.6	73.0		66.5	25.3		70.1	618	52.4
1967	70	16.5	..	44.9	57.8	78.7		69.2	26.5		72.4	130	7.6
			At December			East	West		East	West			
1968	65(3)	15.7(3)	18.8	40.5	52.2	86.2	75.1	69.8	27.7	26.9	70.0	83	18.9
1969	55	14.5	16.2	35.9	46.3	90.9	79.7	64.4	27.9	29.1	67.1	87	26.4
					March								
1970	52	12.8	..	..	40.3	91.5	84.3	63.8	27.2	29.7	65.6	209	7.2
1971	51	11.7	..	..	38.0	93.6	92.9	65.0	28.3	31.0	67.1	626	20.3
1972	54	9.7	..	..	36.1	88.0	89.5	64.0	27.0	29.4	67.3	2,040	7.7
1973	51	10.8	..	..	34.0	..	..	..	29.5		64.4	93	14.4
1974	48	7.4	..	..	30.9	..	..	..	25.1		59.3	1,986	9.4
1975	44	8.7	..	..	31.8	..	..	..	26.5		58.9	104	24.8

General Notes

(i) Sources. For North Wales. Column (a) from Digest of Welsh Statistics; cols. (b) - (f) Reports on Government Action in Wales and Mon. (later just Wales)

For South Wales. Reports on Government Action in Wales and Mon., for cols. 1 and 2 from 1945-51; all other figures are from N.C.B. Annual Report and Statement of Accounts, 1947-1974/5, published till 1971/2 as House of Commons papers and since then published by the N.C.B. The statistics after 1954 are in a separate publication of Statistical Tables issued as vol. II of the Reports and Accounts.

(ii) The figures for 1945-58 relate to all coalmines: those for 1959 onwards relate only to N.C.B. mines. In 1959 the production of private mines in South Wales was about 400,000 tons.

Notes

1. Manpower figures (where available) are an annual average for 1945-46, 1952 and 1956; for 1947-51 they are the average for the last quarter; for 1955 and from 1958 onwards they relate to December; and for 1953-4 and 1957 the figures relate to June.

2. For 1948 and 1949 the O.M.S. figures relate to the last quarter only.

3. The figures for the number of collieries and saleable output relate to South Wales until 1967. Thereafter they relate to the South-Western division of the N.C.B. which includes Somerset and the Forest of Dean. The differences are relatively small: the 1967 figures for the South-Western division, for example, would be 73 collieries with a saleable output of 16.8 m. tons. The figures in the other columns relate to the South-Western division. An indication of the effect of this may be gained by noting that the total number of wage-earners (in thousands) in Somerset and the Forest of Dean was: at end of 1953, 5.9; 1958, 4.9; in March 1963, 1.8; and March 1967, 0.9. In 1966 the division was split into East and West; and in 1972 these were re-joined and the division was re-named South Wales, but there was no change in the area which it covered.

4. The figures mostly relate to N.C.B. mines only. But small licenced mines are included for some headings for some dates (e.g. for output 1945-51) but mostly make no difference. The O.M.S. figures include licenced mines until 1958 and because the numbers employed in licenced mines were large relative to their output, their exclusion leads to a perceptible increase in O.M.S.

COAL 4. Output of Anthracite, South Wales, 1854 - 1974, and U.K., 1894 - 1938

Year	South Wales Output (000s of tons)	U K Output
1854	1,000	..
1855	997.5	..
1856	964.5	..
1859	800.4	..
1865	509.5	..
1866	575.5	..
1888	906.3	..
1890	1,220.9	..
1891	1,258.2	..
1892	1,309.7	..
1893	1,262.9	..
1894	1,550.2	1,795.9
1895	1,761.2	2,072.2
1896	1,785.0	2,077.6
1897	1,803.6	2,129.4
1898	1,805.5	2,112.7
1899	2,113.7	2,418.5
1900	2,203.5	2,523.2
1901	2,254.1	2,565.5
1902	2,596.7	2,922.7
1903	2,572.8	2,901.0
1904	2,626.9	2,962.3
1905	2,789.2	3,112.1
1906	3,042.2	3,377.5
1907	3,498.3	3,850.4
1908	3,731.1	4,080.5
1909	3,914.4	4.259.0
1910	4,032.2	4,379.5
1911	3,992.8	4,350.5
1912	4,353.0	4,696.7
1913	4,833.2	5,194.6
1914	4,370.2	4,719.0
1915	4,393.2	4,712.1
1916	4,318.2	4,644.0
1917	3,484.2	3,799.4
1918	3,518.7	3,811.9
1919	3,935.7	4,236.3
1920	4,232.0	4,539.0
1921	3,199.3	3,470.7
1922	4,485.9	4,822.6
1923	4,873.0	5,282.2
1924	4,971.4	5,425.6
1925	5,566.5	6,126.4
1926	2,527.3	2,876.7
1927	5,747.8	6,286.6
1928	4,852.5	5,463.5
1929	5,595.7	6,287.2
1930	5,568.2	6,306.0
1931	5,043.2	5,747.3
1932	5,692.8	6,482.4
1933	6,127.4	6,928.5
1934	6,133.9	7,000.0
1935	5,874.4	6,694.9
1936	6,003.2	6,439.1
1937	5,870.1	6,246.8
1938	6,053.2	6,219.8
1939	5,785.0	..
1940 (1)	4,908.9	..
1941	3,692.2	..
1942	2,668.5	..
1943	3,504.3	..
1944	3,040.8	..

Year	South Wales Output (million tons)	Average no. of wage-earners (000s)
1945 (2)	2.68	19.4
1946	2.93	19.2
1947	2.99	19.6
1948	2.99	19.2
1949	2.91	18.1
1950	2.83	17.0
1951	2.97	17.2
1952	2.96	17.5
1953	3.00	17.7
1954	3.03	17.8
1955	2.88	17.2
1956	2.84	16.5
1957	2.84	16.7
1958	2.66	16.1
1959	2.49	14.8
1960	2.47	14.5
1961	2.41	14.2
1962	2.77	13.9
1963	2.99	13.3
1964	3.15	13.0
1965	2.69	12.0
1966	2.61	10.5
1967	2.56	9.6
1968	2.38	7.9
1969	2.18	6.9
1970	2.10	6.3
1971	2.12	5.9
1972	1.49	5.6
1973	..	..
1974	1.26	..

General Notes

(i) Sources. 1854-93 from Hunt's Mineral Statistics; 1894-1939 from Mines Inspectors' Reports and F.A. Gibson; 1940- from Min. of Fuel and Power Statistical Digests (later Energy Statistics published by Ministry of Power 1968-69, Ministry of Technology, 1970 Department of Trade and Industry 1971-3; Department of Energy, 1974).

Notes

1. From 1940 onwards the figures relate to 'saleable coal'. The comparable figure for 1940 on the same basis as previously is 5,391.9.

2. From 1945 the output figures are given in millions of tons and includes (in addition to NCB mines) the output of licenced mines from 1947. For 1948-55 the figures relate to calendar years; for 1956 onwards then relate to 52 weeks ending in various dates in December.

COAL 5. Output from Government Open Cast Workings, South Wales 1943 - 72

	Quantity produced (000s tons)	of which the following amount is Anthracite	Numbers employed at end of year(1)
1943	190.3	..	543
1944	390.7	..	810
1945	356.4	..	785
1946	572.6	86.8	775
1947	842.6	234.7	975
1948	1,012.7	222.9	1,142
1949	1,504.7	606.1	1,715
1950	1,712.4	905.1	1,595
1951	1,332.1	616.2	1,420
1952	1,097.0	473.4	1,437
1953	1,240.5	527.0	1,514
1954(2)	1,317.1	767.3	1,408
1955	1,679.9	849.6	1,689
1956	1,643.8	723.5	1,557
1957	1,386.9	620.6	1,713
1958	1,580.5	765.9	1,759
1959	1,529.4	656.1	1,559
1960	1,573.7	719.8	1,442
1961	1,779.1	767.4	1,316
1962	1,341.6	766.1	1,518
1963	1,404.9	832.2	1,682
1964	1,869.6	1,129.9	1,800
1965	1,987.7	1,262.1	2,003
1966	2,336.4	1,609.5	2,187
1967	2,203.7	1,375.5	2,068
1968	2,312.8	1,507.0	1,971
1969	1,980.0	1,396.0	2,036
1970	2,266.0	1,527.0	2,533
1971	3,290.0	1,937.0	2,698
1972	..	1,571.0	..

General Notes

(i) Sources. Ministry of Fuel and Power, Statistical Digest and successors (see Sources for Table 4);

(ii) No figures are available for North Wales which is included in the North Western region. In the editions of the Statistical Digest since 1968 the figure given is not for 'Wales' (i.e. S. Wales) but for the South-Western region which includes all amounts for Somerset and the Forest of Dean.

Notes

1. For 1944, the figures include labour employed on constructional work for railway branches sidings, screens and washeries. For other years up to 1951 the figures exclude labour directly employed by the Government. From 1952 onwards the figures include persons directly employed by the NCB. The 1952 figure comparable to a 1951 basis is 1,349.

2. The figures for 1954 onwards exclude all screening losses, amounting in total to about 2%.

COAL 6. Output and numbers employed, South Wales as a Percentage of the U.K., 1874 - 1975

Year	OUTPUT	NUMBER OF MEN	
	S.W. as % of U.K.	S.W. as % of U.K.	
		Underground	Underground and Surface
1874	13.0	14.5	14.2
1875	10.6	14.9	14.2
1876	12.6	14.5	13.7
1877	12.5	14.6	13.8
1878	13.1	14.8	14.0
1879	13.3	15.3	14.6
1880	14.4	15.6	14.9
1881	14.4	16.2	15.4
1882	14.5	16.4	15.5
1883	15.2	17.2	16.3
1884	15.8	17.6	16.7
1885	15.2	17.9	17.0
1886	15.3	17.8	16.8
1887	16.0	17.9	17.0
1888	16.0	18.3	17.6
1889	15.8	18.6	17.9
1890	16.1	18.7	18.1
1891	16.1	18.8	18.1
1892	17.1	18.5	17.8
1893	18.3	18.3	17.7
1894	17.7	18.8	17.9
1895	17.4	19.2	18.1
1896	17.3	19.3	18.2
1897	17.7	19.5	18.4
1898	13.2	19.4	18.4
1899	18.1	19.4	18.3
1900	17.4	20.1	19.1
1901	17.9	19.8	18.8
1902	18.1	19.9	18.9
1903	18.3	20.1	19.0
1904	18.8	20.5	19.4
1905	18.2	20.5	19.4
1906	18.7	21.1	19.9
1907	18.6	21.5	20.4
1908	19.2	21.7	20.6
1909	19.0	21.4	20.3
1910	18.4	21.5	20.5
1911	18.4	22.0	20.8
1912	19.2	21.9	20.8
1913	19.7	21.9	20.8
1914	20.2	21.8	20.6
1915	19.9	22.5	21.2
1916	20.3	22.6	21.4
1917	19.5	22.7	21.5
1918	20.5	23.0	21.7
1919	20.7	22.8	21.6
1920	20.1	22.8	21.7
1921	18.6	21.2	20.6
1922	20.1	22.0	20.9
1923	19.7	21.7	20.7
1924	19.1	21.4	20.3
1925	18.3	20.1	19.1
1926	16.0	20.4	19.3
1927	18.4	19.7	18.7
1928	18.2	18.7	17.7
1929	18.7	19.5	18.4
1930	18.5	19.5	18.3
1931	16.9	19.2	18.0
1932	16.7	18.6	17.6
1933	16.6	19.0	17.9
1934	15.9	18.7	17.6
1935	15.8	18.1	17.0
1936	14.8	17.4	16.3
1937	15.7	18.2	17.0
1938	15.6	..	17.3
1939	15.3	..	16.8
1940	14.4	..	17.2
1941	13.3	..	16.0
1942	13.1	..	16.1
1943	12.9	..	16.2
1944	12.2	..	15.8
1945	12.1	..	15.5
1946	10.6	..	16.5
1947	11.4	..	16.2
1948	11.4	..	16.0
1949	11.2	..	15.7
1950	11.3	16.0	15.5
1951	11.1	15.9	15.5
1952	11.1	15.8	15.4
1953	11.1	15.8	15.4
1954	11.1	15.7	15.4
1955	10.9	15.5	15.2
1956	10.8	15.1	14.9
1957	10.8	15.0	14.9
1958	10.6	14.8	14.7
1959	10.1	14.4	14.4
1960	10.1	14.3	14.4
1961	8.8	14.1	14.3
1962	9.7	14.2	14.4
1963	n.a.	n.a.	n.a.

Year	OUTPUT	NUMBER OF MEN	
	S.W. as % of U.K.	S.W. as % of U.K.	
		Underground	Underground and Surface
1964	10.1	14.6	14.8
1965	10.0	14.4	14.7
1966	9.5	14.0	14.2
		at December	
1967	10.0	13.7	13.9
1968	9.6	13.4	13.7
1969	9.5	14.0	14.3
1970	9.2	..	13.6
1971	8.8	..	13.3
1972	8.9	..	13.2
1973	8.5	..	12.9
1974	7.6	..	12.7
1975	7.6	..	12.8

General Notes

(i) Sources. F.A. Gibson, op.cit., (see notes to Table 2) for 1874-1937; Wales and Mon. Summary of Government Action for 1938-44; N.C.B. Annual Reports and Accounts, Statistical Tables for 1945 onwards.

(ii) Until 1962 the figures relate to calendar years; after this they relate to the year ending in March of the year given.

Coal ·7. Coal Shipments (Coastal and Foreign) from South Wales ports, 1816-74.

	Coastwise	Foreign	Total		Coastwise	Foreign	Total
1816 (1)	365.6	121.0	486.6	1846	1,694.6	221.5	1,916.1
1817 (1)	413.5	175.7	589.2	1847	1,499.2	258.5	1,757.7
1818 (1)	443.4	148.4	591.8	1848	1,663.9	300.2	1,964.1
1819	602.8	5.6	608.3	1849	1,458.3	328.9	1,787.1
1820	572.9	4.5	577.4	1850	1,500.6	417.5	1,918.1
1821	597.9	3.4	601.3	1851	1,573.8	452.2	2.026.0
1822	649.3	3.8	653.1	1852	1,554.0	556.4	2,110.4
1823	675.0	5.1	680.0	1853	1,865.5	634.2	2,499.7
1824	777.8	4.9	782.6	1854	1,785.9	822.5	2,608.4
1825	726.4	5.3	731.7	1855	1,776.6	1,121.0	2,897.7
1826	835.3	10.7	846.0	1856	1,944.4	1,278.4	3,222.8
1827	770.1	10.3	780.4	1857	2,004.2	1,418.0	3,422.3
1828	831.9	7.0	838.9	1858	1,920.2	1,375.5	3,295.7
1829	..	8.8	..	1859	2,001.9	1,540.8	3,542.7
1830	..	12.9	..	1860	2,238.9	1,719.6	3,958.4
1831	..	19.3	..	1861	2,384.2	1,870.2	4,254.4
1832	..	19.4	..	1862	2,379.0	2,129.8	4,508.8
1833	1,049.3	24.7	1,074.1	1863	2,231.1	2,272.5	4,503.6
1834	..	..	..	1864	2,343.7	2,455.4	4,799.0
1835	1,054.9	39.3	1,094.1	1865	2,425.4	2,411.8	4,837.2
1836	1,066.3	46.1	1,112.4	1866	2,431.7	2,971.9	5,403.6
1837	1,316.2	76.5	1,392.7	1867	2,615.4	3,049.5	5,664.9
1838	1,228.1	65.9	1,294.0	1868	2,298.4	3,217.5	5.515.9
1839	1,307.7	68.5	1,376.2	1869	2,511.1	3,226.8	5,737.9
1840	1,374.4	63.9	1,438.3	1870	2,511.6	3,470.1	5,981.7
1841	1,345.2	63.2	1,408.5	1871	2,494.8	3,207.6	5,702.4
1842	1,453.2	109.8	1,563.0	1872	2,550.7	3,678.6	6,229.3
1843	1,395.7	120.9	1,516.6	1873	2,490.1	3,634.2	6,124.4
1844	1,482.8	232.4	1,715.2	1874	2,270.5	3,992.3	6,262.8
1845	1,657.0	237.9	1,894.8				

General Notes

(i) Source. Royal Commission on Coal, 1871.

Notes

1. The level of foreign shipments for 1816-18 seems implausibly high. Some of these shipments should presumably be classified as coastal and probably represent shipments to Ireland.

COAL 8. Shipments. Cargoes (Foreign and Coastwise) and Bunkers from South Wales ports, and South Wales as a percentage of U.K. shipments, 1874 - 1950

YEAR	CARGOES						BUNKERS		ALL SHIPMENTS AND BUNKERS	
	Foreign		Coastwise		Total Shipments Foreign and Coastwise		Foreign and Coastwise(2)		Foreign and Coastwise	
	South Wales(1)	% of U.K.	South Wales(1)	% of U.K.	South Wales(1)	% of U.K.	Total	% of U.K.	South Wales(1)	% of U.K.
	000s tons		000s tons		000s tons		000s tons		000s tons	
1874	3,977	29.7	2,269	23.7	6,246	27.2	..	..	..	..
1875	3,686	26.4	2,181	20.4	5,867	23.8	..	..	..	..
1876	4,801	30.6	2,418	22.0	7,219	27.1	..	..	..	..
1877	5,061	34.0	2,373	21.7	7,434	28.8	..	..	..	..
1878	5,571	37.1	2,412	21.8	7,984	30.7	..	..	..	..
1879	5,933	37.7	2,534	21.1	8,467	30.5	..	..	..	..
1880	6,894	38.5	2,492	21.2	9,386	31.7	..	..	..	..
1881	7,429	39.6	2,698	22.1	10,127	32.7	..	..	..	..
1882	8,132	40.8	2,750	22.5	10,882	33.9	..	..	..	..
1883	9,319	43.0	3,013	23.3	12,332	35.6	..	..	..	..
1884	9,730	43.5	2,932	22.9	12,661	36.0	..	..	..	..
1885	9,824	43.3	3,055	23.2	12,879	35.9	..	..	..	..
1886	9,445	42.7	3,120	23.1	12,565	35.3	..	..	..	..
1887	10,605	45.6	3,174	23.0	13,779	37.2	..	..	..	..
1888	11,709	45.7	3,015	21.5	14,725	37.1	..	..	..	..
1889	12,146	44.2	2,940	20.7	15,087	36.2	..	..	..	..
1890	12,508	43.5	2,748	19.4	15,255	35.5	..	..	..	..
1891	12,583	42.7	2,983	19.8	15,566	34.9	..	..	..	..
1892	13,186	45.4	3,390	22.6	16,575	37.6	..	..	..	..
1893	12,582	45.4	3,445	21.2	16,026	36.5	..	..	..	..
1894	14,927	47.0	3,734	21.5	18,661	38.0	..	..	..	..
1895	14,652	46.2	3,424	20.9	18,076	37.6	..	..	..	..
1896	15,323	46.5	3,666	21.5	18,989	38.0	2,590	26.1	22,280	36.2
1897	16,419	46.4	3,975	22.5	20,394	38.4	2,715	26.0	23,963	36.6
1898	12,175	34.7	2,732	15.6	14,908	28.4	2,126	18.9	17,803	27.2
1899	18,603	45.2	4,016	22.4	22,619	38.3	3,167	25.9	26,939	36.7
1900	18,457	41.9	3,729	20.8	22,186	35.8	2,646	22.5	25,961	34.2
1901	18,619	44.5	3,759	21.0	22,378	37.4	3,147	23.2	26,715	35.5
1902	19,447	45.1	3,913	20.4	23,360	37.5	3,663	21.3	28,160	34.6
1903	19,881	44.2	4,144	21.5	24,025	37.4	4,086	21.7	29,170	34.4
1904	20,799	45.0	4,221	21.0	25,019	37.7	4,198	21.8	30,548	34.9
1905	20,053	42.2	4,180	20.8	24,233	35.9	4,188	21.4	29,633	33.3
1906	23,401	42.1	4,226	21.3	27,627	36.6	4,437	21.3	33,565	34.0
1907	25,657	40.3	4,216	20.8	29,872	35.6	4,493	21.6	35,989	33.6
1908	25,166	40.2	4,301	21.4	29,468	35.7	4,743	21.9	35,834	33.5
1909	25,365	40.2	4,401	20.7	29,766	35.3	4,758	21.6	36,154	33.2
1910	25,215	40.6	4,398	20.3	29,613	35.4	4,470	20.4	35,702	33.0
1911	25,192	39.0	4,070	18.5	29,262	33.8	4,013	18.5	34,997	31.5
1912	26,104	40.5	3,681	18.2	29,784	35.2	4,235	20.6	35,694	33.1
1913	29,785	40.6	3,411	16.7	33,196	35.4	5,222	22.3	40,604	33.7
1914	24,462	41.4	2,755	15.0	27,216	35.2	4,491	21.5	33,438	33.2
1915	18,599	42.7	1,548	10.1	20,147	34.2	3,739	23.9	25,249	32.9
1916	17,415	45.4	1,124	8.8	18,539	36.3	3,622	24.6	23,664	34.7
1917	19,892	56.8	952	7.9	20,844	44.3	3,162	27.4	25,725	41.9
1918	17,001	53.5	1,111	12.3	18,112	44.4	2,529	25.8	22,176	41.7
1919	20,230	57.4	2,031	15.6	22,261	46.2	3,529	26.5	27,506	42.5
1920	15,470	62.1	5,352	28.6	20,822	47.7	3,547	22.8	26,613	42.1
1921	12,240	49.6	1,774	15.5	14,014	38.8	2,770	22.8	17,583	35.3
1922	25,625	39.9	2,035	14.0	27,660	35.1	4,624	23.2	33,579	32.8
1923	30,035	37.8	1,695	12.9	31,730	34.3	4,399	22.4	37,522	32.0
1924	25,624	41.6	1,737	11.8	27,361	35.8	4,410	23.0	32,954	33.1
1925	21,399	42.1	1,504	10.5	22,903	35.1	3,734	21.0	26,640	32.1
1926	9,279	45.1	635	8.4	9,915	35.2	1,706	20.2	12,167	32.1
1927	22,564	44.0	1,504	9.2	24,069	35.6	4,142	22.7	29,636	33.3
1928	21,389	42.7	1,536	8.9	22,925	34.1	4,009	22.1	28,075	31.5
1929	24,677	40.9	1,581	8.3	26,258	33.1	4,062	22.6	31,695	31.3
1930	23,245	42.3	1,414	7.7	24,658	33.6	3,491	20.4	29,279	31.2
1931	17,986	42.1	1,311	7.1	19,297	31.6	3,067	19.2	23,258	29.0
1932	16,480	42.4	1,252	6.6	17,732	30.7	3,252	21.0	21,897	28.7
1933	16,046	41.1	1,200	6.2	17,246	29.4	3,011	20.3	21,222	27.7
1934	15,901	40.1	1,436	6.7	17,337	28.4	2,987	20.1	21,242	26.9
1935	15,583	40.2	1,715	7.8	17,298	28.5	2,801	20.1	20,972	27.0
1936	13,115	38.0	2,015	8.5	15,130	26.0	2,793	20.9	18,535	24.9
1937	16,172	40.1	2,337	9.6	18,510	28.7	3,068	23.5	22,308	27.6
	(incl bunkers)									
1946	2,570		2,803							
1947	1,062		3,232							
1948	3,883		2,949							
1949	5,219		2,744							
1950	5,328		2,757							

General Notes

(i) Sources. F.A. Gibson (see notes to Table 2), after 1945 N.C.B. Reports and Accounts (see notes to Table 3).

(ii) Strikes in South Wales Coalfield:-

1875 1st January to 31st May.
1879 1st July to 8th July.
1893 1st August to 11th September (partial stoppage).
1898 1st April to 1st September.
1910 November - December (partial stoppage).
1911 1st January to 31st August (partial stoppage).
1912 National Strike, 1st March to 14th April (Minimum Wage).

Notes

1. Excludes shipments of coke and patent fuel.

2. 1896 - 1901 Foreign only.

COAL 9. **Shipments.** Exports of Coal, Coke and Patent Fuel from South Wales ports, 1854 - 1937

YEAR	TOTAL OUTPUT	COAL EXPORTED	COKE (coal equivalent)(1)		PATENT FUEL (coal content)(2)		BUNKER COAL(3)	TOTAL COALS EXPORTED	Quantity remaining for home consumption for all purposes
			Exported	Exports as % of UK	Exported	Exports as % of UK			
	('000 tons)	('000 tons)	('000 tons)		('000 tons)		('000 tons)	('000 tons)	('000 tons)
1854	..	812	6	3.2	..	..	..	818	..
1855	..	1,114	6	2.8	61	72.2	..	1,181	..
1856	..	1,262	15	6.2	45	93.0	..	1,322	..
1857	..	..	..	..	..	..	..	..	..
1858	..	..	..	..	..	..	..	..	..
1859	..	1,522	10	4.4	61	80.6	..	1,592	..
1860	..	1,695	11	4.5	77	84.4	..	1,783	..
1861	..	..	..	..	..	..	..	..	..
1862	..	..	..	..	..	..	..	..	..
1863	..	2,507(4)	..	..	..	..	..	..	..
1864	..	2,297(4)	..	..	..	..	..	..	..
1865	..	2,412(5)	..	..	..	..	..	..	..
1866	..	2,972(5)	..	..	..	..	..	..	..
1867	..	2,999	22	6.5	143	95.5	..	3,165	..
1868	..	3,181	21	6.5	133	99.9	..	3,335	..
1869	..	3,197	18	5.2	154	98.3	..	3,369	..
1870	..	3,463	20	6.0	195	98.1	..	3,678	..
1871	..	3,188	22	6.3	193	97.3	..	3,402	..
1872	..	3,556	22	7.9	201	97.0	..	3,780	..
1873	..	3,612	22	8.3	265	95.1	..	3,899	..
1874	16,491	3,977	25	6.4	270	96.8	..	4,272	12,218
1875	14,173	3,686	11	2.1	227	97.4	..	3,923	10,250
1876	16,972	4,801	24	4.3	250	98.4	..	5,074	11,898
1877	16,911	5,061	45	8.2	176	95.3	..	5,283	11,630
1878	17,417	5,571	45	9.9	180	90.2	..	5,797	11,628
1879	17,819	5,933	67	11.7	286	89.0	..	6,286	11,533
1880	21,166	6,894	88	12.0	329	94.8	..	7,312	13,854
1881	22,234	7,429	65	9.4	334	90.0	..	7,828	14,406
1882	22,817	8,132	88	11.3	431	88.4	..	8,651	14,166
1883	24,975	9,319	66	8.1	505	91.0	..	9,889	15,086
1884	25,552	9,730	65	8.2	445	95.3	..	10,240	15,312
1885	24,343	9,824	100	10.0	434	94.1	..	10,358	13,985
1886	24,204	9,445	114	10.5	457	96.6	..	10,016	14,188
1887	26,046	10,605	124	11.2	476	97.9	..	11,205	14,841
1888	27,355	11,709	174	13.0	471	97.0	..	12,354	15,001
1889	28,064	12,146	125	9.8	596	97.1	..	12,868	15,197
1890	29,415	12,508	173	14.2	585	96.7	..	13,266	16,149
1891	29,993	12,583	233	16.3	639	97.6	..	13,455	16,538
1892	31,207	13,186	254	25.0	704	98.2	..	14,143	17,064
1893	30,155	12,582	150	15.0	626	96.4	..	13,358	16,797
1894	33,418	14,927	179	18.2	631	96.2	..	15,737	17,682
1895	33,040	14,652	174	14.9	601	97.2	..	15,426	17,614
1896	33,868	15,323	137	12.1	548	95.5	2,590	18,599	15,269
1897	35,806	16,419	199	12.2	659	95.9	2,715	19,992	15,814
1898	26,724	12,175	125	9.7	624	94.4	2,126	15,050	11,673
1899	39,870	18,603	187	12.9	933	97.4	3,167	22,889	16,981
1900	39,328	18,457	188	11.5	898	97.5	2,646	22,190	17,138
1901	39,209	18,619	182	13.5	969	99.6	3,147	22,918	16,292
1902	41,306	19,447	149	13.0	942	99.7	3,430	23,968	17,337
1903	42,154	19,881	171	14.3	849	98.7	3,824	24,725	17,430
1904	43,730	20,799	157	12.4	1,106	99.3	3,983	26,645	17,686
1905	43,203	20,053	182	14.1	990	99.2	3,966	25,191	18,012
1906	47,056	23,401	214	15.8	1,231	99.3	4,210	29,056	18,000
1907	49,978	25,657	244	14.9	1,323	99.3	4,300	31,523	18,455
1908	50,227	25,166	261	13.1	1,289	99.5	4,514	31,231	18,996
1909	50,364	25,365	242	12.5	1,305	99.6	4,522	31,433	18,930

1910	48,700	25,215	194	12.0	1,320	99.7	4,224	30,953	17,747
1911	50,201	25,192	185	10.5	1,436	98.9	3,798	30,612	19,589
1912	50,116	26,104	156	9.2	1,402	98.6	4,027	31,688	18,428
1913	56,830	29,785	226	11.0	1,828	98.9	4,994	36,832	19,998
1914	53,880	24,462	216	11.0	1,426	.. (6)	4,423	30,528	23,357
1915	50,453	18,599	269	15.9	1,079	97.9	3,724	23,670	26,782
1916	52,081	17,415	358	17.2	911	.. (6)	3,579	22,263	29,818
1917	48,508	19,892	388	18.1	1,336	97.3	3,118	24,734	23,774
1918	46,717	17,001	123	8.1	1,304	96.3	2,487	20,916	25,801
1919	47,552	20,230	182	7.3	1,484	96.4	3,502	22,124	25,399
1920	46,249	15,470	199	7.0	1,910	94.0	3,277	20,857	25,392
1921	30,564	12,240	69	5.5	680	88.9	2,680	15,669	14,895
1922	50,325	25,625	165	3.9	1,076	97.5	4,428	31,295	19,030
1923	54,252	30,035	547	8.3	956	99.6	4,230	35,768	18,483
1924	51,085	25,624	192	4.1	958	99.8	4,239	31,014	20,071
1925	44,630	21,339	140	4.0	1,036	99.2	3,577	26,153	18,476
1926	20,273	9,279	71	5.6	448	99.0	1,631	11,429	8,843
1927	46,256	22,564	122	4.0	1,212	99.8	4,016	27,914	18,342
1928	43,312	21,389	190	4.4	922	99.2	3,879	26,379	16,933
1929	48,150	24,677	242	4.9	1,105	99.6	3,917	29,941	18,209
1930	45,108	23,245	195	4.7	909	99.7	3,350	27,697	17,411
1931	37,085	17,986	196	5.5	704	99.6	2,935	21,821	15,264
1932	34,874	16,480	235	7.1	676	98.9	3,125	20,516	14,358
1933	34,355	16,046	246	7.2	713	99.6	2,875	19,880	14,475
1934	35,173	15,901	277	8.5	654	99.7	2,841	19,673	15,500
1935	35,025	15,583	237	6.5	635	100.0	2,654	19,109	15,916
1936	33,886	13,115	137	4.0	462	99.0	2,652	16,366	17,520
1937	37,773	16,172	123	3.4	571	94.0	2,926	19,792	17,981

General Notes

(i) Sources. Hunt, Mineral Statistics (for 1854-73); F.A. Gibson, (see Notes to Table 2) (for 1874-1937).

(ii) The exports of coal from South Wales as a percentage of U.K. exports is given in Table 8.

Notes

1. Figures computed on assumption that for each 60 tons of coke exported, 100 tons of coal was used in its manufacture.

2. Patent Fuel is assumed to contain 90 per cent coal, other 10 per cent is mostly pitch.

3. These relate to coal shipped on British and Foreign vessels bound for foreign ports.

4. These are figures given in Hunt, 1864, for 'Total Exports of coal from Severn Ports'.

5. These figures are the total of coal, coke and patent fuel.

6. Not computed because error in source gives a greater figure for exports from South Wales than for exports from all U.K. (including South Wales).

COAL 10. Shipment (foreign and coastwise) from each port (Cardiff, Swansea, Newport, Llanelli, Milford, Neath, Porthcawl, Port Talbot), various dates, 1780-1974

CARDIFF

Year	Shipments Coastwise	Shipments Foreign	Total Shipments
	tons	tons	tons
1816 (1)	177,044	75,199	252,243
1817 (1)	207,753	90,090	297,843
1818 (1)	218,800	95,414	314,214
1819	133,669	670	134,339
1820	85,427	..	85,427
1821	90,252	1,143	91,395
1822	99,066	445	99,511
1823	114,830	2,108	116,938
1824	19,246	467	19,713
1825	24,144	374	13,994
1826	21,683	952	13,500
1827	24,842	406	12,955
1828	30,147	281	30,428
1829	..	131	..
1830	..	711	..
1831	..	726	..
1832	..	1,052	..
1833	138,272	1,521	139,793
1834	..	..	..
1835	123,279	972	124,251
1836	130,989	2,251	133,240
1837	169,248	3,840	173,088
1838	123,614	2,455	126,069
1839	145,057	4,879	149,936
1840	162,283	3,826	166,109
1841	156,407	4,374	160,781
1842	238,319	7,510	245,829
1843	267,303	12,781	280,084
1844	329,569	23,037	352,606
1845	417,831	33,096	450,927
1846	442,065	45,102	487,167
1847	432,726	81,032	513,758
1848	546,961	117,674	664,635
1849	488,772	171,686	660,458
1850	497,695	233,634	731,329
1851	501,002	249,001	750,003
1852	462,243	358,174	820,417
1853	485,713	429,495	915,208
1854	481,353	565,946	1,047,299
1855	468,841	738,587	1,207,428
1856	551,984	846,863	1,398,847
1857	542,571	919,877	1,462,448
1858	592,745	798,741	1,391,486
1859	672,241	966,601	1,638,842

Year	Shipments Coastwise	Shipments Foreign	Total Shipments
	tons	tons	tons
1860	782,002	1,133,086	1,915,088
1861	895,729	1,109,354	2,005,083
1862	884,283	1,329,658	2,213,941
1863	865,260	1,475,698	2,340,958
1864	841,908	1,473,615	2,315,523
1865	901,724	1,452,741	2,354,465
1866	890,585	1,861,683	2,752,268
1867	874,498	1,945,311	2,819,809
1868	787,984	2,156,206	2,944,190
1869	889,212	2,189,460	3,078,672
1870	885,646	2,360,259	3,245,905
1871	861,506	2,039,270	2,900,776
1872	937,451	2,599,401	3,536,852
1873	965,822	2,618,442	3,584,264

Year	COAL			COKE Foreign and Coastwise	PATENT FUEL Foreign and Coastwise
	Coastwise	Foreign	Total		
	'000 tons	'000 tons	'000 tons	'000 tons	'000 tons
1874	837	2,933	3,770	10	72
1875	748	2,725	3,473	4	73
1876	865	3,536	4,401	9	68
1877	788	3,764	4,553	21	70
1878	815	4,076	4,891	20	98
1879	826	4,254	5,080	28	147
1880	865	4,991	5,856	40	160
1881	934	5,456	6,390	27	168
1882	941	5,723	6,663	38	215
1883	1,039	6,720	7,759	28	227
1884	1,004	6,971	7,975	31	205
1885	1,089	7,094	8,183	50	218
1886	1,187	6,630	7,817	69	217
1887	1,193	7,369	8,562	67	237
1888	1,179	8,439	9,618	92	220
1889	1,203	8,997	10,200	76	269
1890	1,230	9,424	10,654	98	236
1891	1,299	9,679	10,978	126	314
1892	1,486	10,255	11,741	145	343
1893	1,575	9,716	11,292	85	287
1894	1,770	11,133	12,903	98	311
1895	1,726	10,906	12,632	83	335
1896	1,880	11,442	15,171	63	324
1897	2,243	12,006	16,207	76	362
1898	1,468	8,817	11,811	55	237
1899	2,338	13,805	18,411	71	434
1900	2,244	13,383	17,519	74	420
1901	2,324	13,801	18,472	65	452
1902	2,398	14,129	19,142	46	389
1903	2,466	14,389	19,721	53	365
1904	2,549	14,905	20,380	42	482
1905	2,566	14,040	19,516	63	400
1906	2,634	15,945	21,660	75	505
1907	2,610	17,356	23,058	93	519
1908	2,753	16,775	22,717	115	561
1909	2,879	17,077	23,236	97	566
1910	2,867	16,958	22,876	90	496
1911	2,644	16,128	21,386	69	591
1912	2,351	17,243	22,421	67	522
1913	1,879	19,282	24,577	105	718
1914	1,362	15,857	20,244	90	532

CARDIFF

Year	COAL Coastwise	COAL Foreign	COAL Total	COKE Foreign and Coastwise	PATENT FUEL Foreign and Coastwise
	'000 tons	'000 tons	'000 tons	'000 tons	'000 tons
1915	566	10,531	13,424	105	344
1916	372	9,230	11,928	172	315
1917	362	13,014	15,423	172	410
1918	387	10,733	14,784	50	419
1919	1,158	12,374	15,832	69	499
1920	3,908	8,772	14,916	69	586
1921	1,053	8,024	10,860	30	247
1922	1,072	15,940	19,835	54(2)	335(2)
1923	1,112	17,817	21,667	265	343
1924	1,106	15,632	19,551	97	404
1925	906	12,762	15,967	70	481
1926	342	5,665	7,040	32	184
1927	799	13,921	17,370	59	452
1928	827	13,419	16,807	92	320
1929	828	14,789	18,143	101	355
1930	742	13,278	16,058	84	323
1931	750	10,267	12,914	112	370
1932	752	9,193	11,757	125	494
1933	722	8,786	11,176	146	457
1934	858	8,542	11,059	171	394
1935	1,124	8,430	11,140	150	468
1936	1,258	6,869	9,834	69	407
1937	1,627	8,516	11,978	..	..

in '000 tons

Year	Coal, Coke and Patent Fuels	Year	Coal, Coke and Patent Fuels	Year	Coal, Coke and Patent Fuels
1938	5,229				
1945	1,120	1955	956	1965	40
1946	1,197	1956	780	1966	7
1947	736	1957	533	1967	14
1948	1,622	1958	394	1968	..
1949	1,588	1959	408	1969	1
1950	1,605	1960	377	1970	..
1951	1,222	1961	331	1971	..
1952	1,514	1962	390	1972	34
1953	1,447	1963	520	1973	4
1954	1,349	1964	228	1974	41

COAL 10. Shipment (foreign and coastwise) from each port (Cardiff, Swansea, Newport, Llanelli, Milford, Neath, Porthcawl, Port Talbot), various dates, 1780-1974

SWANSEA

Year	Shipments Coastwise	Shipments Foreign	Total Shipments
	tons	tons	tons
1780	..	..	64,502
1781	..	..	53,772
1782	..	..	71,597
1783	..	..	70,725
1784	..	..	102,391
1785	..	..	88,624
1786	..	..	90,645
1787	..	..	98,111
1788	..	..	101,412
1789	..	..	113,509
1790	126,288	29,238	157,588
1791	121,409	32,828	154,943
1792	142,214	35,494	179,595
1793	177,294	40,730	218,060
1794	136,627	33,372	169,999
1795	154,242	28,504	182,746
1796	149,139	32,100	181,239
1797	171,041	30,401	202,023
1798	181,573	28,872	211,172
1799	211,748	33,228	244,976

Year	Shipments Coastwise		Shipments Internal and Foreign		Total Shipments	
	Coal	Culm or Anthracite	Coal	Culm or Anthracite	Coal	Culm or Anthracite
	tons		tons		tons	
1816	159,181		29,974		189,155	
1817	167,251		57,784		225,035	
1818	190,022		34,321		224,343	
	tons	tons	tons	tons	tons	tons
1819	99,542	85,063	925	292	100,377	85,355
1820	95,678	135,244	786	267	96,464	135,511
1821	79,776	127,057	1,172	115	80,948	127,172
1822	109,253	115,948	1,535	132	110,788	116,080
1823	107,503	115,622	1,425	113	108,928	115,735
1824	136,801	155,112	1,547	225	138,348	155,337
1825	128,935	104,405	1,423	157	130,358	104,562
1826	130,388	186,408	3,703	353	134,091	186,761
1827	107,035	167,315	3,393	217	110,428	167,532
1828	122,923	165,303	3,552	127	126,475	165,430
1829	..	..	4,924	..	..	..
1830	..	..	6,278	125	..	..
1831	..	..	7,709	304	..	..
1832	..	..	7,963	235	..	..
1833	139,884	246,679	13,000	501	152,884	247,180
1834	..	..	..	..	..	..
1835	136,350	221,782	21,629	2,112	157,979	223,894
1836	163,987	223,357	17,620	904	181,607	224,261
1837	216,540	275,426	34,030	965	250,570	276,391
1838	199,288	276,977	28,230	300	227,518	277,277
1839	227,500	259,292	25,291	393	252,791	259,685
1840	213,790	246,411	32,911	178	246,701	246,589
1841	200,559	249,560	28,781	215	229,340	249,775
1842	226,019	245,222	39,451	571	265,470	245,793
1843	207,299	194,594	35,521	2,200	242,820	196,814
1844	222,481	199,095	34,599	5,700	257,080	204,795
1845	263,568	215,860	39,153	3,986	302,721	219,846
1846	258,297	196,053	35,607	2,928	293,904	198,981
1847	212,970	160,337	42,665	4,050	255,635	164,387
1848	224,325	168,046	39,399	2,715	263,724	170,761
1849	181,050	123,857	34,896	1,742	215,946	125,599
1850	207,298	110,270	38,649	2,232	245,947	112,502

Year	Shipments Coastwise	Shipments Foreign	Total Shipments
	tons	tons	tons
1851	352,247	41,502	393,749
1852	375,182	51,486	426,668
1853	434,406	73,549	507,955
1854	255,894	88,410	344,304
1855	257,598	153,218	410,816
1856	301,255	185,408	486,663
1857	279,407	245,442	524,849
1858	240,700	269,084	509,784
1859	227,620	308,464	536,084
1860	227,675	295,102	522,777
1861	242,112	418,219	660,331
1862	255,521	454,451	709,972
1863	220,175	467,845	688,020
1864	264,023	534,632	798,655

Year	Shipments Coastwise	Shipments Foreign	Total Shipments
	tons	tons	tons
1865	261,586	489,553	751,139
1866	265,688	538,526	804,214
1867	294,033	478,679	772,712
1868	248,042	518,671	766,713
1869	247,074	498,324	745,398
1870	232,831	541,467	774,298
1871	211,505	576,714	788,219
1872	225,919	538,914	764,883
1873	256,228	556,326	812,554

SWANSEA

Year	COAL Coastwise	COAL Foreign	COAL Total	COKE Foreign and Coastwise	PATENT FUEL Foreign and Coastwise
	'000 tons	'000 tons	'000 tons	'000 tons	'000 tons
1874	474	563	1,037	5	236
1875	510	535	1,044	3	191
1876	262	576	838	5	211
1877	251	605	857	4	128
1878	237	642	879	4	101
1879	250	601	851	6	170
1880	249	688	937	8	211
1881	295	647	941	10	207
1882	314	843	1,157	11	266
1883	339	840	1,179	8	336
1884	308	824	1,132	5	298
1885	312	792	1,104	3	250
1886	319	742	1,061	4	243
1887	347	774	1,121	3	242
1888	341	810	1,151	6	262
1889	340	857	1,196	3	341
1890	313	925	1,238	9	364
1891	287	906	1,194	15	350
1892	304	916	1,220	6	376
1893	308	869	1,177	1	361
1894	360	969	1,329	8	342
1895	295	1,108	1,404	18	290
1896	315	1,100	1,692	13	253
1897	327	1,311	1,909	23	332
1898	318	1,379	1,984	14	401
1899	385	1,505	2,225	24	508
1900	320	1,745	2,379	14	504
1901	278	1,664	2,312	18	488
1902	236	1,904	2,560	11	513
1903	306	1,805	2,597	21	459
1904	301	1,654	2,321	23	583
1905	303	1,926	2,589	15	527
1906	293	2,551	3,251	15	607
1907	290	2,896	3,631	19	689
1908	278	2,969	3,728	17	613
1909	309	2,889	3,659	18	644
1910	359	2,711	3,523	13	660
1911	327	2,930	3,718	13	681
1912	332	3,002	3,809	15	728
1913	423	3,511	4,500	16	925
1914	352	2,887	3,742	13	723
1915	205	3,102	3,707	10	638
1916	145	2,649	3,147	9	703
1917	102	2,039	2,494	10	763
1918	163	2,102	2,529	5	715
1919	79	2,342	2,750	2	855

Year	COAL Coastwise	COAL Foreign	COAL Total	COKE Foreign and Coastwise	PATENT FUEL Foreign and Coastwise
	'000 tons	'000 tons	'000 tons	'000 tons	'000 tons
1920	56	1,852	2,231	4	1,160
1921	64	1,357	1,705	3	378
1922	104	2,539	3,167	6(2)	619
1923	73	3,358	3,933	11	578
1924	105	2,912	3,497	6	490
1925	78	2,702	3,202	3	447
1926	39	1,054	1,274	3	230
1927	72	2,671	3,198	2	680
1928	46	2,357	2,849	6	570
1929	63	3,358	3,932	16	702
1930	68	3,246	3,750	8	447
1931	52	2,721	3,155	6	351
1932	49	2,874	3,553	14	258
1933	43	2,913	3,516	10	296
1934	51	2,958	3,551	5	241
1935	42	2,757	3,292	4	86
1936	109	2,539	3,075	3	86
1937	103	3,394	3,953	..	..

in '000 tons

Year	Coal, Coke and Patent Fuels
1938	3,782
1945	874
1946	1,141
1947	557
1948	1,106
1949	1,472
1950	1,950
1951	1,691
1952	1,898
1953	1,630
1954	1,867

Year	Coal, Coke and Patent Fuels
1955	1,868
1956	1,738
1957	1,602
1958	1,225
1959	1,015
1960	1,089
1961	1,360
1962	1,724
1963	2,227
1964	1,822

Year	Coal, Coke and Patent Fuels
1965	1,311
1966	965
1967	786
1968	947
1969	1,304
1970	1,371
1971	949
1972	638
1973	867
1974	1,063

COAL 10. Shipment (foreign and coastwise) from each port (Cardiff, Swansea, Newport, Llanelli, Milford, Neath, Porthcawl, Port Talbot), various dates, 1780-1974

NEWPORT

Year	Shipments Coastwise	Shipments Foreign	Total Shipments
	tons	tons	tons
1797	..	..	6,939
1798	..	..	9,715
1799	..	..	18,375
1800	..	..	32,277
1801	..	..	29,981
1802	..	..	38,813
1803	..	..	36,219
1804	..	..	64,393
1805	..	..	73,823
1806	..	..	89,129
1807	..	..	109,648
1808	..	..	132,316
1809	..	..	148,019
1816[1]			
1817[1]			
1818[1]			
1819	193,662	-	193,662
1820	174,104	711	174,815
1821	211,997	-	211,997
1822	234,573	-	234,573
1823	257,434	-	257,434
1824	374,996	763	375,759
1825	372,456	2,126	374,582
1826	401,319	2,801	404,120
1827	375,671	4,302	379,973
1828	420,964	1,818	422,782
1829	..	1,606	..
1830	..	1,930	..
1831	..	4,698	..
1832	..	5,244	..
1833	384,774	2,609	387,383
1834	..	..	..
1835	443,651	2,823	446,474
1836	415,954	5,578	421,532
1837	480,870	7,183	488,053
1838	430,618	8,745	439,363
1839	470,820	13,035	483,855
1840	482,398	7,256	489,654
1841	506,078	14,788	520,866
1842	503,308	52,445	555,753
1843	495,419	58,694	554,113
1844	469,396	148,881	618,277

Year	Shipments Coastwise	Shipments Foreign	Total Shipments
	tons	tons	tons
1845	485,402	149,800	635,209
1846	493,582	123,595	617,177
1847	436,099	116,098	552,197
1848	429,217	124,885	554,102
1849	402,078	108,705	510,783
1850	426,439	125,245	551,684
1851	451,491	151,668	603,159
1852	451,770	137,489	589,259
1853	450,520	111,888	562,408
1854	506,435	134,555	640,990
1855	474,873	187,647	662,520
1856	494,560	186,882	681,442
1857	522,047	187,338	709,385
1858	475,335	208,043	683,378
1859	513,966	175,245	689,211
1860	629,206	187,591	816,797
1861	617,227	211,199	828,426
1862	585,633	202,888	788,521
1863	547,967	184,288	732,255
1864	609,732	282,016	891,748
1865	639,231	292,700	931,931
1866	659,896	378,032	1,037,928
1867	786,564	398,773	1,185,337
1868	646,212	332,907	979,119
1869	774,093	330,052	1,104,145
1870	798,192	398,394	1,196,586
1871	798,928	369,223	1,168,151
1872	781,538	336,068	1,117,606
1873	780,001	305,520	1,085,521

Year	COAL			COKE Foreign and Coastwise	PATENT FUEL Foreign and Coastwise
	Coastwise	Foreign	Total		
	'000 tons	'000 tons	'000 tons	'000 tons	'000 tons
1874	686	370	1,056	1	..
1875	655	329	983	1	..
1876	791	569	1,360	2	0.4
1877	824	610	1,434	4	0.7
1878	876	756	1,632	5	..
1879	984	927	1,911	8	0.9
1880	869	1,016	1,885	7	..
1881	911	1,149	2,059	4	0.1
1882	898	1,360	2,259	6	0.1
1883	1,000	1,565	2,565	6	0.3
1884	1,052	1,712	2,764	5	0.2
1885	1,132	1,756	2,888	3	16
1886	1,138	1,914	3,051	14	50
1887	1,130	2,277	3,406	12	52
1888	991	2,260	3,251	6	50
1889	923	2,094	3,016	3	56
1890	793	1,982	2,776	3	51
1891	970	1,788	2,758	1	48
1892	1,144	1,810	2,954	3	64
1893	1,104	1,803	2,907	6	51
1894	1,132	2,589	3,721	5	51
1895	895	2,417	3,311	5	45
1896	1,059	2,524	4,036	8	33
1897	989	2,845	4,311	22	36
1898	654	1,736	2,695	5	53
1899	891	2,928	4,374	17	93
1900	770	2,774	3,975	31	76
1901	796	2,619	3,817	20	90
1902	861	2,768	4,098	16	70
1903	917	2,953	4,434	15	36
1904	940	3,145	4,699	19	51
1905	824	3,006	4,432	18	67
1906	779	3,541	4,962	18	119
1907	781	3,803	5,221	16	133
1908	777	3,922	5,414	42	137
1909	775	3,833	5,304	38	119
1910	736	3,774	5,165	21	147
1911	688	4,325	5,658	22	113
1912	674	3,976	5,288	16	125
1913	719	4,679	6,144	16	147
1914	707	4,093	5,459	17	138
1915	569	3,412	4,625	23	46
1916	498	3,467	4,634	18	55
1917	394	3,346	4,300	36	78
1918	432	3,124	4,002	14	86
1919	663	3,655	4,956	28	102

NEWPORT

Year	COAL			COKE Foreign and Coastwise	PATENT FUEL Foreign and Coastwise
	Coastwise	Foreign	Total		
	'000 tons	'000 tons	'000 tons	'000 tons	'000 tons
1920	1,161	2,679	4,449	41	155
1921	544	1,981	2,987	5	89
1922	645	4,777	6,264	20(2)	97(2)
1923	321	5,594	6,653	39	134
1924	382	4,449	5,563	8	115
1925	347	3,871	4,833	9	124
1926	203	1,724	2,198	9	39
1927	489	3,806	4,904	11	154
1928	566	3,742	4,936	14	116
1929	534	4,161	5,292	21	143
1930	482	4,109	5,168	13	131
1931	418	3,125	3,954	8	20
1932	359	2,193	2,942	12	-
1933	349	1,964	2,677	8	41
1934	433	2,008	2,811	10	92
1935	424	2,251	3,033	6	103
1936	496	1,795	2,608	7	137
1937	450	2,368	3,265	..	..

in '000 tons

Year	Coal, Coke and Patent Fuels
1938	3,061
1945(3)	907
1946	867
1947	638
1948	1,598
1949	1,387
1950	1,449
1951	1,302
1952	1,194
1953	1,346
1954	1,362

Year	Coal, Coke and Patent Fuels
1955	1,131
1956	993
1957	766
1958	615
1959	523
1960	346
1961	406
1962	286
1963	449
1964	322

Year	Coal, Coke and Patent Fuels
1965	5
1966	3
1967	4
1968	10
1969	47
1970	70
1971	58
1972	2
1973	-
1974	33

COAL 10. Shipment (foreign and coastwise) from each port (Cardiff, Swansea, Newport, Llanelli, Milford, Neath, Porthcawl, Port Talbot), various dates, 1780-1974

LLANELLI

Year	Total Shipments
	(tons)
1790	2,190
1791	2,219
1792	1,251
1793	1,478
1794	339

Year	Total Shipments
	(tons)
1795	..
1796	300
1797	150
1798	1,040
1799	837

Year	Shipments Coastwise		Shipments Internal and Foreign		Total Shipments	
	Coal	Culm or Anthracite	Coal	Culm or Anthracite	Coal	Culm or Anthracite
	tons		tons		tons	
1816	29,418		15,480		44,898	
1817	38,512		26,527		65,039	
1818	34,570		18,427		52,997	
1819	54,405	7,867	3,696	-	58,101	7,867
1820	57,695	4,823	2,732	22	60,427	4,845
1821	68,262	1,506	925	-	69,187	1,506
1822	70,014	2,167	1,704	-	71,718	2,167
1823	62,366	2,016	1,337	-	63,703	2,016
1824	68,739	5,278	1,890	-	70,629	5,278
1825	72,146	2,981	1,102	-	73,248	2,981
1826	65,557	7,630	2,843	-	68,400	7,630
1827	68,797	5,336	2,025	-	70,822	5,336
1828	70,196	6,594	1,149	-	71,345	6,594
1829	..	..	1,952	..	..	..
1830	..	..	3,819	36	..	36
1831	..	..	5,817	..	..	..
1832	..	..	4,740	..	..	..
1833	78,886	18,441	7,109	..	85,995	18,441
1834	..	..	-	..	..	..
1835	74,919	11,161	11,287	440	86,206	11,601
1836	76,957	8,342	19,759	-	96,716	8,342
1837	101,919	16,323	30,268	-	132,187	16,323
1838	116,061	20,465	25,962	-	142,023	20,465
1839	114,193	27,646	24,890	-	139,083	27,646
1840	151,750	41,019	19,275	-	171,025	41,019
1841	125,151	37,968	15,079	-	140,230	37,968
1842	128,134	41,584	9,802	40	137,936	41,624
1843	127,304	43,304	10,598	-	137,902	43,304
1844	125,074	69,515	19,524	630	144,598	70,145

Year	Shipments Coastwise		Shipments Internal and Foreign		Total Shipments	
	Coal	Culm or Anthracite	Coal	Culm or Anthracite	Coal	Culm or Anthracite
	tons		tons		tons	
1845	145,597	62,995	11,452	-	157,049	62,995
1846	169,006	67,155	13,828	100	182,834	67,255
1847	165,650	38,741	14,178	-	179,828	38,741
1848	192,222	47,664	15,141	110	207,363	47,774
1849	158,160	52,961	11,324	100	169,484	53,061
1850	154,976	56,367	17,049	459	172,025	56,826

Year	Shipments Coastwise	Shipments Foreign	Total Shipments
	(tons)	(tons)	(tons)
1851	219,460	9,785	229,245
1852	214,735	8,838	223,573
1853	245,948	11,573	257,521
1854	266,402	22,502	288,904
1855	287,444	24,118	311,562
1856	297,207	32,876	330,083
1857	333,099	49,818	382,917
1858	280,926	81,831	362,757
1859	285,745	76,366	362,111
1860	284,170	89,996	374,166
1861	278,270	111,103	389,373
1862	265,641	115,021	380,662
1863	220,539	115,700	336,239
1864	252,710	134,669	387,379
1865	245,969	137,196	383,165
1866	201,620	137,735	339,355
1867	209,736	158,904	368,640
1868	180,881	128,689	309,570
1869	154,391	126,833	281,224
1870	174,647	118,454	293,101
1871	161,324	120,664	281,988
1872	165,946	113,298	279,244
1873	149,956	94,314	244,270

LLANELLI

Year	COAL Coastwise	COAL Foreign	COAL Total	COKE Foreign and Coastwise	PATENT FUEL Foreign and Coastwise
	'000 tons	'000 tons	'000 tons	'000 tons	'000 tons
1874	128	96	224	..	..
1875	123	84	207	..	0.01
1876	116	79	194	..	0.4
1877	114	60	174	..	..
1878	123	70	194	..	..
1879	116	70	186	..	..
1880	120	76	196	..	..
1881	110	58	169	..	..
1882	107	65	172	0.03	..
1883	114	49	163	0.03	0.03
1884	136	72	208	0.07	0.01
1885	112	103	215	..	..
1886	88	81	169	..	0.3
1887	87	92	178	0.06	..
1888	83	114	197	0.02	..
1889	88	141	229	..	..
1890	83	132	215	..	..
1891	64	149	214	..	..
1892	50	143	192	..	..
1893	59	127	186	..	..
1894	75	170	245	0.03	..
1895	72	170	241	..	..
1896	84	196	291	..	..
1897	66	179	253	..	0.3
1898	74	185	268	..	..
1899	78	182	269	..	..
1900	64	205	279	0.2	..
1901	64	197	272	1.0	..
1902	68	201	285	..	0.01
1903	66	227	310	0.02	0.008
1904	84	255	363	0.01	..
1905	94	261	377	..	..
1906	91	288	401	..	..
1907	68	200	285	..	..
1908	64	201	284	..	..
1909	59	190	266	..	..
1910	70	187	337	..	..
1911	64	159	236	0.002	..
1912	65	145	222	0.002	..
1913	63	244	326	0.002	..
1914	76	196	291	..	..
1915	36	118	163	..	..
1916	23	151	186	..	0.4
1917	17	134	163	..	..
1918	14	79	100	..	..
1919	18	285	323	..	0.8

Year	COAL Coastwise	COAL Foreign	COAL Total	COKE Foreign and Coastwise	PATENT FUEL Foreign and Coastwise
	'000 tons	'000 tons	'000 tons	'000 tons	'000 tons
1920	51	531	616	..	11
1921	48	229	298	..	5
1922	92	418	548	..	25(2)
1923	107	529	677	1	7
1924	82	379	493	..	..
1925	96	205	321	..	3
1926	33	55	95	..	4
1927	39	192	248	..	-
1928	26	348	398	..	-
1929	26	376	429	..	0.2
1930	28	409	464	..	-
1931	33	438	499	-	0.7
1932	42	495	571	..	-
1933	36	471	537	..	0.02
1934	34	513	582	..	..
1935	58	506	595	..	..
1936	23	477	528	..	..
1937	16	321	355	..	..

COAL 10. Shipment (foreign and coastwise) from each port (Cardiff, Swansea Newport, Llanelli, Milford, Neath, Porthcawl, Port Talbot), various dates, 1780-1974

MILFORD

Year	Total Shipments	Year	Total Shipments
	(tons)		(tons)
1745	1,516	1755	2,517
1746	1,308	1756	3,031
1747	2,175	1757	2,862
1748	1,864	1758	2,020
1749	2,727	1759	1,777
1750	2,439	1760	2,964
1751	2,091	1761	2,636
1752	..	1762	2,221
1753	1,753	1763	3,840
1754	2,867	1764	2,544
		1765	3,122

Year	Shipments Coastwise		Shipments Internal and Foreign		Total Shipments	
	Coal	Culm or Anthracite	Coal	Culm or Anthracite	Coal	Culm or Anthracite
	tons		tons		tons	
1816	-		316		316	
1817	-		1,310		1,310	
1818	-		269		269	
1819	11,807	16,749	-	-	11,807	16,749
1820	11,033	8,851	-	26	11,033	8,877
1821	10,236	8,847	-	42	10,236	8,889
1822	9,693	8,538	-	-	9,693	8,538
1823	7,000	8,214	-	71	7,000	8,285
1824	7,305	10,280	-	-	7,305	10,280
1825	8,772	12,557	-	100	8,772	12,657
1826	8,640	13,653	20	35	8,660	13,688
1827	7,768	13,304	-	-	7,768	13,304
1828	7,400	8,376	24	-	7,424	8,376
1829	..	..	148	-	..	..
1830	..	..	10	-	..	..
1831	..	..	-	-	..	..
1832	..	..	214	-	..	..
1833	12,631	29,773	-	-	12,631	29,773
1834	..	-	-	-	..	..

Year	Shipments Coastwise		Shipments Internal and Foreign		Total Shipments	
	Coal	Culm or Anthracite	Coal	Culm or Anthracite	Coal	Culm or Anthracite
	tons		tons		tons	
1835	15,674	28,068	-	-	15,674	28,068
1836	14,992	31,685	-	-	14,992	31,685
1837	14,252	41,592	102	120	14,354	41,712
1838	18,410	42,651	210	-	18,620	42,651
1839	17,731	45,490	-	-	17,731	45,490
1840	20,954	55,814	372	39	21,326	55,853
1841	16,922	52,589	-	-	16,922	52,589
1842	15,581	54,987	-	-	15,581	54,987
1843	15,428	45,024	312	819	15,740	45,843
1844	22,089	45,605	-	-	22,089	45,605
1845	19,583	46,126	394	-	19,977	46,126
1846	20,939	47,552	288	24	21,227	47,576
1847	17,319	35,394	439	-	17,758	35,394
1848	16,967	38,535	265	-	17,232	38,535
1849	13,684	37,718	411	-	14,095	37,718
1850	16,270	31,288	231	-	16,501	31,288

Year	Shipments Coastwise	Shipments Foreign	Total Shipments
	tons	tons	tons
1851	49,573	269	49,842
1852	50,102	371	50,473
1853	48,627	540	49,167
1854	51,544	1,255	52,799
1855	49,119	292	49,411
1856	47,566	323	47,889
1857	57,364	641	58,005
1858	54,510	..	54,510
1859	46,264	101	46,365
1860	51,351	45	51,396
1861	51,382	540	51,922
1862	56,069	1,575	57,644
1863	44,462	650	45,112
1864	59,777	628	60,405
1865	47,178	878	48,506
1866	42,517	2,478	44,995
1867	48,745	847	49,592
1868	49,824	250	50,074
1869	58,464	..	58,464

COAL 10 contd

MILFORD

Year	Shipments Coastwise	Shipments Foreign	Total Shipments
	tons	tons	tons
1870	46,623	190	46,813
1871	43,306	..	43,306
1872	46,271	388	46,659
1873	44,475	300	44,775

Year	COAL			COKE Foreign and Coastwise	PATENT FUEL Foreign and Coastwise
	Coastwise	Foreign	Total		
	'000 tons	'000 tons	'000 tons	'000 tons	'000 tons
1874	34	0.4	34	..	..
1875	36	..	36	..	0.01
1876	33	..	33	..	..
1877	25	..	25	..	..
1878	33	..	33	..	..
1879	27	..	27	..	..
1880	25	..	25	..	..
1881	25	..	25	..	..
1882	26	..	26	..	..
1883	37	..	37	..	..
1884	33	0.2	33	..	..
1885	35	..	35	..	..
1886	32	0.9	32	..	..
1887	33	0.8	33	..	..
1888	28	0.2	28	..	..
1889	22	2.4	22	..	..
1890	29	2.6	29	..	..
1891	24	3.3	24	..	..
1892	29	5.4	29	..	..
1893	30	5.6	30	..	..
1894	25	4.1	25	..	..
1895	26	1.5	27	..	..
1896	27	1.4	29	..	..
1897	29	2.1	31	..	..
1898	29	3.3	33	..	..
1899	19	0.9	21	..	..
1900	17	1.1	18	0.1	..
1901	16	0.9	33	..	..
1902	16	0.9	159	..	..
1903	20	0.2	172	..	..
1904	26	0.2	138	..	..

Year	COAL			COKE Foreign and Coastwise	PATENT FUEL Foreign and Coastwise
	Coastwise	Foreign	Total		
	'000 tons	'000 tons	'000 tons	'000 tons	'000 tons
1905	23	..	115	..	..
1906	22	0.3	112	..	..
1907	21	0.3	120	..	..
1908	23	0.5	139	..	..
1909	21	0.7	134	..	..
1910	19	0.3	122	..	..
1911	20	0.3	124	..	..
1912	21	0.3	133	..	..
1913	24	0.3	142	..	..
1914	24	..	24	..	..
1915	20	0.3	112	..	..
1916	15	..	60	..	..
1917	15	0.4	50	..	..
1918	13	0.9	52	..	..
1919	11	2.3	88	..	..
1920	15	5.8	175	..	..
1921	9	0.6	109	..	..
1922	11	9	176	..	..
1923	4	18	189	..	..
1924	5	15	180	..	..
1925	6	11	200	..	..
1926	2	2	128	..	..
1927	3	7	201	..	..
1928	4	7	199	..	..
1929	5	9	232	..	..
1930	4	4	236	..	..
1931	2	2	220	..	..
1932	0.8	7	214	..	..
1933	0.5	8	230	..	..
1934	1	14	211	..	..
1935	4	14	199	..	..
1936	4	7	188	..	..
1937	7	11	210	..	..

COAL 10. Shipment (foreign and coastwise) from each port (Cardiff, Swansea, Newport, Llanelli, Milford, Neath, Porthcawl, Port Talbot), various dates, 1780-1974

NEATH

Year	Shipments Coastwise	Shipments Foreign	Total Shipments
	tons	tons	tons
1853	106,185	5,258	111,443
1854	133,077	6,124	139,201
1855	145,865	10,304	156,169
1856	158,945	14,270	173,215
1857	187,827	10,532	198,359
1858	185,574	16,020	201,594
1859	179,694	13,656	193,350
1860	185,310	13,740	199,050
1861	201,920	18,282	220,202
1862	229,173	24,923	254,096
1863	239,744	27,714	267,458
1864	239,949	28,313	268,262
1865	238,038	28,501	266,539
1866	240,981	43,055	284,036
1867	230,320	46,033	276,353
1868	199,281	47,242	246,523
1869	199,696	52,858	252,554
1870	205,903	23,136	229,039
1871	250,994	70,623	321,617
1872	239,815	69,427	309,242
1873	192,276	48,484	240,760

Year	COAL			COKE Foreign and Coastwise	PATENT FUEL Foreign and Coastwise
	Coastwise	Foreign	Total		
	'000 tons	'000 tons	'000 tons	'000 tons	'000 tons
1874	..	..	..	..	..
1875	..	..	..	..	..
1876	210	39	249	0.1	1
1877	214	19	232	..	..
1878	193	19	212	0.09	1
1879	185	53	238	0.02	0.5
1880	192	94	286	..	0.4
1881	223	96	319	..	0.8
1882	236	111	346	0.05	0.2
1883	252	114	366	0.07	0.5
1884	208	115	323	..	0.02

Year	COAL			COKE Foreign and Coastwise	PATENT FUEL Foreign and Coastwise
	Coastwise	Foreign	Total		
	'000 tons	'000 tons	'000 tons	'000 tons	'000 tons
1885	162	53	215	0.2	0.5
1886	143	53	197	0.1	0.3
1887	167	72	239	0.1	..
1888	176	63	239	..	..
1889	193	38	231	..	0.04
1890	182	28	209	3	..
1891	187	36	223	0.4	..
1892	192	44	236	1	0.04
1893	212	51	263	3	..
1894	223	55	278	2	..
1895	193	12	206	2	..
1896	188	52	239	4	0.04
1897	192	65	257	0.7	2
1898	126	40	166	0.1	2
1899	175	84	259	1	1
1900	183	99	282	0.4	..
1901	163	92	255	..	..
1902	197	103	300	..	..
1903	193	100	293	..	..
1904	183	95	278	..	..
1905	223	96	318	..	..
1906	219	92	311	..	..
1907	240	134	374	..	..
1908	204	202	406	..	..
1909	172	154	327	..	..
1910	163	153	316	..	..
1911	163	218	382	..	..
1912	119	123	243	..	..
1913	132	198	331	..	..
1914	Included Port Talbot		..	..	..
1915	"	"	..	..	..
1916	"	"	..	..	..
1917	"	"	..	..	..
1918	"	"	..	..	..
1919	"	"	..	..	..
1920	"	"	..	..	..
1921	"	"	..	..	..

COAL 10. Shipment (foreign and coastwise) from each port (Cardiff, Swansea, Newport, Llanelli, Milford, Neath, Porthcawl, Port Talbot), various dates, 1780-1974

PORTHCAWL

Year	Shipments Coastwise	Shipments Foreign	Total Shipments
	tons	tons	tons
1853	28,281	-	28,281
1854	22,185	-	22,185
1855	20,882	219	21,101
1856	22,569	200	22,769
1857	20,275	35	20,310
1858	23,054	96	23,150
1859	19,900	-	19,900
1860	17,196	-	17,196
1861	16,573	-	16,573
1862	20,548	-	20,548
1863	21,326	-	21,326
1864	16,966	-	16,966
1865	10,419	340	10,759
1866	43,603	900	44,503
1867	90,968	13,976	104,944
1868	108,679	25,221	133,900
1869	116,250	21,648	137,898
1870	137,446	19,392	156,838
1871	142,430	23,203	165,633
1872	133,964	19,297	153,261
1873	91,467	6,561	98,028

Year	COAL Coastwise	COAL Foreign	COAL Total	COKE Foreign and Coastwise	PATENT FUEL Foreign and Coastwise
	'000 tons	'000 tons	'000 tons	'000 tons	'000 tons
1874	98	10	108	0.1	..
1875	87	13	101	0.2	..
1876	100	0.4	101	..	..
1877	99	..	99	..	..
1878	67	0.1	68	0.6	..
1879	67	8	75	0.4	..
1880	91	12	103	0.3	..
1881	108	9	118	0.03	..
1882	138	12	151	0.03	..
1883	145	14	158	0.04	..
1884	108	21	129	0.2	..
1885	130	14	143	0.1	..
1886	133	15	148	0.05	..
1887	133	11	144	..	..
1888	134	13	148	0.04	..
1889	112	11	123	0.05	..
1890	104	10	115	0.4	..
1891	135	16	151	..	..
1892	159	9	167	0.5	..
1893	133	7	140	2	..
1894	132	5	137	0.7	..
1895	106	5	111	..	..
1896	92	4	95	0.1	..
1897	95	3	98	0.1	..
1898	24	2	25	0.08	..
1899	21	..	21	..	..
1900	7	..	7	..	..
1901	7	..	7	..	..
1902	5	..	5	..	..
1903	3	..	3	..	..
1904	..	..	..	..	..

COAL 10. Shipment (foreign and coastwise) from each port (Cardiff, Swansea, Newport, Llanelli, Milford, Neath, Porthcawl, Port Talbot), various dates, 1780-1974

PORT TALBOT

Year	Shipments Coastwise	Shipments Foreign	Total Shipments
	tons	tons	tons
1853	65,831	1,920	67,751
1854	68,988	3,689	72,677
1855	72,010	6,662	78,672
1856	70,330	11,576	81,906
1857	61,638	4,343	65,981
1858	67,396	1,653	69,049
1859	56,459	361	56,820
1860	61,965	..	61,965
1861	80,960	1,495	82,455
1862	82,103	1,271	83,374
1863	71,598	645	72,243
1864	58,608	1,499	60,107
1865	81,265	9,921	91,186
1866	86,764	9,511	96,275
1867	80,563	6,980	87,543
1868	77,498	8,276	85,774
1869	71,900	7,615	79,515
1870	30,331	8,766	39,097
1871	24,817	7,902	32,719
1872	19,822	1,773	21,595
1873	9,924	4,257	14,181

Year	COAL			COKE Foreign and Coastwise	PATENT FUEL Foreign and Coastwise
	Coastwise	Foreign	Total		
	'000 tons	'000 tons	'000 tons	'000 tons	'000 tons
1874	12	5	17	..	0.05
1875	22	0.4	22	0.07	..
1876	41	2	43	0.03	..
1877	57	3	60	0.05	..
1878	68	8	76	..	..
1879	79	21	100	1.1	..
1880	81	17	98	0.6	..
1881	93	14	107	0.6	..
1882	90	18	108	0.4	..
1883	88	17	105	0.3	..
1884	85	14	98	0.5	..
1885	83	13	96	0.7	..
1886	80	9	89	0.9	..
1887	86	10	95	2.2	..
1888	83	9	93	1.1	..
1889	59	8	67	0.2	..
1890	13	3	16	0.3	..
1891	16	6	22	0.08	..
1892	27	4	31	0.03	..
1893	24	2	26	0.02	..
1894	18	1	19	0.03	..
1895	21	2	23	0.03	..
1896	22	4	27	0.3	..
1897	35	8	43	0.01	..
1898	39	14	53	0.4	..
1899	109	97	206	4	..
1900	125	249	374	8	0.03
1901	111	245	356	8	48
1902	132	340	473	18	75
1903	174	406	580	16	93
1904	137	744	1,038	14	117
1905	147	724	1,075	16	107
1906	188	983	1,367	24	138
1907	205	1,267	1,676	24	130
1908	202	1,097	1,523	15	123
1909	186	1,220	1,598	25	124
1910	183	1,432	1,805	24	166
1911	164	1,432	1,771	17	217
1912	119	1,613	1,904	10	192
1913	110	1,869	2,184	9	250
1914(4)	234	1,428	1,827	17	200
1915	153	1,436	1,845	25	173
1916	72	1,919	2,190	16	213
1917	63	1,358	1,579	15	234
1918	101	962	1,173	7	229
1919	102	1,574	1,852	10	189
1920	162	1,631	1,980	8	211
1921	55	649	830	4	94
1922	111	1,941	2,294	19	119
1923	78	2,717	3,009	15	0.1
1924	58	2,228	2,486	7	56
1925	72	1,848	2,116	4	97
1926	16	780	885	1	43
1927	103	1,968	2,290	3	64
1928	67	1,517	1,745	6	18
1929	124	1,983	2,292	10	27

PORT TALBOT

Year	COAL			COKE Foreign and Coastwise	PATENT FUEL Foreign and Coastwise
	Coastwise	Foreign	Total		
	'000 tons	'000 tons	'000 tons	'000 tons	'000 tons
1930	90	2,199	2,474	15	109
1931	56	1,433	1,623	10	16
1932	49	1,717	1,947	10	-
1933	50	1,905	2,122	8	-
1934	59	1,866	2,110	5	0.2
1935	64	1,624	1,840	6	49
1936	124	1,428	1,690	10	4
1937	133	1,562	1,817	..	..

General Notes

(i) Sources. Royal Commission on Coal 1871, iii, Appendices, especially 13-14, 49 and 103-10 for figures up to 1869 and C. Hadfield, The Canals of South Wales and the Border, p.134 for Newport 1797-1809; Coals, Cinders etc. (Sessional Papers), for figures 1870-74; F.A. Gibson, (see note to Table 2), for figures for 1874-1937; Welsh Digest for figures from 1938 onwards.

(ii) For some years the figures given for total shipments in the 1871 report are different (usually only slightly) from the sum of the figures for coastal and foreign shipment. It has been assumed that this represented an arithmetical error on the part of the 1871 commission and the total figures given in the table have been corrected. The years affected are: Cardiff (1828, 1860); Swansea (1823, 1833, 1843, 1861); Newport (1844, 1845, 1867); Port Talbot (1865); Porthcawl (1872).

(iii) From 1874 on the figure given for total coal exports excludes shipments of coke and patent fuel. From 1874 to 1895 it is the sum of the foreign and coastwise shipments and excludes coal shipped as bunkers. From 1896 to 1937 the total is greater than the sum of foreign plus coastwise, the extra amount being accounted for by shipments for ships' bunkers (foreign and coastal). From 1945 a single total is given for coal, coke and patent fuels shipped both foreign and coastwise.

NOTES

1. Figures for Cardiff for 1816-18 include shipment from Newport.

2. Exclude coastwise shipments.

3. Figures for 1945 onwards excludes trade handled by Newport Harbour Commissioners.

4. Port Talbot includes Briton Ferry (Neath) from 1914 onwards.

COAL 11. Colliery deaths, number and rate per 1,000, under-ground and total, South and North Wales (number only), 1853-1974.

	Under-ground Workers					Underground and Surface					
	Number of Deaths			Death Rate per 1,000 Employed(1)		Number of Deaths			Death Rate per 1,000 Employed(1)		Total no. of colliery deaths
	S.W.	U.K.	S.W. as % of U.K.	S.W.	U.K.	S.W.	U.K.	S.W. as % of U.K.	S.W.	U.K.	North Wales
1853	..	..	..	..	..	137	..	..	..	..	20
1854	..	..	..	..	..	128	1,030	12.4	..	..	29
1855	..	..	..	..	..	178	955	18.6	..	..	31
1856	..	..	..	..	..	272	1,027	26.5	..	..	30
1857	..	..	..	..	..	159	1,119	14.2	..	..	21
1858	..	..	..	..	..	171	931	18.4	..	..	22
1859	..	..	..	..	..	160	905	17.7	..	..	12
1860	..	..	..	..	..	289	1,109	26.1	..	..	19
1861	..	..	..	..	..	156	943	16.5	..	..	26
1862	..	..	..	..	..	170	1,238	13.7	..	..	23
1863	..	..	..	..	..	201	998	20.1	..	..	37
1864	..	..	..	..	..	150	963	15.6	..	..	32
1865	..	..	..	..	..	224	1,053	21.3	..	..	22
1866	..	..	..	..	..	173	1,565	11.1	..	..	35
1867	..	..	..	..	..	356	1,260	28.3	..	..	28
1868	..	..	..	..	..	148	1,080	13.7	..	..	55
1869	..	..	..	..	..	226	1,170	19.3	..	..	31
1870	..	..	..	..	..	199	1,046	19.0	..	..	31
1871	..	..	..	..	..	205	1,126	18.2	..	..	30
1872	..	..	..	..	..	200	1,114	18.0	..	..	22
1873	..	..	..	..	..	159	1,669	14.9	..	..	51
1874	165	947	17.4	2.7	2.2	185	1,056	17.5	2.5	1.9	28
1875	174	1,145	15.1	2.8	2.6	188	1,244	15.1			
1876	160	822	19.4	2.8	2.0	176	933	18.8	2.5	2.3	23
1877	153	1,109	13.7	2.7	2.8	160	1,208	13.2	2.6	1.8	35
1878	431	1,327	32.4	7.9	3.4	448	1,413	31.7	2.4	2.4	23
1879	247	902	27.3	4.3	2.3	256	973	26.3	7.0	2.9	31
									3.8	2.0	24
1880	394	1,230	32.0	6.7	3.1	410	1,318	31.1	5.9	2.7	30
1881	178	866	20.5	2.8	2.1	188	954	19.7	2.5	1.9	31
1882	188	1,042	18.0	2.9	2.5	202	1,126	17.9	2.6	2.2	20
1883	204	946	21.5	2.9	2.2	231	1,054	21.9	2.8	2.0	24
1884	223	848	26.2	3.1	2.0	233	942	24.7	2.7	1.8	29
1885	258	1,075	24.0	3.5	2.5	274	1,150	23.8	3.2	2.2	23
1886	181	864	20.9	2.4	2.0	201	953	21.0	2.3	1.8	19
1887	227	916	24.7	3.0	2.1	243	995	24.4	2.7	1.8	20
1888	172	804	21.3	2.1	1.8	194	888	21.8	2.1	1.6	27
1889	183	969	18.8	2.1	2.0	200	1,064	18.7	2.0	1.8	45
1890	445	1,057	42.1	4.7	2.0	462	1,160	39.8	4.2	1.8	22
1891	208	882	23.5	2.0	1.6	238	979	24.3	2.0	1.5	23
1892	321	904	35.5	3.1	1.6	345	982	35.1	2.9	1.4	14
1893	243	940	25.8	2.4	1.7	272	1,060	25.6	2.3	1.5	21
1894	457	1,015	45.0	4.3	1.7	482	1,127	42.7	3.8	1.5	26
1895	220	923	23.8	2.0	1.6	245	1,042	23.5	1.9	1.4	20
1896	270	902	23.9	2.5	1.6	295	1,025	28.7	2.3	1.4	22
1897	203	833	24.3	1.8	1.4	222	930	23.8	1.7	1.3	15
1898	137	779	17.5	1.2	1.3	159	908	17.5	1.2	1.2	20
1899	199	801	24.8	1.7	1.3	217	916	23.6	1.6	1.2	14
1900	214	899	23.8	1.7	1.4	243	1,012	24.0	1.6	1.2	27
1901	300	950	31.5	2.3	1.4	330	1,101	29.9	2.1	1.3	19
1902	243	907	26.7	1.8	1.3	260	1,024	25.3	1.6	1.2	21
1903	226	917	24.6	1.6	1.3	256	1,072	23.8	1.6	1.2	17
1904	233	914	25.4	1.6	1.3	268	1,055	25.4	1.6	1.2	22
1905	407	1,033	39.3	2.8	1.4	440	1,159	37.9	2.6	1.3	15
1906	253	1,007	25.1	1.7	1.4	290	1,142	25.3	1.6	1.2	26
1907	292	1,103	26.4	1.8	1.4	322	1,245	25.8	1.6	1.3	18
1908	252	1,162	21.6	1.4	1.4	282	1,308	21.5	1.3	1.3	11
1909	329	1,321	24.9	1.8	1.6	354	1,453	24.3	1.7	1.4	25
1910	290	1,622	17.8	1.6	1.9	323	1,775	18.1	1.5	1.6	24
1911	285	1,116	25.5	1.5	1.2	313	1,265	24.7	1.4	1.1	20
1912	270	1,101	24.5	1.4	1.2	306	1,276	23.9	1.3	1.1	16
1913	747	1,580	47.2	3.7	1.7	782	1,753	44.6	3.3	1.5	22
1914	335	1,086	30.8	1.6	1.1	377	1,219	30.9	1.6	1.0	19
1915	304	1,167	26.0	1.7	1.5	331	1,297	25.4	1.6	1.3	..
1916	295	1,163	25.3	1.6	1.4	322	1,313	24.5	1.5	1.3	..
1917	325	1,214	26.7	1.7	1.4	366	1,370	26.7	1.6	1.3	..
1918	313	1,277	24.5	1.7	1.6	340	1,401	24.2	1.5	1.3	..
1919	257	1,003	25.6	1.1	1.0	288	1,118	25.7	1.1	0.9	..
1920	256	965	26.5	1.1	1.0	287	1,103	26.0	1.1	0.9	..
1921	160	682	23.4	0.8	0.7	180	756	23.8	0.8	0.7	14
1922	248	999	24.8	1.2	1.1	270	1,105	24.4	1.1	0.9	10
1923	315	1,175	26.8	1.4	1.2	337	1,293	26.0	1.3	1.1	27
1924	296	1,084	27.3	1.4	1.1	318	1,198	26.5	1.2	0.9	25
1925	238	1,020	23.3	1.3	1.1	273	1,128	24.2	1.3	1.0	16
1926	131	573	22.9	0.7	0.6	146	645	22.6	0.7	0.6	17
1927	266	1,028	25.9	1.6	1.2	284	1,121	25.3	1.5	1.1	20
1928	204	885	23.0	1.4	1.2	223	983	22.7	1.3	1.0	16
1929	212	985	21.5	1.4	1.3	227	1,065	21.3	1.3	1.1	16
1930	203	935	21.7	1.4	1.2	224	1,008	22.2	1.3	1.1	17
1931	161	788	20.4	1.2	1.1	169	856	19.7	1.1	1.0	16
1932	168	805	20.9	1.4	1.2	179	877	20.3	1.2	1.0	16
1933	160	749	21.4	1.3	1.2	176	815	21.6	1.2	1.0	11
1934	151	992	15.2	1.3	1.6	163	1,066	15.3	1.2	1.3	277
1935	149	763	19.5	1.4	1.3	161	849	19.0	1.2	1.1	6
1936	138	726	19.0	1.3	1.2	148	784	18.8	1.2	1.0	8
1937	171	781	21.9	1.5	1.2	182	851	21.4	1.3	1.1	7
1938	140	775	18.0	1.2	1.2	154	851	18.1	1.1	1.0	6
1939	151	722	20.9	0.5(1)	0.5	168	783	21.5	0.4(1)	0.4	..

COAL 11. cont.

	Under-ground Workers					Underground and Surface					
	Number of Deaths			Death Rate per 1,000 Employed(1)		Number of Deaths			Death Rate per 1,000 Employed(1)		Total no. of colliery deaths
	S.W.	U.K.	S.W. as % of U.K.	S.W.	U.K.	S.W.	U.K.	S.W. as % of U.K.	S.W.	U.K.	North Wales
1940	174	836	20.8	0.6	0.5	189	923	20.5	0.5	0.4	..
1941	172	838	20.5	0.7	0.6	193	925	20.9	0.6	0.5	..
1942	149	799	18.6	0.6	0.5	160	877	18.2	0.5	0.4	..
1943	125	655	19.1	0.5	0.5	138	713	19.4	0.4	0.4	..
1944	105	573	18.3	0.4	0.4	115	623	18.5	0.4	0.3	..
1945	103	506	20.4	0.5	0.4	114	550	20.7	0.4	0.3	..
1946	94	493	19.1	0.4	0.4	103	543	19.0	0.4	0.3	..
1947	93	584	15.9	0.4	0.4	101	618	16.3	0.4	0.3	..
1948	107	434	24.7	0.5	0.3	112	468	23.9	0.4	0.3	..
1949	87	411	21.2	0.4	0.3	93	460	20.2	0.3	0.3	..
1950	83	447	18.6	0.4	0.3	94	493	19.1	0.4	0.3	..
1951	68	448	15.2	0.3	0.3	79	487	16.2	0.3	0.3	..
1952	77	376	20.5	0.4	0.3	86	420	20.5	0.3	0.2	..
1953	65	344	18.9	0.3	0.3	81	392	20.7	0.3	0.2	..
1954	86	328	26.2	0.4	0.2	93	371	25.1	0.3	0.2	..
1955	88	366	24.0	0.4	0.3	95	425	22.4	0.4	0.2	..
1956	58	295	19.7	0.3	0.2	61	330	18.5	0.2	0.2	..
1957	76	369	20.6	0.4	0.3	81	396	20.5	0.3	0.2	..
1958	68	290	23.4	0.4	0.2	76	327	23.2	0.3	0.2	..
1959	55	326	16.9	0.3	0.3	58	348	16.7	0.3	0.2	..
1960	83	287	28.9	0.6	0.3	85	317	26.8	0.4	0.2	..
1961	31	207	15.0	0.2	0.2	34	235	14.5	0.2	0.2	..
1962	49	233	21.0	0.4	0.2	55	257	21.4	0.3	0.2	..
1963	51	221	23.1	0.4	0.2	59	254	23.2	0.3	0.2	..
1964	34	175	19.4	0.3	0.2	35	198	17.7	0.2	0.2	..
1965	71	194	36.6	0.7	0.3	74	216	34.3	0.5	0.2	..
1966	28	144	19.4	0.3	0.2	32	160	20.0	0.3	0.2	..
1967	16	126	12.7	0.2	0.2	20	151	13.2	0.2	0.2	..
1968	16	105	15.2	0.2	0.2	17	115	14.8	0.2	0.1	..
1969	13	84	15.5	0.2	0.2	18	100	18.0	0.2	0.1	..
1970	19	82	23.2	0.3	0.2	22	91	24.2	0.3	0.1	..
1971	17	66	25.8	0.3	0.1	17	72	23.6	0.2	0.1	..
1972	13	57	22.8	0.3	0.2	14	64	21.9	0.2	0.1	..
1973	9	74	12.2	0.2	0.2	10	80	12.5	0.1	0.1	..
1974	5	..	..	0.1	..	7	..	..	0.1	..	..

General Notes

(i) Sources. Mines Inspectors' Reports 1853 onwards, F.A. Gibson, op.cit., (see notes to Table 2).

Notes

1. From 1939 onwards the death rates are on the basis of number of deaths per 100,000 manshifts.

COAL 12. **Mechanisation.** Number, type and work done by mechanical coal cutters; number of coal conveyers; and amount of electricity used in mines, North Wales and South Wales, 1900-45.

YEAR	Mechanical Coal Cutters								No. of Conveyers used at Coal-face		Electricity in Mines			
	North Wales				South Wales						North Wales		South Wales	
	NO.	of which:- Elec-tric	of which:- Compr-essed Air	Coal cut 000's tons	NO.	of which:- Elec-tric	of which:- Compr-essed Air	Coal cut 000's tons	North Wales	South Wales	Surface 000's H.P.	Under-ground 000's H.P.	Surface 000's H.P.	Under-ground 000's H.P.
1900	..	..	..	..	5(1)	..	..	51	..(1)	..	..	..	..	..
1901	..	..	..	..	5	..	..	16	..	..	..	..	..	..
1902	..	..	..	..	6	-	6	10	..	..	..	..	..	..
1903	..	..	..	..	5	-	5	18	..	..	..	..	..	..
1904	..	..	..	..	9	-	9	41	..	..	..	..	..	..
1905	..	..	..	..	14(2)	3	7	60	..	..	..	..	..	..
1906	..	..	..	..	20	4	16	76	..	..	..	..	..	..
1907	..	..	..	..	28	9	19	167	..	3	..	..	..	..
1908	..	..	..	..	31	14	17	200	..	2	..	..	..	..
1909	..	..	..	..	51	24	27	286	..	7	..	..	..	..
1910	..	..	..	..	107	51	56	560	..	50	..	..	..	..
1911	..	..	..	..	113	43	70	723	..	43	..	..	..	..
1912	..	..	..	..	114	50	64	593	..	47	..	..	71	78
1913	..	..	..	..	115	36	79	640	..	61	..	..	91	91
1914	..	..	..	..	131	44	87	635	..	63	..	..	94	100
1915	..	..	..	..	139	44	95	564	..	105	..	..	110	125
1916	..	..	..	..	136	51	85	650	..	137	..	..	116	115
1917	..	..	..	..	159	69	90	718	..	205	..	..	122	123
1918	..	..	..	..	156	58	98	824	..	214	..	..	126	125
1919	..	..	..	..	182	61	121	897	..	285	..	..	134	133
1920	..	..	..	..	239	72	167	1,077	..	339	..	..	135	138
1921	56	25	31	233	273	67	206	853	1	342	2	4	147	144
1922	79	27	52	422	304	66	238	1,818	2	416	3	5	170	153
1923	97	38	59	694	361	78	283	2,217	5	562	3	6	189	159
1924	140	44	96	816	409	83	326	2,620	13	671	4	7	208	169
1925	129	39	90	816	405	68	337	2,567	21	721	5	8	220	171
1926	123	49	74	616	401	93	308	1,518	45	740	5	8	241	169
1927	146	52	94	1,410	425	88	337	3,212	83	761	6	8	249	172
1928	132	44	88	1,281	401	80	321	3,318	90(3)	772(3)	6	8	256	172
1929	131	45	86	1,456	430	85	345	4,178	94	910	6	8	254	172
1930	121	48	73	1,610	460	76	384	4,329	85	973	6	8	254	172
1931	133	48	85	1,677	484	75	409	4,356	94	932	6	8	257	172
1932	146	57	89	1,632	437	73	364	4,093	118	875	6	8	262	175
1933	114	45	69	1,611	454	87	367	4,402	113	927	6	7	262	176
1934	117	44	73	1,638	472	98	374	5,235	131	966	5	6	269	176
1935	96	40	56	1,506	476	94	382	6,338	116	1,052	6	6	269	179
1936	95	38	57	1,909	482	102	380	7,151	124	1,063	6	7	273	184
1937	85	31	54	2,029	519	102	417	9,151	122	1,207	7	6	280	182
1938	81	27	54	1,881	535	105	430	9,183	125	1,306	7	7	287	190
1939	82	..	..	1,796	548	..	..	9,213	112	1,384	..	..	..	..
1940	81	..	..	1,626	500	..	..	8,573	122	1,401	..	..	..	..
1941	75	..	..	1,740	489	..	..	7,364	121	1,301	..	..	..	..
1942	81	..	..	1,502	495	..	..	7,302	123	1,328	..	..	..	..
1943	86	..	..	1,416	573	..	..	7,613	122	1,426	..	..	..	..
1944	89	..	..	1,571	608	..	..	7,065	80(4)	1,068(4)	8	7	302	196
1945	89	..	..	1,884	612	..	..	7,549	84(4)	1,072(4)	..	..	..	..

General Notes

(i) Sources. Mines Inspectors' Reports and Mines and Quarries General Reports (for 1900-20); Annual Report of Chief Inspector of Mines (for 1921-38); Min. of Fuel and Power, Statistical Digest from 1938, (1943-4 cd. 6538) and Statistical Digest for 1944 (for 1938-44); Min. of Fuel and Power, Suppl. to Statistical Digest, 1945 (for 1945).

(ii) Before 1921 it is not possible to separate out figures for North Wales from those for the Liverpool (later Lancashire, North Wales and Ireland) District of which they formed a part.

Notes

1. For 1900-09 the South Wales figures exclude those for Monmouthshire which was included as part of the Southern District (Kent, Glos., Devon, Somerset and Mons.) for these purposes. From 1910 onwards the figures are for South Wales and Mons. The number of coal-cutters in the Southern District in 1900 was 2 (cutting 10,000 tons) and in 1909, 23 (cutting 94,000 tons); there were 17 coal conveyers in the Southern district in 1909.

2. The report for 1905 does not give information on the motive power used by the four mechanical cutters in the Swansea district.

3. From 1928 onwards the figures relate to conveyers at the coal-face and elsewhere.

4. At the coal-face only.

COAL 13. Mechanisation. Percentage of coal cut and conveyed by machinery (1937-60); and percentage power-loaded (1947-75), South Wales, 1937-75

Year	Percentage of Output			Electric motors Tn. H.P.
	Cut by machinery	Conveyed by machinery	Power loaded	
1937	23.6	38.5	..	..
1947	36.3	64.3	0.4	583
1948	43.0	70.8	..	593
1949	42.0	80.0	..	621
1950	45.8	83.7	0.6	617
1951	47.8	85.3	0.6	623
1952	48.4	86.9	0.7	644
1953	51.1	88.6	1.5	658
1954	53.5	90.8	1.8	706
1955	59.0	92.4	4.0	760
1956	57.9	93.6	9.1	827
1957	62.9	93.7	15.0	868
1958	64.8	93.8	17.4	902
1959	65.2	94.1	19.6	913
1960	70.5	94.6	23.4	907
1961	..	..	35.5	919
1962	..	..	42.1	926
1963	..	..	48.2	..
1964	..	..	54.4	..
1965	..	..	58.2	..
1966	..	..	65.3	..
1967	..	..	72.5	..
1968	..	..	76.8	..
1969	..	..	79.5	..
1970	..	..	84.0	..
1971	..	..	85.6	..
1972	..	..	88.5	..
1973	..	..	..	..
1974	..	..	92.4	..

General Notes

(i) Source. Ministry of Power *Energy Digests*, 1948-1975. Figures are taken from the last digest in which they appear. Some figures are revised three or four times, others not at all. The revisions make for some small differences from figures given in the Statistical tables of the annual N.C.B. reports.

(ii) Figures include Somerset and Forest of Dean and relate to all mines, except that the figures for power-loading relate only to N.C.B. mines.

(iii) Until 1962 the figures relate to calendar years: thereafter to the 52 weeks ending on the last Saturday in March. The figures for 1963 thus relate to the year ending 28 March 1964.

(iv) The percentage is of pithead output until 1960, except for 1937. For 1937 and 1960-74 the percentage is of saleable output.

COAL 14. Prices. Average pit head prices, North Wales and South Wales, 1878-1938, and f.o.b. prices for steam coal (large and small), South Wales, 1840-1934.

F.o.b. price of large steam coal at Cardiff

	s. d.		s. d.		s. d.		s. d.
1840	10 0	1845	8 9	1850	8 6	1855	10 6
1841	10 0	1846	9 6	1851	8 3	1856	9 6
1842	10 0	1847	9 6	1852	8 0	1857	9 3
1843	9 0	1848	9 3	1853	10 6	1858	8 9
1844	9 0	1849	8 9	1854	11 0	1859	8 3
1860	8 3	1865	8 9	1870	9 3	1875	14 3
1861	8 6	1866	8 6	1871	10 6		
1862	8 7	1867	8 6	1872	19 3		
1863	8 9	1868	8 0	1873	23 3		
1864	8 9	1869	8 6	1874	16 11		

Year	Price at pit-head		F.o.b. price South Wales	
	North Wales	South Wales	Large	Small
	s. d.	s. d.	s. d.	s. d.
1875	..	..	10 9.47[1]	..
1876	..	..	9 10.02	..
1877	..	..	(9 1.25	..
1878	9 6	8 0	(	..
1879	10 0	7 3	8 6.74	..
1880	10 6	7 6	8 6	..
1881	..	..	8 11	..
1882	5 3	5 10	9 5	..
1883	5 4	6 3	9 8	..
1884	5 4	6 3	9 10	..
1885	5 2	5 10	9 3	..
1886	5 6	5 1	8 5	..
1887	5 5	5 4	8 0	..
1888	5 4	5 10	8 4	..
1889	6 3	8 0	10 6	..
1890	8 3	10 3	13 0	..
1891	8 0	10 3	13 5	..
1892	7 0	8 9	11 7	..
1893	6 10	7 6	9 7	..
1894	6 5	7 7	10 8	..
1895	6 2	7 2	9 7	..
1896	5 9	6 0	9 2	..
1897	5 9	6 9	9 3	..
1898	6 9	7 1	10 1	..
1899	7 9	8 10	11 1	..
1900	11 6	12 1	15 2	..
1901	9 3	11 8	16 1	..
1902	8 6	10 6	13 7	7 7
1903	7 7	9 5	12 10	6 9
1904	7 5	9 1	12 9	6 4
1905	7 5	8 9	12 0	6 9
1906	7 5	9 4	12 4	7 6
1907	7 11	11 7	14 9	9 2
1908	8 5	11 1	15 8	8 7
1909	8 0	10 9	13 9	7 5
1910	8 2	11 0	14 10	7 7
1911	8 4	11 2	14 9	7 8
1912	8 11	11 2	15 6	8 8
1913	10 0	11 11	16 5	9 8
1914	9 7	11 11	17 6	8 9
1915	12 4	14 7	20 11	12 7
1916	15 6	17 7	24 5	16 5
1917	16 11	20 0	26 11	17 8
1918	20 2	24 4	30 9	20 3
1919	24 7	32 5	41 1	28 2
1920	27 8	49 7	61 5	49 8
1921	26 7	26 6	39 5	16 7
1922	17 5	18 7	26 2	16 1
1923	17 1	20 10	28 0	18 1
1924	17 10	20 6	27 3	16 5
1925	16 6	18 6	25 1	13 3
1926	20 6	17 8	21 11	11 11
1927	14 9	15 9	21 4	12 6
1928	13 1	13 10	18 8	11 6
1929	13 6	14 8	19 0	12 2
1930	13 9	15 2	19 7	12 9
1931	13 10	15 0	19 9	12 3
1932	13 4	15 0	19 11	12 0
1933	12 11	14 10	19 11	11 9
1934	12 11	14 7	20 0	11 9
1935	13 3	14 8	..	..
1936	14 7	15 1	..	..
1937	15 7	16 2	..	..
1938	16 10	18 0	..	..

General Notes

(i) Sources. W.G. Dalziel, The Monmouthshire and South Wales Coal Owners' Association, Cardiff 1895, p.108c for 1840-75; F.A. Gibson, op.cit., see notes to Table 2, for 1875-1934. The pit head prices given by Gibson come from the Mines and Quarries, General Reports for 1880-1920 and then from the Annual Reports of H.M. Chief Inspector of Mines; the f.o.b. prices for South Wales come from the audits taken under the sliding scale and other wages agreements. Pit head prices for 1878-80 are drawn from Hunt's Mineral Statistics.

(ii) In the original sources the prices are given to two decimal places of a penny. They have here been rounded to the nearest old penny.

Notes

1. The price for 1875, a year of rapidly falling prices, is based on an audit covering only the last two months; the 1877-8 average is of prices from January 1877 to March 1888; the 1879 average is based on the average from January to April only.

COAL 15. Costs and Proceeds. Average wage cost, total cost and proceeds, North Wales and South Wales, 1917-74

Year	North Wales(1)			South Wales(4)		
	Wage Cost	Total Cost	Proceeds	Wage Cost	Total Cost	Proceeds
	s. d.	s. d.	s. d.	s. d.	s. d.	s. d.
1917	14 7¼	18 7¾	18 9¼	15 3¾	21 0½	22 1
1918	17 1½	21 10½	20 6½	16 8¾	23 4¼	26 7¼
1919	25 0¼	30 5	25 9¾	23 11½	31 9	36 9¼
1920(2)	28 8	36 2¼	30 11¾	31 10¼	43 2¾	54 2
1921	23 6	31 11¼	29 11¾	24 0½	35 7	29 4½
1922	14 4	20 2½	19 3¾	12 6	19 11¼	20 5
1923	13 10¼	18 7½	18 5¼	13 3	19 8¾	21 10¼
1924	14 10¾	19 8¼	19 2¼	14 3½	20 9¼	21 1¾
1925	14 8½	19 4	17 5	14 6¾	20 11½	18 11¾
1926(3)	14 3¾	18 8¾	15 4¼	14 0½	19 10½	16 7¼
1927	11 5¾	16 7	16 1¾	11 2	16 9½	15 7¾
1928	10 6¾	15 4½	14 3¼	10 2¼	15 5¼	14 0¾
1929	10 3¼	14 10¼	14 8	9 11¾	14 9¾	14 10¼
1930	10 5¼	15 1	14 11¾	10 3¼	15 4½	15 6
1931	10 6¼	15 4¼	15 2½	9 11½	15 2¾	15 3
1932	10 3	15 0½	14 10¼	10 0	15 6½	15 6¾
1933	9 9¾	14 5½	14 5¾	9 10¼	15 5¼	15 3½
1934	9 9¾	14 4½	14 4½	9 9¾	15 1½	15 0
1935	9 9½	14 6	14 7	9 9½	15 2¼	15 1
1936	10 5¼	15 0½	15 9	10 0	15 8	15 7
1937	11 2¾	16 5½	17 0¾	10 9½	16 6¾	16 11¾
1938	11 1.55	16 9.12	17 9.33	11 8.31	18 4.8	18 7.76
1939	11 4.08	16 8.79	18 3.92	12 0.68	18 10.67	19 8.02
1940	13 9.18	20 2.80	21 5.35	14 6.34	22 4.37	22 6.59
1941	16 7.47	24 0.44	25 4.08	17 5.49	26 9.04	27 5.08
1942	19 10.91	27 0.57	27 11.39	21 9.63	30 3.44	30 5.10
1943	22 10.59	29 7.37	30 7.10	24 7.61	32 4.09	33 1.25
1944	27 0.28	36 3.64	35 1.68	29 6.21	43 4.34	36 3.11
	s. d.	s. d.	s. d.	s. d.	s. d.	s. d.
1945	29 6.73	39 4.81	39 11.5	32 10.13	49 4.14	41 9.50
1946	29 7.58	39 9.20	41 3.13	32 7.64	49 5.64	43 2.56
1947	27 0.5	44 5.0	41 6.7	31 10.5	52 11.7	43 4.7
1948	29 0.8	48 2.4	47 5.1	34 8.5	57 0.2	52 2.9
1949	29 2.4	48 10.1	48 11.4	33 4.8	55 0.1	54 6.0
1950	29 1.6	49 3.6	49 10.9	33 0.5	54 6.9	54 9.1
1951	32 6.7	54 6.3	54 0.3	36 5.7	60 6.5	57 7.8
1952	38 2.0	64 6.7	60 11.8	40 8.5	69 7.5	67 2.1
1953	40 4.4	69 6.0	65 10.5	42 2.7	72 6.5	71 0.3
1954	42 2.3	73 9.0	68 8.2	44 7.9	76 9.2	74 9.2
1955	42 8.7	75 5.9	72 8.1	47 11.8	83 4.6	79 4.8
1956	46 6.0	84 9.9	82 9.3	52 0.4	91 6.9	89 8.7
1957	49 11.5	95 0.9	88 7.3	54 7.2	98 5.5	95 10.9
1958	50 2.0	98 0.4	92 4.7	53 10.3	100 5.3	98 9.9
1959	47 5.4	93 5.8	90 7.0	52 8.0	99 6.0	98 6.0
1960	46 8.9	94 0.0	93 2.7	53 10.2	107 3.3	101 7.4
1961	50 4	104 0	99 7	57 2	116 6	108 3
1962	48 1	101 0	107 4	55 3	114 11	110 7
15 months to March						
1964	47 11	102 1	108 6	54 4	113 8	112 2
year ending March						
1965	49 7	108 9	106 4	53 1	115 7	112 2
1966	60 1	135 11	104 2	54 0	123 8	112 8
1967	60 3	132 3	115 4	53 11	125 4	127 4
	East Wales			West Wales		
1968	53 7	115 9	125 10	57 5	133 8	130 2
1969	55 8	125 1	127 1	56 9	138 3	131 9
1970	59 9	138 1	132 9	59 10	150 1	137 3
	£	£	£	£	£	£
1971	3.22	7.63	7.74	2.95	8.23	8.16
1972	3.87	9.93	9.17	3.58	10.85	9.05

in £'s

SOUTH WALES			
Calendar Year	Wage cost	Total cost	Proceeds
1973	..	11.19	9.83
1974	..	13.93	10.42
1975	..	17.72	16.78

General Notes

(i) Sources. Annual Report of Chief Inspector of Mines, for 1921-38; Min. of Fuel and Power, Statistical Digest from 1938 (Cd. 6538, 1943-4), for 1938-1943; Quarterly Statistical Statements on Coal Industry (Sessional papers 1944-6, then published by N.C.B.); N.C.B. Annual Reports and Accounts for 1947-74.

(ii) The figures for 1917-37, 1943 and 1946 have been calculated as a simple average of the quarterly figures. For the other years an annual average figure is given in the sources.

Notes

1. It is frequently not possible to get figures which relate to North Wales on its own. For 1917-19 Ireland is included with North Wales; for 1920 North Wales is included with Lancashire and Cheshire: from 1927-37 North Wales is included with Cumberland, S. Staffs. Shrops., Bristol, Forest of Dean, Somerset and Kent.

2. Before 1920 the figures relate to 'disposable coal', from 1920 on they relate to 'commercially disposable coal'. The main effect is to exclude coal supplied, free or cheap, to miners.

3. The 1926 figures relate only to the first four months.

4. From 1947-67 the figures for South Wales relate to the South Western division of the N.C.B. From 1968-72 separate figures are given for East Wales and West Wales, and from 1973-5 the figures relate to the South Wales division of the N.C.B.

COAL 16. Miscellaneous. The number and annual output of members of the Coal Owners' Association, 1863-1946

Year	Cardiff District		Newport District		Swansea District		Total		Percentage of the Output of the Coalfield
	Members	Output 000s tons	Members	Output 000s tons	Members	Output 000s tons	Members	Output 000s tons	
1863	..	..	..	..	..	..	11	1,623	14.77
1870	..	..	..	..	..	..	13	2,076	15.19
1873	37	6,376	29	3,762	19	1,284	85	11,423	70.59
1874	36	6,130	25	3,704	18	1,209	79	11,044	66.97
1875	34	6,012	25	3,596	15	1,103	74	10,711	75.57
1876	34	6,012	24	3,596	15	1,379	73	10,987	64.73
1877	..	..	..	..	..	..	..	..	..
1878	27	4,162	20	3,135	12	859	59	8,157	46.83
1879	19	5,315	17	3,312	11	1,311	47	9,938	55.77
1880	25	5,663	17	3,320	10	1,277	52	10,261	48.48
1881	25	6,376	18	3,341	10	1,292	53	11,011	49.52
1882	25	6,578	17	3,377	10	1,321	52	11,278	49.42
1883	23	6,694	16	3,379	11	1,329	50	11,403	45.65
1884	25	7,208	16	3,362	10	1,284	51	11,855	46.39
1885	29	7,801	16	3,261	11	1,196	56	12,279	50.44
1886	31	7,887	15	3,258	9	1,082	55	12,228	50.52
1887	32	8,108	16	3,346	10	1,106	58	12,561	48.22
1888	38	9,871	16	4,723	10	1,262	64	15,856	57.96
1889	41	14,155	17	5,114	12	1,647	70	20,917	74.53
1890	42	14,544	16	4,980	12	1,618	70	21,143	71.88
1891	41	15,215	19	5,393	12	1,492	72	22,102	73.69
1892	36	15,320	19	5,973	11	1,526	66	22,820	73.12
1893	34	16,315	18	6,664	9	1,224	61	24,205	80.27
1894	34	16,840	18	6,999	8	1,287	60	25,127	75.19
1895	32	16,949	18	7,137	8	1,291	58	25,377	76.80
1896	32	16,804	18	7,658	7	1,194	57	25,658	75.76
1897	31	17,673	16	7,258	7	1,333	54	26,265	73.35
1898	32	11,027	16	4,101	7	666	55	15,796	59.10
1899	32	20,928	18	8,101	20	2,485	70	31,515	79.04
1900	37	20,673	18	7,795	25	2,924	80	31,392	79.82
1901	37	21,378	17	7,148	26	2,960	76	31,487	80.30
1902	36	22,257	17	7,415	26	3,060	75	32,733	79.24
1903	37	22,930	16	7,875	26	2,928	74	33,734	80.02
1904	37	23,886	16	7,989	27	3,090	75	34,966	79.95
1905	36	23,843	17	7,628	31	3,328	79	34,800	80.55
1906	35	24,438	17	8,513	31	3,747	77	36,699	77.99
1907	35	25,247	19	9,070	30	3,714	79	38,031	76.09
1908	39	27,061	20	8,946	30	3,934	84	39,941	79.52
1909	39	27,590	19	8,724	34	3,927	88	40,242	79.90
1910	39	27,172	19	8,788	35	4,020	89	39,980	82.09
1911	38	26,188	19	9,072	35	4,356	88	39,616	78.87
1912	40	27,816	19	8,802	37	4,044	92	40,663	81.13
1913	47	31,099	21	10,132	34	4,761	98	45,994	80.93
1914	47	30,103	23	9,842	32	4,201	98	44,147	81.93
1915	47	27,919	23	9,522	32	4,594	98	42,036	83.31
1916	50	28,913	22	9,966	33	4,647	101	43,527	83.57
1917	50	29,045	22	8,894	32	3,684	100	41,624	85.81
1918	52	27,407	23	9,184	29	3,865	99	40,457	86.60
1919	54	27,567	24	9,395	31	4,413	104	41,376	87,06
1920	56	25,931	24	11,073	35	4,283	110	41,289	89.27
1921	59	18,256	28	6,882	39	3,344	120	28,482	93.16
1922	59	29,408	28	12,353	36	5,397	118	47,158	93.71
1923	58	31,242	29	12,169	37	6,006	119	50,416	92.93
1924	57	29,225	28	12,125	35	5,979	115	47,328	92.65
1925	55	25,686	28	11,042	37	5,073	115	41,801	93.66
1926	52	11,251	29	5,283	37	2,586	113	19,120	94.31
1927	46	25,652	25	11,860	35	5,987	100	43,498	94.04
1928	42	23,203	25	12,012	30	5,556	91	40,771	94.13
1929	43	26,198	25	12,716	20	6,758	83	45,672	94.85
1930	37	23,842	25	12,519	18	6,809	75	43,170	95.70
1931	36	19,253	25	10,340	16	6,223	72	35,817	96.58
1932	35	18,375	25	8,921	16	6,585	71	33,881	97.15
1933	35	17,920	25	8,635	16	6,895	71	33,451	97.37
1934	34	18,291	25	9,483	16	6,911	70	34,686	98.61
1935	32	18,415	25	9,799	15	6,541	68	34,754	99.23
1936	21	17,549	17	9,123	15	6,517	50	33,189	97.94
1937	22	20,992	16	10,157	14	6,129	49	37,279	98.69
1938	23	19,525	16	10,061	14	6,154	50	35,741	93.60
1939	22	20,038	16	9,838	13	5,983	48	35,860	93.19
1940	22	18,136	15	9,205	14	5,635	48	32,977	92.94
1941	22	15,572	16	8,031	13	4,371	48	27,974	92.94
1942	24	15,257	17	7,518	14	4,442	52	27,217	93.46
1943	24	14,538	17	7,030	14	4,225	52	25,793	93.21
1944	20	13,147	17	6,340	14	3,777	52	23,264	92.98
1945	20	12,315	17	6,036	14	3,283	51	21,634	93.03
1946	20	12,656	17	6,224	14	3,355	51	22,245	

General Notes

(i) Sources. F.A. Gibson, *op.cit.* (see Table 2); and N.L.W. *S.W. Coal-owners' Mss.*, Annual Summaries.

(ii) Before 1870 the organisation was the 'Aberdare Steam Collieries Association'; in 1870 it became the 'South Wales Steam Collieries Association'; in 1873 the 'Monmouthshire and South Wales Collieries Association'; and from 1890 the 'Monmouthshire and South Wales Coal Owners' Association'.

COAL 17. Miscellaneous. Output from Aberdare parish, 1844-74 and Coal carried by the Taff Vale Railway, 1841-1921

Year	Coal carried by Taff Vale Railway Quantity 000s tons	Aberdare Parish Output Quantity 000s tons
1841	42	..
1842	115	..
1843	152	..
1844	188	177
1845	265	193
1846	294	224
1847	360	269
1848	502	396
1849	530	434
1850	594	477
1851	613	556
1852	712	680
1853	874	832
1854	1,025	1,009
1855	1,156	1,204
1856	1,394	1,451
1857	1,469	1,447
1858	1,445	1,408
1859	1,759	1,633
1860	2,133 (1)	1,755
1861	2,297	1,791
1862	2,541	2,214
1863	2,722	2,149
1864	2,842 (1)	2,048
1865	2,855	1,976
1866	3,248	2,186
1867	3,381 (1)	2,052
1868	3,540	2,054
1869	3,810	2,142
1870	3,944	2,071
1871	3,594	1,837
1872	4,214	2,014
1873	4,528	2,055
1874	4,353	1,963
1875	3,777	..
1876	4,879	..
1877	5,171	..
1878	5,614	..
1879	5,849	..
1880	6,894	..
1881	7,279	..
1882	7,699	..
1883	8,615	..
1884	8,865	..
1885	9,251	..
1886	8,560	..
1887	9,506	..
1888	10,429	..
1889	10,677	..
1890	10,813	..
1891	11,361	..
1892	12,006	..
1893	11,343	..
1894	12,581	..
1895	12,383	..
1896	12,916	..
1897	13,869	..
1898	9,913	..
1899	15,805	..
1900	15,356	..
1901	15,779	..
1902	15,900	..
1903	13,876	..
1904	14,280	..
1905	13,953	..
1906	15,097	..
1907	15,574	..
1908	15,339	..
1909	14,949	..
1910	14,465	..
1911	14,213	..
1912	14,475	..
1913	15,683	..
1914	16,873	..
1915	12,885	..
1916	12,905	..
1917	12,012	..
1918	11,937	..
1919	11,486	..
1920	10,805	..
1921	7,799	..

General Notes

(i) Sources. For T.V.R. traffic. Meade, The Coal and Iron Industries of the U.K., for 1841-80; Mineral Statistics (annual parl. papers) for 1881-1919; T.V.R. Report and Statement of Accounts, Dec. 1921, for 1920 and 1921. For output in Aberdare parish, Mineral Statistics.

Notes

1. Hunt's Mineral Statistics differs from Meade for these years. The Hunt figures (000s of tons) are: 1860, 1,926; 1864, 2,710; and 1867, 3,382.

COAL 18. Miscellaneous. Production of Coke and Number of Coke Ovens, 1905 - 1974

Year	Production of Coke (000s tons)		Number of Coke Ovens			
	At Gas Works	At Coke Works	Beehive	Copee and Solway	Others	Total
1905	1,483		446	1,164	308	1,918
1906	1,528		427	1,155	311	1,893
1907	..	..	..	..	..	..
1908	146	1,264	320	1,183	274	1,777
1909	140	1,217	173	992	248	1,413
1910	143	1,368	206	1,065	251	1,522
1911	149	1,299	234	1,016	253	1,503
1912	149	1,228	176	1,036	253	1,465
1913	162	1,538	305	979	172	1,456
1914	157	1,327	222	837	172	1,231
1915	167	1,496	234	852	172	1,258
1916	156	1,747	230	877	172	1,279
1917	187	1,661	200	834	172	1,206
1918	164	1,659	200	851	132	1,183
1919	152	1,261	166	834	101	1,101
1920	164	1,370	..	1,039	90	1,179
1921	119	345	63	664	830	1,557
1922	118	1,043	77	729	470	1,276
1923	135	1,554	77	837	598	1,512
1924	128	1,401	79	869	425	1,373
1925	125	1,271	114	824	296	1,234
1926	144	540	40	316	105	461
1927	127	1,239	100	782	281	1,163
1928	151	1,344	106	810	261	1,177
1929	152	1,690	107	895	278	1,280
1930	140	1,182	108	706	212	1,026
1931	151	702	101	429	190	720
1932	146	900	99	499	134	732
1933	142	994	96	597	65	758
1934	150	1,241	96	683	149	928
1935	154	1,267	103	677	113	893
1936	154	1,660	..	..	..	..
1937	151	1,830	..	..	..	..
1938	..	1,469	..	..	..	..

Year	At Gas Works	At Coke Works	Compound	Regenerative other than Comp.	Others	Total
1944	..	1,733	..	..	..	..
1945	317	1,616	223	413	22	658
1946	..	1,568	..	..	..	..
1947	294	1,544	158	358	18	534
1948	195	1,649	157	369	..	526
1949	221	1,641	157	335	..	492
1950	235	1,668	243	223	..	466
1951	237	2,065	379	243	..	622
1952	207	2,509	434	243	..	677
1953	189	2,767	498	223	..	721
1954	..	2,941	522	223	..	745
1955	..	3,189	695	223	..	918
1956	..	3,923	753	223	..	976
1957	..	4,027	..	..	..	..
1958	..	3,786	..	..	..	..
1959	..	3,852	..	..	..	..
1960	..	4,420	..	..	..	..
1961	..	4,147	..	..	..	..
1962	..	4,151	..	..	..	..
1963	..	4,502	..	..	..	..
1964	..	4,144	..	..	..	..
1965	..	4,019	..	..	..	..
1966	..	4,737	..	..	..	..
1967	..	4,562	..	..	..	..
1968	..	4,776	..	..	..	..
1969	..	4,843	..	..	..	..
1970	..	4,610	..	..	..	..
1971	..	4,635	..	..	..	..
1972	..	3,849	..	..	..	..
1973	..	4,198	..	..	..	..
1974	..	3,644	..	..	..	..

General Notes

(i) Sources. F.A. Gibson, op.cit. (see Table 2) for 1905-37; Energy Statistics, 1938-

Chapter 6
Iron and steel

Iron has been produced in Wales on a small scale over a very long period. The shift from charcoal to mineral fuel, a shift which was gradually being made in Wales over the last third of the eighteenth century, signalled more than a change in technology. It made Welsh pig-iron production significant both in absolute terms and in relation to the output of the United Kingdom, a significance which - though fluctuating - has been maintained over the succeeding two centuries.

The first four tables illustrate different aspects of the production of pig iron in Wales. As is also seen in the preceding and succeeding sections (on Coal and on Lead, copper etc.), dependable figures over this wide range of industrial and mining activities frequently only begin with the publication of Hunt's Mineral Statistics in 1854. However, the earlier figures included here in both Tables 1 and 3 are considered to be useful rough indicators, at least from 1788 onwards. Some of the many uncertainties attaching to them are briefly given below. A much fuller discussion of these, together with indications about the problems of dating the various estimates and suggestions of other possible estimates by which they might be supplemented is available from recent publications.[(1)] This later work under-lines the basic problem confronting all such figures before the mid-nineteenth century: namely, that they suffer from being a discontinuous series covering years which have been decided upon by more or less chance historical factors, but within these constraints the actual information given may be used with a wary confidence. Wary because the concepts which the figures of Table 1 purport to be measuring are themselves elusive. Should a works be included even if it has not produced any iron during a particular year? Can a distinction be made between closure for temporary reasons (strikes, bad trade etc.) and closure on a more permanent basis? At what stage is a dis-used furnace excluded from the number of furnaces built? Is a furnace 'in blast' if it is operative for any part of the year or only if it operates for the whole (or most) of the year? On this last issue it is difficult to know what basis was used for the first thirty years or so during which continuous statistics were kept, but towards the end of the nineteenth century the figure was reached, and made more accurate, by adding the number of months for which each furnace was in blast.

1. See especially, P. Riden, 'The Output of the British Iron Industry before 1870', E.H.R., xxx, 3, 1977; and G. Hammersley, 'The Charcoal Iron Industry and its Fuel, 1540-1750', E.H.R., xxvi, 4, 1973.

Such considerations warn against any attempts to effect casual marriages between Tables 1 and 3 in order to obtain figures for the average sizes of works and furnaces. For any particular year averages so obtained may be mis-leading although the general trend can be confidently indicated.

The iron ore figures (Table 2) are included to show the scale of the Welsh production of this important raw material. In general, the size of the output was relatively modest and some substantial part was obtained from mines whose primary purpose was the production of coal. In addition it is clear, since the iron content of the ore was normally around a third, that as far back as reliable iron ore statistics are available (the mid-nineteenth century) the Welsh iron industry was dependent on some importation of ore.

The types of pig iron and of steel produced in Wales are set out in Tables 4 and 5 respectively, whilst tinplate output is dealt with in Table 6. It needs to be noted that this last-mentioned table relates to the United Kingdom and not to Wales. The justification for its inclusion is that Wales (and, more especially, parts of Monmouthshire and the districts around Swansea and Llanelli) have tended to dominate the British tinplate industry. Already by 1850 over 70 per cent of British tinplate works were in South Wales and the proportion was rapidly increasing and would have been even more marked if expressed in terms of the total number of mills. 'By 1880 tinplate manufacture had become a mainly Welsh industry and in the following decade the preponderance was to become overwhelming.'[(2)]

Tables 7 and 8 attempt to bring together some of the very patchy information which is available on prices in the Welsh iron and tinplate trades.

2. W.E. Minchinton, The British Tinplate Industry, Oxford, 1957, pp. 33-35.

BOOKS AND THESES

J.P. Addis — The Crawshay Dynasty, Cardiff, 1957.

J.P. Addis — The Heavy Iron and Steel Industry in South Wales and Monmouthshire, 1870-1950, Ph.D. thesis, Wales, 1957.

E.H. Brooke — Chronology of the Tinplate Works of Great Britain, Cardiff, 1944.

E.H. Brooke — Appendix to the Chronology of the Tinplate Works of Great Britain, 1665-1949, Cardiff, 1949.

D.L. Burn — The Economic History of Steel Making, 1867-1939, Cambridge, 1940.

D.L. Burn — The Steel Industry, 1939-59, Cambridge, 1961.

W. Davies — General View of the Agriculture and Domestic Economy of South Wales, Vol. 2, 1814.

Griffiths — Guide to the Iron Trade of Great Britain, 1873.

H. Hancocks — History of Tinplate Manufacture in Llanelly, M.A. thesis, Swansea, 1965.

W.E. Hoare & C.S. Hedges, Tinplate, 1945.

J. Lloyd — Early History of Old South Wales Iron Works, 1760-1840, 1906.

R. Meade — The Coal and Iron Industries of the U.K., 1882.

W.E. Minchinton — The British Tinplate Industry, Oxford, 1957.

D. Mushet — Papers on Iron and Steel, 1846.

H.G. Roepcke — Movements of the British Iron and Steel Industry, 1720-1951, University of Illinois, Urbana, 1956.

H. Scrivenor — A History of the Iron Trade, 1854.

E.E. Watkin — The Development of the South Wales Tinplate Industry with special reference to 1919-39, M.A. thesis, Aberystwyth, 1948.

C. Wilkins — History of Iron, Steel, Tinplate and Other Trades of Wales, 1903.

ARTICLES

G. Hammersley — 'The Charcoal Iron Industry and its Fuel, 1540-1760', E.H.R., xxvi, 4, 1973.

P. Riden — 'The Output of the British Iron Industry before 1870', E.H.R., xxx, 3, 1977.

J. Ryan — 'Statistics of Tins and Cans', J.R.S.S., 1952.

R.M. Shone — 'Statistics Relating to the U.K. Iron and Steel Industry', J.R.S.S., 1950.

GOVERNMENT AND OFFICIAL PUBLICATIONS

British Iron and Steel Federation, Statistical Yearbook, 1877- (annual except 1891-1914: published as Annual Report of British Iron Trade Association, 1877-90; Statistical Report of the Iron Steel and Allied Trades Federation of Middlesbrough, 1915-17; then published by the National Federation of Iron and Steel Manufacturers, 1918-33; by B.J.S.F. 1934-65, with slight variations in title; and by B.S.C. 1966- , as Iron and Steel: Annual Statistics.)

Mineral Statistics, 1854-96, (annual: published by the Geological Survey, and edited by R. Hunt, until 1881, from 1882 in sessional papers).

Mines and Quarries General Reports, 1897-1920, (annual: in sessional papers except for 1920 Part 3).

Annual Report of the Chief Inspector of Mines, 1921-38 (annual: published by Board of Trade Mines Department).

Report of the Select Committee on Coal, (S.P. 1873 Vol.X).

Report on Government Action on Wales and Monmouthshire, 1945-6- (annual: in sessional papers; title changed to Wales in 1964).

IRON AND STEEL 1. Iron. Number of works and furnaces, North Wales and South Wales, 1740-1974

A. Number of furnaces: South Wales, by county, 1740-1823

South Wales	1740	1788	1790	1796	1806	1823
Brecon	2	2	1	3	)	8
Carmarthen	1	1	1	1	)47	-
Glamorgan	2	9	11	15	)	37
Monmouth	2	3	10	6	3	27

B. Total number of furnaces, North Wales and South Wales, 1740-1852(1)

Year	North Wales	South Wales
1740	2	7
1788	1	15(2)
1790	..	23(2)
1796	3(4)	25
1800	..	30
1806	4	50
1823	7	72
1825	7	..
1826	7	..

	North Wales		South Wales	
	In Blast	Out	In Blast	Out
1827	12	..	90(3)	..
1828	12	..	..	..
1830	12	..	113(3)	..
1839	13	7	122	5
1840	12	3	132	31
1847	5	6	151	45
1852	6	7	147	50

Year	GLAMORGAN			MONMOUTH			Anthracite			Total South Wales			North Wales		
	No. of Works	Furnaces Built	Furnaces In Blast	No. of Works	Furnaces Built	Furnaces In Blast	No. of Works	Furnaces Built	Furnaces In Blast	No. of Works	Furnaces Built	Furnaces In Blast	No. of Works	Furnaces Built	Furnaces In Blast
1854(5)	34	134	100	..	..	..	14	35	21	48	169	121	7	11	9
1855(6)	17	75	64	16	78	65	11	34	19	44	187	148	7	11	8
1856	20	87	72	17	77	69	11	36	21	48	200	162	6	10	9
1857	20	87	76	18	84	68	11	36	20	49	207	164	8	14	6
1858	20	89	78	18	74	54	11	36	16	49	199	148	8	13	6
1859	19	89	73	19	78	56	11	36	18	49	203	147	8	13	6
1860	19	89	64	19	89	59	11	35	16	49	213	139	8	14	8
1861	17	78	59	19	91	64	9	31	14	45	200	137	8	12	5
1862	17	82	61	19	83	55	9	32	9	45	197	125	8	13	5
1863	17	82	60	19	84	54	9	31	9	45	197	123	8	13	7
1864	17	82	64	19	86	60	8	29	9	44	197	133	9	14	8
1865	18	81	64	19	85	55	8	29	9	45	195	128	9	14	7
1866	18	83	63	19	86	58	7	24	11	44	193	132	5	10	5
1867	16	76	49	19	86	55	7	25	11	42	187	115	4	11	5
1868	16	75	48	19	86	49	6	23	11	41	184	108	4	9	4
1869	18	79	53	17	76	50	6	23	9	41	178	112	3	8	6
1870	17	75	54	17	76	51	6	23	9	40	174	114	3	8	6
1871	16	72	53	16	76	51	5	19	8	37	167	112	3	8	5
1872	16	71	51	13	70	55	2	13	8	31	154	114	5	11	8
1873	16	73	51	12	62	42	2	13	8	30	148	101	5	13	8
1874	16	64	40	13	62	41	2	13	7	31	139	88	4	11	8
1875	16	78	35	13	62	37	2	13	7	31	153	79	4	11	7
1876	15	59	28	13	62	35	2	13	6	30	134	69	4	11	4
1877	15	76	26	13	61	30	2	13	4	30	150	60	4	11	4
1878	15	75	24	13	57	29	2	13	4	30	145	57	4	11	3
1879	15	75	23	12	57	27	1	11	4	28	143	54	4	11	3
1880	15	74	30	12	56	35	1	11	4	28	141	69	4	10	7
1881	16	78	29	12	52	35	1	11	3	29	141	67	4	10	7
1882	16	91	27	12	48	35	1	11	2	29	150	64	4	10	6
1883	9	81	25	10	46	35	-	-	-	19	127	60	3	10	5

IRON AND STEEL 1. Iron contd.

	GLAMORGAN			MONMOUTH			Total South Wales			North Wales		
	No. of Works	Furnaces Built	Furnaces In Blast	No. of Works	Furnaces Built	Furnaces In Blast	No. of Works	Furnaces Built	Furnaces In Blast	No. of Works	Furnaces Built	Furnaces In Blast
1884	11	89	24	8	45	25	19	134	49	2	10	4
1885	12	88	20	8	46	21	20	132	41	3	10	4 1/4
1886	8	80	12 1/4	8	46	19	16	126	31 1/4	3	10	4 1/2
1887	7	79	13 1/2	6	40	20	13	119	33 1/2	3	10	4 1/2
1888	8	79	18	7	41	21	15	120	39	3	10	3 1/2
1889	8	53	17 3/4	7	31	17 3/4	15	84	35 1/2	3	10	6
1890	9	53	16 9/12	6	31	17 11/12	15	84	34 2/3	3	10	4 7/12
1891	8	55	16 5/12	6	33	14 10/12	14	88	31 1/4	3	8	4
1892	6	55	13 5/12	5	32	11 1/4	11	87	24 2/3	2	8	4
1893(7)	6	46	13 5/12	4	33	9 1/12	10	79	22 1/2	2	7	2 2/3
1894	5	41	12	4	32	10 1/4	9	73	22 1/4	2	7	1 3/4
1895	5	43	11 1/2	5	32	9 1/2	10	75	21	2	7	3
1896	5	41	13 5/12	5	32	11 1/4	10	73	24 2/3	2	7	2
1897	5	42	13 1/12	5	32	11	10	74	24 1/12	2	6	3
1898	10	40	9 2/3	7	32	6 10/12	17	72	16 1/2	3	6	3
1899	9	37	15 1/3	7	32	13 1/12	16	69	28 5/12	3	6	3 5/12
1900	9	37	15 7/12	7	33	13 7/12	16	70	29 2/12	3	5	3 3/4
1901	9	37	12 7/12	7	29	6 2/3	16	66	19 1/4	3	6	2 1/2
1902	5	30	12	4	29	7	9	57	19	3	5	3 2/12
1903	5	28	12 1/4	4	27	7 1/12	9	55	19 1/3	2	5	3
1904	5	28	11	5	28	8 2/12	10	56	19 2/12	2	2	2
1905	5	28	11	4	28	8 1/3	9	56	19 1/3	2	3	2 2/3
1906	5	24	11 2/3	4	19	9 7/12	9	43	21 1/4	2	3	3
1907	5	22	10 1/3	5	13	9 1/3	10	35	19 2/3	2	3	2 7/12
1908	5	22	7 1/3	4	12	6 1/3	9	34	13 2/3	2	4	2 5/12
1909	4	21	7	4	12	5 1/3	8	33	12 1/3	2	4	2 10/12
1910	4	21	7	5	12	7 3/4	9	33	14 3/4	2	4	3
1911	4	21	6 2/12	5	12	5 1/2	9	33	11 2/3	2	4	3
1912	4	19	6	5	12	6 1/2	9	31	12 1/2	2	3	3
1913	6	19	6	5	12	6 5/12	11	31	12 5/12	2	3	3
1914	4	19	6	4	12	4 1/4	8	31	10 1/4	2	5	3
1915	4	17	6	4	12	6 2/3	8	29	12 2/3	2	5	2 10/12
1916	4	17	6	4	12	7 1/2	8	29	13 1/2	2	4	3
1917	5	16	7	3	10	8 2/12	8	26	15 2/12	2	4	3
1918	5	16	8	4	10	7 3/4	9	26	15 3/4	2	4	2
1919	5	17	6 2/3	4	10	3 2/12	9	27	9 10/12	2	4	2 1/4
1920	5	17	6	3	12	4.82	8	29	10.82	2	4	2.05

IRON AND STEEL 1. Iron contd.

SOUTH WALES					
		Furnaces			
			In Blast		
Year	No. of Works	Built	Haem-atite	Basic	Total
1920	8	30	9 2/12	1 7/12	10 3/4
1921	8	32	1 5/12	1	2 5/12
1922	8	33	5 11/12	3	8 11/12
1923	8	32	7 1/12	2 10/12	9 11/12
1924	8	33	7 1/12	2 1/2	9 7/12
1925	8	33	6 3/4	1 1/3	8 1/12
1926	8	28	3 2/12	1/3	3 1/2
1927	7	23	7	1	8
1928	7	23	6 3/4	1 5/12	8 2/12
1929	6	21	6 7/12	2 7/12	9 2/12
1930(8)	6	21	3 2/12	1 1/2	4 3/4
1931	6	19	1 1/12	1 1/12	2 2/12
1932	6	20	2 1/12	1 1/4	3 1/3
1933	6	20	1 1/2	2	3 10/12
1934	..	13	2	2	4
1935	5	13	1 10/12	2 2/12	4
1936	5	9	2 13/52	3 13/52	5 30/52
1937	5	9	1 42/52	4 9/52	5 51/52
1938	4	8	0.96	3.90	5.19
1939	4	9	2.00	5.75	7.75
1940	4	9	2.00	5.92	7.92
1941	4	10	1.83	5.75	7.58
1942	4	10	1.58	6.00	7.58
1943	4	10	1.00	6.00	7.00
1944	4	10	1.00	6.00	7.00
1945	4	10	0.98	5.86	6.84
1946	4	11	1.00	5.85	6.85
1947	4	10	0.79	6.04	6.83
1948	4	10	1.56	5.98	7.54
1949	4	10	2.00	5.98	7.98

SOUTH WALES					
		Furnaces			
			In Blast		
Year	No. of Works	Built	Haem-tite	Basic	Total
1950	4	10	1.94	5.98	7.92
1951	4	9	1.04	6.31	7.35
1952	4	10	1.00	7.41	8.41
1953	4	10	1.36	7.13	8.49
1954	4	11	2.00	6.90	8.90
1955	4	11	2.06	7.36	9.42
1956	4	12	1.63	8.50	10.13
1957	4	11	2.00	8.71	10.71
1958	4	12	1.92	8.78	10.78
1959	3	12	0.81	8.94	9.88
1960	3	12	0.81	9.60	10.56
1961	3	12	0.75	9.44	10.25
1962	4	13	0.81	9.67	10.58
1963	4	14	0.79	10.19	11.13
1964	4	14	0.77	10.06	11.09
1965	4	14	0.73	9.73	10.67
1966	4	14	0.71	10.33	11.31
1967	4	14	0.77	10.29	11.17
1968	4	14	0.98	10.10	11.08
1969	4	14	1.25	9.35	10.60
1970(9)	6	17	..	..	13
1971	6	17	..	..	14
1972	6	17	..	..	12
1973	6	17	..	..	13
1974	6	18	..	..	11

General Notes

i) Sources. H. Scrivenor, *A History of the Iron Trade*, 1854 and R. Meade, *The Coal and Iron Industries of the U.K.*, 1882 and W. Davies, *General View of the Agriculture and Domestic Economy of South Wales*, vol. 2, 1814 for 1740 to 1852; *Mineral Statistics* for 1854 to 1914; *Mines and Quarries General Reports* for 1915 to 1920; British Iron and Steel Federation, *Statistical Year Book* 1921- .

Notes

1. Meade (pp. 610, 617, 624, 625) mentions 17 iron works in South Wales in 1796; 19 in 1801; 25 in 1806; 20 in 1823. Also 8 anthracite works in 1848.
2. Of these 7 were charcoal furnaces.
3. These seem to refer to the total number of furnaces, in and out of blast.
4. In Scrivenor, the output of 5 works in N. Wales plus the Dovey works are mentioned, but only 2 furnaces in Denbeigh and 1 at Dovey are given; Meade (pp. 578, 831) gives 5 furnaces in N. Wales and 1 (the Dovey works) in mid-Wales.
5. Glamorgan figure for 1854 includes Brecons. and Mons.
6. From 1855 to 1888 Brecons. figures are included in Mons. After 1872, however, there were virtually no Brecons. furnaces in blast.
7. From 1893 to 1902 Carms. included in Glamorgan. However, apart from a couple of months in 1893, no Carms. furnaces ever seem to have been in blast during these years.
8. For occasional years (1930, 1933, 1936, 1938 and 1958-67) the total is slightly greater than the sum of haematite and basic furnaces in blast, because small quantities were contributed by forge or foundry furnaces.
9. From 1970 the Brymbo (1 furnace) and Shotton (2 furnaces) works in North Wales are included.

IRON AND STEEL 2. Amount and Value of Iron ore mined in North Wales, 1855-1920, and South Wales, 1855-1971

Year	North Wales		South Wales	
	Amount '000s tons	Value £s	Amount '000s tons	Value £s
1855	65.8	..	1,665.5	..
1856	68.5	..	1,784.7	..
1857	150.4	..	1,038.2	..
1858	88.6	35,980	752.2	257,396
1859	87.1	13,499	649.8	204,729
1860	85.1	21,292	630.7	162,431
1861	86.5	22,425	548.2	173,037
1862	54.2	14,275	472.1	149,279
1863	28.3	9,986	420.0	167,493
1864	29.1	9,836	468.4	185,361
1865	98.3	29,475	387.7	128,590
1866	56.7	17,005	368.7	130,041
1867	44.1	12,123	501.2	131,231
1868	36.3	10,536	712.7	192,898
1869	33.5	10,429	715.0	303,107
1870	59.2	20,730	560.1	196,019
1871	51.9	23,349	969.7	543,423
1872	27.8	19,710	1,247.6	744,466
1873	38.3	22,972	943.9	581,385
1874	42.2	22,765	661.6	339,578
1875	42.2	21,092	495.8	247,920
1876	41.0	24,571	560.3	330,256
1877	42.2	25,221	444.6	259,861
1878	43.5	21,739	375.0	185,873
1879	39.3	19,468	352.8	181,787
1880	43.0	21,508	343.9	175,790
1881	26.3	13,140	251.4	129,062
1882	16.6	6,539	204.9	80,547
1883	6.1	2,214	139.0	42,492
1884	3.0	1,026	92.2	32,594
1885	2.6	913	63.3	22,151
1886	2.9	1,013	60.1	21,625
1887	2.7	950	62.8	24,240
1888	0.7	228	57.5	21,759
1889	0.2	81	53.9	26,942
1890	0.5	166	49.9	26,255
1891	..	..	39.9	19,011
1892	-	-	47.1	24,914
1893	-	-	37.3	17,718
1894	0.1	22	36.2	17,574
1895	0.1	17	28.3	13,685
1896	-	-	26.8	12,896
1897	0.1	10	29.0	14,115
1898	0.8	210	12.2	5,712
1899	1.1	381	20.0	9,625
1900	1.2	565	19.6	7,127
1901	1.6	467	16.9	5,400
1902	8.9	2,064	20.0	6,784
1903	0.7	345	20.6	7,897
1904	0.1	59	19.2	7,260
1905	0.8	233	18.5	6,668
1906	0.7	189	21.8	8,408
1907	0.8	299	21.2	8,007
1908	16.9	5,658	21.4	8,424
1909	28.1	8,285	20.9	8,244
1910	15.5	4,073	33.5	19,917
1911	16.5	5,061	46.3	..
1912	15.4	4,514	42.1	..
1913	10.4	3,163	54.6	..
1914	11.3	2,836	69.5	..
1915	23.3	7,822	75.8	..
1916	26.5	12,664	75.3	..
1917	13.9	6,577	70.6	..
1918	17.5	7,839	65.7	..
1919	10.9	4,756	60.6	..
1920	0.2	..	53.9	..

SOUTH WALES	
Year	Amount '000s tons
1921	20.9
1922	74.9
1923	88.5
1924	95.2
1925	103.1
1926	36.1
1927	127.8
1928	182.9
1929	212.9
1930	141.4
1931	18.0
1932	63.1
1933	106.6
1934	147.5
1935	146.7
1936	230.3
1937	260.6
1938	188.2
1939	204.9
1940	232.5
1941	209.6
1942	166.9
1943	125.2
1944	119.7
1945	103.8
1946	100.7
1947	96.5
1948	89.1
1949	102.4

SOUTH WALES	
Year	Amount '000s tons
1950	103.3
1951	97.3
1952	104.8
1953	115.1
1954	118.0
1955	119.9
1956	129.4
1957	125.5
1958	119.6
1959	125.4
1960	120.1
1961	123.7
1962	130.0
1963	140.1
1964	152.8
1965	146.9
1966	148.7
1967	149.3
1968	144.0
1969	136.0
1970	128.9
1971	130.9
1972	89.6
1973	81.7
1974	60.0

General Notes

(i) Sources. Mineral Statistics for figures up to 1920; Meade, op.cit. for 1858-80; Annual Reports of Chief Inspector of Mines, B.I.S.F. Statistical Yearbooks for 1938-69; U.K. Mineral Statistics for 1970 on.

(ii) The sources break the figures down on a county basis. For North Wales, there was some output from Caerns. for 1855-60 and 1900-02, but otherwise until 1907 the output came from Denbs. and Flints. After 1908, however, nearly all output till 1920 came from Caerns. and Merionethshire. In the inter-war years, the only output given for North Wales was a few hundred tons in each of the years 1922, 1937, and 1938. For South Wales, most of the production until 1938 comes from Mon. and Glam. with occasional small amounts from Brec., Carms. and (very little) from Pembs. After 1938, all the output is from Glam.

(iii) The value figures cease in 1920.

IRON AND STEEL 3. Pig-iron production, North Wales 1740-1919, and South Wales, 1740-1974

Year	Production	
	North Wales '000s tons	South Wales '000s tons
1740	0.6	2.0
1788	0.4	12.5
1796	1.3	34.4
1806	2.1(1)	78.0(1)
1823	(2)	182.3
1825	13.1	..
1826	15.8	..
1827	24.0(3)	272.0(3)
1828	25.2	..
1830	25.0	277.6
1839	33.8	453.9(4)
1840		..
1843		
1847	16.1	706.7
1852	30.0	635.0
1854	32.9	750.0
1855	31.4	840.1
1856	47.7	877.2
1857	37.0	970.7
1858	28.2	886.5
1859	27.0	985.3
1860	49.4	969.0
1861	46.7	888.3
1862	31.7	893.3
1863	51.1	847.8
1864	51.1	937.8
1865	51.9	845.0
1866	25.5	925.5
1867	32.8	886.2
1868	37.0	894.3
1869	38.5	801.0
1870	42.7	979.2
1871	41.9	1,045.9
1872	41.5(5)	981.8
1873	67.5	817.8
1874	51.9	714.7

Year	Production	
	North Wales '000s tons	South Wales '000s tons
1875	55.1	541.8
1876	32.7	756.1
1877	26.7	711.0
1878	23.1	741.1
1879	19.0	669.9
1880	57.8	889.7
1881	46.8	911.0
1882	53.1	934.4
1883	39.4	906.3
1884	34.5	851.4
1885	40.3	792.8
1886	35.3	666.6
1887	37.9	767.4
1888	33.3	870.9
1889	68.0	826.4
1890	64.5	824.7
1891	53.7	760.6
1892	45.6	684.0
1893	30.5	680.4
1894	29.8	708.9
1895	41.3	704.7
1896	49.2	780.4
1897	53.3	804.8
1898	58.8	495.3
1899	66.6	929.4
1900	.. (6)	908.1(6)
1901	..	700.1
1902	..	800.3
1903	..	875.6
1904	55.5	804.9
1905	66.3	912.2
1906	73.7	900.3
1907	62.8	928.7
1908	63.6	802.7
1909	77.5	742.9
1910	75.0	787.8
1911	75.0	718.0
1912	44.2(7)	755.9
1913	50.9	889.2
1914	46.1	753.4
1915	33.5	829.0
1916	45.3	855.5
1917	49.0	778.6
1918	44.2	880.7
1919	41.7	598.8

Year	Production South Wales '000s tons
1920(8)	692.0
1921	120.5
1922	595.5
1923	807.6
1924	865.6
1925	788.9
1926	284.1
1927	739.1
1928	852.8
1929	926.5
1930	542.3
1931	279.8
1932	353.5
1933	451.4
1934	491.7
1935	512.8
1936	750.8
1937	814.5
1938	665.0
1939	1,100.7

Year	Production South Wales '000s tons
1940	962.2
1941	805.3
1942	828.9
1943	804.3
1944	777.6
1945	864.0
1946	1,010.9
1947	1,023.8
1948	1,172.7
1949	1,203.0
1950	1,231.7
1951	1,350.7
1952	1,545.1
1953	1,652.5
1954	1,893.9
1955	1,974.7
1956	2,194.9
1957	2,525.5
1958	2,511.1
1959	2,682.3

Year	Production South Wales '000s tons
1960	3,140.8
1961	2,960.6
1962	3,428.2
1963	4,207.1
1964	4,420.3
1965	4,717.6
1966	4,610.6
1967	4,583.3
1968	4,712.1
1969	4,033.6
1970	5,796.5(9)
1971	5,545.4(9)
1972	5,845.4(9)
1973	6,000.0(9)
1974	4,673.4(9)

General Notes

(i) Sources. Scrivenor, op.cit., and Meade, op.cit., for 1740 to 1852; Mineral Stats. for 1854-1920; B.I.S.F. Statistics (various titles), for 1921 onwards.

(ii) The North Wales output is from Denbighs. and Flints. except for small quantities until early nineteenth century from Dovey furnace in Merioneths.

Notes

1. These are the figures given by Scrivenor as being from returns provided by iron-masters for a House of Commons Committee. Meade gives slightly different figures (Appendix II, Table V) and varies these again a little in his text (pp.578 for N. Wales and pp.609, 616 for S. Wales).

2. Scrivenor gives no figure for 1823 for N. Wales. Meade (Appendix II, Table VI) gives 13.1. This is Scrivenor's figure for 1825 and, indeed, Meade (p.579) gives this as output for 1825.

Notes

3. From Meade (p.610) who quotes 'a paper in the Edinburgh Philosophical Magazine'.

4. Scrivenor gives this figure taken from D. Mushet, Papers on Iron and Steel, p.421. Meade (Appendix II, table VII) agrees, but also (p.619) gives a much lesser figure which seems to result (p.623) from excluding 65.8 thousand tons made with anthracite.

5. The British Iron Trades Association Report, 1877, gives N. Wales output in 1872 as 54.7 thousand tons. The Mineral Statistics figure up to this date only mentions Denbighs. and this is presumed to include any Flints. output, which is separately given in 1873. The figures suggest that Flints. output might have been left out for all the years from 1866 to 1872.

6. For 1900-03 inclusive the N. Wales output is included with that for S. Wales.

7. From 1912-19 inclusive the N. Wales figure is for Denbighs. only as the output for Flints. is included with that for Lancs.

8. From 1920 all N. Wales output is included in Lancs.

9. From 1970 the figures relate to all Wales.

IRON AND STEEL 4. Production of pig-iron, by type, South Wales, 1886-1974

'000s tons

Year	Haem-tite	Basic(1)	Others
1886	568.9	80.5	17.2
1887	468.4	288.2	10.9
1888	756.7	90.8	23.4
1889	601.1	218.9	6.4
1890	757.2	51.8	15.8
1891	614.6	95.8	50.1
1892	595.1	65.1	23.8
1893	579.1	71.1	30.3
1894	619.3	65.8	23.7
1895	648.7	33.1	22.9
1896	630.4	122.8	27.3
1897	727.8	58.4	18.6
1898	465.8	16.6	12.9
1899	858.3	56.0	15.1
1900(2)	767.5	93.5	47.1
1901	602.7	60.5	36.8
1902	679.0	68.5	52.8
1903(3)	712.6	92.9	70.1
1912	711.6	44.3	-
1913(4)	631.3	31.6	226.3
1920	623.6	67.1	1.3
1921	97.4	22.7	0.4
1922	420.6	174.6	0.3
1923	617.3	190.3	-
1924	709.6	154.8	1.2
1925	662.2	125.4	1.3
1926	247.5	35.7	0.9
1927	610.6	126.8	1.7
1928	707.2	144.1	1.5
1929	689.1	237.0	0.4
1930	370.4	166.0	5.9
1931	148.0	131.8	-
1932	170.6	182.9	-
1933	171.4	280.0	-
1934	205.6	286.1	-
1935	183.3	329.5	-
1936	239.5	511.3	-
1937	227.1	587.4	-
1938	111.0	554.0	-
1939	232.9	867.8	-

'000s tons

Year	Haem-tite	Basic(1)	Others
1940	207.5	754.7	-
1941	179.9	625.4	-
1942	139.2	689.7	-
1943	146.1	658.2	-
1944	120.3	657.3	-
1945	128.0	736.0	-
1946	144.0	866.9	-
1947	91.2	932.6	-
1948	177.6	995.1	-
1949	215.7	987.3	-
1950	213.4	1,018.3	-
1951	166.7	1,184.0	-
1952	155.8	1,389.3	-
1953	212.9	1,439.6	-
1954	256.6	1,637.3	-
1955	241.3	1,733.4	-
1956	216.4	1,978.5	-
1957	251.6	2,273.9	-
1958	201.5	2,309.6	-
1959	134.4	2,837.9	-
1960	146.3	2,994.5	-
1961	144.2	2,816.4	-
1962	129.7	3,298.5	-
1963	164.1	4,043.0	-
1964	183.5	4,236.8	-
1965	146.9	4,570.7	-
1966	89.2	4,521.4	-
1967	101.6	4,481.7	-
1968	128.9	4,583.2	-
1969	136.1	3,897.5	-
1970	133.9	5,662.5	-
1971	92.0	5,453.4	-
1972	11.6	5,833.8	-
1973		6,000.0	-
1974		4,673.4	-

General Notes

i) Sources. *Mineral Statistics* for 1886-96; *Mines and Quarries General Reports* for 1897-1920; B.I.S.F. *Annual Statistics* (various titles) for 1921-74.

Notes

1. Basic includes 'Ordinary', which is the total of Foundry plus Forge pig-iron. The size of 'Ordinary' is small relative to that of 'Basic'.
2. The figures for 1900-03 inclusive are for both N.Wales and South Wales.
3. From 1904-11 no separate figure is available because Lancs. is included with Denbs. and Glam.
4. No figures available for War years 1914-19.

IRON AND STEEL 5. Production of steel ingots and castings, by type of furnace, 1878-1974, South Wales

'000s tons

Year	Converter	Open-Hearth		Others	Total
		Acid	Basic		
1878	203.6	..		..	..
1879	252.6	85.0		..	337.6
1880	308.2	116.0		..	424.2
1881	384.7	102.0		..	486.7
1882	483.1	129.5		..	612.6
1883	505.0	136.0		..	641.0
1884	387.7	164.8		..	552.5
1885	403.1	201.0		..	604.1
1886	412.2	194.5		..	606.7
1913	..	..		..	1,807.3
1920	286.7	793.3	797.0	7.3	1,884.3
1921	87.2	310.4	453.9	3.0	854.5
1922	230.9	873.9	763.8	5.5	1,873.9
1923	264.3	1,081.4	859.1	7.3	2,212.1
1924	311.6	1,019.0	916.0	8.0	2,254.6
1925	-	820.8	803.1	338.9	1,962.8
1926	-	419.0	355.9	127.2	902.1
1927	-	842.2	759.4	325.7	1,927.3
1928	-	947.1	845.6	365.9	2,158.6
1929	-	947.3	992.1	396.7	2,336.1
1930	-	661.1	714.1	128.0	1,503.2
1931	-	527.0	745.8	1.2	1,274.0
1932	-	590.7	755.4	1.4	1.347.5
1933	-	842.1	925.8	1.6	1,769.5
1934	-	759.3	1,083.9	2.7	1,845.9
1935	-	725.5	1,155.9	1.9	1,883.3
1936	-	755.5	1,662.3	3.9	2.421.7
1937	-	822.0	1,800.1	6.7	2,628.8
1938	0.6	426.0	1,327.0	5.8	1,759.4
1939	207.6	728.1	1,936.5	15.0	2,887.2
1940	251.1	671.4	1,867.6	26.3	2,816.4
1941	206.1	507.8	1,812.0	38.6	2,564.5
1942	231.9	401.3	1,928.1	64.5	2,625.8
1943	228.5	325.8	1,993.6	61.6	2,609.5
1944	228.8	239.1	1,876.8	73.2	2.417.9
1945	232.9	268.5	1,820.4	58.2	2,380.0
1946	241.6	311.9	2,060.9	36.9	2,651.3
1947	233.2	377.0	2,012.7	44.7	2,667.6
1948	271.7	511.4	2,266.3	48.3	3,097.7
1949	276.0	508.0	2,387.2	48.0	3,219.2
1950	289.4	517.7	2,551.9	48.0	3,407.0
1951	295.6	436.5	2,690.5	52.6	3,475.2
1952	285.8	369.2	3,000.4	65.0	3,720.4
1953	302.2	277.9	3,405.2	64.9	4,050.2
1954	310.0	232.3	3,714.7	65.9	4,322.9
1955	335.2	263.8	3,938.7	69.3	4,607.0
1956	361.2	277.6	4,000.6	66.2	4,705.6
1957	377.7	233.6	4,379.0	65.9	5,056.2
1958	344.0	111.3	3,970.6	52.6	4,478.5
1959	446.7	92.4	4,439.4	46.8	5,025.3
1960	848.4	99.1	4,669.6	49.0	5,666.1
1961	960.9	81.3	3,855.2	40.7	4,938.1
1962	1,191.6	44.3	3,796.0	31.7	5,063.6
1963	2,141.7	32.5	3,655.0	35.5	5.864.7
1964	2,501.5	38.8	3,736.2	45.0	6,321.5
1965	2,832.7	37.4	3,861.3	46.2	6.777.6
1966	2,907.4	32.7	3.413.4	38.8	6.392.3
1967	2,938.8	-	3,285.4	45.5	6,269.7
1968	3,154.6	-	3,332.0	48.6	6,535.2
1969	2,734.4	-	3,040.8	52.9	5,828.1
1970	4,225.2	3,794.3		428.7	8,448.1
1971	4,512.4	3,011.5		386.1	7,910.0
1972	5,059.4	3,098.9		415.0	8,573.3
1973	4,810.8	3,172.3		468.0	8,451.1
1974	3,434.2	2,792.5		478.6	6,705.3

General Notes

(i) Sources. For 1878-86 British Iron and Steel Association Statistical Report (annual); figures for later years taken from the equivalent appropriate publication (see Bibliography of this section for details).

IRON AND STEEL 6. Tinplate. Average number of mills working, 1869-1937, and total production, 1834-1974, United Kingdom

Year	Output [1] '000s of Boxes	Ave. number of mills working
1834	180	..
1848	335	..
1851	748	..
1860	1,550	..
1865	1,755	..
1869(2)	2,520	164
1870	2,700	..
1871	3,000	..
1872	3,000	..
1873	3,100	..
1874	3,000	..
1875	3,500	..
1876	3,600	..
1877	4,050	211
1878	4,107	222
1879	5,250	210
1880	6,350	290
1881	6,915	..
1882	7,550	235
1883	7,615	295
1884	8,045	327
1885	8,300	..
1886	8,945	..
1887	9,277	..
1888	10,552	..
1889	11,705	..
1890	11,280	..
1891	12,000	..
1892	11,000	..
1893	11,300	..
1894	10,600	..
1895	10,500	..
1896	9,000	..
1897	9,500	323
1898	9,200	322
1899	10,100	381
1900	10,000 (500)	384
1901	9,500	343
1902	11,350	398
1903	11,350	371
1904	12,800	385

Year	Output [1] '000s of Boxes	Ave. number of mills working
1905	13,350	426
1906	12,900	421
1907	14,080	444
1908	14,000	440
1909	14,746	451
1910	15,546 (777)	489
1911	16,332	542
1912	16,949	533
1913	16,441	527
1914	13,852	487
1915	13,287	471
1916	12,641	423
1917	7,300	299
1918	9,090	315
1919	11,040	436
1920	12,215 (609)	485
1921	6,556	233
1922	13,365	467
1923	16,169	521
1924	16,498	531
1925	13,906	487
1926	11,374	366
1927	16,000	493
1928	17,295	504
1929	17,597 (880)	498
1930	16,288	437
1931	14,348	377
1932	14,945	394
1933	15,334	405
1934	14,959	408
1935	14,164	394
1936	16,495	415
1937	19,101	..
1938	12,200	..
1939	18,388	..
1940	19,536	..
1941	14,394	..
1942	13,564	..
1943	10,642	..
1944	10,416	..
1945	10,236	..
1946	11,680	..
1947	13,272	..
1948	14,708	..
1949	15,014	..
1950	15,272	..
1951	15,138	..

Year	Output '000s tons
1930	814
1934	748
1935	708
1936	815
1937	958
1938	610
1939	919
1940	977
1941	720
1942	678
1943	532
1944	521
1945	512
1946	584
1947	664
1948	735
1949	751
1950	764
1951	757
1952	908
1953	760
1954	..

Year	Output '000s tons
1955	892
1956	918
1957	1,043
1958	1,043
1959	1,104
1960	1,234
1961	1,077
1962	1,199
1963	1,206
1964	1,186
1965	1,212
1966	1,215
1967	1,237
1968	1,253
1969	1,321
1970	1,277
1971(3)	1,258
1972	1,204
1973	1,330
1974	1,195

General Notes

i) Sources. For output: E.H. Brooke, Chronology of the Tinplate works of Great Britain for 1834-1938; J. Ryan, 'Statistics of Tins and Cans', J.R.S.S. 1952, for output in tons, 1900-51; Annual reports on Wales and Mon. for output 1929-52; B.I.S.F. Statistical Yearbooks (various titles) for 1952 onwards. For mills working: Mineral Statistics for 1869-84; Abstract of Labour Statistics for 1897-1936.

Notes

1. The figures in brackets are the equivalent in thousands of long tons.

2. The output figure for 1869 is from Mineral Statistics, which also gives different figures from Brooke for the succeeding years, i.e.,

1870	3,460 ;	1874	2,530 ;	1879	4,250
1871	2,393 ;	1876	2,815 ;	1880	6,000
1872	2,978 ;	1877	4,050 ;		
1873	2,685 ;	1878	4,058 ;		

In general these, at least till the mid-seventies, are under-estimates because of incomplete returns.

3. From 1971 the figures are on a slightly different basis. For comparison the 1966-70 figures on the new basis would be: 1966 1,238 ; 1967 1,284 ; 1968 1,306 ; 1969 1,345; 1970 1,298.

IRON AND STEEL 7. Prices (per ton) Bar Iron (Newport), 1803-23, 1866-77; Bar Iron (London), 1812-40; Pig Iron, 1803-23, 1863-80; Railway Iron, 1843-52; Tinplate Bars, 1913-43.

Year	Bar Iron(1)	Bar Iron(2)	Railway Iron	Pig Iron Foundry	Pig Iron Forge
	£ s d	£ s d	£ s d	£ s d	£ s d
1803	15 0 0	..	..	6 10 0	5 10 0
1804	14 0 0	..	..	6 0 0	5 0 0
1805	16 0 0	..	..	6 10 0	6 0 0
1806	16 0 0	..	..	7 10 0	6 0 0
1807	13 0 0	..	..	6 6 8	5 0 0
1808	14 0 0	..	..	6 10 0	5 6 8
1809	14 0 0	..	..	6 10 0	5 6 8
1810	..	..	..	..	..
1811	13 0 0	..	..	..	..
1812	12 10 0	15 3 4	..	6 0 0	5 6 8
1813	12 10 0	13 16 8	..	6 0 0	5 6 8
1814	13 0 0	14 8 4	..	6 10 0	..
1815	12 0 0	14 3 4	..	..	..
1816	8 0 0	12 11 8	..	..	..
1817	12 0 0	11 2 6	..	6 5 0	..
1818	12 0 0	12 11 8	..	6 10 0	..
1819	11 0 0	12 15 0	..	7 0 0	..
1820	9 0 0	11 3 4	..	5 15 0	5 0 0
1821	8 0 0	9 8 4	..	5 0 0	..
1822	8 0 0	8 11 3	..	5 15 0	..
1823	7 10 0	8 10 0	..	5 0 0	..
1824	..	9 9 2	..	..	..
1825	..	13 4 2	..	..	..
1826	..	10 5 10	..	..	..
1827	..	9 18 4	..	..	..
1828	..	8 12 11	..	..	..
1829	..	7 6 8	..	..	..
1830	..	6 13 9	..	..	..
1831	..	6 3 9	..	..	..
1832	..	6 3 4	..	..	..
1833	..	7 2 11	..	..	..
1834	..	7 8 9	..	..	..

Year	Bar Iron(1)	Bar Iron(2)	Railway Iron	Pig Iron
	£ s d	£ s d	£ s d	£ s d
1835	..	7 0 0	..	..
1836	..	11 1 6	..	..
1837	..	9 11 3	..	..
1838	..	9 14 7	..	..
1839	..	10 5 0	..	..
1840	..	8 13 9	..	..
1841	..	..	..	..
1842	..	..	..	..
1843	..	..	6 9 0	..
1844	..	..	6 14 3	..
1845	..	..	10 15 10	..
1846	..	..	10 6 8	..
1847	..	..	9 0 4	..
1848	..	..	6 2 10	..
1849	..	..	5 4 6	..
1850	..	..	5 0 8	..
1851	..	..	5 11 7	..
1852	..	..	6 0 1	..
1863	..	..	..	3 17 2
1864	..	..	..	4 10 0
1865	..	..	..	4 15 6
1866	6 4 7	..	..	4 8 6
1867	5 14 4½	..	..	4 3 9
1868	5 15 0	..	..	4 0 0
1869	5 15 7	..	..	4 0 0
1870	6 5 0	..	..	4 0 0
1871	6 13 11½	..	..	4 6 7
1872	10 7 11	..	..	6 12 0
1873	11 18 4	..	..	6 10 6
1874	9 14 7	..	..	5 7 6
1875	8 14 4½	..	..	..
1876	6 8 4	..	..	4 2 6
1877	6 0 0	..	..	3 17 6
1878	..	..	..	..
1879	..	..	..	2 17 6
1880	..	..	..	3 13 9

IRON AND STEEL 7. Prices Pig Iron, Bar Iron, Railway Iron contd.

Year	Tinplate Bars		
	£	s	d
1913	5	4	0
1914	4	13	1
1915	7	7	7
1916	10	15	11
1917	10	7	6
1918	10	7	6
1919	13	7	9
1920	24	13	4
1921	11	5	6
1922	7	7	3
1923	9	0	1
1924	8	14	5

Year	Tinplate Bars		
	£	s	d
1925	7	1	10
1926	6	7	6
1927	6	2	10
1928	5	18	3
1929	6	6	7
1930	6	3	9
1931	4	19	2
1932	4	17	6
1933	4	16	3
1934	5	2	10

Year	Tinplate Bars		
	£	s	d
1935	5	5	9
1936	5	17	2
1937	7	3	9
1938	7	15	0
1939	7	10	0
1940	10	0	5
1941	12	2	6
1942	12	2	6
1943	12	2	6

General Notes

i) Sources. Scrivenor, *op.cit.*, p.410 for bars and pig at Newport, 1803-23; *Ibid.*, for South Wales bar iron in London, 1812-40; Br.Iron Trade Ass., *Report*, 1877 for bar iron in Wales, 1866-77; Scrivenor, *op.cit.*, pp. 296, 298 for railway iron, 1843-52; *S.C. on Coal*, 1873 and Addis (Ph.D thesis) p.44 for pig iron, 1863-80; Hoare and Hedges, *Tinplate*, Statistical App., table 8 for tinplate bars, 1913-43.

Notes

1. Refers to the price of Welsh bar iron in Wales. For 1803-23 the price is that at Newport agreed by the Welsh iron-masters. There was no agreed price in 1810 when it was left open 'for everyone to sell as he likes'.

2. Refers to the price of South Wales bar iron in London, which was about 20s a ton higher than the price at Cardiff or Newport. The prices are an annual average of a monthly series. The 1812 price is average of last six months only.

IRON AND STEEL 8. Prices (per box, f.o.b. Swansea). Tinplate, 1827-1943

Year	Price s.	Price d.
1827	40	4
1828	38	7
1829	37	0
1830	33	2½
1831	32	4½
1832	30	5½
1833	34	8
1834	36	8
1835	35	3
1836	44	5
1837	35	6½
1838	33	7½
1839	33	4½
1840	32	10½
1841	32	1
1842	30	2
1843	26	0½
1844	28	5
1845	31	5½
1846	28	8
1847	25	10½
1848	26	4
1849	28	1
1850 (1)	27	9
1851	25	3
1852	23	2
1853	25	9
1854	26	10
1855	26	11
1856	30	5
1857	32	3
1858	25	10
1859	25	6
1860	24	4
1861	21	7
1862	21	4
1863	21	10
1864	23	7
1865	22	5
1866	25	0
1867	23	6
1868	21	10
1869	22	9
1870	21	8
1871	23	0
1872	34	1
1873	32	8
1874	29	1
1875	24	3
1876	20	3
1877	17	8
1878	14	11
1879	17	1½
1880	18	11½
1881	15	9
1882	16	4
1883	16	1½
1884	14	8¼
1885	14	0
1886	12	9¾
1887	13	0
1888	13	0
1889	13	3
1890	14	4
1891	14	4
1892	11	11
1893	11	2½
1894	9	10¾
1895	9	4¾
1896	9	5¼
1897	9	8¼
1898	9	9
1899	13	1
1900	14	4¾
1901	13	1½
1902	12	9
1903	11	6¾
1904	11	5¼
1905	11	11
1906	13	5¼
1907	14	9½
1908	12	5¾
1909	12	3½
1910	13	9¼
1911	14	3½
1912	14	10
1913	13	10½
1914	12	7½
1915	18	2
1916	32	0
1917	30	8
1918	30	3
1919	36	10
1920	59	10
1921	26	6
1922	19	5
1923	23	4
1924	23	8
1925	20	8
1926	20	10½
1927	19	0
1928	18	2
1929	18	6½
1930	17	10½
1931	14	4¼
1932	15	3¾
1933	16	6¾
1934	17	5
1935	18	3½
1936	18	9½
1937	23	5½
1938	21	11¼
1939	23	5½
1940	31	9
1941	31	3
1942	30	9
1943	30	9

General Notes

i) Sources. Minchinton, British Tinplate Industry, p.262 for 1827-50; Brooke, Chronology, for 1849-1943.

Notes

1. Both Minchinton and Brooke give prices for 1849 and 1850. Those in the table are from Minchinton; the comparable prices from Brooke are: 1849 27s 6d; 1850 27s 4d. It is not clear whether the Minchinton prices are f.o.b.

Statistical  Publications

Welsh Office
Y Swyddfa Gymreig

ANNUAL PUBLICATIONS

Digest of Welsh Statistics
Welsh Agricultural Statistics
Farm Accounts in Wales
Environmental Digest for Wales
Commercial and Industrial Floorspace Statistics: Wales
Welsh Local Government Financial Statistics
Road Accidents: Wales
Welsh Housing Statistics
Statistics of Education in Wales
Health and Personal Social Services Statistics for Wales
Mental Health Statistics for Wales
Key Statisitical Indicators for National Health Service Management in Wales
Activities of Social Services Departments
Staff of Social Services Departments
Children in Care or under Supervision Orders in Wales
Residential Accommodation for the Elderly, Younger Physically Handicapped and Blind
Local Authority Social Services Planning Statements for Wales

OTHER PUBLICATIONS

Welsh Social Trends
Welsh Economic Trends
1983 Based Home Population Projections for the Counties of Wales
Welsh Hospital Waiting List Bulletin
Statistics of Road Lengths in Wales
Survey of House Renovation Grants

The above publications can be purchased individually on application to:

Publications Unit, ESS Division, Welsh Office, Cathays Park, Cardiff CF1 3NQ
Prices of the publications can be determined by application to the Publications Unit at the above address. They are post paid, within the United Kingdom, but payment with order is essential.
Alternatively they may be purchased from any of the following bookshops:

University Bookshop
Senghenydd Road
CARDIFF

Galloways
Pier Street
ABERYSTWYTH

Lears Bookshop
13-17 Royal Arcade
CARDIFF

Galloway and Hodgson
25 Holyhead Road
BANGOR

Uplands Bookshop
Gwydr Square, Uplands
SWANSEA

Bernan Associates
Government Publications Service
9730-E George Palmer Highway
Lanham, MD 20706
U.S.A.

Statistical  Enquiries

Welsh Office
Y Swyddfa Gymreig

Statistics for Wales are prepared by Economic and Statistical Services Division of the Welsh Office, based in Cathays Park, Cardiff CF1 3NQ. This publication is one of a series, the others being listed on the previous page.

Additional information is frequently available and advice can be sought from the subject contact points below. A booklet 'Government Statistics: a brief guide to sources' has been prepared by the Central Statistical Office and is available on written application to the Welsh Office publications unit.

Subject	Telephone Cardiff (0222)
Economic statistics	82 5065
Transport statistics	82 5062
Planning statistics	82 5062
Financial statistics	82 4317
Demographic statistics	82 5085
Education statistics	82 5057
Health statistics	82 5066
Housing statistics	82 5061
Personal social services statistics	82 5041
Agricultural statistics	82 5052
General enquiries	82 5087